NATIONAL REGISTER OF PSYCHOTHERAPISTS

NATIONAL REGISTER OF PSYCHOTHERAPISTS

1997

United Kingdom Council for Psychotherapy

London and New York

First published 1996
by Routledge
11 New Fetter Lane, London EC4P 4EE

Simultaneously published in the USA and Canada
by Routledge
29 West 35th Street, New York, NY 10001

©1996 United Kingdom Council for Psychotherapy

Typeset in Gill Sans by Routledge

Printed and bound in Great Britain by
Unwin Brothers Ltd, Old Woking, Surrey

British Library Cataloguing in Publication Data
A catalogue record for this book is available from the British Library

Library of Congress Cataloguing in Publication Data
A catalogue record for this book has been requested

ISBN 0–415–13830–2

TABLE OF CONTENTS

Page

NATIONAL REGISTER OF PSYCHOTHERAPISTS: 1997

FOREWORD
by Michael R. Pokorny

From the Foster Report of 1971 to the launch of the first National Register of Psychotherapists in 1993, the profession of psychotherapy has changed from a state of fragmentation to a cohesive structure containing approximately seventy psychotherapy organisations arranged in eight Sections and representing every known variety of psychotherapy. A description of the process by which this happened has been published (Pokorny M.R.; BJP, Vol.11 (3) pp. 415-21). The purpose was to unite the profession and to regulate it for the benefit of the public. By providing a National Register that is widely available, the United Kingdom Council for Psychotherapy offers the public the opportunity to consult a list of practitioners who are both professionally competent and ethically responsible. Any practitioner who is found guilty of falling below the standards laid down risks having their registration suspended, or made conditional, or even of being struck off the Register. Currently this Register is voluntary, which means that anyone can still call themselves a psychotherapist and can practise and charge fees, even though they may be neither trained, nor skilled, nor regulated. It is for this reason that the United Kingdom Council for Psychotherapy wants to move towards statutory regulation of psychotherapy. This would give proper protection to the public as well as being a basis for regulating the practice of psychotherapists from other European Union countries who wished to move to the United Kingdom. The mutual recognition of qualifications can only occur between European Union countries where legal control of an occupation exists. In the absence of a legal framework, any European Union national can practise in this country. The United Kingdom Council for Psychotherapy continues to be active in the attempts to found a European Association for Psychotherapy that can establish the boundaries of the profession in the European Union.

The United Kingdom Council for Psychotherapy is working towards the introduction of requirements for continuing professional development for registered psychotherapists and continues to review the ethical guidelines and the complaints procedures of the member organisations.

USING THE REGISTER

The *National Register of Psychotherapists* is designed to make it easy to find and contact a psychotherapist in your area. The names, addresses and telephone numbers of registered psychotherapists are listed alphabetically within geographical areas. Each entry includes a brief description of the type of psychotherapy offered and a code denoting the organisation(s) to which the psychotherapist belongs. A list of these codes and the organisations they relate to appears on page xxi. The register also lists practitioners under the organisation(s) to which they belong.

Each of the eight sections of UKCP has a **Flag Statement** outlining its purpose and distinguishing it from the other sections. The **Flag Statements** and a list of organisations belonging to each section appear on pages xvii.

We hope that you will find this register easy to use and that you will write with your comments to:

United Kingdom Council for Psychotherapy
167-69 Great Portland Street, London WIN 5FB
Tel: 0171 436 3002
Fax: 0171 436 3013

Governing Board

Digby Tantam
Chair

Janet Boakes
Honorary Secretary

Michael Pokorny
Chair, Registration Board

Gill Gorell Barnes
Training Standards Officer

Jean Carr
Treasurer

Paul Zeal
External Relations Officer

Talia Levine Bar-Yoseph
Professional Development Officer

Mark Aveline
Institutional Member

Mia Beaumont
Psychoanalytically-based Therapy with Children Section

Ann Casement
Analytical Psychology Section

Tom Chamberlain
Elected Member

Michael Crowe
Royal College of Psychiatrists

John Dinwoodie
Experiential Constructivist Therapies Section

Joan Evans
Humanistic and Integrative Psychotherapy Section

Dennis Flannery
Elected Member

Anne Garland
Behavioural and Cognitive Psychotherapy Section

Susan Lang
Family, Couple, Sexual and Systemic Therapy Section

Georgia Lepper
Elected Member

Christine Lister-Ford
Elected Member

Lesley Murdin
Psychoanalytic and Psychodynamic Psychotherapy Section

Lesley Parkinson
British Psychological Society

Emmy van Deurzen-Smith
Elected Member

Sue Washington
Hypnotherapy Section

Registration Board

Michael Pokorny
Chair

David Winter
Vice-Chair
Experiential Constructivist Therapies Section

Judy Ryde
Honorary Secretary
Humanistic and Integrative Psychotherapy Section

Claire Adams
Institutional Member

Bernard Burgoyne
Psychoanalytic and Psychodynamic Psychotherapy Section

John Burnham
Family, Couple, Sexual and Systemic Therapy Section

Su Börsig
Humanistic and Integrative Psychotherapy Section

Jeremy Holmes
Royal College of Psychiatrists

Juliet Hopkins
Institutional Member

Ray Keedy-Lilley
Hypnotherapy Section

Gordon Law
Humanistic and Integrative Psychotherapy Section

Eileen Orford
Psychoanalytically-based Therapy with Children Section

Tom Sensky
Institutional Member

Maye Taylor
British Psychological Society

Helen Tarsh
Psychoanalytic and Psychodynamic Psychotherapy Section

Michael Whan
Analytical Psychology Section

Chris Williams
Behavioural and Cognitive Psychotherapy Section

Tim Woolmer
Psychoanalytic and Psychodynamic Psychotherapy Section

ETHICAL GUIDELINES

of the United Kingdom Council for Psychotherapy

I. Introduction

1.1 The purpose of a Code of Ethics is to define general principles and to establish standards of professional conduct for psychotherapists in their work and to inform and protect those members of the public who seek their services. Each organisation will include and elaborate upon the following principles in its Code of Ethics.

1.2 All psychotherapists are expected to approach their work with the aim of alleviating suffering and promoting the well-being of their clients. Psychotherapists should endeavour to use their abilities and skills to their client's best advantage without prejudice and with due recognition of the value and dignity of every human being.

1.3 All psychotherapists on the UKCP Register are required to adhere to the Codes of Ethics and Practice of their own organisations which will be consistent with the following statements and which will have been approved by the appropriate UKCP Section.

2. Codes of Ethics

Each member organisation of UKCP must have published a Code of Ethics approved by the appropriate UKCP Section and appropriate for the practitioners of that particular organisation and their clients. The Code of Ethics will include and elaborate upon the following ten points to which attention is drawn here. All psychotherapists on the UKCP Register are required to adhere to the Codes of Ethics of their own organisations.

2.1 **Qualifications:** Psychotherapists are required to disclose their qualifications when requested and not claim, or imply, qualifications that they do not have.

2.2 **Terms, Conditions and Methods of Practice:** Psychotherapists are required to disclose on request their terms, conditions and, where appropriate, methods of practice at the outset of psychotherapy.

2.3 **Confidentiality:** Psychotherapists are required to preserve confidentiality and to disclose, if requested, the limits of confidentiality and circumstances under which it might be broken to specific third parties.

2.4 **Professional Relationship:** Psychotherapists should consider the client's best interest when making appropriate contact with the client's GP, relevant psychiatric services, or other relevant professionals with the client's knowledge. Psychotherapists should be aware of their own limitations.

2.5 **Relationship with Clients:** Psychotherapists are required to maintain appropriate boundaries with their clients and to take care to not exploit their clients, current or past, in any way, financially, sexually or emotionally.

2.6 **Research:** Psychotherapists are required to clarify with clients the nature, purpose and conditions of any research in which the clients are to be involved and to ensure that informed and verifiable consent is given before commencement.

2.7 **Publication:** Psychotherapists are required to safeguard the welfare and anonymity of clients when any form of publication of clinical material is being considered and to obtain their consent whenever possible.

2.8 **Practitioner Competence:** Psychotherapists are required to maintain their ability to perform competently and to take necessary steps to do so.

2.9 **Indemnity Insurance:** Psychotherapists are required to ensure that their professional work is adequately covered by appropriate indemnity insurance.

2.10 Detrimental Behaviour:

(i) Psychotherapists are required to refrain from any behaviour that may be detrimental to the profession, to colleagues or to trainees.

(ii) Psychotherapists are required to take appropriate action in accordance with Clause 5.8 with regard to the behaviour of a colleague which may be detrimental to the profession, to colleagues or to trainees.

3. Advertising

Member organisations of UKCP are required to restrict promotion of their work to a description of the type of psychotherapy they provide.

3.1 Psychotherapists are required to distinguish carefully between self-descriptions, as in a list, and advertising seeking enquiries.

4. Code of Practice

Each Member Organisation of UKCP will have published a Code of Practice approved by the appropriate UKCP Section and appropriate for the practitioners of that particular organisation and their clients. The purpose of Codes of

Practice is to clarify and expand upon the general principles established in the Code of Ethics of the organisation and the practical application of those principles. All psychotherapists on the UKCP Register will be required to adhere to the Codes of Practice of their own organisations.

5. Complaints Procedure

Each Member Organisation of UKCP must have published a Complaints Procedure, including information about the acceptability or otherwise of a complaint made by a third party against a practitioner, approved by the appropriate UKCP Section and appropriate for the practitioners of that particular organisation and their clients. The purpose of a Complaints Procedure is to ensure that practitioners and their clients have clear information about the procedure and processes involved in dealing with complaints. All psychotherapists on the UKCP Register are required to adhere to the Complaints Procedure of their own organisations.

5.1 **Making a complaint:** A client wishing to complain shall be advised to contact the Member Organisation.

5.2 **Receiving a complaint:** A Member Organisation receiving a complaint against one of its psychotherapists shall ensure that the therapist is informed immediately and that both complainant and therapist are aware of the Complaints Procedure.

5.3 **Appeals:** After the completion of the Complaints Procedure within an organisation, an appeal may be made to the Section on grounds of improper procedure.

5.4 **Reference to UKCP Governing Board:** Appeals not resolved by the Section or those where the Section cannot appropriately hear the appeal shall be referred to the Governing Board of UKCP.

5.5 **Reports to UKCP Section:** Where a complaint is upheld the Section shall be informed by the organisation.

5.6 **Report to the UKCP Registration Board:** Member Organisations are required to report to the UKCP Registration Board the names of members who have been suspended or expelled.

5.7 **Complaints upheld and convictions:** Psychotherapists are required to inform their Member Organisations if any complaint is upheld against them in another Member Organisation, if they are convicted of any notifiable criminal offence or if successful civil proceedings are brought against them in relation to their work as psychotherapists.

5.8 **Conduct of colleagues:** Psychotherapists concerned that a colleague's conduct may be unprofessional should initiate the Complaints Procedure of the relevant Member Organisation.

5.9 The resignation of a member of an organisation shall not be allowed to impede the process of any investigation as long as the alleged offence took place during that person's membership.

6. Sanctions

6.1 Psychotherapists who are suspended by, or expelled from, a Member Organisation are automatically deleted from the UKCP Register.

7. Monitoring Complaints

7.1 Member Organisations shall report to the Registration Board annually concerning the number of complaints received, the nature of the complaints and their disposition.

7.2 The Registration Board shall report annually to the Governing Board on the adequacy of Member Organisations' disciplinary procedures.

SECTIONS AND FLAG STATEMENTS

Analytical Psychology Section

Analytical Psychology is a distinct discipline stemming from the work of C.G. Jung.

Central to the viewpoint of this discipline is the idea that unconscious forces and processes both individual and collective are involved in behaviour, in affect, in self-image, and in relations with others.

The implications of this is that by interpretation of clinical material, including dreams and within the analytical setting (especially in the transference/countertransference relationship) hitherto unconscious elements of individual psychology can be brought into consciousness, to the benefit of the patient. The presence of distinct or overt pathology is not essential to the clinical application of analytical psychology since self-discovery and the exploration of the inner world are valuable in their own right.

There is also a role for analytical psychology in social and cultural spheres, as unconscious processes are active therein on a collective level. Analytical psychologists are committed to research and to the development and publication of theory in all the fields mentioned above.

Organisations

Association of Jungian Analysts
The Independent Group of Analytical Psychologists
Society of Analytical Psychology

Behavioural and Cognitive Psychotherapy Section

Behavioural Psychotherapy has the following features:

Theoretically it is derived from learning theories - classical, operant, cognitive, social - and related empirical studies.

It concentrates on behaviour, in the broadest sense, as the key point in evaluation of therapeutic effectiveness. This may include overt behavioural, cognitive, emotional or physiological events.

It involves a behavioural and cognitive analysis of problems followed by systematic alterations to encourage new and more adaptive responses.

It has a technology of methods to make easier and more efficient the acquisition of new skills and the reduction of dysfunctional ways of behaving and thinking.

All aspects of therapy, assessment, goals and process, are made explicit in negotiation with the individual towards a resolution of their particular difficulties.

It incorporates measures of effectiveness.

It can be used to help resolve problems of living for any person irrespective of intelligence insight or other abilities.

Organisation

British Association of Behavioural and Cognitive Psychotherapies

Experiential Constructivist Therapies Section

These contemporary psychotherapies, which are supported by established psychological theories, are based on the underpinning assumption that people construct their own individual ways of seeing the world through their personal experiences of life. Each individual's constructed model of the world is constantly adapted and modified by experience, which in turn influences his or her actions, words, and thoughts.

Therapies of this kind help clients discover more clearly the models through which they represent the world to themselves, overtly or covertly. The emphasis is on adaptive change. Clients are supported in exploring and testing new ways of constructing their world and operating in it, but it is not assumed that any particular way of constructing the world is 'correct'. Changes can occur in small ways at the level of behaviour or more fundamentally at the level of core beliefs and values.

Various techniques and strategies are used which are creative, personally tailored, and involve the client's active participation. The therapeutic process rests on a client-therapist relationship of mutual respect, leading the client to a greater sense of personal control and empowerment. These therapies generally have a specific focus and expect to effect positive change in the short term. Clients may be seen individually or in groups.

Organisations

Association for Neuro-Linguistic Programming
Centre for Personal Construct Psychology

Family, Couple, Sexual and Systemic Therapy Section

Organisations within the group have in common an understanding that symptoms, problems, and difficulties arise in the context of relationships and are to be understood in terms of interactive and systemic processes. The main focus of intervention emerges from these patterns of interaction and the meanings given to them. Given this focus, the members may work with individuals, couples, families, or parts of them, and other significant relationship networks.

Organisations

The Association for Family Therapy
British Association for Sexual and Marital Therapy
The Family Institute, Cardiff
Institute of Family Therapy
Kensington Consultation Centre

Humanistic and Integrative Psychotherapy Section

This Section includes different psychotherapies which approach the individual as a whole person including body, feelings, mind and spirit. Members welcome interdisciplinary dialogue and an exploration of different psychological processes with particular emphasis on integration within the Section. Organisations in this Section practice approaches compatible with the following:

Humanistic Psychotherapy is an approach which tries to do justice to the whole person including body, mind and spirit. It represents a broad range of therapeutic methods. Each method recognises the self-healing capacities of the client and believes that the greatest expert on the client is the client. The humanistic psychotherapist works towards an authentic meeting of equals in the therapy relationship.

Existential Psychotherapy aims at enabling clients to find constructive ways of coming to terms with the challenges of everyday living. The focus is on clients' concrete individual experience of anxiety and distress leading to an exploration of their personal beliefs and value system, in order to clarify and understand these in relation to the specific physical, psychological and socio-cultural context. The experience and influences of the past, present and future are given equal emphasis. The questioning of assumptions and facing up to the possibilities and limitations of living is an important part of this interactive, dynamic and direct approach.

Transpersonal/Psychospiritual Psychotherapy can be defined by its orientation which includes the spiritual dimension rather than the content of therapy. It views the human psyche as having a central core Self or Soul as the centre of identity as well as a personal ego. Psychotherapists draw on a wide range of therapeutic methods towards the uncovering of past psychological material within a context of the individual's potential based on spiritual insight and experience. Within this perspective there is both a movement of the personal centre to the Self and a movement of the Self to manifest its nature through and in the personal centre. Thus therapy includes both repair and individuation.

Integrative Psychotherapy can be distinguished from eclecticism by its determination to show there are significant connections between different therapies, which may be unrecognised by their exclusive proponents. While remaining respectful to each approach, integrative psychotherapy draws from many sources in the belief that no one approach has all the truth. The therapeutic relationship is the vehicle for experience, growth and change. It aims to hold together the dual forces of disintegration and integration, as presented by the psychologically distressed and disabled. The integrative therapeutic experience leads towards a greater toleration of life's experiences and an increase of creativity and service.

Organisations

Association of Cognitive Analytic Therapists
Association of Humanistic Psychology Practitioners
Bath Centre for Psychotherapy and Counselling
British Psychodrama Association
Centre for Counselling and Psychotherapy Education
Chiron Centre for Holistic Psychotherapy
The Gerda Boyesen Centre
The Gestalt Centre, London
Gestalt Psychotherapy Training Institute
Institute for Arts in Therapy and Education
Institute of Psychosynthesis
Institute of Transactional Analysis
Karuna Institute
London Association of Primal Psychotherapists
The Metanoia Institute
The Minster Centre
North Staffs. Association for Psychotherapy
Psychosynthesis and Education Trust

Regent's College School of Psychotherapy and Counselling
Re.Vision
The Sherwood Psychotherapy Training Institute
Spectrum
Stockton Centre for Psychotherapy and Counselling

Hypnotherapy Section

The Hypnotherapy Section subscribes to the following general definitions to arrive at a description of its distinctive therapeutic practice. Hypnosis constitutes a state of relaxation which people enter voluntarily, during which there occurs an altered state of conscious awareness. Psychology is the study of human behaviour, together with an understanding of the motivational forces within individuals, making them respond to stimuli or situations in ways unique to themselves. Psychotherapy applies psychological principles to the treatment of those suffering from disorders of psychological origin, or exacerbated by psychological factors. Hypnotherapy is that branch of psychotherapy which employs hypnosis as the therapeutic medium.

Organisations

British Association for Autogenic Training and Therapy
Centre Training School for Hypnotherapy and Psychotherapy
The National College of Hypnosis and Psychotherapy
The National Register of Hypnotherapists and Psychotherapists
National School of Hypnosis and Psychotherapy

Psychoanalytic and Psychodynamic Psychotherapy Section

Psychoanalytic psychotherapy is based on psychoanalytic practice and theory. It endeavours to reach the underlying, often unconscious, causes of distress. Together with the therapist the patient can explore free associations, memories, phantasies, feelings and dreams, relating to both past and present. In the reliable setting of the therapy (which allows for regression) and in the exploration of the interaction with the therapist, especially within the transference and counter-transference, the patient may achieve a new and better resolution of long-standing conflicts.

Organisations

Association of Arbours Psychotherapists
Association for Group and Individual Psychotherapy
British Association of Psychotherapists
Cambridge Society for Psychotherapy
Centre for Attachment-Based Psychoanalytic Psychotherapy
Centre for Freudian Analysis and Research
Centre for Psychoanalytical Psychotherapy
Centre for the Study of Psychotherapy (University of Kent)
Guild of Psychotherapists
Guildford Centre for Psychotherapy
Hallam Institute of Psychotherapy
Institute of Group Analysis
Institute of Psychotherapy and Counselling
Institute of Psychotherapy and Social Studies
Liverpool Psychotherapy Diploma Organisation (University of Liverpool)

London Centre for Psychotherapy
NAFSIYAT
Northern Association for Analytical Psychotherapy
North West Institute for Dynamic Psychotherapy
Philadelphia Association
Severnside Institute for Psychotherapy
South Trent Training in Dynamic Psychotherapy
Tavistock Marital Studies Institute
University of Leicester Diploma in Psychodynamic Studies
West Midlands Institute of Psychotherapy
Westminster Pastoral Foundation
The Women's Therapy Centre
Yorkshire Association for Psychodynamic Psychotherapy

Psychoanalytically-based Therapy with Children

Therapists in this Section are engaged in long- and short-term work with children who have problems which are not susceptible to the ordinary intervention of parent or school. Psychoanalytic theory is the basis of an understanding of their conscious and unconscious communications in conversation, play, drawings, and educational tasks. The aim of the work is to restore the child to an age-appropriate developmental level by observation and interpretation of his/her behaviour and use of the therapist and the materials within a reliable setting. As children are dependent on adults and the environment they provide, the work includes contact and often treatment of parents and families.

Organisations
   Association of Child Psychotherapists
   Forum for the Advancement of Educational Therapy and
      Therapeutic Teaching

Institutional Members
   Association of University Teachers of Psychiatry
   Tavistock Clinic
   Universities Psychotherapy Association

Special Members

   British Psychological Society
   Royal College of Psychiatrists

Friends of the Council

   British Association of Counselling

ORGANISATION CODES

Code	Organisation
AAP	Association of Arbours Psychotherapists
ACAT	Association of Cognitive Analytic Therapists
ACP	Association of Child Psychotherapists
AFT	The Association for Family Therapy
AGIP	Association for Group and Individual Psychotherapy
AHPP	Association of Humanistic Psychology Practitioners
AJA	Association of Jungian Analysts
ANLP	Association for Neuro-Linguistic Programming
AUTP	Association of University Teachers of Psychiatry
BABCP	British Association for Behavioural and Cognitive Psychotherapies
BAFAT	British Association for Autogenic Training and Therapy
BAP	British Association of Psychotherapists
BASMT	British Association for Sexual and Marital Therapy
BCPC	Bath Centre for Psychotherapy and Counselling
BPDA	British Psychodrama Association
BTC	The Gerda Boyesen Centre
CAPP	Centre for Attachment-Based Psychoanalytic Psychotherapy
CCHP	Chiron Centre for Holistic Psychotherapy
CCPE	Centre for Counselling and Psychotherapy Education
CFAR	Centre for Freudian Analysis and Research
CPCP	Centre for Personal Construct Psychology
CPP	Centre for Psychoanalytical Psychotherapy
CSP	Cambridge Society for Psychotherapy
CSPK	Centre for the Study of Psychotherapy (University of Kent)
CTS	Centre Training School for Hypnotherapy and Psychotherapy
FAETT	Forum for the Advancement of Educational Therapy and Therapeutic Teaching
FIC	The Family Institute, Cardiff
GCL	The Gestalt Centre, London
GCP	Guildford Centre for Psychotherapy
GPTI	Gestalt Psychotherapy Training Institute
GUILD	Guild of Psychotherapists
HIP	Hallam Institute of Psychotherapy
IATE	Institute for Arts in Therapy and Education

Code	Organisation
IFT	Institute of Family Therapy
IGA	Institute of Group Analysis
IGAP	The Independent Group of Analytical Psychologists
IPC	Institute of Psychotherapy and Counselling
IPS	Institute of Psychosynthesis
IPSS	Institute of Psychotherapy and Social Studies
ITA	Institute of Transactional Analysis
KCC	Kensington Consultation Centre
KI	Karuna Institute
LAPP	London Association of Primal Psychotherapists
LCP	London Centre for Psychotherapy
LPDO	Liverpool Psychotherapy Diploma Organisation (University of Liverpool)
MC	Minster Centre
MET	The Metanoia Institute
NAAP	Northern Association for Analytical Psychotherapy
NRHP	The National Register of Hypnotherapists and Psychotherapists
NSAP	North Staffs Association for Psychotherapy
NSHAP	National School of Hypnosis and Psychotherapy
NWIDP	North West Institute for Dynamic Psychotherapy
PA	Philadelphia Association
PET	Psychosynthesis and Education Trust
RCSPC	Regent's College School of Psychotherapy and Counselling
RE.V	Re.Vision
SAP	Society of Analytical Psychology
SCPC	Stockton Centre for Psychotherapy and Counselling
SIP	Severnside Institute for Psychotherapy
SPEC	Spectrum
SPTI	The Sherwood Psychotherapy Training Institute
STTDP	South Trent Training in Dynamic Psychotherapy
TMSI	Tavistock Marital Studies Institute
ULDPS	University of Leicester Diploma in Psychodynamic Studies
WMIP	West Midlands Institute of Psychotherapy
WTC	The Women's Therapy Centre
YAPP	Yorkshire Association for Psychodynamic Psychotherapy

GEOGRAPHICAL LISTING

AVON

Robert Ash
Psychoanalytic Psychotherapist
54 Cotham Road, Cotham, Bristol
BS6 6DW
Tel: Tel: 0117 942 7079
SIP

Shelagh Austin
Psychodrama Psychotherapist
The Garden Flat, 3 Apsley Villas,
Kingsdown Parade, Bristol BS6 5UH
Tel: Tel: 01272 426433
BPDA

Paul Aylard
Psychodynamic Psychotherapist
Heath House Priory Hospital, Off Bell
Hill, Bristol BS16 1EQ
Tel: Tel: 0117 952 5255
YAPP

Hugh Barnes
Family Therapist
Department of Family Psychiatry,
Children's Hospital, St Michael's Hill,
Bristol BS2 8BJ
Tel: Tel: 0117 929 4530
AFT

Kate Barrows
Psychoanalytic Psychotherapist
16 Sydenham Lane, Cotham, Bristol
BS6
Tel: Tel: 0117 944 6681
SIP

Paul Barrows
Child Psychotherapist
Knowle Clinic Child & Adolescent
Service, Broadfield Road, Knowle,
Bristol BS4 2UH
Tel: Tel: 0117 972 4227/0117 973 4989
ACP

Sally Box
Psychoanalytic Psychotherapist
22 Clifton Wood Road, Clifton, Bristol
BS8 4TW
Tel: Tel: 0117 926 2902
SIP

Ray Brown
Psychoanalytic Psychotherapist
15 Nottingham Road, Bishopston,
Bristol BS7 9DH
Tel: Tel: 0117 942 6105
SIP

Robin Gordon Brown
Psychoanalytic Psychotherapist
14 Ambra Vale West, Clifton Wood,
Bristol BS8 4RD
Tel: Tel: 0117 926 2886
BAP, SIP

Misha Carder
Hypno-Psychotherapist
76 Lower Oldfield Park, Bath, Avon
BA2 3HP
Tel: Tel: 01225 313531
NSHAP

Rachel Clyne
Psychosynthesis Psychotherapist
Greengage Cottage, 94 Carling
Cottages, Nr Peasedown St John, Bath,
Avon BA2 8AW
Tel: Tel: 01761 436463
PET

Whiz Collis
Humanistic Psychotherapist
74 York Road, Montpelier, Bristol
BS6 5QF
Tel: 0117 955 9600
AHPP, BCPC

Barbara Cottman
Psychoanalytic Psychotherapist
Church Cottage, Corston, Bath
BA2 9AY
Tel: 01225 336598/01225 825361
BAP, SIP

Paul Cubie
Systemic Psychotherapist
61 Park Road, Staple Hill, Bristol
BS16 5LQ
IFT

Jane Cutler
Psychosynthesis Psychotherapist
66 Dunkerry Road, Windmill Hill,
Bristol BS3 4LA
Tel: 0117 9632 505
IPS

Sheila Davies
Psychoanalytic Psychotherapist
35 Bath Hill, Keynsham, Bristol
BS18 1HJ
Tel: 0117 986 1020
SIP

Erica Day
Humanistic and Integrative
Psychotherapist
2 Fircliff Park, Portishead, Bristol
BS20 9HQ
Tel: 01275 818341
SPEC

George Dewey
Humanistic and Integrative
Psychotherapist
21 Nutgrove Avenue, Bedminster,
Bristol BS3 4QE
Tel: 0117 966 1100
BCPC

Dana Douglas
Psychosynthesis Psychotherapist
Wellspring, Faulkland, Somerset
BA3 5UX
Tel: 01373 834 338
PET

Iain Dresser
Psychoanalytic Psychotherapist
23 Highbury Villas, Kingsdown, Bristol
BS2 8BY
Tel: 0117 923 9038
SIP

Anthony Elman
Humanistic and Integrative
Psychotherapist
143 North Road, Bristol BS6 5AH
Tel: 0117 9247668
BCPC

Suzanne Essex
Family Therapist
Garden Flat, 13 Windsor Road, St
Andrews, Bristol BS6 5BW
Tel: 0117 9422016
AFT

Tish Feilden
Humanistic and Integrative
Psychotherapist
The Barn, Sheephouse Farm, Warleigh,
Bathford BA1 8EE
Tel: 01225 858301
BCPC

Anstice Fisher
Integrative Psychosynthesis
Psychotherapist
9 Eastville, Claremont Road, Bath
BA1 6QN
Tel: 01225 445 653
RE.V

Jane Fossey
Cognitive Behavioural Psychotherapist
15 Mortimer Road, Clifton, Bristol
BS8 4EY
BABCP

Jill Gabriel
Humanistic and Integrative
Psychotherapist
Langridge House, Langridge, Bath,
Avon BA1 9BX
Tel: 01225 338874
SPEC

Fiona Gardner
Psychoanalytic Psychotherapist
8 St Saviour's Terrace, Larkhall, Bath
BA1 6RL
Tel: 01225 319121
SIP

Peter Gardner
Integrative Psychotherapist
Harpers Batch, Linford, Bristol
BS18 8AF
Tel: 01275 472598
RCSPC

Chris Gaskell
Family Therapist
28 Claremont Avenue, Bristol BS7 8JE
IFT

Eva Gell
Psychoanalytic Psychotherapist
36 Cotham Hill, Bristol BS6 6LA
Tel: 0117 923 7434
LCP, WTC, SIP

Pat Gosling
Psychoanalytic Psychotherapist
White Hart Cottage, 38 High Street,
Rode, Somerset BA3 6PA
Tel: 01373 830901/01373 830172 (f)
GUILD, SIP

Sylvia Green
Psychoanalytic Psychotherapist
29 Calton Gardens, Bath BA2 4QG
Tel: 01225 421746
SIP

Judith Gregory
Gestalt Psychotherapist
'Fernlea', Yate Road, Iron Acton, Bristol
BS17 1XY
Tel: 01454 228418
GPTI

Julie Gresty
Core Process Psychotherapist
71 Mendip Road, Bedminster, Bristol
BS3 4BP
Tel: 0117 9637 285
KI

Nicola Guest
Child Psychotherapist
Department of Child & Family
Psychiatry, Downend Clinic,
Buckingham Gardens, Downend,
Bristol BS16 5TW
Tel: 01179 566025
ACP

Herbert Hahn
Psychoanalytic Psychotherapist
Suite 7, 36 Cotham Hill, Bristol
BS6 6LA
Tel: 0117 973 3258
SIP, BAP

David Hamblin
Psychosynthesis Psychotherapist,
Humanistic and Integrative
Psychotherapist
11 Kensington Gardens, Bath BA1 6LH
Tel: 01225 317 272
PET, BCPC

Marie Hanley
Psychoanalytic Psychotherapist
3 Exeter Buildings, Redland, Bristol
BS6 6TH
Tel: 0117 946 6910
LCP, SIP

Bob Harris
Group Analyst
12 Sydenham Road, Bristol BS6 5SH
Tel: 0117 944 1005
IGA

Jon Hastings
Humanistic and Integrative
Psychotherapist
29 Cobourg Road, Montpelier, Bristol
BS6 5HT
Tel: 0117 935 0915
BCPC

Kim Hastings
Humanistic and Integrative
Psychotherapist
42A Upper Cheltenham Place,
Montpelier, Bristol BS6 5HR
Tel: 0117 954 0649
BCPC

Sheila Hawdon
Psychoanalytic Psychotherapist
Ashlands, Belmont Road, Combe
Down, Bath BA2 5JR
Tel: 01225 840420
SIP

Peter Hawkins
Humanistic and Integrative
Psychotherapist
285 Bloomfield Road, Bath BA2 2NU
Tel: 01225 836191
BCPC, AHPP

Judith Higgins
Gestalt Psychotherapist
5 Fairfield Road, Montpelier, Bristol
BS6 5JN
Tel: 0117 924 6320
GPTI

Max Holloway
Integrative Psychotherapist
54 Devonshire Road, Westbury Park,
Bristol BS6 7NL
Tel: 0117 940736
MC

Tone Horwood
Psychoanalytic Psychotherapist
Oriel House, 45 Cotham Road,
Cotham, Bristol BS6 6DN
Tel: 0117 924 7110
IPSS

Gary Hutchinson
Integrative Psychosynthesis
Psychotherapist
33 Apsley Road, Bath BA1 3LP
Tel: 01225 421735
RE.V

Glenys James
Analytical Psychologist-Jungian Analyst
Flat 1, 20 The Belmont, Lansdown,
Bath, Avon BA1 5DZ
Tel: 01380 871818/01225 463324
BAP, SIP

Pat James
Psychoanalytic Psychotherapist
46 North Road, Midsomer Norton,
Bath BA3 2QQ
Tel: 01761 415538
WMIP

Rosie Jeffries
Integrative Psychotherapist
129 Mina Road, St Werburgh's, Bristol
BS2 9YF
Tel: 01179 763818/01179 551471
MET

P H Jezard-Clark
Cognitive Behavioural Psychotherapist
Petherton, 3 Petherton Road,
Hengrove, Bristol BS14 2BP
Tel: 01275 834048
BABCP

Pat Johnson
Integrative Psychotherapist
9b Alpha Road, Southville, Bristol
BS3 1DH
Tel: 0117 9631610
MC

Kunderke Kevlin
Psychosynthesis Psychotherapist
12 Avon Vale, Stoke Bishop, Bristol
BS9 1TB
Tel: 0117 968 7748
PET

Sue Kuhn
Cognitive Analytic Therapist
13 Belgrave Crescent, Bath, Avon
BA1 5JU
Tel: 01225 465846
ACAT

Phil Lapworth
Integrative Psychotherapist
Lilac Cottage, 65 Murhill, Limpley
Stoke, Bath BA3 6HQ
Tel: 01225 722348
ITA, MET

Tim Leighton
Cognitive Analytic Therapist
35 Belvedere, Bath BA1 5HR;
Clouds House, East Knoyle, Nr
Salisbury SP3 6BE
Tel: 01747 830733/01225 447706
ACAT

Clare Lester
Integrative Psychotherapist
17 Lymore Gardens, Oldfield Park,
Bath BA2 1AQ
Tel: 01225 336375
MC

Jennifer Mackewn
Integrative Psychotherapist
11 Prior Park Buildings, Bath, Avon
BA2 4NP
Tel: 01225 426182
GPTI, MET

Angela Markham
Family Therapist
23 Highbury Villas, Kingsdown, Bristol
BS2 8BY
Tel: 0117 239038
AFT

Brendan McLoughlin
Psychoanalytic Psychotherapist
Open House Centre, Manvers Street
Baptist Church, Bath BA1 1JW
Tel: 01225 481297
IPC

Barbara McNamara
Psychoanalytic Psychotherapist
44 Claremont Road, Bishopston,
Bristol BS7 8DH
Tel: 0117 944 4206
SIP

Muriel Mitcheson Brown
Psychoanalytic Psychotherapist
16 Woodstock Road, Redland, Bristol
BS6 7EJ
Tel: 0117 9241 676
SIP, GUILD

Alexander Newman
Analytical Psychologist-Jungian Analyst
Synge House, 15 Fremantle Square,
Cotham, Bristol BS6 5TN
Tel: 0117 923 2366
SAP, SIP

Georgiana Nye
Psychosynthesis Psychotherapist
45 Canynge Road, Clifton, Bristol
BS8 3LH
Tel: 0117 973 3769
PET

Louise Padgett
Core Process Psychotherapist
6 Fenton Road, Bishopston, Bristol
BS7 8ND
Tel: 01179 426 332
KI

Malcolm Parlett
Gestalt Psychotherapist
51 Fernbank Road, Redland, Bristol
BS6 6PX
Tel: 0117 924 0126
GPTI

Linda Patterson
Psychoanalytic Psychotherapist
10 Brookleaze Buildings, Larkhall, Bath
BA1 6RA
Tel: 01225 311163
SIP

Alix Pirani
Individual and Group Humanistic
Psychotherapist
1 Avondale Court, Goodeve Road,
Bristol BS9 1NU
BCPC, AHPP

Sian Pope
NLP Psychotherapist
4 Henbury Road, Westbury-on-Trym,
Bristol BS9 3HJ
Tel: 01179 504869
ANLP

Jane Purkiss
Humanistic and Integrative
Psychotherapist
93 Stackpool Road, Southville, Bristol
BS3 1NX
Tel: 0117 966 2957
BCPC

Christopher Richards
Psychoanalytic Psychotherapist
4 St Ronan's Avenue, Redland, Bristol
BS6 6EP
Tel: 0117 974 4062
GUILD, SIP

Gillian Richardson
Sexual and Marital Psychotherapist
Maycroft Cottage, Highbury Villas,
Kingsdown, Bristol BS2 8BY
BASMT

Alivia Rose
Gestalt Psychotherapist
21 Nutgrove Avenue, Victoria Park,
Bedminster, Bristol BS3 4QE
Tel: 0117 966 1100
GCL

Jill Rowe
Psychoanalytic Psychotherapist
94 St Andrew's Road, Montpelier,
Bristol BS6 5EJ
Tel: 0117 942 1016
SIP

Judy Ryde
Humanistic and Integrative
Psychotherapist
285 Bloomfield Road, Bath BA2 2NU
Tel: 01225 833657
AHPP, BCPC

Anne Selby
Humanistic and Integrative
Psychotherapist
Prospect House, 4 Prospect Place,
Beechen Cliff, Bath BA2 4QP
Tel: 01225 428826
BCPC

Nuala Sheehan
Family Psychotherapist
6 Thomas Street, Bath BA1 5NW
Tel: 01225 334957
IFT

Alison Simmons
Psychodrama Psychotherapist
Lower Hansley Farm, Pool Lane,
Ridgehill, Nr Winford, Bristol
BS18 8BP
Tel: 01275 472264
BPDA

Ilse Sinclair
Sexual and Marital Psychotherapist
19 Whately Court, Whately Road,
Bristol BS8 2PS
Tel: 0117 973 3384
BASMT

David Slattery
Humanistic and Integrative
Psychotherapist
79a Gloucester Road, Bishopston,
Bristol BS7 8AS
Tel: 0117 942 0226
BCPC

Donna Smith
Family Therapist
The Old Rectory, Rode, Nr Bath
BA3 6PR
Tel: 01373 830710
AFT

Gill Smith
Integrative Psychotherapist
Centre for Whole Health, 12 Victoria
Place, Bristol BS3;
18 Governor's House, Stuart Place,
Bath BA2 3RG
Tel: 0117 923 1138/01225 334624
MC

Suzanne Sproston
Psychoanalytic Psychotherapist
7 Hampton Park, Redland, Bristol
BS6 6LG
Tel: 0117 909 4366
SIP, LCP

Paul Stallard
Cognitive Behavioural Psychotherapist
Dept Child & Family Psychiatry, Royal
United Hospital, Coombe Park, Bath
BA1 3NG
Tel: 01225 825075
BABCP

Yvonne Stevens
Cognitive Analytic Therapist
The Carthouse, Crossways Farm,
Heath House, Wedmore, Somerset
BS28 4UG
Tel: 01934 713693
ACAT

Christine Stones
Psychoanalytic Psychotherapist
5 Rutland House, Granby Hill,
Hotwells, Bristol BS8 1BS
Tel: 0117 929 0311
SIP

Jacqueline Stratford
Family Therapist
8 Owen Grove, Henleaze, Bristol
BS9 4EF
AFT

Iris Tute
Psychoanalytic Psychotherapist
46 Eastfield, Bristol BS9 4BE
Tel: 0117 962 4631
SIP

Chris Valentine
Humanistic and Integrative
Psychotherapist
42 Millmead Road, Oldfield Park, Bath
BA2 3JP
Tel: 01225 337372
BCPC

Francis Vine
NLP Psychotherapist
11 Argyle Place, Cliftonwood, Bristol
BS8 4RH
Tel: 0117 927 3205
ANLP

Deborah Webb
Biodynamic Psychotherapist
17 Rockcliffe Road, Bath BA2 6QN
Tel: 01225 461361
BTC

Martin Wells
Transactional Analysis Psychotherapist
11 Clare Road, Cotham, Bristol
BS6 5TB
Tel: 01179 247457
ITA

John Kirti Wheway
Humanistic and Integrative
Psychotherapist
5 Fairfield Road, Bristol BS6 5JN
Tel: 0117 985 0391
BCPC

Jan White
Family Therapist
Rosebank, Silver Street, Congresbury,
Bristol BS19 5EY
AFT

Chris Williams
Analytical Psychologist-Jungian Analyst
8 Stuart Place, Bath BA2 3RQ
Tel: 01225 463054/01225 427705
AJA

Frank Wills
Cognitive Psychotherapist
7 St Matthews Road, Cotham, Bristol
BS6 5TS
Tel: 0117 924 3574
BABCP

Alexandra Wilson
Psychoanalytic Psychotherapist
Flat 7, Abbey House, Abbey Green,
Bath BA1 1NR
Tel: 01225 336591
SIP

John Witt
Humanistic and Integrative
Psychotherapist
2 Fircliff Park, Portishead, Bristol
BS20 9HQ
Tel: 01275 818341
SPEC

Gaila Yariv
Psychoanalytic Psychotherapist
121 York Road, Montpelier, Bristol,
Avon BS6 5QG
Tel: 0117 955 1827
IPC

AYRSHIRE

Zena J Wight
Cognitive Behavioural Psychotherapist
Clinical Psychology Services,
Strathdoon House, 50 Racecourse
Road, Ayr KA7 2UZ
Tel: 01292 285607
BABCP

BEDFORDSHIRE

Eve Adler
Sexual and Marital Psychotherapist
301 Sharpenhoe Road, Streatley, Nr
Luton, Bedfordshire LU3 3PP
BASMT

Geoffrey Brown
Analytical Psychologist-Jungian Analyst
4 Coach House, Bromham Hall,
Bedford MK43 8HH
Tel: 01604 29696/01234 823 880
SAP

Rosemary Budgell
Integrative Psychotherapist
7 Blaydon Road, Luton, Bedfordshire
LU2 0RP
Tel: 01582 20052/01582 488808
RCSPC

Suzanne Clackson
Psychoanalytic Psychotherapist
21 Bradgate Road, Bedford MK40 3DE
Tel: 01234 356996
GUILD

Louise Clare
Psychoanalytic Psychotherapist
11 Warden Abbey, Bedford MK41 0SN
Tel: 01234 267405
GUILD

Anne Codd
Psychoanalytic Psychotherapist
The Old School House, High Street,
Lidlington, Bedfordshire MK43 0RN
Tel: 01525 406300
AGIP

Pauline Gilkes
Hypno-Psychotherapist
1 Mill Cottage, 101 Mill Road,
Sharnbrook, Bedford MK44 1NP
Tel: 01234 871533
NRHP

Chris Hannah
Systemic Psychotherapist
39 Summer Street, Slip End, Luton,
Beds LU1 4BL
Tel: 01582 422578
KCC

Clare Hannah
Systemic Psychotherapist
39 Summer Street, Slip End,
Bedfordshire LU1 4BL
Tel: 01582 422578
KCC

Christine Heath
Child Psychotherapist
Luton Child & Family Psychiatric Clinic,
Liverpool Rd Health Centre, 9 Mersey
Place, Liverpool Road, Luton, Beds
LU1 1HH
Tel: 01582 424 133/01462 700 021
ACP

Sue Hickman
Systemic Psychotherapist
11 Colchester Way, Bedford
MK41 8BG
Tel: 01234 215610/01234 343506
KCC

Anna K Huszcza
Cognitive Behavioural Psychotherapist
Psychology Department, University of
Luton, Park Square, Luton, Beds
LU1 1HJ
Tel: 01582 419880/01582 489302
BABCP

Duncan B Johnson
Hypno-Psychotherapist
12 Aldwyck Court, Riverside Close,
Bedford MK42 9DQ
Tel: 01234 212155
NRHP

Maureen McGuinness
Psychosynthesis Psychotherapist
38 Woodgreen Road, Luton,
Bedfordshire LU2 8BU
Tel: 01582 455681
IPS

Annabelle Paramour
Psychoanalytic Psychotherapist
30 Bushmead Avenue, Bedford
MK40 3QN
Tel: 01234 345553
CSP

Mary Peart
Psychosynthesis Psychotherapist
15 Dorrington Close, The Durlers,
Luton, Bedfordshire LU3 1XL
Tel: 01582 455272
IPS

Janet Philps
Child Psychotherapist
Bedford Child & Family Consultation
Clinic, Union Street Clinic, Union
Street, Bedford MK40 2SH
Tel: 01234 881365/01234 342437
ACP

Anne Rogers
Psychoanalytic Psychotherapist
32a Church End, Renhold, Bedfordshire
MK41 0LU
Tel: 01234 771595
AGIP

Lyn Sims
Family Psychotherapist
162a High Street, Cranfield,
Bedfordshire MK43 0EN
Tel: 01234 750871
AFT

Kitty Warburton
Integrative Psychotherapist
18 The Warren, Clapham, Bedfordshire
MK41 6DW
Tel: 01234 793362/01234 271938
RCSPC

BERKSHIRE

Janet Adams
Attachment-based Psychoanalytic
Psychotherapist
12 Valerie Court, Bath Road, Reading,
Berkshire RG1 6HP
Tel: 01734 676500
CAPP

Elke Asmus
Psychoanalytic Psychotherapist
27 Addington Road, Reading, Berkshire
RG1 5PZ
Tel: 0118 966 5557
LCP

Tamara Burnet-Smith
Humanistic Psychotherapist, Autogenic
Psychotherapist
71 Westfield Road, Caversham,
Reading, Berkshire RG4 8HL
Tel: 01734 479957
AHPP, BAFAT

Patricia Claxton
Psychoanalytic Psychotherapist
c/o Reading Clinic, 10 Eldon Road,
Reading, Berkshire RG1 4DH
Tel: 01734 502022
AGIP

Jane Collins
Sexual and Marital Psychotherapist
Magnolia House, Sunningdale, Ascot,
Berkshire SL5 0LW
BASMT

Jan Cooper
Family Therapist
5 Buckhurst Way, Earley, Reading
RG6 2RL
Tel: 01734 661543
AFT

Lou Corner
Psychoanalytic Psychotherapist
45 Kendrick Road, Reading, Berkshire
RG1 5EA
Tel: 01734 875501
BAP

Murray Cox
Group Analyst
Broadmoor Hospital, Crowthorne,
Berkshire RG11 7EG
Tel: 01344 773111
IGA

Jenny Coxwell-White
Integrative Psychotherapist
113 New Road, North Ascot,
Berkshire SL5 8PZ
Tel: 01344 884142
CCHP

John Eaton
Hypno-Psychotherapist, NLP
Psychotherapist
Waterloo House, 158 London Road,
Newbury, Berkshire RG13 2AX
Tel: 01635 44444
NSHAP, ANLP

Janet Glynn-Treble
Child Psychotherapist
Highlands, Barkham Hill, Barkham,
Wokingham, Berkshire RG11 4TG
Tel: 01734 792320
ACP

Thelma Griffiths
Transpersonal Psychotherapist
40 The Crescent, Reading, Berks
RG6 2NN
Tel: 01734 668092
CCPE

Rex Haigh
Group Analyst
Winterbourne House, 53-55 Argyle
Road, Reading, Berkshire RG7 3UE
Tel: 01734 332205
IGA

Roger Hepburn
Hypno-Psychotherapist
67 Redhatch Drive, Earley, Reading,
Berks RG6 5QN
Tel: 01734 860551
NRHP

Elizabeth Holder
Child Psychotherapist
Hillview, Lower Inkpen, Newbury,
Berks RG15 0DX
Tel: 01488 668544
ACP

Patrick Hughes
Group Analyst
12 Instow Road, Earley, Reading
RG6 2QJ
Tel: 01734 873049
IGA

Camilla Johnson-Smith
Group Humanistic Psychotherapist
Rainbow's End, Cock Lane, Southend
Bradfield, Nr Reading RG7 6HN
Tel: 01734 744650
LCP, AHPP

Jonathan Kanakam
Hypno-Psychotherapist
50 Farnham Road, Slough, Berks
SL1 3TA
Tel: 01753 552976
NSHAP

John J King
NLP Psychotherapist
101 Hillberry, Birch Hill, Bracknell,
Berks RG12 7ZY
Tel: 01344 53736
ANLP

Wendy Klein
Family Therapist
12 St James Close, Pangbourne,
Reading RG8 7AP
Tel: 01734 842856
AFT

Jane Knowles
Group Analyst
7 Albert Road, Caversham, Reading,
Berks RG4 7AN
Tel: 01734 561250/01734 478872
IGA

Reinhard Kowalski
Psychosynthesis Psychotherapist
16 King Edward Street, Slough, Berks
SL1 2QS
Tel: 01753 869755/01753 824134
IPS

Sylvia Mackinnon
Hypno-Psychotherapist
27 Harkness Road, Burnham, Slough,
Berks SL1 7BL
Tel: 01628 665467
NSHAP

David McDonald
Family Psychotherapist
45 Woodlands Road, Sonning
Common, Reading RG4 9TD;
23 Banbury Road, Oxford OX2 6PD
Tel: 01734 722654/01865 56097
IFT

Tony McGregor
Hypno-Psychotherapist
127 Kingsley Close, Shaw, Newbury,
Berkshire RG14 2EB
Tel: 01635 34231
NRHP

Jane Melton
Cognitive Analytic Therapist
46 Clifton Road, Wokingham,
Berkshire, RG41 1NB
Tel: 01189 771409
ACAT

John Parr
Transactional Analysis Psychotherapist
Norcot House, 131 Norcot Road,
Tilehurst, Reading RG30 6BS
Tel: 01734 453388
ITA

Michael Pritchard
Psychoanalytic Psychotherapist
11 Thames Avenue, Reading, Berks
RG1 8DT
Tel: 01734 318810/01734 587749
BAP

Michelle Quoilin-Lebrun
Biodynamic Psychotherapist
4 Mornington Avenue, Finchamstead,
Wokingham, Surrey RG11 4UE
Tel: 01734 730870
BTC

Janet Richards
Psychoanalytic Psychotherapist
35 Bulmershe Road, Reading, Berks
RG1 5RH
Tel: 01734 269545
GUILD

Gina Selby
Personal Construct Psychotherapist
Ships Cottage, Ashford Hill, Newbury,
Berks RG15 8BD
Tel: 01734 811793
CPCP

Patricia Short
Systemic Psychotherapist
72 Addison Road, Reading RG1 8EG
Tel: 01734 590720
KCC

Basil Smith
Psychoanalytic Psychotherapist
95 Northcourt Avenue, Reading, Berks
RG2 7HG
Tel: 01734 874045
SIP, BAP

Laurie Tytel
Analytical Psychotherapist
19 Grosvenor Road, Caversham,
Reading, Berks RG4 0EJ
Tel: 01734 470 625
LCP

Arlene Vetere
Family Therapist
55 The Avenue, Mortimer, Reading
RG7 3QU
Tel: 01734 332393
AFT

Susan Wagstaff
Family Therapist
7 Melrose Avenue, Reading, Berkshire
RG6 2BN
Tel: 01734 666018
AFT

BORDERS

Anne Hunt Overzee
Core Process Psychotherapist
Crookwelcome, Ettrick, Selkirk
TD7 5HT
KI

BUCKINGHAMSHIRE

Ghislaine Adams
Hypno-Psychotherapist
41 London Road, Stony Stratford,
Milton Keynes MK11 1JQ
Tel: 01908 566362
NSHAP

Ivor Antao
Group Analyst
45 Grenville Green, Aylesbury, Bucks
HP21 8HB
IGA

Julie C Beech
Cognitive Psychotherapist
Campbell Centre, Milton Keynes
Hospital, Standing Way, Eaglestone,
Milton Keynes, Bucks MK6 5NG
Tel: 01908 243256
BABCP

Elaine Bollinghaus
Psychoanalytic Marital Psychotherapist
'Loudhams', Burtons Lane, Little
Chalfont, Buckinghamshire HP8 4BS
Tel: 01494 765947
TMSI

Elizabeth Burns
Family Therapist
11 Green End Street, Aston Clinton,
Aylesbury, Bucks HP22 5JE
IFT

Barbara Butcher
Hypno-Psychotherapist
35 Lowfield Way, Hazlemere,
Buckinghamshire HP15 7RR
Tel: 01494 814306
NSHAP

Harriet B Calvert
Psychoanalytic Psychotherapist
Riemore, Bangors Road South, Iver,
Buckinghamshire SL0 0AY
Tel: 01753 630911/01753 631021
LCP

Wendela Clarke
Hypno-Psychotherapist
The Village House, Nicol Road,
Chalfont St Peter, Buckinghamshire
SL9 9ND
Tel: 01753 885618
NRHP

Anne M Dale
Hypno-Psychotherapist
Little Grove, Grove Lane, Chesham,
Buckinghamshire HP5 3QQ
Tel: 01494 776066
NSHAP

Marianne De Groot
Sexual and Marital Psychotherapist
Antlers, 52 Longfield Drive, Amersham,
Buckinghamshire HP6 5HE
BASMT

Jan Galloway
Sexual and Marital Psychotherapist
Gyldernscroft, 1 Henley Road, Marlow,
Bucks SL7 2BZ
BASMT

Carol A Gilboy
Cognitive Behavioural Psychotherapist
C10 (Clinical Psychology Services), The
Campbell Centre, The Hospital
Campus, Eaglestone, Milton Keynes
MK6 5NG
Tel: 01908 243982
BABCP

Pauline Golding
Hypno-Psychotherapist
Kingsgate, 32 The Rowans, Gerrards
Cross, Bucks SL9 8SE
Tel: 01753 883062
NRHP

Susan Harrison
Sexual and Marital Psychotherapist
Briar Patch, Little London Green,
Oakley, Aylesbury, Bucks HP18 9QL
BASMT

Alison Jefferies
Integrative Psychotherapist
The Barn, Love Lane, Iver, Bucks
SL0 9QZ
Tel: 01753 630509
MC

Mary Newson
Psychosynthesis Psychotherapist
The Dower Cottage, 5 Little
Shardeloes, Amersham,
Buckinghamshire HP7 0EF
Tel: 01494 727 141
IPS

Lisa Elaine Palmer
Cognitive Behavioural Psychotherapist
Psychotherapy Dept, Tindal Centre,
Bierton Road, Aylesbury, Bucks
HP20 1HU
Tel: 01296 393363 ext 364
BABCP

Marion Panchkowry
Group Analyst
Bramble Cottage, Dunton, Nr
Buckingham MK18 3LW
Tel: 01296 393 363 x 525/01525 240
083
IGA

Cynthia Pollard
Cognitive Analytic Therapist
Mill End, Mill Lane, Gerrards Cross,
Bucks SL9 8AZ
Tel: 01753 885164
ACAT

Ruth Reay
Family Therapist
Divisional Director, Social Work,
Buckinghamshire College, Queen
Alexandra Road, High Wycombe,
Bucks HP11 2JZ
Tel: 01494 522141
AFT

Michael Reddy
Transactional Analysis Psychotherapist
90 Church Road, Woburn Sands
MK17 8TR
Tel: 01908 584944
ITA

Rachel Reidy
Cognitive Analytic Therapist
Woodbine Cottage, 81 Totteridge
Lane, High Wycombe, Bucks
HP13 7QA;
The Surgery, 65 Desborough Avenue,
High Wycombe, Bucks HP11 2SD
Tel: 01494 526006/01494 527597
ACAT

Elizabeth J Riley
Sexual and Marital Psychotherapist
Field Place, Dunsmore, Wendover,
Bucks HP22 6QH
BASMT

Jeff Roberts
Group Analyst
Hazel Cottage, 42 Stubbs Wood,
Chesham Bois, Bucks HP6 6EX
Tel: 0171 377 7962 0171 935 3103/
01494 726317
IGA

Jane Roy
Sexual and Marital Psychotherapist
10 Faraday Drive, Shenley Lodge,
Milton Keynes MK5 7DA
BASMT

Anne Shearer
Hypno-Psychotherapist
Beechgrove, Broughton, By Biggar,
Lanark MK12 6HQ
Tel: 0141 553 2353
NRHP

Monika Steiner
Psychoanalytic Psychotherapist
13 Lansdown Road, Chalfont St Peter,
Buckinghamshire SL9 9SP
Tel: 01753 882112
IPSS

Andrea Watson
Child Psychotherapist
Aylesbury Child and Family Psychiatric
Service, Brookside, Station Way,
Aylesbury, Bucks
Tel: 01296 394388/01865 243491
ACP

Eleanor Wigglesworth
Child Psychotherapist
Department of Child Mental Health,
High Wycombe Clinic, 56 Amersham
Hill, High Wycombe, Bucks HP13 6PQ
Tel: 01494 535727/01494 881801
ACP

Diana Young
Transpersonal Psychotherapist
Damien House, 23 High Street, Great
Missenden, Buckinghamshire
HP16 9AA
Tel: 01494 866 440
CCPE

CAMBRIDGESHIRE

Evelyn Adey
Psychoanalytic Psychotherapist
8 Aylestone Road, Cambridge
CB4 1HF
Tel: 01223 627311
LCP

Ian Alister
Analytical Psychologist-Jungian Analyst
56 Hertford Street, Cambridge
CB4 3AQ
Tel: 01223 321684
SAP

Pamela Arriens
Psychoanalytic Psychotherapist
3 Middlemoor Road, Whittlesford,
Cambridge CB2 4PB
Tel: 01223 832877/01223 834665 (f)
CSP

Roger Bacon
Psychoanalytic Psychotherapist
112 Canterbury Street, Cambridge
CB4 3QE
Tel: 01223 560262
GUILD

Wendy Bratherton
Analytical Psychologist-Jungian Analyst
34 Rustat Road, Cambridge CB1 3QT
Tel: 01223 240491
SAP

Michael Briant
Psychoanalytic Psychotherapist
Kingfisher Cottage, 1 Church Rate
Walk, Cambridge CB3 9HJ
Tel: 01223 332865/01223 464611
GUILD

Steve Briant
Psychoanalytic Psychotherapist
57 Victoria Road, Cambridge
CB4 3BW
Tel: 01223 327165
CSP

Johanna Brieger
Analytical Psychologist-Jungian Analyst
29 Ventress Farm Court, Cherry
Hinton Road, Cambridge CB1 4HD;
24 Oxford Road, London NW6 5SL
Tel: 0171 328 9430/01223 213639
SAP, BAP

Lee Brosan
Cognitive Behavioural Psychotherapist
Psychiatric Outpatients (S3), Box 175,
Addenbrooke's Hospital, Cambridge
CB2 2QQ
Tel: 01223 217944
BABCP

Jane E Buckley
Analytical Psychologist-Jungian Analyst
92 Grantchester Meadows, Newnham,
Cambridge CB3 9JN
Tel: 01223 352182
BAP

Sally Byford
Biodynamic Psychotherapist
81 Gwydir Street, Cambridge CB1 2LG
Tel: 01223 321436
BTC

Angela Cameron
Integrative Psychotherapist
18 Clare Street, Cambridge CB4 3BY
Tel: 0223 61043
RCSPC

John Carlisle
Analytical Psychologist-Jungian Analyst
Kilderkin, Couldson Lane, Chipstead,
Surrey CB3 3QH
Tel: 017375 53557
SAP

Samantha Carr
Systemic Psychotherapist
17 Muntjac Close, Eaton Socon, St
Neots, Cambridgeshire PE19 3QH
Tel: 0480 474552
KCC

Jenny Corrigall
Psychoanalytic Psychotherapist
10 Willow Walk, Cambridge CB1 1LA
Tel: 01223 361703
CSP

Judy Davies
Psychoanalytic Psychotherapist
12 Barton Road, Cambridge CB3 9JZ
Tel: 01223 515526
CSP

Sedwell Diggle
Analytical Psychologist-Jungian Analyst
92 Canterbury Street, Cambridge
CB4 3QE
Tel: 01223 351310
SAP

Margaret Dyson
Integrative Psychotherapist, Body
Psychotherapist
4 Kimberley Road, Cambridge
CB4 1HH
Tel: 01223 367311
MC

Margaret Farrell
Psychoanalytic Psychotherapist
The Old Stores, 5 High Street,
Grantchester, Cambridge CB3 9NF
Tel: 01223 69894/01223 841255
GUILD, CSP

Maryline Gagnere
Biodynamic Psychotherapist
6 Chalky Road, Great Abington,
Cambridgeshire CB1 6HT
Tel: 01223 893675
BTC

Vicki Gardiner
Analytical Psychologist-Jungian Analyst
35 Walcot Walk, Netherton,
Peterborough PE3 9QF
Tel: 01733 266213
SAP

Valerie Gentry
Psychoanalytic Psychotherapist
30 Hinton Avenue, Cambridge
CB1 4AS
Tel: 01223 212821
CSP

Leila Gordon
Psychoanalytic Psychotherapist
37 Herbert Street, Cambridge
CB4 1AQ
Tel: 01223 367912
CSP

Sarah Greaves
Psychoanalytic Psychotherapist
33 Eltisley Avenue, Cambridge
CB3 9JQ
Tel: 01223 354526
GUILD, CSP

Hazel Guest
Humanistic Psychotherapist
44 Beaufort Place, Thompson's Lane,
Cambridge CB5 8AG
Tel: 01223 369148
AHPP

Liz Guild
Psychoanalytic Psychotherapist
198 Sturton Street, Cambridge
CB1 2DW
Tel: 01223 311042/01223 339166
PA

David Hall
Psychoanalytic Psychotherapist
47 Cavendish Avenue, Cambridge
CB1 4UR
Tel: 01223 249 732
GUILD

Liz Hardy
Psychoanalytic Psychotherapist
90 Tenison Road, Cambridge
CB1 2DW
Tel: 01223 67850
PA

Gillian Harrison
Family Therapist
21 Millington Road, Cambridge
CB3 9HW
IFT

Eric Haynes
Hypno-Psychotherapist
33A Bridewell Road, Cherry Hinton,
Cambridge CB1 4EN
Tel: 01223 214281
NSHAP

Louise Holland
Jungian Child Analyst, Child
Psychotherapist
21 Richmond Road, Cambridge
CB4 3PP
Tel: 01223 353029
SAP, ACP

Jennifer J Hurley
Cognitive Behavioural Psychotherapist
22 Green End, Fen Ditton, Cambridge
CB5 8SX
Tel: 01223 292124/01223 217944
BABCP

Eric Hutchison
Analytical Psychologist-Jungian Analyst
77 Long Road, Cambridge CB2 2HE
Tel: 01223 840381
BAP

Tony Jaffa
Family Therapist
26 Lyndewode Road, Cambridge
CB1 2HN
Tel: 01223 64510
AFT

Mimi Kilgour
NLP Psychotherapist
332 Eastfield Road, Peterborough,
Cambridgeshire PE1 4RA
Tel: 01733 312900
ANLP

Lucy King
Psychoanalytic Psychotherapist
43 Chesterton Road, Cambridge
CB4 3AN
Tel: 01223 367742
CSP, PA

Liebe Klug
Psychoanalytic Psychotherapist
70 Cavendish Avenue, Cambridge
CB1 4UT
Tel: 01223 248959
CSP

Daphne Lambert
Analytical Psychologist-Jungian Analyst
Binfield, 67 High Street, Girton,
Cambridge CB3 0QD
Tel: 01223 276299
SAP, BAP

Clara Lew
Psychoanalytic Psychotherapist
20 Owlstone Road, Cambridge
CB3 9JH
Tel: 01223 356744
CSP

Paul Lewington
Family Therapist
Brookside Family Consultation Clinic,
Douglas House, 18d Trumpington
Road, Cambridge CB2 2AH
Tel: 01223 66501
IFT

Bill Lintott
Group Analyst
7 Haverhill Road, Stapleford,
Cambridge CB2 5BX
Tel: 01223 69894/01223 842008
IGA

Peter Lomas
Psychoanalytic Psychotherapist
41 Beaulands Close, Cambridge
CB4 1JA
Tel: 01223 354851
CSP

Veronica McDouall
Psychoanalytic Psychotherapist
119 Thornton Road, Cambridge
CB3 0NE;
71 Bridge Street, Cambridge CB2 1UR
Tel: 01223 576648/01223 313515
IPC

Michael Miller
Psychoanalytic Psychotherapist
11 Bishops Road, Trumpington, Cambs
CB2 2NQ
Tel: 01223 69894/01223 845030
GUILD

Sian Morgan
Psychoanalytic Psychotherapist
7 Aylestone Road, Cambridge
CB4 1HF
Tel: 01223 363750
CSP, GUILD

Duncan Moss
Cognitive Behavioural Psychotherapist
The Mill House, Brookfields Hospital,
Mill Road, Cambridge CB1 5DZ
Tel: 01223 568956/7/01223 881272
BABCP

Lesley Murdin
Psychoanalytic Psychotherapist
32 Belvoir Road, Cambridge CB4 1JJ;
Flat 11, 115 Westbourne Terrace,
London W2
Tel: 01223 312848/0171 706 8939
IPC

Carol Naughton
Psychoanalytic Psychotherapist
25 Alpha Road, Cambridge CB4 3DQ
Tel: 01223 352871
CSP

Margaret Nelson
Existential Psychotherapist
37 Annesdale, Ely, Cambridgeshire
CB7 4BN
Tel: 01353 662659
RCSPC

Jean Pain
Hypno-Psychotherapist, NLP
Psychotherapist
7 Way Lane, Waterbeach,
Cambridgeshire CB5 9NQ
Tel: 01223 860 356
NRHP, ANLP

James Pollard
Attachment-based Psychoanalytic
Psychotherapist
60 Montague Road, Cambridge
CB4 1BX
Tel: 01223 314398
CAPP

Rosemary Randall
Psychoanalytic Psychotherapist
113 Gwydir Street, Cambridge
CB1 2LG
Tel: 01223 313539
CSP

Alun Reynolds
Humanistic Psychotherapist
12 Orchard Avenue, Cambridge
CB4 2AH
Tel: 01223 461744
AHPP

Carole Robinson
Psychoanalytic Psychotherapist
10 College Crescent, Haslingfield,
Cambridge CB3 7LZ
Tel: 01223 871457
CSP

Glenys Scott
Psychoanalytic Psychotherapist
Hill Farm, 128 Green End, Comberton,
Cambs CB3 7DY
Tel: 01223 262925
GUILD

Vivienne Serpell
Sexual and Marital Psychotherapist
Scotts, High Street, Whittlesford,
Cambridge CB2 4LT
BASMT

Michael J A Simpson
Analytical Psychologist-Jungian Analyst
2 Cottons Field, Dry Drayton,
Cambridge CB3 8DG
Tel: 01954 780558
BAP

Fiona Sinclair
Psychoanalytic Psychotherapist
Kings Cottage, 7 High Street,
Grantchester CB3 9NF
Tel: 01223 844497
PA

Gillian Smith
Psychoanalytic Psychotherapist
5 Alpha Terrace, Trumpington,
Cambridge CB2 2HS
Tel: 01223 842073
CSP

Hanna Taussig
Psychoanalytic Psychotherapist
296 Hills Road, Cambridge CB2 2QG
Tel: 01223 246643
GUILD

Gillian Todd
Cognitive Psychotherapist
6 Hauxton Road, Trumpington,
Cambridge CB2 2LT
Tel: 01223 841151
BABCP

Patricia Touton-Victor
Psychoanalytic Psychotherapist
18 Bateman Street, Cambridge
CB2 1NB
Tel: 01223 64793
PA

Barbara Tregear
Psychodrama Psychotherapist
79 Gough Way, Cambridge CB3 9LN
Tel: 01223 357221
BPDA

Marina Voikhanskaya
Psychoanalytic Psychotherapist
20 Garden Walk, Cambridge CB4 3EN
Tel: 01223 67747
GUILD

Heather Warwick
Sexual and Marital Psychotherapist
31 Sedley Taylor Road, Cambridge
CB2 2PN
Tel: 01223 245380
BASMT

Gill Westland
Humanistic Psychotherapist, Integrative
Psychotherapist
8 Wetenhall Road, Cambridge
CB1 3AG
Tel: 01223 214658
AHPP

CHANNEL ISLANDS

Christopher Farmer
Psychodrama Psychotherapist
La Couture, Belval Road, Vale,
Guernsey, Channel Islands GY3 5LW
Tel: 01841 45334
BPDA

Rosemarie Lucas
Cognitive Behavioural Psychotherapist
La Lourderie, Rue de la Lourderie,
St Clement, Jersey, JE2 6SG
Tel: 01534 852506
BABCP

Maureen Nelson
Sexual and Marital Psychotherapist
Relate, 2 St Mark's Lane, St Helier,
Jersey
BASMT

Miranda O'Donnell
Sexual and Marital Psychotherapist
Le Vieux Rouvet, St Saviours,
Guernsey, GY7 9NB
BASMT

CHESHIRE

Nicholas Benefield
Analytical Psychologist-Jungian Analyst
East House, Tattenhall Hall, Tattenhall,
Nr Chester, Cheshire CH3 9PX
Tel: 01829 770692
BAP

Linda Berman
Psychoanalytic Psychotherapist
'Arncliffe', South Downs Road,
Bowdon, Altrincham, Cheshire
WA14 3DR
Tel: 0161 928 1388
NWIDP

Mary Berry
Sexual and Marital Psychotherapist
24 Leafield Road, Disley, Stockport,
Cheshire SK12 2JF
BASMT

John Bird
Psychoanalytic Psychotherapist
17 Macclesfield Road, Wilmslow,
Cheshire SK9 2AA
Tel: 01625 523292
NWIDP

Dascha Boronat
Group Analyst
5 Victoria Avenue, Cheadle Hulme,
Cheshire SK8 5DJ
Tel: 0161 941 5673/0161 488 4504
IGA

June Brereton
Transactional Analysis Psychotherapist
'Pendene', 116 Stocks Lane,
Stalybridge, Cheshire SK15 2TQ
Tel: 0161 303 7925
ITA

Louise Brooks
Integrative Psychotherapist
10 Hallefield Crescent, Macclesfield,
Cheshire SK11 7BL
NSAP

Joanna Burrows
Family Therapist
3 Mount Pleasant, Rainow, Nr
Macclesfield, Cheshire SK10 5TJ
AFT

Josie Butcher
Family Psychotherapist
Nantwich Health Centre, Beam Street,
Nantwich, Cheshire CW5 5NX
BASMT

Elaine Clarke
Psychoanalytic Psychotherapist
8 Windmill Lane, Preston-on-the-Hill,
Warrington, Cheshire WA4 4AZ
LPDO

Gloria Collins
Psychoanalytic Psychotherapist
Halton Psychotherapy and Family
Services, Thorn Road Clinic, Thorn
Road, Runcorn, Cheshire WA7 5HQ
Tel: 01928 575073
LPDO

Graham Cooper
Psychoanalytic Psychotherapist
Victoria Infirmary, Northwich,
Cheshire CW8 1AW
Tel: 01606 48316/01606 74331
LPDO

Rhoda Dorndorf
Psychoanalytic Psychotherapist
10 Worthington Close, Henbury,
Macclesfield SK11 9NS
LPDO

Kay Farquharson
Sexual and Marital Psychotherapist
Oak Lodge, Windmill Lane, Appleton,
Warrington, Cheshire WA4 5JN
Tel: 01925 262767
BASMT

Freda Fitton
Gestalt Psychotherapist
15 The Beeches, Upton, Chester
CH2 1PE
Tel: 01244 348843
GPTI, MET

Tom Foxen
Cognitive Behavioural Psychotherapist
'Oaklands', 196a Newton Road,
Lowton, Nr Warrington, Cheshire
WA3 2AQ
Tel: 01942 886807/01942 671319
BABCP

Bryan W J Geldeard
Psychoanalytic Psychotherapist
Pine Day Unit, Halton General
Hospital, East Lane, Runcorn, Cheshire
WA7 2DA
Tel: 01928 714567 x 3175
LPDO

Julie Glynn
Psychoanalytic Psychotherapist
3 Fletcher Street, Warrington,
Cheshire WA4 6PY
LPDO

Barbara A Green
Psychoanalytic Psychotherapist
Stockport Psychology Services,
Stepping Hill Hospital, Poplar Grove,
Stockport SK2 7JE
Tel: 0161 419 5793
LPDO

Terence Greenfield
Hypno-Psychotherapist
First Floor, 157 Ashley Road, Hale,
Altrincham, Cheshire WA14 3UW
Tel: 0161 928 3898/0161 929 0361
NRHP

Francesca Hannah
Transactional Analysis Psychotherapist
29a Alan Road, Heaton Moor,
Stockport SK4 4LE
Tel: 0161 431 5968
ITA

Ann Haworth
Psychoanalytic Psychotherapist
Gifford Mount, East Downs Road,
Bowden, Nr Altrincham, Cheshire
WA14 2LG
Tel: 0161 928 7101
LPDO

Robin Hobbes
Transactional Analysis Psychotherapist
6 Clarence Road, Hale, Altrincham,
Cheshire WA15 8SG
Tel: 0161 928 9997
ITA

Jannie Hollins
Child Psychotherapist
Tattenhall Hall, High Street, Tattenhall,
Cheshire CH3 9PX;
Child and Family Support Service,
Adcote House, Colombia Road,
Oxton, Birkenhead, Wirral L43 6TU
Tel: 0151 670 0031/01829 770654
ACP

Patricia Hunt
Psychoanalytic Psychotherapist, Sexual
and Marital Psychotherapist
Rose Cottage, Foxwist Green,
Whitegate, nr Northwich, Cheshire
CW8 2BJ
Tel: 01606 882170
NWIDP, BASMT

Joyce Kilgour
Family Psychotherapist
8 Moss Lane, Bramhall, Stockport
SK7 1EH
Tel: 0161 439 7982
AFT

Kate Kirk
Psychodrama Psychotherapist
222a Chester Road, Helsby, Frodsham,
Warrington, Lancs WA6 0AW
Tel: 01606 852347
BPDA

Nick V Kirkland-Handley
Psychoanalytic Psychotherapist
Dept of Psychological Therapies &
Counselling, Garden Place Clinic,
Sankey Street, Warrington
Tel: 01925 651188 x 3804
LPDO

E Lawrence
Sexual and Marital Psychotherapist
Hillcroft, Park Lane, Little Bollington,
Altrincham, Cheshire WA14 4TH
BASMT

Denis Lee
Family Psychotherapist
9 Thirlmere, Macclesfield, Cheshire
SK11 7XY
Tel: 01625 614115
AFT

Ken Lewis
Cognitive Behavioural Psychotherapist
7 Brown Heath Road, Waverton,
Chester CH3 7PP
Tel: 01244 336774
BABCP

Diana Lilley
Group Analyst
Thorn Lea House, 32 Grappenhall
Lane, Stockton Heath, Warrington
WA4 2AG
Tel: 01925 268322
IGA

Ann Littlewood
Psychodynamic Psychotherapist
69 Oldfield Road, Altrincham, Cheshire
WA14 4BH
HIP

Carol Lucas
Transactional Analysis Psychotherapist
Strathmore House, 18 Derby Road,
Heaton Moor, Stockport, Cheshire
SK4 4NE
Tel: 0161 443 1628
ITA

Helen McCormick
Psychoanalytic Psychotherapist
13 Lyceum Way, Coppenhall, Crewe,
Cheshire CW1 3YF
Tel: 01270 256397
WMIP

Jeannie McIntee
Psychoanalytic Psychotherapist
Chester Therapy Centre, 20 Walpole
Street, Chester CH3 5PT
Tel: 01244 390121
LPDO

Molly McKay
Cognitive Behavioural Psychotherapist
Psychology Department, Warrington
Comm Health Care Trust, Winnick
Hospital, Winwick, Warrington,
Cheshire WA2 8RR
Tel: 01925 655221
BABCP

Stuart McNab
Psychoanalytic Psychotherapist
58 Parkland Close, Appleton Thorn,
Warrington WA4 4RH
Tel: 01925 601622
LPDO

Denis E Neill
Family Therapist
19 Constable Drive, Wilmslow,
Cheshire SK9 2NS
Tel: 01625 526992
AFT

Jaqui Nevin
Psychoanalytic Psychotherapist
Psychology Department, Watling
Street Clinic, Northwich, Cheshire
CW9 5ET
Tel: 01606 45626
LPDO

Sheena Pollet
Psychoanalytic Psychotherapist
Halton Psychotherapy and Family
Services, Thorn Road Clinic, Runcorn,
Cheshire WA7 5HQ
Tel: 01928 575073
LPDO

Kenneth Redgrave
Hypno-Psychotherapist
11 Parker Avenue, Hartford,
Northwich, Cheshire CW8 3AH
Tel: 01606 74874
NRHP

Janette G Sexton
Psychoanalytic Psychotherapist
West Cheshire NHS Trust, West
Cheshire Hospital, Liverpool Road,
Chester
Tel: 01244 365 1000/01244 364 4893
LPDO

Heather Szabo
Psychoanalytic Psychotherapist
7 Water Tower Street, Chester
CH1 2AE
Tel: 01244 348183
LCP

Sue Taberner
Sexual and Marital Psychotherapist
20 Cogshall Lane, Comberbach,
Northwich, Cheshire CW9 6BS
BASMT

Marjorie Thoburn
Sexual and Marital Psychotherapist
White Gables, Vicarage Hill, Helsby,
Cheshire WA6 9AD
BASMT

Sandra Thomas
Psychodynamic Psychotherapist
27 Heath Road, Stockport, Cheshire
SK2 6JJ
HIP

Ann Tunwell
Sexual and Marital Psychotherapist
Waulkmill Cottage, Ingersley Vale,
Bollington, Macclesfield SK10 5BP
BASMT

Linda Van Schoor
Family Psychotherapist
58 St Mary's Road, Sale, Cheshire
IFT

Lynne Webster
Sexual and Marital Psychotherapist
77 Woodford Road, Bramhall,
Stockport, Cheshire SK7 1JR
BASMT

P G Wells
Psychodynamic Psychotherapist
High Trees, Dark Lane, Henbury,
Manchester SK11 8PE
Tel: 01625 420872
LPDO

Enid Whittam
Integrative Psychotherapist
1 Dorfold Way, Upton-by-Chester,
Chester CH2 1QS
NSAP

Verina Wilde
Cognitive Behavioural Psychotherapist
40 Little Aston Close, Macclesfield,
Cheshire SK10 2UE
Tel: 01625 431 483
BABCP

Mary Wilson
Cognitive Behavioural Psychotherapist
3 Back Jodrell Street, New Mills,
Stockport, Cheshire SK12 3HL
Tel: 01663 745219/0850 297276
BABCP

CLEVELAND

Sue Firth
Psychoanalytic Psychotherapist
86 High Street, Great Broughton,
Middlesbrough, Cleveland TS9 7EG
NAAP

Jolien Haveman
Cognitive Psychotherapist
Woodlands Road Clinic, Woodlands
Road, Middlesbrough, Cleveland
TS1 3BL
Tel: 01642 247311
BABCP

Mary B Heller
Psychoanalytic Psychotherapist
Woodlands Road Clinic,
Middlesbrough, Cleveland TS1 3BL
Tel: 01642 247311
NAAP

Marjorie Homer
Integrative Psychotherapist
2 Hebron Road, Middlesbrough,
Cleveland TS5 6RD
Tel: 01642 814270
SCPC

Christine Lister-Ford
Transactional Analysis Psychotherapist,
Integrative Psychotherapist
Stockton Centre for Psychotherapy, 77
Acklam Road, Thornaby-On-Tees,
Cleveland TS17 7BD
Tel: 01642 649004
ITA, MET, SCPC

Doris McColl
Sexual and Marital Psychotherapist
4 Leven Road, Yarm, Cleveland
TS15 9HB
BASMT

Jennifer McNamara
Integrative Psychotherapist
Stockton Centre for Psychotherapy
and Counselling, 77 Acklam Road,
Thornaby-On-Tees, Cleveland
TS17 7BD
Tel: 01642 649004
ITA, MET, SCPC

David Midgley
Transactional Analysis Psychotherapist
13 Barker Road, Linthorpe,
Middlesbrough, Cleveland TS5 5EW
Tel: 01642 821254
ITA

Sue Richardson
Attachment-based Psychoanalytic
Psychotherapist
22 Queens Road, Middlesbrough,
Cleveland TS5 6EE
Tel: 01642 817658
CAPP

Susi Strang
NLP Psychotherapist
Sundial House, 29 High Street, Skelton,
Saltburn by the Sea, Cleveland
TS12 2EF
Tel: 01287 654 175
ANLP

Gerard Szary
NLP Psychotherapist
98 Oxbridge Lane, Stockton on Tees,
Cleveland TS18 4HW
Tel: 01642 678 653
ANLP

Rose Thacker
Transactional Analysis Psychotherapist
17 Leven Street, Saltburn, Cleveland
TS12 1JY
Tel: 0287 622947
ITA

Steve Williams
Cognitive Psychotherapist
The Spinney, Hutton Village,
Guisborough, Cleveland TS14 8EP
Tel: 01287 637416/01287 632206
BABCP

CLWYD

Ian Boardman
Group Analyst
Garden House, Park Street, Denbigh,
Clwyd
Tel: 0174 581 2871/0174 581 5332
IGA

Linda Butler
Cognitive Behavioural Psychotherapist
Child and Family Service, 31 Grosvenor
Road, Wrexham, Clywd LL11 1BS
Tel: 01978 350050
BABCP

Patricia Gillan
Cognitive Behavioural Psychotherapist
North Wales Medical Centre, Queen's
Road, Llandudno, Gwynedd LL30 1UD;
10 Harley Street, London W1N 1AA
Tel: 0171 436 5252/01492 879031
BABCP

L Hughes
Psychoanalytic Psychotherapist
Tan-y-Bondo, 5a Upper Clwyd Street,
Ruthin, Clwyd LL15 1HY
NWIDP

Alun Jones
Psychoanalytic Psychotherapist
3 Park View, Old Wrexham Road,
Gresford, Wrexham LL12 8UB
LPDO

Celia M Prussia
Psychoanalytic Psychotherapist
The Health Centre, Poplar Avenue,
Gresford, Wrexham, Clwyd LL13 8EP
Tel: 01978 852208
LPDO

Jean Stevens
Hypno-Psychotherapist
Holmlea, 48 Clwyd Park, Kinmel Bay,
Rhyl, Clwyd LL18 5HH
Tel: 01745 342544
NRHP

Christine Uden
Transactional Analysis Psychotherapist
Ty Gwyn, Pentrellyncymmer,
Cerrigydrudion, Corwen Clwyd
LL21 9TU
Tel: 0149 082 639
ITA

Anne Wheeler
Psychoanalytic Psychotherapist
North East Wales Inst of Higher
Education, Postal Point 11, Plas Coch,
Mold Road, Wrexham, Clwyd
LL11 2AW
Tel: 01978 290666
LPDO

Beck Williams
Behavioural Psychotherapist
19 Berry Street, Conwy, Gwynedd
LL32 8DG
Tel: 01492 580612
BABCP

CORNWALL

Suzanne Coombs
Psychoanalytic Psychotherapist
'Garth', Steeple Lane, Trelyon Downs,
Cornwall TR26 2AP
Tel: 01736 795032
GUILD

William Cramer
Psychodrama Psychotherapist
Trevillick Cottage, Trevillick, Tintagel,
Cornwall PL34 0DN
Tel: 01840 770691
BPDA

Fay Fransella
Personal Construct Psychotherapist
The Sail Loft, Mulberry Quay, Market
Strand, Falmouth, Cornwall TR11 3HD
Tel: 01326 314871
CPCP

Jeanne Gimblett
Cognitive Behavioural Psychotherapist
Highland Cottage, St Breward, Bodmin,
Cornwall PL30 4NU
Tel: 01208 850597
BABCP

Roz Grigg
Core Process Psychotherapist
10 North Hill Park, St Austell,
Cornwall PL25 4BJ
Tel: 01726 61675
KI

Christine Hammond-Small
Psychoanalytic Psychotherapist
Tredavoe Lodge, Tredavoe, Penzance,
Cornwall TR20 8TN
Tel: 01872 75757/01736 331868
BAP

Mark Hayward
Family Therapist
Little Clicker, Horningtops, Liskeard,
Cornwall PL14 3QA
Tel: 01503 4822
AFT

Amanda Hodd
Family Therapist
5 Ashmead, Grampound Road, Truro,
Cornwall TR2 4DH
AFT

Peter Hudson
Family Therapist
Child and Family Centre, Treliske
Hopital, Truro, Cornwall
Tel: 01872 75757
AFT

Paul David Kemp
Cognitive Behavioural Psychotherapist
Trevillis House, Lodge Hill, Liskeard,
Cornwall PL14 4EN
Tel: 01579 343097
BABCP

Michael King
Family Therapist
8 Amble Road, Callington, Cornwall
PL17 7QE
Tel: 01579 82216
AFT

John Payne
Psychoanalytic Psychotherapist
Greenscombe House, Luckett,
Callington, Cornwall PL17 8LF
Tel: 01579 370149
GUILD

Susan Rees
Child Psychotherapist, Jungian Child
Analyst
An Skyber, Trevithal, Near Paul,
Penzance, Cornwall TR1 6UQ
Tel: 01736 731973
ACP, SAP

Malcolm Retallick
Gestalt Psychotherapist
48 Molesworth Street, Wadebridge,
Cornwall PL27 7DP
Tel: 01208 812048
GPTI

Michael Sever
Hypno-Psychotherapist
'Veritas', 25 Polwithen Drive, Carbis
Bay, St Ives, Cornwall TR26 2SP
Tel: 01736 798399
NRHP

Kevin J Simpson
Psychoanalytic Psychotherapist
Cornwall & Isle of Scilly Learning
Disability Tst, 57 Pydar Street, Truro
TR1 2SS
Tel: 01208 79525
LPDO

Andy S Thornton
Cognitive Behavioural Psychotherapist
Trengweath, Penryn Street, Redruth,
Cornwall TR15 2SP
Tel: 01209 219232
BABCP

John Trewhella
Hypno-Psychotherapist
Castle Gayer, Leys Lane, Marazion,
Cornwall TR17 0AQ
Tel: 01736 711548
NRHP

Jean White
Psychoanalytic Psychotherapist
Greenscombe House, Luckett, Nr
Callington, Cornwall PL17 8LF
Tel: 01579 370 149
GUILD

Gillian Wilson
Child Psychotherapist
Elderbush Cottage, Longstone,
St Mabyn, Bodmin, Cornwall PL30 3BY
Tel: 01208 84439
ACP

COUNTY DURHAM

Mary A Allinson
Cognitive Behavioural Psychotherapist
Teesdale Community Health Services,
Victoria Road, Barnard Castle, Co
Durham DL12 8HT
Tel: 01833 637795
BABCP

Stephen Lawrence Clarke
Cognitive Behavioural Psychotherapist
The Derwent Clinics, Bede House,
Shotley Bridge Hospital, Consett, Co
Durham DH8 0NB
Tel: 01207 583583 x 4660/4069
BABCP

Margaret Cooper
Psychoanalytic Psychotherapist
2 Manor Close, Shincliffe Village,
County Durham DH1 2NS
Tel: 091 386 5818
NAAP

Pim Draper
Cognitive Behavioural Psychotherapist
Department of Psychology, Darlington
Memorial Hospital, Hollyhurst Road,
Darlington DL3 6HX
Tel: 01325 352515
BABCP

Richard Errington
NLP Psychotherapist
Chapel House, The Green, Aycliffe
Village, Co Durham DL5 6LU
Tel: 01325 314835
ANLP

Barbara Gilbert
Psychoanalytic Psychotherapist
68 Gurney Valley, Bishop Auckland, Co
Durham DL14 3RW
NAAP

Karolyn Hurren
Psychoanalytic Psychotherapist
Bede House, Shotley Bridge General
Hos, Consett DH8 0NB
Tel: 01207 503456
NAAP

Julia Loudon
Sexual and Marital Psychotherapist
Department of Clinical Psychology, The
Memorial Hospital, Hollyhurst Road,
Darlington, Co Durham DL3 6HX
BASMT

Carolyn Matthews
Psychoanalytic Psychotherapist
University Health Services, 42 Old
Elvet, Durham DH1 3JF
Tel: 0191 386 5081
NAAP

Christine Stanbury
Psychoanalytic Psychotherapist
CNS (Psychiatry), Bede House,
Derwent Clinic, Shotley Bridge Gen
Hospital, Consett, Co Durham
DH8 0NB
Tel: 01207 503456
NAAP

Pauline Watson
Psychoanalytic Psychotherapist
Shotley Bridge Hospital, Shotley Bridge,
Co Durham
Tel: 01207 284 0774
NAAP

CUMBRIA

Monica Baynes
Psychoanalytic Psychotherapist
5 Stainbank Green, Brigsteer Road,
Kendal, Cumbria LA9 5RP
Tel: 01539 740605
LPDO

Shanti Cole
Hypno-Psychotherapist
'Four Winds', Church Hill, Arnside,
Cumbria, LA5 0DQ
Tel: 01524 762524
NSHAP

Beth Conroy
Psychosynthesis Psychotherapist
Fern Cottage, 7 Causeway End, Levens,
Nr Kendal, Cumbria LA8 8PW
Tel: 01539 60188
IPS

Mary Cox
Transactional Analysis Psychotherapist
Cambrai House, Calderbridge,
Seascale, Cumbria CA20 1DH
Tel: 01946 841239
ITA

Angus Forsyth
Cognitive Behavioural Psychotherapist
104 Greenacres, Wetheral, Carlisle,
Cumbria CA4 8LD
Tel: 01228 561786
BABCP

Gillian Kelly
Gestalt Psychotherapist, Body
Psychotherapist
Dillygarth, Loughrigg, Ambleside,
Cumbria LA22 9HF
Tel: 01539 433903
CCHP

Peter Kenny
Psychoanalytic Psychotherapist
26 Spital Park, Kendal, Cumbria
LA9 6HG
Tel: 01539 720572
WMIP

Joan Longford
Psychoanalytic Psychotherapist
Dr Howarth's Unit, Garlands Hospital,
Carlisle CA1 3SX
Tel: 01228 31081
NAAP

Jane McQuillin
Transactional Analysis Psychotherapist
31 Prince's Street, Ulverston, Cumbria
LA12 7NQ
Tel: 01229 584250
ITA

John Newson
Analytical Psychologist-Jungian Analyst
Hebblethwaite Hall, Cautley, Sedbergh,
Cumbria LA10 5LX
Tel: 01539 621307
AJA

Brenda Leo Tiller
Hypno-Psychotherapist
Yewthwaite, 135 Burneside Road,
Kendal, Cumbria LA9 6EB
Tel: 01539 733633
NSHAP

Ian Tod
Psychoanalytic Psychotherapist
The Brough Medical Centre, Brough,
Nr Kirby Stephen, Cumbria CA17 4AY
Tel: 017683 71143
NAAP

DERBYSHIRE

Frank Daniels
NLP Psychotherapist
103 Hands Road, Heanor, Derbyshire
DE7 7HB
Tel: 01773 532195
ANLP

Brian Denness
Psychoanalytic Psychotherapist
Department of Psychotherapy (NHS),
Temple House, Mill Hill Lane, Derby
DE3 6SA
Tel: 01332 364512
STTDP

G E Evans
Sexual and Marital Psychotherapist
34 Hockley Lane, Wingerworth,
Chesterfield S42 6QG
BASMT

Hugh Fox
Family Therapist
15 Quarry Lane, Matlock, Derbyshire
DE4 5LG
Tel: 01629 56431
AFT

Barry Greatorex
Cognitive Behavioural Psychotherapist
Clinical Psychology Services, Kingsway
Hospital, Derby DE22 3LZ
Tel: 01332 624 592
BABCP

Hilary Howell
Systemic Psychotherapist
Woods Cottage, Main Road, Brailsford,
Derby DE6 3DA
FIC

Michael Johnson
NLP Psychotherapist
5 Glenthorne Close, Chesterfield,
Derbyshire S40 3AR
Tel: 01246 273002
ANLP

Sue Jones
Systemic Psychotherapist
27 Queen Street, Glossop, Derbyshire
SK13 8EL
FIC

Peter Leakey
NLP Psychotherapist
16 Cromwell Road, Chesterfield,
Derbyshire S40 4TH
Tel: 01246 232765
ANLP

Brendan McMahon
Psychoanalytic Psychotherapist
Derby Dept of Psychotherapy (NHS),
Temple House, Mill Hill Lane, Derby
DE23 6SA
Tel: 01332 364512
STTDP

Jillian Parkinson
Transactional Analysis Psychotherapist
19 Chapel Street, Measham,
Derbyshire DE12 7JD
Tel: 01530 272772
ITA

Gary Robinson
Systemic Psychotherapist
2 Foxcroft, Sunny Bank, Tibshelf,
Derbyshire DE55 5QR
FIC

Nigel Runcorn
Psychoanalytic Psychotherapist
Department of Psychotherapy, Temple
House, Mill Hill Lane, Derby DE23 6SA
Tel: 01332 364512
STTDP

Thomas Schroeder
Psychoanalytic Psychotherapist
Derby Dept of Psychotherapy (NHS),
Temple House, Mill Hill Lane, Derby
DE23 6SA
Tel: 01332 364 512
STTDP, WMIP

Nicholas Michael Serieys
Cognitive Behavioural Psychotherapist
14 Balmoral Close, Littleover, Derby
DE23 6DY
Tel: 01332 362082/0973 520550
BABCP

David Smith
Psychoanalytic Psychotherapist
Derby Dept of Psychotherapy (NHS),
Temple House, Mill Hill Lane, Derby
DE23 6SA
Tel: 01332 364512
STTDP

Janet Smith
Psychoanalytic Psychotherapist
Dept of Psychotherapy, Temple House,
Mill Hill Lane, Derby, DE23 6SA
Tel: 01332 364512
NWIDP

Jon Taylor
Cognitive Behavioural Psychotherapist
55 Church Street, Littleover, Derby,
DE23 6GF
Tel: 01332 272434/01283 543368
BABCP

Belinda Walsh
Cognitive Behavioural Psychotherapist
Clinical Psychology Department,
Walton Hospital, Whitecotes Lane,
Chesterfield S40 3HN
Tel: 01246 277271 x 5520
BABCP

Clare Watson
Psychoanalytic Psychotherapist
Derby Department of Psychotherapy
(NHS), Temple House, Mill Hill Lane,
Derby DE3 6SA
Tel: 01332 364512
STTDP

DEVON

Yon Anjali
Core Process Psychotherapist
7 Kings Orchard, Bridgetown, Totnes,
Devon TQ9 5BX
Tel: 01803 867 402
KI

P K Armbruster
Child Psychotherapist
Young Peoples' Centre, Mount Gould
Hospital, Plymouth, Devon PL4 7QD
Tel: 01752 272320/01822 840162
ACP

Rita Benor
Autogenic Psychotherapist
May Cottage, 19 Fore Street,
Bishopsteighton, South Devon
TQ14 9QR
Tel: 01626 779218
BAFAT

Mary Boston
Child Psychotherapist
Marina, Golf Links Road, Westward
Ho, Bideford, Devon EX39 1HH
Tel: 01237 470424
ACP

Richard Buckland
Child Psychotherapist
Plymouth Child & Family Consultation
Service, Erme House, Mount Gould
Hospital, Plymouth, Devon PL4 7QD
Tel: 01752 272360/01752 881260
ACP

John Campbell-Beattie
Hypno-Psychotherapist
Rosemary Hill, 64A Underlane,
Plymstock, Plymouth PL9 9JZ
Tel: 01752 484265
NRHP

Sarah Clevely
Transactional Analysis Psychotherapist
10 Bartholomew Terrace, Exeter,
Devon EX4 3BW
Tel: 01392 432952
ITA

Susannah Darling Khan
Gestalt Psychotherapist
6 Weston House, Weston Lane,
Totnes, South Devon TQ9 6LB
Tel: 01803 864950
GCL

Julian David
Analytical Psychologist-Jungian Analyst
Luscombe Farm, Buckfastleigh, Devon
TQ11 0JD
Tel: 0171 351 5728/01364 642373
IGAP

Jenny Dawson
Gestalt Psychotherapist
36 Raleigh Road, Exmouth, Devon
EX8 2SB
Tel: 01395 269076
GPTI

Ros Draper
Systemic Psychotherapist
Ivy House, 15 Church Lane, Moorhaven
Village, Devon PL21 0EX
Tel: 01752 698 056
IFT

Pat Dyehouse
Psychoanalytic Psychotherapist
Hazel Tor Barn, Lower Soar, Soar Mill
Cove, Malborough, Kingsbridge, Devon
TQ7 3DS
Tel: 01548 561450
AAP

Mary Etherington
Transactional Analysis Psychotherapist
2 Culm Lea, Cullompton, Devon
EX15 1NJ
Tel: 01884 33812
ITA

Heather Geddes
Educational Therapist
Alfington House, Church Lane,
Alfington, East Devon EX11 1PE
Tel: 01404 850329
FAETT

Angelika Golz
Humanistic Psychotherapist
Dart House, 20 Bridgetown, Totnes,
Devon TQ9 5BA
Tel: 01803 862805
AHPP

Judith Henshaw
Transactional Analysis Psychotherapist
Ollivers, Halsfordwood Lane,
Nadderwater, Nr Exeter EX4 2LD
Tel: 01392 811416
ITA

Julie Hewson
Transactional Analysis Psychotherapist
Iron Mill, Oakford, Tiverton, Devon
EX16 9EN
Tel: 0139 85379
ITA

Ian Hoare
Humanistic and Integrative
Psychotherapist
36 Raleigh Road, Exmouth, Devon
EX8 2SB
Tel: 01395 269076
BCPC

Barbara Hodges
Psychodrama Psychotherapist
Seymour House, 62 Lipson Road,
Plymouth, Devon PL4 8RH
Tel: 01752 661730
BPDA

Jeremy Holmes
Psychoanalytic Psychotherapist
The Old Rectory, Stoke Rivers,
Barnstaple EX32 7LB
Tel: 01598 710291
SIP

Nicole Jones
Psychoanalytic Psychotherapist
57 Thornton Hill, Exeter, Devon
Tel: 01392 54408
SIP

David Kalisch
Core Process Psychotherapist,
Humanistic Psychotherapist
Garden Cottage, Bushy Park, Knowle
Hill, Budleigh Salterton, Devon
EX9 7AL
Tel: 01395 442079
KI, AHPP

Marcia Karp
Psychodrama Psychotherapist
Holwell Centre, East Down,
Barnstaple, N Devon EX31 4NZ
Tel: 01271 850267
BPDA

Petra Kerridge
Psychosynthesis Psychotherapist
36 Clarence Street, Dartmouth, Devon
TQ6 9NW
Tel: 01803 832 457
PET

Roslyn Langdon
Humanistic Psychotherapist
6 Western Terrace, Collins Road,
Totnes, Devon TQ9 5PP
Tel: 01803 865806
AHPP

Dorothy Langley
Psychodrama Psychotherapist
Hanningfields, Warborough Hill,
Kenton, Exeter, Devon EX6 8LR
Tel: 01626 890433
BPDA

Philip Lewis
NLP Psychotherapist
33 Northfield Road, Oakhampton,
Devon EX20 1BB
Tel: 01837 54061
ANLP

Maxine Linnell
Core Process Psychotherapist
6 Pengilly Way, Hartland, Nr Bideford,
Devon EX39 6HR
Tel: 01237 441691
KI

Lorne Loxterkamp
Child Psychotherapist
Family Consultancy, Health Centre,
Vicarage Street, Barnstaple, North
Devon EX32 7BT
Tel: 01271 71761/01271 814901
ACP

Sean Maloney
Core Process Psychotherapist
1 Orchard Terrace, Tuckenham, Totnes,
Devon TQ9 7EJ
Tel: 01803 732 264
KI

Judith Mills
NLP Psychotherapist
Higher Thatch, Ebford Lane, Ebford,
Exeter, Devon EX3 0QX
Tel: 01392 873984
ANLP

Jill Moore
Sexual and Marital Psychotherapist
3 Marlow Close, Shiphay, Torquay,
Devon TQ2 6DQ
BASMT

Jon Munsey
Psychodrama Psychotherapist
11 Auction Way, Woolfardisworthy, Nr
Bideford, N Devon
Tel: 01237 472379
BPDA

Heather Musker
Core Process Psychotherapist
The Linhay, Lake Gardens, Maudlin
Road, Totnes, Devon TQ9 5EX
Tel: 01803 863 979
KI

Elizabeth Nicholson
Psychoanalytic Psychotherapist
18 St Brannocks Park Road, Ilfracombe,
Devon EX34 8HX
Tel: 01271 864003
GUILD

Eileen Nightingale
Psychosynthesis Psychotherapist
'Sidside', Packhorse Close, Sidford,
Sidmouth, Devon EX10 9RR
Tel: 01395 579221
PET

Joanna North
Core Process Psychotherapist
16 Granary Lane, Budleigh Salterton,
Devon EX9 6JD
Tel: 01395 225315
KI

Lena Pehrsson-Tatham
Psychoanalytic Psychotherapist
Maynards, Cornworthy, Totnes, South
Devon TQ9 7HB
Tel: 01803 732733
SIP, GUILD

Frederic Riley
Sexual and Marital Psychotherapist
'Curlew Cottage', Coombe Road,
Ringmore, Shaldon, South Devon
TQ14 0EX
BASMT

Zuleika Robertson
Psychoanalytic Psychotherapist
6 Prospect Park, Exeter, Devon
EX4 6NA
Tel: 013924 30162
GUILD

Mary Roddick
Family Therapist
Coombe Farm, Christow, Exeter
EX6 7NR
Tel: 01647 52553
AFT

Anna Scott Hayward
NLP Psychotherapist
16 Brunswick Terrace, Torquay, Devon
TQ1 4AE
Tel: 01803 323885
ANLP

Vivienne Seymour Clark
Psychoanalytic Psychotherapist
25 Brooklands, Bridgetown, Totnes,
Devon TQ9 5AR
Tel: 01803 864976/01803 862319
CSP

Franklyn Sills
Core Process Psychotherapist
Natsworthy Manor, Widecombe-in-
the-Moor, Newton Abbot, Devon
TQ13 7TR
Tel: 01647 221 457
KI

Maura Sills
Core Process Psychotherapist
Natsworthy Manor, Widecombe-in-
the-Moor, Newton Abbot, Devon
TQ13 7TR
Tel: 01647 221 457
KI

Ken Sprague
Psychodrama Psychotherapist
Holwell Centre, East Down,
Barnstaple, North Devon EX31 4NZ
Tel: 01271 850267
BPDA

John Stathers
Core Process Psychotherapist
Henacre House, Rack Park Road,
Kingsbridge, Devon TQ7 1DQ
Tel: 01548 857 567
KI

Joan Swallow
Integrative Psychotherapist
Bridge House, Culmstock, Cullompton,
Devon EX15 3JJ
Tel: 01884 840513
MC

Peter Tatham
Psychoanalytic Psychotherapist,
Analytical Psychologist-Jungian Analyst
Maynards, Cornworthy, Totnes, South
Devon TQ9 7HB
Tel: 01803 732733
IGAP, SIP

Helen Taylor
Personal Construct Psychotherapist
56 Clamperdown Terrace, Exmouth,
Devon EX8 1EQ
Tel: 01395 267615
CPCP

Alyss Thomas
Core Process Psychotherapist
River Cottage, Bow Road,
Harbertonford, Totnes, Devon
TQ9 7TJ
Tel: 01803 732 751
KI

Joy Thompson
Group Analyst
The Palace, Exeter, Devon EX1 1HY
Tel: 01392 72362
IGA

Stephen Tyrrell
Hypno-Psychotherapist
53 Farm Hill, Exeter, Devon EX4 2LW
Tel: 01392 424432
NRHP

Barbara Ward
Psychosynthesis Psychotherapist
3 Wheelwright Court, Walkhampton,
Yelverton, Devon PL20 6LA
Tel: 01822 855 619
PET

Judith Warin
Cognitive Analytic Therapist
41 Thornton Hill, Exeter, Devon
EX4 4NR
Tel: 01392 403446
ACAT

Gay Watson
Core Process Psychotherapist
Coombery, Tuckenhay, Totnes, Devon
TQ9 7EP
Tel: 01803 732 272
KI

Wendy Webber
Core Process Psychotherapist
Cutteridge Farm, Whitestone, Exeter,
Devon EX4 2HE
Tel: 01392 811203
KI

Felicity Weir
Child Psychotherapist
The Day Unit, Child & Family
Consultation Service, 187 Newton
Road, Torquay, Devon TQ2 7AJ
Tel: 01626 872966/01803 615980
ACP

Sylvia Wheadon
Psychodrama Psychotherapist
16 Clampitt Road, Ippleden, Newton
Abbot, Devon TQ12 5TE
Tel: 01803 813443
BPDA

Angela Willow
Core Process Psychotherapist
1 Orchard Terrace, Tuckenhay, Totnes,
South Devon TQ9 7EJ
Tel: 01803 732264
KI

Sandra Wooding
Psychodrama Psychotherapist
Lower Cator Farmhouse, Lower Cator,
Widecombe-in-the-Moor, Devon
TQ13 7TX
Tel: 01364 621239
BPDA

Maureen Wright
Psychodrama Psychotherapist
Thornlea, Town Lane, Woodbury, Nr
Exeter, Devon EX5 1NB
Tel: 01395 32001
BPDA

Denise Yeldham
Psychoanalytic Psychotherapist
Liesse, Grange Road, Buckfast, South
Devon TQ11 0EH
Tel: 01364 642189
BAP

DORSET

Madeleine Adam
Psychoanalytic Psychotherapist
Rose Cottage, Tarrant Keyneston,
Blandford Forum, Dorset DT11 9JE
Tel: 01258 480778
LCP

Stella Bellis
Child Psychotherapist, Analytical
Psychologist-Jungian Analyst
West Dorset Children's Centre,
Damers Road, Dorchester, Dorset
DT1 2JY;
Brookfield, Bettiscombe, Bridport,
Dorset DT6 6HP
Tel: 01305 254713/01308 868191
ACP, BAP

Gerald A Bennett
Cognitive Behavioural Psychotherapist
20 Newstead Road, Bournemouth,
Dorset BH6 3HJ
Tel: 01202 431090
BABCP

Susan Elizabeth Clarke
Cognitive Psychotherapist, Cognitive
Analytic Therapist
Clinical Psychology Services,
Branksome Clinic, Layton Road,
Parkstone, Poole, Dorset BH12 2BJ
Tel: 01202 735300
BABCP, ACAT

Peter Hardwick
Family Psychotherapist
Child & Family Guidance, Child
Development Centre, Poole General
Hospital, Poole, Dorset BH15 2AB
Tel: 01202 675100
IFT

Philip Kelly
Cognitive Behavioural Psychotherapist
25 Granville Road, Weymouth, Dorset
DT4 0BQ
Tel: 01305 786905/01305 779027
BABCP

Jo Lacy-Smith
Humanistic and Integrative
Psychotherapist
2 Ackerman Road, Dorchester, Dorset
DT1 1NZ
Tel: 01305 266721
BCPC

Nancy Logue
Sexual and Marital Psychotherapist
Halves House, 132 East Street, Corfe
Castle, Dorset BH20 5EH
Tel: 01929 481163
BASMT

Jennifer Long
Cognitive Psychotherapist
Branksome Clinic, Layton Road,
Parkstone, Poole, Dorset BH12 2BJ
Tel: 01202 760193/01202 735300
BABCP

Rosie March-Smith
Humanistic and Integrative
Psychotherapist
Manor Cottage, Buckland Newton,
Dorchester, Dorset DT2 7BX
Tel: 01300 345385
AHPP, BCPC

Chris Newbery
Humanistic and Integrative
Psychotherapist
12 St George's Avenue, Weymouth,
Dorset DT4 7TU
Tel: 01305 786172
AHPP, BCPC

Dorothy Ostler
Systemic Psychotherapist
White Lodge, 255 Sandbanks Road,
Lilliput, Poole, Dorset BH14 8EY
FIC

Laurie Phillips
Psychoanalytic Psychotherapist
11 Viking Way, Mudeford,
Christchurch, Dorset BH23 4AQ
Tel: 01425 276417
AGIP

Martin Robinson
Analytical Psychologist-Jungian Analyst,
Psychoanalytic Psychotherapist
White Hill Farmhouse, Stoke Wake, Nr
Blandford Forum, Dorset DT11 0HF;
Studio E, 49 The Avenue, London
NW6
Tel: 0181 459 5442/01258 817301
AJA, SIP

Joanne Sones
Child Psychotherapist
West Dorset Childrens' Centre,
Damers Road, Dorchester, Dorset
DT1 2JY
Tel: 01305 254713/01202 736591
ACP

Michael Sones
Child Psychotherapist
Child, Adolescent & Family Mental
Health Service, Poole General Hospital,
Longleat Road, Poole, Dorset
Tel: 01202 442741/01202 661671 (f)
ACP

Malathi Venki
Cognitive Behavioural Psychotherapist
11 William Road, Queens Park,
Bournemouth, Dorset BH7 7BB
Tel: 01202 394927
BABCP

Sheila Wildash
Psychoanalytic Psychotherapist
10 Fairway Drive, Northmoor Park,
Wareham, Dorset BH20 4SG
Tel: 01929 553097
AGIP

Gill Wiltshire
Cognitive Behavioural Psychotherapist
61 Lowther Road, Bournemouth,
Dorset BH8 8NW
Tel: 01202 398233
BABCP

Jacqueline Withers
Cognitive Behavioural Psychotherapist
Community Alcohol Team, 16-18
Tower Road, Boscombe, Bournemouth
BH1 4LB
Tel: 01202 443200
BABCP

DUMFRIESHIRE

Alasdair Macdonald
Family Therapist
3 Ardwil Gardens, Lockerbie,
Dumfrieshire, Scotland DG11 2EN
Tel: 01576 204107
AFT

DYFED

Richard Appleton
Family Therapist
47 Cilddewi Park, Johnstown,
Carmarthen, Dyfed SA31 3HP
AFT

Sue Gagg
Systemic Psychotherapist
13 Gardde, Llwynhendy, Llanelli, Dyfed
SA14 9NH
FIC

Pamela Gaunt
Transpersonal Psychotherapist
Bach Y Gaunt, Velindre, Llandysul,
Dyfed SA44 5HX
Tel: 01559 371427
CCPE

Helen F Macdonald
Behavioural Psychotherapist
Psychotherapy Department, St David's
Hospital, Carmarthen, Dyfed
SA31 3HB
Tel: 01267 237481 x 4650
BABCP

EAST SUSSEX

Stephen Arcari
Group Analyst
9/11 Rutland Gardens, Hove, East
Sussex BN3 5PA
Tel: 01273 778383 x 162
IGA

John Bannon
Transpersonal Psychotherapist
Flat 1, 20 Denton Road, Eastbourne,
East Sussex BN20 7ST
Tel: 01323 643819
CCPE

Maureen Rahima Bannon
Transpersonal Psychotherapist
Flat 1, 20 Denton Road, Eastbourne,
East Sussex BN20 7ST
Tel: 01323 643819
CCPE

Mary Barnett
Psychoanalytic Psychotherapist
33 Southdown Avenue, Brighton, East
Sussex BN1 6EH
Tel: 01273 506258
GUILD

Jill Barry
Psychoanalytic Psychotherapist
Stonerunner Cottage, Rye Harbour,
East Sussex TN31 7TT
Tel: 01227 455308/01797 224351
GUILD

Joanna Beazley-Richards
Transactional Analysis Psychotherapist,
Integrative Psychotherapist
2 Quarry View, Whitehill Road,
Crowborough, East Sussex TN6 1JT
Tel: 01892 655195
ITA, MET

Peter Bishop
Family Psychotherapist
34 Clifton Terrace, Brighton, East
Sussex BN1 3HB
IFT

Colin M Blowers
Cognitive Behavioural Psychotherapist
Glenside, Wincombe Road, Brighton,
East Sussex BN1 5AR;
The Priory Hospital, Priory Lane,
Roehampton, London SW15 5JJ
Tel: 01273 504980/0181 876 8261
BABCP

David Bott
Family Therapist
Little Norlington Farmhouse,
Norlington Lane, Ringmer, Brighton
BN8 5SG
Tel: 01273 812943
AFT

Elizabeth Bowman
Hypno-Psychotherapist
Ridgeway, High Hurstwood, nr
Uckfield, East Sussex TN22 4BE
Tel: 01825 732273
NSHAP

Sue Bradbury
Psychodrama Psychotherapist
18 Hanover Crescent, Brighton
BN2 2BP
BPDA

Clare Brennan
Psychoanalytic Psychotherapist, Group
Analytic Psychotherapist
The Merchant House, English Passage,
Cliffe High Street, Lewes, East Sussex
BN7 2AP
Tel: 01273 479157
WTC, LCP

Cornelia Brosskamp
Biodynamic Psychotherapist
72 Westbourne Gardens, Hove, East
Sussex BN3 5PQ
Tel: 01273 385228
BTC

Michael Burton
Psychoanalytic Psychotherapist
Brackley, 11A Harrington Road,
Brighton, Sussex BN1 9RE
Tel: 01273 678156/01273 502923
GUILD

Barbara Chilton
Hypno-Psychotherapist
4 Ashburnham Road, Eastbourne, East
Sussex BN21 2HU
Tel: 01323 638558
NRHP

Tosin Clairmonte
Group Analyst
Hillview, 1 Hope Villas, Highcross,
Rotherfield, East Sussex TN6 3QD
Tel: 0189 285 2997
IGA

Barbara Cole
Humanistic Psychotherapist
4 Offham Terrace, Lewes, East Sussex
BN7 2QP
Tel: 01273 473113
AHPP

Susan Conway
NLP Psychotherapist
154a Church Road, Hove, East Sussex
BN3 2DL
Tel: 01273 559680
ANLP

Christine Cox
Hypno-Psychotherapist
8 Combermere Road, St Leonards on
Sea, East Sussex TN38 0RR
Tel: 01424 424797
NRHP

A S B Crosby
Personal Construct Psychotherapist
Hindleap Corner, Priory Road, Forest
Row, East Sussex RH18 5JF;
4 Sandringham Court, Dufour's Place,
London W1
Tel: 01342 824545
CPCP

Guy Dargert
Humanistic Psychotherapist
175 Preston Drove, Brighton, East
Sussex BN1 6FN
Tel: 01273 557503
AHPP

Tom Davey
Integrative Psychotherapist
Counselling and Psychotherapy
Department, University of Sussex,
Falmer, Brighton BN1 9RW
Tel: 01273 678156/01273 674417
RCSPC

Hanora Desmond
Transpersonal Psychotherapist
30 The Esplanade, Seaford, East Sussex
BN25 1JJ
Tel: 01323 490 721
CCPE

Rosemary Dixon-Nuttall
Group Analytic Psychotherapist
1 Coronation Cottages, Western Road,
Crowborough, East Sussex TN6 3EX
Tel: 01892 663192
IPC

Alec John Duncan-Grant
Cognitive Behavioural Psychotherapist
28 Falmer Avenue, Saltdean, Brighton,
East Sussex BN2 8FG
Tel: 01903 820672/01273 300556
BABCP

Heiner Eisenbarth
Biodynamic Psychotherapist
72 Westbourne Gardens, Hove, East
Sussex BN3 5PO
Tel: 01273 385228
BTC

Rosalind Field
Integrative Psychotherapist
Flat 2, 9 Lewes Crescent, Brighton
BN2 1FH
Tel: 01273 677721
MC

Matthew Forster
Psychoanalytic Psychotherapist
Church Cottage, Barcombe, Lewes,
Sussex BN8 5TW
Tel: 01273 400484
GUILD

Jessica Fox
Psychoanalytic Psychotherapist
Flat 2, Adelaide Court, 15 Adelaide
Crescent, Hove, E Sussex BN3 2JF
Tel: 01273 732177
LCP

Marianne Fry
Gestalt Psychotherapist
5 Green Hedges, Langham Road,
Robertsbridge, East Sussex TN32 5EP
Tel: 01580 882259
GPTI

Eogain Gallagher
Psychoanalytic Psychotherapist
8 Tivoli Crescent, Brighton BN1 5ND
Tel: 01273 887332
LCP

Betty Gilbert
Analytical Psychologist-Jungian Analyst
24 Braybon Avenue, Brighton, East
Sussex BN1 8HG
Tel: 01273 502767
BAP

Lynne Goddard
Transactional Analysis Psychotherapist
137 Montgomery Street, Hove, East
Sussex BN3 5FP
Tel: 01273 202721
ITA

Inger Gordon
Systemic Psychotherapist
31 Castlefields, Hartfield, East Sussex
TN7 4JA
Tel: 01892 770651
KCC

Jill Gordon
Analytical Psychologist-Jungian Analyst
27 Paddock Road, Lewes, East Sussex
BN7 1UU
Tel: 01273 471 267
SAP

Anne Megan Griffiths
Psychoanalytic Psychotherapist
Bedford Cottage, 36 Prince Edward
Road, Lewes, Sussex BN7 1BE
Tel: 01273 478365
GUILD

Mark Hardcastle
Cognitive Behavioural Psychotherapist
10 Wannock Avenue, Eastbourne, East
Sussex BN20 9RS
Tel: 01323 483988/01323 440022
BABCP

Kit Haxby
Psychoanalytic Psychotherapist
28 Withdean Road, Brighton, Sussex
BN1 5BL
Tel: 01273 554027
LCP

Sue Holland
Psychosynthesis Psychotherapist
12 Shawcross House, 235-7 Preston
Road, Brighton BN1 6SW
Tel: 01273 563098
IPS

Margaret Hueting
NLP Psychotherapist
31 Elm Grove, Hampden Park,
Eastbourne, East Sussex BN22 9NN
Tel: 01323 511150
ANLP

Lesley Ironside
Psychoanalytic Psychotherapist, Child
Psychotherapist
35 Clermont Terrace, Brighton, East
Sussex BN1 6SJ
Tel: 01273 709660
ACP

Helen Jones
Biodynamic Psychotherapist
113 Roundhill Crescent, Brighton,
Sussex BN2 3FQ
Tel: 01273 609519
BTC

Ros Jones
Transpersonal Psychotherapist
Southover Cottage, Southover High
Street, Lewes, East Sussex BN7 1HT
CCPE

Jerome Devakumar Joseph
Cognitive Psychotherapist
Gilgal, 17 Nyetimber Hill, Brighton,
East Sussex BN2 4TL
Tel: 01273 706084/01903 820672
BABCP

Catherine Kaplinsky
Analytical Psychologist-Jungian Analyst
Mill Brook, Barcombe Mills, Nr Lewes,
East Sussex BN8 5BP
Tel: 01273 401167/01273 400663 (f)
SAP

Florangel Lambor
Psychoanalytic Psychotherapist
82 Hythe Road, Brighton, Sussex
BN1 6JS
Tel: 01273 774421
CPP

Rushi Ledermann
Analytical Psychologist-Jungian Analyst
10 Hove Park Road, Hove, East Sussex
BN3 6LA
Tel: 01273 508328
SAP, BAP

Jennifer Leeburn
Psychoanalytic Psychotherapist
12 Priory Crescent, Lewes, East Sussex
BN7 1HP
Tel: 01273 476444
BAP

Wendy Lidster
Sexual and Marital Psychotherapist
2 St James's Place, Brighton, Sussex
BN2 1RS
BASMT

Marie Little
Psychoanalytic Psychotherapist
29 Kings Drive, Eastbourne, East
Sussex BN21 2NX
Tel: 01323 649656
IPSS

Mollie Love
Group Analytic Psychotherapist
162 Warren Road, Woodingdean,
Brighton BN2 6DD
Tel: 01273 607529
LCP

Nancy MacKenzie
Group Analyst
18 Wolston Bury Road, Hove, Sussex
BN3 6EJ
Tel: 01273 678156/01273 736740
IGA

Susan Marshall
Integrative Psychotherapist
Moat Mill Farm, Newick Lane, Mayfield,
East Sussex TN20 6RF
Tel: 01435 873483
RCSPC

Helen Masani
Educational Therapist
7 Clare Road, Lewes, East Sussex
BN7 1PN
FAETT

Peter A Masani
Analytical Psychologist-Jungian Analyst
7 Clare Road, Lewes, E Sussex
BN7 1PN
Tel: 01273 474800
BAP

Paula McLeod
Biodynamic Psychotherapist
68 Stanley Road, Brighton, East Sussex
BN1 4NH
Tel: 01273 383429
BTC

Richard Morgan-Jones
Psychoanalytic Psychotherapist
25 Lewes Road, Eastbourne, East
Sussex BN21 2BY
Tel: 01323 647531
LCP

Geoff Mothersole
Integrative Psychotherapist
6 Albert Road, Brighton, East Sussex
BN1 3RL
Tel: 01273 738677
MET, ITA

Jean Mulvey
Analytical Psychologist-Jungian Analyst
Aldsworth, Lewes Road, Ringmer, East
Sussex BN8 5ER
Tel: 01273 812944
SAP

Christine Nicholson
Psychoanalytic Psychotherapist
42 Temple Street, Brighton BN1 3BH
Tel: 01273 202178
LCP

Jane Parkinson
Attachment-based Psychoanalytic
Psychotherapist
53 Wilbury Avenue, Hove, Sussex
BN3 6GH
Tel: 01273 734410
CAPP

Prue Rankin-Smith
Core Process Psychotherapist
18 South Street, Lewes, Sussex
BN7 2BP
Tel: 01273 473244
KI

Michael Richards
Psychoanalytic Psychotherapist
64 Southover High Street, Lewes, East
Sussex BN7 1JA
Tel: 01273 478244
IPC

Madeleine J Richardson
Sexual and Marital Psychotherapist
33 Mandalay Court, London Road,
Brighton BN1 8QU
Tel: 01273 504385
BASMT

Judy Robinson
Psychoanalytic Psychotherapist
St Laurence House, Falmer, Brighton
BN1 9PG
Tel: 01273 606928
GUILD

Jas Ananda Salamander
Transpersonal Psychotherapist
24 Lancaster Road, Brighton, Sussex
BN1 5DG
CCPE

Peter Sanders
Transactional Analysis Psychotherapist
39 Burry Road, St Leonards-on-Sea,
East Sussex TN37 6QZ
Tel: 01424 429053
ITA

Jonathan Smerdon
Transpersonal Psychotherapist
34 Lower Market Street, Hove, East
Sussex
CCPE

Sarah Soutar
Psychoanalytic Psychotherapist
Star Breweries Workshops and Studio,
Castle Ditch Lane, Lewes BN7 1YJ
Tel: 01273 486782
AGIP

Kate Springford
Psychoanalytic Psychotherapist
21 St Anne's Crescent, Lewes, East
Sussex
Tel: 01273 473125
GUILD

Moya Tomlinson
Sexual and Marital Psychotherapist
53 Southover High Street, Lewes, East
Sussex BN7 1JA
BASMT

Clare Tredgold
Psychoanalytic Psychotherapist
13 Florence Road, Brighton, Sussex
BN1 6DL
Tel: 01273 502112
LCP

Jane Turner
Core Process Psychotherapist
120 Vale Avenue, Patcham, Brighton
BN1 8YF
Tel: 01273 566590
KI

Pat Vallely
Transpersonal Psychotherapist
41 The Cliff, Roedean, Brighton, East
Sussex BN2 5RF
Tel: 01273 691 162
CCPE

Corrie Van Halm
Transactional Analysis Psychotherapist
St John's Lodge, Burgh Hill, Etchingham,
East Sussex TN19 7PE
Tel: 01580 860 780
ITA

Diane Waller
Group Analytic Psychotherapist
11a Richmond Road, Brighton
BN2 3RL
Tel: 0171 919 7230/7237/
01273 685 852
LCP

Dawn Ward
Hypno-Psychotherapist
Lake View, 5 Harbour Barn,
Winchelsea Beach, E Sussex TN36 4LR
Tel: 01797 226890
NSHAP

Jane Whistler
Autogenic Psychotherapist
Pond Cottage, Henley Down, Catsfield,
Battle, East Sussex TN33 9BN;
41c The Cut, Waterloo SE1 8LF
Tel: 01323 833913/01424 830422
0171 207 4907
BAFAT

Yvete Wiener
Analytical Psychologist-Jungian Analyst
Gate House, Horse Shoe Lane, Beckley
nr Rye, East Sussex TN31 6RL
Tel: 01797 260759/01797 260287
BAP

Robert Withers
Analytical Psychologist-Jungian Analyst
113 Freshfield Road, Brighton
BN2 5BR;
The Rock Clinic, 270 Eastern Road,
Brighton BN2 5TA
Tel: 01273 621841/01273 671729
SAP

EAST YORKSHIRE

Paul Blackburn
Systemic Psychotherapist
Psychological Services, Westwood
Hospital, Beverley, East Yorkshire
Tel: 01482 875875
IFT

EDINBURGH

Jean B Bechhofer
Behavioural Psychotherapist
51 Barnton Park View, Edinburgh
EH4 6HH
Tel: 0131 339 4083
BABCP

Caroline Blair
Cognitive Psychotherapist
Young People's Unit, Edinburgh Health
Care NHS Trust, Royal Edinburgh
Hospital, Morningside Place EH10 5HF
Tel: 0131 447 4847/0131 537 46364
BABCP

Nick Child
Family Therapist
8 Lee Crescent, Portobello, Edinburgh
EH15 1LW
Tel: 0131 669 2184
AFT

Bobbie Fraser
Sexual and Marital Psychotherapist
Sexual Problems Clinic, Western Gen
Hospital (NHS Trust), Crewe Road,
Edinburgh EH4 2XU
BASMT

Christopher Freeman
Cognitive Behavioural Psychotherapist
Department of Psychotherapy, Cullen
Centre, Royal Edinburgh Hospital,
Morningside Pk, Edinburgh EH10 5HF
Tel: 0131 537 6599
BABCP

Maggie Gray
Cognitive Behavioural Psychotherapist
Cullen Centre, 29 Morningside Park,
Edinburgh EH10 5HF
Tel: 0131 447 2011 x 4797
BABCP

Eira Hamilton
Sexual and Marital Psychotherapist
8 Duddingston Crescent, Edinburgh
EH15 3AS
BASMT

Mary Anne Maclellan Hart
Hypno-Psychotherapist
3 Sciennes Road, Edinburgh EH9 1LE
Tel: 0131 668 3051
NRHP

Penelope Holland
Analytical Psychologist-Jungian Analyst
16 Calton Hill, Edinburgh EH1 3BJ
Tel: 0131 547 4285/2
BAP

Helen Kennedy
Gestalt Psychotherapist
7 Sciennes Gardens, Edinburgh
EH9 1NR
Tel: 0131 667 6257/0131 228 3841
GPTI

Laila Kjellstrom
Psychodrama Psychotherapist
16 Roseneath Place, Edinburgh
EH9 1JB
Tel: 0131 229 3310
BPDA

Jane Kunkler
Cognitive Behavioural Psychotherapist
Department of Health Psychology,
Astley Ainslie Hospital, 133 Grange
Loan, Edinburgh EH9 2HL
Tel: 0131 537 9000 x 49128/
0131 667 3454
BABCP

Alison M McFarlane
Cognitive Behavioural Psychotherapist
Cullen Centre, 29 Morningside Park,
Edinburgh EH10 5HF
Tel: 0131 537 6797
BABCP

Frances Milne
Analytical Psychologist-Jungian Analyst
4 Lennox Street, Edinburgh EH4 1QA
Tel: 0131 332 8049
IGAP

Harry Milton
Hypno-Psychotherapist
14 House O'Hill Road, Edinburgh
EH4 2AP
Tel: 0131 332 6363
NRHP

Bani Shorter
Analytical Psychologist-Jungian Analyst
9 South East Circus Place, Edinburgh
EH3 6TJ
Tel: 0131 225 1297
IGAP

Susan Sibley
Child Psychotherapist
SIHR, 56 Albany Street, Edinburgh
EH1 3QR
Tel: 0131 556 0924/0131 556 2612 (f)
ACP

David B Steven
Hypno-Psychotherapist
Bruntsfield Centre, 16 Granville
Terrace, Edinburgh EH10 4PQ
Tel: 0131 229 7823
NRHP

Guinevere Williams
Gestalt Psychotherapist
4 East Brighton Crescent, Portobello,
Edinburgh EH15 1LR
Tel: 0131 657 3496
GPTI

ESSEX

Janet Anderson
Child Psychotherapist
Harlow Child and Family Consultation
Service, Galen House Clinic, Fourth
Avenue, Harlow, Essex CM20 1DW
Tel: 01279 425371/0181 530 2378
ACP

Jane Arundell
Group Analytic Psychotherapist
Dukes Priory Hospital, Stump Lane,
Springfield, Chelmsford, Essex
CM1 5SJ;
49 Alfred Road, Brentwood, Essex
CM14 4BT
Tel: 01245 345345/01277 224618
IPC

Chris Beighton
Sexual and Marital Psychotherapist
Marital Counselling Service, 150 The
Maples, Harlow, Essex CM19 4RD
BASMT

Jane Bingham
Psychoanalytic Psychotherapist
Moulsham Mill, Parkway, Chelmsford,
Essex CM2 7PX
Tel: 01245 252414/01702 558969
IPC

Bryan Boswood
Group Analyst
Burnside, Ingatestone Road,
Blackmore, Ingatestone, Essex
CM4 0NZ
Tel: 0171 935 3103/01277 821309
IGA

Irene Brankin
Psychosynthesis Psychotherapist
14 Lynton Road, Hadleigh, Essex
SS7 2QQ
Tel: 01702 555420
PET

Stewart Britten
Jungian Child Analyst, Child
Psychotherapist
The Rows, Layer de la Haye,
Colchester, Essex CO2 0EU
Tel: 01206 738299
ACP

Graham Bull
Psychoanalytic Psychotherapist
64 Brathwaite Avenue, Romford, Essex
RM7 0DS
Tel: 01708 753 037
CFAR

Katherine Cameron
Psychoanalytic Psychotherapist
57 Castle Street, Saffron Walden, Essex
CB10 1BD
Tel: 01799 527449
IPSS

Mark Philip Chandler
Cognitive Behavioural Psychotherapist
Westcliffe Community Care Centre,
Balmoral Road, Westcliffe-on-Sea,
Essex SS0 7DN
Tel: 01702 393344
BABCP

Maureen Chapman
Psychoanalytic Psychotherapist,
Analytical Psychologist-Jungian Analyst
The Rectory, Theydon Mount, Epping,
Essex CM16 7PW;
27 Beryl Road, Hammersmith, London
W6 8JS
Tel: 01992 578723/0181 748 0718
BAP, IPC

Margaret Clark
Psychoanalytic Psychotherapist
Linscott House, Flat D, Russell Road,
Buckhurst Hill, Essex IG9 5QE
Tel: 0181 504 6128
LCP

Marie Conyers
Psychoanalytic Psychotherapist
Crushes Manor House, 247 Rayleigh
Road, Hutton, Nr Brentwood, Essex
CM13 1PJ
Tel: 01277 232585
LCP

Kay Coussens
Integrative Psychotherapist
42 Glenwood Drive, Gidea Park,
Romford, Essex RM2 5AS
Tel: 01708 755384
MC

Carol Crouch
Integrative Psychotherapist
Woodside, 61 Russell Road, Buckhurst
Hill, Essex IG9 5QF
Tel: 0181 504 0059
RCSPC

Elizabeth A Deeble
Cognitive Behavioural Psychotherapist
Psychology Dept, Goodmayes Hospital,
Barley Lane, Goodmayes, Essex
IG3 8XJ
Tel: 0181 983 8000 x 2260
BABCP

Naomi Elton
Systemic Psychotherapist
Child and Family Consultation Service,
42 London Road, Braintree, Essex
CM7 2LQ
Tel: 01376 553263/01376 327079 (f)
KCC

Karl Figlio
Psychoanalytic Psychotherapist
24 Rosebery Avenue, Colchester, Essex
CO1 2UJ
AGIP

Almuth-Maria Fox
Integrative Psychotherapist
101 Hadleigh Road, Leigh-on-Sea, Essex
SS9 2LY
Tel: 01277 840668/01702 72634
RCSPC

Derek Gale
Humanistic Psychotherapist
The Gale Centre, Stable Cottage,
Whitakers Way, Loughton, Essex
IG10 1SQ
Tel: 0181 508 9344
AHPP

Sharon Gilbert
Psychosynthesis Psychotherapist
128 Meads Lane, Seven Kings, Ilford,
Essex IG3 8PE
Tel: 0181 590 3850
PET

Joan Goring-Avery
Hypno-Psychotherapist
19A Station Road, Thorpe Bay, Essex
SS1 3JY
Tel: 01702 587 506
NSHAP

Eve Grainger
Child Psychotherapist
Barking & Dagenham Child & Family
Consult Service, 31 Woodward Road,
Dagenham, Essex RM9 4SJ
Tel: 0181 592 4445/0181 348 5457
ACP

John Gravelle
Integrative Psychotherapist
8 Gordon Road, Chelmsford, Essex
CM2 9LL
Tel: 01245 491795
MC

Angela Greenwood
Educational Therapist
34 Sea View Road, Leigh on Sea, Essex
SS9 1AT
Tel: 01702 73540
FAETT

Jamie G H Hacker Hughes
Cognitive Behavioural Psychotherapist
Sunnyside, King Street, Maldon, Essex
CM9 5DY
Tel: 01621 850211/01708 464244
BABCP

Linda Harvey
Cognitive Analytic Therapist
Norbrook, Eastwick, Nr Harlow, Essex
CM20 2QX
Tel: 01279 410 435
ACAT

Devam Hendry
Psychosynthesis Psychotherapist
14 Home Close, Harlow, Essex
CM20 3PD
Tel: 01279 414470
PET

Peter Hood
Analytical Psychologist-Jungian Analyst
Appletree Cottage, The Street, Feering,
Colchester, Essex CO5 9QH
Tel: 01206 579190/01376 571478
BAP

Faridoon Hormasji
Hypno-Psychotherapist
2A Cross Road, Romford, Essex
RM7 8AT
Tel: 01708 764740
NRHP

Christina Howtone
Hypno-Psychotherapist
139 Sevenoaks Close, Harold Hill,
Essex RM3 7EF
Tel: 01708 373175
NSHAP

Margaret Hurst
Child Psychotherapist
North Essex Child & Family
Consultation Service, Rannoch Lodge,
146 Broomfield Road, Chelmsford,
Essex CM1 1RN
Tel: 01245 354188/0181 989 6740
ACP

Beverley Jenkins
Psychoanalytic Psychotherapist
4 Towneley Cottages, Tysea Hill,
Stapleford Abbotts, Essex RM4 1JP
Tel: 01708 377327
LCP

Janice Johnstone
Hypno-Psychotherapist
10 De Bohun Court, Saffron Walden,
Essex CB10 2BA
Tel: 01799 524123
NRHP

Margaret Kendrick
Hypno-Psychotherapist
3 Seaview Parade, Maylandsea, Essex
CM3 6EL
Tel: 01621 742745
NSHAP

Daniel Kwei
Gestalt Psychotherapist
6 Brentwood Place, Sawyers Hall Lane,
Brentwood, Essex CM15 9DN
Tel: 01277 226834
GPTI, MET

Annie Lau
Family Psychotherapist
Child Guidance Clinic, Loxford Hall,
Loxford Lane, Ilford, Essex IG1 2PL
Tel: 0171 478 7211
IFT

Jo-Ann Lewis
Psychoanalytic Psychotherapist
6 Fairview Gardens, Woodford Green,
Essex IG8 7DJ
Tel: 0181 559 1318
AGIP

Trevor J Mathews
Cognitive Behavioural Psychotherapist
1 Moat Edge Gardens, Billericay, Essex
CM12 0NJ
Tel: 01277 631554/01245 351441
BABCP

David Millar
Child Psychotherapist
Colchester Child & Family
Consultation Service, Stanwell House,
Stanwell Street, Colchester, Essex
CO2 7DL
Tel: 01206 579190/01206 768211
ACP

Susan Moses
Psychoanalytic Psychotherapist
3 Harlings Grove, Waterloo Lane,
Chelmsford, Essex CM1 1YQ
Tel: 01245 354318
IPC

Michael Neenan
Cognitive Behavioural Psychotherapist
36 Shearers Way, Boreham, Essex
CM3 3AE
Tel: 01245 468262/01245 351441
BABCP

Michael Parker
Group Analyst
6 Vicarage Road, Chelmsford, Essex
CM2 9PG
Tel: 01277 840263/01245 609656
IGA

Joyce Penn
Hypno-Psychotherapist
213 York Road, Southend-on-Sea,
Essex SS1 2RU
Tel: 01702 462191
NRHP

Dusan Potkonjak
Psychodrama Psychotherapist
Warley Hospital, Warley Hill,
Brentwood, Essex CM14 5HQ
Tel: 01277 217299
BPDA

Maeja Raicar
Attachment-based Psychoanalytic
Psychotherapist
8 Feering Road, Billericay, Essex
CM11 2DR
Tel: 01277 654351
CAPP

Michelle Reynolds
Psychoanalytic Psychotherapist
Whitehall, Elmdon, Essex CB11 4NH
Tel: 01763 838800
LCP

Paul Rice
Behavioural Psychotherapist
Blackwater House, 81 Riverside Way,
Kelvedon, Colchester, Essex CO5 9LX
Tel: 01376 571515/01708 464238
BABCP

Sandra Rix
Sexual and Marital Psychotherapist
Coopers, Coopers Hill, Ongar, Essex
CM5 9EG
BASMT

Mardi Robinson
Group Analyst
The Cottage, Mill Street, Polestead,
Colchester, Essex CO6 5AD
Tel: 01206 263104
IGA

Noel F Sawyer
Cognitive Behavioural Psychotherapist
Chelmsford & Essex Centre, New
London Road, Chelmsford, Essex;
Dukes Priory Hospital, Stump Lane,
Springfield Green, Chelmsford
CM1 5SJ
Tel: 01245 287440
BABCP

Kay Schreiber
Systemic Psychotherapist
18 Brunswick Road, Southend-on-Sea,
Essex SS1 2UH
Tel: 0702 611 973
KCC

Michael Scott
Group Analyst
20 Thornwood, Colchester, Essex
CO4 5LR
Tel: 01255 220226/01206 854965
IGA

Ruth M Seglow
Child Psychotherapist
Barking & Dagenham Child & Family
Consult Service, 31 Woodward Road,
Dagenham, Essex RM9 4SJ
Tel: 0181 340 9145/0181 592 4445
ACP

David Shrimpton
Psychodynamic Psychotherapist
Oakleigh, Church Road, Wickham
St Paul, Essex CO9 2PN
Tel: 01787 269594
WMIP

Richard Smith
Transpersonal Psychotherapist
15 Squirrel's Field, Myland Gate, Mill
Road, Colchester, Essex
Tel: 01206 844 032
CCPE

Patricia Steel
Hypno-Psychotherapist
56 Burnway, Emerson Park,
Hornchurch, Essex RM11 3SG
Tel: 01708 472573
NRHP

Alan Talbot
Analytical Psychologist-Jungian Analyst
Belchers, The Street, High Easter, Nr
Chelmsford, Essex CM1 4PW
Tel: 01245 231603
SAP

Peter Tapang
Family Therapist, Family
Psychotherapist
23 Joydon Drive, Chadwell Heath,
Romford, Essex RM6 4ST
Tel: 0181 556 2450
IFT

Chris Teng
Systemic Psychotherapist
33 Furrowfelde, Kingswood, Basildon,
Essex SS16 5HA
Tel: 01268 533 911 x 3835/
01268 533769
KCC

Joan Thompson
NLP Psychotherapist
31 Priory Crescent, Prittlewell,
Southend-on-Sea, Essex SS2 6JY
Tel: 01702 613828
CPCP, ANLP

Margaret Togher
Systemic Psychotherapist
52 Kenwood Gardens, Gants Hill, Ilford
IG2 6YQ
Tel: 0181 535 6818/0181 550 7436
KCC

Joanna Trosh
Cognitive Behavioural Psychotherapist
Behavioural Psychotherapy Dept,
Chelmsford and Essex Centre, New
London Road, Chelmsford CM2 0QH
Tel: 01245 287440
BABCP

David Tune
Body Psychotherapist
59 Glebe Road, Tiptree, Essex
CO5 0TD
Tel: 01621 817932
CCHP, AHPP

Steven Walker
Family Psychotherapist
15 Granville Close, West Bergholt,
Essex CO6 3LQ
Tel: 01206 242160
AFT

Anne Welsh
Psychosynthesis Psychotherapist
Blacksmith's Cottage, Clavering, Nr
Saffron Walden, Essex CB11 4QL
Tel: 0181 202 4525
IPS

Bernard Westcott
Group Analyst
67 Somerset Road, Laindon, Basildon,
Essex SS15 6PP
Tel: 01268 411032
IGA

Ann Whatley
Family Therapist
Ansden, 9 Colehills Close, Clavering,
Saffron Walden, Essex CB11 4QY
Tel: 01799 550807
AFT

Eleanor Wheeley
Systemic Psychotherapist
Cromwell House, 7 Cromwell Avenue,
Billericay, Essex CM12 0AE
BASMT

David Wilmot
Family Psychotherapist
Poplar Cottage, Chapel Road,
Ridgewell, Essex CO9 4RZ
Tel: 01440 785377
IFT

Paul Woodcraft
Cognitive Behavioural Psychotherapist
Chelmsford and Essex Centre, New
London Road, Chelmsford, Essex
CM2 0QH
Tel: 01245 287440
BABCP

Nicola Woodward
Child Psychotherapist
Redbridge Child & Family Consultation
Centre, Loxford Hall, Loxford Lane,
Ilford, Essex IG1 2PL
Tel: 0181 347 6831/0181 478 7211
ACP

Kenneth Wright
Psychoanalytic Marital Psychotherapist
4 Mill Street, Nayland, Colchester,
Essex CO6 4HU
Tel: 01206 262234
TMSI

FIFE

Joyce Agnew
Personal Construct Psychotherapist
Citra, Cupar Road, Ceres, Cupar, Fife,
Scotland KY15 5LP
Tel: 01334 828340
CPCP

Rosemary Braid
Humanistic and Integrative
Psychotherapist
Channel Farm, Kinross, Scotland
KY13 7HD
Tel: 01592 840 236
AHPP

Neil Harrington
Cognitive Behavioural Psychotherapist
Clinical Psychology Department,
Stratheden Hospital, Cupar, Fife
KY15 5RR
Tel: 01334 657443/01334 652611
BABCP

Clare Petrie
Transpersonal Psychotherapist
Earlsneuk, Chapel Green, Earlsferry,
Leven, Fife KY9 1AD
Tel: 01333 330853
CCPE

Jack Tollan
Hypno-Psychotherapist
'Redcroft', 27 Andrew Lang Crescent,
St Andrews, Fife KY16 8LY
Tel: 01334 478457
CTS

FIFE & CENTRAL

Kay Kennedy
Individual and Group Humanistic
Psychotherapist
15 High Station Road, Falkirk FK1 5LP
Tel: 01324 621930
AHPP

Katherine Young
Cognitive Behavioural Psychotherapist
20 Kellie Place, Alloa,
Clackmannanshire, Scotland
FK10 2DW
Tel: 01786 434000 x 7841/
01259 314623
BABCP

GLAMORGAN

Barrie Aldridge
Integrative Psychotherapist
Creigfan, Graig Penllyn, Cowbridge,
South Glamorgan, South Wales
CF7 7RT
Tel: 01443 482896/01446 773202
RCSPC

John Brett
Systemic Psychotherapist
3 Springfield, Horton, South Gower,
West Glamorgan SA3 1LQ
FIC

Paul David Gwyn Harris
Cognitive Behavioural Psychotherapist
102 Glynhir Road, Pontardulais,
Swansea, West Glamorgan SA4 1PU
Tel: 01792 561155 x 6588/
01792 884 952
BABCP

Jenny Thomas
Transactional Analysis Psychotherapist
The Highlands, Old Llantrisant Road,
Tonyrefail, Mid Glamorgan CF39 8YU
Tel: 01443 676579
ITA

GLASGOW

Helen Bates
Family Therapist
12 Skaterigg Drive, Glasgow G13 1SR
AFT

Mari E Brannigan
Cognitive Behavioural Psychotherapist
Dept of Clinical Psychology, Stobhill
Hospital, 133 Balornock Road,
Glasgow G21 3UW
Tel: 0141 201 3607
BABCP

Teresa Brown
Psychodrama Psychotherapist
Stoneleigh, 48 Clevedon Drive,
Kelvinside, Glasgow G12 0MU
Tel: 0141 334 8908
BPDA

Barbara Carruthers
Humanistic Psychotherapist
115 Dowanhill Street, Glasgow
G12 9EQ
Tel: 0141 357 3371
AHPP

Jim Christie
Group Analyst
The Garnethill Centre Ltd, 28 Rose
Street, Glasgow G3 6RE
Tel: 0141 333 0730/0141 357 5676
IGA

Grace Coia
Hypno-Psychotherapist
10 Carment Drive, Glasgow G41 3PP
Tel: 0141 632 6663
NRHP

George Crawford
Child Psychotherapist
Scottish Institute of Human Relations,
13 Park Terrace, Glasgow, Scotland
Tel: 0131 556 0924/0141 332 0011
ACP

Jane Ellwood
Psychoanalytic Psychotherapist, Child
Psychotherapist
Flat 1 / Left, 53 Fergus Drive, North
Kelvinside, Glasgow G20 6AQ;
Dept of Child & Family Psychiatry,
Royal Hospital for Sick Children,
Yorkhill, Glasgow G3
Tel: 0141 531 6106/0141 946 7030
LCP, ACP

Angela Hamilton
Psychoanalytic Psychotherapist
The Garnethill Centre, 28 Rose Street,
Glasgow G3 6RE
Tel: 0141 333 0730
LPDO

Wallace Hamilton
Child Psychotherapist, Psychoanalytic
Psychotherapist
17 Schaw Drive, Bearsden, Glasgow,
Scotland G61 3AT
Tel: 0141 942 1226
ACP, BAP

Christine Retson Hogg
Hypno-Psychotherapist
26 Westbourne Crescent, Bearsden,
Glasgow G61 4HD
Tel: 0141 942 5286
NRHP

Anne J A Hume
Cognitive Behavioural Psychotherapist
101 Parkville Drive, Burnside Park,
Blantyre, Lanarkshire G72 0LF
Tel: 01698 711405
BABCP

Hetty MacKinnon
Autogenic Psychotherapist
An Airigh, 20 Borden Road, Glasgow
G13 1QX
Tel: 0141 959 3230
BAFAT

J G Robinson
Child Psychotherapist
Department of Child & Family
Psychiatry, Royal Hospital for Sick
Children, Glasgow, Scotland
Tel: 0141 201 0000/0141 620 0651
ACP

Wilson Russell
Group Analyst
The Garnethill Centre, 28 Rose Street,
Glasgow G3 6RE
Tel: 0141 333 0730/0131 447 6038
IGA

Martin S Turner
Cognitive Behavioural Psychotherapist
Larkfield Centre, Garngaber Avenue,
Lenzie, Glasgow G66 3UG
Tel: 0141 776 7100
BABCP

GLOUCESTERSHIRE

Eve Adams
Integrative Psychosynthesis
Psychotherapist
Lantern Cottage, Stockend, Edge,
Stroud GL6 6PN
Tel: 01452 813355
RE.V

James Agar
Transactional Analysis Psychotherapist
c/o South Cotswold Psychotherapy
Centre, Red House Farm, Westrip
Lane, Westrip, Stroud, Glos GL5 4PL
Tel: 01453 750716
ITA

Kay Allan
Psychoanalytic Psychotherapist
111 Promenade, Cheltenham,
Gloucestershire GL50 1NW
Tel: 01242 252902
IPC, SIP

Cecilia Batten
Psychoanalytic Psychotherapist
58 Leckhampton Road, Cheltenham,
Gloucestershire GL53 0BG
Tel: 01242 22222 x 4241/01242 521768
SIP, BAP

William Burritt
Analytical Psychologist-Jungian Analyst
1 Merestones Drive, The Park,
Cheltenham GL50 2SU
Tel: 01242 244744
IGAP

Paula Carter
Sexual and Marital Psychotherapist
Clutters, 11-12 Great Rissington,
Cheltenham, Gloucestershire
GL54 2LR
BASMT

John Cross
Psychoanalytic Psychotherapist
The Old Coach House, Lye Lane,
Cleeve Hill, Cheltenham, Glos
Tel: 01204 621200
AGIP

Gerard Cutner
Psychoanalytic Psychotherapist
Chelholm Flat 1, Lansdown Road,
Cheltenham GL51 6PU
Tel: 01242 527376
BAP

Miranda Davies
Child Psychotherapist, Jungian Child
Analyst
Hillslie House, Littleworth, Amberley,
Stroud, Gloucestershire GL5 5AN;
Severnside Institute of Psychotherapy,
11 Orchard Street, PO Box 47, Bristol
BS10 7BZ
Tel: 0117 950 0255/01453 873 552
ACP, SAP, SIP

Johanna Maria Diepeveen
Psychosynthesis Psychotherapist
Highfield Cottage, Ocker Hill,
Randwick, Stroud, Gloucestershire
GL6 6HY
Tel: 01453 764215
IPS

Barbara Docker-Drysdale
Psychoanalytic Psychotherapist
2 Popes Court, Whelford, Fairford,
Glos GL7 5JP
Tel: 01285 712728
SIP

Lea K Elliott
Psychoanalytic Psychotherapist
18 Eldorado Road, Cheltenham, Glos
GL50 2PT
Tel: 01242 518642
WMIP, SIP

Frances Emeleus
Sexual and Marital Psychotherapist
1 Church Cottages, Notgrove,
Cheltenham, Glos GL54 3BT
BASMT

Anne Goodrich
Psychoanalytic Psychotherapist
6 Wychbury Close, Leckhampton,
Cheltenham, Glos GL53 0HT
Tel: 01242 262526
IPC

David Gowling
Transactional Analysis Psychotherapist
The Red House Farm, Westrip Lane,
Westrip, Stroud, Glos GL5 4PL
Tel: 01453 836277
ITA, MET

Jane Gracie
Psychoanalytic Psychotherapist
10 Somerford Road, Cirencester,
Gloucestershire GL7 1TN
Tel: 01285 650143
SIP

Annie Grocott
Psychoanalytic Psychotherapist
20 Moorend Crescent, Leckhampton,
Cheltenham, Gloucestershire
GL53 0EL
Tel: 01242 572290
GUILD, SIP

Kelvin Hall
Humanistic and Integrative
Psychotherapist
Cherry Tree Cottage, Shortwood,
Nailsworth, Glos GL6 0SB
Tel: 01453 833 861
BCPC

Nick Hedley
Psychosynthesis Psychotherapist
Highfield Cottage, Ocker Hill,
Randwick, Stroud, Gloucestershire
GL6 6HY
Tel: 01453 750131
IPS

Patricia Hoogh-Rowntree
Analytical Psychologist-Jungian Analyst
Ivy Cottage, Church Lane, Sapperton,
Nr Cirencester, Gloucestershire
GL7 6LQ
Tel: 01285 760209
BAP

Frances Lacey
Transactional Analysis Psychotherapist
The Red House Farm, Westrip Lane,
Westrip, Stroud, Glos GL5 4PL
Tel: 01453 750716
ITA, MET

Barbara Luthy
Humanistic and Integrative
Psychotherapist
College Farm, Beacon Lane, Haresfield,
Glos GL10 3ES
Tel: 01452 720934
BCPC, AHPP

June McOstrich
Psychosynthesis Psychotherapist
Forge House, Kemble, Gloucestershire
GL7 6AD
Tel: 01285 770 538
IPS

Cass Moggridge
Psychodrama Psychotherapist
Priory Mill, Kelmscott Road, Lechlade,
Glos GL7 3HB
Tel: 01367 25334
BPDA

Elizabeth Morris
Humanistic and Integrative
Psychotherapist
Buckholdt House, The Street,
Frampton on Severn, Gloucestershire
GL7 7ED
Tel: 01462 741106
AHPP

Stephen Morris
Psychoanalytic Psychotherapist
53 Slad Road, Stroud, Glos GL5 1QT
Tel: 01453 750765
SIP

Karen O'Hara
Integrative Psychotherapist, Body
Psychotherapist
F23, The Old Convent, Beeches Green,
Stroud, Glos
Tel: 01452 813261
CCHP

Carmen Reynal
Analytical Psychologist-Jungian Analyst
Keyneton Hayes, Upper Slaughter,
Gloucestershire GL54 2JG;
31 Warnborough Road, Oxford
OX2 6JA
Tel: 01865 511063/01451 821947
IGAP

Elizabeth Seigal
Psychoanalytic Psychotherapist
Westbourne, 43 Middle Street, Stroud,
Glos GL5 1DZ
Tel: 01453 751114
SIP, BAP

Mary Silmon
NLP Psychotherapist
66 Elmbridge Road, Gloucester
GL2 0PB
Tel: 01452 414976
ANLP

Claire Skailes
Analytical Psychotherapist
5 Fairview Terrace, Wallsquarry,
Brimscombe, Stroud GL5 2PB
Tel: 01453 885229
WMIP

Lyn Stephens
Psychoanalytic Psychotherapist
9 Montpellier Grove, Cheltenham,
Gloucestershire GL50 2XB
Tel: 01242 521945
AGIP

Deirdre Sutton-Smith
Group Analyst, Psychoanalytic
Psychotherapist
'Book End Cottage', Amberley,
Gloucester GL5 5AJ
Tel: 01179 441005/01435 872786
IGA, WTC

Penny Thomas
Humanistic and Integrative
Psychotherapist
6 Wallow Green, Horsley, Nailsworth,
Stroud GL6 0PB
Tel: 01453 833752
BCPC

Shona Ward
Transactional Analysis Psychotherapist
South Cotswold Centre, Red House
Farm, Foxmoor Lane, Glos GL5 4PL
Tel: 01453 750716
ITA

Judy Watkins
Psychoanalytic Psychotherapist
Broadwell, Church Road,
Leckhampton, Cheltenham GL51 5XX
Tel: 01242 580214
GUILD

GRAMPIAN

David D Howie
Hypno-Psychotherapist
9B Millburn Street, Aberdeen,
Grampian AL11 6SS
Tel: 01224 574190
NRHP

Christiane Kohler
Hypno-Psychotherapist
51 Cairngrassie Circle, Portlethen,
Aberdeen AB1 4TZ
Tel: 01224 781747
NSHAP

Enno Kuttner
Family Therapist
Royal Aberdeen Children's Hospital,
Cornhill Road, Aberdeen AB9 2ZG
Tel: 01224 681818
AFT

Malcolm MacPherson
Psychoanalytic Psychotherapist
15 Crollshillock Place, Newtonhill,
Stonehaven, Kincardineshire AB3 2RF;
15/17 Belmont Street, Aberdeen
AB1 1JR
Tel: 01224 620495/01569 730963
NAAP

Ken Sawyer
Hypno-Psychotherapist
31 Cairngrassie Circle, Portlethen,
Aberdeen AB1 4TZ
Tel: 01224 781452
CTS

GWENT

Jan Hillman
Sexual and Marital Psychotherapist
The Darlin, Llangattock-Vibon-Avel,
Monmouth, Gwent NP5 4NG
BASMT

Jo Morgan
Hypno-Psychotherapist
6 Silver Birch Close, Roman Reach,
Caerleon, Gwent NP6 1RX
Tel: 01633 420847
NSHAP

John Plowman
Hypno-Psychotherapist
22 Goldcroft Common, Caerleon,
Newport, Gwent NP6 1NG
Tel: 01633 420095
NRHP

GWYNEDD

Keith Fearns
Cognitive Behavioural Psychotherapist
Llys Deinol, Garth Road, Bangor,
Gwynedd LL57 2SE
BABCP

Sheila Jenkins
Cognitive Behavioural Psychotherapist
Arfon Mental Health Centre, 26
College Road, Bangor, Gwynedd
LL57 4AN
Tel: 01248 370137
BABCP

Allen Langley
Hypno-Psychotherapist
Bryn Hyfryd, Lon St Ffraid, Trearddur
Bay, Holyhead, Anglesey LL65 2UD
Tel: 01407 861258
NRHP

Adam May
Hypno-Psychotherapist
Cefn Cana, Llanddaniel Fab, Gaerwen,
Ynys Mon LL60 6EF
Tel: 01248 421015
NRHP

Madeline Osborn
Psychoanalytic Psychotherapist
Hergest Unit, Ysbyty Gwynedd,
Bangor, Gwynedd LL57 2PW
Tel: 01248 384038
NWIDP

Ian Rickard
Cognitive Behavioural Psychotherapist
Green Oak, Pentre Du, Betws y coed
LL24 0BU
Tel: 01248 682682/01690 710647
BABCP

HAMPSHIRE

Louise Anthias
Family Therapist
Old School House, Knapp Lane,
Ampfield, Romsey, Hants SO51 9BT
IFT

Brian Attridge
Core Process Psychotherapist
Flat 1, 16 Victoria Grove, Southsea,
Hampshire PO5 1NE
Tel: 01705 863266
KI

Melloney Atuahene
NLP Psychotherapist
15 St Peters Road, Basingstoke,
Hampshire RG22 6TD
Tel: 01256 841184
ANLP

Anne Baring
Analytical Psychologist-Jungian Analyst
White Lodge, Grange Park, Alresford,
Hants SO24 9TG
Tel: 01962 732744
AJA

Jan D Beach
Cognitive Behavioural Psychotherapist
G Block, Royal Naval Hospital, Haslar,
Gosport, Hants PO12 2AA
Tel: 01705 584255 x 2421
BABCP

Ross Bennett
Humanistic and Integrative
Psychotherapist
Kwanti, Jermyns Lane, Ampfield,
Romsey, Hampshire SO51 0QA
Tel: 01794 368012
SPEC

Eileen Berry
Group Analyst
4 Eastgate Street, Winchester, Hants
SO23 8EB
Tel: 01962 854439
IGA

Nicholas J Black
Cognitive Behavioural Psychotherapist
Clinical Psychology Service, Royal
Hampshire County Hospital, Romsey
Road, Winchester SO22 5DG
Tel: 01962 824351/01962 824418
BABCP

Daphne Boddington
Sexual and Marital Psychotherapist
Coopers Bridge Farm, Bramshott,
Liphook, Hants GU30 7RF
BASMT

Jane Bould
Psychodrama Psychotherapist
17 Tudor Avenue, Emsworth,
Hampshire PO10 7UG
Tel: 01705 814545
BPDA

Sue Brock
NLP Psychotherapist
4 Paddock Fields, Old Basing,
Basingstoke, Hampshire RG24 7DB
Tel: 01256 26176
ANLP

Dianna Carruthers
Humanistic and Integrative
Psychotherapist
Portsmouth Natural Health &
Psychotherapy Centre, 20 Landport
Terrace, Portsmouth, Hampshire
PO1 2RG
Tel: 01705 830558
SPEC

Adrian Childs-Clarke
Cognitive Behavioural Psychotherapist
Psychological Therapies Service,
Department of Psychiatry, Royal South
Hants Hospital, Graham Road,
Southampton SO14 0YG
Tel: 01703 634288 x 2536
BABCP

Isabel Clarke
Cognitive Behavioural Psychotherapist
Psychological Therapies Service,
Department of Psychiatry, Royal South
Hants Hospital, Southampton, SO14
0YG
Tel: 01703 825531/01703 552546
BABCP

Andrea Clifford
Educational Therapist
Osborne House, Kingsley, Hampshire
GU35 9LW
Tel: 01420 476042
FAETT

S Clifton
Sexual and Marital Psychotherapist
3 Hermitage Gardens, Waterlooville,
Hampshire PO7 7PR
BASMT

Peter J Coles
Cognitive Behavioural Psychotherapist
Park Way Centre, Park Way, Havant,
Hampshire PO9 1HH
Tel: 01705 471661
BABCP

Brian Copley
Cognitive Behavioural Psychotherapist
Marchwood Priory Hospital, Hythe
Road, Marchwood, Southampton,
Hants SO4 4WU
Tel: 01703 840044
BABCP

Josephine Dahle
Humanistic and Integrative
Psychotherapist
Grove Natural Therapy Centre, 22
Grosvenor Road, Highfield,
Southampton, SO13 1RT
Tel: 01703 582245
SPEC

Mo Daniels
Psychodrama Psychotherapist
14 Sir Georges Road, Southampton,
Hampshire SO1 3AT
Tel: 01703 227778
BPDA

Paula Dyer
Sexual and Marital Psychotherapist
11 Basingbourne Close, Fleet, Hants
GU13 9TF
Tel: 01252 628744
BASMT

Enid Edgeley
Transpersonal Psychotherapist
59 St Chads Avenue, North End,
Portsmouth, Hants PO2 0SD
CCPE

Madeleine Everington
Psychoanalytic Psychotherapist
Hamesford House, East Harting,
Petersfield, Hants GU31 5LY
Tel: 01730 825383
LCP

Felicity Fincham
Cognitive Behavioural Psychotherapist
1 Hope Cottage, Little Shore Lane,
Bishops Waltham, Southampton, SO32
1ED
Tel: 01489 893753/01703 475247
BABCP

Anne Francis
Psychoanalytic Psychotherapist
1 Orchard Close, Epsom Road,
Guildford, Surrey GU12 PR
Tel: 01483 69177
AGIP, GCP

Patricia Glasspool
Hypno-Psychotherapist
12 Hocombe Drive, Chandlers Ford,
Eastleigh, Hants, SO53 5QE;
Southgate Natural Therapy Clinic,
Ground Floor, 13 Southgate Street,
Winchester, Hants SO23 9DZ
Tel: 01962 866903/01703 255678
NRHP

Peter Goold
Personal Construct Psychotherapist
Coudray House, Herriard, Nr
Basingstoke, Hants RG25 2PN
CPCP

P Kenneth Gordon
Cognitive Behavioural Psychotherapist
Winchester & Eastleigh Healthcare,
NHS Trust, Psychology Services, St
Paul's Hospital, Winchester SO22 5AA
Tel: 01962 860661 x 2094
BABCP

Margaret Greaves
Humanistic and Integrative
Psychotherapist
85 Park Road, Chandler's Ford,
Eastleigh, Hampshire, SO53 1GJ
Tel: 01703 263604
SPEC

Peter Gregory
Sexual and Marital Psychotherapist
19 Chatsworth Road, Boyatt Wood,
Eastleigh, Hampshire, SO50 4PE
Tel: 01703 617990
BASMT

Rosalie Gurr
Sexual and Marital Psychotherapist
The Old Village Stores, Braishfield,
Romsey, Hampshire SO51 0PQ
BASMT

Linda Hall
Transpersonal Psychotherapist
The Maples, Lingmala Grove, Church
Crookham, Fleet, Hants GU13 0JW;
Mayan Pathways, 3 Bank Place,
Porthmadog, Gwynedd LL49 9AA
CCPE

Peter Hatswell
Psychoanalytic Psychotherapist
'Stillions', 3 Windmill Hill, Alton, Hants
GU34 2RY
Tel: 01420 82385
GUILD, GCP

Valerie Hatswell
Psychoanalytic Psychotherapist
Stillions, 3 Windmill Hill, Alton,
Hampshire GU34 2RY
Tel: 01420 82385
GCP

Gillian Isaacs Hemmings
Psychoanalytic Psychotherapist
Levers, North Lane, South Harting,
Petersfield, Hants GU31 5NW
Tel: 01730 825 226
LCP

Beatrice Hook
Group Analyst
31 Southview Road, Shirley,
Southampton SO15 5JD
Tel: 01703 496488
IGA

John Hook
Group Analyst
31 Southview Road, Shirley,
Southampton SO15 5JD
Tel: 01703 496488
IGA

Christine M Hooper
Family Therapist
'Ellesmere', The Crescent, Romsey,
Hampshire SO51 7NG
IFT

Vera M Hopkins
Psychodynamic Psychotherapist
'Oak Wood', 4 The Grange, Everton,
Lymington, Hants, SO41 0ZR
Tel: 01590 643335
HIP

Paul Jackson
Sexual and Marital Psychotherapist
66 Middle Brook Street, Winchester,
Hampshire SO23 8DQ
BASMT

Sue Lethbridge
Psychoanalytic Psychotherapist
16 Bannerman Road, Petersfield,
Hampshire GU32 2HQ
Tel: 01730 264056
AGIP, GCP

Maureen Lever
Integrative Psychotherapist
77 Hill Head Road, Hill Head, Fareham,
Hants PO14 3JP
Tel: 01329 662891
RCSPC

Gwenda Lippitt
Psychoanalytic Psychotherapist
Loyal Cottage, 3 The Street, Old
Basing, Nr Basingstoke, Hants
RG24 0BH
Tel: 01256 21178
CPP

Aidan Lunt
Psychoanalytic Psychotherapist
The Firs, 1 Barrs Wood Road, New
Milton, Hampshire BH25 5HS
Tel: 01425 610398
NWIDP

Sue Malone
Systemic Psychotherapist
Tresco, Forest Road, Liss Forest,
Hampshire GU33 7BL
BASMT

Cherrith A Marshall
Systemic Psychotherapist
'Sunnyside', Blissford Cross, Blissford,
Fordingbridge, Hants SP6 2JG
FIC

Angela Martin
Sexual and Marital Psychotherapist
27 Edgar Road, Winchester, Hants
SO23 9TN
BASMT

Helen P Matthews
Cognitive Behavioural Psychotherapist
Western Community Hospital, Walnut
Grove, Millbrook, Southampton, SO16
4XE
Tel: 01703 475400
BABCP

Brigitte McAndrew
Psychoanalytic Psychotherapist
46 Cleveland Road, Southsea PO5 1SG
Tel: 01705 861090
AAP

Terry Moore
NLP Psychotherapist
58 Northern Parade, Portsmouth,
Hampshire PO2 8NE
Tel: 01705 645774
ANLP

Josephine Mulvey
Sexual and Marital Psychotherapist
Flat 2, 106 Christchurch Road,
Winchester, Hampshire SO23 9TG
BASMT

Turid Nyhamar
Child Psychotherapist
72 Stoney Lane, Weeke, Winchester,
Hampshire SO22 6DP
Tel: 01962 883316
ACP

Michael O'Connor
Systemic Psychotherapist
136 Alexandra Road, Farnborough,
Hampshire GU14 6RN
Tel: 01276 692211/01252 515053
KCC

David Percy
Psychoanalytic Psychotherapist
10 Nightingale Close, Winchester,
Hants SO22 5QA
Tel: 01962 877962
GUILD

Barbara Plant
Sexual and Marital Psychotherapist
Theydon, Sarum Road, Winchester,
Hants SO22 5QT
BASMT

David Porter
Psychoanalytic Psychotherapist
161 Hursley Road, Chandlers Ford,
Eastleigh, Hants SO53 1JH
Tel: 01703 269603
IPC

Barbara Quin
Psychodrama Psychotherapist
9 Campbell Road, Southsea, Hampshire
PO5 1RH
Tel: 01705 294818
BPDA

Keith Reed-Jones
Transactional Analysis Psychotherapist,
Integrative Psychotherapist
4a Brading Avenue, Southsea,
Portsmouth, Hants PO4 9QJ
Tel: 01705 877792
MET

Marina Remington
Cognitive Behavioural Psychotherapist
Psychological Therapies Service, Dept
of Psychiatry, Royal South Hants
Hospital, St Mary's Rd, Soton
SO14 0YG
Tel: 01703 825531
BABCP

Margaret Robinson
Systemic Psychotherapist
Merryways, Owslebury, Winchester,
Hants SO21 1LP
IFT

Gillian Rose-Smith
Humanistic and Integrative
Psychotherapist
1 Riverview, Longmoor Road,
Greatham, Nr Liss, Hants GU33 6AE
Tel: 01420 538628
SPEC

Susan M Ross
Cognitive Behavioural Psychotherapist
Clinical Psychology Department,
Department of Psychiatry, Royal South
Hants Hospital, Southampton
SO14 6HW
Tel: 01703 230130/01702 825531
BABCP

Val Rubie
Attachment-based Psychoanalytic
Psychotherapist
17 Adam Close, Baughurst, Hampshire
RG26 5HG
Tel: 01734 811948
CAPP

Rosemary Russell
Psychoanalytic Psychotherapist
Finches, Hastards Lane, Selbourne,
Hampshire GU34 3LB
Tel: 01420 511367
BAP

Gill Salter
Humanistic and Integrative
Psychotherapist
The Grove Centre, 22 Grosvenor
Road, Southampton
Tel: 01703 582 245
SPEC

Brigitte Scott
Biodynamic Psychotherapist
4 Park Lane, Alderholt, Fordingbridge,
Hants SP6 3AJ
Tel: 01425 652577
BTC

E John Seymour
Psychoanalytic Psychotherapist
Racton, 36 Breach Avenue, Emsworth,
Hants PO10 8NB
Tel: 01243 373608
GCP

Rick Stanwood
Psychoanalytic Psychotherapist
34 St David's Road, Southsea,
Hampshire PO5 1QN
Tel: 01705 793983
AGIP, GCP

Quentin Stimpson
Transpersonal Psychotherapist
3 Grove Cottages, Gordon Road,
Fareham, Hampshire PO16 7TD
Tel: 01329 826 621
CCPE

Eva Stolte
Psychoanalytic Psychotherapist
34 St David's Road, Southsea, Hants
PO5 1QN
Tel: 01705 793983
AGIP, GCP

Barry Stone
Systemic Psychotherapist
'Acorns', 29 Forest Dean, Fleet,
Hampshire GU13 8TT
KCC

Jan Symes
Systemic Psychotherapist
Butts Cottage, The Butts, Alton,
Hampshire GU34 1RD
BASMT

Tony Taylor
Psychoanalytic Psychotherapist
9 Radford Gardens, Basingstoke, Hants
RG21 3NS
Tel: 01256 466308
IPSS

Jose von Buhler
Sexual and Marital Psychotherapist
33 High Street, Farnborough, Hants
GU14 6ES
Tel: 0836 240990/01252 543973
BASMT

HEREFORDSHIRE

John Aston
Integrative Psychotherapist
Stonebow Unit, County Hospital,
Hereford HR1 2ER
Tel: 01432 355444 x 5572/
01989 740232
RCSPC

Mervyn Brunt
Transactional Analysis Psychotherapist
Willow Glen, 19 Clive Street, Hereford
HR1 2SB
Tel: 01432 342789
ITA

Kiki Crean
Child Psychotherapist
Hereford Child & Family Guidance
Centre, Gaol Street, Hereford
HR1 1SA
Tel: 01432 273977/01432 357351
ACP

Christopher Fenton
Psychoanalytic Psychotherapist
The Leys, Aston, Kingsland,
Leominster, Herefordshire HR6 9PU
Tel: 01568 708632
IPC

Barbara Forryan
Psychoanalytic Psychotherapist
5 Dormington Drive, Tupsley, Hereford
HR1 1SA;
Hereford Child & Family Guidance,
Health Clinic, Gaol Street, Hereford
HR1 1SA
Tel: 01432 357351/01432 268937
SIP, WMIP

Fiona Palmer Barnes
Analytical Psychologist-Jungian Analyst
Rock Cottage, Newton St Margaret's,
Herefordshire HR2 0QW
Tel: 01981 510613
AJA

Paula Jacobs
Transpersonal Psychotherapist
The Wren's Nest, Brampton Road,
Madley, Hereford
CCPE

HERTFORDSHIRE

Margaret Adcock
Family Psychotherapist
1 Cunningham Hill Road, St Albans,
Hertfordshire
IFT

Eleanor Anderson
Systemic Psychotherapist
9 Money Hill Road, Rickmansworth,
Hertfordshire WD3 2EE
Tel: 0181 969 2488 x 3633
KCC

Charles D Bactawar
Cognitive Behavioural Psychotherapist
5 Aubrey Avenue, London Colney,
St Albans, Hertfordshire AL2 1NE
Tel: 01727 824870
BABCP

Gillian Ballance
Analytical Psychologist-Jungian Analyst
30 Westminster Court, St Albans,
Hertfordshire AL1 2DX
Tel: 01727 858361
SAP, BAP

Sara Barratt
Systemic Psychotherapist
26 Bushey Grove Road, Bushey,
Hertfordshire WD2 2JQ
Tel: 01923 817247
IFT

Iris Berger
Sexual and Marital Psychotherapist
18 Chalk Lane, Cockfosters, Barnet,
Hertfordshire EN4 9HJ
BASMT

Peter Berry
Psychoanalytic Psychotherapist
9 Sandridgebury Lane, St Albans,
Hertfordshire AL3 6DD
Tel: 01727 830196
GUILD

Judith Bevan
Systemic Psychotherapist
14 Cranfield Crescent, Cuffley,
Hertfordshire EN6 4EA
Tel: 01707 873874
KCC

Jane Bird
Autogenic Psychotherapist
18 Holtsmere Close, Garston,
Watford, Hertfordshire WD2 6NG
Tel: 01923 675501
BAFAT

Julia Buckroyd
Psychoanalytic Psychotherapist
41 Harlesden Road, St Albans,
Hertfordshire AL1 4LE
Tel: 01727 867465
GUILD

Don Busolini
Hypno-Psychotherapist
45 Valley Road, Welwyn Garden City,
Hertfordshire AL8 7DH
Tel: 01707 330557
NSHAP

Sue Byng-Hall
Family Psychotherapist
Child and Family Psychiatric Clinic,
Marlowes Health Centre, Hemel
Hempstead, Hertfordshire
Tel: 01442 259132
IFT

David Clendon
Psychoanalytic Psychotherapist
1 Docklands, Pirton, Hitchin,
Hertfordshire SG5 3QF
Tel: 01462 712741
GUILD

Gillian Clover
Psychosynthesis Psychotherapist
19 Chapel Street, Tring, Hertfordshire
HP23 6BL
Tel: 01442 825706
IPS

Vivienne Cobden
Group Analytic Psychotherapist
53 Little Bushey Lane, Bushey, Herts
WD2 3SD
Tel: 0181 950 4301
IPC

Barbara Cohen
Family Therapist
57 Valley Road, Chorleywood,
Hertfordshire WD3 4DT
Tel: 01923 773984
AFT

Leila Collins
Integrative Psychotherapist
2 King Edward Road, Barnet,
Hertfordshire EN5 5AP
Tel: 0171 288 5296/0181 440 9776
RCSPC

Sheila Cromwell
NLP Psychotherapist
Monkhams Cottage, Aimes Green,
Galley Hill, Waltham Abbey, Essex
EN9 2AU
Tel: 01992 893405
ANLP

Deborah Cullinan
Child Psychotherapist
209 Ebberns Road, Hemel Hempstead,
Herts HP3 9RD
Tel: 01727 867184/01442 251743
ACP

Dorothy Daniell
Psychoanalytic Psychotherapist
17 Crossfell Road, Leverstock Green,
Hemel Hempstead, Hertfordshire
HP3 8RF
Tel: 01442 254766
LCP

Gillian Darcy
Psychoanalytic Psychotherapist
32 Ripon Way, Borehamwood,
Hertfordshire WD6 2HS
Tel: 0181 207 1314
CFAR

Arna Davis
Analytical Psychologist-Jungian Analyst
7 Sherwoods Road, Watford,
Hertfordshire WD1 4AY
Tel: 01923 224819
BAP

Valerie Davis
Biodynamic Psychotherapist
39 Vesta Avenue, St Albans, Herts
AL1 2PE
Tel: 01727 853823
BTC

Jude Egan
Systemic Psychotherapist
33 North Road, Berkhamstead,
Hertfordshire HP4 3DU
Tel: 01442 864045
KCC

Martin Eldon
NLP Psychotherapist
Broomfield Cottage, The Heath,
Hatfield Heath, Herts CM22 7DZ
Tel: 01279 731649
ANLP

Michael Evans
Psychoanalytic Psychotherapist
Old White Horse, Francis Road, Ware,
Herts SG12 9EZ
Tel: 01920 462101
CSP

John Eveson
Child Psychotherapist
North Herts Consultation Clinic,
Southgate Health Centre, Stevenage,
Herts SG1 1HB
Tel: 01438 781406/7/0181 441 5313
ACP

Merlyn Falkowska
Biodynamic Psychotherapist
'Sibden', Pipers Hill, Gt Gaddesden,
Herts HP1 3BY
Tel: 01442 64203
BTC

Ann Fausset
Systemic Psychotherapist
21 Royal Oak Lane, Pirton, Near
Hitchin, Herts SG5 3QT
KCC

Janet Fitzsimmons
Psychoanalytic Psychotherapist
29 Calvert Road, Barnet, Hertfordshire
EN5 4HH
Tel: 0181 449 3868
LCP

Annie Fox
Transpersonal Psychotherapist
41 Bendysh Road, Bushey,
Hertfordshire WD2 2HZ
CCPE

Jackie Gerrard
Psychoanalytic Psychotherapist
'Julay', 39 Lodge Avenue, Elstree, Herts
WD6 3NA
Tel: 0181 207 5019
LCP

Brunhild Gourlay
Analytical Psychologist-Jungian Analyst
2 Pendley Bridge Cottages, Tring
Station, Herts HP23 5QU
Tel: 01442 822206
SAP

Kevin Gournay
Behavioural Psychotherapist
14 Cassandra Gate, Cheshunt, Herts
EN8 0XE
Tel: 01992 446817/0181 882 8191
BABCP

Anne Gray
Psychoanalytic Psychotherapist
55 Watford Road, St Albans, Herts
AL1 2AE
Tel: 01727 852669
GUILD

Angela Gruber
Transpersonal Psychotherapist
204 Nevells Road, Letchworth, Herts
SG6 4TZ
Tel: 01462 671 553
CCPE

Gaye Gunton
Integrative Psychotherapist
106 Oaklands Avenue, Oxhey,
Watford, Hertfordshire WD1 4LW
Tel: 01923 241626
RCSPC

Michal Gurion
Child Psychotherapist
North Herts Consultation Clinic,
Southgate Health Centre, Stevenage,
Herts SG1 1HB
Tel: 0181 881 0026/01438 781406/7
ACP

Kim Hamilton
Psychoanalytic Psychotherapist
222 Hagden Lane, Watford,
Hertfordshire WD1 8LS
Tel: 01923 212230
AGIP

Dianne Harris
Analytical Psychologist-Jungian Analyst
6 Whitelands Avenue, Chorleywood,
Rickmansworth, Herts WD3 5RD
Tel: 01923 283600
BAP

Susan Harrison-Mayor
Integrative Psychotherapist
86 Handside Lane, Welwyn Garden
City, Herts AL8 6SJ
Tel: 01707 320782
MC

Pam Harvey
Systemic Psychotherapist
42 Barleycroft Road, Welwyn Garden
City, Hertford AL8 6JU
KCC

Peter Honig
Family Therapist
Hope Cottage, 77 Orchard Road,
Melbourn, Hertfordshire SG8 6BB
Tel: 01763 261696
IFT

Margot Huish
Sexual and Marital Psychotherapist
96 Hadley Road, New Barnet, Herts
EN5 5QR
BASMT

David Humphreys
Family Therapist
12 Pinelands, Bishops Stortford, Herts
CM23 2TE
IFT

George Ikkos
Group Analyst
Barnet General Hospital, Psychiatric
Unit, Wellhouse Lane, Barnet, Herts
EN5 3DJ
Tel: 0181 440 5111/0171 372 1311
IGA

Joe Jacobs
Child Psychotherapist
Watford Child & Family Clinic, 130
Hempstead Road, Watford, Herts
Tel: 01923 229272/0171 433 1927
ACP

Eileen Jamieson
Family Therapist
4a Hubbards Road, Chorleywood,
Herts WD3 5JJ
Tel: 01923 282965
AFT

Nasim Kanji
Autogenic Psychotherapist
147 Hampermill Lane, Oxhey,
Hertfordshire WD1 4PH
Tel: 01923 225402
BAFAT

Suna Kilich-Walpole
Psychoanalytic Psychotherapist
9 Nascot Street, Watford, Herts
WD1 3RB
Tel: 01923 447587
LCP

Madeleine King
Systemic Psychotherapist
31 Meadowbank, Hitchin, Herts
SG4 0HY
Tel: 01992 465042/01462 432179
KCC

Robert Kirkwood
Analytical Psychologist-Jungian Analyst
7 Avenue Road, St Albans, Herts
AL1 3QG
Tel: 01727 867466
SAP

Heather Law
Psychoanalytic Psychotherapist
344 Whippendell Road, Watford, Herts
WD1 7PD
Tel: 01923 231174
IPSS

John Leary-Joyce
Gestalt Psychotherapist
64 Warwick Road, St Albans, Herts
AL1 4DL
Tel: 01727 864806
GCL

Judith Leary-Tanner
Gestalt Psychotherapist
64 Warwick Road, St Albans, Herts
AL1 4DL
Tel: 01727 864806
GCL

Deena Marcus
Psychosynthesis Psychotherapist
4A Alston Road, Barnet, Herts
EN5 4ET
Tel: 0181 441 8353
IPS

Shirley Marks-Pinfold
Sexual and Marital Psychotherapist
'Rhondda', Barnet Lane, Elstree, Herts
WD6 3RH
BASMT

Caroline Maudling
Gestalt Psychotherapist
7 Holwell Court, Hertford Road,
Essendon, Nr Hatfield, Hertfordshire
AL9 5RE
Tel: 01582 462601
SPTI, GPTI

Anita McCann
Child Psychotherapist
Barnet Child & Family Consultation
Service, Vale Drive Child Guidance
Clinic, Vale Drive, Barnet EN5 2ED
Tel: 0181 440 8668/0171 538 3698
ACP

Damian McCann
Family Psychotherapist, Family
Therapist
35 Hart Road, St Albans, Herts
AL1 1NF
IFT

Meryl McCartney
Child Psychotherapist
Marlowes Health Centre, Marlowes,
Hemel Hempstead, Herts HP1 1HE
Tel: 01442 228632/0181 9502590
ACP

Judith McConnach
Psychoanalytic Psychotherapist
Priory Cottage, 174 High Road, Bushey
Heath, Herts WD2 1NP
Tel: 0181 950 5121
LCP

Belinda Milani
Systemic Psychotherapist
Westfield, Gardener's Cottage, Grubb's
Lane, Nr Hatfield, Herts AL9 6EF
Tel: 01992 465042/01707 659326
KCC

Richard Mitchell
Individual and Group Humanistic
Psychotherapist
31 Chiswell Green Lane, St Albans,
Herts AL2 3AJ
Tel: 01727 851251
AHPP

Sue Morgan-Williams
Existential Psychotherapist
16 Kingsland Way, Ashwell, Herts
SG7 5PZ
Tel: 01462 743296
RCSPC

Peter A Morris
Cognitive Behavioural Psychotherapist
112 Folly Lane, St Albans, Herts
AL3 5JH
Tel: 01727 836961
BABCP

Barbara Morrison
Integrative Psychotherapist
35 Dury Road, Hadley Green, Barnet
EN5 5PU
Tel: 0181 440 8735
MC

Zenobia Nadirshaw
Cognitive Behavioural Psychotherapist
Harperbury Hospital, Harper Lane,
Radlett, Herts WD7 9HQ
Tel: 01923 854861 ext 4230
BABCP

Alan Naylor-Smith
Psychoanalytic Psychotherapist
2 Fishery Passage, Horsecroft Road,
Hemel Hempstead, Hertfordshire
HP1 1RF
Tel: 01442 24730
GUILD

Sue Pallenberg
Sexual and Marital Psychotherapist
110 High Street, Sandridge, St Albans,
Hertfordshire AL4 9BY
BASMT

Meriel A Parr
Integrative Psychotherapist
'Derwood', Todds Green, Stevenage,
Herts SG1 2JE
Tel: 01438 748478/01438 361491
RCSPC

Chris Pawson
Biodynamic Psychotherapist
10 Hunters Park, Berkhamsted,
Hertfordshire HP4 2PT
Tel: 01442 862029
BTC

Sheila Pawson
Biodynamic Psychotherapist
10 Hunters Park, Berkhamstead, Herts
HP4 2PT
Tel: 01442 862029
BTC

Helen Payne
Humanistic Psychotherapist
1 The Wick, High Street, Kimpton,
Herts SG4 8SA
Tel: 01438 833440
AHPP

Margery Pike
Family Therapist
19d Hill Street, St Albans, Herts
AL3 4QS
IFT

Christine Pinch
Autogenic Psychotherapist
37 Ramsbury Road, St Albans,
Hertfordshire AL1 1SN
Tel: 01727 851574
BAFAT

Sue Pople
Group Analytic Psychotherapist
37 Lancaster Avenue, Hadley Wood,
Barnet, Hertfordshire EN4 0ER;
Enfield Counselling Service, St Paul's
Centre, 102A Church Street, Enfield,
Middlesex
Tel: 0181 367 2333/0181 440 4642
IPC

Maria E Pozzi
Child Psychotherapist
Consultation Clinic for Children,
Families, & Young People, Southgate,
Stevenage, Herts SG1 1HB
Tel: 01438 781406/0181 340 6167
ACP

Elizabeth Richardson
Analytical Psychologist-Jungian Analyst
43 Barleycroft Road, Welwyn Garden
City, Herts AL8 6JX
Tel: 01707 336696
BAP

Marion Rickett
Psychoanalytic Psychotherapist
15 George Street, Old Town, Hemel
Hampstead, Herts HP2 5HJ
Tel: 01442 61712
GUILD

Nicole Rossotti
Personal Construct Psychotherapist
Redbourn, Nr St Albans, Herts
AL3 7DU
CPCP

Joseph Sadowski
Child Psychotherapist
20 The Ridings, Thorley Park, Bishop's
Stortford, Hertfordshire CM23 4EH
Tel: 01279 507864
ACP

Ruth Selwyn
Child Psychotherapist, Psychoanalytic
Psychotherapist
Marlowes Health Centre, Marlowes,
Hemel Hempstead, Herts HP1 1HE;
2 Edis Street, London NW1 8LG
Tel: 01442 228632/0171 722 2558
ACP, LCP

Peggy Sherno
Gestalt Psychotherapist
22 Garden Row, Hitchin, Herts
SG5 1QD
Tel: 01462 432439
GCL

Anna Sladden
Analytical Psychologist-Jungian Analyst
45 Kings Road, Berkhamsted, Herts
HP4 3BJ
Tel: 01442 862072
BAP

Robin Sproul-Bolton
Group Analyst
c/o Shrodell's Unit, Watford General
Hospital, Vicarage Road, Watford,
Herts WD1 8HD
Tel: 01923 244366 x 447 or x 250
IGA

Nick Spyropoulos
Child Psychotherapist
74 Normandy Road, St Albans, Herts
AL3 5PW
Tel: 01727 54402
ACP

Linda Stacey
Psychosynthesis Psychotherapist
218 Stanstead Road, Bishops Stortford,
Herts CM23 2AR
Tel: 01279 504048
PET

Sandra Steel
Integrative Psychotherapist
10 Abbotts Park, London Road,
St Albans, Herts AL1 1TW
Tel: 01727 830378
MC

Beverley Stobo
Psychoanalytic Psychotherapist
12 Cole Green Lane, Welwyn Garden
City, Herts AL7 3PW
Tel: 01707 332665
WTC

Geoffrey Thiel
Transpersonal Psychotherapist
17 Browning Road, Harpenden, Herts
AL5 4TS
Tel: 01582 764579
CCPE

Chris Thorman
Personal Construct Psychotherapist
115 Pickford Hill, Harpenden, Herts
AL5 5HJ
Tel: 01582 712454
CPCP

S Timmann
Hypno-Psychotherapist, Transpersonal
Psychotherapist
16 Brackendene, Bricket Wood,
St Albans, Hertfordshire AL2 3SX
Tel: 01923 672880
NRHP, CCPE

Susan Tompkins
Psychoanalytic Psychotherapist
43 Ridge Lea, Hemel Hempstead, Herts
HP1 2AZ
Tel: 01442 249919
IPC

Susan Wax
Psychoanalytic Psychotherapist
10 Watling Street, Radlett, Herts
WD7 7NH
Tel: 01923 856147
BAP

Ann Webb
Systemic Psychotherapist
30 Royal Oak Lane, Pirton, Hitchin,
Herts SG5 3QT
KCC

Michael Whan
Analytical Psychologist-Jungian Analyst
39 Common Lane, Batford, Harpenden,
Hertfordshire AL5 5BT
Tel: 01582 763062
IGAP

Maria Wheeler
Systemic Psychotherapist
64 Gloucester Road, New Barnet,
Hertfordshire EN5 1NB
Tel: 0181 440 8693
KCC

Julia Wigglesworth
Systemic Psychotherapist
10 Stanhope Road, St Albans, Herts
AL1 5BL
KCC

David Winter
Personal Construct Psychotherapist
Psychology Department, Barnet
Healthcare NHS Trust, Napsbury
Hospital, Nr St Albans AL2 IAA
Tel: 01727 823333
CPCP

Bernard Wooder
Core Process Psychotherapist
17 Farrant Way, Borehamwood,
Hertfordshire WD6 4TE
Tel: 0181 207 3457
KI

Ralph Woolf
Psychoanalytic Psychotherapist
3 Burywick, Beeson End, Harpenden,
Hertfordshire AL5 2AD
Tel: 01582 761472
LCP

HIGHLAND

Yvonne G Edmondstone
Cognitive Behavioural Psychotherapist
Craig Dunain Hospital, Inverness
IV3 6JU
Tel: 01463 234001
BABCP

Alison Sheriffs
Psychosynthesis Psychotherapist
Sluie Lodge, Dunphail, Forres, Moray,
Scotland IV36 0QG
Tel: 01309 611 263
PET

Courtenay Young
Humanistic Psychotherapist
c/o Findhorn Foundation, Findhorn,
Forres, Moray, Scotland IV36 OTZ
Tel: 01309 690251
AHPP

ISLE OF WIGHT

Peter Elliott
Cognitive Behavioural Psychotherapist
Island Clinical Psychology Service, The
Gables, Halberry Lane, Fairlee,
Newport, Isle of Wight PO30 2ER
Tel: 01983 521464
BABCP

Theresa Hendra
Family Therapist
Family Centre, Atkinson Drive,
Newport, Isle of Wight PO30 2LS
Tel: 01983 525790/01983 522919 (f)
IFT

Roma Jacques
Transpersonal Psychotherapist
5 Dower House, 80 Mitchell Avenue,
Ventnor, Isle of Wight PO38 IDS
Tel: 01983 856 365
CCPE

Fiona Kennedy
Cognitive Behavioural Psychotherapist
The Gables, Halberry Lane, Newport,
Isle of Wight PO30 2ER
Tel: 01983 525326
BABCP

Miranda Passey
Child Psychotherapist
Department of Child & Family
Psychiatry, 7 Pyle Street, Newport, Isle
of Wight
Tel: 01983 523602/01983 531312
ACP

Dave Simon
Family Therapist
21 Ashey Road, Ryde, Isle of Wight
PO33 2UW
Tel: 01983 614795
AFT

Eve White
Psychodrama Psychotherapist
Home Cottage, Gunville West,
Newport, Isle of Wight PO30 5LL
Tel: 01983 822912
BPDA

ISLES OF SCILLY

Christopher Reeves
Child Psychotherapist
Gorseacre, West Polberro, St Agnes,
Cornwall TR5 0ST
Tel: 01872 552092
ACP

KENT

Paul T Alexander
Cognitive Behavioural Psychotherapist
Ticehurst Clinic, 76 Castle Street,
Canterbury, Kent CT1 2QD
Tel: 01227 452171
BABCP

Christine Alnuaimi
Family Therapist
Child & Family Adolescent Service,
Glendinning House, 11 Bromley
Common, Bromley, Kent BR2 9LS
Tel: 0181 460 5593
AFT

Nickie Bamber
Psychoanalytic Psychotherapist
Monckton Manor, Mountain Street,
Chilham, Kent CT4 8DQ
Tel: 01227 730767
LCP

Mary Banks
Psychoanalytic Psychotherapist
Fernside Lodge, 6 Rosemount Drive,
Bickley, Bromley, Kent BR1 2LQ
Tel: 0181 776 4365/0181 467 1405
BAP

Z Bhunnoo
Behavioural Psychotherapist
305 Maidstone Road, Bridgewood,
Chatham, Kent ME5 9SE
Tel: 01233 643407/01634 861440
BABCP

Adrian Blake
Hypno-Psychotherapist
93 Birkbeck Road, Sidcup, Kent
DA14 4DJ
Tel: 0181 300 5465
NRHP

Graeme Blench
Integrative Arts Psychotherapist
Kenfield Cottage, Kenfield Hall,
Petham, Nr Canterbury, Kent
Tel: 01227 700775
IATE

Derek Blows
Analytical Psychologist-Jungian Analyst
2 Blackmoor House, Roodlands Lane,
Four Elms, Edenbridge, Kent TN8 6PG
Tel: 01732 700 770
SAP

Marie Botha
Group Analytic Psychotherapist
70 Bradbourne Road, Sevenoaks, Kent
TN13 3QA
Tel: 01732 455903
IPC

Anne Bousfield
Systemic Psychotherapist
10 Mandeville Road, Canterbury, Kent
CT2 7HB
Tel: 01233 612678
IFT

Suzanne Boyd
Transactional Analysis Psychotherapist
The Old Farm House, Biddenden Road,
Fittenden, Cranbrook, Kent TN17 2BE
Tel: 01580 852414
ITA

Elisabeth Brindle
Sexual and Marital Psychotherapist
Milestones, Packhorse Road,
Sevenoaks, Kent TN13 2QP
BASMT

Valerie Bucknall
Attachment-based Psychoanalytic
Psychotherapist
26 Burnt Ash Lane, Bromley, Kent
BR1 4DH
Tel: 0181 290 6817
CAPP

Carol Bunker
Psychoanalytic Psychotherapist
Ivy Cottage, The Lees, Boughton
Aluph, Ashford, Kent TN25 4JB
Tel: 01233 620000
CSPK

Nigel Bunker
Psychoanalytic Psychotherapist
Ivy Cottage, The Lees, Boughton
Aluph, Ashford, Kent TN25 4JB
Tel: 01233 620000
CSPK

Mary Cairns
Psychoanalytic Psychotherapist
39 Chapel Lane, Blean, Canterbury,
Kent CT2 9HE
Tel: 01227 472439
CSPK

Diana Cant
Child Psychotherapist
Breeches Field Oast, Egerton, Kent
TN27 9HA
Tel: 01233 503954/01233 756552
ACP

Carol Carsley
Integrative Psychotherapist
Boulders, Beckenham Place Park,
Beckenham, Kent BR3 2BP
Tel: 0181 650 7264/0181 658 8181
RCSPC

Alan Cartwright
Psychoanalytic Psychotherapist
Little Yockletts, Duckpit Lane,
Waltham, Canterbury, Kent CT4 5PZ
Tel: 01227 700849
CSPK

Kate Cartwright
Psychoanalytic Psychotherapist
Little Yockletts, Duckpit Lane,
Waltham, Canterbury, Kent CT4 5PZ
Tel: 01227 700849
CSPK

Geraldine Causton
Systemic Psychotherapist
5 Westfield Road, Beckenham, Kent
BR3 4EU
Tel: 0181 289 0183/0181 650 7965
KCC

David Challender
Family Therapist
Lardergate, 29a The Precincts,
Canterbury, Kent CT1 2EP
Tel: 01227 700067
AFT

Christine Clark
Group Analytic Psychotherapist
Lydens, 28 Pembury Road, Tonbridge,
Kent TN9 2HX
Tel: 01732 352637
IPC

Linda Coutts
Hypno-Psychotherapist
4 Ashleigh Gardens, Headcorn, Kent
TN27 9TW
Tel: 01622 890720
NSHAP

Jeremiah Cronin
Psychoanalytic Psychotherapist
54 School Lane, Blean, Canterbury,
Kent CT2 9JA;
Deanwood Drive, Parkwood, Rainham,
Kent ME8 9PG
Tel: 01634 377396/01227 471694
GUILD

Diane Cunningham
Psychoanalytic Psychotherapist
Willow Farm House, Upper
Harbledown, Nr Canterbury, Kent
Tel: 01227 768131
AGIP, CSPK

Valerie Cunningham
Integrative Psychotherapist
19 Birling Road, Tunbridge Wells, Kent
TN2 5LX
Tel: 01892 529903
ITA, MET

Bernadette Curwen
Cognitive Behavioural Psychotherapist
Gravesend CMHT, 6 High Street,
Gravesend, Kent DA11 0BQ
Tel: 01474 534200
BABCP

Hazel Darnley
Psychoanalytic Psychotherapist
Dove Cot, Anvil Green, Waltham,
Canterbury, Kent CT4 7EU
Tel: 01227 700752
CSPK

Peggy Davies
Transactional Analysis Psychotherapist
11 Oakhurst Close, Walderslade, Kent
ME5 9AN
Tel: 01634 861262
MET, ITA

Joyce Dawson
Psychoanalytic Psychotherapist
23 Mapledene, Kemnal Road,
Chislehurst, Kent BR7 6LX;
246a High Street, Bromley, Kent
BR1 1PQ
Tel: 0181 295 1558
IPC

Moira Doolan
Family Therapist
27 Barnmead Road, Beckenham, Kent
BR3 1JF
Tel: 0181 676 8495
AFT

Dorothy M Duck
Hypno-Psychotherapist
Fairhaven, Station Road, Pluckley,
Ashford, Kent TN27 0Q2
Tel: 01233 840263/0171 920 0514
NSHAP

Kathleen Duguid
Child Psychotherapist
Child & Family Adolescent Service,
Ravensbourne Trust, Glendinning
House, 11 Bromley Common, Kent
BR2 9LS
Tel: 0181 460 5593
ACP

Nancy M Farley
Cognitive Behavioural Psychotherapist
Hayes Grove Priory Hospital, Prestons
Road, Hayes, Kent BR2 7AS
Tel: 0181 462 7722
BABCP

Daphne Fraser
Transpersonal Psychotherapist
Herne Bay, Kent
Tel: 01227 740 580
CCPE

David Freeman
Analytical Psychologist-Jungian Analyst
222 Mackenzie Road, Beckenham, Kent
BR3 4SJ
Tel: 0181 659 0108
AJA

Christopher Gausden
Hypno-Psychotherapist
Alsirat, 1 Village Green Way, Biggin Hill,
Kent TN16 3NB
Tel: 01959 540601
NRHP

Eliott Green
Transactional Analysis Psychotherapist
9a Turnbury Avenue, Walderslade,
Chatham, Kent ME5 9EH
Tel: 01634 868809
ITA

Gillian Hayhurst
Systemic Psychotherapist
26 Wood Rise, Petts Wood,
Orpington, Kent
Tel: 01689 819 749/0181 310 6570
KCC

Christopher Headon
Sexual and Marital Psychotherapist
79 Goodhart Way, West Wickham,
Kent BR4 0ET
BASMT

Philip J Hewitt
Psychoanalytic Psychotherapist
27 Barnmead Road, Beckenham, Kent
BR3 1JF
Tel: 0181 963 1099/0181 402 2984
BAP

Rene Hiestand
Cognitive Behavioural Psychotherapist
Deal Mental Health Centre, Bowling
Green Lane, Deal, Kent CT14 9HF
Tel: 01304 381321
BABCP

John Hills
Family Therapist
47 St Augustines Road, Canterbury,
Kent CT1 1XR
Tel: 01227 452155
AFT

Ruth Hirons
Psychoanalytic Psychotherapist
1 Lavender Bank, Beesfield Lane,
Farningham, Dartford, Kent DA4 0DA
Tel: 01622 727997/01322 862629
BAP

Margaret Jones
Psychoanalytic Psychotherapist
Mill Cottage, 120 Heathfield Road,
Keston, Kent BR2 6BA
Tel: 01689 853881
GUILD

Pamela Jones
Hypno-Psychotherapist
25 Harrow Way, Weavering,
Maidstone, Kent ME14 5TU
Tel: 01622 739266
NSHAP

Bridget Kelly
Psychoanalytic Psychotherapist
54 Beacon Drive, Bean, nr Dartford,
Kent DA2 8BG
Tel: 01474 705171
AAP

Katalin Lanczi
Psychoanalytic Psychotherapist
37 Preston Lane, Faversham, Kent
ME13 8LG
Tel: 01795 590653
AAP

John Lee
Group Analyst
The Rectory, Chiddingstone,
Edenbridge, Kent TN8 7AH
Tel: 01892 870478
IGA

Rob Leiper
Psychoanalytic Psychotherapist
Huntley Cottage, 122 Wateringbury
Road, East Malling, Kent ME19 6JD
Tel: 01622 690944/01732 842349
BAP, CSPK

Graham Lennox
NLP Psychotherapist
72 Queens Road, Tankerton,
Whistable, Kent CT5 2JQ
Tel: 01227 273042
ANLP

Liisa Lettington
Cognitive Analytic Therapist
9 Waldegrave Road, Bickley, Bromley,
Kent BR1 2JP;
The Campshill Surgery, Campshill
Road, London SE13 6QU
Tel: 0181 852 1384/0181 467 5513
ACAT

Melanie Lewin
Transactional Analysis Psychotherapist
2 Railway Cottages, Railway Hill,
Barham, Nr Canterbury CT4 6PZ
Tel: 01227 831757
ITA

Sean McCoy
Cognitive Behavioural Psychotherapist
1 Sussex Road, West Wickham, Kent
BR4 0JX
Tel: 0181 777 9837/01622 686123
BABCP

Penny Mendelssohn
Family Therapist
The Coach House, Uckfield Lane,
Hever, Nr Edenbridge, Kent TN8 7LQ
Tel: 01732 862865
AFT

Susan Morrish
Transactional Analysis Psychotherapist
Savannah, Sheerwater Road, Elmstone,
Canterbury, Kent CT3 1HJ
Tel: 0227 721 783
ITA

Jean P Murton
NLP Psychotherapist
The Belmont Centre, 46 Belmont
Road, Ramsgate, Kent CT11 7QG
Tel: 01843 587929
ANLP

David W Nicholson
Analytical Psychologist-Jungian Analyst
The Coach House, Handley Green, Bull
Lane, Chislehurst, Kent BR7 6NX
Tel: 0181 859 8327/0181 467 9297
BAP

Renee O'Sullivan
Integrative Psychotherapist
31 Herald Walk, Knight's Manor,
Dartford DA1 5ST
Tel: 0322 276577
RCSPC

Lesley Palgrave
Cognitive Analytic Therapist
2 Gainsborough Square, Bexleyheath,
Kent DA6 8BU
Tel: 0181 301 2793
ACAT

Niki Parker
Child Psychotherapist
Child and Adolescent Mental Health
Service, 18 Crook Log, Bexleyheath,
Kent BR6
Tel: 0181 303 4786/0181 693 3805
ACP

Mary M Penwarden
Child Psychotherapist
Lenworth Clinic, Dept of Child &
Family Psychiatry, 329 Hythe Road,
Ashford, Kent TN24 0QE
Tel: 0171 351 9429/01233 629875
ACP

Marriane Phillips
Psychoanalytic Psychotherapist
104 Petts Wood Road, Petts Wood,
Orpington, Kent BR5 1LE
Tel: 01689 821 971
AAP

Frances Rae
Systemic Psychotherapist
21 Court Road, Tunbridge Wells
TN4 8EB
Tel: 01892 543025
KCC

Bill Reading
Psychoanalytic Psychotherapist
1 Denstead Oast, Chartham Hatch,
Canterbury, Kent CT4 7SH
Tel: 01227 730808
CSPK

Ann Riding
Psychoanalytic Psychotherapist
32 Cromwell Road, Canterbury, Kent
CT1 3LE
Tel: 01227 462511
CSPK

Nick Riding
Psychoanalytic Psychotherapist
32 Cromwell Road, Canterbury, Kent
CT1 3LE
Tel: 01227 462511
CSPK

Pauline Roberts
Psychoanalytic Psychotherapist
2 Knoll Road, Bexley, Kent DA5 1AZ
Tel: 01322 553807
IPC

Lesley A Rogers
Cognitive Behavioural Psychotherapist
202 Lower Higham Road, Gravesend,
Kent DA12 2NN
Tel: 01474 534200/01474 363584
BABCP

Gail Rowland
NLP Psychotherapist
7 Lower Green Road, Pembury,
Tunbridge Wells, Kent TN2 4DZ
Tel: 01892 825640
ANLP

Robin Royston
Analytical Psychologist-Jungian Analyst
The Red House, Stonewall Park Road,
Langton Green, Tunbridge Wells, Kent
Tel: 01892 863858
AJA

Maggie Schaedel
Psychoanalytic Psychotherapist
The Spinney Cottage, Knockholt Road,
Halstead, Sevenoaks, Kent TN14 7EX
Tel: 01959 532510
CSPK, AAP

Maureen Shaw
Psychoanalytic Psychotherapist
20 Westbere Lane, Westbere,
Canterbury, Kent CT2 0HH
Tel: 01227 710505
CSPK

Susan Diane Smith
Hypno-Psychotherapist
The Bromley Stress Management
Centre, 42 East Street, Bromley, Kent
BR1 1QW
Tel: 0181 402 5421
NRHP

John Spalding
Psychoanalytic Psychotherapist
32 Aldermary Road, Bromley, Kent
BR1 3PH
Tel: 0181 464 8292
AGIP

Penny Spearman
Psychoanalytic Psychotherapist
106 George Lane, Hayes, Kent
BR2 7LQ
Tel: 0171 937 6956/0181 462 8703
LCP

Alice Stevenson
Transactional Analysis Psychotherapist
Upper Green, Sandhurst, Hawkhurst,
Kent TN18 5JX
Tel: 01580 850361
ITA

Sue Swift
Transactional Analysis Psychotherapist
83 Mount Ephraim, Tunbridge Wells,
Kent TN4 8BS
Tel: 01892 545065
ITA

Anne Tonge
Psychoanalytic Psychotherapist
8 Dartford Road, Sevenoaks, Kent
TN13 3TQ
Tel: 01732 452046
IPC

Maria Totman
Psychosynthesis Psychotherapist
209A Bexley Road, Northumberland
Heath, Erith, Kent DA8 3EU
Tel: 01322 334139
IPS

Joy K Toyne
Hypno-Psychotherapist
Oast Meadow, Burrs Hill, Brenchley,
Tonbridge, Kent TN12 7AT
Tel: 01892 723799
NRHP

Frances Truscott
Child Psychotherapist
9 Sandown Close, Sandown Park,
Tunbridge Wells, Kent TN2 4RL
Tel: 01892 822093
ACP

Claude Tse
Behavioural Psychotherapist
Dillywood Corner, Dillywood Lane,
Higham, Rochester ME3 7NT
Tel: 01634 717601
BABCP

Daphne Tully
Sexual and Marital Psychotherapist
6 Monkton Gardens, Cliftonville,
Margate, Kent CT9 3HN
BASMT

Heidy Twelvetrees
Gestalt Psychotherapist, Humanistic
Psychotherapist
27 Nurstead Road, Bexley Heath, Kent
DA8 1LS
Tel: 01322 449239
GCL, AHPP

Douglas Van-Loo
Family Psychotherapist
Drug & Alcohol Team, Royal Victoria
Hospital, Radnor Park Avenue,
Folkstone, Kent CT19 5BL
Tel: 01303 850202
IFT

Leslie Virgo
Integrative Psychotherapist
The Rectory, Skibbs Lane, Chelsfield,
Kent BR6 7RH
Tel: 01689 825749
MC

David Walker
Group Analyst
Dairy Cottage, 17 Dower House
Crescent, Southborough, Kent
TN4 0TT
Tel: 01892 520239
IGA

Yvonne Warren
Integrative Psychotherapist
The Archdeaconry, Rochester, Kent
ME1 1SX
Tel: 01634 842527
RCSPC

Anne Waters
Transactional Analysis Psychotherapist
Benton Cottage, Dingleden, Benenden,
Kent TN17 4JX
Tel: 01580 240169
ITA

Rosemary Westcott
Psychoanalytic Psychotherapist
235 Southlands Road, Bromley
BR1 2EG
Tel: 0181 854 9008
GUILD

Diana Whitmore
Psychosynthesis Psychotherapist
Southfield, Leigh, Nr Tonbridge, Kent
TN11 8PJ
Tel: 0171 403 2100
PET

Veronica Wilson
Integrative Arts Psychotherapist
Park Farmhouse, Kirkwood Avenue,
Woodchurch, Ashford, Kent TN26 3SE
Tel: 01233 860593
IATE

Roe Woodroffe
Integrative Psychosynthesis
Psychotherapist
38 Prospect Road, Tunbridge Wells,
Kent TN2 4SH
Tel: 01892 543 596
RE.V

LANCASHIRE

Janet Applegarth
Psychoanalytic Psychotherapist
'Elleswood', Hollins Lane, Arnside, Via
Carnforth, Lancashire LA5 0EG
Tel: 01524 761005
LPDO

Lynda Arkwright
Psychoanalytic Psychotherapist
Calderstones, Chestnut Drive, Mitton
Road, Whalley, Clitheroe, Lancs
BB6 9PE
NWIDP

Freda Ashworth
Hypno-Psychotherapist
Mulsanne, 16 Harefield Drive,
Heywood nr Rochdale, Lancashire
OL10 1RN
Tel: 01706 368193
NRHP

Margaret Black
Hypno-Psychotherapist
24 Stopford Court, Sparth Road,
Clayton-le-Moors, Lancashire
Tel: 01254 389 494
NSHAP

E Veronica (Vicky) Bliss
Cognitive Behavioural Psychotherapist
Chorley & S Ribble NHS Trust, Clinical
Psychology Service, Eaves Lane
Hospital, Chorley, Lancashire PR6 0TT
Tel: 01257 245542
BABCP

J G Callaghan
Psychoanalytic Psychotherapist
7 Alford Close, Breightmet Drive,
Bolton BL2 6NR
Tel: 01204 387065
LPDO

John Casson
Psychodrama Psychotherapist
62 Shaw Hill Bank Road, Greenfield,
Saddleworth, Oldham, Lancashire
OL3 7LE
Tel: 01457 877161
BPDA

Maria Cornell
Psychoanalytic Psychotherapist
Hillside, Dept of Clinical Psychology,
Lancaster Moor Hospital, Quernmore
Road, Lancaster LA1 3JR
Tel: 01524 586400
NWIDP

Paddy Crossling
Systemic Psychotherapist
9 Parkfield Road, Grasscourt, Oldham
OL4 4JG
FIC

Marjorie Curtis
Hypno-Psychotherapist
'Johnswood', Ridgmont Drive,
Horwich, Bolton BL6 6RR
Tel: 01204 696127
CTS

Adrienne Cutner
Hypno-Psychotherapist
28 Tithebarn Hill, Glasson Dock,
Lancaster LA2 0DQ
Tel: 01524 752080
CTS

Mary Eminson
Family Therapist
Child and Family Services, Bolton
Hospitals NHS Trust, Minerva Road,
Farnworth, Bolton BL4 0JR
AFT

Rufus Fagbadegun
Group Analyst
Elton Grange Farm, Elton Vale Road,
Bury, Lancs BL8 2RZ
Tel: 01282 773321/0161 763 3833
IGA

Mary Ferguson
Psychoanalytic Psychotherapist
Psychiatric Outpatient Department,
Royal Oldham Hospital, Rochdale
Road, Oldham OL1 2JH
Tel: 0161 627 8330
LPDO

Helen Haworth
Psychoanalytic Psychotherapist
Adelphi House Psychotherapy Unit, 12
Queen Street, Blackpool, Lancs
FY1 1PD
Tel: 01253 28653
NWIDP

Malcolm Judkins
Psychoanalytic Psychotherapist
Adelphi House Psychotherapy Unit, 12
Queen Street, Blackpool, Lancs
FY1 1PD
Tel: 01253 28653
NWIDP

Gundi Kiemle
Psychoanalytic Psychotherapist
NACTU (North)/Bolton Centre for
Sexual Health, Bolton General
Hospital, Minerva Road, Farnworth,
Bolton BL4 0JR
Tel: 01204 390988
LPDO

Kirsten Lamb
Psychoanalytic Psychotherapist
Department of Clinical Psychology,
Bolton General Hospital, Minerva
Road, Farnworth, Bolton BL4 0SR
LPDO

Claire Leggatt
Psychoanalytic Psychotherapist
2 Lindow Square, Lancaster LA1 1SE
Tel: 01524 383822
AGIP

Eileen MacAlister
Group Analyst
14 Oulder Hill Drive, Rochdale,
Greater Manchester OL11 5LB
Tel: 01706 45883
IGA

Anne Maguire
Analytical Psychologist-Jungian Analyst
17 Wellington Street, St John's,
Blackburn BB1 8AF;
23 Harley Street, London W1N 1DA
Tel: 01254 59910 0171 436 5262/01254
55433
IGAP

Claire Maguire
Psychoanalytic Psychotherapist
17 Hutchinson Road, Norden,
Rochdale OL11 5TX;
Department of Clinical Psychology,
314-316 Oldham Road, Royston
OL2 5AS
Tel: 0161 624 0420 x 5350
LPDO

Olivera Markovic
Family Therapist
Psychology Department, 1 Albert
Road, Preston PR2 8PG
AFT

Kathryn May
Sexual and Marital Psychotherapist
29 Albert Street, Padiham, Burnley,
Lancashire BB12 8HE
BASMT

Sue McAllister
Psychoanalytic Psychotherapist
Preston Psychotherapy Service, 1
Albert Road, Fulwood, Preston, Lancs
PR2 4PJ
Tel: 01772 787197
NWIDP

Meg McCaldin
Hypno-Psychotherapist
2 Aldcliffe Mews, Aldcliffe, Lancaster
LA1 5BT
Tel: 01524 61553
NSHAP

Barbara Moon
Hypno-Psychotherapist
90 Watkin Road, Clayton-le-Woods,
Chorley, Lancashire PR6 7PX
Tel: 01257 275169
CTS

Ann Morris
Psychoanalytic Psychotherapist
44 Lindeth Road, Silverdale, Carnforth,
Lancs LA5 0TX
Tel: 01524 701 533
NAAP

Nicholas Pamphlett
Transactional Analysis Psychotherapist
97 Woone Lane, Clitheroe, Lancashire
BB7 1BJ
Tel: 01200 429450
ITA

Julie Ross
Psychoanalytic Psychotherapist
Clinical Psychology Service, Eaves Lane
Hospital, Eaves Lane, Chorley,
Lancashire PR6 0TT
Tel: 01257 245537
LPDO

Patrick Savage
Family Therapist
9 Gregson Way, Fulwood, Preston,
Lancs PR2 4WY
Tel: 01772 702933
AFT

Peter J D Savage
Hypno-Psychotherapist
c/o National College, 12 Cross Street,
Nelson, Lancs BB9 7EN
Tel: 01282 699378
NRHP

Helen Sheldon
Psychoanalytic Psychotherapist
Department of Clinical Psychology,
Bolton General Hospital, Minerva
Road, Farnworth, Bolton, Lancashire
BL4 0JR
Tel: 01204 390831
NWIDP

Dave Spenceley
Transactional Analysis Psychotherapist
41 Brookdale, Lower Healy, Rochdale,
Lancs OL12 0SS
Tel: 01706 30136
ITA

Graham S Spratt
Cognitive Behavioural Psychotherapist
Dept of Clinical Psychology, Billinge
Hospital, Billinge, Wigan WN5 7ET
Tel: 01695 626181
BABCP

John Sudbury
Psychodynamic Psychotherapist
139 Calderbrook Road, Littleborough,
Lancs OL15 9JW
HIP

Graeme Summers
Transactional Analysis Psychotherapist
49 Westbourne Road, Lancaster
LA1 5DX;
2A Jackson Close, Lancaster, Lancs
LA1 5EY
Tel: 01524 39443
MET, ITA

Elizabeth Taylor
Hypno-Psychotherapist
5 Stonefold, Rising Bridge, Accrington
BB5 2DP
Tel: 01706 210404
CTS

Michael Turton
Gestalt Psychotherapist
Preston Therapy Centre, 57 Garstang
Road, Preston, Lancs PR1 1LB
Tel: 01772 886994
GPTI

LEICESTERSHIRE

Valerie Vora
Sexual and Marital Psychotherapist
196 Manchester Road, Westhoughton,
Bolton BL5 3LA
BASMT

Stuart Walsh
Psychodrama Psychotherapist
4 Woodlea, Church Road, Todmorden
OL14 8EZ
Tel: 01706 819873
BPDA

Sue Washington
Hypno-Psychotherapist
145 Chapel Lane, Longton, Preston
PR4 5NA
Tel: 01772 617663
CTS

Peter M J Wesson
Hypno-Psychotherapist
Complementary Health Centre, 12
Tenterden Street, Bury, Lancashire
BL9 0EG
Tel: 0161 763 1660
NRHP

Peter Wilkin
Psychoanalytic Psychotherapist
414 Manchester Road, Rochdale, Lancs
OL11 4PE
Tel: 01706 344206
LPDO

LEICESTERSHIRE

James Bailey
Psychoanalytic Psychotherapist
Leicester Psychotherapy Dept (NHS),
Humberstone Grange Clinic,
Thurmaston Lane, Leicester LE5 0TA
Tel: 0116 246 0505
STTDP

John Barker
Psychoanalytic Psychotherapist
Highways, Main Street, Cold Newton,
Leicestershire LE7 9DA
Tel: 0116 259 5205
WMIP

Teresa J Black
Psychoanalytic Psychotherapist
212 Brookside, Burbage, Hinchley,
Leicester LE10 2TW
NWIDP

Eric Button
Personal Construct Psychotherapist
Dept of Clinical Psychology, Psychiatric
Dept, Leicester General Hospital,
Gwendolen Road, Leicester LE5 4PW
CPCP

James Craig
Psychoanalytic Psychotherapist
16 The Yews, Stoughton Park, Oadby,
Leicestershire LE2 5EF
Tel: 0116 271 4722
LCP

Naomi Curry
Psychoanalytic Psychotherapist
Leicester Psychotherapy Dept (NHS),
Humberstone Grange Clinic,
Thurmaston Lane, Leicester LE5 0TA
Tel: 0116 246 0505
STTDP

Rebecca Dalgarno
Cognitive Behavioural Psychotherapist
Cognitive Behavioural Dept, Psychiatric
Dept, Leicester General Hospital,
Gwendolen Rd, Leicester LE5 4PW
Tel: 0116 258 4765
BABCP

Dilys Davies
Cognitive Analytic Therapist
8 Church Lane, Quorn, Loughborough,
Leicestershire LE12 8DP
Tel: 01203 350111/01509 413866
ACAT

Guy Deans
Sexual and Marital Psychotherapist
9 St Philips Road, Leicester LE5 5TR
BASMT

Peter Delves
NLP Psychotherapist
13A Allandale Road, Leicester
LE2 2DA
Tel: 01162 709701
ANLP

Peter Dent
Psychodynamic Psychotherapist
40 Leicester Road, Hinckley,
Leicestershire LE10 1LS
Tel: 01455 633400
ULDPS

Geraldine Gould
Hypno-Psychotherapist
22 High Street, Lutterworth, Leicester
LE17 4AD
Tel: 01455 556808
NSHAP

Anthony Grainger
Analytical Psychologist-Jungian Analyst
Fern Bank, 173 Avenue Road, Leicester
LE2 3EB
Tel: 0116 270 5278
BAP

Janet Hills
Integrative Psychotherapist, Body
Psychotherapist
4 Storer Road, Loughborough,
Leicestershire LE11 5EQ
Tel: 01509 235948
CCHP

Hazel Hirst
Transactional Analysis Psychotherapist
Making Changes, 64 St Mary's Road,
Market Harborough, Leicestershire;
142 Knighton Fields Road East,
Knighton Fields, Leicester LE2 6DR
Tel: 0116 270 9727
ITA

Joan Hurd
Psychoanalytic Psychotherapist
18 St John's Chambers, Ashwell Street,
Leicester LE1 6JL
Tel: 0116 254 5451
PA

Michael Jacobs
Psychodynamic Psychotherapist
12 Manor Road Extension, Oadby,
Leicester LE2 4FF
Tel: 0116 271 8469
ULDPS

Sue Jewson
Psychodynamic Psychotherapist
42 Laureston Drive, Stoneygate,
Leicester
ULDPS

Richard Jones
Psychoanalytic Psychotherapist
Leicester Psychotherapy Dept (NHS),
Humberstone Grange Clinic,
Thurmaston Lane, Leicester LE5 0TA
Tel: 0116 246 0505
STTDP

Liz MacKenzie
Integrative Psychotherapist
69 Dulverton Road, Leicester LE3 0SE
Tel: 0116 233 4726
GPTI

Mary Morton
Psychoanalytic Psychotherapist
Leicestershire Psychotherapy
Department, Humberstone Grange
Clinic, Thurmastone Lane, Leicester
LE5 0TA
Tel: 0116 246 0505
STTDP

Anita Mountain
Transactional Analysis Psychotherapist
105 Burgess Road, Aylestone, Leicester
LE2 8QL
Tel: 01162 833886
ITA

George J Porter
Hypno-Psychotherapist
2 The Oval, Oadby, Leicester LE2 5JB
Tel: 0116 271 8089
NSHAP

Joan Rayson
Sexual and Marital Psychotherapist
9 Mountbatten Road, Oakham, Rutland
LE15 6LS
BASMT

Gillean Russell
Psychoanalytic Psychotherapist
Fremantle Flat, Wistow Hall, Nr Great
Glen, Leicester LE8 0QF
Tel: 01162 593419
IPC

Joy Schaverien
Analytical Psychotherapist
1 The Square, South Luffenham,
Oakham, Leics LE5 8NS
Tel: 01780 720117
WMIP

Jenny Strang
Psychodynamic Psychotherapist
University of Leicester Counselling
Service, 161 Welford Road, Leicester
LE2 6BF
Tel: 0116 255 2550
ULDPS

Tonie Vass
Psychoanalytic Psychotherapist
1 Brookfield Cottages, Holt Yard,
Drayton Road, Medbourne, Market
Harborough, Leic
Tel: 01858 833
AGIP

Moira Walker
Psychodynamic Psychotherapist
12 Manor Road Extension, Oadby,
Leicester LE2 4FF
Tel: 0116 271 8469
ULDPS

Chris Whyte
Psychoanalytic Psychotherapist
Leicestershire Dynamic Psychotherapy
Service, Humberstone Grange,
Thurmaston Lane, Leicester LE5 0TA
Tel: 0116 246 0505
STTDP

Sherly Williams
Psychoanalytic Psychotherapist
31 Kingsway Road, Evington, Leicester,
Leics LE5 5TN
Tel: 0116 273 7713
IPC, WMIP, ULDPS

LINCOLNSHIRE

Nicky Buckley
Psychoanalytic Psychotherapist
Lincoln Department of
Psychotherapyo, 1 St Anne's Road,
Lincoln LN1 5RA
Tel: 01522 512000
AAP, WTC

Ian Clegg
Hypno-Psychotherapist
5 Richards Avenue, Lincoln,
Lincolnshire LN6 8SJ
Tel: 01522 688142
NSHAP

Patricia East
Psychodynamic Psychotherapist
Frogs Leap, 615 Newark Road, Lincoln
LN6 8SA
Tel: 01522 681510
ULDPS

Geoff Fisk
Psychoanalytic Psychotherapist
Lincoln Dept of Psychotherapy (NHS),
1 St Anne's Road, Lincoln LN1 5RA
Tel: 01522 51200
STTDP

Jean Flannery
Psychoanalytic Psychotherapist
8 Church Drive, Lincoln LN6 7AX
AGIP

Alan Hassall
Integrative Psychotherapist
'Cobblers', 34 High Street, Navenby,
Lincoln LN5 0DZ
NSAP

Jean Headworth
Psychoanalytic Psychotherapist
Glenbrooke, 5 Morden Close,
Metheringham, Lincoln LN4 0TA
STTDP

Lynda Miller
Psychoanalytic Psychotherapist
8 Meynell Avenue, Lincoln LN6 7UT
AGIP

Sheila Norton
Psychoanalytic Psychotherapist
Lincoln Department of Psychotherapy
(NHS), 1 St Anne's Road, Lincoln
LN1 5RA
Tel: 01522 512000
STTDP

Janet Sutherland
Biodynamic Psychotherapist
4 St Andrews Street, Heckington,
Sleaford, Lincs NG34 9RE;
137 Grosvenor Avenue, London
N5 2NH
Tel: 01529 61571
BTC

Alan Thomson
Personal Construct Psychotherapist
Highfield House, Glentham, Lincoln
LN2 3EU
Tel: 01673 878508
CPCP

LONDON CENTRAL

Michelle Altman
Cognitive Behavioural Psychotherapist
262 Shakespeare Tower, Barbican,
London EC2Y 8DR
Tel: 0171 628 9719
BABCP

Naona Beecher-Moore
Psychosynthesis Psychotherapist,
Humanistic Psychotherapist
3 Temple Gardens, Middle Temple
Lane, London EC4 9AU
Tel: 0171 353 2101
PET, AHPP

Dora Black
Family Psychotherapist
Camden and Islington NHS Trust, Child
and Family Services, 73 Charlotte
Street, London W1P 1LB
Tel: 0171 436 9000
IFT

David Boadella
Humanistic Psychotherapist, Group
Humanistic Psychotherapist
BCM Chesil, London WC1N 3XX
Tel: 0181 342 0444
AHPP

Charmian Bollinger
Sexual and Marital Psychotherapist
124 Montagu Mansions, London
W1H 1LA
BASMT

Robert Bor
Family Therapist
Psychology Department, City
University, Northampton Square,
London EC1V 0HB
Tel: 0171 477 8523
IFT

Mary Buckley
Cognitive Behavioural Psychotherapist
National Hospital for Neurology &
Neurosurgery, Queen's Square,
London WC1N 3BG
Tel: 0171 837 3611 x 3406
BABCP

Ron Cushion
Systemic Psychotherapist
c/o Institute of Family Therapy, 43 New
Cavendish Street, London W1M 7RG
Tel: 01626 875875 x 2216
IFT

Brian Davidson
Autogenic Psychotherapist
86 Harley Street, London W1N 1AE
Tel: 0171 580 4188
BAFAT

Kieron Deahl
NLP Psychotherapist
McIntyre Centre, 29 Crawford Street,
London W1H 1PL
Tel: 0171 419 9657
ANLP

Sue Draney
Psychoanalytic Psychotherapist
Flat 1, Clare Court, Judd Street,
London WC1
Tel: 0171 833 4156
GUILD

Ora Dresner
Child Psychotherapist, Psychoanalytic
Psychotherapist
Camden Psychotherapy Unit,
Instrument House, 207/215 Kings
Cross Road, London WC1X 9DB;
17 St Georges Road, London
NW11 0LU
Tel: 0171 837 5628/0181 458 6763
ACP, LCP

Hella Ehlers
Psychoanalytic Psychotherapist
Flat 12, Byron Court, 26 Mecklenburgh
Square, London WC1N 2AF
Tel: 0171 278 2212
AAP

Guy Gladstone
Psychoanalytic Psychotherapist,
Individual and Group Humanistic
Psychotherapist
The Open Centre, 188 Old Street,
London EC1V 9FR
Tel: 0181 549 9583
IPSS, AHPP

Danya Glaser
Family Psychotherapist
Consultant Child Psychiatrist, Dept of
Psychological Medicine, Great Ormond
Street Hospital, London WC1N 3JH
Tel: 0171 829 8679
IFT

Alice Greene
Autogenic Psychotherapist
86 Harley Street, London W1N 1AE
Tel: 0171 580 4188
BAFAT

Suzanne Harper
NLP Psychotherapist
140 Harley Street, London W1N 1AH
Tel: 0171 224 3387
ANLP

Jill Hodges
Child Psychotherapist
Great Ormond Street Hospital, Dept
of Psychological Medicine, Great
Ormond Street, London WC1N 3JH
Tel: 0171 829 8679/0181 809 2834
ACP

Anthony James
Family Psychotherapist
c/o IFT, 43 New Cavendish Street,
London W1M 7RG
Tel: 0171 703 6333
IFT

Martin Jelfs
Humanistic and Integrative
Psychotherapist
53 New Cavendish Street, London
W1M 7RF
Tel: 0973 504121
AHPP

Matthew Kalitowski
Hypno-Psychotherapist
44 Midhope House, Whidborne Street,
London WC1H 8HH
Tel: 0171 916 3681
NSHAP

Jane Knight
Analytical Psychologist-Jungian Analyst
16 Gower Mews Mansions, London
WC1E 6HR
Tel: 0171 580 7520
SAP

Davina Lilley
Group Analyst
13a Chadwell Street, London EC1R
IGA

Patricia Lloyd
Sexual and Marital Psychotherapist
3 De Walden Street, London W1M 7PJ
Tel: 0171 224 6872
BASMT

Judith Green Loose
Child Psychotherapist
6 Montagu Square, London W1H 1RA
Tel: 0171 224 6028/0171 935 0802
ACP

Jeanne Magagna
Child Psychotherapist
Great Ormond Street Hospital for
Children, Dept of Psychological
Medicine, Great Ormond Street,
London WC1N 3JH
Tel: 0171 829 8679/0171 829 8657 (f)
ACP

David Oldman
Psychoanalytic Marital Psychotherapist
The Counselling Partnership, 5 Albert
Mansions, Luxborough Street, London
WIM 3LN;
5 Buckland Court, Buckland, Surrey
RH3 7EA
Tel: 0171 487 3766/01737 844079
TMSI

Michael Perring
Integrative Psychotherapist, Sexual and
Marital Psychotherapist
114 Harley Street, London WIN IAG;
La Tuque, 33220 Ste Foy La Grande,
SW France
Tel: 0171 935 5651
MET, BASMT

Malcolm Pines
Group Analyst
The Group-Analytic Practice, 88
Montagu Mansions, London WIH ILF
Tel: 0171 935 3103
IGA

Marlene Robinson
Child Psychotherapist
PPCS, 14 Devonshire Place, London
WI
Tel: 0171 935 0640
ACP

Michael Seear
NLP Psychotherapist
86 Harley Street, London WIN IAE
Tel: 0171 580 3256
ANLP

Deborah Sussman
Child Psychotherapist
University College Hospital, Cleveland
Street, London WI
Tel: 0171 380 0717 x 2265/0171 431
3545
ACP

Peter Wilson
Child Psychotherapist
Young Minds, 2nd Floor, 102-108
Clerkenwell Road, London ECIM 5SA
Tel: 0171 336 8445/0181 883 6370
ACP

Laurie Jo Wright
Attachment-based Psychoanalytic
Psychotherapist
16 Bingham Place, London WIM 3FH
Tel: 0171 486 2608
CAPP

LONDON EAST

Martin Adams
Existential Psychotherapist
84 Middleton Road, London E8 4LN
Tel: 0171 254 2707
RCSPC

Percy Aggett
Family Therapist, Systemic
Psychotherapist
69 Glenarm Road, London E5 0LY
IFT

Carol Anson
Systemic Psychotherapist
7 Upper Walthamstow, Walthamstow,
London E17 3QG
Tel: 0181 521 7932
KCC

Paul Atkinson
Psychoanalytic Psychotherapist
6A St Mark's Rise, London E8 2NJ
Tel: 0171 241 2506
GUILD

Gill Bannister
Psychoanalytic Psychotherapist
78 Lichfield Road, Bow, London E3 5AL
Tel: 0181 981 2244
IPC

Helen Bender
Child Psychotherapist
Child & Family Consultation Centre,
Royal London Hospital, London E1 1BB
Tel: 0171 377 7390/0181 445 4798
ACP

Tricia Bickerton
Psychoanalytic Psychotherapist
86 Eleanor Road, Hackney, London E8
Tel: 0171 249 2770
GUILD

Sharon Bond
Systemic Psychotherapist
34 Belton Road, London E7 9PF
Tel: 0181 809 5577/0181 472 6234
KCC

John Boulton
Psychoanalytic Psychotherapist
39 Shearsmith House, Hindmarsh
Close, Cable St, London E1
Tel: 0171 265 0091
CPP

Marion Brion
NLP Psychotherapist
59 Osborne Road, London E7 0PJ
Tel: 0181 534 5494
ANLP

Suesanne Burgess
Hypno-Psychotherapist
64 Queenswood Gardens, Wanstead,
London E11 3SF
Tel: 0181 530 4413
NSHAP

Maggie Burlington
Psychosynthesis Psychotherapist
68 Devonshire Road, London E17 8QJ
Tel: 0181 521 3269
PET

Sandy Chapman
Analytical Psychologist-Jungian Analyst
148 Millfields Road, London E5 0AD
Tel: 0181 986 3792
BAP

Natalie Collins
Psychoanalytic Psychotherapist
133 Larkshall Road, North Chingford,
London E4 6PE
Tel: 0181 529 4986
GUILD

Anita Colloms
Child Psychotherapist
Lower Clapton Child Guidance Clinic,
36 Lower Clapton Road, London
E5 0PQ
Tel: 0181 986 7351/0171 607 1640
ACP

Rebecca Cooper
Humanistic Psychotherapist
99 Eleanor Road, London E8 1DN
Tel: 0171 254 7186
AHPP

Philip Cox
Psychoanalytic Psychotherapist
63 Somerset Road, London E17 8QN
AGIP

Joan Crawford
Integrative Psychosynthesis
Psychotherapist
68 Devonshire Road, London E17 8QJ
Tel: 0181 521 3269
RE.V

Clare Crombie
Gestalt Psychotherapist
103 Wellington Row, London E2 7BN
GCL

Grazyna Czubinska
Psychoanalytic Psychotherapist
10 Flamborough Street, London
E14 7LS
Tel: 0171 790 6737
IPC

Catherine Daniel
Educational Therapist
11b Grosvenor Road, London
E11 2EW
Tel: 0181 530 4866
FAETT

Anna David
Integrative Psychotherapist
22B Montague Road, Hackney, London
E8 2HW
Tel: 0171 923 1019
RCSPC

Linda Dawson
Child Psychotherapist
Wellington Way Centre, 1A Wellington
Way, London E3 4NE;
6 Thompson Road, London SE22 9JR
Tel: 0181 693 6455/0181 980 3510
ACP, SAP

Margaret Drew
Integrative Psychotherapist
1d Mount View Road, Chingford,
London E4 7EF
Tel: 0181 524 7079
RCSPC

Rosemary Duffy
Child Psychotherapist
Newham Child and Family
Consultation Service, 84 West Ham
Lane, London E15 4PT
Tel: 0171 263 7743/0181 534 5608
ACP

Margaret Fagan
Psychoanalytic Psychotherapist
26 Poole Road, London E9 7AE
Tel: 0181 533 0709
AAP

Shirley Faruki
Hypno-Psychotherapist
38 Pulteney Road, South Woodford,
London E18 1PS
Tel: 0181 989 6734
NRHP

Ann Froshaug
Analytical Psychotherapist
196 Queensbridge Road, London
E8 4QE
Tel: 0171 254 4041
LCP

Pamela Gawler-Wright
Hypno-Psychotherapist
34 Grove Road, Bow, London E3 5AX
Tel: 0181 983 9699/0181 983 9701
NSHAP

Jenny Gibson
Transactional Analysis Psychotherapist
36 Morecambe Close, Beaumont
Square, Stepney Green, London
E1 4NH
Tel: 0171 790 4784
MET, ITA

Elizabeth Good
Integrative Psychotherapist
38 Addison Road, Wanstead, London
E11 2RG
Tel: 0181 201 8526/0181 989 6529
RCSPC

Simon Good
Psychoanalytic Psychotherapist
38 Addison Road, London E11 2RG
Tel: 0181 989 6529
GUILD

John Goodchild
Psychoanalytic Psychotherapist
2 Diamond House, Roman Road,
London E3 5QP
Tel: 0181 980 2849
LCP

Deborah Goodes
Psychoanalytic Psychotherapist
28 Brettenham Road, London E17 5BA
Tel: 0171 375 1052/0181 531 6389
AAP

Kati Gray
Psychoanalytic Psychotherapist
30 Skelton Road, London E7 9NJ
Tel: 0181 471 8016
GUILD

Celia Harding
Psychoanalytic Psychotherapist
36 Richmond Road, Leytonstone,
London E11 4BU
Tel: 0181 556 5089
IPC

Biljana Harling
Transactional Analysis Psychotherapist
Flat 4, 57 Clapton Common, Stamford
Hill, London E5 9AA
Tel: 0181 806 9508
ITA, MET

John Henderson
Child Psychotherapist
Newham Child & Family Consultation
Service, 252 Katherine Road, London
E7 8PW
Tel: 0181 552 5171/0181 340 2275
ACP

Steve Herington
Family Psychotherapist
7 Upper Walthamstow Road, London
E17 3QG
Tel: 0181 521 7932
IFT

Hazel Hickson
Attachment-based Psychoanalytic
Psychotherapist
85 Godwin Road, Forest Gate, London
E7 0LW
Tel: 0181 555 6040
CAPP, WTC

Astrid Hoang
Group Analytic Psychotherapist
40 Spruce Hills Road, Walthamstow,
London E17 4LD;
Westminster Pastoral Foundation, 23
Kensington Square, London W8 5HN
Tel: 0181 527 7258/0171 937 6956
IPC

John Holden
Psychoanalytic Psychotherapist
16 Rhondda Grove, Bow, London
E3 5AP
Tel: 0181 980 8628
IPC

Richard Huson
Psychosynthesis Psychotherapist
Flat 7, Sugar Loaf Walk, London E2 0JQ
Tel: 0181 981 2428
IPS

Glenys Jacques
Gestalt Psychotherapist
15 Kemey's Street, Homerton, London
E9 5RQ
Tel: 0181 533 2948
GPTI

Dave Jones
Humanistic and Integrative
Psychotherapist
8 Forest Glade, Leytonstone, London
E11 1LU
Tel: 0181 989 6565
AHPP

Ros Kane
Psychoanalytic Psychotherapist
15 Matcham Road, London E11
Tel: 0181 555 5248
GUILD

Agnes Keane
Transpersonal Psychotherapist
29 Dunton Road, Leyton, London
E10 7AF
CCPE

Madeleine Knowles
Family Therapist
Newham Child & Family, Consultation
Service, 252 Katherine Road, London
E7 8PW
Tel: 0181 552 5171
IFT

Michael Lamprell
Psychoanalytic Psychotherapist
36 Richmond Road, Leytonstone,
London E11 4BU
Tel: 0181 556 5089
IPC

Kathleen Lyons
Psychosynthesis Psychotherapist
Mazenod House, 62 Chamber Street,
London E1 8BL
Tel: 0171 680 0756
PET

Julius Malkin
Cognitive Behavioural Psychotherapist
Professional Development Foundation,
21 Limehouse Cut, 46 Morris Road,
London E14 6NQ
Tel: 0181 340 2692/0171 987 2805
BABCP

Philip Messent
Family Psychotherapist
The Emanuel Miller Centre, The Health
Centre, Gill Street, London E14
Tel: 0171 515 6633
IFT

Stirling Moorey
Cognitive Behavioural Psychotherapist
Hackney Hospital, Homerton High
Street, London E9 6BE
Tel: 0181 919 8777
BABCP

Allan Morris
Family Therapist
Emmanuel Miller Centre, Gill Street,
London E14
Tel: 0171 515 6633
IFT

Denise Nelson
Sexual and Marital Psychotherapist
216 Carr Road, Lloyd Park, London
E17 5EW
Tel: 0181 812 2847
BASMT

Judith Nesbit
Psychoanalytic Psychotherapist
32 Thornby Road, London E5 9QL
AGIP

Elizabeth O'Driscoll
Psychoanalytic Psychotherapist
13 Hillstowe Street, London E5 9QY
AGIP

Carmen O'Leary
Group Analyst
14 Queen's Grove Road, London
E4 7PT
Tel: 0181 919 5555 x 8630/
0181 529 3536
IGA

Renos Papadopoulos
Analytical Psychologist-Jungian Analyst
20 Woodriffe Road, London E11 1AH
Tel: 0181 556 3180
IGAP

Rosalind Pearmain
Psychoanalytic Psychotherapist
69 Gordon Road, Wanstead, London
E11 2RA
Tel: 0181 989 8891
GUILD

Stef Pixner
Integrative Psychotherapist
94 Colvestone Crescent, Hackney,
London E8 2LJ
Tel: 0171 254 6216
MC

Rene Plen
Systemic Psychotherapist
57 Mayola Road, London E5 0RE
BASMT

Tammy Ratoff
Psychoanalytic Psychotherapist
80 Melford Road, Leytonstone, London
E11 4PS
Tel: 0181 558 0622
LCP

John Renwick
Transactional Analysis Psychotherapist
41 Evelyn Road, Walthamstow, London
E17 9HE
Tel: 0181 521 2364
MET

John Rowan
Individual and Group Humanistic
Psychotherapist
79 Pembroke Road, Walthamstow
Village, London E17 9BB
Tel: 0181 521 4764
AHPP

Tricia Scott
Individual and Group Humanistic
Psychotherapist
8 Shrubland Road, London E8 4NN
Tel: 0171 254 4490
AHPP

Christine Shearman
Integrative Psychotherapist
24 Hollybush Hill, London E11 1PP
Tel: 0181 989 5206
ITA, MET, GPTI

Alan Shuttleworth
Child Psychotherapist
Walthamstow Child & Family
Consultation Service, Shernhall Street,
London E17 3EA
Tel: 0181 509 0424/0181 883 7908
ACP

John Slade
Integrative Psychotherapist
86 Clifden Road, London E5 0LN
Tel: 0181 986 6855
MC

Gwynnedd Somerville
Psychoanalytic Psychotherapist
23 Mornington Grove, London E3 4NS
Tel: 0181 983 1085
IPC

Lyndsay Spendelow
Integrative Psychotherapist
9 Mountague Place, Poplar, London
E14 0EX
Tel: 0956 235995/0171 987 2275
RCSPC

Judy Stevenson
Child Psychotherapist, Jungian Child
Analyst
Child & Family Consultation Centre,
Royal London Hospital, Whitechapel,
London E1 1BB;
Garden Flat, 83 St Quintin Avenue,
London W10 6PB
Tel: 0171 377 7390/0181 968 5991
ACP, SAP

Marion Stiasny
Child Psychotherapist
Newham Child & Family Consultation
Service, 84 West Ham Lane, London
E15 4PT
Tel: 0171 372 5222/0181 534 5608
ACP

Elisabeth Sutherland
Psychosynthesis Psychotherapist
50 Blondin Street, Bow, London
E3 2TR
Tel: 0181 981 1553
PET

Mary Taylor
Psychoanalytic Psychotherapist
118 Glenarm Road, Hackney E5 0NA
Tel: 0181 986 1108
LCP

Guinevere Tufnell
Family Psychotherapist
Child & Family Consultation Service,
Shernhall Street, London E17 3EA
Tel: 0181 509 0424
IFT

Catherine Urwin
Child Psychotherapist
Emanuel Miller Centre, The Health
Centre, 11 Gill Street, London
E14 8HQ
Tel: 0171 515 6633/0181 802 8593
ACP

Susan Vas Dias
Child Psychotherapist, Attachment-
based Psychoanalytic Psychotherapist
69 Gordon Road, London E18 1DT;
Diagnostic Unit, Queen Elizabeth Hosp
for Children, Hackney Road, London
E2 8PS
Tel: 0171 739 8422 x 6425/
0181 505 7481
ACP, CAPP

David Vincent
Group Analyst
15 Draycot Road, Wanstead, London
E11 2NX
Tel: 0181 535 6899/0181 989 6028
IGA

Tony Yates
Group Analytic Psychotherapist
7 Queensdown Road, London E5 8NN
Tel: 0181 985 2053
IPC

LONDON NORTH

Elisabeth Abrahams
Integrative Psychotherapist
57 Holdenhurst Avenue, Finchley,
London N12 0JA
Tel: 0181 346 7104
MC

Jan Abram
Psychoanalytic Psychotherapist
18 Ridge Road, London N8 9LG
Tel: 0181 292 8584
AAP

Susanna Abse
Psychoanalytic Marital Psychotherapist
17 Muswell Avenue, Muswell Hill,
London N10 2EB
Tel: 0181 883 5746
TMSI

Gisela Albrecht
Psychoanalytic Psychotherapist
45 Ashley Road, London N19 3AG
Tel: 0171 281 1265
IPC

Sandra Alexander
Sexual and Marital Psychotherapist
39 Outram Road, London N22 4AB
BASMT

Tamara Alferoff
Transpersonal Psychotherapist
London N19 3BG
Tel: 0171 272 3589
CCPE

Brenda Allan
Family Psychotherapist
61 Woodland Rise, London N10 3UN
Tel: 0181 444 0851
AFT

Paul Allsop
Humanistic and Integrative
Psychotherapist, Gestalt
Psychotherapist
Spectrum, 7 Endymion Road, London
N4 1EE
Tel: 0181 883 3246
SPEC

Talal Alrubaie
Hypno-Psychotherapist
2nd Floor, 41 Denison Close, East End
Road, East Finchley, London N2 0JU
Tel: 0181 444 9567
NSHAP

Olivia Amiel
Psychoanalytic Psychotherapist
16 Elms Avenue, London N10 2JP
Tel: 0181 444 0396
GUILD

Elizabeth Anderson
Psychoanalytic Psychotherapist
140 Muswell Hill Road, London
N10 3JD
Tel: 0181 444 2507
AGIP

Robert Andry
Psychoanalytic Psychotherapist
44 Cholmeley Crescent, London
N6 5HA
Tel: 0181 340 7293
LCP, BAP

Ofra Anker
Psychosynthesis Psychotherapist
13 Oldfield Mews, London N6 5XA
Tel: 0181 341 1759
IPS

Alicia Arendar
Psychoanalytic Psychotherapist
12 Freegrove Road, London N7 9JN
Tel: 0171 607 4346
LCP

Seema Ariel
Psychoanalytic Psychotherapist
22 Durham Road, London N2 9DN
Tel: 0181 883 7386
AGIP

Brian Arnold
Sexual and Marital Psychotherapist
27 North Grove, London N6 4SH
BASMT

Katherine Arnold
Child Psychotherapist, Psychoanalytic
Psychotherapist
57 Cecile Park, Crouch End, London
N8 9AX;
Child and Family Department,
Tavistock Clinic, 120 Belsize Lane,
London NW3 5BA
Tel: 0121 449 9552/0181 340 2922
ACP, CPP

Rosemary Arnold
Psychoanalytic Psychotherapist
3 Stanmore Road, London N15
Tel: 0181 889 7335
GUILD

Lia Ashby
Humanistic and Integrative
Psychotherapist, Transpersonal
Psychotherapist
Spectrum, 7 Endymion Road, London
N4 1EE
Tel: 0181 348 3006
SPEC

Corinne Aves
Child Psychotherapist
33 Hamilton Crescent, Palmers Green,
London N13 5LN
Tel: 0181 245 1946
ACP

Racheli Azgad
Psychoanalytic Psychotherapist
67 Dollis Road, London N3 1RD
Tel: 0181 346 1525
PA

Adrienne Baker
Integrative Psychotherapist
16 Sheldon Avenue, Highgate, London
N6 4JT
Tel: 0181 340 5970/0171 487 7644
RCSPC

Tessa Balogh Henghes
Child Psychotherapist
92 Highgate Hill, London N6 5HE
Tel: 0181 348 7731
ACP

Afrakuma Bannerman
Analytical Psychologist-Jungian Analyst
22 Jansons Road, London N15 4JU
Tel: 0181 800 3771
BAP

Vivien Bar
Psychoanalytic Psychotherapist,
Lacanian Analyst
5 Stanmore Road, London N15 3PR
Tel: 0181 889 5925
GUILD, CFAR, WTC

Gina Barker
Humanistic Psychotherapist
50 Burma Road, London N16 9BJ
Tel: 0171 275 8002
AHPP

Gillian Barratt
Psychoanalytic Psychotherapist, Group
Analyst
19 Clifton Road, London N8 8JA
Tel: 0181 451 8424/0181 348 1735
IGA, BAP

Anne Barry
Integrative Psychotherapist
43 Dukes Avenue, Muswell Hill,
London N10 2PX
NSAP

Francesca Bartlett
Child Psychotherapist
Child and Adolescent Mental Health
Team, Haringey Healthcare NHS Trust,
St Ann's Hospital, London N15 3TH
Tel: 0181 442 6467/0171 226 9933
ACP

Mia Beaumont
Educational Therapist
13 Highbury Terrace, London N5 1UP
Tel: 0171 226 8103
FAETT

Dale Beckett
NLP Psychotherapist
18 Ockendon Road, Islington, London
N1 3NP
Tel: 0171 704 9999
ANLP

Jennifer Beddington
Analytical Psychologist-Jungian Analyst
39 Waterlow Road, London N19 5NJ
Tel: 0171 263 3551
BAP

Harold Behr
Group Analyst
81 Gordon Road, London N3 1ER
Tel: 0181 965 5733/0181 440 1451/
0181 346 8323
IGA

Angela Bennett
Analytical Psychologist-Jungian Analyst
6 Cyprus Road, London N3 3RY
Tel: 0181 349 2073
BAP

Patrick Bentley
Systemic Psychotherapist
44 Sydney Road, London N10 2RL
Tel: 0181 809 5577/0181 883 9943
KCC

Marie Beresford
Psychosynthesis Psychotherapist
153c Brecknock Road, Tufnell Park,
London N19
Tel: 0171 267 7643
IPS

Joseph Berke
Psychoanalytic Psychotherapist
5 Shepherd's Close, London N6 5AG
Tel: 0181 348 4492
AAP

Sally Berry
Psychoanalytic Psychotherapist
11 Cecile Park, London N8 9AX
Tel: 0181 340 5161
AAP, WTC

Vibha Bhatt
Psychoanalytic Psychotherapist
85 Sydney Road, London N8 0ET
Tel: 0181 348 9313
GUILD

Vicky Bianco
Family Therapist
16 Willow Bridge Road, Canonbury,
London N1 2LA
IFT

John H Bierschenk
Analytical Psychologist-Jungian Analyst
58 Queen's Avenue, London N10 3NU
Tel: 0181 883 3567
AJA

Tessa Bilder
Transpersonal Psychotherapist
61 Huntingdon Road, London N2 9DX
Tel: 0181 444 5289
CCPE

Linda Binnington
Psychoanalytic Marital Psychotherapist
6 Tyndale Terrace, Canonbury Lane,
London N1 2AT
TMSI

Heather Bowman
Integrative Psychotherapist
9 Leadale Road, Stamford Hill, London
N16 6BZ
Tel: 0181 800 8476
MC

Jo Bownas
Systemic Psychotherapist
4 Clyro Court, Tollington Park, London
N4 3AQ
Tel: 0171 263 1897
KCC

Catrin Bradley
Child Psychotherapist
Hackney Child & Family Consultation
Service, Woodbury Down Unit, John
Scott Health Centre, Green Lanes,
London N4 2NU
Tel: 0181 809 5577/0181 444 4733
ACP

Jonathan Bradley
Child Psychotherapist, Psychoanalytic
Psychotherapist
Child and Family Department,
Tavistock Clinic, 120 Belsize Lane,
London NW3 5BA
Tel: 0171 435 7111/0181 477 4733
ACP, CPP

Rex Bradley
Humanistic and Integrative
Psychotherapist
Spectrum, 7 Endymion Road, London
N4 1EE
Tel: 0181 341 2277
SPEC

Marion Brady
Psychoanalytic Psychotherapist
11 Priory Road, London N8 8LH
Tel: 0181 340 3992
BAP

Eleanor Braterman
Hypno-Psychotherapist
36E Portland Rise, London N4 2PP
Tel: 0181 802 9206
NSHAP

Anna Brave-Smith
Attachment-based Psychoanalytic
Psychotherapist, Psychoanalytic
Psychotherapist
59 Holmesdale Road, London N6 5TH
Tel: 0181 340 9137
IPSS, CAPP

Damian Brennan
Personal Construct Psychotherapist
4 Hornsey Rise, London N19 5SB
Tel: 0171 263 6138
CPCP

Stan Brennan
Humanistic and Integrative
Psychotherapist
Spectrum, 7 Endymion Road, London
N4 1EE
Tel: 0181 340 9690
SPEC

Clive Britten
Analytical Psychologist-Jungian Analyst
10 Priory Avenue, Crouch End, London
N8 7RN
Tel: 0181 340 2539
SAP

Sara Brown
Psychoanalytic Psychotherapist
6 Carlingford Road, Turnpike Lane,
London N15
Tel: 0181 889 3464
AGIP

Elizabeth Browne
Analytical Psychologist-Jungian Analyst
15 Bisham Gardens, Highgate, London
N6 6DJ
Tel: 0181 340 3838
SAP

Bernard Burgoyne
Lacanian Analyst
5 Stanmore Road, London N15 3PR
Tel: 0181 889 5925
CFAR

Ellora Polly Burridge
Educational Therapist
34 Mercers Road, London N19 4PJ
Tel: 0171 272 2069
FAETT

Susie Burrows
Transpersonal Psychotherapist
64a St John's Grove, London N19 5RP
Tel: 0171 272 7892
CCPE

Dennis R Bury
Personal Construct Psychotherapist,
Cognitive Behavioural Psychotherapist
47 Mayfield Road, Hornsey, London
N8 9LL
Tel: 0181 348 9181
CPCP, BABCP

Christel Buss-Twachtmann
Psychoanalytic Marital Psychotherapist
75 Cromwell Avenue, London N6
Tel: 0181 341 1358
TMSI

Catherine ByGott
Analytical Psychologist-Jungian Analyst
28 Cornwall Avenue, London N2 4DA
Tel: 0181 881 0929
AJA

Dorothy Byrne
Analytical Psychologist-Jungian Analyst
16 Elm Park Road, London N3 1EB
Tel: 0181 346 7748/0181 371 0202 (f)
SAP

Anna Cameron
Psychoanalytic Psychotherapist
37 Orpington Road, Winchmore Hill,
London N21 3PD
Tel: 0181 482 0787
AAP

Rod Cameron
Psychoanalytic Psychotherapist
37 Orpington Road, Winchmore Hill,
London N21 3PD
Tel: 0181 482 0787
AAP

David Campbell
Systemic Psychotherapist
5 Tivoli Road, London N8 8RE
IFT

Aileen Campbell Nye
Analytical Psychologist-Jungian Analyst
The Garden Flat, 25 Penn Road,
London N7 9RD
Tel: 0171 609 4364
IGAP

Christina Campbell-Thomson
Psychoanalytic Psychotherapist
21 Sussex Way, London N7 6RT
Tel: 0171 272 7767
AAP

Nicholas Carolan
Psychoanalytic Psychotherapist
55 Horsham Avenue, North Finchley,
London N12 9BG
Tel: 0181 361 4512
LCP

Jules Cashford
Analytical Psychologist-Jungian Analyst
136 Cloudesley Road, London N1 0EA
Tel: 0171 278 6468
AJA

Anne Casimir
Educational Therapist
50 Brookfield, Highgate West Hill,
London N6 6AT
Tel: 0171 340 6655
FAETT

Sean Cathie
Psychoanalytic Psychotherapist
23 Brookfield Mansions, Highgate West
Hill, London N6 6AS
Tel: 0181 340 6603
IPC

Paul Caviston
Psychoanalytic Psychotherapist
54 Leswin Road, London N16 7NH
Tel: 0171 254 7188
PA

Laurena Chamlee-Cole
NLP Psychotherapist
38 Middle Lane, London N8 8PG
Tel: 0181 340 8156
ANLP

Philip Chandler
Psychoanalytic Psychotherapist
31 Huntingdon Road, London N2
Tel: 0181 444 3509
GUILD

Praxoulla Charalambous
Psychoanalytic Psychotherapist
48 Old Park Road, Palmers Green,
London N13 4RE
Tel: 0181 886 8488
LCP, WTC

Anne Chatfield
Group Analyst
88 Woodland Gardens, Muswell Hill,
London N10 3UB
Tel: 0181 883 4085
IGA

Jacques China
Psychoanalytic Psychotherapist
54 Compton Road, London N1 1EJ
Tel: 0171 354 1533
GUILD

Elphis Christopher
Analytical Psychologist-Jungian Analyst
35 Wood Vale, London N10 3DJ
Tel: 0181 883 0085
BAP

Jennifer Clifford
Psychoanalytic Psychotherapist
10 Alwyne Place, London N1 2NL
Tel: 0171 354 3930
IPC

David Cohen
Psychoanalytic Psychotherapist
48 Burma Road, Stoke Newington,
London N16 9BH
Tel: 0171 249 4917
LCP

Maggie Cohen
Child Psychotherapist
Neonatal Intensive Care Unit,
Whittington Hospital, Highgate,
London N19 5NF
Tel: 0171 485 4999
ACP

Sylvia Cohen
Psychoanalytic Psychotherapist
11 Clifton Avenue, London N3 1BN
Tel: 0181 343 4097
GUILD

Nancy Cohn
Child Psychotherapist, Psychoanalytic
Psychotherapist
108 Dartmouth Park Hill, London
N19 5HT;
Basildon Child Guidance Clinic, Great
Oaks, Basildon, Essex SS14 1EH
Tel: 01268 523355/0171 272 3529
GUILD, ACP

Mireille Colahan
Family Therapist
25 Huntingdon Street, London N1 1BS
Tel: 0171 607 5453
AFT

Howard Cooper
Psychoanalytic Psychotherapist
37 Lansdowne Road, London N3
Tel: 0181 349 3891
AGIP

Jillian Cooper
Existential Psychotherapist
24 Rocliffe Street, London N1 8DT
Tel: 0171 253 1651
RCSPC

Sara Cooper
Psychoanalytic Psychotherapist
37 Lansdowne Road, London N3 1ET
Tel: 0181 349 3891
GUILD

Terry Cooper
Humanistic and Integrative
Psychotherapist, Body Psychotherapist
Spectrum, 7 Endymion Road, London
N4 1EE
Tel: 0181 341 2277/0181 340 0426 (f)
SPEC

Tom Cooper
Humanistic and Integrative
Psychotherapist
57a Umfreville Road, London N4 1RZ;
C/ - 305A Glenfield Road, Glenfield,
Auckland, New Zealand
Tel: 0181 348 8658/09 480 7801
SPEC

Ronald Cosmo Luckcock
Hypno-Psychotherapist
110a Alexandra Park Road, Muswell
Hill, London N10 2AE
Tel: 0181 444 7348
NSHAP

Susan Coulson
Child Psychotherapist
Hornsey Rise Child Guidance Unit,
Beaumont Rise, London N19 3YU
Tel: 0171 530 2444/0181 348 5726
ACP

Jeni Couzyn
Psychoanalytic Psychotherapist
30 Chestnut Avenue, London N8 8NY
Tel: 0181 340 5697
GUILD

Susan Cowan-Jenssen
Primal Psychotherapist
West Hill House, 6 Swains Lane,
Highgate, London N6 6QU
Tel: 0171 267 9616
LAPP

Bill Critchley
Integrative Psychotherapist, Gestalt
Psychotherapist
1 Northolme Road, London N5 2UZ
Tel: 0171 354 0745
MET, GPTI

Julia Crowley
Psychoanalytic Psychotherapist
2 Marlow Court, 6-8 The Grove,
Finchley, London N3 1QW
Tel: 0181 346 1337
IPC

Catherine Crowther
Analytical Psychologist-Jungian Analyst,
Family Psychotherapist
50 Leconfield Road, London N5 2SN
Tel: 0171 226 3112
IFT, SAP

Farhad Dalal
Group Analyst
51 Evering Road, Stoke Newington,
London N16 7PU
Tel: 0171 249 5118
IGA

Heather Daniel
Psychoanalytic Psychotherapist
13 Trinity Road, East Finchley, London
N2 8JJ
Tel: 0181 369 3273
IPC

Orpa Daniels
Psychoanalytic Marital Psychotherapist
4 Shortgate, Woodside Park, London
N12 7JP
Tel: 0181 445 8117
TMSI

Susan Daniels
Psychoanalytic Psychotherapist
9 Finsbury Park Road, London N4 2LA
Tel: 0171 359 5965
IPSS

Liv Darling
Psychoanalytic Psychotherapist
c/o 1 Fairbridge Road, London
N19 3EW
Tel: 0171 272 7013
AGIP

Marie-Laure Davenport
Psychoanalytic Psychotherapist
28 Onslow Gardens, London N10 3JU
Tel: 0181 444 4695
PA, WTC

Ann David
Integrative Psychotherapist
5 Hill Close, London NW11 7JP
Tel: 0181 458 8768
ITA, MET

Polly de Boer
Systemic Psychotherapist
137 Hornsey Park Road, London
N8 0JX
Tel: 0181 888 9433
KCC

Felicity de Zulueta
Group Analyst
17 Westhill Court, Millfield Lane,
London N6
IGA

Gianni Dianin
Psychoanalytic Psychotherapist
24 Morley Avenue, Wood Green,
London N22 6LY
Tel: 0171 928 9500/0181 888 7338
AAP

Yair Domb
Child Psychotherapist
36 Dresden Road, London N19 3BD
Tel: 0181 366 9139/0171 272 3894
ACP

Gill Doust
Humanistic and Integrative
Psychotherapist
1 Duckett Road, London N4 1BJ
Tel: 0181 341 9168
SPEC

Christine Driver
Psychoanalytic Psychotherapist
71 Umfreville Road, London N4 1RZ
Tel: 0181 340 3324
IPC

Nick Duffell
Psychosynthesis Psychotherapist
128a Northview Road, Hornsey,
London N8 7LP
Tel: 0181 905 5937
IPS

Jenny Dunn
Psychoanalytic Psychotherapist
3 Monsell Road, London N4 2EF
Tel: 0171 354 2100
GUILD

Mark Dunn
Cognitive Analytic Therapist
49 Princes Avenue, Wood Green,
London N22 4SB
Tel: 0171 955 4822/0181 888 9629
ACAT

Jane Dutton
Family Therapist
97 Foulden Road, London N16 7UH
Tel: 0171 249 3993
IFT

Barbara Eccles
Child Psychotherapist
Child and Adolescent Mental Health
Team, Haringey Healthcare NHS Trust,
St Ann's Hospital, London N15 3TH
Tel: 0181 442 6737/0181 442 6467
ACP

Susan Egert
Psychoanalytic Psychotherapist
136 Winston Road, London N16 9LJ
Tel: 0171 254 0526
GUILD

Sue Einhorn
Group Analyst, Psychoanalytic
Psychotherapist
37 Stanhope Gardens, London N4 1HY
Tel: 0171 607 2789/0181 800 7247
IGA, WTC

Hetty Einzig
Psychosynthesis Psychotherapist
42 Norcott Road, London N16 7EL
Tel: 0171 843 6099
PET

Susan Eisen
Psychoanalytic Psychotherapist
53 Benthal Road, London N16 7AR
Tel: 0181 806 8703
GUILD

Penny Elder
Psychoanalytic Psychotherapist
24 Muswell Road, Muswell Hill, London
N10 2BG
Tel: 0181 883 3399
LCP

Zack Eleftheriadou
Integrative Psychotherapist
Flat 19, High Sheldon, Sheldon Avenue,
London N6 4NJ
Tel: 0171 263 4130/0181 342 8685
RCSPC

Lois Elliott
Psychoanalytic Psychotherapist
6 Church Lane, London N8 7BU
Tel: 0181 348 8419
AAP

Mary Lynne Ellis
Psychoanalytic Psychotherapist
78 Huddleston Road, London N7 0EG
Tel: 0171 263 2410
PA

Michael Ellis
Gestalt Psychotherapist, Humanistic
Psychotherapist
5a Cromartie Road, London N19 3SJ
Tel: 0171 263 4778
GCL, AHPP

Louise Emanuel
Child Psychotherapist
Child & Adolescent Mental Health
Team, Haringey Healthcare NHS Trust,
St Ann's Hospital, London N15 3TH
Tel: 0181 442 6467/0181 348 7032
ACP

Carole Epstein
Child Psychotherapist
Child Line, Royal Mail Building, Studd
Street, London N1 0QW
Tel: 0171 239 1000/0181 444 8481
ACP

Frances Epstein
Integrative Psychotherapist
156 Gladesmore Road, London
N15 6TH
Tel: 0181 802 0761
RCSPC

Sheila Ernst
Group Analyst, Psychoanalytic
Psychotherapist
53 Manor Road, London N16 5BH
Tel: 0181 800 7371
IGA, WTC

Ruth Erskine
Family Psychotherapist
12 Priory Avenue, London N8 7RN
Tel: 0181 340 4642
IFT

Em Farell
Integrative Psychotherapist
26 Freegrove Road, London N7 9RQ
Tel: 0171 700 0330/0171 607 8306
RCSPC

Caroline Fawkes
Psychoanalytic Psychotherapist
90 Woodland Gardens, London
N10 3UB
Tel: 0181 372 0728
AAP

Marilyn Feldberg
Psychosynthesis Psychotherapist
21 Clifton Avenue, London N3 1BN
Tel: 0181 349 9429
PET

Wendy Feldman
Child Psychotherapist
5 Cholmeley Crescent, Highgate,
London N6 5EZ
Tel: 0171 340 0878/0181 340 0463 (f)
ACP

Geoff Ferguson
Psychoanalytic Psychotherapist
113 Wargrave Avenue, London
N15 6TX
Tel: 0181 802 4353
LCP

Nathan Field
Analytical Psychologist-Jungian Analyst,
Analytical Psychotherapist
14 Talbot Road, Highgate, London
N6 4QR
Tel: 0181 341 0904
LCP, BAP

Rosalind Finlay
Analytical Psychologist-Jungian Analyst
31 Hampstead Lane, London N6 4RT
Tel: 0181 340 6211
AJA

Marj Fleming
Attachment-based Psychoanalytic
Psychotherapist
7 Wyndham Crescent, London N19
Tel: 0171 281 1079
CAPP

Elisabeth Flinspach
Integrative Psychotherapist
50c Albert Road, Finsbury Park,
London N4 3RP;
2 The Syke, Brigstock, Kettering,
Northamptonshire NN14 3HR
Tel: 01536 373 058/0171 263 2098
MC

Susan Ford
Psychoanalytic Psychotherapist
48 Crayford Road, London N7 0ND
Tel: 0171 609 4800
AAP

Laura Forti
Psychoanalytic Psychotherapist
38 Berkeley Road, London N8 8RU
Tel: 0181 348 6933
AAP

Jackie Fosbury
Cognitive Analytic Therapist
29 Carysfort Road, Stoke Newington
N16 9AA
Tel: 0171 249 9994
ACAT

Loretta Fox
Psychosynthesis Psychotherapist
1 Helen Court, Hendon Lane, Finchley,
London N3 3SX
Tel: 0181 349 0448
PET

Glenda Fredman
Systemic Psychotherapist
44 Glenwood Road, London N15 3JU
KCC

Sue Freeman
Psychoanalytic Psychotherapist
5a Winchester Road, London
N6 5HW
Tel: 0181 348 8889
IPC

Elizabeth Gee
Analytical Psychologist-Jungian Analyst
22 Wood Vale, London N10 3DP
Tel: 0181 883 3479
SAP, BAP

Hugh Gee
Analytical Psychologist-Jungian Analyst
22 Wood Vale, London N10 3DP
Tel: 0181 883 3479
SAP, BAP

Irene Gee
Family Therapist
41 Eastern Road, London N2 9LB
Tel: 0181 444 9832
IFT

Gillie Gilbert
Biodynamic Psychotherapist
27 Sandringham Gardens, North
Finchley, London N12 0NY
Tel: 0181 445 8424
BTC

Phyllis Goldblatt
Psychoanalytic Psychotherapist
104 Southwood Lane, London N6 5SY
Tel: 0181 348 4125
GUILD

Sylvia Golden
Integrative Psychotherapist
27 Thornhill Road, London N1 1JR
Tel: 0171 586 5959 x 3992/0171 700
2674
RCSPC

Lesley Goodman
Psychoanalytic Psychotherapist
73 Huddleston Road, London N7 0AE
Tel: 0171 700 2563
BAP

Kate Goslett
Psychoanalytic Psychotherapist
83 Axminster Road, London N7 6BS
Tel: 0171 272 8322
IPSS

Marion Gow
Psychoanalytic Psychotherapist
76b Inderwick Road, London N8 9JY
Tel: 0181 347 8748
GUILD, WTC

Hilary Graham
Family Therapist
19 Cornwallis Road, London N19 4LP
Tel: 0171 263 6001
AFT

Judy Graham
Humanistic Psychotherapist
9 Highbury Crescent, London N5 1RN
Tel: 0171 700 7532
AHPP

Margaret Granowski
Integrative Psychotherapist
191 Brecknock Road, London
N19 5AB
Tel: 0171 485 5274
MC

Rosamund Grant
Psychoanalytic Psychotherapist
84 Raleigh Road, London N8 0JA
Tel: 0181 341 7339
GUILD, WTC

Nigel Gray
Body Psychotherapist, Integrative
Psychotherapist
72 Blake Road, Bounds Green, London
N11 2AH
Tel: 0181 368 2778
CCHP

Margaret Green
Psychoanalytic Psychotherapist
158a Stapleton Hall Road, London
N4 4QJ
Tel: 0171 263 3775/0181 340 4182
AAP, WTC

Cyril Green-Thompson
Hypno-Psychotherapist
4 Alexandra National House, 330
Seven Sisters Road, London N4 2PF
Tel: 0181 802 7103
NSHAP

David Grey
Psychoanalytic Psychotherapist
16a Beatty Road, London N16 8EB
Tel: 0171 249 7859
IPSS

Sheila Griffiths
Systemic Psychotherapist
22 Church Crescent, London
N10 3ND
Tel: 0181 883 2262
KCC

Grete Gross
Autogenic Psychotherapist
21 Walfield Avenue, London N20 9PS
Tel: 0171 445 8275
BAFAT

Stephen Gross
Analytical Psychologist-Jungian Analyst
5 Barnard Hill, London N10 2HB
Tel: 0181 444 0598
BAP

Vivienne Gross
Systemic Psychotherapist, Family
Psychotherapist
5 Barnard Hill, Muswell Hill, London
N10 2HB
Tel: 0181 809 5577/0181 444 0598
KCC, IFT

Madeleine Guppy
Psychoanalytic Psychotherapist
82 Hertford Road, London N2 9BU
Tel: 0181 883 4442
LCP

Gideon Hadary
Child Psychotherapist
Child and Adolescent Mental Health
Team, Haringey Healthcare NHS Trust,
St Ann's Hospital, London N15 3TH
Tel: 0181 442 6467/0181 459 3881
ACP

Orna Hadary
Psychoanalytic Psychotherapist
31 Templars Crescent, London
N3 3QR
Tel: 0181 459 3881/0181 346 0594
CPP

Guy Hall
Psychoanalytic Psychotherapist
13 Falkland Avenue, London N3 1QR
Tel: 0181 343 0069
AAP

Kirsty Hall
Psychoanalytic Psychotherapist
134 Dukes Avenue, London N10 2QB
Tel: 0181 883 9681
AAP

William Halton
Child Psychotherapist
10 Lincoln Road, London N2 9DL
Tel: 0181 444 7497
ACP

Dorothy Hamilton
Psychoanalytic Psychotherapist
1 Fairbridge Road, London N19 3EW
Tel: 0171 272 7013
AGIP

Paule Hamilton-Duckett
Psychoanalytic Psychotherapist
91 Priory Road, London N8 8LY
Tel: 0181 340 9720
IPC

Maureen Hancock
Gestalt Psychotherapist, Humanistic
Psychotherapist
233 Biddestone Road, London N7 9UE
Tel: 0171 700 3298
GCL, AHPP

Sr M Letizia Hannon
Educational Therapist
53 Bethune Road, London N16 5EE
Tel: 0181 802 3430
FAETT

Georgina Hardie
Psychoanalytic Psychotherapist
26 Anson Road, London N7 0RD
Tel: 0171 609 5750
BAP

Judy Hargreaves
Humanistic and Integrative
Psychotherapist
Spectrum, 7 Endymion Road, London
N4 1EE
Tel: 0181 749 1964
SPEC

Ki Harley
Transactional Analysis Psychotherapist
25 Grove Avenue, Finchley Central,
London N3 1QS
Tel: 0181 349 9827
ITA, MET

Anita Harper
Psychoanalytic Psychotherapist,
Transpersonal Psychotherapist
62 Highgate Hill, London N19 5NQ
Tel: 0171 263 2005
IPSS, CCPE

Eric Harper
Lacanian Analyst
Flat 4, 82 Stapleton Hall Road, London
N4
Tel: 0181 348 6112
CFAR

Tirril Harris
Psychoanalytic Psychotherapist
6 Tufnell Park Road, London N7 0DP
Tel: 0171 272 9235
LCP, BAP

Jane Harrison
Psychosynthesis Psychotherapist
24 Endymion Road, London N4 1EE
Tel: 0181 802 2649
IPS

Wendy Hartman
Psychoanalytic Psychotherapist
19 Baalbec Road, Highbury Fields,
London N5 1QN
Tel: 0171 226 4775
IPC

Nicola Haskins
Transpersonal Psychotherapist
Highbury, London N5
Tel: 0171 226 6680
CCPE

Elisabeth Heismann
Systemic Psychotherapist
Upper Street Counselling Centre, 309
Upper Street, London N1 2TU
Tel: 0171 354 0043
KCC

Judith Hemming
Gestalt Psychotherapist
79 Ronalds Road, London N5 1XB
Tel: 0171 359 3000
GPTI

Pauline Henderson
Integrative Psychotherapist
51 Evering Road, London N16 7PU
Tel: 0171 249 5118
MC

Dinea Henney
Psychoanalytic Psychotherapist
38 Swains Lane, London N6 6QR
Tel: 0171 267 2375
BAP

Helen High
Educational Therapist, Child
Psychotherapist
7 Hillside Gardens, London N6 5SU;
c/o BAP, 37 Mapesbury Road, London
NW2 4HJ
Tel: 0181 340 7037
FAETT, ACP

Alison Hilder
Child Psychotherapist
Canonbury Child Guidance Unit, River
Place Health Centre, River Place,
London N1 2DE
Tel: 0171 278 2088/0171 530 2940
ACP

Ruth Hiller
Analytical Psychologist-Jungian Analyst
20 Canonbury Park North, London
N1 2JT
Tel: 0171 226 3723
IGAP

Jo Hogg
NLP Psychotherapist
AILMS, 27 Maury Road, London
N16 7BP
Tel: 0181 806 6165
ANLP

Gisele Holender
Psychoanalytic Psychotherapist
36 Dresden Road, London N19 3BD
Tel: 0171 272 3894
LCP

Stevie Holland
Attachment-based Psychoanalytic
Psychotherapist
7 Cheverton Road, London N19 3BB
Tel: 0171 281 3190
CAPP

Avril Hollings
Humanistic and Integrative
Psychotherapist
Spectrum, 7 Endymion Road, London
N4 1EE
Tel: 0181 341 7214
SPEC

Carol Holmes
Integrative Psychotherapist
76 Mountview Road, London N4 4JR
Tel: 0181 487 7428/0181 348 7457
RCSPC

Paul Holmes
Psychodrama Psychotherapist
87 Carleton Road, London N7 0EZ
Tel: 0171 700 5778
BPDA

John Hosking
Attachment-based Psychoanalytic
Psychotherapist
58 Woodlands Gardens, London
N10 3UA
Tel: 0181 444 3664
CAPP

Carolyn Howell
Transpersonal Psychotherapist
21 Millington House, Stoke Newington
Church Street, London N16 9JA
Tel: 0171 241 2817
CCPE

Inge Hudson
Group Analyst, Psychoanalytic
Psychotherapist
22 Scarborough Road, Stroud Green,
London N4 4LT
Tel: 0171 281 1710
IGA, WTC

Pauline Hudson
Systemic Psychotherapist
68 Tetherdown, Muswell Hill, London
N10 1NG
Tel: 0181 883 7662
KCC

Ann Hughes
Psychoanalytic Psychotherapist
92 Hemingford Road, London N1 1DD
Tel: 0171 607 0803
GUILD

Harold Humphries
Psychoanalytic Psychotherapist
c/o AGIP, 1 Fairbridge Road, London
N19 3EW
Tel: 0171 272 7013
AGIP

Maggie Hunt
Psychosynthesis Psychotherapist
79 Grange Park Avenue, London
N21 2LN
Tel: 0181 360 1024
PET

Hannah Hurst
Attachment-based Psychoanalytic
Psychotherapist
62 Winston Road, London N16 9LT
Tel: 0171 254 7288
CAPP

Antonia Inlander
Psychoanalytic Psychotherapist
c/o AGIP, 1 Fairbridge Road, London
N19 3EW
AGIP

Di Iveson
Family Psychotherapist
77 Muswell Avenue, London N10 7EH
Tel: 0181 883 5731
IFT

Eve Jackson
Analytical Psychologist-Jungian Analyst
54 Eade Road, London N4 1DH
Tel: 0181 800 1418
IGAP

Romey Jacobson
Systemic Psychotherapist
Flat 3, 24 Weston Park, London N8 9TJ
Tel: 0181 347 8904/
01279 444455 x 7278
KCC

Marianne Jacoby
Analytical Psychologist-Jungian Analyst
44 Stokes Court, Diploma Avenue,
London N2 8NX
Tel: 0181 444 1447
BAP

Lyn C Jennings
Educational Therapist
25 Hoodcote Gardens, London
N21 2NG
Tel: 0181 360 5423
FAETT

Einar D Jenssen
Primal Psychotherapist
West Hill House, 6 Swains Lane,
Highgate, London N6 6QU
Tel: 0171 267 9616
LAPP

Bryan Jobbins
Psychoanalytic Psychotherapist
220 Stapleton Hall Road, London
N4 4QR
Tel: 0181 341 3286
LCP

Angela Joyce
Psychoanalytic Psychotherapist
25 Drylands Road, London N8 9HN
Tel: 0181 341 9429/0181 348 6320
GUILD

Leonor Juarez
Psychoanalytic Psychotherapist
144A Mercers Road, London N19 4PU
Tel: 0171 272 1929
IPSS

Stewart Katzman
Analytical Psychologist-Jungian Analyst
35 Creighton Avenue, Muswell Hill,
London N10 1NX
Tel: 0181 444 0724
SAP

David L Kay
Analytical Psychologist-Jungian Analyst
The End House, 56 Hendon Avenue,
Finchley, London N3 1UH
Tel: 0181 346 3320
SAP

Ray Keedy-Lilley
Hypno-Psychotherapist
28 Finsbury Park Road, London N4 2JX
Tel: 0171 226 6963
NSHAP

Michael Kelly
Psychoanalytic Psychotherapist, Group
Analyst
132 Stapleton Hall Road, London
N4 4QB
Tel: 0181 340 9597
AAP, IGA

Angela Kenny
Psychoanalytic Psychotherapist
128 Nevill Road, London N16 0SX
Tel: 0171 254 8558
AGIP

Miranda Kenny
Analytical Psychologist-Jungian Analyst
63 Maury Road, Stoke Newington,
London N16 7BJ
Tel: 0181 806 9202
BAP

Judi Keshet-Orr
Individual and Group Humanistic
Psychotherapist, Sexual and Marital
Psychotherapist
28 Woodland Gardens, London
N10 3UA
Tel: 0181 444 9217
BASMT, AHPP

Inge Kessel
Humanistic and Integrative
Psychotherapist
1 Uplands Road, Crouch End, London
N8 9NN
Tel: 0181 348 2315
BCPC

Lee Kidd
Psychoanalytic Psychotherapist
91 Priory Road, London N8 8LY
Tel: 0181 348 1433
IPC

Mary Kingsley
Transpersonal Psychotherapist
c/o 19 Cranley Gardens, London
N10 3AA;
Rivers Edge, 2 Woodland View,
Lynbridge, North Devon EX35 6BE
Tel: 01598 753347/0181 444 4229
CCPE

Jane Kitto
Psychoanalytic Psychotherapist
Flat 1, 2 The Park, London N6 4EU
Tel: 0181 348 6506
LCP

Richard Klein
Lacanian Analyst
17 Granville Road, London N4 4EJ
Tel: 0181 347 5304
CFAR

Valerie Knowles
Psychoanalytic Psychotherapist
1 Florence Villas, Holmesdale Road,
London N6 5TJ
Tel: 0181 348 3251
IPC

Jasna Kostic
Primal Psychotherapist
West Hill House, 6 Swains Lane,
Highgate, London N6 6QU
Tel: 0181 800 6952
LAPP

Yig Labworth
Core Process Psychotherapist,
Humanistic and Integrative
Psychotherapist
9 Eastwood Road, Muswell Hill,
London N10 1NL
Tel: 0181 444 8506
KI, BCPC

Martine Lafargue
Primal Psychotherapist
60 Windermere Road, London
N10 2RG
Tel: 0181 444 8201
LAPP

Regine Lallah
Psychoanalytic Psychotherapist
2 Greville Lodge, 40 Avenue Road,
London N6 5DP
Tel: 0181 340 9943
IPC

Patricia Land
Psychoanalytic Psychotherapist
4 Scholefield Road, Islington N19 3EX
Tel: 0171 272 6077
WTC

Richard Lang
Integrative Psychotherapist
87B Cazenove Avenue, London
N16 6BB
Tel: 0181 806 3710
MC

Myrna Lazarus
Family Therapist
30 Jackson's Lane, Highgate, London
N6 5SX
AFT

Tsafi Lederman
Biodynamic Psychotherapist
7 Arkansas House, New Orleans Walk,
London N19 3SJ
Tel: 0171 263 8551
BTC

Alessandra Lemma
Integrative Psychotherapist
43 Tavistock Terrace, London N19 4BZ
Tel: 0171 380 7897/0171 281 6719
RCSPC

Georgia Lepper
Analytical Psychologist-Jungian Analyst
99 Sotheby Road, London N5 2UT
Tel: 0171 226 9353
SAP

Muriel Letts
Psychoanalytic Psychotherapist
2 Queens Avenue, London N20 0JE
Tel: 0181 445 2888
IPSS

Bernd Leygraf
Humanistic Psychotherapist, Sexual and
Marital Psychotherapist
Flat 4, 69 High Street, London
N8 7QG;
3 Highcroft, North Hill, London
N6 4RD
Tel: 0181 342 9956
BASMT, AHPP

Lauren Liebling
Biodynamic Psychotherapist
6 Crescent Street, Barnsbury, London
N1 1BT
Tel: 0171 700 3995
BTC

Martin Little
Systemic Psychotherapist
23 Woodberry Grove, Finchley,
London N12 0DN
KCC

Maria Loret de Mola
Child Psychotherapist
12 Herons Lea, Sheldon Avenue,
London N6 4JT
Tel: 0181 340 7415
ACP

Olivia Lousada
Psychodrama Psychotherapist
14 Allerton Road, London N16 5UJ
Tel: 0181 802 5284
BPDA

Renee Mallardo
Hypno-Psychotherapist
Pure Balance Mind & Body Centre, 1A
Leicester Mews, Leicester Road, East
Finchley, London N2 9DJ
Tel: 0181 883 4316
NRHP

Peter Mark
Group Analyst
14 Montenotte Road, Shepherd's Hill,
London N8 8RL
Tel: 0171 357 0867/0181 341 3395
IGA

Gaby Marks
Psychoanalytic Psychotherapist
87 Kingsley Way, London N2 0EL
Tel: 0181 455 9783
LCP

Antoinette Marshall
Psychoanalytic Psychotherapist
73 Alexandra Park Road, London
N10 2DG
Tel: 0181 444 9357
IPSS

Carol Marshallsay
Psychoanalytic Psychotherapist
32 Priory Avenue, Hornsey, London
N8 7RN
Tel: 0181 340 0169
LCP

Nicholas Marshallsay
Analytical Psychologist-Jungian Analyst
32 Priory Avenue, Hornsey, London
N8 7RN
Tel: 0181 340 0169
BAP

Stephen Martin
Child Psychotherapist
22 Blythwood Road, London N4 4EU
Tel: 0171 272 5090
ACP

Robert Mayer
Family Therapist
22 Montague Road, London N8 9PJ
IFT

Jessica Mayer-Johnson
Group Analyst
26 St Paul's Place, London N1 2QG
Tel: 0171 359 4925
IGA

Henrietta Mayne
Analytical Psychologist-Jungian Analyst
16 Birchington Road, London N8 8HP
Tel: 0181 340 5156
BAP

Stewart McCafferty
Systemic Psychotherapist
14 Hyde Park Gardens, London
N21 2PN
Tel: 0956 377685
KCC

John McClure
Cognitive Behavioural Psychotherapist
Grovelands Priory Hospital, The
Bourne, Southgate, London N14 6RA
Tel: 0181 882 8191
BABCP

Jennifer McDonnell
Psychoanalytic Psychotherapist
25 Talbot Road, Highgate N6 4QS
Tel: 0181 348 0374
LCP

Colin McGee
Psychoanalytic Psychotherapist
24 Palace Road, Crouch End, London
N8 8QJ
Tel: 0181 348 1848
IPSS

Maggie McKenzie
Humanistic and Integrative
Psychotherapist
Spectrum, 7 Endymion Road, London
N4 1EE
Tel: 0181 341 2277
SPEC

Bryce McKenzie-Smith
Psychoanalytic Psychotherapist
34 North Crescent, London N3 3LL
Tel: 0181 346 7353
AGIP

Mary McKeon
Psychoanalytic Psychotherapist
219 Fox Lane, Palmers Green, London
N13 4BB
Tel: 0181 886 0766
IPC

Ann McNair
Systemic Psychotherapist
29 Halstead Road, Winchmore Hill,
London N21 3DY
Tel: 0181 360 2942
KCC

Delcia McNeil
Humanistic and Integrative
Psychotherapist
Flat 2, 56 Queens Avenue, London
N10 3NU
Tel: 0181 442 0391
SPEC

Betty Mead
Psychoanalytic Psychotherapist
13 St Marks Mansions, 60 Tollington
Park, London N4 3QZ
AGIP

David Mellows
Psychoanalytic Psychotherapist
34 Curzon Road, London N10 2RA
Tel: 0181 883 6230
LCP

Hilary Mellows
Psychoanalytic Psychotherapist
34 Curzon Road, London N10 2RA
Tel: 0181 883 6230
LCP

Hans Jorg Messner
Primal Psychotherapist
West Hill House, 6 Swains Lane,
Highgate, London N6 6QU
Tel: 0171 267 9616
LAPP

Oriel Methuen
Humanistic and Integrative
Psychotherapist, Gestalt
Psychotherapist
Spectrum, 7 Endymion Road, London
N4 1EE
Tel: 0181 883 3246
SPEC

Ann L Meza
Transpersonal Psychotherapist
25 Crane Grove, London N7 8LD
Tel: 0171 607 6805
CCPE

Jess Michael
Attachment-based Psychoanalytic
Psychotherapist
8 Perth Road, Finsbury Park, London
N4 3HB
Tel: 0171 281 1871
CAPP

Ann Miller
Family Psychotherapist
55 Woodlands Avenue, London
N3 2NS
Tel: 0171 624 8605
IFT

Ori Miller
Transpersonal Psychotherapist
3 Chindit House, Aden Terrace,
London N16 9EB
Tel: 0171 249 2525
CCPE

Penny Miller
Attachment-based Psychoanalytic
Psychotherapist
3 Carysfort Road, Stoke Newington,
London N16 9AA
Tel: 0171 249 7846
CAPP

Isabel Montero
Psychoanalytic Psychotherapist
55 Birley Road, London N20 0HB
Tel: 0181 446 2581
AAP, WTC

Aslan Mordecai
Psychoanalytic Psychotherapist
76 Grove Avenue, London N10 2AN
Tel: 0181 883 9665
BAP

Kay Mordecai
Psychoanalytic Psychotherapist
76 Grove Avenue, London N10 2AN
Tel: 0181 883 9665
BAP

Anne Morgan (Mhlongo)
Group Analyst
126a Wilberforce Road, London
N4 2SU
Tel: 0171 354 0436
IGA

Elspeth Morley
Psychoanalytic Psychotherapist,
Psychoanalytic Marital Psychotherapist
43 Highbury Place, London N5 1QL
Tel: 0171 359 2282
BAP, TMSI

Robert Morley
Psychoanalytic Psychotherapist,
Psychoanalytic Marital Psychotherapist
43 Highbury Place, London N5 1QL
Tel: 0171 359 2282
BAP, TMSI

Shosh Morris
Psychoanalytic Psychotherapist
23C Milner Square, London N1 1TL
Tel: 0171 359 0258
GUILD

Richard Morrison
Humanistic and Integrative
Psychotherapist
Spectrum, 7 Endymion Road, London
N4 1EE
Tel: 0181 348 6546
SPEC

Gillian Morton
Educational Therapist
Flat 5, 17 Haslemere Road, London
N8 9QP
Tel: 0181 340 5686
FAETT

Alan Mulhern
Analytical Psychologist-Jungian Analyst
30 Danvers Road, London N8 7HH
Tel: 0181 348 9809
AJA

Graham Music
Integrative Psychotherapist
2 Avenell Road, Finsbury Park, London
N5 1DP
Tel: 0171 359 4403
MC

Piers Myers
Integrative Psychotherapist
94A Bethune Road, London N16 5BA
Tel: 0181 802 9290
RCSPC

Julia Naish
Humanistic and Integrative
Psychotherapist
Spectrum, 7 Endymion Road, London
N4 1EE
Tel: 0181 341 2277
SPEC

Trinidad Navarro
Psychoanalytic Psychotherapist
Garden Flat, 13 Christchurch Road,
London N8 9QL
Tel: 0181 889 6921/0181 348 9244
AAP

Annie Nehmad
Cognitive Analytic Therapist
65 Northwold Road, London N16 7DS
Tel: 0181 806 5025
ACAT

Zah Ngah
Child Psychotherapist
Child and Adolescent Mental Health
Team, Haringey Healthcare NHS Trust,
St Ann's Hospital, London N15 3TH
Tel: 0181 442 6467/0171 359 8283
ACP

Amelie Noack
Analytical Psychologist-Jungian Analyst
The Garden Flat, 213 Tufnell Park
Road, London N7 OPX
Tel: 0171 609 8380
AJA

Jane Noble
Psychoanalytic Psychotherapist
54 Redston Road, London N8 7HE
Tel: 0181 348 2801
GUILD

Marsha Nodelman
Primal Psychotherapist
West Hill House, 6 Swains Lane,
Highgate, London N6 6QU
Tel: 0171 267 9616
LAPP

Noreen O'Connor
Psychoanalytic Psychotherapist
78 Huddleston Road, London N7 0EG
Tel: 0171 263 2410
PA, GUILD

Margaret D Ohene
Systemic Psychotherapist
16 Wilton Road, Muswell Hill, London
N10 1LS
Tel: 0181 442 6000 x 4281/0181 444
9662
KCC

Christopher Owen
Hypno-Psychotherapist
Pure Balance Mind & Body Centre, 1A
Leicester Mews, Leicester Road, East
Finchley, London N2 9DJ;
38 Victoria Road, London N22 4XD
Tel: 0181 883 4316
NRHP

Simona Panetta-Crean
Analytical Psychologist-Jungian Analyst
Flat 1, 10 Cromartie Road, London
N19 3SJ
Tel: 0171 263 7244
SAP

Rosie Parker
Psychoanalytic Psychotherapist
17 Archibald Road, London N7 0AN
Tel: 0171 700 2097
IPC

Val Parks
Psychoanalytic Psychotherapist
18 Rosemary Avenue, Finchley, London
N3 2QN
Tel: 0181 349 1214
IPC

Stuart Paterson
Humanistic and Integrative
Psychotherapist, Body Psychotherapist
Spectrum, 7 Endymion Road, London
N4 1EE
Tel: 0181 342 9594
SPEC

Anna Patterson
Humanistic and Integrative
Psychotherapist
Spectrum, 7 Endymion Road, London
N4 1EE
Tel: 0181 341 2277
SPEC

George Pearce
Psychoanalytic Psychotherapist
288 Park Road, London N8 8JY
Tel: 0181 340 1233
AAP

Sharon Pettle
Systemic Psychotherapist
10 Priory Avenue, Crouch End, London
N8 7RN
Tel: 0181 340 2539
IFT

Judith Philo
Analytical Psychologist-Jungian Analyst
194 Tufnell Park Road, London N7 0EE
Tel: 0171 263 1952
BAP

Rachel Pick
Child Psychotherapist
2 Beresford Terrace, Highbury, London
N5 2DH
Tel: 0181 584 6301/0171 359 2461
ACP

Keith Pickstock
Psychosynthesis Psychotherapist
105 Clissold Crescent, Stoke
Newington, London N16 9AS
Tel: 0171 254 4975
PET

Stella Pierides
Psychoanalytic Psychotherapist
15 Victoria Road, London N4 3SH
Tel: 0171 272 5957
AAP

Edna Pimentel
Humanistic Psychotherapist
41 Springcroft Avenue, London N2 9JH
Tel: 0181 883 0511
AHPP

Robin Piper
Psychoanalytic Psychotherapist, Group
Analytic Psychotherapist
148 Mercers Road, London N19 4PX
Tel: 0171 272 4002
LCP

Eduardo Pitchon
Child Psychotherapist, Psychoanalytic
Psychotherapist
Lubavitch Foundation, 107/115
Stamford Hill Road, London N16;
10 Cholmley Gardens, Fortune Green
Road, London NW6
Tel: 0171 800 0022/0171 435 0496
ACP, LCP

Ruth Pitman
Psychoanalytic Psychotherapist
21 Southwood Avenue, London
N6 5SA
Tel: 0181 341 2608
BAP

Patricia Polledri
Psychoanalytic Psychotherapist
2 Southview, 162 Oakleigh Road South,
London N11 1HE
Tel: 0181 368 1475
CPP

Fern Presant
Integrative Psychotherapist
22 Osbaldeston Road, London
N16 7DP
Tel: 0181 806 8119
MC

Kay Preston
Group Analytic Psychotherapist
53 Curzon Road, Muswell Hill, London
N10 2RB
Tel: 0181 883 9051
IPC

Marty Radlett
Existential Psychotherapist
46 Noel Road, London N1
Tel: 0181 868 5836
RCSPC

Elizabeth Ram
Psychoanalytic Psychotherapist
12 Uplands Road, London N8 9NL
Tel: 0181 340 4240
LCP

Judith Rea
Psychoanalytic Psychotherapist
11 Anson Road, London N7 0RB
Tel: 0171 607 0546
GUILD

Tim Read
Group Analyst
28 St John's Villas, London N19 3EG
Tel: 0171 636 8333 x 3306/7/
0171 263 8965
IGA

Sue Rennie
Integrative Arts Psychotherapist
23 Eastern Road, London N22 4DD
Tel: 0181 888 9487
IATE

Martine Renoux
Integrative Psychotherapist
4 Canning Crescent, London N22 5SR
Tel: 0181 889 9980
MC

Lynette Rentoul
Psychoanalytic Psychotherapist
27 Pages Hill, Muswell Hill, London
N10 1PX
Tel: 0171 872 3021/0181 883 3687
BAP

Sue Rhind
Psychosynthesis Psychotherapist
35 Long Lane, Church End, Finchley,
London N3 2PS
Tel: 0181 343 4325
IPS

Val Richards
Psychoanalytic Psychotherapist
28 Ravensdale Avenue, London
N12 9HT
Tel: 0181 445 6120
GUILD, IPSS

Sheila Ritchie
Psychoanalytic Psychotherapist
18b Alexandra Grove, London N4 2LF
Tel: 0181 802 2908
WTC, AGIP

Sylvia Roberts
Systemic Psychotherapist
12 Redston Road, Haringey, London
N8 7HJ
Tel: 0181 340 6336
KCC

Letizia Romano
Transpersonal Psychotherapist
Flat 6, Avenue Hall, 2 Avenue Road,
London N6 5DN
CCPE

Liza Romisch-Clay
Integrative Psychotherapist
7 Rookfield Close, London N10 3TR
Tel: 0181 883 6575
RCSPC

Maria Rosen
Psychoanalytic Psychotherapist
40 Priory Gardens, London N6
Tel: 0181 348 0597
LCP

Jenner Roth
Humanistic and Integrative
Psychotherapist
Spectrum, 7 Endymion Road, London
N4 1EE
Tel: 0181 341 2277
SPEC

Alan Rowan
Lacanian Analyst
16 Claigmar Gardens, London N3 2HR
CFAR

Dorothy Rowe
Personal Construct Psychotherapist
The Garden Flat, 40 Highbury Grove,
London N5 2AG
Tel: 0171 354 3498
CPCP

Robert Royston
Psychoanalytic Psychotherapist
82 Tufnell Park Road, London N7 0DT
Tel: 0171 263 8600
LCP

Marion Russell
Humanistic and Integrative
Psychotherapist
Garden Flat, 68 Pyrland Road, London
N5 2JD
Tel: 0171 704 6761
SPEC

Mary Jane Rust
Psychoanalytic Psychotherapist
45a Uplands Road, London N8 9NN
Tel: 0181 341 1583
WTC

Joanna Ryan
Psychoanalytic Psychotherapist
26 Kyverdale Road, London N16 7AH
Tel: 0181 802 1641
PA

Tom Ryan
Psychoanalytic Psychotherapist
11 Cecile Park, London N8 9AX
Tel: 0181 292 8908/0181 340 5161
AAP

Patsy Ryz
Child Psychotherapist
Dept of Child and Adolescent
Psychiatry, North Middlesex Hospital,
Sterling Way, London N18 1QX
Tel: 0181 887 4231/0181 349 2263
ACP

Marie-Christine Réguis
Psychoanalytic Psychotherapist
36 Warrender Road, London N19 5EF
Tel: 0171 263 8105
AAP

Andrea Sabbadini
Psychoanalytic Psychotherapist
38 Berkeley Road, London N8 8RU
Tel: 0181 340 2936
AAP

Miriam Salles
Biodynamic Psychotherapist
38 Onslow Gardens, London N10 3JU
Tel: 0181 444 4595
BTC

Adam Saltiel
Psychoanalytic Psychotherapist
35 Corbyn Street, London N4 3BY
Tel: 0171 272 2796/0171 281 9375
AAP

Andrew Samuels
Analytical Psychologist-Jungian Analyst
148 Mercers Road, London N19 4PX;
17 Archibald Road, London N7 0AN
Tel: 0171 272 1292/0171 609 6211
SAP

Carole Samuels
Psychoanalytic Psychotherapist
14 Deansway, East Finchley N2 0JF
Tel: 0181 883 7823
LCP

Sue Saville
Psychoanalytic Psychotherapist
9 Twyford Avenue, East Finchley,
London N2 9NU
Tel: 0181 442 1442
IPC

John Schlapobersky
Psychoanalytic Psychotherapist, Group
Analytic Psychotherapist
5 Southwood Lawn Road, London
N6 5SD
Tel: 0181 348 6475
LCP

Tamar Schonfield
Psychoanalytic Psychotherapist
71 Woodland Rise, London N10 3UN
Tel: 0181 365 3226
AAP

Marilyn Selby
Educational Therapist
34 Arden Road, London N3 3AN
Tel: 0181 349 2507
FAETT

Adriana Seradi
Psychoanalytic Psychotherapist
27 Hertford Road, London N2 9BX
Tel: 0181 444 7885
AGIP

Adella Shapiro
Integrative Psychotherapist
41a Fairmead Road, London N19 4DG
Tel: 0171 272 5868
MC

Pury Sharifi
Analytical Psychologist-Jungian Analyst
27 Fortismere Avenue, London
N10 3BN
Tel: 0171 262 1366/0181 444 8234
BAP

Belinda Sharp
Psychoanalytic Psychotherapist
54 Park Drive, London N21 2LS
Tel: 0181 360 6020
IPC

Mannie Sher
Psychoanalytic Psychotherapist
17 Templars Crescent, London
N3 3QR
Tel: 0181 349 9399/0181 346 5294
BAP

H Shivakumar
Analytical Psychologist-Jungian Analyst
16 Elm Park Road, London N3 1EB
Tel: 0181 346 7748
SAP

Gloria Simmons
Systemic Psychotherapist
'Timbers', 64 Manor Drive,
Whetstone, London N20 0DU
Tel: 0181 361 3740
KCC

Monty Simmons
Psychoanalytic Psychotherapist
64 Manor Drive, Whetstone N20 0DU
Tel: 0181 361 3740
LCP

Gail Simon
Systemic Psychotherapist
41 Lealand Road, London N15 6JS
KCC

Jonathan Smith
Psychoanalytic Psychotherapist
59 Holmesdale Road, London N6 5TH
Tel: 0181 340 9137
IPSS

Margaret E Smith
Systemic Psychotherapist
40 Vallance Road, Wood Green,
London N22 4UB
Tel: 0181 809 5577/0181 889 0358
KCC

Peter Smith
Psychoanalytic Psychotherapist
52 Lorne Road, London N4 3RU
Tel: 0171 263 0505
AAP

Ruthie Smith
Psychoanalytic Psychotherapist
63 Lothair Road South, London
N4 1EN
Tel: 0181 341 5438
WTC

Hannah Solemani
Psychoanalytic Psychotherapist
82 Cecile Park, London N8 9AU
Tel: 0181 341 1612
AAP

Clare Soloway
Integrative Psychotherapist
14 Wilton Road, Muswell Hill, London
N10 1LS
Tel: 0181 442 0928
MC

Brenda Squires
Psychosynthesis Psychotherapist
7 Elm Grove, London N8 9AH
Tel: 0181 341 1315
PET

Yvonne Stein
Family Therapist
48 Finchley Park, North Finchley,
London N12 9JL
Tel: 0181 446 4913
AFT

Kate Stevenson
Systemic Psychotherapist
28 Lanchester Road, Highgate, London
N6 4TA
Tel: 0181 442 1430
KCC

Angus Stewart
Psychoanalytic Psychotherapist
44 Etheldene Avenue, London
N10 3QH
Tel: 0181 883 9247
LCP

Joy Stovell
Psychoanalytic Psychotherapist
42A Athenaeum Road, Whetstone,
London N20 9AH
Tel: 0181 446 2434
IPSS

Ricardo Stramer
Psychoanalytic Psychotherapist
19 Cascade Avenue, London N10 3PT
Tel: 0171 586 4262/0181 883 1170
BAP, LCP

Gillian Stuart
Analytical Psychologist-Jungian Analyst
68 Tottenham Lane, Crouch End,
London N8 7EE
Tel: 0181 341 6477
AJA

Margot Sunderland
Gestalt Psychotherapist, Integrative
Arts Psychotherapist
'Terpsichore', 70 Cranwich Road,
London N16 5JD
Tel: 0181 809 5866/0171 704 2534
IATE, GPTI, MET

Alison Swan Parente
Child Psychotherapist, Psychoanalytic
Psychotherapist
The Women's Therapy Centre, 6/9
Manor Gardens, London N7 6LA;
Welbeck Abbey, Welbeck, Worksop,
Nottinghamshire S80 3LN
Tel: 01909 531054/0171 263 6200
ACP, WTC

Richard Swynnerton
Integrative Psychotherapist
11 Links View, Dollis Road, Finchley
Central, London N3 1RN
Tel: 0181 349 1604
RCSPC

Sue SÜnkel
Psychoanalytic Psychotherapist
1 Foxham Road, London N19 4RR
Tel: 0171 281 5193
IPSS

Richard Tan
Psychoanalytic Psychotherapist
4 Ingram Road, East Finchley, London
N2 9QA
Tel: 0181 883 2820
CPP

Harvey Taylor
Psychoanalytic Psychotherapist
318 Long Lane, East Finchley, London
N2 8JP
Tel: 0171 272 7013
AGIP, LCP

Shoshi Terry
Integrative Psychotherapist, Body
Psychotherapist
22b Uplands Road, Crouch End,
London N8 9NL
Tel: 0181 340 7168
CCHP

Harriet Thistlethwaite
Psychoanalytic Psychotherapist
63 Mercers Road, London N19 4PS
Tel: 0171 272 5984
LCP

Lennox Thomas
Psychoanalytic Psychotherapist
278 Seven Sisters Road, Finsbury Park,
London N4 2HY
Tel: 0181 263 4130/0181 995 4362
BAP

Paul Thompson
Psychoanalytic Psychotherapist
10 Huntingdon Road, London N2 9DU
Tel: 0181 444 0795
LCP

Steven Ticktin
Existential Psychotherapist
29 Churchgarth, Pemberton Gardens,
London N19 5RN
Tel: 0171 272 9214/0171 272 2474
RCSPC

Penny Tillett
Educational Therapist
2 The Drive, Fordington Road, London
N6 4TD
Tel: 0181 444 7073
FAETT

Eileen Toibin
Psychoanalytic Psychotherapist
92 Palmerston Crescent, Palmers
Green, London N13 4HN
Tel: 0181 881 1468
LCP

Gethsimani Vastardis
Child Psychotherapist
Canonbury Child Guidance Unit, River
Place Health Centre, River Place,
London N1 2DE
Tel: 0171 530 2940/0181 340 3840
ACP

David Veale
Cognitive Behavioural Psychotherapist
Grovelands Priory Hospital, The
Bourne, Southgate, London N14 6RA
Tel: 0181 882 8191
BABCP

Maurice Veale
Gestalt Psychotherapist, Individual and
Group Humanistic Psychotherapist
148 Corbyn Street, Finsbury Park,
London N4 3DB
Tel: 0171 263 4079
GCL

Rolf Veling
Psychoanalytic Psychotherapist
12 Cromwell Close, London N2 0LL
Tel: 0181 444 0533
LCP

Julia Vellacott
Psychoanalytic Psychotherapist
4 Compton Terrace, London N1 2UN
Tel: 0171 359 2831
LCP

Paul Vernon
Psychoanalytic Psychotherapist
46B Ferntower Road, London N5 2JH
Tel: 0171 359 4943/0181 806 6046
BAP, LCP

Margot Waddell
Psychoanalytic Psychotherapist, Child
Psychotherapist
5 Cardozo Road, London N7 9RJ;
Child & Family Department, Tavistock
Clinic, 120 Belsize Lane, London
NW3 5BA
Tel: 0171 607 3492/0171 435 7111
WTC, ACP

Judy Walker
Systemic Psychotherapist
MHCOP, Whittington Hospital,
Archway Wing A8, Highgate Hill,
London N19 5NF
Tel: 0171 288 5629
KCC

Hilary Waterfield
Psychoanalytic Psychotherapist
160 Albion Road, London N16 9JS
Tel: 0171 263 4130/0171 923 1947
AAP

Sarah Craven Webster
Humanistic and Integrative
Psychotherapist
Spectrum, 7 Endymion Road, London
N4 1EE
Tel: 0181 340 9690
SPEC

Tara Weeramanthri
Family Therapist
12c Petherton Road, London N5 2RD
Tel: 0171 226 2731
AFT

Gwyn Whitfield
Systemic Psychotherapist
41 Lealand Road, London N15 6JS
Tel: 0181 809 7218
KCC

Sonia Whittle
Psychoanalytic Psychotherapist
6 Church Lane, Crouch End, London
N8 7BU
Tel: 0181 348 8419
AAP

Christina Wieland
Psychoanalytic Psychotherapist
50 Fernleigh Road, London N21 3AL
Tel: 0181 886 0232
AGIP

Huguette Wieselberg
Family Therapist
8 Broughton Avenue, London N3 3ER
IFT

Avril Wigham
Psychosynthesis Psychotherapist
119 Grosvenor Avenue, Highbury,
London N5 2NL
Tel: 0181 354 1603
PET

Gillian Wilce
Psychoanalytic Psychotherapist
3 Farleigh House, 25/27 Halton Road,
London N1 2EL
Tel: 0171 354 2942
GUILD

Kate Williams
Humanistic and Integrative
Psychotherapist
101 Bounds Green Road, London
N22 4DF
Tel: 0181 888 7927
SPEC

Susan Williams
Analytical Psychologist-Jungian Analyst
64b Rokesly Avenue, Crouch End,
London N8 8NH
Tel: 0181 340 6020
AJA

Ian Williamson
Jungian Child Analyst, Child
Psychotherapist
53 Bouverie Road, London N16 0AH
Tel: 0181 802 9189/0181 809 3549
SAP, ACP

Serena Willmott
Analytical Psychologist-Jungian Analyst
127 Dynevor Road, London N16 0DA
Tel: 0181 348 7711/0171 254 5915
BAP

Susan Willmott
Humanistic and Integrative
Psychotherapist
Spectrum, 7 Endymion Road, London
N4 1EE
Tel: 01494 758069
SPEC

Carol Wilson
Integrative Psychotherapist
88 Talbot Road, London N6 4RA
Tel: 0181 348 1988
RCSPC

Jilian Wilson
Child Psychotherapist, Psychoanalytic
Psychotherapist
Department of Child & Adolescent
Psychiatry, North Middlesex Hospital,
Sterling Way, London N18 1QX;
74 Dukes Avenue, London N10 2PU
Tel: 0181 887 4231/0181 883 6370
ACP, BAP

Michael Wilson
Psychoanalytic Psychotherapist
258A Caledonian Road, London N1
Tel: 0171 278 0845
GUILD

Rob Wood
Psychoanalytic Psychotherapist
19 Baalbec Road, London N5 1QN
Tel: 0171 226 4775
IPC

Therese M-Y Woodcock
Child Psychotherapist
4 Earlham Grove, Wood Green,
London N22 5HJ;
Developmental Psychiatry Section, Uni
of Cambridge, Douglas House, 18B
Trumpington Road, Cambridge
CB2 2AH
Tel: 01223 336098/01223 324661 (f)
ACP

Chrysoula Worrall
Psychoanalytic Psychotherapist
15 Gresley Road, London N19 3LA
Tel: 0171 272 4133
GUILD

Vivienne Wynant
Psychosynthesis Psychotherapist
1 Blythwood Road, Islington, London
N4 4EU
Tel: 0171 272 0780
PET

Margot Young
Integrative Psychotherapist
132 Highbury Hill, London N5 1AT
Tel: 0171 704 8876
MC

Robert M Young
Psychoanalytic Psychotherapist
26 Freegrove Road, London N7 9RP
Tel: 0171 607 8306
IPSS

LONDON NORTH WEST

Stella Acquarone
Psychoanalytic Psychotherapist, Child
Psychotherapist
Parent Infant Clinic, 27B Frognal,
London NW3;
Tetherdown Child & Family
Consultation Centre, 13 Tetherdown,
London N10 1ND
Tel: 0171 433 3112/0181 442 6467
LCP, ACP

Mary Adams
Psychoanalytic Psychotherapist
25 Denning Road, London NW3
Tel: 0171 435 2707
WTC

Hella Adler
Analytical Psychologist-Jungian Analyst
19 Burgess Hill, London NW2 2DD
Tel: 0171 435 7424
AJA

Bobbie Akinboro-Cooper
Child Psychotherapist
Child and Family Unit, Park Royal
Mental Health Unit, Acton Lane,
London NW10 7NS
Tel: 0181 788 1642/0181 453 2357
ACP

Sylvia Albrighton
Integrative Psychotherapist, Body
Psychotherapist
28 Marley Walk, Lennon Road, London
NW2 4PX
Tel: 0181 452 2201
CCHP

V V Alexander
Analytical Psychologist-Jungian Analyst
75D Belsize Park Gardens, London
NW3 4JP
Tel: 0171 586 1629
SAP

Lesley Allen
Systemic Psychotherapist
Marlborough Family Service, 38
Marlborough Place, St John's Wood,
London NW8 0PG
Tel: 0171 624 8605
KCC

Jenny Altschuler
Family Therapist
Tavistock Clinic, 120 Belsize Lane,
London NW3
Tel: 0171 435 7111
AFT

Anne Alvarez
Child Psychotherapist
Children & Families Department,
Tavistock Clinic, 120 Belsize Lane,
London NW3 5BA
Tel: O71 435 7111/0171 435 2424
ACP

Michael Anderton
Analytical Psychologist-Jungian Analyst
100 Harvist Road, London NW6 6HL
Tel: 0181 960 4780
IGAP

Biddy Arnott
Analytical Psychologist-Jungian Analyst,
Group Analyst
21 Constantine Road, London
NW3 2LN
Tel: 0171 267 1732
SAP, IGA

A R Arthur
Psychoanalytic Psychotherapist
23 College Crescent, London
NW1 0XH
Tel: 0171 388 6990
WMIP

Jill Ashley
Family Psychotherapist
40 Falkland Road, London NW5 2DX
Tel: 0171 267 9032
IFT

Lesley Austin
Integrative Psychotherapist
48 Carlton Hill, London NW8 0ES
Tel: 0171 624 6862
RCSPC

Neil Austin
Psychoanalytic Psychotherapist
Flat 2, 20 Maresfield Gardens, London
NW3 5SX
Tel: 0171 431 1395
AAP

Debbie Bandler Bellman
Child Psychotherapist
34 Solent Road, London NW6 1TU
Tel: 0171 794 3519
ACP

Talia Levine Bar-Yoseph
Integrative Psychotherapist
18a Heriot Road, London NW4 2DG
Tel: 0181 202 6678
GPTI, MET

Tessa Baradon
Child Psychotherapist
Anna Freud Centre, 21 Maresfield
Gardens, London NW3 5SH
Tel: 0171 794 2313/0181 883 9308
ACP

Monica Bard
Psychoanalytic Psychotherapist
29 Fellows Road, London NW3 3DX
Tel: 0171 722 3148
LCP

Ruth Barnett
Psychoanalytic Psychotherapist
73 Fortune Green Road, London
NW6 1DR
Tel: 0171 431 0837
LCP

Jean Barrett
Psychoanalytic Psychotherapist
31 Harvard Court, Honeybourne Road,
London NW6 1HL
Tel: 0171 435 3166
GUILD

Parizad Bathai
Integrative Psychotherapist
Flat C, 85 Melrose Avenue, London
NW2 4LR
Tel: 0181 208 1095
MC

Audrey Battersby
Psychoanalytic Psychotherapist
83 Belsize Lane, London NW3 5AU
Tel: 0171 722 2784
GUILD

Gay Baynes
Psychoanalytic Psychotherapist
56 Aberdare Gardens, London
NW6 3QD
Tel: 0171 624 1728
IPC

Amely Becker
Gestalt Psychotherapist, Individual and
Group Humanistic Psychotherapist
26A Gayton Road, London NW3 1TY
Tel: 0171 794 2821
GCL, AHPP

Claire Bellenis
Hypno-Psychotherapist
68 Haverstock Hill, London NW3 2BE
Tel: 0171 485 6997
NSHAP

Haydene Benjamin
Child Psychotherapist
7 Turners Wood, London NW11 6TD
Tel: 0181 455 2065
ACP

Pauline Benson
Cognitive Behavioural Psychotherapist
54 Hendon Hall Court, Parson Street,
London NW4 1QY
Tel: 0181 203 6060
BABCP

Arnon Bentovim
Family Psychotherapist
12 Falcon Lodge, London NW3 7LD
IFT

Bice Benvenuto
Lacanian Analyst
23 Primrose Gardens, London
NW3 4UJ
Tel: 0171 586 0992
CFAR

Bernadine Bishop
Psychoanalytic Psychotherapist
7 Patshull Road, London NW5 2JX
Tel: 0171 485 4911
LCP

David Black
Analytical Psychologist-Jungian Analyst
30 Cholmley Gardens, Aldred Road,
London NW6 1AG
Tel: 0171 435 9192
AJA

Roger Bland
Integrative Psychotherapist
17 Park Road, London NW1 6XN
Tel: 0171 373 2014/0171 813 2145
RCSPC

Evanthe Blandy
Child Psychotherapist, Psychoanalytic
Psychotherapist
2 Montrose Avenue, Queens Park,
London NW6 6LB
Tel: 0181 960 3040/0181 964 3813
ACP, GUILD

Anita Blum
Sexual and Marital Psychotherapist
18 Foscote Road, London NW4 3SD
BASMT

Arna Blum
Psychoanalytic Psychotherapist
72 Balcombe Street, London
NW1 6NE;
Abbey Cottage, Sutton Courtenay,
Abingdon, Oxford OX14 4AF
Tel: 0171 262 9474/01235 848719
IPC

Valerie Bonnefin
Autogenic Psychotherapist
83 Nottingham Terrace, London
NW1 4QE
Tel: 0171 486 6367
BAFAT

Su Borsig
Integrative Psychotherapist
90 Harvist Road, London NW6 6HL
Tel: 0181 964 2719
MET

Paula Boston
Family Psychotherapist
10 Temple Grove, London NW11 7UA
IFT

Nigel Burch
Psychoanalytic Psychotherapist
Flat 1, 1a Laurier Road, London
NW5 1SD
Tel: 0171 267 2785
AAP

Charlotte Burck
Family Therapist, Systemic
Psychotherapist
Senior Clinical Lecturer in Social Work,
Tavistock Clinic, London NW3 5BA
Tel: 0171 435 7111
IFT

Alex Burns
Psychoanalytic Psychotherapist
Garden Flat, 31 Denning Road, London
NW3 1ST
Tel: 0171 435 5369
IPSS

Mary V Burton
Psychoanalytic Psychotherapist
Flat 1, 40 Belsize Park, London
NW3 4EE
Tel: 0171 586 9708
WMIP

Diana Butt
Family Psychotherapist, Family
Therapist
19 Priory Road, London NW6 4NN;
West London Health Care Trust, Child
& Family Consultation Service,
Windmill Lodge, Uxbridge Road,
Southall UB1 3EU
Tel: 0181 845 5766
IFT

John Byng-Hall
Family Psychotherapist
Tavistock Clinic, 120 Belsize Lane,
London NW3 5BA
Tel: 0171 435 7111
IFT

Carola Byring
Biodynamic Psychotherapist
Upper Maisonette, 19 Princess Road,
London NW1 8JR
Tel: 0171 483 1976
BTC

Jennifer Caccia
Psychoanalytic Psychotherapist
Top Flat, 132 Goldhurst Terrace,
London NW6 3HR
Tel: 0171 328 5779
LCP

Donald Campbell
Child Psychotherapist
Portman Clinic, 8 Fitzjohns Avenue,
London NW3 5NA
Tel: 0171 794 8262/0171 722 7573
ACP

Elizabeth Campbell
Psychoanalytic Psychotherapist
2 Provost Road, London NW3 4ST
Tel: 0171 722 7573
GUILD

Maria Canete
Group Analyst
57 Hamlet Square, London NW2 1SR
Tel: 0181 450 5167
IGA

Rosemarie Carapetian
Hypno-Psychotherapist
15 Ingham Road, West Hampstead,
London NW6 1DG
Tel: 0171 794 7608
NRHP

Theresa Carlson
Transpersonal Psychotherapist
2 Ainger Mews, London NW3 3AZ
CCPE

Richard Carvalho
Analytical Psychologist-Jungian Analyst
51 Woodsome Road, London
NW5 1SA
Tel: 0171 482 1187
SAP

Prudence Cave
Psychoanalytic Psychotherapist
4 Marty's Yard, 17 Hampstead High
Street, London NW3 1PX
Tel: 0171 284 1578
AAP

Deborah Cazalet
Psychoanalytic Psychotherapist
Flat 1, 12 Abercorn Place, London
NW8 9XP
Tel: 0171 286 6024
IPC

Lynn Champion
Child Psychotherapist
Flat 3, 12 Rosslyn Hill, London
NW3 1PH
Tel: 0171 431 7508
ACP

Lilian Chandwani
Psychoanalytic Psychotherapist
18 Park Drive, London NW11 7SP
Tel: 0181 458 8204
IPSS

Claire Chappell
Educational Therapist
46 Princess Road, London NW1 8JL
Tel: 0171 722 9716
FAETT

Anne Charvet
Systemic Psychotherapist
60 Compayne Gardens, London
NW6 3RY
Tel: 0171 836 6633 x 2284/
0171 328 4174
KCC

Giselle China
Psychoanalytic Psychotherapist
24B South Hill Park Gardens, London
NW3 2TG
Tel: 0171 435 6361
IPSS

Conny Christmann
NLP Psychotherapist
147 Bathurst Gardens, London
NW10 5JJ
Tel: 0181 968 4894
ANLP

Jo Ann Clapp
Psychoanalytic Psychotherapist
42A Arkwright Road, Hampstead,
London NW3 6BH
Tel: 0171 435 4205
IPC

Christopher Clulow
Psychoanalytic Marital Psychotherapist
TMSI, Tavistock Centre, 120 Belsize
Lane, London NW3 5BA
Tel: 0171 435 7111
TMSI

Andrew Cockburn
Analytical Psychotherapist
30 Southway, Hampstead Garden
Suburb, London NW11 6RU
Tel: 0181 731 7887
LCP

Pauline Cohen
Child Psychotherapist
Anna Freud Centre, 21 Maresfield
Gardens, London NW3 5SH
Tel: 0171 794 2313/0171 794 6046
ACP

Vivienne Cohen
Group Analyst
8 Linnell Drive, London NW11 7LT
Tel: 0181 455 4781
IGA

Jeffrey Collis
Sexual and Marital Psychotherapist
27 Station Road, London NW10 4UP
BASMT

Warren Colman
Psychoanalytic Marital Psychotherapist
TMSI, Tavistock Centre, 120 Belsize
Lane, London NW3 5BA;
65 Gurney Court Road, St Albans,
Herts AL1 4QU
Tel: 0171 435 7111/01727 810337
TMSI

Christopher Connolly
Psychosynthesis Psychotherapist
28a Hampstead High Street, London
NW3 1QA
Tel: 0171 794 4066
PET

Jim Conwell
Integrative Psychotherapist
2 Kemplay Road, London NW3 1SY
Tel: 0171 435 7477
MC

Alan Cooklin
Family Psychotherapist
Huntley Centre, Cappa Street, London
NW1;
89 Southwood Lane, London N6 5TB
Tel: 0171 387 9300 x 5043
IFT

Hilary Cooper
Psychoanalytic Psychotherapist
14 Dartmouth Road, London
NW2 4EU
Tel: 0181 208 3349
PA

Robin Cooper
Psychoanalytic Psychotherapist
14 Dartmouth Road, London
NW2 4EU
Tel: 0181 208 3349
PA

Beta Copley
Child Psychotherapist
25 Pilgrims Lane, London NW3 1SX
Tel: 0171 794 4780
ACP

Marie Costello
Psychoanalytic Psychotherapist
18 Maresfield Gardens, Hampstead,
London NW3 5SX;
47a Golders Green Road, Golders
Green, London NW11
Tel: 0171 431 8159
IPC

Theresa Coulter
Psychoanalytic Psychotherapist
Flat 30, 35-36 Belsize Square, London
NW3 4HL
Tel: 0171 794 7930
IPSS

Stephen Crawford
Psychoanalytic Psychotherapist
27 St Margarets Road, Kensal Green,
London NW10 5PY
Tel: 0181 968 9168
IPC

Dave Crisp
NLP Psychotherapist
30A The Loning, Colindale, London
NW9 6DR
Tel: 0181 200 4944
ANLP

Lynne Cudmore
Psychoanalytic Marital Psychotherapist,
Analytical Psychologist
TMSI, Tavistock Centre, 120 Belsize
Lane, London NW3 5BA;
70 Mill Hill Road, London W3 8JJ
Tel: 0171 435 7111/0181 993 1534
TMSI

Barbara Dale
Family Psychotherapist
Tavistock Clinic, 120 Belsize Lane,
London NW3 5BA
Tel: 0171 435 7111
IFT

Kevin Daly
Cognitive Behavioural Psychotherapist
54 Yale Court, Honeybourne Road,
West Hampstead, London NW6 1JQ
Tel: 0171 431 1794
BABCP

Diana Daniell
Psychoanalytic Marital Psychotherapist,
Psychoanalytic Psychotherapist
23 College Crescent, London
NW3 5LL
Tel: 0171 794 9782
TMSI, BAP

Didier Danthois
Biodynamic Psychotherapist
Upper Maisonette, 19 Princess Road,
London NW1 8JR
Tel: 0171 483 1976
BTC

Adele Davide
Analytical Psychologist-Jungian Analyst
49 Llanvanor Road, Child's Hill, London
NW2 2AR
Tel: 0181 458 2667
AJA

Jennifer Davids
Child Psychotherapist
Anna Freud Centre, 21 Maresfield
Gardens, London NW3 5SH
Tel: 0171 794 2313/0171 372 3403
ACP

Helen Davis
Integrative Psychotherapist, Body
Psychotherapist
73 Staverton Road, London
NW2 5HA;
The Minster Centre, Unit 1/2 Drakes
Courtyard, 291 Kilburn High Road,
London NW6 7JR
Tel: 0171 372 4940/0181 451 7802
MC

Dilys Daws
Psychoanalytic Psychotherapist, Child
Psychotherapist
43 Heath Hurst Road, London
NW3 2RU;
Child and Family Department,
Tavistock Clinic, 120 Belsize Lane,
London NW3 5BA
Tel: 0171 435 7111/0171 435 9248
ACP, BAP

Neil Dawson
Family Psychotherapist
Marlborough Family Service, 38
Marlborough Place, London NW8 0PJ
Tel: 0171 624 8605
IFT

Penelope de Haas
Analytical Psychologist-Jungian Analyst
10 Maresfield Gardens, London
NW3 5SU
Tel: 0171 431 7055/0171 435 0513
SAP

Patrick de Mare
Group Analyst
5 Holly Place, London NW3 6QU
Tel: 0171 794 3171
IGA

Judith Dell
Humanistic Psychotherapist
45 Litchfield Way, London NW11 6NU
Tel: 0181 458 7893
AHPP

Marika Denton
Group Analyst, Psychoanalytic
Psychotherapist
11 Oakhill Avenue, London NW3 7RD
Tel: 0171 435 2086
IGA, WTC

Adrian Dickinson
Analytical Psychotherapist
84a Hillfield Road, West Hampstead,
London NW6 1QA
Tel: 0171 435 9079
LCP

Damini Angeli Diyaljee
Hypno-Psychotherapist
Flat 6, 346 Finchley Road, Hampstead,
London NW3 7AJ
Tel: 0171 431 4943
NRHP

Wendy Dobbs
Psychoanalytic Psychotherapist
12 Bocastle Road, London NW5 1EG
AGIP

Anne Doggett
Psychoanalytic Psychotherapist
57 Dartmouth Park Road, London
NW5 1SL
Tel: 0171 485 6723
AAP

Geri Dogmetchi
Psychoanalytic Psychotherapist
18 Spencer Rise, London NW5 1AP
Tel: 0171 485 2883
IPSS

Damien Doorley
Analytical Psychologist-Jungian Analyst
75 Goldhurst Terrace, London
NW6 3HA
Tel: 0171 624 6524
AJA

Jenny Dover
Educational Therapist
11 Gainsborough Gardens, London
NW3 1BJ
Tel: 0171 794 6510
FAETT

Emilia Dowling
Family Psychotherapist
The Tavistock Clinic, 120 Belsize Lane,
London NW3 5BA
Tel: 0171 435 7111
IFT

Gwynneth Down
Family Therapist
c/o IFT, 24-32 Stephenson Way,
London NW1 2HX
IFT

Windy Dryden
Cognitive Psychotherapist
14A Winchester Avenue, London
NW6 7TU
Tel: 0171 328 9687
BABCP

Marc Du Ry
Lacanian Analyst
172a Camden Road, London NW1 9HJ
Tel: 0171 267 9669
CFAR

Helene Dubinsky
Child Psychotherapist
Child and Family Department,
Tavistock Clinic, 120 Belsize Lane,
London NW3 5BA
Tel: 0171 435 7111/0171 794 5047
ACP

Alexander Duddington
Analytical Psychologist-Jungian Analyst
18 East Heath Road, London NW3 1AJ
Tel: 0171 435 2301
AJA

Nicola Dunn
Integrative Psychotherapist
53 Shirlock Road, London NW3 2HR
Tel: 0171 284 2497
MC

Arif Dyrud
Psychosynthesis Psychotherapist
41 Barker Drive, Elm Village, Camden
Town, London NW1 0JG
Tel: 0171 388 9865
PET

Marje Eagles
Group Analyst
107 Frognal, Hampstead, London
NW3 6SR
Tel: 0181 954 6745/0171 431 1465
IGA

Marjorie Eagles
Psychoanalytic Psychotherapist
107 Frognal, Hampstead, London
NW3 6SR
Tel: 0181 954 6745/0171 431 1465
LCP

Judith Easter
Psychoanalytic Psychotherapist
77 Torbay Road, London NW6 7DU
Tel: 0171 328 6250
GUILD

Rose Edgcumbe
Child Psychotherapist
Anna Freud Centre, 21 Maresfield
Gardens, London NW3 5SH
Tel: 0171 794 2313/0171 794 6506 (f)
ACP

Dagmar Edwards
Gestalt Psychotherapist
28 Blenheim Gardens, London
NW2 4NS
GPTI

Barbara Elliott
Group Analyst
36 Dennington Park Road, London
NW6 1BD
Tel: 0171 794 6014
IGA

Anne Elton
Systemic Psychotherapist
63 Parliament Hill, London NW3 2TB
IFT

Ricky Emanuel
Child Psychotherapist
Dept of Child & Adolescent Psychiatry,
Royal Free Hospital, Pond Street,
London NW3 2QG
Tel: 0171 794 0500 x 5819/0181 348
7032
ACP

Archibald Erskine
Psychoanalytic Psychotherapist,
Analytical Psychotherapist
130 Walm Lane, London NW2 4RT
Tel: 0181 452 9251
LCP, BAP

Joan Evans
Psychosynthesis Psychotherapist
Institute of Psychosynthesis, 65A
Watford Way, Hendon, London
NW4 3AQ
Tel: 0181 202 4525
IPS

Roger Evans
Psychosynthesis Psychotherapist
Institute of Psychosynthesis, 65A
Watford Way, Hendon, London
NW4 3AQ
Tel: 0181 202 4525
IPS

Arturo Ezquerro-Adan
Group Analyst
57 Hamlet Square, London NW2 1SR
Tel: 0171 435 7111/0181 450 5167
IGA

Alexandra Fanning
Psychoanalytic Psychotherapist
46 Westbere Road, London NW2 3RU
Tel: 0171 794 4010/0171 435 5712 (f)
AAP

Nina Farhi
Psychoanalytic Psychotherapist
11 North Square, London NW11 7AB
Tel: 0181 455 5329
GUILD

Antonio Fazio
Psychoanalytic Psychotherapist
35 The Park, London NW11 7ST
Tel: 0181 455 6855
LCP

Tom Feldberg
Psychoanalytic Psychotherapist
24 Brookfield Park, London NW5 1ER
Tel: 0171 267 2577
IPSS

John Fentiman
Transpersonal Psychotherapist
8 Mortimer Court, Abbey Road,
London NW8 9AB
Tel: 0171 266 5610
CCPE

Heidi Ferid
Psychoanalytic Psychotherapist,
Attachment-based Psychoanalytic
Psychotherapist
20 South Hill Park, Hampstead, London
NW3 2SB
Tel: 0171 549 9583/0171 794 9130
IPSS, CAPP

Valentina Fernandez
Cognitive Behavioural Psychotherapist
360 Finchley Road, London NW3 7AJ
Tel: 0171 433 1643
BABCP

Geraldine Festenstein
Group Analyst
8 Briardale Gardens, London
NW3 7PP
Tel: 0171 435 2741
IGA

Berthe Ficarra
Psychoanalytic Psychotherapist
7 Estelle Road, London NW3 2JX
Tel: 0181 482 3399
GUILD

Mike Fielder
Psychoanalytic Psychotherapist
Top Flat, 41 Buckland Crescent,
London NW3 5DJ
Tel: 0171 794 2652/0171 722 2589
PA

James V Fisher
Psychoanalytic Marital Psychotherapist,
Psychoanalytic Psychotherapist
TMSI, Tavistock Centre, 120 Belsize
Lane, London NW3 5BA
Tel: 0171 435 7111/0171 435 2707
TMSI, BAP

Ann Foden
Analytical Psychologist-Jungian Analyst
23 College Crescent, Swiss Cottage,
London NW3 5LL
Tel: 0181 568 0074
BAP

Jane Foley
Integrative Psychotherapist
168 Regents Park Road, London
NW1 8XN
Tel: 0171 722 5165
MC

Angela Foster
Psychoanalytic Psychotherapist
14 Hoveden Road, London NW2 3XD
Tel: 0181 450 2713
LCP

Frank Franklyn
Psychoanalytic Psychotherapist
26 Sydney Grove, Hendon, London
NW4 2EH
Tel: 0181 202 7546
IPSS

Diane Frazer
Psychoanalytic Psychotherapist
9 Greyhound Road, London
NW10 5QH
Tel: 0181 969 9675
AGIP

Joe Friedman
Psychoanalytic Psychotherapist
Top Flat, 41 Buckland Crescent,
London NW3 5DJ
Tel: 0171 722 5077
PA

Debbie Friedman-Kempson
Psychosynthesis Psychotherapist
1189a Finchley Road, London
NW11 0AA
Tel: 0181 458 5760
IPS

Richard P W Fry
Family Therapist
4 Plympton Avenue, Brondesbury,
London NW6 7TJ
Tel: 0181 451 3359
AFT

Susan Fyvel
Family Therapist
59 Broomleigh Street, London
NW6 1QQ
AFT

Steve Gans
Psychoanalytic Psychotherapist
The Diorama, 34 Osnaburgh Street,
London NW1
Tel: 0171 916 5433
PA

Audrey Gavshon
Child Psychotherapist
Anna Freud Centre, 21 Maresfield
Gardens, London NW3 5SH
Tel: 0171 794 2313/0181 348 0276
ACP

Sheryle Geen
Integrative Psychotherapist
95b Leighton Road, London NW5 2QJ
Tel: 0171 482 4537
MC

Dorothy George
Integrative Psychotherapist
610 Jacqueline House, 52 Fitzroy Road,
London NW1 8UA
Tel: 0171 586 8862
RCSPC

Pamela George
Psychoanalytic Psychotherapist
Flat 1, 2 Inglewood Road, London
NW6 1QZ
Tel: 0171 794 1588
LCP

Golshad Ghiaci
Psychoanalytic Psychotherapist
Flat B, 20 Lady Somerset Road, London
NW5 1UP
Tel: 0171 485 4379
PA

Katarina Gildebrand
Transactional Analysis Psychotherapist,
Integrative Psychotherapist
17 Midland Terrace, London
NW2 6QH
Tel: 0181 450 6802
ITA, MET

Douglas Gill
Psychoanalytic Psychotherapist
34 Osnaburgh Street, London
NW1 3ND
Tel: 0171 916 5429
PA

Bonnie Gold
Group Analyst
18 Manor Hall Avenue, Hendon,
London NW4 1NX
Tel: 0181 203 2279
IGA

Lavinia Gomez
Integrative Psychotherapist
21 Mill Lane, London NW6 1NT
Tel: 0171 794 5308
MC

Liz Good
Psychoanalytic Psychotherapist
47a Golders Green Road, London
NW11 8EL
Tel: 0181 208 8526
AGIP

Paul Gordon
Psychoanalytic Psychotherapist
74 Victoria Road, London NW6 6QA
Tel: 0171 624 3053/0171 624 4529
IPSS, PA

Gill Gorell Barnes
Family Psychotherapist
Tavistock Clinic, 120 Belsize Lane,
London NW3 5BA
Tel: 0171 435 7111/0181 348 9029
IFT

Carry Gorney
Systemic Psychotherapist
43 Spencer Rise, London NW5 1AR
Tel: 0171 583 2652/0171 267 6619
KCC

Arlene Gorodensky
Integrative Psychotherapist
The Lodge, 47 Belgrave Gardens,
London NW8 0RE
Tel: 0171 372 5181
RCSPC

Iona Grant
Psychoanalytic Psychotherapist
75 Fleetwood Road, London
NW10 1NR
Tel: 0181 452 4479
AAP, WTC

Esther Green
Analytical Psychologist-Jungian Analyst
20 Marlborough Mansions, Cannon
Hill, London NW6 1JR
Tel: 0171 435 7039
SAP, WTC

Viviane Green
Child Psychotherapist
Marlborough Family Service,
Marlborough Place, London NW8
Tel: 0171 624 8605/0171 435 4960
ACP

Sheena Grunberg
Child Psychotherapist
Tavistock Clinic, 120 Belsize Lane,
London NW3 5BA
Tel: 0171 435 7111/0171 267 1379
ACP

John F Guilfoyle
Sexual and Marital Psychotherapist
40 Brooksville Avenue, Queen's Park,
London NW6 6TG
BASMT

Roger Hacker
Psychoanalytic Psychotherapist
5 Chalcot Gardens, London NW3 4YB
Tel: 0171 586 4144
AAP

Ann Haine
Psychoanalytic Psychotherapist
Flat B, 96 Fortess Road, London
NW5 2HJ
Tel: 0171 267 8936
LCP

Stephen Haine
Psychoanalytic Psychotherapist
Flat B, 96 Fortess Road, London
NW5 2HJ
Tel: 0171 267 8936
AGIP

Jeff Halperin
Analytical Psychologist-Jungian Analyst
Clinical Psychology Department, Royal
Free Hospital, Hampstead, London
NW3 2QG
Tel: 0171 794 0500 x 3672/
0181 882 2904
BAP

Lesley Hampson
Humanistic Psychotherapist
21 South Hill Park, London NW3 2ST
Tel: 0171 435 5536
GCL

Carol Hanson
Child Psychotherapist
Kilburn Child & Family Team, Kilburn
Square Health Clinic, Kilburn Square,
London NW6 6PS
Tel: 0171 625 5115/0181 348 7565
ACP

Michael Harding
Existential Psychotherapist
24 Birchington Court, West End Lane,
London NW6 4PB
Tel: 0171 328 1823
RCSPC

Nahum Harlap
Integrative Psychotherapist
5a Northgate, Prince Albert Road,
London NW8 7RD
Tel: 0171 586 4228
RCSPC

Olivia Harvard-Watts
Psychoanalytic Psychotherapist
44 Woodsome Road, London NW5
Tel: 0171 485 6582
GUILD

Natasha Harvey
Psychoanalytic Psychotherapist
Flat 5, 130 Fellows Road, London
NW3 3JH
Tel: 0171 483 4649
IPC

Susan Haxell
Analytical Psychologist-Jungian Analyst
24 Dyne Road, London NW6 7XE
Tel: 0171 372 6503
SAP

Jane Haynes
Analytical Psychologist-Jungian Analyst
32 Priory Terrace, London NW6 4DH
Tel: 0171 624 2981
SAP

John Heaton
Psychoanalytic Psychotherapist
Top Flat, 41 Buckland Crescent,
London NW3 5DJ
Tel: 0171 722 7428/0171 435 5574
GUILD

Anne Heavey
Family Therapist
North West London Mental Health
NHS Trust, 255 North Circular Road,
Brent Park, London NW10 0JQ
IFT

Karen Hedley
Psychosynthesis Psychotherapist
2 Exeter Road, London NW2 4SP
Tel: 0181 450 6564
IPS

John Henry
Attachment-based Psychoanalytic
Psychotherapist
27 Elm Grove, London NW2 3AE
Tel: 0181 452 8865
CAPP

Zdenka Hermann
Psychoanalytic Psychotherapist
14 Fawley Road, London NW6 1SH
Tel: 0171 435 3158
LCP

Edward Herst
Analytical Psychologist-Jungian Analyst
9 Fitzroy Road, London NW1 8TU
Tel: 0171 722 1661/0171 586 0361 (f)
SAP, BAP

Judy Hildebrand
Family Therapist, Systemic
Psychotherapist
Tavistock Clinic, 120 Belsize Lane,
London NW3 5AB
Tel: 0171 435 7111
IFT

Malka Hirsch-Napchan
Psychoanalytic Psychotherapist
22 Broomsleigh Street, West
Hampstead, London NW6 1QH
Tel: 0171 794 3406
CPP

Ray Holland
Integrative Psychotherapist
25 Greenhill Road, Harlesden, London
NW10 8UD
Tel: 0181 961 7874
CCHP

Kirsti E Holm
Hypno-Psychotherapist
871a Finchley Road, London
NW11 8RR
Tel: 0181 202 3654
NSHAP

Betty Anne Holtrop
Integrative Psychotherapist
Flat 1, 170 Goldhurst Terrace, London
NW6 3HN
Tel: 0171 328 7641
MC

Anne Hooper
Sexual and Marital Psychotherapist
179c Haverstock Hill, London NW3
BASMT

Earl Hopper
Psychoanalytic Psychotherapist, Group
Analyst
11 Heath Mansions, The Mount, Heath
Street, London NW3 6SN
Tel: 0171 435 2053/0171 435 4350
IGA, BAP

Ann Horne
Child Psychotherapist
Portman Clinic, 8 Fitzjohns Avenue,
London NW3 5NA
Tel: 0171 794 8262/0181 673 6486
ACP

Gaie Houston
Gestalt Psychotherapist
8 Rochester Terrace, London
NW1 9JN
Tel: 0171 485 9265
GCL

Angela Howard
Psychoanalytic Psychotherapist
37 Loudoun Road, London NW8 0NE
Tel: 0171 624 2788/0171 624 1709
GUILD

Judith Hubback
Analytical Psychologist-Jungian Analyst
4 Provost Road, London NW3 4ST
Tel: 0171 586 4341
SAP

Margaret Humphrey
Psychoanalytic Psychotherapist
36 Bartholomew Villas, London
NW5 2LL
Tel: 0171 482 3744
BAP

Anne Hurry
Child Psychotherapist, Psychoanalytic
Psychotherapist
Anna Freud Centre, 21 Maresfield
Gardens, London NW3 5SH;
Garden Flat, 15 Lambolle Road,
London NW3 4HS
Tel: 0171 794 2313/0171 794 1762
ACP, BAP

Sylvia Hutchinson
Group Analyst
2 St Gabriel's Road, London NW2 4RY
Tel: 0171 431 2693/0181 450 2791
IGA

Sacha Alexi Irwin
Educational Therapist
9 Johnston Terrace, London NW2 6QJ
Tel: 0181 450 5274
FAETT

Zelda Isaacson
Integrative Psychotherapist
19 Windermere Avenue, London
NW6 6LP
Tel: 0181 960 5121
RCSPC

Silvia Jacon
Integrative Psychotherapist, Body
Psychotherapist
32 West Heath Drive, London
NW11 7QH
Tel: 0181 731 8486
CCHP

Jo James
Integrative Arts Psychotherapist
17 Mackeson Road, Hampstead,
London NW3 2LU
Tel: 0171 267 0188
IATE

Charlotte Jarvis
Child Psychotherapist
Adolescent Department, Tavistock
Clinic, 120 Belsize Lane, London
NW3 5BA
Tel: 0171 435 7111/0171 226 0623
ACP

Riva Joffe
Psychoanalytic Psychotherapist
6 Peploe Road, Queens Park, London
NW6 6EB
Tel: 0181 969 0288
IPSS

John Jolliffe
Attachment-based Psychoanalytic
Psychotherapist
Flat 4, Laurier Court, Laurier Road,
London NW5 1SE
Tel: 0171 284 4334
CAPP

Janet Jones
Psychoanalytic Psychotherapist
1A Exeter Road, London NW2 4SJ
Tel: 0181 452 5860
IPC

Dorothy Judd
Child Psychotherapist, Psychoanalytic
Psychotherapist
TMSI, Tavistock Centre, 120 Belsize
Lane, London NW3 5BA;
20 Mount Pleasant Road, London
NW10 3EL
Tel: 0171 435 7111/0181 459 1118
ACP, CPP, TMSI

Fagie Kadish
Psychoanalytic Psychotherapist
1b Alverstone Road, London NW2 5JS
Tel: 0181 451 1559
LCP

Brett Kahr
Integrative Psychotherapist
3 Greenhill, Prince Arthur Road,
London NW3 5UB
Tel: 0171 435 2955
RCSPC

Myron Kaplan
Psychoanalytic Psychotherapist
1 Clarence Gate Gardens, Glentworth
Street, London NW1
Tel: 0171 724 3062
AGIP

Caro Kelly
Gestalt Psychotherapist
CHOICE Psychotherapy Practice, 18a
Heriot Road, Hendon, London
NW4 2DG
Tel: 0181 223 0680
GPTI, MET

Jennifer Kenrick
Child Psychotherapist
Child and Family Department,
Tavistock Clinic, 120 Belsize Lane,
London NW3 5BA
Tel: 0171 435 7111/0171 352 2525
ACP

Marilyn Kernoff
Psychosynthesis Psychotherapist
Flat 3, 64 Aberdare Gardens, London
NW6 3QD
Tel: 0171 624 0587
PET

Olya Khaleelee
Psychoanalytic Psychotherapist
10 Golders Rise, London NW4 2HR
Tel: 0181 202 7097
LCP

Mavis Klein
Transactional Analysis Psychotherapist
1 Estelle Road, London NW3 2JX
Tel: 0171 267 0784
ITA

Michael Knight
Cognitive Analytic Therapist
Garden Flat, 66 Belsize Park, London
NW3 4EH;
CCG, 24 Buckingham Gate, London
SW1E 6LB
Tel: 0171 828 1123/0171 722 9007
ACAT

Valli Kohon
Child Psychotherapist
31 Beechcroft Avenue, London
NW11 8BJ
Tel: 0171 435 8338
ACP

Sebastian Kraemer
Family Psychotherapist
Tavistock Clinic, 120 Belsize Lane,
London NW3 5BA
Tel: 0171 435 7111
IFT

Sue Krzowski
Psychoanalytic Psychotherapist
Flat 8, Embassy House, West End Lane,
West Hampstead, London NW6 2NA
Tel: 0171 328 5057
GUILD, WTC

Edna Kyrie
NLP Psychotherapist
1 Cecil Rhodes House, Goldington
Street, London NW1 1UG
Tel: 0171 388 7763
ANLP

Maggie La Tourelle
NLP Psychotherapist
58 Leverton Street, Kentish Town,
London NW5 2NU
Tel: 0171 485 4215
ANLP

M Laport-Steuerman
Child Psychotherapist
34 Ornan Road, London NW3 4QB
Tel: 0171 435 4376
ACP

Barbara Latham
Psychoanalytic Psychotherapist
Top Flat, 41 Buckland Crescent,
London NW3 5DJ
Tel: 0171 722 7428
PA

Virginia Katharine Lawlor
Integrative Psychotherapist
43 Shirlock Road, London NW3 5UB
Tel: 0973 353 702
RCSPC

Catherine Leder
Humanistic Psychotherapist,
Biodynamic Psychotherapist
12a Ravenshaw Street, London
NW6 1NN
Tel: 0171 794 2995
AHPP

Heather E Lee Messner
Primal Psychotherapist
18 Laurier Road, London NW5 1SH
Tel: 0181 348 8989
LAPP

Pam Lehrer
Psychoanalytic Psychotherapist
Heath Riding, 32 Wildwood Road,
London NW11 6XB
Tel: 0181 458 8750
IPSS

Jackie Levitsky
Psychoanalytic Psychotherapist
95 Willifield Way, London NW11 6YH
Tel: 0181 455 6413
LCP

Patricia D Levitsky
Integrative Psychotherapist
37 Arkwright Road, London NW3 6BJ
Tel: 0171 435 0816/01494 812219
GPTI

Colette Levy
Psychoanalytic Psychotherapist
52 Springfield Road, St John's Wood,
London NW8 0QN;
Flat 3, Hamilton Court, London
W9 1QR
Tel: 0171 624 4777/0171 289 5044
IPC

Vivienne Lewin
Psychoanalytic Psychotherapist
24 Estelle Road, London NW3 2JY
Tel: 0171 485 5123
LCP

Meira Likierman
Child Psychotherapist, Psychoanalytic
Psychotherapist
5 Downshire Hill, London NW3 1NR;
Child and Family Department,
Tavistock Clinic, 120 Belsize Lane,
London NW3 5BA
Tel: 0171 435 7111/0171 435 9888
ACP, LCP

Roger Linden
Psychoanalytic Psychotherapist
6 Nugent Terrace, Off Abercorn Place,
St Johns Wood, London NW8 9QB
Tel: 0171 289 3216
IPC

Roger Linden
NLP Psychotherapist
6 Nugent Terrace, Abercorn Place, St
John's Wood, London NW8 9QB
Tel: 0171 289 3216
ANLP

Sophie Linden
Psychoanalytic Psychotherapist
9A Kings Gardens, West End Lane,
London NW6 4PU
Tel: 0171 625 6396
LCP

Caroline Lindsey
Psychotherapist (Family & Systemic)
23 Gresham Gardens, London NW11;
Tavistock Clinic, 120 Belsize Lane,
London NW3
Tel: 0181 455 2882
IFT

Michael Lodrick
Psychoanalytic Psychotherapist
12 Stratford Villas, London NW1 9SG
Tel: 0171 267 9845
IPC

Gaynor Lovell
Systemic Psychotherapist
90 Canfield Gardens, London
NW6 3EE
Tel: 0171 624 6190
KCC

James Low
Cognitive Analytic Therapist, Sexual
and Marital Psychotherapist
78B Princess Road, London NW6 5QX
Tel: 0171 732 1342/0171 328 4450
BASMT, PA, ACAT

Francesco Lunardon
Psychoanalytic Psychotherapist
69 Hamilton Road, London
NW10 1NH
Tel: 0181 450 5332
AAP

Mary Lynch
Child Psychotherapist
Child and Family Department,
Tavistock Clinic, 120 Belsize Lane,
London NW3 5BA
Tel: 0171 435 7111/0181 748 8942
ACP

Helena Lövendal-Sörensen
Psychosynthesis Psychotherapist
18b North End Road, London
NW11 7LP
Tel: 0181 905 5937
IPS

Catherine MacGregor
Psychosynthesis Psychotherapist
24 Harley Road, Hampstead, London
NW3 3BN
Tel: 0181 969 3587
IPS

Danuza Machado
Lacanian Analyst
14 Eton Hall, Eton College Road,
London NW3 2DW
Tel: 0171 722 7383
CFAR

Begum Maitra
Analytical Psychologist-Jungian Analyst
38 Nant Road, London NW2 2AT
Tel: 0171 221 4656/0181 458 2510
AJA

Michael Mallows
NLP Psychotherapist
Power 2, 37 Layfield Road, Hendon,
London NW4 3UH
Tel: 0181 202 3373
ANLP

Gertrud Mander
Psychoanalytic Psychotherapist
24 Chalcot Crescent, London
NW1 8YD
Tel: 0171 722 0033
IPC

Claire Manifold
Integrative Psychotherapist
23 Lawn Road, London NW3 2XR
Tel: 0181 853 2395/0171 586 3077
RCSPC

Cordelia Mansall
Integrative Psychotherapist
75 Callcott Road, Kilburn, London
NW6 7EE
Tel: 0171 328 1048
RCSPC

Mario Marrone
Psychoanalytic Psychotherapist, Group
Analyst
75 Minster Mews, Minster Road,
London NW2 3SJ
Tel: 0171 794 4498/0171 431 3912 (f)
LCP, IGA

Christine Martin
Child Psychotherapist
Child & Family Unit, Park Royal Mental
Health Unit, Acton Lane, London
NW10 7NS
Tel: 0171 272 5090/0181 453 2357
ACP

Philippa Marx
Group Analytic Psychotherapist
88 Olive Road, Cricklewood, London
NW2 6UP
Tel: 0181 450 3385
IPC

Barry Mason
Family Psychotherapist, Systemic
Psychotherapist
Institute of Family Therapy, 24-32
Stephenson Way, London NW1 2HX
Tel: 0171 391 9150
IFT

Ian McDermott
NLP Psychotherapist
7 Rudall Crescent, London NW3 1RS
Tel: 0181 442 4133
ANLP

Paul McDermott
Transpersonal Psychotherapist
64 Fleet Road, Hampstead, London
NW3 2QT
CCPE

Patricia McEvoy
Systemic Psychotherapist
31 Cholmley Gardens, Aldred Road,
Hampstead, London NW6 1AG
Tel: 0171 431 8729
KCC

Brenda McHugh
Family Psychotherapist
Marlborough Family Service, 38
Marlborough Place, London NW8 0PJ
Tel: 0171 624 8605
IFT

Julienne McLean
Analytical Psychologist-Jungian Analyst
Flat 21, Christchurch Court, 171
Willesden Lane, London NW6 7XF
Tel: 0181 451 5255
AJA

Mando Meleagrou
Child Psychotherapist, Psychoanalytic
Psychotherapist
Tavistock Mulberry Bush Day Unit, 33
Daleham Gardens, London NW3;
Flat 4, 137-139 Gloucester Terrace,
London W3
Tel: 0181 452 5182/0171 794 3353
ACP, WTC

Sheila Melzak
Child Psychotherapist
Medical Foundation, 96-98 Grafton
Road, London NW5
Tel: 0171 284 4321/0171 226 2895
ACP

Annette Mendelsohn
Child Psychotherapist
Department of Child & Adolescent
Psychiatry, Royal Free Hospital, Pond
Street, London NW3 2QG;
Royal Free Hospital, Pond Street,
London NW3 2QG
Tel: 0171 794 0500 x 5819/
0171 794 8708
ACP

William Meredith-Owen
Analytical Psychologist-Jungian Analyst
6 Holly Mount, London NW3 6SG;
Boscobel, Hatton Rock, Stratford upon
Avon, Warwickshire CV37 0NU
Tel: 01789 292740/0171 794 4764
SAP

Gillian Miles
Psychoanalytic Psychotherapist
37 Prospect Road, London NW2 2JU
Tel: 0171 794 7501/0171 435 7111
BAP

John Andrew Miller
Psychoanalytic Psychotherapist
22 Fitzjohns Avenue, London NW3
Tel: 0171 435 1079
AGIP

Lisa Miller
Child Psychotherapist
Child & Family Department, Tavistock
Clinic, 120 Belsize Lane, London
NW3 5BA
Tel: 0171 435 7111
ACP

Martin Miller
Child Psychotherapist
2 Dunstan Road, London NW11 8AA
Tel: 0171 435 3418
ACP

Riva Miller
Systemic Psychotherapist
Royal Free Hospital, Pond Street,
London NW3 2QC
Tel: 0171 794 0500
IFT

Malcolm Millington
Psychoanalytic Marital Psychotherapist
TMSI, The Tavistock Centre, 120
Belsize Lane NW3 5BA
Tel: 0171 435 7111
TMSI

Adele Mittwoch
Psychoanalytic Psychotherapist, Group
Analyst
1 Chesterford Gardens, London
NW3 7DD
Tel: 0171 435 8589
BAP, LCP, IGA

Elizabeth Model
Child Psychotherapist
Anna Freud Centre, 21 Maresfield
Gardens, London NW3 5SH
Tel: 0171 794 2313/0171 794 6506 (f)
ACP

Lucia Moja-Strasser
Existential Psychotherapist
144A Abbey Road, London NW6 4SR
Tel: 0171 487 7406/0171 372 6407
RCSPC

Julia Moore
Integrative Psychotherapist
192 Fordwych Road, London
NW2 3NX
Tel: 0181 452 9933
MC

H Morgan
Analytical Psychologist-Jungian Analyst
35 Bertie Road, London NW10 2LJ
Tel: 0181 459 2642
BAP

Mary Morgan
Psychoanalytic Marital Psychotherapist
TMSI, Tavistock Centre, 120 Belsize
Lane, London NW3 5BA;
191 Mornington Road, Leytonstone,
London E11 3DT
Tel: 0171 435 7111/0181 558 8929
TMSI

Monique Morris
Psychoanalytic Psychotherapist
35 Highcroft Gardens, London NW11
Tel: 0181 455 4306
GUILD

Ruth Muffett
Analytical Psychologist-Jungian Analyst
39 Belsize Square, London NW3 4HL
Tel: 0171 794 9854
SAP

Elizabeth Nabarro
Psychoanalytic Psychotherapist
58 Croftdown Road, London
NW5 1EN
Tel: 0171 485 3597
GUILD

Omar Nafie
Systemic Psychotherapist
21 Viceroy Court, 58-74 Prince Albert
Road, London NW8 7PP
KCC

Robin Nagle
Child Psychotherapist
13 Carlingford Road, London
NW3 1RY
Tel: 0171 435 6038
ACP

Gill Nathan
Group Analyst
31 Langland Gardens, London
NW3 6QE
Tel: 0171 794 7136
IGA

Charles Neal
Humanistic and Integrative
Psychotherapist
North End Practice, 8a Burghley Road,
Kenton Town, London NW1 0XB
Tel: 0171 387 6758
SPEC

Kathleen Newton
Analytical Psychologist-Jungian Analyst
25c Fitzjohn's Avenue, London
NW3 5JY
Tel: 0171 435 7923
SAP

Veronica Norburn
Psychoanalytic Psychotherapist
18a Tanza Road, London NW3 2UB
Tel: 0171 794 8697
IPSS

Susan Norrington
Psychoanalytic Psychotherapist
6a Lady Somerset Road, London
NW5 1UT
Tel: 0171 284 1818
LCP

Elizabeth Noyes
Cognitive Behavioural Psychotherapist
33 Downside Crescent, London
NW3 2AN
Tel: 0171 794 8321/0171-794 8321
BABCP

Lesley O'Callaghan
Integrative Psychotherapist
53 Okehampton Road, London
NW10 3EN
Tel: 0181 830 1912
MC

Susan O'Cleary
Psychoanalytic Psychotherapist
Flat 2, 20 Maresfield Gardens, London
NW3 5SX
Tel: 0171 431 1395
AAP

Victoria O'Connell
Psychoanalytic Psychotherapist
93 Chevening Road, London NW6
Tel: 0181 960 1065
LCP

Len O'Connor
Family Therapist
33c Belsize Square, London NW3 4HL
Tel: 0171 431 0292
IFT

Haya Oakley
Psychoanalytic Psychotherapist
62 Upper Park Road, London
NW3 2UX
Tel: 0171 722 1628
GUILD, PA

Silvia Oclander Goldie
Child Psychotherapist
Child and Family Department,
Tavistock Clinic, 120 Belsize Lane,
London NW3 5BA
Tel: 0171 435 7111/0171 485 6558
ACP

Andrew Odgers
Attachment-based Psychoanalytic
Psychotherapist
36b South Hill Park, London NW3 2SJ
Tel: 0171 431 0687
CAPP

Elizabeth Oliver-Bellasis
Child Psychotherapist
Child and Family Department,
Tavistock Clinic, 120 Belsize Lane,
London NW3 5BA
Tel: O71 435 7111/0171 485 6998
ACP

Felicia Olney
Psychoanalytic Marital Psychotherapist
TMSI, Tavistock Centre, 120 Belsize
Lane, London NW3 5BA
Tel: 0171 435 7111
TMSI

Susie Orbach
Psychoanalytic Psychotherapist
2 Lancaster Drive, London NW3 4HA
Tel: 0171 794 8226
WTC, LCP

Eileen Orford
Child Psychotherapist
30 Regents Park Road, London
NW1 7TR
Tel: 0171 485 4012
ACP

Vanja Orlans
Gestalt Psychotherapist, Integrative
Psychotherapist
28 Blenheim Gardens, London
NW2 4NS
Tel: 0181 208 1235
GPTI, AHPP

Tom Ormay
Psychoanalytic Psychotherapist
113 Goldhurst Terrace, London
NW6 3HA
Tel: 0171 625 6576
AGIP, CPP, LCP

Jane Palmer
Integrative Psychotherapist
31b Wrottesley Road, London
NW10 5UT
Tel: 0181 961 8076
MC

Shanti Parslow
Family Psychotherapist
Marlborough Family Service, 38
Marlborough Place, London NW8
Tel: 0181 960 0880
IFT

Marianne Parsons
Child Psychotherapist
Anna Freud Centre, 21 Maresfield
Gardens, London NW3 5SH
Tel: 0171 794 2313/0171 624 0600
ACP

Anna-Maria Patalan
Group Analyst
4 Somerton Road, London NW2 ISA
Tel: 0181 450 1630
IGA

Diana Paulson
Family Therapist
34 Alma Street, London NW5 3DH
IFT

Hara Pepeli
Lacanian Analyst
55 Dartmouth Park Road, London
NW5
Tel: 01268 735555 x 352
CFAR

Rosine Perelberg
Family Psychotherapist
35 Hodford Road, London NW11 8NL
Tel: 0171 624 8605
IFT

Linda Peters
Psychoanalytic Psychotherapist
6 Sandwell Crescent, West Hampstead,
London NW6 1PN
Tel: 0171 435 5414
IPC

Corinna Peterson
Analytical Psychologist-Jungian Analyst
107A Hamilton Terrace, London
NW8 9QY
Tel: 0171 286 3995
SAP

Desmond Picard
Psychoanalytic Psychotherapist
33 Sheaveshill Avenue, London
NW9 6SD
Tel: 0181 367 8844/0181 200 5486
BAP

Patrick Pietroni
Analytical Psychologist-Jungian Analyst
57 Fitzroy Road, London NW8 9QY
Tel: 0171 586 4430
SAP

Sue Platt
Integrative Psychotherapist
6 Marion Road, Mill Hill, London
NW7 4AN
Tel: 0181 959 6560
MC

Michael Pokorny
Psychoanalytic Psychotherapist, Group
Analytic Psychotherapist
167 Sumatra Road, London NW6 1PN
Tel: 0171 431 4693/0171 794 4010
AGIP, LCP

Elena Pollard
Psychoanalytic Psychotherapist
82 Christchurch Avenue, London
NW6 7PE
Tel: 0181 459 1945
LCP

Ruth Porter
Psychoanalytic Psychotherapist
6 Raglan Street, London NW5 3DA
Tel: 0171 485 2889
GUILD

Angela Powell
Psychoanalytic Psychotherapist
30 Deacon Road, London NW2 5QH
Tel: 0171 435 2151/0181 830 3773
WTC, AAP

Sheila Powell
Analytical Psychologist-Jungian Analyst
18 Elaine Grove, London NW5 4QG
Tel: 0171 485 4801
BAP

Kevin Power
Group Analytic Psychotherapist
7 Coverdale Road, London NW2 4DB
Tel: 0181 830 2791
LCP

Werner Prall
Integrative Psychotherapist
61 Riffel Road, Willesden Green,
London NW2 4PG
Tel: 0181 452 9438
CCHP

Kristiane Preisinger
Humanistic and Integrative
Psychotherapist
14 Richborough Road, London
NW2 3LU
Tel: 0181 452 6703
MC, AHPP

Michael Preisinger
Humanistic Psychotherapist
14 Richborough Road, London
NW2 3LU
Tel: 0181 452 6703
AHPP

Annie Price
Psychoanalytic Psychotherapist
6 Montpelier Grove, London
NW5 2XD
Tel: 0171 482 3220
AGIP

Jane Puddy
Gestalt Psychotherapist
78 Tennyson Road, London NW6 7SB
Tel: 0171 624 9109
GCL

Eilish Quinn
Psychoanalytic Psychotherapist
c/o LCP, 19 Fitzjohns Avenue, London
NW3 5JY
Tel: 0171 482 7149
LCP

Judith Rabin
Existential Psychotherapist
33 West Heath Drive, London
NW11 7QG
Tel: 0181 201 8765/0181 458 1007
RCSPC

Norman Rabin
Psychoanalytic Psychotherapist
33 West Heath Drive, London
NW11 7QG
Tel: 0181 458 1007
IPSS

Patricia Radford
Child Psychotherapist
Anna Freud Centre, 21 Maresfield
Gardens, London NW3 5SH
Tel: 0171 794 2313/0171 435 4265
ACP

Francesca Raphael
Integrative Arts Psychotherapist
36 Kingsley Road, London NW6 7RT
Tel: 0171 624 3146
IATE

Hilde Rapp
Psychoanalytic Psychotherapist
21 Priory Terrace, London NW6 4DG
Tel: 0171 625 4287
IPSS

Verity Ravensdale
Psychoanalytic Psychotherapist
2 Gloucester Crescent, London
NW1 7DS
Tel: 0171 485 4514
AAP

Celia Read
Psychoanalytic Psychotherapist
31 St Albans Road, London NW5 IRG
Tel: 0171 485 0256
LCP

Joseph Redfearn
Analytical Psychologist-Jungian Analyst
Garden Flat, 38 Frognal, London
NW3 6AG;
16 Tower Street, Brightlingsea, Essex
CO7 0AL
Tel: 0120 630 5374/0171 794 6116
SAP, GUILD

Leon Redler
Psychoanalytic Psychotherapist
c/o Diorama Arts, 34 Osnaburgh
Street, London NW1
Tel: 0171 916 5191
PA

Joan Reggiori
Analytical Psychologist-Jungian Analyst
7 Merton Rise, London NW3 3EN
Tel: 0171 601 8107/0171 722 8687
BAP

Susan Reid
Child Psychotherapist
Child & Family Department, Tavistock
Clinic, 120 Belsize Lane, London
NW3 5BA
Tel: 0171 435 7111/0171 435 0467
ACP

Herta Reik
Group Analyst
7 Oakhill Park Mews, London
NW3 7LH
Tel: 0171 794 7517
IGA

Mirjana Renton
Child Psychotherapist
Child & Family Department, Tavistock
Clinic, 120 Belsize Lane, London
NW3 5BA
Tel: 0171 435 7111/0171 387 2842
ACP

Maria Rhode
Child Psychotherapist
Child & Family Dept, Tavistock Clinic,
120 Belsize Lane, London NW3 5BA
Tel: 0171 435 7111/0171 221 6263
ACP

Diana Richards
Psychoanalytic Psychotherapist
71 The Avenue, London NW6 7NS
Tel: 0181 459 3180
BAP

Gabrielle Rifkind
Group Analyst
39 Lancaster Grove, London
NW3 4HB
Tel: 0171 794 9914
IGA

Chris Robertson
Integrative Psychosynthesis
Psychotherapist
8 Chatsworth Road, London
NW2 4BN
Tel: 0181 451 2165
RE.V

Ewa Robertson
Integrative Psychosynthesis
Psychotherapist
Re.Vision, 8 Chatsworth Road, London
NW2 4BN
Tel: 0181 451 2165
RE.V

Hazel Robinson
Psychoanalytic Psychotherapist
75A Hartland Road, London
NW6 6BH
Tel: 0171 624 0877
GUILD

Estelle Roith
Psychoanalytic Psychotherapist
7 Hogarth Hill, London NW11 6AY
Tel: 0181 455 1514
LCP

G Romm-Bartfeld
Psychoanalytic Psychotherapist
28 Bentick Close, Prince Albert Road,
London NW8
Tel: 0171 483 4854/0171 458 9611
CPP

Kevin Rose
Psychoanalytic Psychotherapist
37 Ashbourne Avenue, London
NW11 0DT
Tel: 0181 455 5936
IPSS

J E Rosenthall
Psychoanalytic Marital Psychotherapist
TMSI, Tavistock Centre, 120 Belsize
Lane, London NW3 5BA
Tel: 0171 435 7111
TMSI

Priscilla Roth
Child Psychotherapist
Child and Family Department,
Tavistock Clinic, 120 Belsize Lane,
London NW3 5BA
Tel: 0171 435 7111/0171 586 3775
ACP

Ruth Roth
Humanistic and Integrative
Psychotherapist
16 Oman Avenue, London NW2 6BG
Tel: 0181 452 7376
MC, BCPC

Richard Rusbridger
Child Psychotherapist
27 Normanby Road, London
NW10 1BU
Tel: 0181 452 1880/0181 830 6743 (f)
ACP

Malcolm Rushton
Analytical Psychologist-Jungian Analyst
Flat 3, 13 Belsize Grove, London
NW3 4UX
Tel: 0171 722 1989
SAP

Julian Russell
NLP Psychotherapist
Pace Personal Development Ltd, 86
South Hill Park, London NW3 2SN
Tel: 0171 794 0960
ANLP

Margaret Rustin
Child Psychotherapist
Child & Family Department, Tavistock
Clinic, 120 Belsize Lane, London
NW3 5BA
Tel: 0171 435 7111/0181 452 9276
ACP

Stanley Ruszczynski
Psychoanalytic Marital Psychotherapist
TMSI, Tavistock Centre, 120 Belsize
Lane, London NW3 5BA
Tel: 0171 435 7111
TMSI

Joel Ryce-Menuhin
Analytical Psychologist-Jungian Analyst
85 Canfield Gardens, London
NW6 3EA
Tel: 0171 624 6930
IGAP

Jean Scarlett
Psychoanalytic Psychotherapist
3 Byron Villas, Vale of Heath, London
NW3 1AR
Tel: 0171 435 2362
LCP, BAP, GCP

Morton Schatzman
Psychoanalytic Psychotherapist
35 Croftdown Road, London
NW5 1EL
Tel: 0171 267 0304
AAP

Margot Schiemann
Integrative Psychotherapist
17b Frognal, London NW3 6AR
Tel: 0171 431 1810
MC

Maureen Schild
Psychosynthesis Psychotherapist
11 Christchurch Avenue, London
NW6 7QP
Tel: 0181 451 4772
IPS

Anneliese Schnurmann
Child Psychotherapist
Flat 5, 11 Netherall Gardens, London
NW3 5RN
Tel: 0171 435 9315
ACP

Joe Schwartz
Attachment-based Psychoanalytic
Psychotherapist
2 Lancaster Drive, London NW3 4HA
Tel: 0171 794 8226
CAPP

Barbara Segal
Child Psychotherapist
Kingsbury Child & Family Centre,
Kingsbury Community Unit, Honeypot
Lane, London NW9 9QY
Tel: 0181 451 8424/0181 722 7844
ACP

Eva Seligman
Analytical Psychologist-Jungian Analyst,
Psychoanalytic Marital Psychotherapist
9 Hillcrest Avenue, London NW11 0EP
Tel: 0181 458 4566
SAP, TMSI

Merkel Sender
Educational Therapist
43 Southway, London NW11 6RX
Tel: 0181 455 6194
FAETT

Irena Bruna Seu
Psychoanalytic Psychotherapist
40 King's Road, London NW10 2BP
Tel: 0181 459 3423
AAP

Ann Shearer
Analytical Psychologist-Jungian Analyst
26 Lambolle Place, London NW3 4PG
Tel: 0171 794 4913
IGAP

Maureen Sheehan
Analytical Psychologist-Jungian Analyst
29 Golders Gardens, London
NW11 9BP;
Royal Free Hospital
Tel: 0171 794 0500 x 3672/0181 458
7909
SAP

Arthur Sherman
Analytical Psychologist-Jungian Analyst
14B Springfield Court, 41 Eton Avenue,
London NW3 3ER
Tel: 0171 431 1175
SAP

Diana Shmukler
Integrative Psychotherapist,
Transactional Analysis Psychotherapist
23a Bracknell Gardens, Hampstead,
London NW3 7EE
Tel: 0171 431 9031
SPTI, ITA

Carl M Silverman
Analytical Psychologist-Jungian Analyst
34 Douglas Road, London NW6
Tel: 0171 912 0803
AJA

Keith Silvester
Psychosynthesis Psychotherapist
51 Cranhurst Road, London NW2 4LL
Tel: 0171 722 8183
IPS

Tina Simmonds
Integrative Psychotherapist
14 Park Avenue, London NW11 7SJ
Tel: 0181 455 9102
MC

Valerie Sinason
Child Psychotherapist
Children & Families Department,
Tavistock Clinic, 120 Belsize Lane,
London NW3 5BA
Tel: O71 435 7111/0171 433 1754
ACP

Robin Skynner
Group Analyst
8 South Square, Hampstead Garden
Suburb, London NW11 7AL
Tel: 0181 458 4085
IGA

Carole Smith
Psychoanalytic Psychotherapist
86 Canfield Gardens, London
NW6 3EE
Tel: 0171 624 5271
IPSS

Gerrilyn Smith
Family Psychotherapist
Institute of Family Therapy, 24-32
Stephenson Way, London NW1 2HX
IFT

Judith Smith
Psychoanalytic Psychotherapist
59 Greenside Road, London
NW12 9JZ
Tel: 0181 743 9096/01225 447089
LCP, SIP

Hester Solomon
Analytical Psychologist-Jungian Analyst
262c Finchley Road, London
NW3 7AA
Tel: 0171 794 7402/0171 794 6230
BAP

Rosemary Southan
Psychoanalytic Psychotherapist
24 Glebe Road, London SW13 0EA
Tel: 0181 876 2808
BAP, LCP

John Southgate
Attachment-based Psychoanalytic
Psychotherapist
12 Nassington Road, London
NW3 2UD
Tel: 0171 433 1263
CAPP

Edna Sovin
Psychoanalytic Psychotherapist
74 Corringham Road, London
NW11 7EG
Tel: 0181 455 0868
LCP

Liz Specterman
Psychosynthesis Psychotherapist
26 Priory Terrace, West Hampstead,
London NW6 4DH
Tel: 0171 624 8569
PET

Marlene Spero
Group Analyst
10 Turner Close, London NW11 6TU
Tel: 0181 458 8109/0181 905 5703 (f)
IGA

Josefine Speyer
Humanistic Psychotherapist
20 Heber Road, London NW2 6AA
Tel: 0171 208 0670
AHPP

Lawrence Spurling
Psychoanalytic Psychotherapist
4 Marty's Yard, 17 Hampstead High
Street, London NW3 1QW
Tel: 0171 431 5471
GUILD

Natalie Spyer
Psychoanalytic Psychotherapist
38 Temple Fortune Lane, London
NW11 7UD
Tel: 0181 455 3050
IPSS

Anthony Stadlen
Existential Psychotherapist,
Psychoanalytic Psychotherapist
64 Dartmouth Park Road, London
NW5 1SN
Tel: 0171 485 3896
LCP, RCSPC

Barbara Stafford
Psychoanalytic Psychotherapist
14 Shirlock Road, London NW3 2HS
Tel: 0171 485 9224
LCP

Miriam Steele
Child Psychotherapist
Anna Freud Centre, 21 Maresfield
Gardens, London NW3 5SH
Tel: 0171 794 2313/0171 624 8500
ACP

Peter Stehle
Existential Psychotherapist
2 The Clock Tower, Holly Hill, 49
Heath Street, London NW3 6UD
Tel: 0171 431 6155
RCSPC

Janine Sternberg
Child Psychotherapist
Tavistock Mulberry Bush Day Unit, 33
Daleham Gardens, London NW3
Tel: 0171 794 3353/0171 794 6505
ACP

Bruce Stevenson
Body Psychotherapist, Integrative
Psychotherapist
23 Nightingale Road, London
NW10 4RG
Tel: 0181 961 7802
CCHP

John Stewart
Psychoanalytic Psychotherapist
51 Hendale Avenue, Hendon, London
NW4 4LP
Tel: 0181 203 9079
IPC

Angela Steyn
Group Analytic Psychotherapist
5 Denman Drive, London NW11 6RE
Tel: 0181 458 1214
IPC

Yael Stobezki
Transpersonal Psychotherapist
Flat E, 46 Fairhazel Gardens, London
NW6 3SJ
Tel: 0171 328 9015
CCPE

Anthony Stone
Humanistic and Integrative
Psychotherapist
7 Westholm, London NW11 6LH
Tel: 0181 455 0794
SPEC

Martin Stone
Analytical Psychologist-Jungian Analyst
Flat 1, 62 Rosslyn Hill, London
NW3 1ND
Tel: 0171 794 8445/0171 435 6072
AJA

Miriam Stone
Psychoanalytic Psychotherapist
39 Parliament Hill, London NW3 2TA
Tel: 0171 435 6072
IPC

Sandra Stone
Child Psychotherapist
8 Alma Square, London NW8 9QD
Tel: 0171 435 4184
ACP

Freddie Strasser
Existential Psychotherapist
99 West Heath Road, Hampstead,
London NW3 7TN
Tel: 0181 455 0118
RCSPC

Anita Sullivan
Individual and Group Humanistic
Psychotherapist
143 Melrose Avenue, London
NW2 4LY
Tel: 0181 450 2107
AHPP

Christopher Sullivan
Psychosynthesis Psychotherapist
143 Melrose Avenue, London
NW2 4LY
Tel: 0181 450 2107
PET

Ann Syz
Child Psychotherapist
Howard House, 30 Belsize Avenue,
London NW3 4AU
Tel: 0171 431 4430/0171 722 2121
ACP

Idonea Taube
Educational Therapist
15 Church Row, London NW3
Tel: 0171 485 2119
FAETT

Mary Taylor
Systemic Psychotherapist
39 Dartmouth Park Road, London
NW5 1SU
Tel: 0171 485 5719/0171 485 0602 (f)
KCC

Caroline Taylor-Thomas
Psychoanalytic Psychotherapist
9 Hayland Close, London NW9 0LH
Tel: 0181 200 1609
IPC

Rita Testa
Child Psychotherapist
Department of Child & Adolescent
Psychiatry, Royal Free Hospital, Pond
Street, London NW3 2QG
Tel: 0171 794 0500 x 5819/0171 794
6819
ACP

Nigel Thomas
Cognitive Behavioural Psychotherapist
Charter Nightingale Hospital, 11-19
Lisson Grove, London NW1 6SH
Tel: 0171 723 1987
BABCP

Jean Thomson
Analytical Psychologist-Jungian Analyst
1 Beatty Street, London NW1 7LN
Tel: 0171 388 5508
SAP

Heather Townsend
Psychoanalytic Psychotherapist
3B Healey Street, London NW1 8SR
Tel: 0171 482 0994
PA

Carlien van Heel
Biodynamic Psychotherapist
Flat 4, 1a Laurier Road, London
NW5 1SD
Tel: 0171 485 2922
BTC

Arturo Varchevker
Psychoanalytic Psychotherapist
Flat 3, 36 Platts Lane, London
NW3 7NT
Tel: 0171 435 3969
LCP

Christopher Vincent
Psychoanalytic Marital Psychotherapist,
Psychoanalytic Psychotherapist
TMSI, Tavistock Centre, 120 Belsize
Lane, London NW3 5BA;
Wellington Cottage, 18 Victoria Street,
Slough SL1 1PR
Tel: 0171 435 7111/01753 822 892
BAP, TMSI

Peter Wanless
Integrative Psychotherapist
Flat 1, 170 Goldhurst Terrace, London
NW6 3HN
Tel: 0171 328 7641
MC

Eve Warin
Psychoanalytic Psychotherapist
22 Churchill Road, London NW5 1AN
Tel: 0171 485 4238
BAP

Eileen Watkins Seymour
NLP Psychotherapist
Ravenscroft Centre, 6 Ravenscroft
Avenue, London NW11 0RY
Tel: 0181 455 3743
ANLP

Lindsay Watson
Lacanian Analyst
95 Parliament Hill Mansions, Lissenden
Gardens, London NW5 1NB
Tel: 0171 485 1274
CFAR

Bilha Weider
Family Psychotherapist
4 Cranbourne Gardens, London
NW11 0HP
Tel: 0181 455 6668
AFT

Hildegard Weinrich
Analytical Psychologist-Jungian Analyst
38 Cranhurst Road, London NW2 4LP
Tel: 0181 450 0537
IGAP

Karen Weixel-Dixon
Integrative Psychotherapist
36 Courthope Road, London
NW3 2LD
Tel: 0171 485 1515
RCSPC

Lindsay Wells
Psychoanalytic Psychotherapist
Flat 19, Brondesbury Court, 235
Willesden Lane, London NW2 5RR
Tel: 0181 886 0232
AGIP

Jean Wetherell
Analytical Psychologist-Jungian Analyst
31 Brondesbury Road, London
NW6 6BA
Tel: 0171 328 1135
BAP

Meredith Wheeler
Transpersonal Psychotherapist
51 Queens Crescent, London
NW5 3QG
CCPE

Kate White
Attachment-based Psychoanalytic
Psychotherapist
12 Nassington Road, London
NW3 2UD
Tel: 0171 433 1263
CAPP

Anastasia Widdicombe
Psychoanalytic Psychotherapist, Child
Psychotherapist
75 Albert Street, London NW1 7LX;
Barnet Child & Family Consultation
Service, Edgware General Hospital,
Edgware, Middx HA8 0AD
Tel: 0171 387 4288/0181 905 6679
ACP, BAP

Jan Wiener
Analytical Psychologist-Jungian Analyst
24 Dyne Road, London NW6 7XE
Tel: 0171 328 6888/0171 625 1428 (f)
SAP

Gerhard Wilke
Group Analyst
75 St Gabriels Road, London
NW2 4DU
Tel: 0181 450 0469
IGA

Gianna Williams
Child Psychotherapist
Child and Family Department,
Tavistock Clinic, 120 Belsize Lane,
London NW3 5BA
Tel: 0171 435 7111/0181 455 5682
ACP

Isca Wittenberg
Child Psychotherapist
Child & Family Department, Tavistock
Clinic, 120 Belsize Lane, London
NW3 5BA
Tel: 0171 435 7111/0181 455 4344
ACP

Gillian Woodman-Smith
Psychoanalytic Psychotherapist, Child
Psychotherapist
62 Albert Street, London NW1 7NR
Tel: 0171 388 5987
ACP, BAP, LCP

John Woods
Child Psychotherapist, Group Analyst
The Young Abusers Project, The
Tavistock Centre, 120 Belsize Lane,
London NW3 5BA;
21 Hillfield Road, London NW6 1QD
Tel: 0171 431 7931/0171 794 6276
ACP, IGA

Marion Yass
Psychoanalytic Marital Psychotherapist
5a Templewood Avenue, London
NW3 7UY
Tel: 0171 794 2221
TMSI

Vernon Yorke
Psychoanalytic Psychotherapist
189 Goldhurst Terrace, London
NW6 3ER
Tel: 0171 624 3002
LCP

Vega Zagier Roberts
Psychoanalytic Psychotherapist
23 College Crescent, London
NW3 3LL
Tel: 0171 431 3312
LCP

Marie Zaphiriou Woods
Child Psychotherapist
Anna Freud Centre, 21 Maresfield
Gardens, London NW3 5SH
Tel: 0171 794 2313/0171 794 6276
ACP

Hindle Zinkin
Analytical Psychologist-Jungian Analyst
25A Maresfield Gardens, London
NW3 5SD
Tel: 0171 435 9219
BAP

LONDON SOUTH EAST

Tessa Adams
Psychoanalytic Psychotherapist
122 Erlanger Road, London SE14
Tel: 0171 358 0018
GUILD

Nigel Alabaster
Family Psychotherapist
Greenwich Child Guidance Service,
Plumstead Health Centre, Tewson
Road, London SE18 1BH
Tel: 0181 855 9254
AFT

Gina M V Alexander
Analytical Psychologist-Jungian Analyst
10 Shooters Hill Road, London
SE3 7BD
Tel: 0181 858 4758
BAP

Shakir Ansari
Cognitive Analytic Therapist
10 Ivy Court, 109 Lee Road,
Blackheath, London SE3 9EA
Tel: 0171 955 4822/0181 852 5248
ACAT

Sonia Appleby
Psychoanalytic Psychotherapist
12 Arran Road, Catford, London
SE6 2NL
Tel: 0181 698 6575
LCP

Coral Atkins
Psychoanalytic Psychotherapist
167 Kennington Road, London
SE11 6SF
Tel: 0171 582 4663
GUILD

Peter Atwood
Family Therapist, Systemic
Psychotherapist
317b Upland Road, East Dulwich,
London SE22 0DL
IFT

Anthony Ayres
Psychoanalytic Psychotherapist
37 Donaldson Road, London SE18 3JZ
Tel: 0181 856 1542
GUILD

Hilary Beard
Cognitive Analytic Therapist
4 Grangewood Terrace, Grange Road,
South Norwood, London SE25 6TA
Tel: 0171 928 9292/0181 771 4475
ACAT

Frances Bell
Analytical Psychologist-Jungian Analyst
296 Commercial Way, Peckham,
London SE15 1QN
Tel: 0171 732 9709
AJA

Lesley Bennett
Psychoanalytic Psychotherapist
167 Brockley Rise, Forest Hill, London
SE23 1NL
Tel: 0181 690 7537
IPSS

Patricia Bishop
Psychoanalytic Psychotherapist
156 Westcombe Hill, Blackheath,
London SE3 7DH
Tel: 0181 293 1995
IPSS

Judith Black
Hypno-Psychotherapist
31 Merritt Road, Crofton Park, London
SE4 1DT
Tel: 0181 691 1168
NSHAP

Sandra Black
Psychoanalytic Psychotherapist
112 Friern Road, London SE22 0AX
Tel: 0181 693 7524
IPSS

John Bland
Cognitive Behavioural Psychotherapist
92 Tuam Road, Plumstead Common,
London SE18 2QU
Tel: 0181 856 4970/0181 473 5937
BABCP

Valerie Blomfield
Psychosynthesis Psychotherapist
12 Woodlands Park Road, Greenwich,
London SE10 9XD
Tel: 0181 853 0772
PET

Janet Boakes
Group Analyst
134 Grove Lane, Denmark Hill, London
SE5 8BP
Tel: 0181 672 1255
IGA

Stephen Bray
NLP Psychotherapist
13 Harrogate Court, Droitwick Close,
Sydenham Hill, London SE26 6TL
Tel: 0181 693 3719
ANLP

Charlie Brittain
Transpersonal Psychotherapist
120 Sandyhill Road, London SE18 7BA
CCPE

Beverly Brooks
Cognitive Analytic Therapist
15 Cibber Road, Forest Hill, London
SE23 2EF;
GHN Limited, 16 Hanover Square,
London W1R 9AJ
Tel: 0171 493 5239/0181 699 8836
ACAT

Ann Bruce
Analytical Psychologist-Jungian Analyst
54 Uffington Road, London SE27 0ND
Tel: 0181 670 3783
SAP

Linda Buckingham
Child Psychotherapist
Forest Hill Child Guidance Clinic, 203
Stanstead Road, London SE23 1HU
Tel: 0181 690 3488/0171 435 3166
ACP

Faye Carey
Psychoanalytic Psychotherapist
15 Holly Grove, London SE15 5DF
Tel: 0171 639 1075
LCP

Charles Caruana
Psychoanalytic Psychotherapist
Flat 6, 50 New Cross Road, London
SE14 5BD
Tel: 0171 277 7402
AGIP

Diana Chandler
Psychosynthesis Psychotherapist
22 St Lukes Close, Woodside, London
SE25 4SX
Tel: 0181 656 9209
IPS

Karen Chessell
Psychoanalytic Psychotherapist
329 Upland Road, East Dulwich,
London SE22 0DL
Tel: 0181 299 2890
IPSS

Dorel Cleminson
Integrative Psychotherapist
36 Seymour Gardens, Brockley,
London SE4 2DN
Tel: 0171 358 9661
RCSPC

Richard Cleminson
Biodynamic Psychotherapist
64 Sunderland Road, Forest Hill,
London SE23 2PY
Tel: 0181 699 0096
BTC

Andrea Clough
Psychosynthesis Psychotherapist
37 Harefield Road, Brockley, London
SE4 1LW
Tel: 0181 692 7171 x 2248
IPS

Margaret Cochrane
Analytical Psychologist-Jungian Analyst
100 Erlanger Road, London SE14 5TH
Tel: 0171 732 0606/0181 858 9800
BAP

Ann Combes
Group Analytic Psychotherapist
53 South Norwood Hill, South
Norwood, London SE25 6BX
Tel: 0181 771 2057
IPC

Susan Corneck
Psychoanalytic Psychotherapist
41 Creek Road, London SE8 3BU
Tel: 0181 694 0221
AGIP

Jan Cousins
Child Psychotherapist
Greenwich Child & Family
Consultation Service, Chevening Road,
London SE10 0LB
Tel: 0181 853 2651/2631/
0171 482 4923
ACP

Pauline Cowmeadow
Cognitive Analytic Therapist
45 Beauval Road, Dulwich, London
SE22 8UG
Tel: 0171 955 4279/0181 693 1812
ACAT

Gordon Cree
Cognitive Behavioural Psychotherapist
12 Allenby Road, Forest Hill, London
SE23 2RQ
Tel: 0181 291 1597
BABCP

Michael Crowe
Sexual and Marital Psychotherapist
Maudsley Hospital, Denmark Hill,
London SE5 8AZ
Tel: 0171 703 6333/0181 777 4823
BASMT

Annalee Curran
Cognitive Analytic Therapist
108 Norwood Road, Herne Hill,
London SE24 9BB
Tel: 0171 703 3988/0181 674 8702
ACAT

Peter Dawson
Transpersonal Psychotherapist
8a Peabody Buildings, Camberwell
Green, London SE5 7BD
Tel: 0171 708 5399
CCPE

Alicia Deale
Cognitive Behavioural Psychotherapist
Academic Dept of Psychological
Medicine, Kings College Hospital,
Denmark Hill, London SE5 9RS
Tel: 0171 346 3014
BABCP

Barbara Kathleen Dearnley
Psychoanalytic Marital Psychotherapist
186 Court Lane, London SE21 7ED
Tel: 0181 693 2603
TMSI

Lindsey D Denford
Cognitive Behavioural Psychotherapist
Three Tuns House, Guy's Hospital, 117
Borough High Street, London SE1 1NP
Tel: 0171 955 8843
BABCP

Ursula Deniflee
Biodynamic Psychotherapist
30 Syles House, The Cut, London
SE1 8DP
Tel: 0171 401 3582
BTC

Elizabeth Dodge
Family Therapist
Psychotherapy Section, Institute of
Psychiatry, De Crespigny Park,
Denmark Hill, London SE5 8AF
Tel: 0181 919 3196
IFT

Hilary Dowber
Psychoanalytic Psychotherapist
14 Dalrymple Road, London SE4 2BH
Tel: 0181 691 3070
IPSS

John Doyle
Psychosynthesis Psychotherapist
6 Rommany Court, Gipsy Road,
London SE27 9QX
Tel: 0181 761 5514
IPS

Alan Dupuy
Personal Construct Psychotherapist
Flat 6, Quarry Court, 2 Dunstans
Grove, London SE22 0HJ
Tel: 0181 693 5769
CPCP

Stella Egert
Family Psychotherapist
183 Rosendale Road, West Dulwich,
London SE21 8LW
Tel: 0181 670 3417
IFT

Clive Eiles
Psychoanalytic Psychotherapist
133 Rushkin Park House, Champion
Hill, London SE5 8TL
Tel: 0171 274 8142
AAP

Ivan Eisler
Family Therapist
Institute of Psychiatry, De Crespigny
Park, Denmark Hill, London SE5 8AF
Tel: 0171 919 3184
IFT

Isabelle Ekdawi
Systemic Psychotherapist
4 Rye View Maisonettes, The Gardens,
East Dulwich, London SE22 9QB
Tel: 0181 472 4661 x 5091
KCC

Sandra A Elliott
Cognitive Behavioural Psychotherapist
Psychology Dept, School of Social
Science, Avery Hill Road, Eltham,
London SE9 2HB
BABCP

Victoria Elliott
Child Psychotherapist
Plumstead Child Guidance Unit,
Plumstead Health Centre, Tewson
Road, London SE18 1BH
Tel: 0181 244 4732/0181 855 9254
ACP

Judith Erskine
Attachment-based Psychoanalytic
Psychotherapist
45a Tremaine Road, Anerley, London
SE20 7UA
Tel: 0181 659 2465
CAPP

David Findlay
Integrative Psychosynthesis
Psychotherapist
207 Waller Road, Telegraph Hill,
London SE14 5LX
Tel: 0171 639 9732
RE.V

Judith Firman
Psychosynthesis Psychotherapist
Psychosynthesis & Education Trust, 92-
94 Tooley Street, London SE1 2TH
Tel: 0171 403 2100
PET

Linda Fisher
Cognitive Behavioural Psychotherapist
CFS Research Unit, The Rayne
Institute, 123 Coldharbour Lane,
London SE9 9NU
Tel: 0171 737 4000 x 4096/
0171 346 3363
BABCP

Robert W K Fleming
Child Psychotherapist
Department of Child & Adolescent
Psychiatry, 35 Black Prince Road,
Kennington, London SE11 6JJ
Tel: 0171 793 7113
ACP

Joan Fletcher
Humanistic and Integrative
Psychotherapist
171 Algernon Road, Lewisham, London
SE13 7AP
Tel: 0181 690 8987
SPEC

Margaret Gardiner
Psychoanalytic Psychotherapist
3 Collins Square, off Tranquil Vale,
Blackheath, London SE3 0BT
Tel: 0181 318 1693
AGIP

Sheila Gordon
Psychoanalytic Psychotherapist
West Side Row, 222 South Norwood
Hill, London SE25 6AS
Tel: 0181 771 7074
LCP

Olga Gracia
Psychosynthesis Psychotherapist
25 Elmers Road, Woodside, South
Norwood, London SE25 5DS
Tel: 0181 654 7108
PET

Mary Griffin
Sexual and Marital Psychotherapist
Out-Patient Department, Maudsley
Hospital, Denmark Hill, London
SE5 8AZ
BASMT

Janet Haddington
Psychoanalytic Psychotherapist
2a Bromar Road, Camberwell, London
SE5 8DL
Tel: 0181 962 4167
AAP

Thomasz Hanchen
NLP Psychotherapist
55 Cressingham Road, Lewisham,
London SE13 5AQ
Tel: 0181 318 3102
ANLP

Pauline Hancock
Psychosynthesis Psychotherapist
Flat 1, 194 Peckham Rye, East Dulwich,
London SE22 9QA
Tel: 0181 299 1767
PET

Dorothy Hanna
Psychosynthesis Psychotherapist
74 Auckland Hill, West Norwood,
London SE27 9QQ
Tel: 0181 761 2855
IPS

Helena Hargaden
Transactional Analysis Psychotherapist,
Integrative Psychotherapist
Southside, 43 Brockley Park, London
SE23 1PT
Tel: 0181 690 3175
MET, ITA

Christopher Hauke
Analytical Psychologist-Jungian Analyst
4a Nelson Road, Greenwich, London
SE10 9JB
Tel: 0181 690 7014/0181 858 9800
SAP

Fran Hedges
Systemic Psychotherapist
213 New Cross Road, London
SE14 5UH
Tel: 0171 358 0518
KCC

Evelyn R Hendry
Cognitive Behavioural Psychotherapist
York Clinic, Guy's Hospital, London
SE1 1NP
Tel: 0171 955 4933
BABCP

Sarah Holden
Group Analyst
15 Auckland Hill, West Norwood,
London SE27 9PF
Tel: 0181 672 9911 x 42236/
0181 473 3038
IGA

Daphne Hort
Psychoanalytic Psychotherapist
36 Alanthus Close, Lee Green, London
SE12 8RE
Tel: 0181 852 6914
GUILD

Coral Howard
Systemic Psychotherapist
47 Thorpewood Avenue, Sydenham,
London SE26 4BY
Tel: 0181 244 0724
KCC

Heather Howard
Psychoanalytic Psychotherapist
83 Blackheath Park, London SE3 0EU
Tel: 0181 852 6564
IPSS

Carol Hughes
Child Psychotherapist
Belgrave Dept of Child and Family
Psychiatry, Kings College Hospital,
Denmark Hill, London SE5 9RS
Tel: 0171 346 3219/01795 531605
ACP

Brian Jacobs
Family Therapist, Systemic
Psychotherapist
Maudsley Hospital, Denmark Hill,
London SE5 8AZ
Tel: 0171 703 6333
IFT

Christopher James
Family Therapist
39 Northbrook Road, London
SE13 5QT
IFT

Hugh Jenkins
Systemic Psychotherapist
83 Hurstbourne Road, Forest Hill,
London SE23 2AQ
IFT

Merryn Jones
Group Analytic Psychotherapist
8 Broadwall, London SE1 9QE
Tel: 0171 401 2393
IPC

Anna Kerr
Psychoanalytic Psychotherapist
3 Talbot Place, London SE3 0TZ
Tel: 0181 852 1751
GUILD

Jack Kerridge
Psychoanalytic Psychotherapist
96 Langton Way, London SE3 7TD
Tel: 0181 305 1287
GUILD

Christine King
Hypno-Psychotherapist
13 Blackheath Village, Blackheath,
London SE3 9LA
Tel: 0181 305 2317
NRHP

Alan Kirby
Humanistic Psychotherapist
29a Adamsrill Road, Sydenham, London
SE26 4AJ
Tel: 0181 291 3515
AHPP

Josephine Klein
Psychoanalytic Psychotherapist
58 Roupell Street, London SE1 8TB
Tel: 0171 928 5747
LCP, BAP

Marianna Koeppelmann
Psychosynthesis Psychotherapist
73 Lawnside, Blackheath, London
SE3 9HL
Tel: 0171 318 0792
PET

Peter Lang
Systemic Psychotherapist
40 Rosenthorpe Road, London
SE15 3EG
KCC

Susan Lang
Systemic Psychotherapist
40 Rosenthorpe Road, London
SE15 3EG
KCC

Monica Langdon
Psychoanalytic Psychotherapist
6 Upwood Road, London SE12 8AA
Tel: 0181 318 0110
AGIP

Monica Lanyado
Child Psychotherapist
30 Brookway, Blackheath, London
SE3 9BJ
Tel: 0181 852 1521/0181 297 0528 (f)
ACP

Judith Lask
Family Therapist
99 Underhill Road, London SE22 0QR
IFT

Joan M Lee
Analytical Psychologist-Jungian Analyst
69 Beaconsfield Road, London SE3 7LG
Tel: 0181 313 6095/0181 858 3133
BAP

Gareth Leeming
Psychoanalytic Psychotherapist
Flat 8, 82 Wickham Road, Brockley,
London SE4 1LS
Tel: 0181 469 0666
IPC

Hilary Lester
Humanistic Psychotherapist
235 Barry Road, East Dulwich, London
SE22 0JU
Tel: 0181 299 4368
AHPP

Joan Longley
Psychoanalytic Psychotherapist
Lavender Cottage, 9b Tudor Road,
London SE19 2UH
Tel: 0181 768 0224
AGIP

Karina Lovell
Cognitive Behavioural Psychotherapist
Psychological Treatment Unit, 99
Denmark Hill, Maudsley Hospital,
London SE5 8AZ
Tel: 0171 919 3458
BABCP

Judith Lowe
NLP Psychotherapist
6 Denman Road, London SE15 5NP
Tel: 0171 7082358
ANLP

Laurie Macdonald
NLP Psychotherapist
24 Robinscroft Mews, Greenwich,
London SE10 8DN
Tel: 0181 691 6513
ANLP

David Mann
Psychoanalytic Psychotherapist
134 Westwood Park, London
SE23 3QH
Tel: 0181 699 6498
GUILD

Jennifer Marsh
Psychoanalytic Psychotherapist
96 Elfindale Road, Herne Hill, London
SE24 9NW
Tel: 0171 274 3467
GUILD

Edward Martin
Analytical Psychologist-Jungian Analyst
17 Honor Oak Rise, London SE23 3QY
Tel: 0181 699 2303
SAP

Marilyn Mathew
Analytical Psychologist-Jungian Analyst
46 Dovercourt Road, Dulwich, London
SE22 8ST
Tel: 0181 693 2009
BAP

Brian Lawrence Maunder
Psychoanalytic Psychotherapist
Badgers' Oak, 12 Chinbrook Road,
Grove Park, London SE12 9TH
Tel: 0181 851 5702
IPC

Moira McCutcheon
Child Psychotherapist
Camberwell Child Guidance Centre,
Lister Health Centre, 1 Camden
Square, Peckham Road, London
SE15 5LA
Tel: 0171 701 7371
ACP

Brendan Nicholas McLoughlin
Cognitive Behavioural Psychotherapist
Behavioural Psychotherapy Unit, 99
Denmark Hill, Maudsley Hospital,
London SE5 8AZ
Tel: 0171 919 2101
BABCP

Gladeana McMahon
Cognitive Behavioural Psychotherapist
11 Streetfield Mews, Blackheath Park,
London SE3 0ER
Tel: 0181 852 4854
BABCP

Penny McMillan
Attachment-based Psychoanalytic
Psychotherapist
32 Congers House, Bronze Street,
London SE8 3DT
Tel: 0181 691 7199
CAPP

Sylvia Mears
Psychoanalytic Psychotherapist
5 Quentin Road, Blackheath SE13 5DG
Tel: 0181 852 0399
LCP

Fiona Miles
Psychosynthesis Psychotherapist
104 Humber Road, Blackheath, London
SE3 7LX
Tel: 0181 858 7338
PET

Gerry Millar
Psychosynthesis Psychotherapist
38 Argosy House, Windlass Place,
London SE8 3QZ
Tel: 0171 254 9202
IPS

Wendy Monticelli
Psychoanalytic Psychotherapist
19 Brunswick Quay, Rotherhithe,
London SE16 1PU
Tel: 0171 231 4309
IPC

Brenda Morris
Personal Construct Psychotherapist
31 Lewisham Park, London SE13 6QZ
CPCP

Diana Mukuma
Gestalt Psychotherapist
Flat 3, 194 Kennington Lane, London
SE11 5DL
Tel: 0171 735 5442
GPTI

Susan Murphy
Integrative Psychotherapist
4 Egremont Road, London SE27 0BH
Tel: 0171 937 6956/0181 670 6139
RCSPC

Jack Nathan
Psychoanalytic Psychotherapist
356 Upland Road, London SE22 0DP
Tel: 0181 299 3779
LCP

Alison Newbigin
Integrative Psychotherapist
48 Surrey Square, London SE17 2JX
Tel: 0171 703 9544
MC

Madeleine Oakley
Psychoanalytic Psychotherapist
Camberwell Child Guidance, Lister
Health Centre, London SE15 5LA
Tel: 0171 701 7371
IPSS

Shan Palanisamy
Cognitive Behavioural Psychotherapist
55 Eastgate Close, Thamesmead,
London SE28 8PL
Tel: 0181 311 5983/0181 855 8886
BABCP

Stephen Palmer
Cognitive Behavioural Psychotherapist
Centre for Stress Management, 156
Westcombe Hill, Blackheath, London
SE3 7DH
Tel: 0181 293 4114
BABCP

Judy Parkinson
Psychoanalytic Psychotherapist
48 Newlands Park, Sydenham, London
SE26 5NE
Tel: 0181 659 5001
IPC

Jack Pawsey
Psychoanalytic Psychotherapist
20 Addington Square, London SE5 7JZ
Tel: 0171 701 8920
IPC

Jonathan Pedder
Psychoanalytic Psychotherapist
Maudsley Hospital, Denmark Hill,
London SE5 8AZ
AUTP

Sheila Peters
Hypno-Psychotherapist
102A Holmesdale Road, South
Norwood, London SE25 6JF
Tel: 0181 653 4242
NRHP

Sue Phillips
Analytical Psychologist-Jungian Analyst
88 Lancaster Avenue, London
SE27 9EB
Tel: 0181 761 8591
BAP

Eliana Pinto
Psychoanalytic Psychotherapist
20 Shelbury Road, London SE22 0NL
Tel: 0181 299 0983
LCP

Polly Plowman
Integrative Psychosynthesis
Psychotherapist
Flat 2, 14 Trinity Church Square,
London SE1 4HU
Tel: 0171 403 4854
RE.V

Marie Pompe
Psychoanalytic Psychotherapist
102 Alleyn Road, London SE21
Tel: 0181 670 6388
AGIP

Susan Price
Psychoanalytic Psychotherapist
15 Boyne Road, London SE13 5AL
Tel: 0181 318 4410
GUILD

Christopher Rance
Group Analyst
43 Rosendale Road, Dulwich, London
SE21 8DY
Tel: 0181 670 5023
IGA

Ferga Robinson
Cognitive Behavioural Psychotherapist
44 Brockwell Park Gardens, Herne Hill,
London SE24 9BJ
Tel: 0181 674 2359
BABCP

Cynthia Rogers
Group Analyst
178 Turney Road, Dulwich, London
SE21 7JL
Tel: 0171 274 4655
IGA

Fiona Ross
Analytical Psychologist-Jungian Analyst
17 Honor Oak Rise, London SE23 3QY
Tel: 0181 699 2303
SAP

Peter Ruddell
Cognitive Behavioural Psychotherapist
Centre for Rational Emotive BT, 156
Westcombe Hill, Blackheath, London
SE3 7DH
Tel: 0181 293 4114
BABCP

Boris Rumney
Psychoanalytic Psychotherapist
1 Foxes Dale, London SE3 9BD
Tel: 0181 852 9015
GUILD

Sue Ryall
Integrative Psychosynthesis
Psychotherapist
17 Montague Avenue, London SE4 1YP
Tel: 0181 692 3084
RE.V

Brigitte Ryley
Biodynamic Psychotherapist
Flat 1, 39a Glengarry Road, London
SE22 8QA
Tel: 0181 693 6953
AHPP

Gillian Salmon
Educational Therapist
46 Pepys Road, London SE14 5SB
Tel: 0171 639 3062
FAETT

Julia Sarkic
Hypno-Psychotherapist
5A Howard Road, London SE20 8HQ
Tel: 0181 778 9524
NRHP

Anthony Seigal
Sexual and Marital Psychotherapist
148 Woodwarde Road, London
SE22 8UR
BASMT

Margaret Sheehan
Analytical Psychologist-Jungian Analyst
17 St Aidan's Road, London SE22 0RP
Tel: 0181 299 2456
SAP

Deanne Sherriff
Cognitive Behavioural Psychotherapist
92 Tuam Road, Plumstead Common,
London SE18 2QU
Tel: 0181 473 5937/0181 855 8886
BABCP

Christopher Shingler
Psychosynthesis Psychotherapist
37 Harefield Road, Brockley, London
SE4 1LW
Tel: 0181 691 5303
IPS

David L Smith
Integrative Psychotherapist
8 Brenchley Gardens, Forest Hill,
London SE23 3QS
Tel: 0171 487 7406/0181 699 6687
RCSPC

Norah Smith
Analytical Psychologist-Jungian Analyst
15 Domett Close, Champion Hill,
London SE5 8AR
Tel: 0171 326 0649
SAP

Trevor E L Smith
Cognitive Behavioural Psychotherapist
22 Pleydell Avenue, Upper Norwood,
London SE19 2LP
Tel: 0956 810 585/0181 993 7892
BABCP

Val Smith
Group Analyst
38 Edgehill Road, Sheffield SE7 1SP
Tel: 01742 660677/01742 588489
IGA

Mary Spence
Systemic Psychotherapist
85 St John's Place, London SE3 7JW
Tel: 0181 853 2389
KCC

Ernesto Spinelli
Existential Psychotherapist
69 Oglander Road, East Dulwich
SE15 4DD
Tel: 0171 487 7406/0181 693 9332
RCSPC

Martin Stanton
Psychoanalytic Psychotherapist
40 Circus Street, Greenwich, London
SE10 8SN
Tel: 0181 853 0302
LCP

Maire Stedman
Family Psychotherapist
11 Lamerton Street, Greenwich,
London SE8 3PL
IFT

Lilly Stuart
Transactional Analysis Psychotherapist
106 Heathwood Gardens, Charlton,
London SE7 8ER
Tel: 0181 854 3606
ITA

Claire Tanner
Cognitive Analytic Therapist
26 Vancouver Road, Forest Hill,
London SE23 2AF
Tel: 0181 699 7996
ACAT

Nick Topliss
Family Therapist
162 Kilmorie Road, Forest Hill, London
SE23 2SR
IFT

Paola Valerio-Smith
Analytical Psychologist-Jungian Analyst
29 Marmora Road, East Dulwich,
London SE22 0RX
Tel: 0181 693 8421
BAP

Emmy van Deurzen-Smith
Existential Psychotherapist
4 Kings Garth Mews, Forest Hill,
London SE23 3TZ
Tel: 0171 487 7443/0181 699 2860
RCSPC

Paul van Heeswyk
Child Psychotherapist
Bloomfield Clinic, Guys Hospital, St
Thomas Street, London SE1 9RT
Tel: 0171 955 4581/0171 622 6493
ACP

Karin-Marie Wach
Psychoanalytic Psychotherapist
2 Pottery Street, Cherry Garden Pier,
London SE16 4PH
Tel: 0171 252 3947
AAP

Kathleen Waters
Family Therapist
15a Colfe Road, Forest Hill, London
SE23 2ES
IFT

Christine Watson
Sexual and Marital Psychotherapist
36 Alleyn Road, London SE21 8AL
BASMT

J P Watson
Sexual and Marital Psychotherapist
UMDS Div of Psychiatry, Guy's
Hospital, London SE1 9RT
BASMT

John Way
Jungian Child Analyst
72 Alleyn Road, Dulwich, London
SE21 8AH
Tel: 0181 670 5315
SAP

Jeremy White
Group Analyst
4a Spenser Road, Herne Hill, London
SE24 0NR
Tel: 0171 733 0834
IGA

Gerti Wilford
Family Therapist
The Belgrave Dept of Child & Family
Psychiatry, King's College Hospital,
Bessemer Road, London SE5
AFT

Michael Wilkins
Systemic Psychotherapist
178 Turney Road, Dulwich, London
SE21 7JL
KCC

Ruth M Williams
Cognitive Behavioural Psychotherapist
Department of Psychology, Institute of
Psychiatry, De Crespigny Park, London
SE5 8AF
Tel: 0171 919 3242
BABCP

James Wilson
Psychoanalytic Psychotherapist
18 Dovercourt Road, East Dulwich,
London SE22 8ST
LCP

Mary Wilson
Analytical Psychologist-Jungian Analyst
46 Erlanger Road, New Cross, London
SE14 5TG
Tel: 0171 639 1867
SAP

Suzanne Winders
Psychoanalytic Psychotherapist
21B Holmdene Avenue, London
SE24 9LB
Tel: 0171 274 7517
IPC

Frances Mary Wooster
Psychoanalytic Psychotherapist
28 Holly Grove, London SE15 5DF
Tel: 0171 635 0448
GUILD

LONDON SOUTH WEST

Shafika Abbasi
Psychoanalytic Psychotherapist, Group
Analyst
2 Tunley Road, London SW17 7QJ
Tel: 0181 675 0235
IGA, LCP, BASMT

Stephen Adams-Langley
Integrative Psychotherapist
24 Fairmount Road, London SW2 2BL
Tel: 0171 701 0769/0181 678 0473
RCSPC

Ana Aguirregabiria
Psychodrama Psychotherapist
8d Peterborough Villas, Bagley Lane,
London SW6 2AT
Tel: 0181 570 1582
BPDA

Nadia Allawi
Psychoanalytic Psychotherapist
Woolborough House, 40 Roedean
Crescent, Roehampton, London
SW15 5JU
Tel: 0181 876 4182
IPSS

Chriso Andreou
Child Psychotherapist
The Adolescent Community Team, 32b
York Road, London SW11 3QJ
Tel: 0181 871 7767/0171 263 2206
ACP

Elizabeth Andrew
Psychoanalytic Psychotherapist
3 Camp View, Wimbledon, London
SW19 4UL
Tel: 0181 947 2732
IPC

C Ruth Archer
Psychoanalytic Psychotherapist
8 Roundacre, Inner Park Road,
Wimbledon, London SW19 6DB
Tel: 0181 788 5128
IPC

Derick Armstrong
Analytical Psychologist-Jungian Analyst
15 Cheyne Court, Flood Street,
London SW3 5TP
Tel: 0171 352 5185
IGAP

Loukas Athanasiadis
Cognitive Behavioural Psychotherapist
Flat 10D, Austen House, St George's
Grove, Strathdon Drive, London
SW17 0PZ
Tel: 01811 672 9911 x 429
BABCP

Okeke Azu-Okeke
Psychoanalytic Psychotherapist
118 Streatham Vale, London
SW16 5TB
Tel: 0181 764 8894
BAP

Tricia Barnes
Sexual and Marital Psychotherapist
7 Grange Park Place, Thurstan Road,
Wimbledon, London SW20 0EE
BASMT

Deike Begg
Psychosynthesis Psychotherapist
21 Condray Place, London SW11 3PE
Tel: 0171 978 7749
PET

Ean Begg
Analytical Psychologist-Jungian Analyst
21 Condray Place, Battersea Church
Road, London SW11 3PE
Tel: 0171 978 4761
IGAP

Jocelyn Berger
Integrative Psychotherapist
15 Sandgate Lane, London SW18 3TP
Tel: 0181 874 0763
RCSPC

Sally Kemmis Betty
Systemic Psychotherapist
30 Lillian Road, Barnes, London
SW13 9JG
KCC

Keith Bibby
Hypno-Psychotherapist
49 Klea Avenue, Clapham South,
London SW4 9HG
Tel: 0181 673 6311
NSHAP

Desmond Biddulph
Analytical Psychologist-Jungian Analyst
3A Gilston Road, London SW10 9SJ
Tel: 0171 351 3800/0171 351 3054 (f)
SAP

Diana Birkitt
Psychoanalytic Psychotherapist
95 Elspeth Road, London SW11 1DP
Tel: 0181 228 9738
CPP

Wolf Blomfield
Psychoanalytic Psychotherapist
123 Hambalt Road, London SW4 9EL
Tel: 0181 673 5342
LCP, BAP

Antonia Boll
Analytical Psychologist-Jungian Analyst
51 Coniger Road, London SW6 3TB
Tel: 0171 736 0226
AJA

Sheila Borges
Integrative Psychotherapist
71 Mantilla Road, London SW17 8DY
Tel: 0181 767 6595
MC

Sasha Brookes
Psychoanalytic Marital Psychotherapist,
Psychoanalytic Psychotherapist
44a Bramham Gardens, London
SW5 0HQ
Tel: 0171 370 4689
TMSI, AAP

Marie-Noël (Billie) Buckley
Psychoanalytic Psychotherapist
6 Trevor Place, Knightsbridge, London
SW7 1LA
Tel: 0171 581 3987/0171 589 1763 (f)
IPC

John Burnard
Analytical Psychologist-Jungian Analyst
12 Madeira Road, London SW16 2DF
Tel: 0181 677 9819
SAP

Joan Burnett
Psychoanalytic Psychotherapist
91 Chelverton Road, London
SW15 1RW
Tel: 0181 789 9934
BAP

Catherine Butler
Personal Construct Psychotherapist
30 Cumberland Gardens, London
SW13 0AG
Tel: 0181 878 3017
CPCP

John Butler
Hypno-Psychotherapist
37 Orbain Road, Fulham, London
SW6 7JZ
Tel: 0171 385 1166
NRHP

Christine Campbell
Integrative Psychotherapist
33 Montepelier Walk, London
SW7 1JG
Tel: 0171 402 2272/0171 581 3374
RCSPC

Anne Chancer
Psychoanalytic Psychotherapist
35 Temple Sheen Road, London
SW14 7QF
Tel: 0181 876 1523
GUILD

Kathleen Chimera
Family Psychotherapist
186 Ribblesdale Road, London
SW16 6QS
Tel: 0181 677 4996
IFT

Miles Clapham
Psychoanalytic Psychotherapist
12 Jelf Road, London SW2 1BH
Tel: 0171 274 7778
PA

John Clay
Analytical Psychologist-Jungian Analyst
17 Aldebert Terrace, London
SW8 1BH
Tel: 0171 793 7560/0171 735 3886
BAP

Cairns Clery
Family Therapist
50 Girdwood Road, Southfields,
London SW18 5QS
Tel: 0181 788 7523
AFT

Elaine Clifton
Integrative Psychotherapist
Flat 3, 55 Onslow Square, London
SW7 3LR
Tel: 0171 581 0387
MET

Jane Coleridge
Psychoanalytic Psychotherapist
85 Erpingham Road, London SW15
Tel: 0181 785 9891
GUILD

Prophecy Coles
Psychoanalytic Psychotherapist
18 Spencer Road, London SW18 2SW
Tel: 0171 738 0195
LCP

Walter Coles
Educational Therapist
18 Spencer Road, Wandsworth,
London SW18 2SW
Tel: 0171 738 2455
FAETT

Louise Colson
Cognitive Behavioural Psychotherapist
The Priory Hospital, Priory Lane,
Roehampton, London SW2 4XQ
Tel: 0181 674 0305/0181 876 8261
BABCP

Ann Conlon
Psychoanalytic Psychotherapist
10 Neville Court, 35 Weir Road,
London SW12 0NU
Tel: 0181 675 1590
LCP

Ita Coronas
Gestalt Psychotherapist, Humanistic
Psychotherapist
37 Barkston Gardens, London
SW5 0ER
Tel: 0171 373 3989
AHPP, GCL, GPTI

Marilyn Corry
Psychoanalytic Psychotherapist
20 Bemish Road, Putney, London
SW15 1DG
Tel: 0181 789 3668
LCP

John Costello
Analytical Psychologist-Jungian Analyst
122 Lupus Street, London SW1V 4AN
Tel: 0171 834 1708
IGAP

Valerie Coumont Graubart
Integrative Psychotherapist
18 Laitwood Road, Balham, London
SW12 9QL;
64 Moor End Road, Mellor, Stockport,
Cheshire SK6 5PT
Tel: 0181 265 5504/061 427 6799
MC

Susie Courtault
Psychoanalytic Psychotherapist
8 Clifford Avenue, London SW14 7BS
Tel: 0181 876 3552
IPSS

Andrew Culliss
Psychoanalytic Psychotherapist
55 Trelawn Road, Brixton, London
SW2 1DH
Tel: 0171 326 4773
IPSS

Arminal Dare-Bryan
Psychoanalytic Psychotherapist
15 Melrose Road, Southfields, London
SW18 1ND
Tel: 0181 874 3138
IPC

Emerald Davis
Attachment-based Psychoanalytic
Psychotherapist
64 Lyndhurst Avenue, Norbury,
London SW16 4UF
Tel: 0181 764 6740
CAPP

Asun de Marquiegui
Sexual and Marital Psychotherapist
Clapham Common Clinic, 1st Floor,
151-153 Clapham High Street, London
SW4 7SS
BASMT

Cara Denman
Analytical Psychologist-Jungian Analyst
23 Lawrence Street, London SW3 5NF
Tel: 0171 352 9559
IGAP

Francesca Denman
Cognitive Analytic Therapist
24 Lawrence Street, Chelsea SW3 5NF
Tel: 0171 352 1851
ACAT

Suzanne Dennis
Integrative Psychosynthesis
Psychotherapist
54 Baldry Gardens, London SW16 3DJ
Tel: 0181 679 3572
RE.V

Rosemary Dighton
Sexual and Marital Psychotherapist,
Systemic Psychotherapist
30 Burghley Road, Wimbledon, London
SW19 5HW;
Claremont House, 44 High Street,
Wimbledon Village, London
SW19 5AU
Tel: 0181 946 0706/0181 946 1097
BASMT, KCC

Laura Donington
Core Process Psychotherapist
39 Blenkarne Road, London
SW11 6HZ
Tel: 0171 228 1107
KI

Lynne Drummond
Cognitive Behavioural Psychotherapist
Department of Mental Health Sciences,
St George's Hospital Medical School,
Cranmer Terrace, London SW17 0RE
Tel: 0181 725 5561
BABCP

Simon Du Plock
Existential Psychotherapist
Flat 1, 7 Macaulay Road, Clapham Old
Town, London SW4 0QP
Tel: 0171 487 7406/0171 498 6597
RCSPC

Marjory Edgell
Hypno-Psychotherapist
23 Crescent Grove, London SW4 7AF
Tel: 0171 622 4755
NRHP

Judith Edwards
Child Psychotherapist
Wandsworth Town Child and Family
Clinic, 7 Ram Street, London
SW18 1TJ
Tel: 0171 727 8759/0181 870 0161
ACP

Michael Edwards
Analytical Psychologist-Jungian Analyst
7c Carlton Drive, London SW15 2BZ
Tel: 0181 788 5699
IGAP

Patricia Eglin
Integrative Psychotherapist
36 Turret Grove, London SW4 0ET
Tel: 0171 738 8554/0171 978 1180
RCSPC

Eddie Farmer
Psychoanalytic Psychotherapist
122 Hambalt Road, Clapham Park,
London SW4 9EJ;
Rowleth Edge, Gunnerside, Richmond,
North Yorkshire DL11 6JP
Tel: 0181 673 2044/01748 886 500
IPC

Peter Fleming
Humanistic Psychotherapist
15 Killyon Road, London SW8 2XS
Tel: 0171 720 4499
AHPP

Linda Freeman
Analytical Psychologist-Jungian Analyst
20 Ensor Mews, London SW7 3BT
Tel: 0171 370 2327
IGAP

Victoria G Fuller
Analytical Psychologist-Jungian Analyst,
Group Analyst
10 Onslow Gardens, London SW7 3AP
Tel: 0171 584 7939
SAP, IGA

Rus Gandy
Biodynamic Psychotherapist
5 Avenue Mansions, Battersea, London
SW11 5SL
Tel: 0171 223 4269
BTC

Fiorella G Gatti-Doyle
Personal Construct Psychotherapist
Flat 2a, Sloane Avenue Mansions,
Sloane Avenue, London SW3 3JF
Tel: 0171 584 9589
CPCP, RCSPC

Tony Glanville
Gestalt Psychotherapist
66 Valleyfield Road, London
SW16 2HU
Tel: 0181 769 5536
GPTI

Godfrey Godfrey-Issacs
Analytical Psychotherapist
105 Christchurch Road, East Sheen,
London SW14 7AT
Tel: 0181 876 5223
LCP

Ellen Golden
Child Psychotherapist
William Harvey Centre, 313-315
Cortis Road, London SW15 6XG
Tel: 0181 450 0624/0181 788 0074
ACP

Virginia Gordon
Systemic Psychotherapist
79 Medfield Street, Roehampton,
London SW15 4JY
Tel: 0181 788 3126
KCC

Nancy Graham
Family Therapist
54 Heythorp Street, Southfields,
London SW18 5BN
IFT

Roberta Green
Group Analyst
41 Woodlawn Road, Fulham, London
SW6 6BQ
Tel: 0181 846 7898/0171 385 3408
IGA

John Greenwood
Psychoanalytic Psychotherapist
98 White Hart Lane, London
SW13 0QA
Tel: 0181 876 2080
AAP

Shaun Growney
NLP Psychotherapist
Flat C, 15 Sangora Road, Battersea,
London SW11 1RL
Tel: 0171 924 7327
ANLP

Pamela Gulliver
Psychoanalytic Psychotherapist
6 Cardinal Place, Putney, London
SW15 1NX
Tel: 0181 785 7149
IPC

Paul Harlow
Analytical Psychologist-Jungian Analyst
39 Bradbourne Street, London
SW6 3TF
Tel: 0171 736 4271
SAP

Melanie Hart
Psychoanalytic Psychotherapist
13 Sibella Road, London SW4 6JA
Tel: 0171 622 7814
LCP

Trevor Hartnup
Child Psychotherapist
William Harvey Centre, 313-315
Cortis Road, London SW15 6XG
Tel: 0181 788 0074/0181 287 0620
ACP

Michael Hayes
Psychosynthesis Psychotherapist
Digby Stuart College, Roehampton
Institute London, Roehampton Lane,
London SW15 5PH
Tel: 0181 878 9863
IPS

Caroline Helm
Child Psychotherapist
Queen Marys University Hospital,
Roehampton Lane, London SW15 5PN
Tel: 0181 789 6611 x 2051
ACP

Lindy Henny
Group Analytic Psychotherapist
Colne Denton, 106 Cheyne Walk,
London SW10 0DG
Tel: 0171 352 3977
IPC

Marika Henriques
Humanistic Psychotherapist
54 Campbell Court, Gloucester Road,
London SW7 4PD
Tel: 0171 584 9793
GUILD, AHPP

Nini Hitchman
Psychosynthesis Psychotherapist
4 First Avenue, Mortlake, London
SW14 8SR
Tel: 0181 876 9056
PET

Peter Hollis
Family Psychotherapist
20 Rydal Road, London SW16 1QN
Tel: 0181 460 5593/0181 677 5776
IFT

Ann Hopwood
Analytical Psychologist-Jungian Analyst
127 Grandison Road, London
SW11 6LT
Tel: 0171 924 5171/0171 228 9130
SAP

Irene Howard
Analytical Psychologist-Jungian Analyst
103 Hurlingham Road, London
SW6 3NL
Tel: 0171 736 3924
BAP, LCP

David Howell
Analytical Psychologist-Jungian Analyst
7 Malcolm Road, Wimbledon, London
SW19 4AS
Tel: 0181 946 7178
SAP

Margaret Hunter
Child Psychotherapist
Brixton Child Guidance, 19 Brixton
Water Lane, London SW2 1NU
Tel: 0171 274 5459/0171 737 4140 (f)
ACP

Sonia Ingram
Group Analyst
10 Pelham Place, London SW7 2NH
Tel: 0171 581 5033
IGA

Susan Irving
Psychoanalytic Psychotherapist
33 Greyhound Lane, Streatham
Common, London SW16 5NP
Tel: 0181 769 7988
BAP

Joy Isaacs
Psychoanalytic Psychotherapist
105 Christchurch Road, East Sheen,
London SW14 7AT
Tel: 0181 876 5223
LCP

Judith Jackson
Child Psychotherapist
Lincoln Centre & Institute of
Psychotherapy, 19 Abbeville Mews, 88
Clapham Park Road, London SW4 7BX
Tel: 0171 978 1545/0181 346 0379
ACP

Emily Jacob
Sexual and Marital Psychotherapist
16 Avenue Gardens, East Sheen,
London SW14 8BP
Tel: 0181 878 5835
BASMT

Eileen Jarvis
Systemic Psychotherapist
52 Frewin Road, London SW18 3LP
Tel: 0181 870 0037
KCC

David Jones
Humanistic Psychotherapist
39 Blenkarne Road, London
SW11 6HZ
Tel: 0171 223 7020
AHPP

Pamela Keane
Transpersonal Psychotherapist
234 Worple Road, West Wimbledon,
London SW20 8RH
Tel: 0181 946 8522
CCPE

Babs Kirby
Humanistic Psychotherapist
194 Ferndale Road, London SW9 8AH
Tel: 0171 733 2748
AHPP

Nicholas Kitson
Psychoanalytic Psychotherapist
65 Church Road, Wimbledon, London
SW19 5DQ
Tel: 0181 682 6306/0181 944 9951
LCP

Peter John Kolb
Cognitive Behavioural Psychotherapist
Cottage Day Hospital, Springfield
Hospital, Glenburnie Road, Tooting,
London SW17 0QT
Tel: 0181 672 9911 ext 42973
BABCP

Marianne Kolbuszewski
Integrative Psychotherapist
187 Latchmere Road, Battersea,
London SW11 2JZ
Tel: 0171 228 1560
MC

Pedro Kujawski
Analytical Psychologist-Jungian Analyst
12 Guthrie Street, London SW3 6NU
Tel: 0171 352 6203
IGAP

Ann E Kutek
Analytical Psychologist-Jungian Analyst
32 Lillie Road, London SW6 1TN
Tel: 0171 937 6224/0171 385 4299
BAP

Margaret Lawrence
Psychoanalytic Psychotherapist
14 Lancaster Gardens, Wimbledon,
London SW19
Tel: 0181 946 8223
GUILD

Sandy Layton
Child Psychotherapist
91 Ravensbury Road, London
SW10 4RX
Tel: 0181 879 1442/0181 947 4485 (f)
ACP

Sara Leon
Integrative Arts Psychotherapist,
Humanistic Psychotherapist
46 Appach Road, Brixton, London
SW2 2LB
Tel: 0181 244 9390
IATE, AHPP

Richard Lewis
Integrative Psychotherapist
63 Franciscan Road, London
SW17 8EA
Tel: 0171 635 5039/0181 672 5035
MC

Mary Lister
Analytical Psychologist-Jungian Analyst
138 Brudenell Road, London
SW17 8DF
Tel: 0181 672 1554
BAP

Del Loewenthal
Psychoanalytic Psychotherapist
70 Kenilworth Avenue, London
SW19 7LR
Tel: 0181 947 7085
PA

Philippa Lubbock
Gestalt Psychotherapist
16 Cabul Road, London SW11 2PN
Tel: 0171 228 4175
GPTI

Duncan Macdiarmid
Analytical Psychologist-Jungian Analyst
26 Liston Road, London SW4 0DF
Tel: 0171 652 5815/0171 498 3553 (f)
SAP

Valerie Magner
Integrative Psychotherapist
203 Crowborough Road, London
SW17 9QE
Tel: 0181 672 8569
MET

Marie Maguire
Psychoanalytic Psychotherapist
20B The Pavement, London SW4 0HY
Tel: 0171 622 2434
GUILD, WTC

Marietta Marcus
Analytical Psychologist-Jungian Analyst
16 Sunbury Avenue, East Sheen,
London SW14 8RA
Tel: 0181 876 1040
BAP, LCP

Michal Margalit
Psychoanalytic Psychotherapist
58 Lessar Avenue, London SW4 9QH
Tel: 0181 673 6059
LCP

Desa Markovic
Systemic Psychotherapist
3 Markham Place, London SW3 3JX
Tel: 0171 584 7923
KCC

Frances Marling
Psychosynthesis Psychotherapist
6 Kenilworth Avenue, Wimbledon,
London SW19 7LW
Tel: 0181 946 4063
PET

Patricia Marsden
Psychoanalytic Psychotherapist
48 Wandle Road, London SW17 7DW
Tel: 0181 767 0563
IPC

Alexsandra Mastilovic
Systemic Psychotherapist
55 Cloudesdale Road, London
SW17 8ET
KCC

Robin McGlashan
Analytical Psychologist-Jungian Analyst
102 Westway, Raynes Park, London
SW20 9LS
Tel: 0181 542 2125
SAP

Savi McKenzie-Smith
Child Psychotherapist
Brixton Child Guidance, 19 Brixton
Water Lane, London SW2 1NU
Tel: 0171 274 5459/0171 794 6819
ACP

Gaynor McManus
Systemic Psychotherapist
35 Sutherland Street, London
SW1V 4JU
Tel: 0171 834 3113
KCC

Rosaleen Meaden
Psychoanalytic Psychotherapist
78 Ringford Road, London SW18 1RR
Tel: 0181 870 0743
IPC

Julia Mikado
Child Psychotherapist
Wandsworth Town Child & Family
Clinic, 7 Ram Street, London
SW18 1TJ
Tel: 0181 870 0161/0181 871 0978 (f)
ACP

Irene Milburn
Psychoanalytic Psychotherapist
33 Boscobel Place, London SW1W 9PE
Tel: 0171 235 3533
GUILD

Sylvia Millier
Psychoanalytic Psychotherapist
Flat 8, 34 Longridge Road, London
SW5 9SJ
Tel: 0171 373 7937
IPC

Ruth Mitchell
Sexual and Marital Psychotherapist
41 Nassau Road, London SW13 9QF
BASMT

Stephen Munt
Humanistic Psychotherapist
279 Sheen Lane, London SW14 8RN
Tel: 0181 876 9023
AHPP

Beatrice Musgrave
Group Analytic Psychotherapist
Flat 7, 416 Wimbledon Park Road,
London SW19 6PW
Tel: 0181 789 7208
IPC

Sue Nappez
Transpersonal Psychotherapist
147 The High, Streatham High Road,
London SW16 1HD
Tel: 0181 769 5101
CCPE

Lalage Neal
Psychoanalytic Psychotherapist
2 Rossdale Road, Putney, London
SW15 1AD
Tel: 0181 780 3171
IPC

Patricia Neate
Systemic Psychotherapist
2 Daylesford Avenue, Putney, London
SW15 5QR
Tel: 0181 876 1902
KCC

Maja O'Brien
Psychoanalytic Psychotherapist
50 Archbishops Place, London
SW2 2AJ
Tel: 0181 671 1870
BAP

James O'Neill
Psychoanalytic Psychotherapist
20 Elms Crescent, London SW4 8RA
Tel: 0171 622 0607
PA

Christine Oliver
Systemic Psychotherapist
3 Beverley Gardens, Barnes, London
SW13 0LZ
Tel: 0181 878 3601
KCC

Mary Parker
Humanistic and Integrative
Psychotherapist
66 Brixton Water Lane, London
SW2 1QB
Tel: 0171 274 6531
AHPP

Phil Parkinson
Transpersonal Psychotherapist
Tooting Bec, London SW17
Tel: 0181 767 7464
CCPE

Lesley Pavincich
Psychoanalytic Psychotherapist
20 Rydal Road, London SW16 1QN
Tel: 0181 677 5776
AAP

Adrianna Penalosa
Systemic Psychotherapist
52 Fullerton Road, London SW18 1BX
Tel: 0181 883 8562/0181 874 8608
KCC

Sandy Penniceard
Psychoanalytic Psychotherapist
8 Loxley Road, London SW18 3LJ
Tel: 0181 874 1569
IPC

Roderick Peters
Analytical Psychologist-Jungian Analyst
55 Clancarty Road, London SW6 3AH;
'Weavers', Ewhurst Green, Surrey
GU6 7RR
Tel: 01483 278481/0171 736 7256
SAP, BAP

Juliette Pollitzer
Transactional Analysis Psychotherapist
Flat 5, 64 Rutland Gate, London
SW7 1PJ
Tel: 0171 584 4951
ITA

John Priestley
Analytical Psychologist-Jungian Analyst
32 Atheldene Road, Earlsfield, London
SW18 3BW
Tel: 0181 871 2848
BAP

Mary Quaine
Psychoanalytic Psychotherapist
12 Marius Mansions, Marius Road,
London SW17 7QG
Tel: 0181 673 0548
IPC

Asher Quinn
Transpersonal Psychotherapist
22 Fawe Park Road, Putney;
Little Venice, London
Tel: 0181 874 6955
CCPE

Margaret Ramage
Sexual and Marital Psychotherapist
14 Tenham Avenue, London SW2 4XR
BASMT

R S Rani
Cognitive Behavioural Psychotherapist
Behavioural/Cognitive Psychotherapy
Unit, Cottage Day Hospital, Springfield
Hospital, 61 Glenburnie Rd, London
SW17 7DJ
Tel: 0181 682 6548
BABCP

Caroline Raymond
Hypno-Psychotherapist
4 Clare Court, Grosvenor Hill,
Wimbledon Village, London
SW19 4RZ
Tel: 0181 947 0962
NRHP

Paula Reardon
Integrative Psychotherapist
Flat 5, The Willows, 83 Vincent Square,
London SW1P 2PF
Tel: 0171 332 8302/0171 834 7288
RCSPC

Peter Reder
Systemic Psychotherapist
80 Madrid Road, Barnes, London
SW13 9PG
KCC

Marguerite Reid
Child Psychotherapist
Dept of Child & Adolescent Mental
Health, Chelsea & Westminster
Hospital, Fulham Road, London SW10
Tel: 0171 746 8616/0171 946 0647
ACP

Jennie Reuvid
Sexual and Marital Psychotherapist,
Autogenic Psychotherapist
26 Birley Street, Battersea, London
SW11 5XF
Tel: 0171 223 9236
BASMT, BAFAT

Paulina Reyes
Child Psychotherapist
Wandsworth Town Child & Family
Clinic, 7 Ram Street, London
SW18 1TJ
Tel: 0181 994 7529/0181 870 0161
ACP

Wendy Rose
Transpersonal Psychotherapist
86 Florence Road, London SW19 8TJ
Tel: 0181 540 3124
CCPE

Susie Sanders
Transpersonal Psychotherapist
11 Thurloe Square, London SW7 2TA
CCPE

Margaret Savill
Systemic Psychotherapist
29 Falcon Grove, Battersea, London
SW11 2SS
Tel: 0171 223 8330
KCC

Lynn-Ella Schofield
Psychoanalytic Psychotherapist
105 Warwick Way, London
SW1V 1QL
Tel: 0171 821 0518
GUILD

Chuck Schwartz
Analytical Psychologist-Jungian Analyst
7c Carlton Drive, London SW15 2BZ
Tel: 0181 789 0301/01822 860236
IGAP

Jennifer Silverstone
Psychoanalytic Psychotherapist
58 Alderney Street, London
SW1V 4EX
Tel: 0171 932 0858/0171 834 7891
LCP

Ian Simpson
Group Analyst
195 Fallsbrook Road, Streatham,
London SW16 6DY
Tel: 0171 926 7304/0181 769 1469
IGA

Rachid Smail
Cognitive Behavioural Psychotherapist
European Medical Centre, 31-39
Harrington Road, London SW7 3HQ
Tel: 0171 584 0150
BABCP

Imogen Smallwood
Integrative Psychotherapist
98 Bonneville Gardens, London
SW4 9LE
Tel: 0181 675 6836
RCSPC

Anne Smith
Psychoanalytic Psychotherapist
39 Dornton Road, Balham, London
SW12 1NB
Tel: 0181 675 3098
GUILD

Nick Smith
Family Psychotherapist
9 Lindesfarne Road, Wimbledon,
London SW20 0NW
Tel: 0181 947 5839
IFT

Penelope Smyly
Transpersonal Psychotherapist
13a Fieldhouse Road, London
SW12 0HL
Tel: 0181 673 6190
CCPE

Randa Snow
Psychoanalytic Psychotherapist
130 Ifield Road, London SW10 9AF
Tel: 0171 373 2202
IPC

Brian Snowdon
Analytical Psychologist-Jungian Analyst
25 Knollys Road, London SW16 2JJ
Tel: 0181 769 1424
SAP

Janet Spencer
Analytical Psychologist-Jungian Analyst
7a Carlton Drive, London SW15 3BZ
Tel: 0181 789 3727
IGAP

Terri Spy
Integrative Psychotherapist
12 Derwent Road, London SW20 9NH
Tel: 0181 330 4045
AHPP

Dorothee Steffens
Analytical Psychologist-Jungian Analyst
30 Thurloe Square, London SW7 2SD
Tel: 0171 589 5996
SAP

Karen Stobart
Analytical Psychologist-Jungian Analyst
7 Grafton Mansions, Venn Street,
London SW4 0AY
Tel: 0171 720 5206
SAP

Jean Stokes
Psychoanalytic Psychotherapist,
Analytical Psychologist-Jungian Analyst
5 Sispara Gardens, Southfields, London
SW18 1LG
Tel: 0181 874 6631
IPC, AJA

Amarilla Stracey
Integrative Psychotherapist, Body
Psychotherapist
22 Elms Crescent, London SW4 8RA
Tel: 0171 720 4601
CCHP

Cassandra Struthers
Psychoanalytic Psychotherapist
31 Cambridge St, London SW1
Tel: 0171 834 3475
AGIP

Barbara C Swinburne
Cognitive Behavioural Psychotherapist
BCPU, 1st Floor, Cottage Day Hospital,
Springfield Hospital, 61 Glenburnie Rd,
London SW17 7DJ
Tel: 0181 672 9911 x 42637
BABCP

Britt Tajet-Foxell
Cognitive Behavioural Psychotherapist
Eton House, 23 Sudbourne Road,
London SW2 5AE
Tel: 0171 733 8348
BABCP

Alannah Tandy (Pilbrow)
Psychosynthesis Psychotherapist
25 Lamont Road, London SW10 OHR
Tel: 0171 352 9540
PET

Daniel Tanguay
Biodynamic Psychotherapist
Flat 1, Langley Mansions, Langley Lane,
London SW8 1TJ
Tel: 0171 582 4287
BTC

Jane Taylor
Sexual and Marital Psychotherapist
136 Sutherland Grove, London
SW18 5QN
Tel: 0181 780 9890
BASMT

Margaret Tholstrup
Integrative Psychotherapist
10 Parkmead, London SW15 5BS
Tel: 0181 789 0090
MET

Molly Tuby
Analytical Psychologist-Jungian Analyst
60 Stanhope Gardens, London
SW7 5RF
Tel: 0171 373 0892
IGAP

Annie Turner
Systemic Psychotherapist
81 Pendle Road, London SW16 6RX
Tel: 0181 677 5026
IFT

Mary J Walker
Child Psychotherapist
Dept of Child Psychiatry, Lanesborough
Wing, St George's Hospital, Blackshaw
Road, London SW17 0QT
Tel: 0181 725 3715/0181 664 7296
ACP

Sandra Walline
Analytical Psychologist-Jungian Analyst
26 Disraeli Road, London SW15 2DS
Tel: 0181 785 9647
SAP

Benjamin J Wallis
Analytical Psychologist-Jungian Analyst
Christ Church Flat, Cabul Road,
London SW11 2PN
Tel: 0171 350 0851
BAP

Sue Walrond-Skinner
Family Therapist
78 Stockwell Park Road, London
SW9 0DA
AFT

Aine Walsh
Psychoanalytic Psychotherapist
56c Sarsfeld Road, Balham, London
SW12 8HN
Tel: 0181 767 8997
IPC

Gordon Watson
Psychoanalytic Psychotherapist
19b Thornton Hill, London SW19 4HU
Tel: 0181 947 3512
PA

Anne Webster
Psychoanalytic Psychotherapist
92 Rossiter Road, Balham, London
SW12 9RX
Tel: 0181 673 5150/0181 675 1397
IPC

Virginia West
Cognitive Analytic Therapist
37 Blenkarne Road, London
SW11 6HZ
ACAT

H White
Psychodynamic Psychotherapist
La Retraite, 17 Tooting Bec Road,
London SW17 8BS
Tel: 0181 767 7659
WMIP

Eric Whitton
Humanistic Psychotherapist
31 Ovington Street, Chelsea, London
SW3 2JA
Tel: 0171 584 8819
AHPP

Frances Wilks
Integrative Psychotherapist
115 Alderney Street, London
SW1V 4HE
Tel: 0171 477 8260/0171 834 9264
RCSPC

Averil Williams
Analytical Psychologist-Jungian Analyst
78 Kenilworth Avenue, London
SW19 7LR
Tel: 0181 946 6857
SAP

Norman Wilson
Sexual and Marital Psychotherapist
16 Lower Common South, Putney,
London SW15 1BP
BASMT

Teresa Wilson
Systemic Psychotherapist
55 Cloudesdale Road, London
SW17 8ET
Tel: 0181 675 7848
KCC

Angela Wilton
Cognitive Analytic Therapist
27F Bramham Gardens, London
SW5 0JE
Tel: 0171 373 7520
ACAT

Jenny Wimshurst
Systemic Psychotherapist
St Peter's Vicarage, 21 Plough Road,
London SW11 2DE
Tel: 0171 228 8027
KCC

Kenneth Wingrove-Gibbons
Hypno-Psychotherapist
10 Greycoat Place, Victoria, London
SW1P 1SB
Tel: 0171 222 1888
NRHP

Jeremy Woodcock
Family Therapist
36 Ursula Street, Battersea, London
SW11 3DW
Tel: 0171 652 6365
IFT

James Wright
Psychoanalytic Psychotherapist
50 Burnfoot Avenue, Fulham, London
SW6 5EA;
Three Chimneys, Crown Lane, Orford,
Woodbridge IP12 2NB
Tel: 0171 385 6279/01394 450497
IPC

Charlotte Wynn-Parry
Integrative Psychotherapist
11a Moring Road, London SW17 8DN
Tel: 0181 672 9258
MC

Sarah Young
Integrative Psychotherapist
29 Felden Street, London SW6 5AE
Tel: 0171 731 1120
RCSPC

LONDON WEST

Patricia Allen
Analytical Psychologist-Jungian Analyst,
Psychoanalytic Psychotherapist
34 Thornfield Road, London W12 8JQ
Tel: 0181 749 5027
BAP, LCP

Caroline Armstrong
Biodynamic Psychotherapist
22 Bolton Road, London W4 3TB
Tel: 0181 994 0951
BTC

Lynn Arnold
Integrative Psychotherapist
296 Westbourne Park Road, London
W11 1EH
Tel: 0171 727 0688
MC

Yiannis Arzoumanides
Integrative Psychotherapist
218D Rundolph Avenue, London
W9 1PF
Tel: 0171 328 8955
RCSPC

Alexandra Asseily
NLP Psychotherapist
13 Addison Road, London W14 8DJ
Tel: 0171 602 1402
ANLP

James Astor
Analytical Psychologist-Jungian Analyst,
Jungian Child Analyst
Flat 3, 6 Ladbroke Square, London
W11 3LX
Tel: 0171 229 8707/0171 727 5759
SAP, ACP, BAP

Jan Baker
Integrative Psychotherapist
30 Beaconsfield Road, Ealing, London
W5 5JE
Tel: 0181 840 3849
MC

James Bamber
Group Analyst, Analytical Psychologist-
Jungian Analyst
115 Ladbroke Grove, Notting Hill,
London W11 1PG
Tel: 0171 727 6368
IGA, AJA

Peter Barham
Psychoanalytic Psychotherapist
23 Randolph Crescent, London
W9 1DP
Tel: 0171 289 4026
GUILD

Elizabeth Barker
Biodynamic Psychotherapist
82 Esmond Road, Chiswick, London
W4 1JF
Tel: 0181 994 6101
BTC

Harika Basharan
Transpersonal Psychotherapist
9 Fletcher Road, Chiswick, London
W4 5AT
Tel: 0181 995 3836
CCPE

Stefanie Baum
Biodynamic Psychotherapist
1 Grafton Road, London W3 6PB;
146 Lynton Road, London W3 9HH
Tel: 0181 992 4941
BTC

Agnes Beguin
Psychoanalytic Psychotherapist
Flat 3, 88 Holland Park, London
W11 3RZ
Tel: 0171 727 9448
IPC

Lorna Berger
Psychoanalytic Psychotherapist
122 St Albans Avenue, Chiswick,
London W4 5JR
Tel: 0171 937 6956/0181 995 2468
BAP

Irene Bloomfield
Psychoanalytic Psychotherapist
3 Marlborough, 38/40 Maida Vale,
London W9 1RW
Tel: 0171 286 8265
AGIP

Miranda Blum
Integrative Psychotherapist
104 Rannoch Road, London W6 9SW
Tel: 0181 741 5445
RCSPC

Joachim Boening
Integrative Psychotherapist, Body
Psychotherapist
1 Studley Grange Road, Hanwell,
London W7 2LU
Tel: 0181 579 2993
CCHP

Michaela Boening
Integrative Psychotherapist, Body
Psychotherapist
1 Studley Grange Road, Hanwell,
London W7 2LU
Tel: 0181 579 2993
CCHP

Camilla Bosanquet
Analytical Psychologist-Jungian Analyst
34E Upper Montagu Street, London
W1H 1RP;
Wyndside, Ryarsh, West Malling, Kent
ME19 5LB
Tel: 01732 842351/0171 262 3899
SAP, GUILD

Willie Botterill
Personal Construct Psychotherapist
39 Hammersmith Grove, London
W6 0NE
Tel: 0181 748 2894
CPCP

Victoria Botwood
Psychoanalytic Psychotherapist
34 Brook Green, London W6 7BL
Tel: 0171 603 5277
BAP

Ebba Boyesen
Biodynamic Psychotherapist
Acacia House, Centre Avenue, London
W3 7JX
Tel: 0171 743 2437
BTC

Gerda Boyesen
Biodynamic Psychotherapist
Acacia House, Centre Avenue, London
W3 7JX
Tel: 0171 743 2437
BTC

Mona Lisa Boyesen
Biodynamic Psychotherapist
Acacia House, Centre Avenue, London
W3 7JX
Tel: 0171 743 2437
BTC

George Bright
Analytical Psychologist-Jungian Analyst
176 Holland Road, London W14 8AH
Tel: 0171 602 4655/0171 371 6425 (f)
SAP

Dennis Brown
Group Analyst
The Group-Analytic Practice, 88
Montagu Mansions, London W1H 1LF
Tel: 0171 935 3103/0181 458 1435
IGA

Margaret Browne
Integrative Psychotherapist
11 Audley Road, London W5
Tel: 0181 985 0861 x 2013/0181 932
2784
RCSPC

Maureen Browne
Integrative Psychotherapist, Body
Psychotherapist
16 Cavendish Avenue, Ealing, London
W13 0JQ
Tel: 0181 998 1168
CCHP

Claire Bruas-Jaquess
Analytical Psychologist-Jungian Analyst
23 Greenside Road, London W12 9JQ
Tel: 0181 749 3389
SAP

Jackie Buckler
Sexual and Marital Psychotherapist
9 Melon Place, Kensington Church
Street, London W8 4DE
BASMT

Diana Buirski
Transpersonal Psychotherapist
Basement Flat, 3 Essendine Road,
London W9 2LS
Tel: 0171 289 9368
CCPE

Jane Bunster
Analytical Psychologist-Jungian Analyst,
Jungian Child Analyst
Parkside Clinic, 63-65 Lancaster Road,
London W11 1QG;
93 Tufnell Park Road, London N7 0PS
Tel: 0171 221 4656/0171 607 8468
SAP, ACP

Todd Butler
Gestalt Psychotherapist
37 Madeley Road, Ealing, London
W5 2LS
Tel: 0181 998 9390
GPTI, MET

Pietro Cardile
Transactional Analysis Psychotherapist
10E Cumberland Park, Acton, London
W3
Tel: 0181 993 0177
ITA

Ann Casement
Analytical Psychologist-Jungian Analyst
5 Kensington Park Gardens, London
W11 2HB
Tel: 0171 727 8218
AJA

Carola Chataway
Systemic Psychotherapist
66 Maida Vale, London W9 1PR
Tel: 0171 624 4052
KCC

Sangamithra U D Choudree
Cognitive Analytic Therapist
3 Millwood Street, London W10 6EH
Tel: 0181 740 3036/0181 969 9527
ACAT

Catherine Clancy
Psychoanalytic Psychotherapist
48 Sutton Court Road, Chiswick,
London W4 4NL
Tel: 0181 994 6732
IPC

John Clare
Psychoanalytic Psychotherapist
15 Waldeck Road, Strand-on-the-
Green, London W4 3NL
Tel: 0181 747 3213
IPSS

Petruska Clarkson
Individual and Group Humanistic
Psychotherapist, Transactional Analysis
Psychotherapist
12 North Common Road, Ealing,
London W5 2QB
Tel: 0181 579 3531/0181 567 0388
MET, GPTI, AHPP

Marion Cochlin
Analytical Psychologist-Jungian Analyst
41 Antrobus Road, London W4 5HY
Tel: 0181 995 2560
BAP

Christine Cochrane
Analytical Psychologist-Jungian Analyst,
Psychoanalytic Psychotherapist
10 Kensington Church Walk, London
W8 4NB
Tel: 0171 937 4225
BAP, LCP

Stephen Cogill
Group Analyst
60 Ranelagh Road, London W5 5RP
Tel: 0181 932 1212 0181 993 7892/
0181 566 1771
IGA

Ingrid Coltart
Analytical Psychologist-Jungian Analyst
76 Castellain Mansions, Castellain
Road, London W9 1HA
Tel: 0171 286 8486
SAP

Jenny Craddock
Analytical Psychotherapist
36 Clifton Gardens, London W9 1AU
Tel: 0973 386 176/0171 286 2812
LCP

Gabrielle Crockatt
Child Psychotherapist
Parkside Clinic, 63-65 Lancaster Road,
London W11 1QG
Tel: 0171 221 4656/0181 969 4006
ACP

Didi Crook
Biodynamic Psychotherapist
15 Powis Court, 29-39 Powis Square,
London W11 1JQ
Tel: 0171 221 4912
BTC

Penelope Daintry
Gestalt Psychotherapist
83 Stile Hall Gardens, London W4 3BT
Tel: 0181 995 4531
GPTI, MET

Caroline Dalal
Systemic Psychotherapist
1 Wolverton Gardens, Hammersmith,
London W6 7DQ
Tel: 0181 846 7806
KCC

Peggy Dalton
Personal Construct Psychotherapist
20 Cleveland Avenue, Chiswick,
London W4 1SN
Tel: 0181 994 7959
CPCP

Alan Danks
Psychoanalytic Psychotherapist
33 Park Road, Chiswick, London
W4 3EY
Tel: 0181 994 3131
IPC

Maggie Davidge
Gestalt Psychotherapist
36 Newburgh Road, Acton, London
W3 6DQ
Tel: 0181 993 0868
GCL

J Keith Davies
Psychoanalytic Psychotherapist
64B Hadyn Park Road, London
W12 9AG
Tel: 0181 740 5130
IPSS

Joyce Davis
Analytical Psychologist-Jungian Analyst
66 South Edwardes Square, London
W8 6HL
Tel: 0171 602 6348
IGAP

Heather de Leon
Psychoanalytic Psychotherapist
11 Whitehall Gardens, London
W4 3LT
Tel: 0181 741 0661/0181 994 2930
PA

Judith Dear
Analytical Psychotherapist
Flat 6a, Douglas House, 6 Maida Vale,
London W2
Tel: 0171 724 4036
LCP

Diana Dennis
Analytical Psychologist-Jungian Analyst
32 Bourdon Street, London W1X 9HX
Tel: 0171 629 6537/01580 291218
BAP

Marisa Dillon Weston
Group Analyst
23 Rusthall Avenue, London W4 1BW
Tel: 0181 994 6749
IGA

John Dinwoodie
NLP Psychotherapist
68 Fielding Road, London W4 1HL
Tel: 0181 995 0384
ANLP

Gillian Donaldson
Integrative Psychotherapist
Flat 2, 7 Tring Avenue, London
W5 3QA
Tel: 0181 992 3177
MET

Alicja Drewnowska
Integrative Psychotherapist, Body
Psychotherapist
7C Dorville Crescent, London W6
Tel: 0181 846 9889
CCHP

Moira Duckworth
Analytical Psychologist-Jungian Analyst
17 Perryn Road, London W3 7LR
Tel: 0181 743 1990
AJA

Alyce Faye Eichelberger Cleese
Child Psychotherapist
43 Holland Park Mews, London
W11 3SP
Tel: 0171 221 5394
ACP

Bernd Eiden
Integrative Psychotherapist, Body
Psychotherapist
26 Eaton Rise, Ealing, London W5 2ER
Tel: 0181 997 5219
CCHP, AHPP

Judith Elkan
Child Psychotherapist
St Mary's Department of Child
Psychiatry, 17 Paddington Green,
London W2 1LQ
Tel: 0171 723 1081/0181 455 8845
ACP

Dena Elliott
Integrative Psychotherapist, Humanistic
Psychotherapist
7 Grove Road, Acton W3 6AW
Tel: 0181 993 0523
CCHP, AHPP

Meg Errington
Psychoanalytic Psychotherapist
19 Hanover Court, Uxbridge Road,
London W12 9EP
Tel: 0181 740 1981
IPC

Anthony F Fagan
Transpersonal Psychotherapist
PO Box 624, St Charles Square,
London W10 6EA
Tel: 0181 964 3800
CCPE

Angela Fell
Integrative Psychotherapist
87 Rothschild Road, London W4 5NT
Tel: 0181 994 6206
MC

Sue Fish
Integrative Psychotherapist
13 North Common Road, Ealing,
London W5 2QB
Tel: 0181 458 8768
GPTI, MET, ITA

Susan Fisher
Analytical Psychologist-Jungian Analyst
5 Connaught Close, London W2 2AD
Tel: 0171 262 6189
BAP

Brenda Foguel
Group Analyst
Flat 14, 11 Hyde Park Gardens, London
W2 2LU
Tel: 0171 262 2522
IGA

Jennifer Forssander
Transpersonal Psychotherapist
27 Bathurst Mews, London W2 2SB
Tel: 0171 402 0290
CCPE

Alfred Fox
Transpersonal Psychotherapist
23A Fitzgeorge Avenue, London
W14 0SY
Tel: 0171 603 7777
CCPE

Lynett Fraser
Psychoanalytic Psychotherapist
6 Hereford House, Links Road, London
W3 0HX
Tel: 0181 993 1380
LCP

Martin Freeman
Psychoanalytic Psychotherapist
2 Clarendon Place, London W2 2NP
Tel: 0171 262 3693
LCP, BAP

Caroline Fry
Psychoanalytic Psychotherapist
56 Elers Road, London W13 9QD
Tel: 0181 579 6582
GUILD

Anne Furneaux
NLP Psychotherapist
New Life Potential, 4 Delamere Road,
Ealing, London W5 3JR
Tel: 0181 567 9759
ANLP

Evan George
Family Psychotherapist
Brief Therapy Practice, 4d Shirland
Mews, London W9 3DY
Tel: 0181 968 0070
IFT

Melanie Gibson
Psychoanalytic Psychotherapist
99 Vicarage Court, Vicarage Gate,
Kensington, London W8 4HQ
Tel: 0171 937 6280
IPC

Maria Gilbert
Integrative Psychotherapist
PO Box 2512, London W5 2QG
Tel: 0181 579 2505/0181 998 9866
MET, ITA, GPTI

Maureen Gledhill
Psychoanalytic Psychotherapist
93 Harley Street, London W1N 1DF
Tel: 0171 935 1163/0181 455 7211
LCP, CPP

Liza Glenn
Analytical Psychologist-Jungian Analyst,
Group Analyst
38 Chepstow Road, London W2 5BE;
Group Analytic Practice, 88 Montagu
Mansions, London W1H 1LF
Tel: 0171 935 3103/0171 229 6399
IGA, SAP

Geraldine Godsil
Analytical Psychologist-Jungian Analyst
60 Ealing Park Gardens, London
W5 4EU
Tel: 0181 560 9744/0181 568 0144
BAP

Francoise Golden
Psychoanalytic Psychotherapist
29 Park Close, Ilchester Place, London
W14 8NH
Tel: 0171 371 3687
LCP

John Goldman
Sexual and Marital Psychotherapist
22 De Walden Street, London
W1M 7PH
Tel: 0171 486 5148
BASMT

Ian Gordon-Brown
Transpersonal Psychotherapist
Centre for Transpersonal Psychology, 7
Pembridge Place, London W2 4XB
Tel: 0171 727 6412
PET

Rosemary Gordon-Montagnon
Analytical Psychologist-Jungian Analyst
26 Montagu Square, London W1H 1RE
Tel: 0171 935 1232/0171 486 3187 (f)
SAP, BAP

Carole Grace
Existential Psychotherapist
170 Valetta Road, London W3 7TP
Tel: 0181 743 8096
RCSPC

Bob Grant
Psychoanalytic Psychotherapist
72 Sinclair Road, London W14 0NJ
Tel: 0171 603 0529
AAP

Maurice Greenberg
Group Analyst
53 Rowan Road, London W6 7DT
Tel: 0171 387 4411/0171 603 5425
IGA

Frances Greenfield
Core Process Psychotherapist
14 Highlever Road, London W10 6PS
Tel: 0181 960 2530
KI

Pamela Griffiths
Transpersonal Psychotherapist
10 Livingstone Mansions, Queens Club
Gardens, London W14 9RW
CCPE

Nellie Hadzianesti
Analytical Psychologist-Jungian Analyst
Flat 11, 1 Stanley Gardens, London
W11 2ND
Tel: 0171 727 5303
BAP

Nigel Hamilton
Transpersonal Psychotherapist
Beauchamp Lodge, 2 Warwick
Crescent, London W2 6NE
Tel: 0171 266 3006
CCPE

Linda Harakis
Psychoanalytic Psychotherapist
40 Mattock Lane, London W13 9NS
Tel: 0181 579 2367
LCP

Michele Harris
Biodynamic Psychotherapist
126 Rainville Court, Rainville Road,
London W6 9HJ
Tel: 0171 385 3570
BTC

Nelly Hatzianesti
Analytical Psychologist-Jungian Analyst
Flat 2, 1 Stanley Gardens, London
W2 2ND
Tel: 0171 727 5303
BAP

Brigitte Haupts
Transpersonal Psychotherapist
64 Kensington Gardens Square,
Bayswater, London W2 4DG
Tel: 0171 221 2501
ACAT, CCPE

Susan Hauser
Biodynamic Psychotherapist
20 Goldsmith Road, London W3 6PX
Tel: 0181 992 9586
BTC

Karin Heinitz
Biodynamic Psychotherapist
c/o Gerda Boyesen Centre, Acacia
House, Centre Avenue, London
W3 7JX
Tel: 01843 591290/01227 273580
BTC

Andrew Henderson
Integrative Psychotherapist
178 Lancaster Road, London
W11 1QU
Tel: 0171 229 6790
MET

Agnes Birgit Heuer
Analytical Psychologist-Jungian Analyst,
Individual and Group Humanistic
Psychotherapist
13 Mansell Road, London W3 7QH
Tel: 0181 749 4388
AHPP, BAP

Gottfried Heuer
Analytical Psychologist-Jungian Analyst,
Individual and Group Humanistic
Psychotherapist
13 Mansell Road, London W3 7QH
Tel: 0181 749 4388
AJA

Robert Hinshelwood
Psychoanalytic Psychotherapist
18 Artesian Road, London W2 5AR
Tel: 0171 229 2855
LCP

Paul Hitchings
Integrative Psychotherapist
132 Princes Avenue, Acton, London
W3 8LT
Tel: 0181 992 3736
MET

Lynne Holmes
Body Psychotherapist, Holistic
Psychotherapist
21 Woodfield Crescent, London
W5 1PD
Tel: 0181 997 0942
CCHP

Roger Horrocks
Individual and Group Humanistic
Psychotherapist
5 West Kensington Mansions, North
End Road, London W14 9PE
Tel: 0171 385 4091
AHPP

Flora Hoskin
Gestalt Psychotherapist
25 Rothschild Road, Chiswick, London
W4 5HT
Tel: 0181-995 7440
GCL

Chris Iveson
Family Therapist
The Brief Therapy Practice, 4d Shirland
Mews, London W9 3DY
Tel: 0181 968 0070
IFT

Cecilia Jarvis
Psychosynthesis Psychotherapist
11 Walmer Gardens, Ealing, London
W13 9TS
Tel: 0181 567 1331
PET

Natasha Jenner
Child Psychotherapist
5 Chepstow Court, Chepstow
Crescent, London W11 3ED
Tel: 0171 221 4656 ext 143
LCP

Jenny Jennings
Transpersonal Psychotherapist
46 Holland Park, London W11 3RS
CCPE

Ellie Johnson
Systemic Psychotherapist
51a Faraday Road, London W10 5SF
Tel: 0181 968 0510
IFT

Philip Joyce
Gestalt Psychotherapist
2 Richmond Road, Ealing, London
W5 5NS
Tel: 0181 567 9217
GPTI, MET

Maggie Kafton
Transpersonal Psychotherapist
5A Ladbroke Gardens, London
W11 2PT
Tel: 0171 221 8717
CCPE

Alexandra Karan
Psychoanalytic Psychotherapist
47 Lanark Road, London W9 1DE
Tel: 0171 286 7090
GUILD

Anne Kearns
Gestalt Psychotherapist, Integrative
Psychotherapist
83 Stilehall Gardens, Chiswick, London
W4 3BT
Tel: 0181 995 4531
MET, GPTI

Duncan Kegerreis
Group Analyst
67 Addison Gardens, London
W14 0DT
Tel: 0181 870 1061/0171 603 9609
IGA

Susan Kegerreis
Child Psychotherapist
67 Addison Gardens, London
W14 0DT
Tel: 0171 603 9609/0171 823 1225
ACP

Michael Kennedy
Lacanian Analyst
55 St Quintin Avenue, London
W10 6NZ
Tel: 0181 968 3769
CFAR

Wendy Kennett-Brown
Systemic Psychotherapist
30 Amherst Road, Ealing, London
W13 8LT
Tel: 0181 997 2975
KCC

William Kinbacher
Transpersonal Psychotherapist
c/o 2 Warwick Crescent, London
W2 6NE
CCPE

Diana Kinder
Group Analyst
23 Woodville Gardens, London
W5 2LL
Tel: 0181 997 1207
IGA

Achim Korte
Biodynamic Psychotherapist
c/o Gerda Boyesen Centre, Acacia
House, Centre Avenue, London
W3 7JX
Tel: 0171 837 6960
BTC

Lyn Lamplough
Transpersonal Psychotherapist
41 Craven Avenue, Ealing, London
W5 2SY
Tel: 0181 579 9955
CCPE

James Lawley
NLP Psychotherapist
1 Lauderdale Road, Maida Vale, London
W9 1LT
Tel: 0171 289 8626
ANLP

Graham Lee
Psychoanalytic Psychotherapist
21 Poplar Grove, London W6 7RF
Tel: 0171 603 1021
AGIP

Norman Leitman
Integrative Psychotherapist
37 Madeley Road, Ealing, London
W5 2LS
Tel: 0181 998 9390
MET, RCSPC

Mary Levens
Psychodrama Psychotherapist
16 Bristol Mews, Little Venice, London
W9 2JF
Tel: 0171 286 8251
BPDA

Brigitte Leveque
Integrative Psychotherapist
7 Rivercourt Road, London W6 9LD
Tel: 0181 748 9656
RCSPC

Derek Linker
Analytical Psychologist-Jungian Analyst
Flat 4, 175 Sussex Gardens, London
W2 2RH
Tel: 0171 262 7318
SAP

Ray Little
Transactional Analysis Psychotherapist
16 Hatfield Road, Chiswick, London
W4 1AF
Tel: 0181 994 2905
ITA

Britta Lloyd
Analytical Psychologist-Jungian Analyst
1 Lansdowne Road, London W11 3AL
Tel: 0171 727 7567/0171 727 0768
BAP

Josephine Lock
Integrative Psychotherapist
Garden Flat, 74 Elgin Avenue, London
W9 2HB
Tel: 0171 286 4996
MC

Susan Loden
Psychoanalytic Psychotherapist
20 Clarendon Road, London W11 3AB
Tel: 0171 727 2551
BAP

Dorothy Luciani
Child Psychotherapist
17 Wimpole Street, London
W1M 7AD
Tel: 0171 436 1144
ACP

Jochen Lude
Integrative Psychotherapist, Body
Psychotherapist
26 Eaton Rise, Ealing, London W5 2ER
Tel: 0181 997 5219
CCHP, AHPP

Dorrie MacLean
Psychoanalytic Psychotherapist,
Analytical Psychologist-Jungian Analyst
139 West Kensington Court, London
W14 9AD
Tel: 0171 603 3284
IPC, BAP

Veronika Marlow
Analytical Psychologist-Jungian Analyst
Flat 2, 29 Auriol Road, London
W14 0SP;
5 School Lane, Kenilworth,
Warwickshire CV8 2GU
Tel: 01926 512611/0171 602 4453
SAP

Martin Marlowe
Cognitive Analytic Therapist
Flat 6, 7 St Stevens Crescent,
Bayswater, London W2
Tel: 0171 727 6440
ACAT

Chandra Masoliver
Psychoanalytic Psychotherapist
Flat 15, Argyll Mansions, Hammersmith
Road, London W14 8QG
Tel: 0171 602 1525
AAP

Kikan Massara
Integrative Psychotherapist
115 St Mary's Mansions, St Mary's
Terrace, London W2 1SZ
Tel: 0171 262 7870
RCSPC

Carol Matthews
Psychoanalytic Psychotherapist
122 St Albans Avenue, Chiswick,
London W4 5JR;
Myrtle Farm, Shurton Stogursey,
Bridgwater, Somerset TA5 1QE
Tel: 0181 995 2468/01278 732587
IPC, SIP

Teresa McCreanor
Group Analytic Psychotherapist
65a Randolph Avenue, London
W9 1DW
Tel: 0171 286 6435
LCP

Dennis McEldowney
Psychoanalytic Psychotherapist
39 Leythe Road, Acton, London
W3 8AW
Tel: 0181 993 1559
IPSS

Andy McKeown
Integrative Psychotherapist
13 Madeley Road, London W5;
also practice address in Somerset
MET

Oliver McShane
Analytical Psychologist-Jungian Analyst
Knightsbridge House, 229 Acton Lane,
London W4 5DD;
33 Foliot Street, London W12 0BQ
Tel: 0181 742 7596/0181 743 6784
SAP

Christine Mead
Psychosynthesis Psychotherapist
10 Faroe Road, London W14 0EP
Tel: 0171 602 0401
IPS

Steven Mendoza
Psychoanalytic Psychotherapist
34 Thornfield Road, London W12 8JQ
Tel: 0181 749 5027
LCP

Sallie Mercer
Family Psychotherapist
8 Beconsfield Road, London W5 5JE
Tel: 0181 567 7043
IFT

Beth Miller
Analytical Psychologist-Jungian Analyst
48 New Cavendish Street, London
W1M 7LE
Tel: 0171 486 4843
SAP

Louise Mitchell
Sexual and Marital Psychotherapist
2 Littlewood Close, West Ealing,
London W13
BASMT

Richard Mizen
Analytical Psychologist-Jungian Analyst
46 Castlebar Road, Ealing, London
W5 2DD
Tel: 0181 997 9180/0181 810 8378
SAP

Norah Moore
Analytical Psychologist-Jungian Analyst
31 Weymouth Mews, London
W1N 3FN;
7 Weald Way, Caterham, Surrey
CR3 6EL
Tel: 01883 342191/0171 580 4055
SAP

Anni Moorhouse
Systemic Psychotherapist
21 Convent Gardens, London W5 4UT
Tel: 0181 568 2900
IFT

Flavia Morante
Psychoanalytic Psychotherapist
65 Victoria Road, London W8 5RH
Tel: 0171 602 6647
IPSS

Clare Morris
Personal Construct Psychotherapist
65 Braybrook Street, London
W12 0AL
CPCP

Nuala Muldoon
Integrative Psychotherapist
2 Denbigh Road, Ealing, London
W13 8PX
Tel: 0181 998 1725
RCSPC

Katherine Murphy
Integrative Psychotherapist
29 Stilehall Gardens, Chiswick, London
W4 3BS
Tel: 0181 747 1041
MET

John Murray
NLP Psychotherapist
The Boadicea, Lower Mall, London
W6 9DJ
Tel: 0181 741 4407
ANLP

Antje Netzer-Stein
Child Psychotherapist
St Mary's Department of Child
Psychiatry, 17 Paddington Green,
London W2 1LQ
Tel: 0181 771 5523/0171 723 1081
ACP

Rudolph Oldeschulte
Child Psychotherapist
c/o Child & Family Consultation
Centre, 1 Wolverton Gardens, London
W6 7DQ
Tel: 0181 846 7806
ACP

Anne Page
Analytical Psychologist-Jungian Analyst
67 Black Lion Lane, London W6 9BG
Tel: 0181 748 8892
SAP

Gabrielle Parker
Systemic Psychotherapist
34 Heathstar Road, London W12 0RA
KCC

Jean Pearson
Analytical Psychologist-Jungian Analyst
120 Church Road, London W7 3BE
Tel: 0181 933 6451
BAP

Adam Phillips
Child Psychotherapist, Psychoanalytic
Psychotherapist
99 Talbot Road, London W11 2AT;
Child & Family Consultation Centre, 1
Wolverton Gardens, London W6
Tel: 0181 846 7807
ACP, GUILD

Allan Pimentel
Transpersonal Psychotherapist
c/o CCPE, Beauchamp Lodge, 2
Warwick Crescent, London W2 6NE
Tel: 0171 266 3006
CCPE

Angela Plotel
Hypno-Psychotherapist
168A Coningham Road, Shepherds
Bush, London W12 8BY
Tel: 0181 740 4674
NRHP

Robert Poole
Group Analytic Psychotherapist
59/61 Ladbroke Grove, London
W11 3AT
Tel: 0171 727 9551
LCP

Barry D Proner
Analytical Psychologist-Jungian Analyst,
Jungian Child Analyst
83 Strand-on-the-Green, London
W4 3PU
Tel: 0181 995 8319
ACP, BAP

Karen Proner
Psychoanalytic Psychotherapist, Child
Psychotherapist
Child and Family Department,
Tavistock Clinic, 120 Belsize Lane,
London NW3 5BA
Tel: 0171 435 7111/0171 435 7057 (f)
LCP, ACP

Sandra Ramsden
Child Psychotherapist
Department of Child Psychiatry,
Middlesex Hospital, North House,
Cleveland Street, London W1N 8AA
Tel: 0171 380 9089/0181 444 8337
ACP

Harvey Ratner
Family Psychotherapist
Brief Therapy Practice, 4D Shirland
Mews, London W9 3DY
Tel: 0181 968 0070
IFT

Jane Read
Sexual and Marital Psychotherapist
6 Cambridge Road North, Chiswick,
London W4 4AA
BASMT

Keith Reed
Analytical Psychologist-Jungian Analyst
8 Wilton Avenue, London W4 2HY
Tel: 0181 994 3978
SAP

Eric Rhode
Psychoanalytic Psychotherapist, Child
Psychotherapist
28 Holland Park, London W11 3TA
Tel: 0171 221 6263
LCP, ACP

Anne Richardson
Transpersonal Psychotherapist
London W4 5EH
Tel: 0181 994 5969
CCPE

Sue Robinson
Psychoanalytic Psychotherapist
7 Richford Street, London W6 7HH
Tel: 0181 749 7785
GUILD

Hilary C A M Rodger
Psychoanalytic Psychotherapist
Flat 1, 140 Portland Road, London
W11 4LX
Tel: 0181 229 9388
IPC

Maggie Rogers
Psychoanalytic Psychotherapist
137 Fielding Road, Chiswick, London
W4 1DA
Tel: 0181 994 3580
IPSS

Miroslava Ross
Child Psychotherapist
Maisonette 1, 16 Bristol Gardens, Little
Venice, London W9
Tel: 0171 289 6759
ACP

Rosette Rozenburg
Psychoanalytic Psychotherapist
56 Cleveland Mansions, Widley Road,
London W9 2LB
Tel: 0171 286 7005
AGIP

Heiner Schuff
Psychoanalytic Psychotherapist
119 Elgin Avenue, London W9 2NR
Tel: 0171 286 9225
LCP

Janice Scott
Gestalt Psychotherapist
2 Oak Cottages, Green Lane, Hanwell,
London W7 2PE
Tel: 0181 840 4886
GPTI, MET

Juliet Sharman
Psychoanalytic Psychotherapist
209 Hammersmith Grove, London
W6 0NP
Tel: 0181 749 0270
IPC

Meg Sharpe
Analytical Psychologist-Jungian Analyst
The Group Analytic Practice, 88
Montagu Mansions, London W1H 1LF
Tel: 0171 935 3103/3085/
0171 794 0210
SAP

Dolores Sheridan
Transpersonal Psychotherapist
53 Matlock Court, Kensington Park
Road, London W11 3BS
Tel: 0171 221 0331
CCPE

Sue Sherwin-White
Child Psychotherapist
Child & Family Consultation Centre, 1
Wolverton Gardens, London W6
Tel: 0181 846 7807/0171 278 2188
ACP

Ellen Attracta Shields
Integrative Psychotherapist
26 Fairlea Place, Woodfield Road,
London W5 1SP
Tel: 0181 810 4552
RCSPC

Sunita Shipton
Biodynamic Psychotherapist
132 Kings Street, London W6 0QU
Tel: 0181 748 2061
BTC

Peter Shoenberg
Psychoanalytic Psychotherapist
Flat E, 30 Pembridge Villas, London
W11 3EL;
Department of Psychological Medicine,
University College Hospital, Gower
Street, London WC1E 6AU
Tel: 0171 387 9300 x 8584
BAP

Rosa Shreeves
Humanistic and Integrative
Psychotherapist, Integrative Arts
Psychotherapist
24 Strand-on-the-Green, London
W4 3PH
Tel: 0181 995 5904
SPEC

Dave Sichel
Integrative Psychotherapist
194 Sutton Court Road, Chiswick,
London W4 3HR
Tel: 0181 995 7175
MC

Charlotte Sills
Transactional Analysis Psychotherapist,
Integrative Psychotherapist
2 Richmond Road, London W5 5NS
Tel: 0181 567 9217
ITA, MET

Charmian Skinner
Psychoanalytic Psychotherapist
6 Ruston Mews, London W11 1RB;
27 Beryl Road, Hammersmith, London
W6 8JS
Tel: 0171 792 2145/0171 748 0718
IPC

Jonathan Smith
Gestalt Psychotherapist
36 Newburgh Road, London W3 6DQ
Tel: 0181 993 0868
GCL

Milica Sobat
Child Psychotherapist
Maisonette 2, 16 Bristol Gardens, Little
Venice, London W9
Tel: 0171 289 6759
ACP

Barbara Somers
Transpersonal Psychotherapist
Centre for Transpersonal Psychology, 7
Pembridge Place, London W2 4XB
Tel: 0171 727 6412
PET

Ann Ngan Soo
Educational Therapist
75 Rosebank Road, Hanwell, London
W7 2EW
Tel: 0181 579 7910
FAETT

Clover Southwell
Biodynamic Psychotherapist
3 Bulstrode Street, London W1M 5FS
Tel: 0171 935 5107
BTC

Shirley Spitz
Integrative Psychotherapist
Flat 4, 2 Hyde Park Gardens, London
W2 2LT
Tel: 0171 706 4930
SPTI

Pamela Stang
Psychoanalytic Psychotherapist
3 Irving Mansions, Queens Club
Gardens, London W14 9SL
Tel: 0171 385 4476
IPC

Elizabeth Stanley
Sexual and Marital Psychotherapist
82 Harley Street, London W1N 1AE
BASMT

Gill Straker
Integrative Psychotherapist
Sherwood Psychotherapy Training
Institute, Thiskney House, 2 St James
Terrace, Nottingham NG1 6FW
Tel: 0115 924 3994
SPTI, MET

Michael Sunderland
Psychoanalytic Psychotherapist
3 Elgin Mews South, London W9 1JZ
Tel: 0171 289 1330
LCP

Pauline Sutcliffe
Family Psychotherapist
Flat 1, 95 Oxford Gardens, London
W10 5UN
Tel: 0171 792 1229
IFT

Karin Syrett
Analytical Psychologist-Jungian Analyst
27 Royal Crescent, London W11 4SN
Tel: 0171 602 0864
AJA

Kasia Szymanska
Cognitive Behavioural Psychotherapist
83 Felix Road, Ealing, London
W13 0NZ
Tel: 0181 579 6757
BABCP

Kerry Thomas
Analytical Psychologist-Jungian Analyst
93 Blenheim Crescent, London
W11 2EQ
Tel: 01908 654527/0171 727 8572
BAP

Penny Tompkins
NLP Psychotherapist
1 Lauderdale Road, Maida Vale, London
W9 1LT
Tel: 0171 289 8626
ANLP

Julia Tugendhat
Systemic Psychotherapist
35 Westbourne Park Road, London
W2 5QD
Tel: 0171 727 3315
KCC

Jan-Floris Van der Wateren
Biodynamic Psychotherapist
52 Blenheim Crescent, London
W11 1NY
Tel: 0171 221 6221
BTC

Lorraine Walker
Analytical Psychologist-Jungian Analyst
1 Helen House, Gunnersbury Lane,
London W3 3HZ
Tel: 0181 993 2084
IGAP

Eileen Walsh
NLP Psychotherapist
7 Montgomery Road, Chiswick,
London W4 5LZ
Tel: 0181 995 1934
ANLP

Barbara Warner
Family Therapist
41 Wallingford Avenue, London
W10 6PZ
IFT

Lesley Wells
Psychoanalytic Psychotherapist
1 Hart Grove, London W5 3NA
Tel: 0181 992 4920
GUILD

Penny Wigram
Psychoanalytic Psychotherapist
2 Clarendon Place, London W2 2NP
Tel: 0171 723 8925
IPC

Claerwen Williams
Integrative Psychotherapist
14 Hartswood Road, London
W12 9NQ
Tel: 0181 451 6162/0181 743 7823
RCSPC

Ruth Windle
Analytical Psychologist-Jungian Analyst
203c Ladbroke Grove, London
W10 6HQ
Tel: 0181 960 7304
BAP

Christine Yawetz
Sexual and Marital Psychotherapist
2 Aubrey Road, Campden Hill, London
W8 7JJ
BASMT

Ali Zarbafi
Psychoanalytic Psychotherapist
30 Magnolia Road, Strand-on-the-
Green, Chiswick, London W4 3QW
Tel: 0181 747 0408
IPSS

Nicholas Zinovieff
Existential Psychotherapist
74 Hazledene Road, London W4 3BJ
Tel: 0181 995 5265
RCSPC

LOTHIANS

Geraldine Bienkowski
Cognitive Behavioural Psychotherapist
Psychology Department, St John's
Hospital, Howden, Livingston, Scotland
EH54 6PP
Tel: 01506 419666 x 4570
BABCP

Thomas M Brown
Cognitive Behavioural Psychotherapist
9 Maidlands, Linlithgow, West Lothian
EH49 6AG
Tel: 01506 419666
BABCP

MANCHESTER

Joy Appleby
Gestalt Psychotherapist, Integrative
Psychotherapist
3 The Beeches, West Didsbury,
Manchester M20 2BG
Tel: 0161 445 0766
GPTI

Claire Bacha
Group Analyst
20 Kersal Road, Prestwich, Manchester
M25 8SJ
Tel: 0161 773 0409/0161 301 1904
IGA

Anne Bannister
Psychodrama Psychotherapist
Glebe Cottage, Church Road, Mellor,
Stockport SK6 5LX
Tel: 0161 427 3307
BPDA

Gillian Barnett
Psychoanalytic Psychotherapist
University of Manchester, Student
Health Services, Crawford House,
Precinct Centre, Oxford Road,
Manchester M13 9QS
Tel: 0161 275 2859
NWIDP

Susan Benbow
Systemic Psychotherapist
SCOPE, Carisbrooke Resource Centre,
Wenlock Way, Gorton, Manchester
M12 5LF
FIC

Nagy R Bishay
Cognitive Behavioural Psychotherapist
North Manchester General Hospital,
Crumpsall, Manchester M8 6RL
Tel: 0161 653 4294/0161 720 2034
BABCP

Shaun Brookhouse
Hypno-Psychotherapist
Richmael House, 25 Edge Lane,
Chorlton, Manchester M21 9JH
Tel: 0161 881 1677
CTS

M Buckley
Psychoanalytic Psychotherapist
Macartney House, Psychotherapy
Service, Beech Mount, Rochdale Road,
Manchester M9 1XS
Tel: 0161 205 7555
NWIDP

Robert Cooke
Transactional Analysis Psychotherapist
454 Barlow Moor Road, Chorlton,
Manchester M21 1BQ
Tel: 0161 862 9456
ITA

Jan Costa
Psychodrama Psychotherapist
6 Bethel Avenue, Failsworth,
Manchester M35 0AG
Tel: 0161 794 0874
BPDA

Sarah Davenport
Psychoanalytic Psychotherapist
Dept of Rehabilitation, Harrop House,
Salford NHS Trust, Bury New Road,
Manchester M25 3BL
Tel: 0161 773 9121
NWIDP

Jim Davis
Transactional Analysis Psychotherapist
7 Talbot Road, Ladybarn, Manchester
M14 6TA
Tel: 0161 225 2556
ITA

Judi Egerton
Psychoanalytic Psychotherapist
Dept of Psychiatry, Withington
Hospital, West Didsbury, Manchester
M20 2LR
Tel: 0161 447 4327/4661
LPDO

Don Feasey
Psychoanalytic Psychotherapist
16 Raynham Avenue, Didsbury,
Manchester M20 6BW
Tel: 0161 445 3612
WMIP

Mark Gabbay
Psychoanalytic Psychotherapist
Department of General Practice,
University of Manchester, Rusholme
Health Centre, Walmer St, Manchester
M14 5NP
LPDO

Jaya Gowrisunkur
Psychoanalytic Psychotherapist
Gaskell House, Department of
Psychotherapy, Swinton Grove,
Manchester M13 0EU
Tel: 0161 273 2762
NWIDP

Else Guthrie
Psychoanalytic Psychotherapist
The Rawnsley Building, Department of
Psychiatry, Manchester Royal Infirmary,
Oxford Road, Manchester M13 9BX
Tel: 0161 276 5365
NWIDP

Kate Hellin
Psychoanalytic Psychotherapist
The Red House Psychotherapy Service,
78 Manchester Road, Swinton,
Manchester M27 5FG
Tel: 0161 794 0875
NWIDP

Robert Hobson
Psychoanalytic Psychotherapist
Gaskell House Psychotherapy Service,
Manchester Royal Infirmary, Swinton
Grove, Manchester M13 0EU
Tel: 0161 273 2762
NWIDP

Alan Horne
Psychoanalytic Psychotherapist
Psychotherapy Centre, Manchester
Royal Infirmary, Gaskell House,
Swinton Grove, Manchester M13 0EU
Tel: 0161 273 2762
NWIDP

Lynette Hughes
Psychoanalytic Marital Psychotherapist
c/o Winnicott Centre, 195-97
Hathersage Road, Manchester M13 0JE
Tel: 0161 248 9494
TMSI

Keith Hyde
Psychoanalytic Psychotherapist
The Red House Psychotherapy Service,
78 Manchester Road, Swinton,
Manchester M27 1FG;
5 Devonshire Road, Salford M6 8HY
Tel: 0161 794 0875/0161 789 4393
NWIDP

Toni-Lee Isaac
Hypno-Psychotherapist
81 Palatine Road, Didsbury,
Manchester M20 9LJ
Tel: 0161 446 1070
CTS

Elisabeth Jackson
Gestalt Psychotherapist
Manchester Gestalt Centre, 7 Norman
Road, Rusholme, Manchester M14 5LF
Tel: 0161 257 2202
GPTI

Malcolm Kay
Psychodrama Psychotherapist
45 Chadwick Road, Eccles, Manchester
M30 0WU
Tel: 0161 788 0490
BPDA

Susan Lendrum
Psychoanalytic Psychotherapist
Flat 1, Parkfield Road South,
Manchester M20 6DA
Tel: 0161 434 9709
NWIDP

Maria A Lever
Cognitive Behavioural Psychotherapist
Palliative Care Counselling Service,
Ordsall Health Centre, Belfort Drive,
Salford M5 3PP
Tel: 0161 872 2004 x 161/
01204 493914
BABCP

Marion Lindsay
Psychoanalytic Psychotherapist
Macartney House Psychotherapy
Service, Beechmount, Harpurhey,
Manchester M9 1XS
LPDO

Sarah Littlejohn
Integrative Psychotherapist
2 Limefield Terrace, Levenshulme,
Manchester M19 2EP
Tel: 0161 225 5349
MC

Sandra Lobel
Sexual and Marital Psychotherapist
30 Longton Avenue, Withington,
Manchester M20 3JN
BASMT

Sydney Lobel
Sexual and Marital Psychotherapist
30 Longton Avenue, Withington,
Manchester M20 3JN
BASMT

Frank Margison
Psychoanalytic Psychotherapist,
Transactional Analysis Psychotherapist
Dept of Psychotherapy, Manchester
Royal Infirmary, Gaskell House,
Swinton Grove, Manchester M13 0EU
Tel: 0161 273 2762
NWIDP

Graeme McGrath
Psychoanalytic Psychotherapist
Department of Psychotherapy, Gaskell
House, Swinton Grove, Manchester
M13 0EU
Tel: 0161 273 2762
NWIDP

Joan Meredith
Psychodynamic Psychotherapist
11 Shaftesbury Road, Manchester
M8 0WL
HIP

Lesley Mitchell
Psychoanalytic Psychotherapist
Macartney House Psychotherapy
Service, Beech Mount, Rochdale Road,
Harpurhey, Manchester M9 1XS
Tel: 0161 205 7555
NWIDP

John Monk-Steel
Transactional Analysis Psychotherapist
119 Old Road, Failsworth M35 0GD
Tel: 0161 681 6200
ITA

Elisabeth Perriollat Munro
Psychoanalytic Psychotherapist
43 Pine Grove, Eccles, Manchester
M30 9JB
Tel: 0161 281 8416
AAP

Jane Nicholson
Psychoanalytic Psychotherapist
Gaskell House, Psychotherapy Service,
Swinton Grove, Manchester M13 0EU
Tel: 0161 275 5221
NWIDP

Peter Philippson
Gestalt Psychotherapist
Manchester Gestalt Centre, 7 Norman
Road, Rusholme, Manchester M14 5LF
Tel: 0161 257 2202
GPTI

Nick Poole
NLP Psychotherapist
386 Kingsway, Burnage, Manchester
M19 1PL
Tel: 0161 432 8624
ANLP

Stephen Potter
Psychoanalytic Psychotherapist
Uni of Manchester & UMIST
Counselling Service, Crawford House,
Manchester M13 9QS
Tel: 0161 275 2864
LPDO

Alan Prodgers
Psychoanalytic Psychotherapist
The Red House Psychotherapy Service,
78 Manchester Road, Swinton,
Manchester M27 5FG
Tel: 0161 794 0875
NWIDP

Jean Rawsthorne
Psychoanalytic Psychotherapist
Gaskell House, Department of
Psychotherapy, Swinton Grove,
Manchester M13 0EU
Tel: 0161 273 2762
NWIDP

Rev A Rhodes
Psychoanalytic Psychotherapist
Chaplaincy, Manchester Royal
Infirmary, Oxford Road, Manchester
M13 9WL
Tel: 0161 276 4726
NWIDP

Albert Sawyer
Hypno-Psychotherapist
5 Lyndene Avenue, Roegreen, Worsley,
Manchester M28 4RJ
Tel: 0161 727 8551/0161 799 5537
NSHAP

Celia Scanlon
Psychodrama Psychotherapist
Hampden House, 2-4 Palahue Road,
Withington, Manchester M20 3JA
BPDA

Ronald Siddle
Cognitive Behavioural Psychotherapist
Dept of Clinical Psychology,
Withington Hospital, West Didsbury,
Manchester M20 8LR
Tel: 0161 447 4846
BABCP

Joyce Stableford
Hypno-Psychotherapist
16 Thompson Road, Denton,
Manchester M34 2PS
Tel: 0161 336 2353
CTS

Adrian Sutton
Psychoanalytic Psychotherapist
Child & Family Service, Winnicott
Centre, Hathersage Road, Manchester
M13 0JE
Tel: 0161 248 9494
NWIDP

Maye Taylor
Psychodynamic Psychotherapist
Psychology and Speech Pathology,
Manchester Metropolitan University,
Elizabeth Gaskell Campus, Hathersage
Rd Manchester M13 0JA
Tel: 0161 247 2573/0161 442 3417
NWIDP

Esme Towse
Psychoanalytic Psychotherapist
Hampden House Psychotherapy
Centre, 2-4 Palatine Road, Didsbury,
Manchester M20 3JA
Tel: 0161 445 2099/3389
NWIDP

Maggie Towse
Psychoanalytic Psychotherapist
Macartney House Psychotherapy
Service, Beech Mount, Rochdale Road,
Manchester M9 1XS
Tel: 0161 205 7555
NWIDP

Christine Verduyn
Family Therapist
Dept of Clinical Psychology, Royal
Manchester Children's Hospital,
Hospital Road, Pendlebury, Manchester
M27 4HA
AFT

Jeni Webster
Family Psychotherapist
Mathematics Building, Manchester
University, Oxford Road, Manchester
M13 9PL
Tel: 0161 275 5220
AFT

Paul Wilkins
Psychodrama Psychotherapist
Manchester Metropolitan University,
Centre for Human Communication,
799 Wilmslow Road, Didsbury,
Manchster M20 8RR
Tel: 0161 860 4437
BPDA

MERSEYSIDE

Bill Barnes
Psychoanalytic Psychotherapist
Liverpool Psychotherapy &
Consultation Service, Mossley Hill
Hospital, Park Avenue, Liverpool
L18 8BU
Tel: 0151 250 6046
LPDO

Edith Bergel
Psychoanalytic Psychotherapist
41 Menlove Gardens West, Liverpool
L18 2ET
Tel: 0151 722 5936
LPDO

Paul Bielicz
Psychoanalytic Psychotherapist
33 St George's Road, Waterloo,
Liverpool L22 1RA
Tel: 0151 920 8905
NWIDP

Suzanne Blundell
Child Psychotherapist
Crosby Hall, Little Crosby, Liverpool
L23 4UA
Tel: 0151 924 8590/0171 435 3599 (f)
ACP

Tom Bolton
Hypno-Psychotherapist
161A Manor Road, Wallasey, Wirral,
Merseyside L44 0EN
Tel: 0151 638 6706
NRHP

Sandra Bryson
Psychoanalytic Psychotherapist, Family
Therapist
59 Vaughan Road, Wallasey, Merseyside
L45 1LJ
Tel: 0151 639 7830
AFT, LPDO

Anthony Cawley
Hypno-Psychotherapist
44 Wellesley Road, Liverpool,
Merseyside L8 3SU
Tel: 0151 727 1485
NRHP

Sue Clements-Jewery
Sexual and Marital Psychotherapist
79 Ampthill Road, Liverpool L17 9QN
BASMT

Paul Dickinson
Psychoanalytic Psychotherapist
Liverpool Psychotherapy &
Consultation Service, Mossley Hill
Hospital, Park Avenue, Liverpool
L18 8BU
Tel: 0151 250 6128
LPDO

Elizabeth Doyle
Psychoanalytic Psychotherapist
18 Dunraven Road, Little Neston,
South Wirral L64 9QU
Tel: 0151 336 4692
LPDO

Delia Essex
Psychoanalytic Psychotherapist
The Counselling Service, Liverpool
University, 14 Oxford Street, Liverpool
L7 7BL
Tel: 0151 794 3304
LPDO

Paul Foster
Psychoanalytic Psychotherapist
c/o University of Liverpool Counselling
Services, 14 Oxford Street, Liverpool
L7 7BW
Tel: 0151 794 3304
LPDO

Michael Göpfert
Psychoanalytic Psychotherapist
Liverpool Psychotherapy &
Consultation Service, Mossley Hill
Hospital, Park Avenue, Liverpool
L18 8BU
Tel: 0151 250 6128
LPDO

Patricia Hagan
Psychoanalytic Psychotherapist
District Psychology Service, Whiston
Hospital, Prescot, Merseyside L35 5DR
Tel: 0151 430 1321
LPDO

Sheila L L Hamilton
Psychoanalytic Psychotherapist
Department of Clinical Psychology,
Oakdale Unit, Fazakerley Hospital,
Longmoor Lane, Liverpool L9 7AL
Tel: 0151 529 3249
LPDO

Anne Hardman
Hypno-Psychotherapist
22 Lawton Road, Rainhill, Merseyside
L35 0PP
Tel: 0151 426 1795
CTS

Peter Harmsworth
Family Psychotherapist
Barnardos Family Therapy Service,
Mornington Terrace, 29 Upper Duke
Street, Liverpool L1 9DY
Tel: 0151 709 0540
AFT

Jean Hazlehurst
Hypno-Psychotherapist
Grange Hall, Blackhorse Hill, West
Kirby, Merseyside L48 7EF
Tel: 0151 625 1809
NRHP

Begum Hendrickse
Sexual and Marital Psychotherapist
25 Riverbank Road, Heswall,
Merseyside L60 4SQ
BASMT

Robert Higgo
Psychoanalytic Psychotherapist
Lakeside Clinic, Orphan Drive,
Liverpool L6 7UN
Tel: 0151 250 3000
LPDO

Jane Jameson Milner
Gestalt Psychotherapist
15 Princes Park Mansions, Liverpool
L8 3SA
Tel: 0151 727 5501/0151 707 1311
GPTI

Caroline Jones
Sexual and Marital Psychotherapist
4A Greenfields Avenue, Bromborough,
Wirral L62 6DD
BASMT

Judith Jones
Sexual and Marital Psychotherapist
Irby Farm, Thingwall Road, Irby, Wirral
L61 3UA
BASMT

Paul Stephen Keenan
Cognitive Behavioural Psychotherapist
Dept of Psychiatry, Clatterbridge
Hospital, Bebington, Wirral,
Merseyside L63 4JY
Tel: 0151 334 4000 x 4028/0151 327
5867
BABCP

Des Kennedy
Gestalt Psychotherapist
Shalom, 36 Hillside Road, West Kirby,
Wirral L48 8BB
Tel: 0151 625 9839
GPTI, MET

Helen Marks
Systemic Psychotherapist
8 Salisbury Road, Liverpool L19 0PJ
FIC

Susan Martin
Hypno-Psychotherapist
10 Moss Lane, Orrell Park, Liverpool
L9 8AJ
Tel: 0151 525 1043
CTS

Sheila Mattison
Psychoanalytic Psychotherapist
16 Countisbury Drive, Liverpool
L16 0JJ
Tel: 0151 722 9482
LPDO

Eileen McAleer
Integrative Psychotherapist
Flat 6, 80-82 Egerton Street, Wallasey,
Merseyside L45 2LT
Tel: 051 639 7816
RCSPC

Damien McVey
Hypno-Psychotherapist
12 Rodney Street, Liverpool L1 2TE
Tel: 0151 709 1900
CTS

Julia Nelki
Family Therapist
Dept of Psychological Medicine, RLCH
(Myrtle St Hospital), Myrtle Street,
Liverpool
AFT

Pierce J O'Carroll
Cognitive Behavioural Psychotherapist
Liverpool John Moores University,
Centre for Psychology, Trumean Street,
Liverpool L3 2ET
Tel: 0151 231 4233
BABCP

Christopher Pitt
Family Therapist
Barnardos Family Therapy Service,
Mornington Terrace, 29 Upper Duke
Street, Liverpool L1 9DY
Tel: 0151 709 0540
AFT

Charlie Scott
Psychoanalytic Psychotherapist
Psychology Service, Wirral Community
Healthcare (NHS), St Catherines
Comm Hospital, Birkenhead,
Merseyside L42 0RQ
Tel: 0151 604 7276
LPDO

Michael Scott
Cognitive Behavioural Psychotherapist
39 Hayles Green, Liverpool L25 4SG
Tel: 0151 428 6846
BABCP

Geraldine Sharples
Psychoanalytic Psychotherapist
Psychology Service, Whiston Hospital,
Prescot, Merseyside L35 5DR
Tel: 0151 430 1321
LPDO

G C Shetty
Psychoanalytic Psychotherapist
Psychiatry Department, Ashworth
Hospital, Parkbourn, Maghull, Liverpool
L31 1HW
Tel: 0151 473 0303
LPDO

Flo M F Smith
Psychoanalytic Psychotherapist
Wirral Community Healthcare Trust,
Saint Catherines Hospital, Church
Road, Birkenhead, Wirral L42 0RQ
Tel: 0151 678 7272
LPDO

Margaret Smith
Psychoanalytic Psychotherapist
13 St Anthony's Road, Blundellsands,
Liverpool L23 8TN
Tel: 0151 931 5194
LPDO

June Stewart
Psychoanalytic Psychotherapist
Sunnyside, Reeds Brow, Rainford,
St Helens WA11 8PD
LPDO

Patsy Taylor
Psychoanalytic Psychotherapist
University of Liverpool, Counselling
Service, 14 Oxford Street, Liverpool
L7 7BL
Tel: 0151 794 3304
LPDO

Julie Wetherill
Group Analyst
6 Waverley Grove, Prenton, Wirral
L49 9PU
Tel: 01928 575073/0151 608 7442
IGA

Pete Woodall
Psychoanalytic Psychotherapist
South Liverpool Child & Family
Consultation Team, T Ward, Alder Hey
Childrens Hospital, Eaton Road,
Liverpool L12 2AP
LPDO

A E Woods
Psychoanalytic Psychotherapist
Occupational Therapy/Physiotherapy
Department, Whiston Hospital,
Prescot, Merseyside L35 5DR
Tel: 0151 430 1131
LPDO

Rae Woodward
Psychoanalytic Psychotherapist
Saint Catherine's Hospital, Church
Road, Birkenhead, Wirral L42 0LQ
Tel: 0151 604 7276
LPDO

MIDDLESEX

Helena Alder
Integrative Psychotherapist
35 Chiltern View Road, Uxbridge,
Middlesex UB8 2PF
Tel: 01895 257900
MC

Jacqueline Ardeman
Family Therapist
44 Stanmore Hill, Stanmore, Middlesex
HA7 3BN
Tel: 0181 954 1462
AFT

Jenny Averbeck
Transpersonal Psychotherapist
310 Hoe Lane, Enfield, Middlesex
EN1 4JW
CCPE

Jocelyn Avigad
Systemic Psychotherapist
26 Rosecroft Walk, Pinner, Middlesex
HA5 1LL
IFT

Raymond Blake
Group Analyst
31 Upper Grotto Road, Twickenham,
Middlesex TW1 4NG
Tel: 0171 352 7026/0181 892 9494
IGA

Elizabeth Bostock
Psychoanalytic Psychotherapist
1 Selborne Gardens, Greenford,
Middlesex UB6 7PD
Tel: 0181 998 2883
LCP, BAP

Lesley Brown
Integrative Psychosynthesis
Psychotherapist, Gestalt
Psychotherapist
'Brightwater', Dunally Park,
Shepperton, Middlesex TW17 8LJ
Tel: 01932 220590
MET, GPTI, RE.V

Clare Brunt
Individual and Group Humanistic
Psychotherapist
97 Warren Road, Whitton,
Twickenham, Middlesex TW2 1DJ
Tel: 0181 755 0353
AHPP

Monica Burton
Hypno-Psychotherapist
18 Beechwood Avenue, South Harrow,
Middlesex HA2 8BY
Tel: 0181 422 0402
NSHAP

Helen Carroll
Integrative Psychosynthesis
Psychotherapist
St Dominics, 39 Rushout Road, Kenton,
Harrow HA3 0AS
Tel: 0181 907 3908
RE.V

Stanley Chandler
Hypno-Psychotherapist
Shandon, Poplar Close, Pinner,
Middlesex HA5 3PZ
Tel: 0181 868 1372
NRHP

Tony Clapp
Psychoanalytic Psychotherapist
10 Willow Road, Enfield, Middlesex
EN1 3NE
Tel: 0181 366 7338
LCP

Nita Clark
Analytical Psychologist-Jungian Analyst
16 Bellfield Avenue, Harrow Weald,
Middlesex HA3 6SX
Tel: 0181 421 1879
AJA

Evelyn Cleavely
Psychoanalytic Marital Psychotherapist
8 Cox's Avenue, Grange Farm, Upper
Halliford, Shepperton, Middlesex
TW17 8TE
Tel: 01932 789088
TMSI

Cassie Cooper
Personal Construct Psychotherapist
12 Coniston Court, High Street,
Harrow on the Hill, Middlesex
HA1 3LP
Tel: 0181 423 9386
CPCP

Suzanne Cooper
Holistic Psychotherapist, Body
Psychotherapist
5 Lawrence Road, Pinner, Middlesex
HA5 1LH
Tel: 0181 866 1521
CCHP

Ursula Cornish
Family Psychotherapist, Family
Therapist
Pharmacia House, Prince Regent Road,
Hounslow, Middlesex TW3 1NE
Tel: 0181 572 1180
IFT

Anita Courtman
Psychosynthesis Psychotherapist
252 St Margarets Road, Twickenham,
Middlesex TW1 1PR
Tel: 0181 893 2324
PET

Verena Crick
Child Psychotherapist
Barnet Child & Family Consultation
Service, Edgware General Hospital,
Edgware, Middlesex HA8 0AD
Tel: 0181 905 6679/0171 431 1761
ACP

Anne Cussins
Psychoanalytic Psychotherapist
55a Pope's Avenue, Strawberry Hill,
Twickenham, Middlesex TW2 5TD
Tel: 0181 898 1366
IPSS

MIDDLESEX

Lesley Day
Integrative Psychotherapist
41 Ailsa Avenue, St Margarets,
Twickenham, Middlesex TW1 1NF
Tel: 0181 892 2076
MET

Michael Day
Systemic Psychotherapist, Family
Therapist
1 Burtons Road, Hampton Hill
TW12 1DB
Tel: 0181 977 7280
AFT, KCC

Sally Day
Psychoanalytic Psychotherapist
27 Trafalgar Road, Twickenham, Middx
TW2 5EJ
Tel: 0181 894 1609
IPC

Paul Dean
Individual and Group Humanistic
Psychotherapist, Integrative Arts
Psychotherapist
74 Lincoln Avenue, Twickenham,
Middlesex TW2 6NP
Tel: 0181 898 2522
IATE, AHPP, MET

Sally Dean
Psychoanalytic Psychotherapist
74 Lincoln Avenue, Twickenham,
Middlesex TW2 6NP
Tel: 0181 898 2522
IPC

Christine Deering
Psychoanalytic Psychotherapist
6a Murray Road, Northwood,
Middlesex HA6 2JY
Tel: 01923 823790
LCP, NAAP

Ruth Fasht
Group Analyst
'Gayton', 23 Aylmer Drive, Stanmore,
Middlesex HA7 3EJ
Tel: 0181 954 4710
IGA

Albina Fitzgerald-Butler
Hypno-Psychotherapist
'Ivy Cottage', Ealing Road, Northolt
Village, Middx UB5 6AA
Tel: 0181 841 4092
NRHP

Liliana Gilli
Psychosynthesis Psychotherapist
16 Clovelly Close, Ickenham, Middlesex
UB10 8PT
Tel: 01895 677405
PET

Claire Glasscoe
Family Psychotherapist
Children & Families Consultation
Service, West London Healthcare NHS
Trust, Windmill Lodge, Uxbridge Road,
Southall, Middx UB1 3EU
IFT

Pam Goldstein
Systemic Psychotherapist
18 Hazledene Drive, Pinner, Middlesex
HA5 3NJ
Tel: 0181 429 1640
KCC

Deidre Gordon
Core Process Psychotherapist
19 Sudbury Court Drive, Harrow,
Middlesex HA1 3SZ
Tel: 0181 904 6488
KI

Graham Gorman
Hypno-Psychotherapist
33 Westholme Gardens, Ruislip, Middx
HA4 8QJ
Tel: 01895 633753
NRHP

Thomas Goss
Psychosynthesis Psychotherapist
Anzac Cottage, Hill End Road,
Harefield, Middlesex UB9 6LH
Tel: 01895 824811
PET

June Green
Psychoanalytic Psychotherapist
'Redholme', 15 Ducks Hill Road,
Northwood, Middx HA6 2NW
Tel: 01923 824858
IPSS

Michael Harari
Analytical Psychologist-Jungian Analyst,
Child Psychotherapist
15 Woodside Road, Northwood,
Middlesex HA6 3QE
Tel: 01923 825880
SAP, ACP

Liesel Hearst
Group Analyst
78 Elm Park, Stanmore, Middlesex
HA7 4BQ
Tel: 0181 440 1451/0181 954 7999
IGA

Anita Hobbs
Sexual and Marital Psychotherapist
89 Syon Park Gardens, Osterley,
Middlesex TW7 5NF
Tel: 0181 568 4967
BASMT

Ralph Horton
Psychoanalytic Psychotherapist
99 Church Road, Ashford, Middlesex
Tel: 01784 252459
AGIP

Wendy Kingsnorth
Psychoanalytic Psychotherapist
91 First Avenue, Bush Hill Park, Enfield
EN1 1BW
Tel: 0181 363 3821
IPC

Claudius Kokott
Integrative Psychotherapist, Body
Psychotherapist
19 Clitherow Road, Brentford, Middx
TW8 9JT
Tel: 0181 568 0589
CCHP

Michael Kulyk
Hypno-Psychotherapist
313 Martindale Road, Hounslow,
Middlesex TW4 7HG
Tel: 0181 570 3795
NRHP

Bernie Laschinger
Attachment-based Psychoanalytic
Psychotherapist
27 Chalkhill Road, Wembley Park,
London HA9 9DS
Tel: 0181 904 2176
CAPP

Penny Lewis
Systemic Psychotherapist
10 Haweswater House, Summerwood
Road, Isleworth, Middlesex TW7 7QL
Tel: 0956 934825/0181 891 4867/0956
KCC

Tina Lucas
Group Analyst
24 Montpelier Row, Twickenham,
Middlesex TW1 2NQ
Tel: 0181 892 6584
IGA

Maria Lynch
Analytical Psychologist-Jungian Analyst
34 Abbotsmede Close, Strawberry Hill,
Twickenham TW1 4RL
Tel: 0181 891 4242
BAP

Veronica Marsden
Gestalt Psychotherapist
59 Manor Lane, Sunbury on Thames
TW16 5EB
Tel: 01932 786147
GCL

Brandy Martin
Transpersonal Psychotherapist
1 Amhurst Gardens, Isleworth, Middx
TW7 6AW
CCPE

Greta Mattar
Hypno-Psychotherapist
14 Chestnut Manor Close, Staines,
Middlesex TW18 1AQ
Tel: 01784 464567
NRHP

Monica Meinrath
Group Analyst
31 Bushey Park Gardens, Teddington,
Middlesex TW11 0LQ
Tel: 0181 977 2242
IGA

Beckie Menckhoff
Analytical Psychologist-Jungian Analyst
23 The Chase, Eastcote, Pinner,
Middlesex HA5 1SJ
Tel: 01895 250741/0181 866 9093
BAP

Suzanne Michaud-Lennox
Psychoanalytic Psychotherapist
20 Heming Road, Edgware, London
HA8 9AE
Tel: 0181 952 2418
IPSS

Bahman Mostaeddi
Child Psychotherapist
Ealing Hospital, Windmill Lodge,
Uxbridge Road, Southall, Middlesex
UB1 3EU
Tel: 0181 340 8864
ACP

David Newns
Transpersonal Psychotherapist
110 Waterloo Road, Uxbridge,
Middlesex UB8 2QY
Tel: 01895 467046
CCPE

Giuliana Norsa
Child Psychotherapist
Enfield Child & Family Service, 8
Dryden Road, Enfield EN1 2PP
Tel: 0181 360 6771
ACP

Christopher Perry
Analytical Psychologist-Jungian Analyst
64 Sidney Road, St Margarets,
Twickenham TW1 1JR
Tel: 0181 892 3126
SAP, BAP

Julie Petrie-Kokott
Integrative Psychotherapist, Body
Psychotherapist
19 Clitherow Road, Brentford,
Middlesex TW8 9JT
Tel: 0181 568 0589
CCHP

Asha Phillips
Child Psychotherapist
11 Fallowfield, Stanmore, Middlesex
HA7 3DF
Tel: 0181 954 4909
ACP

Barbara Pokorny
Psychoanalytic Psychotherapist
28 Glendale Gardens, Wembley, Middx
HA9 8PS
Tel: 0181 904 7878
LCP

Glyn Powell
NLP Psychotherapist
67 Waldegrave Road, Teddington,
Middlesex TW11 8LA
Tel: 0181 943 9215
ANLP

Diane Rees-Roberts
Psychoanalytic Psychotherapist
12 Cambridge Crescent, Teddington,
Middlesex TW11 8DY
Tel: 0181 977 7282
IPC

Susan Ricketts
Child Psychotherapist
48 Sherland Road, Twickenham,
Middlesex TW1 4HD
Tel: 01703 284352
ACP

Janet Rimmer
Psychosynthesis Psychotherapist
Northlands, 24 Parkfield Gardens,
Harrow, Middlesex HA2 6JR
Tel: 0181 863 1931
PET

June Roberts
Psychoanalytic Psychotherapist
57 St Margaret's Road, Twickenham
TW1 2LL
Tel: 0181 891 1205
IPSS

Wendy Schaffer-Fielding
Child Psychotherapist
Barnet Child & Family Consultation
Service, Child Guidance Centre, East
Road, Burnt Oak, Edgware, Middx
HA8 0BT
Tel: 0181 359 3801/0181 445 5614
ACP

Daphne Seaman
Sexual and Marital Psychotherapist
29 Manor Way, North Harrow,
Middlesex HA2 6BZ
BASMT

Thomas R Shortall
Cognitive Behavioural Psychotherapist
309 Carr Road, Northolt, Middlesex
UB5 4RW
Tel: 0181 966 7000 x 299/
0181 864 1482
BABCP

Judy Shuttleworth
Child Psychotherapist
Enfield Child & Family Service, Avenue
House, 8 Bycullah Avenue, Enfield
EN2 8DW
Tel: 0181 367 8844/0181 883 7908
ACP

Iris Singer
Attachment-based Psychoanalytic
Psychotherapist
1 Fairfield Avenue, Edgware, Middlesex
HA8 9AG
Tel: 0181 952 3931
CAPP

Cheryl Sklan
Psychoanalytic Psychotherapist
9 Dorset Drive, Edgware, Middlesex
HA8 7NT
Tel: 0181 381 1709/0181 952 3743
BAP

David Stafford
Psychoanalytic Psychotherapist
19 Thorpe Road, Staines, Middlesex
TW18 3HD
Tel: 0956 340655/01784 451647
AAP

Frances Stearman
Psychoanalytic Psychotherapist
20 South Road, Twickenham, Middx
TW2 5NU
Tel: 0181 977 1658
LCP

Susan Storring
Child Psychotherapist
Barnet Child & Family Consultation
Service, Child Guidance Centre, East
Road, Burnt Oak, Edgware, Middlesex
HA8 0BT
Tel: 0181 445 5539/0181 359 3801
ACP

Robert I Sutherland
Hypno-Psychotherapist
69 Sherwood Avenue, Greenford,
Middlesex UB6 OPQ
Tel: 0181 864 8795
NRHP

Joanna Swift
Psychoanalytic Psychotherapist
5 Beresford Avenue, Twickenham,
Middlesex TW1 2PY
Tel: 0181 892 4722
PA

Jill Taylor
Biodynamic Psychotherapist
65 Mereway Road, Twickenham,
Middlesex TW2 6RF;
Idol Lane, London EC3R 5DD
Tel: 0181 898 2805
BTC

Bill Thorndycraft
Group Analytic Psychotherapist
90 Court Way, Twickenham, Middlesex
TW2 7SW;
St Thomas Psychotherapy Dept, Dept
of Psychiatry, St Thomas Hospital,
London SE1 7EH
Tel: 0181 892 4376/
0171 928 9292 x 2272
IPC

Barbara Traynor
Transactional Analysis Psychotherapist
24 Bristow Road, Hounslow, Middlesex
TW3 1UP
Tel: 0181 570 9438/0181 572 0650
ITA, MET

Salley Vickers
Psychoanalytic Psychotherapist
5 The Butts, Brentford, Middlesex
TW8 8BJ
Tel: 0181 560 6490
GUILD

Liz Wadland
Family Therapist
Wembley Vicarage, 3 Crawford
Avenue, Wembley, London HA0 2HX
Tel: 0181 902 0273
AFT

John Ward
Psychoanalytic Psychotherapist
123 Amyand Park Road, Twickenham
TW1 3HN
Tel: 0181 570 5200
AGIP

Ann Wells
Child Psychotherapist
Uxbridge Child & Adolescent Mental
Health Service, 26 Bennetts Yard,
Lancaster Road, Uxbridge, Middlesex
UB8 1JH
Tel: 01892 56521/4/0181 452 3804
ACP

Sarah Weston
Analytical Psychologist-Jungian Analyst
19 Belmont Road, Twickenham,
Middlesex TW2 5DA
Tel: 0181 755 0133/0181 898 4388
BAP

Patricia Wheeler
Psychoanalytic Psychotherapist
30a Wolsey Road, Ashford, Middlesex
TW15 2RB
Tel: 01784 246611
LCP

Max Wilkins
Humanistic Psychotherapist
29c Broom Road, Teddington,
Middlesex TW11 9PG
Tel: 0181 977 3577
CCHP

Pamela Wolfe
Psychosynthesis Psychotherapist
48 Fairacres, Ruislip, Middlesex
HA4 8AW
Tel: 01845 631 094
IPS

NORFOLK

Remy Aquarone
Psychoanalytic Psychotherapist
11 Pottergate, Norwich NR2 1DS
Tel: 01603 633115
LCP

Simon Burton
Systemic Psychotherapist
17 Eade Road, Norwich
Tel: 01603 421950 x 421961/
01603 667072
KCC

Raymond F Docking
Systemic Psychotherapist
1 Kettlewell Lane, King's Lynn, Norfolk
PE30 1PW
Tel: 01553 767520
KCC

Christine Ender
Psychosynthesis Psychotherapist
8 Russell Terrace, Trowse, Norwich
NR14 8TQ
Tel: 01603 626 831
IPS

Ursula Harben
Systemic Psychotherapist
29 Unthank Road, Norfolk NR2 2PB
Tel: 01603 630681
KCC

Sally Hart
Humanistic Psychotherapist
26 Grant Street, Norwich NR2 4HA
Tel: 01603 623795
AHPP

Elizabeth Hoare
Systemic Psychotherapist
Roydon Hall, Diss, Norfolk IP22 3XL
Tel: 01379 642155
KCC

Jacqui Hughes
Gestalt Psychotherapist
62 Unthank Road, Norwich NR2 2RN
Tel: 01603 625090
GPTI

Nicholas Irving
Transactional Analysis Psychotherapist
22 Lynn Road, Hillington, Kings Lynn,
Norfolk PE30 6DD
Tel: 01485 600987
ITA

Patricia Kerkham
Psychoanalytic Psychotherapist
Banklands, Clenchwarton, King's Lynn,
Norfolk PE34 4DB
Tel: 01553 773854
IPSS

Jon Little
Integrative Psychotherapist
14 Central Close, Hethersett, Norwich
NR9 3ER
Tel: 01603 810946
RCSPC

Elspeth McAdam
Systemic Psychotherapist
89 St Leonard's Road, Norwich
NR1 4JF
Tel: 01603 421 978/01603 622 440
KCC

Jean Mundy
Biodynamic Psychotherapist
7 Caystreward, Great Yarmouth,
Norfolk NR30 4AS
Tel: 01493 850867
BTC

Peg Nunneley
Biodynamic Psychotherapist
The Dial House, Foulsham, Dereham,
Norfolk NR20 4RT
Tel: 0136 284 4216
BTC

Jane Polden
Psychoanalytic Psychotherapist
16 Catton Grove Road, Norwich
NR3 3NH
AGIP

Francois Reynolds
NLP Psychotherapist
8 Town Close Road, Norwich, Norfolk
NR2 2NB
Tel: 01603 622542
ANLP

Susan Richardson
Hypno-Psychotherapist
25 Cypress Close, Taverham, Norwich,
Norfolk NR8 6QG
Tel: 01603 861019
NRHP

Paddie Smith
Integrative Psychotherapist, Body
Psychotherapist
'Coppers', 20b St Nicholas Place,
Sheringham, Norfolk NR26 8LF
Tel: 01263 825346
CCHP

Dorothea Elizabeth West
Psychoanalytic Psychotherapist
Trotters, Edgefield Hall Farm, Norwich
Road, Edgefield, Norfolk NR24 2RS
Tel: 01263 713 799
IPC

Jonathan Whines
Gestalt Psychotherapist
62 Unthank Road, Norwich NR2 2RN
Tel: 01603 663186
GPTI

Mary Wilkinson
Systemic Psychotherapist
Yew Tree Cottage, Stocks Hill,
Bawburgh, Norwich NR9 3LL
Tel: 01603 811456
KCC

Martyn Wood-Bevan
Group Analytic Psychotherapist
St Augustine's Psychotherapy Practice,
39 Exchange Street, Norwich, Norfolk
NR2 1DP;
Ipswich Psychotherapy & Counselling
Centre, 25 St Margarets Green,
Ipswich, Suffolk IP4 2BN
Tel: 01603 633791/01473 216559
IPC

Rosemary Wood-Bevan
Integrative Psychotherapist
Bede Cottage, 26 St Augustines Street,
Norwich NR3 3BZ
Tel: 01603 633791
MC

NORTH HUMBERSIDE

Nancy Blake
NLP Psychotherapist
102 Park Avenue, Princes Avenue, Hull
HU5 3ET
Tel: 01482 447765
ANLP

G N Bolsover
Psychoanalytic Psychotherapist, Family
Psychotherapist
6A Station Road, Brough, Nr Hull, East
Yorkshire HU15 1DX
Tel: 01482 665412
HIP, IFT, YAPP

Michael Wang
Cognitive Behavioural Psychotherapist
Deptartment of Psychology, University
of Hull, Cottingham Road, Hull
HU6 7RX
BABCP

NORTH YORKSHIRE

Liz Bulmer
Transactional Analysis Psychotherapist
7a Belgrave Crescent, Harrogate,
North Yorkshire HG2 8HZ
Tel: 01423 508281
ITA

C W Burdett
Cognitive Behavioural Psychotherapist
37 Broomfield Avenue, Northallerton,
North Yorkshire DL7 8RH
Tel: 01609 771 528/01325 743 566
BABCP

Leslie Davidoff
Psychoanalytic Psychotherapist
18 Broadway West, Fulford, York
YO1 4JJ
Tel: 01904 621866
IPSS

Suzanne Davidoff
Hypno-Psychotherapist
18 Broadway West, Fulford, York
YO1 4JJ
Tel: 01904 621866
NRHP

Graeme Farquharson
Group Analyst
'Oaklands', 4 Aislabie Close,
Clotherholme Road, Ripon, North
Yorkshire HG4 2DD
Tel: 01628 668645/01765 608452 (f)
IGA

Sarah Greening
Integrative Psychotherapist
5 South Parade, Northallerton, North
Yorkshire DL7 8SE
Tel: 01607 776680
SCPC

Rima Handley
Psychosynthesis Psychotherapist
34 St James Green, Thirsk, North
Yorkshire YO7 1AG
Tel: 0191 490 0274
PET

Bridget Hester
Psychoanalytic Psychotherapist
The Old Rectory, Crayke, York
YO6 4TA
Tel: 01347 821593
YAPP, LPDO

Helen Jones
Personal Construct Psychotherapist
58 Aldwark, York YO1 2BU
Tel: 01904 630 517
CPCP

Marlene Jones
Family Therapist
18 Guards Court, Burniston Road,
Scarborough
IFT

David Kennard
Group Analyst, Psychodynamic
Psychotherapist
24 St Oswalds Road, Fulford, York
YO1 4PF;
The Retreat, York YO1 5BN
Tel: 01904 412551/01904 633415
IGA, YAPP

Christine Kennett
Gestalt Psychotherapist
38 Millfield Road, York YO2 1NQ
Tel: 01904 638623
SPTI

Gill Martin
Psychodynamic Psychotherapist
34 The Old Village, Huntington, York
YO3 9RB
Tel: 01904 750285
YAPP

Una McCluskey
Psychodynamic Psychotherapist, Family
Therapist
Dept of Social Policy & Social Work,
University of York, Heslington, York
YO1 5DD;
The Yews, Waplington Hall,
Allerthorpe, York YO4 4RS
Tel: 01759 302104
YAPP, AFT

Liza Miller
Family Therapist
10 St Oswald's Road, Fulford, York
YO1 4PF
Tel: 01904 633417
AFT

Graham Payne
Psychoanalytic Psychotherapist
Dept of Mental Health, Friarage
Hospital, Northallerton DL6 1JG
Tel: 01609 779911
NAAP

Helen Proudley
Sexual and Marital Psychotherapist
Doxford House, 73 Front Street,
Sowerby, Thirsk, N Yorks YO7 1JP
BASMT

Stephen Reilly
Psychodynamic Psychotherapist
Bootham Park Hospital, York YO3 7BY
Tel: 01904 610777 x 4018
YAPP

Robert Tyson
Gestalt Psychotherapist
Forge House, 65 High Street, Snainton,
Scarborough, North Yorkshire
YO13 9AL
Tel: 01723 859265
GPTI

Heward Wilkinson
Integrative Psychotherapist
25 Mayville Avenue, Scarborough,
Yorks YO12
Tel: 01723 376246
SPTI

Kate Wilkinson
Gestalt Psychotherapist, Integrative
Psychotherapist
25 Mayville Avenue, Scarborough,
Yorks YO12
Tel: 01723 376246
SPTI

Ewa Wojiechowska
Group Analyst
'Oaklands', 4 Aislabie Close,
Clotherholme Road, Ripon, North
Yorkshire HG4 2DD
Tel: 01765 604982
IGA

NORTHAMPTONSHIRE

Barry Bowen
Family Therapist
76 St Peter's Avenue, Kettering,
Northants NN16 0HB
Tel: 01536 515476
AFT

Alec Clark
Family Therapist
280 Wellingham Road, Rushden,
Northants NN10 9XP
Tel: 01933 386354
AFT

Christine Hamblin
Analytical Psychologist-Jungian Analyst
23 Woodford Street, Northampton
NN1 5EN
Tel: 01604 37681/01604 30115
SAP

Terry Lear
Group Analyst
140 St George's Avenue, Northampton
NN2 6JF
Tel: 01604 713616
IGA

Clive G Long
Cognitive Behavioural Psychotherapist
St Andrews Hospital, Billing Road,
Northampton NN1 5DG
Tel: 01604 29696
BABCP

Peter Marsden-Allen
Family Therapist
33 Alfred Street, Rushden,
Northamptonshire NN10 9YS;
The Crescent Family Centre, 11-12
Highbury Crescent, Islington, London
N5 1RN
Tel: 0171 4774130/01933 411476
AFT

Pamela Milne
Cognitive Behavioural Psychotherapist
St Andrew's Hospital, Billing Road,
Northampton NN1 5DG
Tel: 01604 29696 x 580
BABCP

Helen M O'Neill
Cognitive Behavioural Psychotherapist
Occupational Therapy Dept, St
Andrews Hospital, Northampton
NN1 5DG
Tel: 01604 29696 x 533
BABCP

Julie Roberts
Group Analyst
4 Clumber Drive, Edgemont Grange,
Northampton NN3 3NX
Tel: 01604 412376
IGA

Jenny Sprince
Child Psychotherapist
Thornby Hall, Peper Harrow
Foundation, Northampton
Tel: 01604 740001/0171 241 2911
ACP

Harry Tough
Group Analyst
102 Church Way, Weston Favell,
Northampton NN3 3BQ
Tel: 01604 28984
IGA

NORTHERN IRELAND

Jarlath Benson
Psychosynthesis Psychotherapist,
Psychoanalytic Psychotherapist
The Belfast Counselling and Training
Centre, Office 22, 40 Victoria Street,
Belfast, Northern Ireland BT1 4QB
Tel: 01232 242597
IPS

Avril Brown
Sexual and Marital Psychotherapist
113 University Street, Belfast,
Northern Ireland BT7 1HP
Tel: 01247 873908
BASMT

Mary Cairns
Psychoanalytic Psychotherapist
171 Barnett's Road, Belfast, N Ireland
BT5 7BG
Tel: 01232 489 422
AAP

Stephen Coulter
Family Therapist
8 Five Acres, Portadown, N Ireland
BT63 5UH
Tel: 01762 337113
AFT

Terry Cromey
Cognitive Behavioural Psychotherapist
'Brakken', 43 Sheridan Drive, Helen's
Bay, Co Down, N Ireland BT19 1LB
Tel: 01247 853473/01247 454276
BABCP

P Davis
Psychoanalytic Psychotherapist
28 Brookvale Avenue, Belfast
BT14 6BW
Tel: 01232 744676
WMIP

Ian G Hanley
Cognitive Behavioural Psychotherapist
7 Lynnehurst Drive, Comber, Co
Down, Northern Ireland BT23 5LN
Tel: 01247 873644
BABCP

Marie Kenny
Family Therapist
Child, Adolescent & Family
Consultation Centre, 30a/b Station
Road, Antrim BT41 4BS
AFT

Ruth Lawson
Cognitive Behavioural Psychotherapist
52A Church Street, Newtownards, Co
Down, Northern Ireland BT23 4AL
Tel: 01247 820660
BABCP

Noel McCune
Family Psychotherapist
Child and Family Clinic, Psychiatric
Department, Craigavon Area Hospital,
Craigavon BT63 5QQ
Tel: 01762 334444
AFT

NORTHUMBERLAND

William Brough
Psychoanalytic Psychotherapist
Holeyn Hall, Wylam, Northumberland
Tel: 01661 852 535
NAAP

Iain Cameron
Psychoanalytic Psychotherapist
Poplars Annexe, Cherry Knowle
Hospital, Ryhope, Sunderland
Tel: 0191 569 9415
NAAP

Patricia Marshall
Psychoanalytic Psychotherapist
St Georges Hospital, Morpeth,
Northumberland
Tel: 01670 512121
NAAP

Jan McGregor-Hepburn
Psychoanalytic Psychotherapist
Post Office Cottage, Station Bank,
Mickley, Stocksfield, Northumberland
Tel: 01661 842727
LCP, NAAP

Susan Proctor
Psychoanalytic Psychotherapist
St Georges Hospital, Morpeth,
Northumberland
Tel: 01670 512121
NAAP

Amanda Stafford
Psychoanalytic Psychotherapist
10 West Lawn, Ashbrooke, Sunderland
SR2 7HW
Tel: 0191 522 6913
NAAP

NOTTINGHAMSHIRE

Judith Anderson
Analytical Psychotherapist
115 Main Street, East Bridgford,
Nottingham NG13 8NH;
Clinical Science Building, Leicester
Royal Infirmary, PO Box 65, Leicester
LE2 7LX
Tel: 01949 20871
WMIP

Mark Aveline
Psychoanalytic Psychotherapist
Nottingham Psychotherapy Unit
(NHS), St Ann's House, 114
Thorneywood Mount, Nottingham
NG3 2PZ
Tel: 0115 962 7891
STTDP

George Bassett
Gestalt Psychotherapist
c/o SPTI, 2 St James Terrace,
Nottingham NG1 6FW
Tel: 0115 961 7911
SPTI

Diane Beechcroft
Transactional Analysis Psychotherapist
178 Harrington Drive, Lenton,
Nottingham NG7 1JH
Tel: 01159 414378
ITA

David C Blore
Cognitive Behavioural Psychotherapist
Millbrook Mental Health Unit, Kings
Mill Centre, Mansfield Road, Sutton-in-
Ashfield, Notts NG17 4JT
Tel: 01623 785050 x 3428/
01623 784773
BABCP

Carolyn Brown
Gestalt Psychotherapist
10 Hampden Grove, Beeston,
Nottingham NG9 1FG
Tel: 0115 925 9083
SPTI

Pat Bryant
Gestalt Psychotherapist
6 Clumber Avenue, West Bridgeford,
Nottingham NG2 6DQ
Tel: 0115 924 3606
SPTI

Raymond T Challis
Hypno-Psychotherapist
Adam House Medical Centre, 85-91
Derby Road, Sandicare, Nottingham
NG10 5HZ
Tel: 0115 960 6116
NRHP

Janine Cherry-Swaine
Child Psychotherapist
Thorneywood Child & Adolescent
Psychiatry Unit, Porchester Road,
Mapperley, Nottingham NG3 6LF
Tel: 01159 587888/01159 529479 (f)
ACP

Sonia Coats
Sexual and Marital Psychotherapist
The Orchards, Church Lane,
Attenborough, Nottinghamshire
NG9 6AS
BASMT

Penny Cooper
Sexual and Marital Psychotherapist
25 Cresta Gardens, Mapperley,
Nottingham NG3 5GD
BASMT

Gitta Drury
Gestalt Psychotherapist
c/o SPTI, 2 St James Terrace,
Nottingham NG1 6FW
Tel: 0115 924 3994
SPTI

Katie Dunn
Behavioural Psychotherapist
32A George Road, West Bridgford,
Nottingham NG2 7QG
Tel: 0115 945 5990
BABCP

Richard Erskine
Integrative Psychotherapist
c/o 31 Foxhill Road, Burton Joyce,
Nottingham NG14 5DB
Tel: 0115 924 3994
SPTI

Ken Evans
Integrative Psychotherapist
The Sherwood Psychotherapy Training
Institute, Thiskney House, 2 St James
Terrace, Nottingham NG1 6FW
Tel: 0115 924 3994
SPTI, GPTI, MET

Mairi M Evans
Transactional Analysis Psychotherapist
The Sherwood Psychotherapy Training
Institute, Thiskney House, 2, St James
Terrace, Nottingham NG1 6FW
Tel: 0115 924 3994
SPTI

Andrew Fookes
Gestalt Psychotherapist
17 Brancaster Close, Cinderhill,
Nottingham NG6 8SL
Tel: 0115 927 2940
SPTI, GPTI

William Galbreath
Gestalt Psychotherapist
25 George Road, West Bridgeford,
Nottingham NG2 6DQ
Tel: 0115 945 5290
SPTI

Michael Gent
Hypno-Psychotherapist
14 Sherwood Road, Rainworth,
Mansfield, Notts NG21 0LJ
Tel: 01623 796251
NRHP

Hilary E Graham
Hypno-Psychotherapist
25 George Road, West Bridgford,
Nottingham NG2 7PT
Tel: 01159 455290
NRHP

Ian Greenway
Gestalt Psychotherapist
2 St James's Terrace, Nottingham
NG1 6FW
Tel: 0115 924 3994
GPTI

David J Hannigan
Cognitive Behavioural Psychotherapist
Dept of Behavioural Psychotherapy,
Nottingham Psychotherapy Unit, 114
Thorneywood Mount, St Anns,
Nottingham NG3 2PZ
Tel: 0115 952 9458/013784 98220
BABCP

Deborah Hindle
Child Psychotherapist
Thornywood Child & Adolescent
Psychiatry Unit, Porchester Road,
Mapperley, Nottingham NG3 6LF
Tel: 01159 587888/01949 20719
ACP

Rosemary Hutchby
Gestalt Psychotherapist
c/o The Sherwood Psychotherapy
Training Institute, Thiskney House, 2 St
James Terrace, Nottingham NG1 6FW
Tel: 01949 20998
SPTI

Paul Keenan
Transactional Analysis Psychotherapist
7 Manvers Road, West Bridgford,
Nottingham NG2 6DJ
Tel: 0115 960 6082
ITA

Adrienne Lee
Transactional Analysis Psychotherapist
2 Castle Grove, The Park, Nottingham
NG7 1DN
Tel: 01159 473296
ITA

Helen Lee
Psychoanalytic Psychotherapist
Nottingham Psychotherapy Dept
(NHS), St Ann's House, 114
Thorneywood Mount, Nottingham
NG3 2PZ
Tel: 0115 962 7891
STTDP

Ann Morley
Psychoanalytic Psychotherapist
(Jungian)
36 Crosby Road, West Bridgford,
Nottinghamshire NG13 8DW
Tel: 0115 914 0256
WMIP

(Jennifer) Ruth Nathan
Gestalt Psychotherapist
4 Blackacre, Burton Joyce, Nottingham
NG14 5BS
Tel: 0115 931 4275
GPTI, MET

Susan Phillips
Integrative Psychotherapist,
Transactional Analysis Psychotherapist
1 Orchard Close, Southwell,
Nottingham NG25 0DY
Tel: 01636 813 794
MET, ITA

Sheila Pigott
Gestalt Psychotherapist
St Paul's House, Boundary Road, West
Bridgeford, Nottingham NG2 7DB
Tel: 01159 223492
SPTI

Bernard Ratigan
Psychoanalytic Psychotherapist
Nottingham Psychotherapy Dept
(NHS), St Ann's House, 114
Thorneywood Mount, Nottingham
NG3 2PZ
Tel: 0115 962 7891
STTDP

Stephen Regel
Cognitive Behavioural Psychotherapist
Nottingham Natural Health Centre,
354 Mansfield Road, Nottingham
NG5 2EF
Tel: 0115 960 8855
BABCP

Paul Richards
NLP Psychotherapist
Flat 2, 12a Alexandra Street, Sherwood
Rise, Nottingham NG5 1AY
Tel: 0115 985 7372
ANLP

Jonathan Salisbury
Psychodrama Psychotherapist
21 Church Drive, Arnold, Nottingham
NG5 2AS
Tel: 01602 200470
BPDA

Deborah Short
Gestalt Psychotherapist
SPTI, 2 St James Terrace, Nottingham
NG1 6FW
Tel: 0115 924 3994
SPTI

Cora Smith
Integrative Psychotherapist
Sherwood Psychotherapy Training
Institute, Thiskney House, 2 St James
Terrace, Nottingham NG1 6FW
Tel: 0115 924 3994
SPTI

June Stephens
Gestalt Psychotherapist
22 The Paddocks, London Road,
Newark, Nottingham NG24 1SS
Tel: 01636 73456
SPTI

Erika Stern
Integrative Psychotherapist
The Sherwood Psychotherapy Training
Institute, Thiskney House, 2 St James
Terrace, Nottingham NG1 6FW
Tel: 0115 924 3994
SPTI

Ian Stewart
Transactional Analysis Psychotherapist
Old School House, Kingston on Soar,
Nottingham NG11 0DE
Tel: 01509 673569
ITA

Jeannie Thompson
Psychodrama Psychotherapist
21 Church Drive, Arnold, Nottingham
NG5 2AS
Tel: 01602 200470
BPDA

David A Toms
Psychodynamic Psychotherapist
The Manor House, Main Street,
Aslockton, Nottinghamshire
NG13 9AL
Tel: 01949 850374
WMIP

Catriona Walker
Psychoanalytic Psychotherapist
Nottingham Psychotherapy Unit, St
Ann's House, Thorneywood Mount,
Nottingham NG3 2PZ
Tel: 0115 962 7891
STTDP

Keltie Ward
Sexual and Marital Psychotherapist
64 Musters Road, West Bridgford,
Nottingham NG2 7PR
BASMT

Jackie Watts
Integrative Psychotherapist
Sherwood Psychotherapy Training
Institute, Thiskney House, 2 St James
Terrace, Nottingham NG1 6FW
Tel: 0115 924 3994
SPTI

Myra Woolfson
Psychodynamic Psychotherapist
87 Sherwood Vale, Mapperley,
Nottingham NG5 4EB
HIP

Gill Wyatt
Transactional Analysis Psychotherapist,
Integrative Psychotherapist
100 Gertrude Road, West Bridgford,
Notts NG2 5DB
Tel: 01159 821 834
ITA, MET

Raymond Young
Psychoanalytic Psychotherapist
Nottingham Psychotherapy Unit
(NHS), St Ann's House, 114
Thorneywood Mount, Nottingham
NG3 2PZ
Tel: 0115 962 7891
STTDP

OXFORDSHIRE

Patricia M Allen
Transactional Analysis Psychotherapist
33 Butts Road, Horspath, Oxford
OX33 1RJ
Tel: 01865 872388
ITA

Peter Amies
Cognitive Psychotherapist
77 Victoria Road, Summertown,
Oxford OX2 7QG;
31 Wood Street, Swindon SN1 4AN
Tel: 01865 556322/01793 491917
BABCP

Pamela Armitage
Psychoanalytic Psychotherapist
Flat 1, 9 Northmoor Road, Oxford
OX2 6UW
Tel: 01865 58068
GUILD

Steve Bagnall
Family Therapist
Advent House, Manor Court, Kingham,
Oxfordshire OX7 6YZ
Tel: 01608 659 075
IFT

Linda Bloch
Group Analyst
33 Manor Road, South Hinskey, Oxford
OX1 5AS
Tel: 01865 730733
IGA

Kirsten Blow
Family Therapist
2 Woodlands, Mill End, Kidlington,
Oxon OX5 2ER
Tel: 01865 842407
AFT

Maire Brankin
NLP Psychotherapist
19 Norham Road, Oxford OX2 6SF
Tel: 01865 310320
ANLP

Madelyn Brewer
Psychoanalytic Psychotherapist
38 Rectory Road, St Clements, Oxford
OX4 1BU
Tel: 01865 725588
PA

Robin Brown
Psychoanalytic Psychotherapist
23 Alexandra Road, Oxford
Tel: 01865 242400
SIP

Jane Campbell
Group Analyst
227 Kennington Road, Kennington,
Oxford OX1 5PG
Tel: 01865 735519/01865 730347
IGA

Margaret Campbell
Psychoanalytic Psychotherapist
Kiln House, Church Road, Sanford on
Thames OX4 4XZ
Tel: 01865 779556
CFAR

Jean Carr
Analytical Psychologist-Jungian Analyst
12 Windsor Street, Headington,
Oxford OX3 7AP
Tel: 01865 750796
BAP

Joyce Chesterton
Transactional Analysis Psychotherapist
3 Beech House, Ancastle Green,
Henley-on-Thames, Oxon RG9 1UL
Tel: 01491 577726
ITA

Mary Coghlan
Analytical Psychologist-Jungian Analyst
12 Bickerton Road, Headington,
Oxford OX3 7LS
Tel: 01865 61859
SAP

Alexander Coren
Psychoanalytic Psychotherapist
86 Church Way, Iffley, Oxford
OX4 4EF
Tel: 01865 270300/01865 717974
BAP

Gwyn Daniel
Family Therapist
8 Chalfont Road, Oxford OX2 6TH
Tel: 01865 311518
IFT

Marie De'ath
Sexual and Marital Psychotherapist
48 Hermitage Road, Abingdon, Oxon
OX14 5RW
BASMT

Sue Douglas
Humanistic and Integrative
Psychotherapist
Fawler Barn, Kingston Lisle, Nr
Wantage, Oxon OX12 9QJ
Tel: 0136 782 562
BCPC

Mary Duhig
Psychoanalytic Psychotherapist
The Stable Flat, The Old Vicarage,
Little Milton, Oxon OX4 7QB
Tel: 01844 279841
PA

Louise Elwell
Cognitive Analytic Therapist
57 Western Road, Grandpont, Oxford
OX1 4LF
Tel: 01865 724685
ACAT

Daniel Fordwour
Psychoanalytic Psychotherapist
39 Stapleton Road, Headington,
Oxford OX3 7LX
Tel: 01865 741 061
LCP

Michael Gage
Sexual and Marital Psychotherapist
West Street Surgery, 12 West Street,
Chipping Norton, Oxon
BASMT

Sally Gell
Educational Therapist
98 Tower Hill, Witney, Oxon OX8 5ES
Tel: 01993 705547
FAETT

Liana Guy
Psychoanalytic Psychotherapist
33 Marlborough Road, Oxford
OX1 4LW
Tel: 01865 251 812
GUILD

Monica Hanaway
Integrative Psychotherapist
79 Fairacres Road, Iffley Fields, Oxford
OX4 1TQ
Tel: 01865 815690/01865 246905
RCSPC

Gordon Harris
Analytical Psychologist-Jungian Analyst
Hillside, 72 Honey Lane, Cholsey,
Wallingford, Oxon OX10 9NJ
Tel: 01491 651 271/01491 652 840 (f)
BAP, SIP

Peter Haworth
Psychodrama Psychotherapist
8 Rahere Road, Cowley, Oxford
OX4 3QG
Tel: 01865 747604
BPDA

Claudia Herbert
Cognitive Behavioural Psychotherapist
The Oxford Consulting Group, New
Road, Woodstock, Oxfordshire, OX20
1PD
Tel: 01993 813313
BABCP

Penny Hill
Psychoanalytic Psychotherapist
17 Norreys Avenue, Oxford OX1 4ST
Tel: 01865 722259
PA

Michael Hobbs
Group Analyst
Dept of Psychotherapy, Warneford
Hospital, Warneford Lane, Headington,
Oxford OX3 7JX
Tel: 01865 226331
IGA

Pauline Hodson
Psychoanalytic Marital Psychotherapist
14 Brookside, Headington, Oxford
OX3 7PJ
Tel: 01865 62991
TMSI

Peter Hutchinson
Psychodrama Psychotherapist
95 Sunningwell Road, Oxford OX1 4SY
Tel: 01865 246194
BPDA

Penny Jaques
Psychoanalytic Psychotherapist
7 Stanley Road, Oxford OX4 1QY
Tel: 01865 724141
BAP

Linda Johnston
Family Therapist
62 Sadlers Court, Abingdon, Oxon
OX14 2PA
Tel: 01235 530274
AFT

David Jones
Psychoanalytic Psychotherapist
23 Alexandra Road, Oxford OX2 0DD
Tel: 01865 202904
LCP

Jacqueline Keating
Analytical Psychologist-Jungian Analyst
Abbots Piece, Church Lane, Islip
OX5 2TA
Tel: 01865 376162
IGAP

Gillie King
Psychodrama Psychotherapist
12 The Green, Cuddesdon, Oxford
OX33 9JZ
Tel: 01865 873721
BPDA

Jean Knox
Analytical Psychologist-Jungian Analyst
209 Woodstock Road, Oxford
OX2 7AB
Tel: 01865 515550
SAP

Christine K Chemann
Psychoanalytic Psychotherapist
3 Northmoor Road, Oxford
OX2 6UW
Tel: 0865 515160
AGIP

Margaret Landale
Integrative Psychotherapist, Body
Psychotherapist
Mill House, Mill Lane, Dyers Hill,
Charlbury, Oxon OX7 3QG
Tel: 01608 810485
CCHP

Marianna Lutyens
Psychoanalytic Psychotherapist
99 Woodstock Road, Oxford
OX2 6HL;
Richmond House, 235 Upper
Richmond Road, London SW15 6SN
Tel: 01865 331104
IPC

Nick Luxmoore
Psychodrama Psychotherapist
176 Divinity Road, Oxford OX4 1LR
Tel: 01865 245510
BPDA

Catharine Mack Smith
Child Psychotherapist
White Lodge, Osler Road, Oxford
OX3 9BJ
Tel: 01865 62878
ACP

Mira Malovic-Yeeles
Analytical Psychologist-Jungian Analyst
30 Haywards Road, Oxford OX2 8LW
Tel: 01865 226312/01865 56686
BAP

Sheila Millard
Group Analyst
78 Cumnor Hill, Oxford OX2 9HU
Tel: 01865 862 224
IGA

John Miller
Analytical Psychologist-Jungian Analyst
19 Stanley Road, Cowley, Oxford
OX4 1QY;
24 Oxford Road, London NW6
Tel: 0171 328 9430/01865 725203
AJA

Philippa Morrison
Existential Psychotherapist
Church Wing, The Old Rectory,
Church Street, Somerton, Bicester,
Oxfordshire OX6 4NB
Tel: 0171 262 5050 x 3555/
01869 346770
RCSPC

Derry Murphy
Personal Construct Psychotherapist
35 Home Close, Wooton, Oxon
CPCP

Kenneth Newman
Analytical Psychologist-Jungian Analyst
Pinewood, Fox Lane, Boars Hill,
Oxford OX1 5DR
Tel: 01865 326300
IGAP

Ruth Nissim
Family Therapist
Dores Cottage, 17 High Streetl,
Finstock, Oxon OX7 3DA
Tel: 01993 868 147
AFT

Jane Orton
Humanistic and Integrative
Psychotherapist
28 Bloxham Road, Banbury,
Oxfordshire OX16 9JN
Tel: 01295 262626
BCPC

Patrick Parry-Okeden
Psychoanalytic Psychotherapist
Turnworth, Little Blenheim, Yarnton,
Oxford OX5 1LX
Tel: 01865 376446
BAP

Barbara Porter
Transactional Analysis Psychotherapist
Silver Birches, Kingwood Common,
Henley-on-Thames, Oxon RG9 5LR
Tel: 01491 628609
MET

Andrew Powell
Group Analyst, Psychoanalytic
Psychotherapist
Dept of Psychotherapy, Warneford
Hospital, Warneford Lane, Headington,
Oxford OX3 7JX;
Bramley Cottage, 2 Crown Lane,
Dorchester on Thames, Oxon
OX10 7L
Tel: 01865 741717/01865 341715
IGA, BAP, BPDA

John E Ralphs
Psychoanalytic Psychotherapist
209 Woodstock Road, Oxford
OX2 7AB
Tel: 01865 515550
BAP

Davina Rendall
Sexual and Marital Psychotherapist
5 Abberbury Avenue, Iffley Village,
Oxford OX4 4EU
BASMT

Philip Roys
Psychoanalytic Psychotherapist
Dormer House, Horton Cum Studley,
Oxford OX33 1BB
Tel: 01865 351175
BAP

Elizabeth Ryan
Sexual and Marital Psychotherapist
The Old Stores, Wellshead Lane,
Harwell, Oxon OX11 0HD
BASMT

Carole Shadbolt
Transactional Analysis Psychotherapist
11 Alexandra Square, Chipping
Norton, Oxon OX7 5HL
Tel: 01608 644748
MET, ITA

Doreen Shewan
Psychoanalytic Psychotherapist
19 Stanley Road, Oxford OX4 1QY
Tel: 01865 725203
SIP

Fiona Simpson
Transactional Analysis Psychotherapist
Longbarn, 22 St Georges Road,
Wallingford, Oxon OX10 8HP
Tel: 01491 833018
ITA

Julia Sleeper
Psychoanalytic Psychotherapist
42 Lonsdale Road, Oxford OX2 7EW
Tel: 01865 311394
LCP

Eva Smith
Cognitive Analytic Therapist
9 Western Road, Oxford OX1 4LF
Tel: 01865 724 351
ACAT

Michael Soth
Integrative Psychotherapist, Body
Psychotherapist
16 Riverside Road, Oxford OX2 0HU
Tel: 01865 723613
CCHP

Frances Sparkes
Personal Construct Psychotherapist
Finches, Hilltop Lane, Chinnor,
Oxfordshire OX9 4BH
Tel: 01844 351411
CPCP

Elizabeth Standish
Psychoanalytic Psychotherapist
14 Park Crescent, Abingdon, Oxon
OX14 1DF
Tel: 01235 528806
SIP

Theresa Staunton-Soth
Holistic Psychotherapist
16 Riverside Road, Oxford OX2 0HU
Tel: 01865 723613
CCHP

F Beaumont Stevenson
Group Analyst
Chaplain's Office, Littlemore Hospital,
Littlemore, Oxford OX4 1SW
Tel: 01865 778911
IGA

Jill Steward
Psychoanalytic Psychotherapist
Cobstone Mill Farmhouse, Turville,
Henley-on-Thames, Oxon RG9 6QL
Tel: 01491 638250
IPC

Sabina Strich
Group Analyst
1 Folly Bridge Court, Thames Street,
Oxford OX1 1SW
Tel: 01865 251741
IGA

Susie Taylor
Psychodrama Psychotherapist
St Brelades, 15 Swinbourn Road,
Littlemore, Oxford OX4 4PQ
Tel: 01865 454932
BPDA

Simon Thomson
Psychodrama Psychotherapist
41b Church Street, Ardington, Oxon
OX12 8QA
Tel: 01491 35098
BPDA

Gill Williams
Psychodrama Psychotherapist
121 Southfield Road, Oxford
OX4 1NY
Tel: 01865 246589
BPDA

Wendy Winter
Transpersonal Psychotherapist
Birdcage Cottage, 61 Newland, Witney,
Oxon OX8 6JN
CCPE

PERTHSHIRE & ANGUS

Christina H Coyle
Cognitive Behavioural Psychotherapist
65 Bruce Road, Downfield, Dundee
DD3 8LW
Tel: 01382 833780
BABCP

Stephen Michael Gray
Cognitive Behavioural Psychotherapist
13 Station Terrace, Invergowrie,
Dundee DD2 5DS
Tel: 01382 561292/01382 828046
BABCP

Hanne Malcolm
Hypno-Psychotherapist
29 Bell Street, Tayport, Fife DD6 9AP
Tel: 01382 553596
NRHP

Richard Victor Morton
Cognitive Behavioural Psychotherapist
40 Carlogie Road, Carnoustie, Angus,
Scotland DD7 6EY
Tel: 01382 580441 ext 4965/
01241 853002
BABCP

Henry B Stewart
Cognitive Behavioural Psychotherapist
43 Provost Reid's Road, Montrose,
Angus DD10 8DZ
Tel: 01356 622291 x 152/01674 673823
BABCP

John S Swan
Cognitive Behavioural Psychotherapist
80 Seafield Road, Dundee DD1 4NA
Tel: 01382 202448
BABCP

Peter J Walters
Behavioural Psychotherapist
26 Terrace Road, Carnoustie, Tayside
DD7 7AF
Tel: 01382 580441/01241 856086
BABCP

Fiona Wilson
Cognitive Behavioural Psychotherapist
Clayholes, Balmachie Road, Carnoustie,
Angus DD7 6LA
Tel: 01241 855378
BABCP

Kath Yates
Psychodynamic Psychotherapist,
Integrative Psychotherapist
Blairs Farm, Trinity Gask, Madderty,
Auchterarder, Perthshire PH3 1LL
Tel: 01764 683385
WMIP, NSAP

Jessie Zentler
Psychoanalytic Psychotherapist
53 Henrietta St, Avoch, Ross-shire,
Scotland
AGIP

POWYS

Julie G Biggs
Hypno-Psychotherapist
Stingwern Cottage, Brooks,
Welshpool, Powys SY21 8QS
Tel: 01686 640853
NRHP

Jenny Hill
Psychoanalytic Psychotherapist
Harpton Gardens, New Radnor, Powys
LD8 2RE
Tel: 01554 350698
WMIP

Kathleen Mary Howes
Cognitive Behavioural Psychotherapist
Y Bwthyn, Battle, Brecon, Powys,
Wales LD3 9RN
Tel: 01874 623638
BABCP

Susan Peace
Hypno-Psychotherapist
The Peace Clinic, Cwm Meillion,
Llangammarch Wells, Powys LD4 4EN
Tel: 01591 620339
NRHP

John Pugh
Hypno-Psychotherapist
Forest Lodge, Cascob, Presteigne,
Powys LD8 2NT
Tel: 01547 560232
NRHP

Hilary Thompson
Psychosynthesis Psychotherapist
Ffridd Cottage, Abermule,
Montgomery, Powys SY15 6JH
Tel: 01686 630 439
IPS

H Wright
Psychoanalytic Psychotherapist
Gwinllan, Y-Maes, Rhayader, Powys
LD6 5DE
Tel: 01597 810821
WMIP

SHEFFIELD

Lily Barker
Psychodynamic Psychotherapist
14 Southbourne Road, Sheffield
S10 2QN
HIP

Judy Bennison
Psychodynamic Psychotherapist
Moorland View Farm, Commonside
Road, Barlow, Derbyshire S18 5SJ
HIP

Juliet Berry
Psychodynamic Psychotherapist
Cobb Barn, Smalldale, Bradwell,
Derbyshire, via Sheffield S30 2JQ
HIP

John Blackburn
Cognitive Behavioural Psychotherapist
Specialist Psychotherapy Services,
Brunswick House, 299 Glossop Road,
Sheffield S10 2HL
Tel: 0114 271 6901
BABCP

Polly Blacker
Psychodynamic Psychotherapist
32 Havelock Street, Sheffield S10 2FP
HIP

Joady Brennan
Personal Construct Psychotherapist
Centre for Psychotherapeutic Studies,
University of Sheffield, 16 Claremont
Crescent, Sheffield S10 2TA
Tel: 0114 276 8555 x 4970
CPCP

Peter R F Clarke
Psychodynamic Psychotherapist
90 Crimicar Lane, Sheffield S10 4FE
HIP

Stephen Colver
Psychoanalytic Psychotherapist,
Psychodynamic Psychotherapist
41 Bannerdale Road, Millhouses,
Sheffield S7 2DJ
Tel: 0114 258 5521
GUILD, YAPP

Faye Cooper
Sexual and Marital Psychotherapist
Whiteley Wood Clinic, Woofinden
Road, Sheffield S10 3TL
BASMT

Brian Daines
Psychodynamic Psychotherapist, Sexual
and Marital Psychotherapist
16 Rangeley Road, Sheffield, South
Yorkshire S6 5DW
BASMT, YAPP

Carole Dale
Psychodrama Psychotherapist
99 Meersbrook Park Road, Sheffield
S8 9FP
Tel: 0114 258 8088
BPDA

John De Carteret
Psychodynamic Psychotherapist
The Quaker Community, Water Lane,
Bamford, Sheffield S30 2DA
HIP

Helen Drucquer
Analytical Psychotherapist
84 Southgrove Road, Sheffield
S10 2NQ
HIP

David Edwards
Psychodynamic Psychotherapist
Centre for Psychotherapeutic Studies,
University of Sheffield, 16 Claremont
Crescent, Sheffield S10 2TA
HIP

Lynda Ellis
Psychoanalytic Psychotherapist
16 East Grove Road, Sheffield
S10 2NN
HIP

Louise Embleton-Tudor
Integrative Psychotherapist
Temenos, 13a Penrhyn Road, Hunter's
Bar, Sheffield S11 8UL
Tel: 0114 266 3931
MC

Rita Garlovsky
Psychoanalytic Psychotherapist
41 Oakhill Road, Sheffield S7 1SJ
Tel: 0114 258 7910
GUILD

Pauline Garvin-Crofts
Hypno-Psychotherapist
Tether's End, 630 Abbey Lane,
Whirlow, Sheffield S11 9NA
Tel: 0114 236 8307
NRHP

Anita Guiton
Psychodynamic Psychotherapist
SHARE Psychotherapy Agency, 176
Crookesmoor Road, Sheffield S6 3FS
HIP

Ray Haddock
Group Analyst, Analytical
Psychotherapist
108 Totley Brook Road, Dore, Sheffield
S17 3QU
Tel: 01742 716890/01742 716893 (f)
IGA

Ruth Hallam-Jones
Sexual and Marital Psychotherapist
123 Ecclesall Road South, Ecclesall,
Sheffield S11 9PJ
BASMT

Andrew Harvey
Cognitive Behavioural Psychotherapist
705 Ecclesall Road, Hunters Bar,
Sheffield S11 8TG
Tel: 0114 268 5456/0114 271 6890
BABCP

Patricia A Hunt
Psychodynamic Psychotherapist
Share Psychotherapy Agency, 176
Crookesmoor Road, Sheffield S6 3FS
HIP

Tim Kendall
Psychoanalytic Psychotherapist,
Psychodynamic Psychotherapist
Centre for Psychotherapeutic Studies,
University of Sheffield, 16 Claremont
Crescent, Sheffield S10 2TA
HIP

Alan Lidmila
Psychoanalytic Psychotherapist
371 Fulwood Road, Sheffield S10 3BS;
University of Sheffield, Centre for
Psychotherapeutic Stud, 16 Claremont
Crescent, Sheffield S10 2TA
Tel: 0114 266 2115
YAPP, HIP

Patrick A Loftus
Psychodynamic Psychotherapist
114 Industry Street, Walkley, Sheffield
S6 2WX
HIP

David Loxley
Psychodynamic Psychotherapist
193 Crimicar Lane, Sheffield S10 4EH
HIP

Norman D Macaskill
Cognitive Behavioural Psychotherapist
52 Linden Avenue, Sheffield S8 0GA
Tel: 0114 281 7561
BABCP

Enid MacNeill
Psychodynamic Psychotherapist
21 Knaresborough Road, Sheffield
S7 2LA
HIP

Pamela Mann
Psychodynamic Psychotherapist
Cobb Barn, Smalldale, Bradwell,
Derbyshire, via Sheffield S30 2JQ
HIP

Myra Marshall
Psychodynamic Psychotherapist
11 Rutland Park, Broomhill, Sheffield
S10 2PB
HIP

John McAuley
Analytical Psychotherapist
SHARE Psychotherapy Agency, 176
Crookesmoor Road, Sheffield S6 3FS
HIP

Lisa Mettam
Cognitive Behavioural Psychotherapist
Specialist Psychotherapy Services,
Brunswick House, 299 Glossop Road,
Sheffield S10 2HL
Tel: 0114 234 2332/0114 271 6890
BABCP

Carol Mohamed
Psychoanalytic Psychotherapist
136 Crookesmoor Road, Sheffield,
South Yorkshire S6 3FS
Tel: 0114 281 6686
WTC

Jane Monach
Psychodynamic Psychotherapist
Cocked Hat Cottage, 100 Bolehill Lane,
Crookes, Sheffield S10 1SD
HIP

M C Moore
Sexual and Marital Psychotherapist
Goatscliff Farm, Stoke Grindleford, Via
Sheffield S30 1HW
BASMT

John E D Oram
Psychodynamic Psychotherapist
12 Montgomery Road, Sheffield
S7 1LQ
HIP

Glenys Parry
Cognitive Analytic Therapist
Psychology Services, Sheffield Health
Authority, Argyll House, Williamson
Road, Sheffield S11 9AR
Tel: 0114 271 6652/01433 621757
ACAT

Angie Perrett
Sexual and Marital Psychotherapist
53 Endowood Road, Sheffield S7 2LY
BASMT

Susan Pethen
Psychodynamic Psychotherapist
62 Brincliffe Edge Road, Sheffield
S11 9BW
HIP

Deborah Pickvance
Psychodynamic Psychotherapist
108 Carr Road, Sheffield S6 2WZ
HIP

Beryl Ann Rayner
Analytical Psychotherapist
5 Sherwood Chase, Totley Brook Road,
Sheffield S17 3QT
HIP

Thomas N Ricketts
Cognitive Behavioural Psychotherapist
299 Glossop Road, Sheffield S10 2HL
Tel: 0114 271 6890
BABCP

Margaret Rosemary
Gestalt Psychotherapist
3 Strathtay Road, Greystones, Sheffield
S11 7GU
Tel: 0114 266 0229
GPTI

Angela Rosenfeld
Group Analyst
78 Carr Road, Walkley, Sheffield
S6 2RW
Tel: 01742 752157/01742 330523
IGA

Gwyneth Sampson
Sexual and Marital Psychotherapist
Whiteley Wood Clinic, Woofinden
Road, Sheffield S10 3TL
BASMT

Geraldine Shipton
Psychodynamic Psychotherapist
7 Psalter Lane, Sheffield S11 8YL
HIP

Digby Tantam
Psychodynamic Psychotherapist, Group
Analyst
Centre for Psychotherapeutic Studies,
16 Claremont Crescent, Sheffield
S10 2TA
Tel: 0114 282 4931
IGA, NWIDP

Pat Thomson
Psychodynamic Psychotherapist
35 Slayleigh Avenue, Sheffield S10 3RA
HIP

Margaret Todd
Psychodynamic Psychotherapist
16 Prospect Road, Coal Aston,
Dronfield, Sheffield S18 6EA
HIP

Keith Tudor
Transactional Analysis Psychotherapist
13A Penrhyn Road, Hunter's Bar,
Sheffield S11 8UL
Tel: 0114 266 3931
MET, ITA

Sheila Vipan
Psychodynamic Psychotherapist
Echo Gate, Foolow Road, Eyam, via
Sheffield S30 1QS
HIP

Jean Willowes
Psychodynamic Psychotherapist
79 Highton Street, Walkey, Sheffield
S6 3TQ
HIP

Llynwen Wilson
Sexual and Marital Psychotherapist
25 Meadow Bank Avenue, Sheffield
S7 1PB
BASMT

Kevan R Wylie
Sexual and Marital Psychotherapist
Whiteley Wood Clinic, Woofinden
Road, Sheffield S10 3TL
BASMT

SHROPSHIRE

Sonia Bliss
Psychodynamic Psychotherapist
31 Port Hill Gardens, Shrewsbury,
Shropshire SY3 8SB
Tel: 01743 232745
WMIP

Michael Foulkes
Systemic Psychotherapist
14 Greenfields Drive, Bridgenorth,
Shropshire WV16 9JR
FIC

Margaret Fox
Family Therapist
The Child and Family Service, Bourne
House, Radbrook Centre, Radbrook
Road, Shrewsbury SY3 9BL
Tel: 01743 232837
AFT

Gill Goodwillie
Systemic Psychotherapist
'Invergarry', 15 North Hermitage, Belle
Vue, Shrewsbury SY3 7JW
Tel: 01743 249 194
KCC

Linda M Hoag
Psychoanalytic Psychotherapist
(Jungian)
Rose Cottage, Wrockwardine, Nr
Wellington, Telford TF6 5DG
Tel: 01952 244803
WMIP, GUILD

Sharon Matthews
Cognitive Behavioural Psychotherapist
Beech Ward, Shelton Hospital,
Shropshire Mental Health NHS Trust,
Bicton Heath, Shrewsbury SY3 8DN
Tel: 01743 261276
BABCP

Elizabeth Morgan
Sexual and Marital Psychotherapist
70 Kingston Drive, London Road,
Shrewsbury, Shropshire SY2 6SJ
BASMT

Alexander R Nuthall
Cognitive Behavioural Psychotherapist
The Mount, 1 Haygate Road,
Wellington, Telford, Shropshire
TF1 1QX
Tel: 01952 641580
BABCP

Chris Purnell
Attachment-based Psychoanalytic
Psychotherapist
Fern Cottage, 5 St Luke's Road,
Doseley, Telford, Shropshire TF4 3BE
Tel: 01952 503523
CAPP

Margaret Spencer
Psychoanalytic Psychotherapist
44 Underdale Road, Shrewsbury,
Shropshire SY2 5DT
Tel: 01743 232103
WMIP

Helen Thorley
Psychoanalytic Psychotherapist
Black Firs, Birks Drive, Ashley Heath,
Near Market Drayton, Shropshire
TF9 4PQ
Tel: 01630 672636
LPDO

SOMERSET

Vivian Broughton
Gestalt Psychotherapist
49 Witham Friary, Near Frome,
Somerset BA11 5HF
Tel: 01749 850661
GPTI, MET

Bernard Dinneen
Hypno-Psychotherapist
16 Great Ostry, Shepton Mallet,
Somerset BA4 5TT
Tel: 01749 346652
NSHAP

Sue Gottlieb
Psychoanalytic Psychotherapist
Babbs Farm, Westhill Lane, Watchfield,
Highbridge, Somerset TA9 4RF
Tel: 01278 793244
SIP, LCP

Jane Gotto
Humanistic and Integrative
Psychotherapist
The Terrace, Therapy and Natural
Health Centre, 35 Staplegrove Road,
Taunton, Somerset TA3 7JR
Tel: 01823 338968
SPEC

Elisabeth Holdaway
Sexual and Marital Psychotherapist
Godney House, Godney, Nr Wells,
Somerset BA5 1RX
BASMT

Jill Hopkins
Psychoanalytic Psychotherapist
Badger's Hay, Kingston St Mary,
Taunton TA2 8HU
Tel: 01823 451656
SIP, GUILD

Patricia Howe
Psychosynthesis Psychotherapist
27 Roman Way, Glastonbury, Somerset
BA6 8AB
Tel: 01458 833864
PET

Gisela Lockie
Integrative Psychotherapist, Body
Psychotherapist
16 Fowler Street, Taunton, Somerset
TA2 6JB
Tel: 01823 323240
CCHP

John Mitchell
Gestalt Psychotherapist
49 Witham Friary, Near Frome,
Somerset BA11 5HF
Tel: 01749 850661
GPTI, MET

Kate Nowlan
Psychoanalytic Psychotherapist
Lanswood, 10 Lansdown Place, Frome,
Somerset BA11 3HP;
Wessex Counselling Service, Fairfield
House, King Street, Frome BA11 1BH
Tel: 01373 464919/01373 453137
IPC

Will Parfitt
Psychosynthesis Psychotherapist
27 Roman Way, Glastonbury, Somerset
BA6 8AB
Tel: 01458 833864
PET

Rose Persson
Group Analytic Psychotherapist
Ham Manor, Ham Lane, Shepton Mallet
BA4 5JR;
St Augustine's Medical Practice, 495
Bath Road, Saltford BS18 3HQ
Tel: 01749 342141/01225 873245
IPC

Harry Procter
Personal Construct Psychotherapist
Petrel House, Broadway Park,
Bridgwater, Somerset TA6 5YA
Tel: 01278 446909
CPCP

Andrew Pullin
Group Analyst
85 Weymouth Road, Frome, Somerset
BA11 1HJ
Tel: 01373 472170
IGA

Sigurd Reimers
Family Therapist
179 Cheddon Road, Taunton, Somerset
TA2 7AH
FIC

Louise Robinson
Humanistic and Integrative
Psychotherapist
38 Belvedere Road, Taunton, Somerset
TA1 1HD
Tel: 01823 353009
MC

Michael Scovell
Psychoanalytic Psychotherapist
63 Summerland Avenue, Minehead,
Somerset TA24 5BW
Tel: 01643 706675
SIP

Adrian Tait
Psychoanalytic Psychotherapist
13 Haines Hill, Taunton, Somerset
TA1 4HN
Tel: 01823 321588
GUILD

Madeleine Thomas
Cognitive Behavioural Psychotherapist
Ashford Lodge, Cannington,
Bridgwater, Somerset TA5 2NL
Tel: 01823 432136/01278 671595
BABCP

Abigail Wedderkopp
Psychoanalytic Psychotherapist
Anstey Place, 8A St James Street,
Munton, Somerset
Tel: 01278 732306
SIP

Nigel Wellings
Psychoanalytic Psychotherapist
Well Cottage, Kingwestern Road,
Chalton MacKnell, Nr Somerton,
Somerset
AGIP

Roger Wells
Psychoanalytic Psychotherapist
Prioryfield House, 20 Canon Street,
Taunton, Somerset TA1 1SW
Tel: 01392 79317
GUILD

Nigel Williams
Individual and Group Humanistic
Psychotherapist, Lacanian Analyst
38 Belvedere Road, Taunton, Somerset
TA1 1HD
Tel: 01823 337069
MC, AHPP

Raymond Young
Transpersonal Psychotherapist
Gough House, East Compton, Shepton
Mallet BA4 4NR
Tel: 01749 346 539
CCPE

Paul Zeal
Psychoanalytic Psychotherapist
12 Elm Grove, Taunton, Somerset
TA1 1EG
Tel: 01823 323099/01823 323860 (f)
PA, SIP

SOUTH GLAMORGAN

Anne Brazier
Family Therapist
Centre for Training in Clinical
Psychology, Whitchurch Hopital,
Whitchurch, Cardiff CF4 7XB
AFT

Jon Chatham
Family Therapist
Preswylfa Child and Family Centre,
Clive Road, Canton, Cardiff
Tel: 01222 344489
AFT

Brenda Cox
Systemic Psychotherapist
The Family Institute, 105 Cathedral
Road, Cardiff CF1 9PH
FIC

Mairlis Davies
Family Therapist
Preswylfa Child & Family Centre, Clive
Road, Canton, Cardiff CF5 1GN
AFT

Jan Dryden
Humanistic and Integrative
Psychotherapist
22 Talbot Street, Cardiff CF1 9BW
Tel: 01222 238076
SPEC

Jeffrey Faris
Systemic Psychotherapist
56 Richards Terrace, Cardiff CF2 1RX
FIC

Jeremy Hazell
Psychoanalytic Psychotherapist
9 Fairleigh Road, Pontcanna, Cardiff
CF1 9JT
Tel: 01222 345832
SIP, BAP

Elsa Jones
Systemic Psychotherapist
The Natural Health Clinic, 98
Cathedral Road, Cardiff CF1 9LP
IFT

Julie Lowe
Existential Psychotherapist
32 Victoria Park Road East, Canton,
Cardiff, Wales CF5 1EH
Tel: 01222 340376
RCSPC

Trish Mylan
Systemic Psychotherapist
Ty Caehir, Peterston-Super-Ely, Cardiff
CF5 6LH
FIC

Barbara Parsons
Family Therapist
Preswylfa Child & Family Centre, Clive
Road, Canton, Cardiff CF5 1GN
AFT

Mark Rivett
Family Therapist
6 Severn Grove, Canton, Cardiff
CF1 9EN
Tel: 01222 382266
AFT

Helen Rowlands
Integrative Psychotherapist
32 Kingsland Crescent, Barry, South
Glamorgan, CF63 4JQ
Tel: 01446 740517
MET

Philippa Seligman
Systemic Psychotherapist
22 West Orchard Crescent, Llandaff,
Cardiff CF5 1AR
Tel: 01222 561491
AFT, KCC

Eddy Street
Systemic Psychotherapist
19 Velindre Road, Whitchurch, Cardiff
FIC

Jim Wilson
Systemic Psychotherapist
86 Donald Street, Roath, Cardiff
CF2 4TR
FIC

SOUTH HUMBERSIDE

Susan Emm
Transpersonal Psychotherapist
The Rectory, Church Lane, North
Thoresby, Lincs DN36 5QG
Tel: 01472 840029
CCPE

SOUTH YORKSHIRE

Illana Cariapa
Cognitive Behavioural Psychotherapist
Dept of Child & Family Psychiatry,
Chatham House, Doncaster Gate,
Rotherham S65 1DJ
Tel: 01709 824808/9
BABCP

J Heather Caulfield
Psychodynamic Psychotherapist
35 Barrie Grove, Hellaby, Rotherham
S66 8HG
HIP

Gillian Donohoe
Cognitive Behavioural Psychotherapist
Department of Behavioural
Psychotherapy, Doncaster Royal
Infirmary, Armthorpe Road, Doncaster
DN2 5LT
Tel: 01302 366666 x 3214
BABCP

Ingolf Gudjonsson
Psychodynamic Psychotherapist
Adult Psychology & Psychotherapy
Services, Doncaster Royal Infirmary,
Armthorpe Road, Doncaster DN2 5LT
YAPP, HIP

Mary Lea
Behavioural Psychotherapist
Mental Health Unit, Rotherham Dist
General Hospital, Moorgate,
Rotherham S60 2UD
Tel: 01709 820000 x 6032
BABCP

Enid MacNeill
Psychodrama Psychotherapist
21 Knaresborough Road, Sheffield
S72 LA
Tel: 01142 364349
BPDA

Eileen F Smith
Psychodynamic Psychotherapist
First Floor Flat, Hooton Pagnell Hall,
Hooton Pagnell, Doncaster DN5 7BW
HIP

Pat Townsend
Cognitive Behavioural Psychotherapist
16 Marina Rise, Darfield, Barnsley,
South Yorks S73 9PT
Tel: 01226 340024/01977 606506
BABCP

Christine M J Wright
Cognitive Behavioural Psychotherapist
Dept of Behavioural Psychotherapy,
Doncaster Royal Infirmary, Armthorpe
Road, Doncaster DN4 7DT
Tel: 01302 366666 x 3214
BABCP

STAFFORDSHIRE

Megan Adams
Hypno-Psychotherapist
Hawthorn Cottage, Church Farm,
Church Road, Dosthill, Tamworth,
Staffs B77 1LU
Tel: 01827 281233
NSHAP

Nabil Anees
Psychoanalytic Psychotherapist
3 Cooke Close, Penkridge, Stafford
ST19 5SL
Tel: 01785 715595
WMIP

Graham Breeze
Integrative Psychotherapist
87 Basford Bridge Lane, Cheddleton,
Nr Leek, Staffordshire ST13 7EQ
NSAP

Sue Brough
Psychoanalytic Psychotherapist,
Integrative Psychotherapist
38 Gable Croft, Lichfield, Staffordshire
WS14 9RY
Tel: 01543 264282
WMIP, NSAP

Suzy Challis
Psychoanalytic Psychotherapist
Department of Clinical Psychology,
City General Hospital, Newcastle
Road, Stoke-on-Trent ST4 6QG
Tel: 01782 718929
LPDO

Alison Clegg
Sexual and Marital Psychotherapist
The Dower House, Bonehill,
Tamworth, Staffordshire B78 3HX
BASMT

Enid Corker
Psychoanalytic Psychotherapist
Ambleside, 55 The Avenue, Harpfields,
Stoke-on-Trent ST4 6BT
Tel: 01782 662655
AGIP

J A Crisp
Psychodynamic Psychotherapist
Ranellie, Tinkers Lane, Brewood,
Staffordshire ST19 9DD
Tel: 01902 850481
WMIP

Himanshu Ghadiali
Analytical Psychologist-Jungian Analyst
The Elms, 65/67 Asbourne Road,
Derby DE12 3FS;
Kingsway Hospital, Kingsway, Derby
DE22 3LZ
Tel: 01332 624558/01332 739782
SAP

Rita Ghent
Integrative Psychotherapist
7 Tolkien Way, Hartshill Road,
Hartshill, Stoke on Trent, Staffordshire
NSAP

Mary Goodman
Family Therapist
Greenlow Bank, Butterton, Nr Leek,
Staffordshire ST13 7TD
Tel: 01538 304340
AFT

Pete Gray
Family Psychotherapist
33 Church Lane, Oulton, Nr Stone,
Staffs ST15 8UB
Tel: 01785 819217
AFT

Sharon Hallard
Group Analyst
Hay House Farm, Belmont Road,
Ipstones, Staffs ST10 2JR
Tel: 01538 266834
IGA

Pam Horrocks
Psychodynamic Psychotherapist
36 Station Road, Alsager, Stoke on
Trent ST7 2PD
Tel: 01270 877284
ULDPS

Cathy Moxon
Integrative Psychotherapist
18 Hartington Street, Wolstanton,
Newcastle under Lyme, Staffordshire
ST5 8DR
NSAP

Theresa Moyes
Cognitive Behavioural Psychotherapist
Psychology Department, St George's
Hospital, Corporation Street, Stafford
ST16 3AG
Tel: 01785 57888 x 5656
BABCP

Adrian Newell
Cognitive Psychotherapist
Clinical Psychology Service, St George's
Hospital, Corporation Street, Stafford
ST16 3AG
Tel: 01785 57888 x 5429/
0121 354 1392
BABCP

R Niblett
Psychodynamic Psychotherapist
12 Spring Road, Lichfield, Staffs
WS13 6BQ
Tel: 01543 264 860
WMIP

James Osborne
Family Therapist
12 Near Ridding, Gnosall, Stafford
ST20 0DP
FIC

Nicola Overs
Personal Construct Psychotherapist
Roache House Farm, Upper Hulme,
Leek, Staffs ST13 8UB
Tel: 01538 300517
CPCP

Shirley Wheeley
Psychoanalytic Psychotherapist
(Jungian)
70 Fecknam Way, Lichfield, Staffs
WS13 6AN
Tel: 01543 264801
WMIP, GUILD

Margaret Wiles
Integrative Psychotherapist
18 Cornwall Avenue, Clayton,
Newcastle under Lyme, Staffordshire
ST5 3DJ
NSAP

SUFFOLK

Tessa Allen
Psychoanalytic Psychotherapist
63 Victoria Road, Woodbridge, Suffolk
IP12 1EL
Tel: 01394 388654
NWIDP

James Atkinson
Analytical Psychologist-Jungian Analyst
Cotton Hall, Rectory Road, Kedington,
Suffolk CB9 7QN
Tel: 01440 61690
SAP

Rosalind Bowers
Psychoanalytic Psychotherapist
Yew Tree Farm, Sweffling,
Saxmundham, Suffolk IP17 2BU
Tel: 0171 628 8966/0172 878 538
GUILD

Christopher Coulson
Individual and Group Humanistic
Psychotherapist
PO Box 12, Woodbridge, Suffolk
IP12 4QG
Tel: 01394 388222
AHPP

Ian Craib
Group Analytic Psychotherapist
Mill House, Kitchen Hill, Bulmer Road,
Sudbury, Suffolk CO10 7EZ
Tel: 01787 310210
LCP

Sylvia Cullum
Sexual and Marital Psychotherapist
Briar Hill, Aldringham, Leiston, Suffolk
IP16 4QL
BASMT

Keith Faull
Family Therapist
46 Oxford Road, Ipswich, Suffolk
IP4 1NL
AFT

Elizabeth McCormick
Cognitive Analytic Therapist
East Friars, Dunwich, Suffolk
IP17 3DW
Tel: 0172 873 672
ACAT

Terry Mohan
NLP Psychotherapist
20 Nelson Road, Bury St Edmunds,
Suffolk IP33 3AG
Tel: 01284 701505
ANLP

Penny Parks
NLP Psychotherapist
Mount Pleasant, Debenham,
Stowmarket, Suffolk IP14 6PT
Tel: 01728 860490
ANLP

Denis Payne
Analytical Psychologist-Jungian Analyst
The Crooked House, Darsham, Nr
Saxmundham, Suffolk IP17 3RN
Tel: 01728 668 705
AJA

Frances Reader
Sexual and Marital Psychotherapist
The Old Rectory, 100 Seckford Street,
Woodbridge, Suffolk IP12 4LZ
BASMT

Ruth Whittaker
Sexual and Marital Psychotherapist
Low Farm, Westleton, Saxmundham,
Suffolk IP17 3BT
BASMT

SURREY

Eileen Aird
Psychoanalytic Psychotherapist
Hillcroft College, South Bank, Surbiton,
Surrey KT6 6DF
Tel: 0181 399 2688
NAAP

Anne Ashley
Analytical Psychologist-Jungian Analyst
Timmynoggy House, 49 Godstone
Road, Purley, Surrey CR8 2AN
Tel: 0181 660 3099
SAP

Bronwen Astor
Psychoanalytic Psychotherapist
Tuesley Manor, Godalming, Surrey
GU7 1UD;
25 Cadogan Place, London SW1X 9SA
Tel: 01483 417281
AGIP, GCP

Marie Baines
Group Analytic Psychotherapist
46 Crescent Road, Kingston upon
Thames, Surrey KT2 7RG
Tel: 0181 546 7049
IPC

Moke Baker
Psychoanalytic Psychotherapist
59 Hillside Road, Ashtead, Surrey
KT21 1RZ
Tel: 01372 275885
IPC

Ruth Baker
Integrative Psychotherapist
Chestnut Bend, Grub Street,
Limpsfield, Surrey RH8 0SH
Tel: 01883 717995
RCSPC

Eva Bayley
Psychosynthesis Psychotherapist
125 Addison Road, Guildford, Surrey
GU1 3QE
Tel: 01483 31552
PET

Margaret Beer
Psychoanalytic Psychotherapist
7 Fabyc House, Cumberland Road,
Kew Gardens, Surrey TW9 3HH
Tel: 0181 940 7353
IPC

Margaret Bennett
Family Therapist
285 Kings Road, Kingston, Surrey
KT2 5JJ
Tel: 0181 546 9785
IFT

Radha Bhat
Group Analyst
8 Godson Road, Waddon, Croydon,
Surrey CR0 4LT
Tel: 0181 460 5593/0181 686 2908
IGA

Renate Blackwood
Psychoanalytic Psychotherapist
7 Esher Park Avenue, Esher, Surrey
KT10 9NP
Tel: 01372 462852
LCP, GCP

Cherry Boa
Cognitive Analytic Therapist
3 Holmesdale Road, Kew Gardens,
Richmond, Surrey TW9 3JZ
Tel: 0171 928 9292/0181 940 0486
ACAT

Roger Boff
Hypno-Psychotherapist
88 Ingleboro Drive, Purley, Surrey
CR8 1EF
Tel: 0181 668 1128
NSHAP

Jan Bolton
Systemic Psychotherapist
214 Gordon Avenue, Camberley,
Surrey GU15 2NT
Tel: 01276 64625
KCC

Pauline Brassington
Sexual and Marital Psychotherapist
Maldon Lodge, Crawley Ridge,
Camberley, Surrey GU15 2AD
BASMT

Jenny Bridge
Integrative Psychotherapist
569 Upper Richmond Road West,
Richmond, Surrey TW10 5DX
Tel: 0181 878 7388/0181 878 2658
ITA

Gillian A Brown
Family Psychotherapist
29 Mountside, Guildford, Surrey
GU2 5JD
Tel: 01483 504360
AFT

Toni Brown
Cognitive Psychotherapist
1c Headley Close, West Ewell, Epsom,
Surrey KT19 9JA
Tel: 0181 391 1316
BABCP

Valerie Browne
Psychoanalytic Psychotherapist
22 Ruskin Avenue, Kew, Richmond,
Surrey TW9 4DJ
Tel: 0181 878 9803
IPC

Sarah-Jill Buchanan
Autogenic Psychotherapist
Hastings, Pennymead Drive, East
Horsley, Surrey KT24 5AH
Tel: 01483 284497
BAFAT

Birgit Bukovics-Heiller
Transactional Analysis Psychotherapist,
Integrative Psychotherapist
6 Green Lane, Cobham, Surrey
KT11 2NN
Tel: 01932 867549
ITA

Malcolm Bush
Sexual and Marital Psychotherapist
35 Crossways, South Croydon, Surrey
CR2 8JQ
BASMT

Patrick J Byrne
Family Psychotherapist
Child Guidance Clinic, Victoria House,
Southbridge Place, Croydon CR0 4HA
Tel: 0181 686 0393
IFT

Brede Carr
Psychoanalytic Psychotherapist
9 Chepstow Rise, Croydon, Surrey
CR0 5LX
Tel: 0181 667 0970
IPC

Helen Carroll
Humanistic Psychotherapist
25A St Barnabas Road, Sutton, Surrey
SM1 4NP
Tel: 0181 643 1439
AHPP

Martha Carvajal-Ogden
Biodynamic Psychotherapist
103 Richmond Hill Court, Richmond,
Surrey TW10 6BG
Tel: 0181 940 4726
BTC

Michael Channon
Psychoanalytic Psychotherapist
2 Fabyc House, Cumberland Road,
Kew, Richmond, Surrey TW9 3HH
Tel: 0181 940 1092
IPC

Freni Chinoy
Child Psychotherapist
Sutton Child & Family Clinic, Robin
Hood Lane Health Centre, Camden
Road, Sutton, Surrey SM1 2SH
Tel: 0181 770 6781/0181 949 1995
ACP

Margaret Clark
Psychoanalytic Psychotherapist
11 The Broadway, Manor Lane, Sutton,
Surrey SM1 4BU;
26 Woodcote Avenue, Wallington,
Surrey SM6 0QY
Tel: 0181 661 0007/0181 669 8772
SAP

Hans W Cohn
Existential Psychotherapist
7 Fabyc House, Cumberland Road,
Kew, Surrey TW9 3HH
Tel: 0181 940 3748
RCSPC

Hazel Danbury
Psychoanalytic Psychotherapist
16 Lynton Road, New Malden, Surrey
KT3 5EE
Tel: 0181 942 2374
BAP

Ann Davies
Psychoanalytic Psychotherapist
The Old Dog Kennel, Hill House,
Woodside Road, Chiddingfold,
Godalming GU8 4RF
Tel: 01428 683102
AGIP

Laurie Day
Integrative Psychotherapist
34 St Stephens Avenue, Ashtead,
Surrey KT21 1PL
Tel: 01372 272670
MET

Patricia de Berker
Psychoanalytic Psychotherapist
Ferndown Cottage, 3 Hillier Road,
Guildford, Surrey
Tel: 01483 504554
LCP, GCP

Paul de Berker
Psychoanalytic Psychotherapist
Ferndown Cottage, 3 Hillier Road,
Guildford, Surrey
Tel: 01483 504554
LCP, GCP, BAP

Mark Dearnley
Systemic Psychotherapist
St Paul's Vicarage, 278 Hook Road,
Hook, Chessington, Surrey KT9 1PF
Tel: 0181 397 3521
KCC

Pat Dooley
Psychoanalytic Psychotherapist
43 Guildford Road, Croydon, Surrey
CR0 2HL;
7 Woburn Close, Frimley, Camberley,
Surrey GU16 5NU
Tel: 0181 683 1041/01276 681684
IPC

Deirdre Dowling
Child Psychotherapist
Cassel Hospital, Ham Common,
Richmond, Surrey TW10 7JF
Tel: 0181 390 4548/0181 940 8181
ACP

Alexandre Dubinsky
Child Psychotherapist
Richmond Child & Family Consultation
Centre, Windham Road Clinic,
Windham Road, Richmond TW9 2HP
Tel: 0181 940 4775/0171 794 5047
ACP

Jennifer Duckham
Analytical Psychologist-Jungian Analyst
7 Upper Park Road, Kingston-upon-
Thames, Surrey KT2 5LB
Tel: 0181 546 4173
SAP

Sally Duncan
Sexual and Marital Psychotherapist
1 George Denyer Close, Pathfields,
Haslemere, Surrey GU27 2BH
BASMT

Andrea Dykes
Analytical Psychologist-Jungian Analyst
Fox Glade, Bunch Lane, Haslemere,
Surrey GU27 1ET
Tel: 01428 652363
AJA

Andrea K Edeleanu
Cognitive Behavioural Psychotherapist
Dept of Clinical Psychology, Buryfields
Clinic, Lawn Road, Guildford, Surrey
GU2 5AZ
Tel: 01483 64635 x 214
BABCP

Robert J Edelmann
Cognitive Behavioural Psychotherapist
Dept of Psychology, University of
Surrey, Guildford, Surrey GU2 5XH
Tel: 01483 300800 x 2483
BABCP

Ray Evans
Personal Construct Psychotherapist
6 Fabyc House, Cumberland Road,
Kew, Richmond, Surrey TW9 3HH
Tel: 0181 940 1597
CPCP

Tricia Evans
Sexual and Marital Psychotherapist
38 Blackborough Road, Reigate, Surrey
RH2 7BX
BASMT

Erica Filby
Family Therapist
East Surrey Priority Care NHS Trust,
Child & Family Consultation Service,
Oxted, Surrey RH8 0BQ
Tel: 01883 714 361/01273 564275
IFT

Patrick Fleming
Psychoanalytic Psychotherapist
Highfield House, Philpot Lane,
Cobham, Surrey GU24 8HE
Tel: 01276 8402
LCP

Richard France
Cognitive Behavioural Psychotherapist
The Medical Centre, Yateley,
Camberley, Surrey GU17 7LS
Tel: 01252 870737/01252 872333
BABCP

Pat Freeman
Family Therapist
5 Shaftesbury Road, Richmond upon
Thames, Surrey TW9 2LD
Tel: 0181 948 7197
AFT

Lena Furst
Psychoanalytic Psychotherapist
313 Ewell Road, Surbiton, Surrey
KT6 7BX
Tel: 01932 872010 x 3307/
0181 390 7800
BAP

Alegra Garner
Analytical Psychologist-Jungian Analyst
1 Bank Lane, Kingston upon Thames,
Surrey KT2 5AZ
Tel: 0181 541 3141
SAP

Brian Glaister
Cognitive Behavioural Psychotherapist
135 Foxley Lane, Purley, Surrey
CR8 3HR
Tel: 0181 660 7465
BABCP

Elma Golsworthy
Cognitive Behavioural Psychotherapist
Little France, Greendene, East Horsley,
Surrey KT24 5RD
Tel: 01483 283537
BABCP

Ewa Gottesman
Group Analyst
'Foxbreak', 28 Courts Mount Road,
Haslemere, Surrey GU27 2PP
Tel: 01428 642483
IGA

Robert Gottesman
Psychoanalytic Psychotherapist
Foxbreak, 28 Court Mount Road,
Haslemere, Surrey GU27 2PP
Tel: 01428 642483
LCP

Myrna Gower
Family Therapist
Cranford, 14 The Crest, Surbiton,
Surrey KT5 8JZ
Tel: 0181 399 2012
AFT

Juliet Grayson
NLP Psychotherapist
268 Canbury Park Road, Kingston,
Surrey KT2 6LG
Tel: 0181 974 5573
ANLP

Francoise Grimshaw
Personal Construct Psychotherapist
Purley, Surrey
Tel: 0181 660 0338
CPCP

Virginia Grosser
Psychoanalytic Psychotherapist
19 Lancaster Park, Richmond, Surrey
TW10 6AB
Tel: 0181 940 4414
GUILD

Robert Hart
Analytical Psychologist-Jungian Analyst
12 Grange Mansions, Kingston Road,
Ewell Village, Surrey KT17 2AD
Tel: 0181 393 4675
BAP

Beth Hashemi
Psychoanalytic Psychotherapist
7 Nightingale Road, Guildford, Surrey
GU1 1ER
Tel: 01483 563135
IPC, GCP

Pamela Hayes
NLP Psychotherapist
Sancroft, Hoe Lane, Abinger Hammer,
Nr Dorking, Surrey RH5 6RH
Tel: 01306 730070
ANLP

Marlene Heap
Analytical Psychologist-Jungian Analyst
53 Hazelwood Grove, Sanderstead,
Surrey CR2 9DW
Tel: 0181 657 1128
SAP

John Heatley
Group Analyst
West Dene Cottage, Midhurst Road,
Haslemere, Surrey GU27 2PT
Tel: 01428 654265
IGA

Anita Heavens
Psychoanalytic Psychotherapist
60 Melfort Road, Thornton Heath,
Surrey
AGIP

Korinna Hedinger-Farrell
Body Psychotherapist, Integrative
Psychotherapist
36 Woodbines Avenue, Kingston,
Surrey KT1 2AY
Tel: 0181 255 3468
CCHP

June Henley
Family Therapist
Walwood House, Park Road, Banstead,
Surrey SM7 3ER
Tel: 01737 352626
IFT

Rachael Hewett
Transactional Analysis Psychotherapist
Flat 4, 83 Mt Ararat Road, Richmond,
Surrey TW10 6PL
Tel: 0181 940 8010
ITA

Harriet Holve
Psychoanalytic Psychotherapist
11 Littleworth Common Road, Esher,
Surrey KT10 9UE
Tel: 01372 464529
GCP

Jean Hopwood
Analytical Psychotherapist
Waverley, Somerswey, Shalford,
Guildford GU4 8EQ
Tel: 01483 568669
GCP

Michael Hopwood
Analytical Psychotherapist
Waverley, Somerswey, Shalford,
Guildford GU4 8EQ
Tel: 01483 568669
GCP, LCP

Marjorie Hudson
Psychoanalytic Psychotherapist
108 Great Tattenhams, Epsom, Surrey
KT18 5SE
Tel: 01737 353211
IPC, GUILD

Fakhir Hussain
Integrative Psychotherapist
Flat 7, Kingswood Court, Marchmont
Road, Richmond, Surrey TW10 6EU
Tel: 0181 948 4551
MC

Dennis Hyde
Integrative Psychotherapist
'Hawkchurch', 32 Amis Avenue, New
Haw, Addlestone, Surrey KT15 3ET
Tel: 01932 345526
MC

Nida Ingham
Autogenic Psychotherapist
Heath Cottage, Pitch Hill, Ewhurst, Nr
Cranleigh, Surrey GU6 7NP
Tel: 01483 277333
BAFAT

Sally Jakobi
Analytical Psychologist-Jungian Analyst
Bench House, Ham Street, Richmond,
Surrey TW10 7HR
Tel: 0181 940 9059
SAP

Jinnie Jefferies
Psychodrama Psychotherapist
15 Audley Road, Richmond, Surrey
TW10 6EY
Tel: 0181 948 5595
BPDA

Arthur Jonathan
Existential Psychotherapist
'The Jays', 27 Aultone Way, Sutton,
Surrey SM1 3LD
Tel: 0171 487 7406/0181 641 1601
RCSPC

Alan Jones
Humanistic Psychotherapist
3 Bushey Road, Sutton, Surrey
SM1 1QR
Tel: 0181 641 1792
AHPP

Margaret Peggy Jones
Analytical Psychologist-Jungian Analyst
52 The Vineyard, Richmond, Surrey
TW10 6AT
Tel: 0181 948 8478/0181 948 1083
SAP

Joyce Keith
Sexual and Marital Psychotherapist
The Links House, The Warren,
Ashstead, Surrey KT21 2SN
BASMT

Robert Lafon
Family Therapist
26 Hardman Road, Kingston upon
Thames, Surrey KT2 6RH
IFT

Christine Lawson
Psychoanalytic Psychotherapist
19 The Vineyard, Richmond, Surrey
TW10 6AQ
Tel: 0181 940 7184
PA

Elizabeth Leiper
Gestalt Psychotherapist
75 Larchwood Drive, Englefield Green,
Egham, Surrey TW20 0SL
Tel: 01784 438478
GPTI, MET

Ruth Lewis
Systemic Psychotherapist
One Oak, Knoll Road, Godalming,
Surrey GU7 2EJ
Tel: 01483 415 700
KCC

Stuart Lieberman
Family Therapist, Psychoanalytic
Psychotherapist
Dept of Psychiatry, Ridgewood Centre,
Mental Health Unit, Surrey GU16 5QE;
Pines House, Pines Road, Fleet, Hants
Tel: 01276 692919 x 5307/
01252 613994 071 672 1255
IFT, CPP

Shirley Lingard
Systemic Psychotherapist
Rosemead, Churt, Nr Farnham, Surrey
GU10 2NX
Tel: 01252 724044/01428 712206
KCC

Suzanne Looms
NLP Psychotherapist
28 Kingscote Road, Croydon, Surrey
CR0 7DN
Tel: 0181 656 1518
ANLP

Valerie Lynch
Psychoanalytic Psychotherapist
11 Telford Court, Clandon Road,
Guildford, Surrey GU1 2EA
Tel: 01483 562204
GCP

Christopher MacKenna
Analytical Psychologist-Jungian Analyst,
Psychoanalytic Psychotherapist
Hascombe Rectory, Godalming, Surrey
GU8 4JA
Tel: 01483 208362
BAP, GCP

Norma Anderson Maple
Cognitive Analytic Therapist, Group
Analyst
25 Burlington Avenue, Kew, Richmond,
Surrey TW9 4DF
Tel: 0181 878 5244/0181 876 3977
ACAT, IGA

Janet Marshall
Autogenic Psychotherapist
12 Churchfields Avenue, Weybridge,
Surrey KT13 9YA
Tel: 01932 821721
BAFAT

Jill Marshall
Hypno-Psychotherapist
6 Perryfield Way, Richmond, Surrey
TW10 7SP
Tel: 0181 948 1573
NRHP

Vivien Marshall
Psychoanalytic Psychotherapist
29 Dale Road, Purley, Surrey CR8 2ED
Tel: 0181 668 0557
IPC

Brian Maxwell
Group Analyst
98 Leatherhead Road, Chessington,
Surrey KT9 2HY
Tel: 0181 397 3971
IGA

Cynthia Maynerd
Family Psychotherapist, Family
Therapist
15 Smoke Lane, Reigate, Surrey
RH2 7HJ
Tel: 01737 242051
IFT

Patricia McKeown
Transpersonal Psychotherapist
97 Firs Close, Mitcham, Surrey
CR4 IAX
Tel: 0181 286 1606
CCPE

Lisa Morice
Child Psychotherapist
Cassel Hospital, Ham Common,
Richmond, Surrey TW10 7JF
Tel: 0181 940 8181/0181 940 4199
ACP

Michael Morice
Child Psychotherapist
Child and Family Consultation Service,
Richmond Royal Hospital, Kew Foot
Road, Richmond, Surrey
Tel: 0181 940 4199/0181 332 4490
ACP

Lesleen Mountjoy
Hypno-Psychotherapist
16 Middle Bourne Lane, Lower Bourne,
Farnham, Surrey GU10 3NE
Tel: 01252 725574
NRHP

June Mycroft-Miles
Sexual and Marital Psychotherapist
8 Sunny Rise, Caterham on the Hill,
Surrey CR3 5PR
BASMT

Pat O'Brien
Family Psychotherapist
'Corner Cottage', Abinger Lane,
Abinger Common, Dorking, Surrey
RH5 6JH
IFT

Nadia O'Connor
Transpersonal Psychotherapist
8 Queens Road, Thames Ditton, Surrey
KT7 0QX
CCPE

Tricia O'Dell
Psychoanalytic Psychotherapist
Lichfield, 161 New Haw Road,
Addlestone, Weybridge, Surrey
KT15 2DP
Tel: 01932 851897
IPC, GCP

Christopher J O'Neill
Hypno-Psychotherapist
14 Chapelfields, Charterhouse Road,
Godalming, Surrey GU7 2DX
Tel: 01483 414437
NSHAP

Lynda Osborne
Gestalt Psychotherapist
Crossways, 8 Lancaster Avenue,
Farnham, Surrey GU9 8JY
Tel: 01252 724403
GPTI, MET

Peter Owtram
Psychoanalytic Psychotherapist
14 Busbridge Lane, Godalming, Surrey
GU7 IPU
Tel: 01483 417443
BAP, GCP

Karen Partridge
Systemic Psychotherapist
I Woodside Road, Kingston upon
Thames, Surrey KT2 5AT
Tel: 0181 472 4661 x 5091
KCC

Cathy Pearman
Psychosynthesis Psychotherapist
'Tzaneen', Blackhorse Road, Woking,
Surrey GU22 ORE
Tel: 01483 232030
IPS

Paul Pengelly
Psychoanalytic Marital Psychotherapist
Abraham Cowley Unit (NHS),
Holloway Hill, Lyne, Chertsey, Surrey
KT16 0AE;
17 Arlington Gardens, London
W4 4EZ
Tel: 01932 872010/0181 747 0795
TMSI

Brenda Peover
Psychoanalytic Psychotherapist
Melrose Villa, Jocelyn Road, Richmond,
Surrey TW9 2TJ
Tel: 0181 940 5574
LCP

Ajit Perera
Cognitive Behavioural Psychotherapist
18 Manor Road, Merstham, Redhill,
Surrey RH1 3LT
Tel: 01737 642275/01737 782931
BABCP

Belinda Pethick
Psychoanalytic Psychotherapist
71 Kew Green, Richmond, Surrey
TW9 3AH
Tel: 0181 940 2426
LCP

Sheila Pratt
Psychoanalytic Psychotherapist
44 East Meads, Onslow Village,
Guildford, Surrey GU2 5SP
Tel: 01483 572 093
GUILD, WMIP, GCP

Lois Prichard
Transpersonal Psychotherapist
7 Rowan Court, Queens Road,
Kingston-upon-Thames, Surrey
CCPE

Marie-Louise Rabe
Psychoanalytic Psychotherapist
23 Addiscombe Court Road, Croydon
CR0 6TT
Tel: 0181 656 7954
AAP

Rosamund Reid
Psychoanalytic Psychotherapist
The Cottage, Ivy Lane, Woking, Surrey
GU22 7BY
Tel: 01483 764146
GCP

Hilary Reynolds
Psychoanalytic Psychotherapist
I I The Waldrons, Oxted, Surrey
RH8 9DY;
Flat 5, 130 Fellows Road, London
NW3 3JH
Tel: 01883 712783/0171 483 4649
IPC

Jane Ridley
Sexual and Marital Psychotherapist
77 Church Road, Richmond, Surrey
TW10 6LX
Tel: 0181 940 7678
BASMT

Nigel A Sage
Cognitive Behavioural Psychotherapist
W Surrey & N Hants Psychology, 2
Barossa Road, Camberley, Surrey
GU15 4JE
Tel: 01276 66772
BABCP

Audrey Sandbank
Family Therapist
30 Beech Road, Reigate, Surrey
RH2 9NA
Tel: 01737 221347
AFT

Jean Scott-Chinnery
Cognitive Behavioural Psychotherapist
173 Southway, Guildford, Surrey
GU2 6DJ
Tel: 01483 502787/0973 338310
BABCP

Michael Sevitt
Group Analyst
7 Upper Park Road, Kingston-upon-
Thames, Surrey KT2 5LB
Tel: 01372 729 136/0181 546 4173
IGA

Brian Sheldon
Cognitive Behavioural Psychotherapist
Horton Building, Royal Holloway
College, University of London, Egham,
Surrey TW20 0EX
Tel: 01784 443681/01249 658991
BABCP

Angela Sheppard-Fidler
Systemic Psychotherapist
3 Sunnybank, Epsom, Surrey KT18 7DY
Tel: 01372 727 200
KCC

Patricia Snowden
Sexual and Marital Psychotherapist
15 Hookfield, Epsom, Surrey KT19 8JQ
BASMT

Gordon Starte
Analytical Psychologist-Jungian Analyst
Northwood, Seale Lane, Puttenham,
Nr Guildford, Surrey GU3 1AX
Tel: 01483 810542/01483 811271
AJA

David Stembridge
Psychoanalytic Psychotherapist
10 Lismore Road, South Croydon,
Surrey
Tel: 0181 688 3947
LCP

Helen Tarsh
Psychoanalytic Marital Psychotherapist
Wentworth House, The Green,
Richmond upon Thames, Surrey
TW9 1PB
Tel: 0181 948 1913
TMSI

Suzanne Thornton
Integrative Psychotherapist
Ivy Cottage, Clockhouse Lane, Egham,
Surrey TW20 8PF
Tel: 01784 433480
RCSPC

Jay Upton
Psychoanalytic Psychotherapist
2 Eversfield Road, Kew, Richmond,
Surrey TW9 2AP
Tel: 0181 940 9263
GUILD

Yvonne Vallins
Psychoanalytic Psychotherapist
21 Hardwicke Road, Reigate, Surrey
RH2 9HJ
Tel: 01737 247 608
GUILD

Helen Veasey
Psychoanalytic Psychotherapist
8 Hilgay Close, Guildford, Surrey
GU1 2EN
Tel: 01483 38077
GUILD

Norma Wallace
Integrative Psychotherapist
100 Grosvenor Road, Langley Vale,
Epsom Downs, Surrey KT18 6JB
Tel: 01372 274779
MET

Michael Walton
Integrative Psychotherapist
18 Fern Close, Frimley, Camberley
GU16 5QV
Tel: 01276 27151
RCSPC

Vivien Webber
Psychoanalytic Psychotherapist
6 Catherine Drive, Richmond, Surrey
TW9 2BX
Tel: 0181 332 9834
LCP

Norman Webster
Cognitive Behavioural Psychotherapist
48 Merrivale Gardens, Woking, Surrey
GU21 3LX
Tel: 01483 723650
BABCP

Heather Williams
Psychosynthesis Psychotherapist
76 Deerings Road, Reigate, Surrey
RH2 0PN
Tel: 01737 240638
PET

Sally Willis
Group Analyst
50D Maple Road, Surbiton, Surrey
KT6 4AE
Tel: 0181 399 3334
IGA

Vivienne Wilmot
Psychoanalytic Psychotherapist
'Ithaca', 62 Petworth Road, Haslemere,
Surrey GU27 3AU
Tel: 01428 643912
GCP

James Wilson
Group Analyst
3 Fairbriar Court, Hereford Close,
Epsom, Surrey KT18 5BZ
Tel: 01372 735735 x 6299/
01372 720023
IGA

Margarita Wood
Child Psychotherapist
13 Uxbridge Road, Kingston-upon-
Thames, Surrey KT1 2LH
Tel: 0181 546 4668/0181 547 3419 (f)
ACP

Joan Woodhill
Biodynamic Psychotherapist
4 Calinwark Drive, Camberley, Surrey
GU15 3TX
Tel: 01276 22255
BTC

Bernadette Woolmer
Psychoanalytic Psychotherapist
79 North Road, Kew, Richmond,
Surrey TW9 4HQ
Tel: 0181 878 1259
BAP

Tim Woolmer
Group Analyst
79 North Road, Richmond, Surrey
TW9 4HQ
Tel: 0171 937 6956/0181 878 1259
IGA

Annette Wotton
Psychoanalytic Psychotherapist
White Cottage, 100 Dorking Road,
Chilworth, Surrey GU4 8NS
AGIP

Hymie Wyse
Integrative Psychotherapist
47 Ashcombe Road, Carshalton, Surrey
SM5 3ET
Tel: 0181 647 8568
MC

Melanie Yallop
Psychoanalytic Psychotherapist
11 Mount Pleasant, Weybridge, Surrey
KT13 8EP
Tel: 01932 844688
IPC, GCP

TYNE & WEAR

Jenny Biancardi
Psychodrama Psychotherapist
94 St Georges Terrace, Jesmond,
Newcastle Upon Tyne NE2 2DL
Tel: 0191 281 6243
BPDA

Pat Black
Psychoanalytic Psychotherapist
Reg Dept of Psychotherapy, Claremont
House, Royal Victoria Infirmary,
Newcastle NE2 4AA
NAAP

Ivy-Marie Blackburn
Cognitive Behavioural Psychotherapist
Newcastle Cognitive Therapy Centre,
Collingwood Clinic, St Nicholas
Hospital, Gosforth, Newcastle
NE3 3XT
Tel: 0191 213 0151
BABCP

David Brazier
Psychodrama Psychotherapist
Quannon House, 53 Grosvenor Place,
Jesmond, Newcastle Upon Tyne
NE2 2RE
Tel: 0191 281 5592
BPDA

Alison Cookson
Psychoanalytic Psychotherapist
Claremont House, Royal Victoria
Infirmary, Newcastle NE2 4AA
Tel: 0191 232 5131
NAAP

Paul Cromarty
Cognitive Behavioural Psychotherapist
Cognitive & Behavioural Therapies
Centre, Collingwood Clinics, Gosforth,
Newcastle upon Tyne NE3 3XT
Tel: 0191 223 2601
BABCP

Mary Dobson
Psychoanalytic Psychotherapist
10 Meadway, Forest Hall, Newcastle
upon Tyne NE12 9RB
Tel: 0191 266 6501
NAAP

Beckett Ender
Psychosynthesis Psychotherapist
21 Ebor Street, Heaton, Newcastle,
Northumberland NE6 5DL
Tel: 0191 281 8500
IPS

Anne Garland
Cognitive Behavioural Psychotherapist
Newcastle Cognitive Therapy Centre,
Collingwood Clinic, Gosforth,
Newcastle upon Tyne NE3 3XT
Tel: 0191 223 2509
BABCP

Timothy P Gillett
Cognitive Behavioural Psychotherapist
Sir Martin Roth Young Peoples Unit,
Newcastle General Hospital, Westgate
Road, Newcastle upon Tyne NE4 6BE
Tel: 0191 273 0404/0191 226 1734 (f)
BABCP

Diana Jansen
Psychoanalytic Psychotherapist
The Cottage, Dalton, Newcastle upon
Tyne NE18 5AA
Tel: 01661 886200
NAAP, CPP

Carolyn H John
Cognitive Behavioural Psychotherapist
11 Tankerville Terrace, Jesmond,
Newcastle upon Tyne NE2 3AH
Tel: 0191 281 0411
BABCP

Carlotta Johnson
Psychoanalytic Psychotherapist
Fordwich House, Hepscott, Nr
Morpeth, Northumberland NE61 6LN
Tel: 0607 514129
GUILD, NAAP

Frank Johnson
Psychoanalytic Psychotherapist
Fordwich House, Hepscott, Nr
Morpeth, Northumberland NE61 6LN
Tel: 0607 515 119
NAAP

Jo Reed Kendal
Psychoanalytic Psychotherapist
20/22 Fenham Road, Fenham,
Newcastle NE4 5PB
Tel: 0191 273 6973
NAAP

Charles Lund
Psychoanalytic Psychotherapist
Claremont House, Off Framlington
Place, Newcastle NE2 4AA
Tel: 0191 232 5131
NAAP

Janet Mahmood
Psychoanalytic Psychotherapist
11 Roseworth Avenue, Gosforth,
Newcastle upon Tyne NE3 1NB
Tel: 0191 285 7463
NAAP

Gordon Moore
Cognitive Behavioural Psychotherapist
Plessy Acute Therapy Centre, Stanley
Street, Blyth, Northumberland
NE2 4DE
Tel: 01670 355344
BABCP

Shirley P Morgan
Psychoanalytic Psychotherapist
Feversham School, Hexham Road,
Wallbottle NE15 8HW
Tel: 0191 229 0111
NAAP

William Morgan
Cognitive Psychotherapist
Department of Social Policy, 5th Floor
Claremont Bridge Building, University
of Newcastle, Newcastle NE1 7RU
Tel: 0191 222 7540
BABCP

Ashleigh Phoenix
Psychoanalytic Psychotherapist
Dryden Road Hospital, Dryden Road,
Gateshead
Tel: 0191 478 2388
NAAP

Alex Reed
Systemic Psychotherapist
29 Hallstile Bank, Hexham,
Northumberland NE46 3PQ
KCC

Jan Scott
Cognitive Behavioural Psychotherapist
University Dept Psychiatry, Royal
Victoria Infirmary, Newcastle Upon
Tyne NE1 4LP
Tel: 0191 227 5073
BABCP

Marc A Serfaty
Cognitive Behavioural Psychotherapist
University Dept of Psychiatry, Leazes
Wing, Royal Victoria Infirmary,
Richardson Road, Newcastle upon
Tyne NE1 4LP
Tel: 0191 232 5131
BABCP

Lindsay Shrubsole
Psychoanalytic Psychotherapist
David Grieve House, Headlam Street,
Byker NE6 2DX
Tel: 0191 224 2717
NAAP

Sally Standart
Cognitive Psychotherapist
Newcastle Cognitive Therapy Centre,
Collingwood Clinic, St Nicholas
Hospital, Gosforth, Newcastle
NE3 3XT
Tel: 0191 223 2509
BABCP

Dianne P Wilcox
Cognitive Behavioural Psychotherapist
50 Sunlea Avenue, Cullercoats, North
Shields, Tyne and Wear NE30 3DT
BABCP

WARWICKSHIRE

C Abberley
Psychodynamic Psychotherapist
5 Highcroft Crescent, Old Milverton
Road, Leamington Spa, Warwickshire
CV32 6BN
Tel: 01926 336066
WMIP

Erica Alexander
Family Therapist
5 Lloyd Close, Hampton Magna,
Warwick CV35 8SH
FIC

James Barrett
Psychoanalytic Psychotherapist
(Jungian)
45 Clarendon Road, Leamington Spa,
Warwickshire CV32 4SQ
Tel: 01926 316178
WMIP, LCP

Paula Burns
Psychoanalytic Psychotherapist
30 Langton Road, Rugby, Warwickshire
CV21 3UA
Tel: 01788 536446
IPSS

Brenda Hill
Sexual and Marital Psychotherapist
93 High Street, Bidford-on-Avon,
Warwickshire B50 4BD
Tel: 01789 773192
BASMT

Marilyn Howe
Sexual and Marital Psychotherapist
The Hawthorns, 25 Edyvean Close,
Bilton, Rugby, Warwickshire
CV22 6LD
BASMT

Brian Kiely
Cognitive Behavioural Psychotherapist
Psychology Department, Combe
House, George Eliot Hospital,
Nuneaton CV10 7DJ
Tel: 01203 350111
BABCP

Irene Lacey
Family Therapist
16 Keytes Lane, Barford, Warwick
CV35 8EP
AFT

Janet McNaught
Sexual and Marital Psychotherapist
Professional Counselling Services, The
Cloisters, Lower Leam Street,
Leamington Spa, Warwicks CV31 1DJ
Tel: 01926 882521
BASMT

Marion Myers
Psychodynamic Psychotherapist
44 St Mary's Road, Leamington Spa,
Warks CV31 1JP
Tel: 01926 425403
WMIP

P John Nicholas
Psychoanalytic Psychotherapist
(Jungian)
41 Portland Street, Leamington Spa
CV32 5EY
Tel: 01926 452891
WMIP

Murray Ryburn
Systemic Psychotherapist
34 North Villiers Street, Leamington
Spa, Warwicks CV32 5XY
KCC

Roy Watson
Psychodrama Psychotherapist
17 Albion Street, Kenilworth,
Warwickshire CV8 2FX
Tel: 01926 56574
BPDA

WEST MIDLANDS

Sally Baldwin
Psychoanalytic Psychotherapist
c/o 39 Daventry Road, Coventry
Tel: 01203 501 573
LCP

M A Beedie
Psychodynamic Psychotherapist
Bushey Fields Hospital, Bushey Fields
Road, Russells Hall, Dudley DY1 2LZ
Tel: 01384 252243
WMIP

Janice Birtle
Psychoanalytic Psychotherapist
Uffculme Clinic, Queensbridge Road,
Moseley, Birmingham B13 8QD
Tel: 0121 442 4545
WMIP

A R Bond
Psychodynamic Psychotherapist
Uffculme Clinic, Queensbridge Road,
Moseley, Birmingham B13 8QD
Tel: 0121 442 4545
WMIP

Jillyan Bray
Psychodynamic Psychotherapist
26 Maney Hill Road, Sutton Coldfield,
West Midlands B72 1JL
Tel: 0121 354 2403
WMIP

John Burnham
Systemic Psychotherapist
74 Park Hill, Moseley, Birmingham
B13 8DS
Tel: 0121 442 4545 x 331/0121 449
6760
KCC

Jane Calvert
Psychoanalytic Psychotherapist
48 Hartopp Road, Four Oaks, Sutton
Coldfield, Birmingham
Tel: 0121 323 4233
WMIP

Sonia Carlish
Psychoanalytic Psychotherapist
8 Moor Green Lane, Moseley,
Birmingham B13 8ND
Tel: 0121 449 0544
WMIP

Martin Cole
Sexual and Marital Psychotherapist
40 School Road, Moseley, Birmingham
B13 9SN
Tel: 0121 449 0892
BASMT

Grahame F Cooper
Psychoanalytic Psychotherapist, Sexual
and Marital Psychotherapist
6 Clarence Road, Moseley, Birmingham
B13 9SX
Tel: 0121 449 2308
BASMT, WMIP

Peter Cummins
Personal Construct Psychotherapist
Psychology Department, Adams Ward,
Gulson Hospital, Gulson Road,
Coventry CV1 2HR
Tel: 01203 844 061
CPCP

M Curran
Psychodynamic Psychotherapist
20 Bloomfield Road, Moseley,
Birmingham B13 9BY
Tel: 0121 449 0384
WMIP

Mahendra Singh Dayal
Psychoanalytic Psychotherapist
All Saints Hospital, Birmingham
B18 5SD
Tel: 0121 455 7986
WMIP

Elizabeth Anne Doggart
Cognitive Behavioural Psychotherapist
97 Wood Lane, Harborne, Birmingham
B17 9AY
Tel: 0850 990711/0121 427 7292
BABCP

Fiona Fox
Psychodynamic Psychotherapist
Chillington Farm, Codsall Wood,
Wolverhampton WV8 1RB
Tel: 01902 850269
WMIP

Cath Gilliver
Psychodynamic Psychotherapist
Uffculme Clinic, Queensbridge Road,
Birmingham B13 8QD
WMIP

S Gladwell
Psychodynamic Psychotherapist
Uffculme Clinic, Queensbridge Road,
Moseley, Birmingham B13 8QD
Tel: 0121 442 4545
WMIP

Patricia Goodyear
Psychoanalytic Psychotherapist
139 Knightlow Road, Harborne,
Birmingham B17 8PY
Tel: 0121 429 2364
WMIP

S Handy
Cognitive Behavioural Psychotherapist
60 Hamilton Avenue, Harborne,
Birmingham B17 8AR
Tel: 0121 427 4380
BABCP

Gerald A Harris
Hypno-Psychotherapist
77 Highbridge Road, Sutton Coldfield,
West Midlands B73 5QE
Tel: 0121 355 5278
NRHP

Nina Harris
Child Psychotherapist
Oaklands Centre, Selly Oak Hospital,
Raddlebarn Road, Birmingham B29 6JB
Tel: 0121 627 8231/0121 427 9546
ACP

T A Harvey
Psychoanalytic Psychotherapist
6 Clarence Road, Moseley, Birmingham
B13 9SX
Tel: 0121 449 2308
WMIP

Jane Hawksley
Sexual and Marital Psychotherapist
156 High Street, Henley-in-Arden,
Warwickshire B95 5BN
BASMT

Val Hill
Psychodynamic Psychotherapist
17 Brown's Court, Wake Green Park,
Moseley, Birmingham B13 9XU
Tel: 0121 449 7426
WMIP

A Kahn
Psychodynamic Psychotherapist
26 Wentworth Road, Harborne,
Birmingham B17 9SG
Tel: 0121 427 1434
WMIP

Laurence Kingsley
Psychoanalytic Psychotherapist
131a Alcester Road, Birmingham
B13 8JP
Tel: 0121 449 8122
WMIP

Raymond Lightbown
Sexual and Marital Psychotherapist
8 Woodlands Farm Road, Birmingham
B24 0PG
BASMT

Iris Linn
Hypno-Psychotherapist
32 Clive Road, Pattingham, Nr
Wolverhampton, West Midlands
WV6 7BY
Tel: 01902 701023
NRHP

Helen Lloyd
Psychoanalytic Psychotherapist
65 Blakedown Road, Halesowen
B63 4NG
Tel: 0121 501 3194
WMIP

Ian Lowery
Psychoanalytic Psychotherapist
Flat 8, 1 Melton Drive, Edgbaston,
Birmingham B15 2NB
Tel: 0121 440 2438
WMIP

I D Mackenzie
Psychoanalytic Psychotherapist
20 Bloomfield Road, Moseley,
Birmingham B13 9BY
Tel: 0121 449 0384
WMIP

David Male
Psychoanalytic Psychotherapist
81 Belle Vue, Wordsley, Nr
Stourbridge, W Midlands DY8 5DB
Tel: 01384 278761
WMIP

G May
Psychoanalytic Psychotherapist
62 Chadbrook Crest, Richmond Hill
Road, Edgbaston, Birmingham
B15 3RN
Tel: 0121 455 7327
WMIP

James McDonald
Psychoanalytic Psychotherapist
20 Greenfields Road, Wombourne,
Staffs WV5 0HP
Tel: 01902 893512
WMIP

Linda Morgan
Hypno-Psychotherapist
53 Wheeler Street, Stourbridge, West
Midlands DY8 1XL
Tel: 01384 836453
NSHAP

Ian Rory Owen
Integrative Psychotherapist
Psychology Department, University of
Wolverhampton, Lichfield Street,
Wolverhampton WV1 1DJ
Tel: 01902 28525
RCSPC

Margaret Randall
Psychoanalytic Psychotherapist
46 Queenswood Road, Moseley,
Birmingham B13 9AX
Tel: 0121 449 6884
WMIP

Robert W Rentoul
Analytical Psychotherapist
Woodhill, Ormes Lane,
Wolverhampton WV6 8LL
Tel: 01902 758504
WMIP

M J Reynolds
Analytical Psychotherapist
16 Bantock Court, Broad Lane,
Bradmore, Wolverhampton WV3 9DA
WMIP

Jenny Robinson
Transactional Analysis Psychotherapist
32 Grove Avenue, Moseley,
Birmingham B13 9RY
Tel: 0121 449 2284
ITA

Sylvia Rose
Transactional Analysis Psychotherapist
58 Oxford Road, Moseley, Birmingham
B13 9ES
Tel: 0121 449 2822
ITA

Geraldine Roy
Psychoanalytic Psychotherapist
174 Walmley Road, Sutton Coldfield
B76 8PY
Tel: 0121 351 1651
WMIP

A M Ryan
Psychodynamic Psychotherapist
The Barn, West Trescott Farm,
Bridgnorth Road, Wolverhampton
WV6 3EU
WMIP

Bebe Speed
Analytical Psychotherapist, Systemic
Psychotherapist
c/o West Midlands Institute of
Psychotherapy, Uffculme Clinic,
Queensbridge Road, Birmingham
B13 8QD;
Moseley, Birmingham B13 8DT
Tel: 0121 449 8503
WMIP, FIC

Jenny Stokes
Psychoanalytic Psychotherapist
51 Greenhill Road, Moseley,
Birmingham B13 9SU
Tel: 0121 449 1247
WMIP

Vivienne Taylor
Psychoanalytic Psychotherapist
146 Malt House Lane, Earlswood,
Solihull, West Midlands B94 5SD
Tel: 01564 702992
WMIP

Anthony Tilney
Transactional Analysis Psychotherapist
63 Victoria Road, Sutton Coldfield,
West Midlands B72 1SN
Tel: 0121 354 4042
ITA

Harold Tonks
Psychodynamic Psychotherapist
10 Cadell Court, 78 Cambridge Road,
Birmingham B13 9UG
Tel: 0121 449 8461
WMIP

Michael Townend
Cognitive Behavioural Psychotherapist
Solihull Health Care, 20 Union Road,
Solihull, West Midlands B91 3EF
Tel: 0121 711 7171 x 2222
BABCP

Brian Truckle
Child Psychotherapist, Psychoanalytic
Psychotherapist
Oaklands Centre, Selly Oak Hospital,
Raddlebarn Road, Birmingham B29 6JB;
96 Park Hill, Moseley, Birmingham
B13 8DS
Tel: 0121 627 8231/0121 449 3180
ACP, WMIP

Shirley Truckle
Child Psychotherapist, Psychoanalytic
Psychotherapist
Birmingham Trust for Psychoanalytic
Psychotherapy, 96 Park Hill,
Birmingham B13 8DS
Tel: 0121 627 8231/0121 553 1665
ACP, WMIP

Brenda Mary Tweed
Transactional Analysis Psychotherapist
148 Sir Hiltons Road, West Heath,
Birmingham B31 3NW
Tel: 0121 477 2420
ITA

Fiona Vallance
Psychodynamic Psychotherapist
St Paul's Convent, Selly Park,
Birmingham B29 7LL
Tel: 0121 472 0245
WMIP

S Van Marle
Psychoanalytic Psychotherapist
18 St Mary's Road, Birmingham
B17 0HA
Tel: 0121 442 4545
WMIP

Athina Villia-Gosling
Analytical Psychotherapist
1075 Bristol Road, Selly Oak,
Birmingham B29 6LX
Tel: 0121 472 6587
WMIP

Jean Way
Psychoanalytic Psychotherapist
4 Carisbrooke Road, Edgbaston,
Birmingham B17 8NW
Tel: 0121 429 3307
WMIP

Sue Wheeler
Psychodynamic Psychotherapist
17 Cambridge Road, Moseley,
Birmingham B13 9UE
Tel: 0121 444 3201
WMIP

Linda Winkley
Child Psychotherapist, Psychoanalytic
Psychotherapist
Oaklands Centre, Selly Oak Hospital,
Raddlebarn Road, Birmingham B29 6JB
Tel: 0121 627 8231/0121 554 1977
ACP, WMIP

Sue Wood
Sexual and Marital Psychotherapist
Heathlands Consulting Rooms, 130-132 Worcester Street, Stourbridge, West Midlands DY8 1BA
Tel: 01384 372987
BASMT

Joan Woodward
Psychodynamic Psychotherapist
61 Selly Wick Drive, Selly Park, Birmingham B29 7JQ
Tel: 0121 472 3055
WMIP

Robin Yapp
Cognitive Behavioural Psychotherapist
97 Wood Lane, Harborne, Birmingham, West Midlands B17 9AY
Tel: 0121 427 7292
BABCP

WEST SUSSEX

Mary Addenbrooke
Psychoanalytic Psychotherapist
The Vicarage, Colgate, Horsham, West Sussex RH12 4SZ
Tel: 01293 851826/01293 851362
SAP, GUILD

Peter Addenbrooke
Analytical Psychologist-Jungian Analyst
The Vicarage, Colgate, Horsham, West Sussex RH12 4SZ
Tel: 01293 851362
SAP

Janet Aldridge
Integrative Psychotherapist
64 Stocks Lane, East Wittering, West Sussex PO20 8NJ
Tel: 01243 670924
RCSPC

Kathleen Ayres
Hypno-Psychotherapist
6 Marshall Avenue, Bognor Regis, West Sussex PO21 2TJ
Tel: 01243 822263
NRHP

Rosemary Bardelle
Biodynamic Psychotherapist
1 Copper Hall Close, Rustington, West Sussex BN16 3RZ
Tel: 01903 850050
BTC

Eva Coleman
Integrative Psychotherapist
Lattenbells, Farm Lane, Ditching, Hassocks, West Sussex BN6 8DR
Tel: 01273 622886/01273 844142
RCSPC

Patricia Coussell
Psychoanalytic Marital Psychotherapist
Flat 5, Farebrothers, Church Street, Warnham, West Sussex RH12 3DZ
Tel: 01403 274484
TMSI

John Davidson
Cognitive Behavioural Psychotherapist
Greenwoods, Selsey Road, Sidlesham, Chichester, W Sussex PO20 7LR
Tel: 01444 441881/01243 641436
BABCP

Paul E Davis
Cognitive Behavioural Psychotherapist
The Summit, 22 Sudley Road, Bognor Regis, West Sussex PO21 1ER
Tel: 01243 869234
BABCP

Claude Esposito
Family Psychotherapist
Smiles Cottage, 47 High Street, Ardingly, West Sussex RH17 6TB
Tel: 01444 892 497
IFT

Richard Evans
Gestalt Psychotherapist
Brook House, Quay Meadow, Bosham, West Sussex PO18 8LY
Tel: 01243 573475
GPTI

John C Field
Cognitive Analytic Therapist
64 Wickham Hill, Hurstpierpoint, West Sussex BN6 9NP
Tel: 01273 834716/01273 843012
ACAT

Kitty Hagenbach
Transpersonal Psychotherapist
Nenthorne West, Hammerwood Road, Ashurst Wood, West Sussex RH19 3RU;
also at St Johns Wood NW8, and Fulham SW6
Tel: 01342 823461
CCPE

Elizabeth Hancock
Psychoanalytic Psychotherapist
Holly Cottage, 30 Summerhill Drive, Hurstwood, Felpham, W Sussex PO22 6AS
Tel: 01243 586591
GUILD

Linda Herdman
Cognitive Behavioural Psychotherapist
Bedale Mental Health, 1 Glencathara Road, Bognor Regis, West Sussex PO21 2SF
Tel: 01243 841041
BABCP

Christine Hillman
Psychosynthesis Psychotherapist
2 The Old Convent, East Grinstead, West Sussex RH19 3RS
Tel: 01343 315097
PET

Ursula Kiernan
Psychoanalytic Psychotherapist
13 Manor Close, Storrington, West Sussex RH20 4LF
Tel: 01903 743289
IPSS

Christine Le Brun
Integrative Psychotherapist
28 Oving Road, Chichester, West Sussex PO19 4EN
Tel: 01243 531440
RCSPC

Ann Orbach
Psychoanalytic Psychotherapist
19 New Park Road, Chichester, W Sussex PO19 1XH
Tel: 01243 783667
GUILD

Dorothy Palmer
Sexual and Marital Psychotherapist
Carriers, Lewes Road, Lindfield, West Sussex RH16 2LE
BASMT

R G Peckitt
Cognitive Behavioural Psychotherapist
Shelley House, 59 Nyewood Lane, Bognor Regis, West Sussex PO21 2SQ
BABCP

William Reavley
Cognitive Behavioural Psychotherapist
79 Whyke Road, Chichester, West Sussex PO19 2HU
Tel: 01243 531455/01243 787970
BABCP

Ivan Thorpe
Integrative Psychotherapist
20 Hailsham Road, Worthing, West
Sussex BN11 5PA
Tel: 01903 830057/01903 299075
RCSPC

Jim Walker
Psychoanalytic Psychotherapist
Westlake, Broad Street, Cuckfield,
West Sussex RH17 5LL
Tel: 01444 440204
IPSS

Marcus West
Analytical Psychologist-Jungian Analyst
Redleaf, 22 Steep Lane, Findon, West
Sussex BN14 0UE
Tel: 01903 877039/01903 874140
SAP

Margaret Wilkinson
Analytical Psychologist-Jungian Analyst
Wren Cottage, 15 Little Paddocks,
Ferring, West Sussex BN12 5NH
Tel: 01903 243037
SAP

WEST YORKSHIRE

James Anderson
Psychodynamic Psychotherapist
Brackley House, High Street, Holme-
on-Spalding Moor, York YO4 4AA
Tel: 01430 860106
YAPP

Susanna Bailey
Psychoanalytic Psychotherapist
'Highgate', off Street Lane, Leeds
LS8 1DF
YAPP

Kate Bonner
Psychodynamic Psychotherapist
17 Launds, Rochdale Road, Golcar,
Huddersfield HD7 4NN
Tel: 0484 654508
YAPP

Christine Bostock
Psychodynamic Psychotherapist
1 Hawthorn House, Regent Street,
Leeds LS7 4PE
Tel: 0113 269 7194
HIP, YAPP

Stephen Burr
Cognitive Behavioural Psychotherapist
The Cottage Clinic, 95 Bierley Lane,
Bradford, West Yorkshire BD4 6AW
Tel: 01274 684045
BABCP

Lesley Cann
Psychodynamic Psychotherapist
Lynfield Mount Hospital, (Bradford
CMHT), Bradford BD9 6DP
Tel: 01274 363233
YAPP

Kate Carr
Analytical Psychologist-Jungian Analyst
5a Westgate, Otley, West Yorkshire
LS21 3AT
Tel: 01943 467030/01943 467001
BAP, YAPP

Isobel Conlon
Psychoanalytic Psychotherapist,
Analytical Psychotherapist
The Women's Counselling and Therapy
Service, Oxford Chambers, Oxford
Place, Leeds LS1 3AP;
15 Ash Grove, Headingley, Leeds
LS6 1AX
Tel: 0113 245 5725/0113 275 1958
NWIDP, YAPP

Mary Courtney
Psychodynamic Psychotherapist
St James's University Hospital, Beckett
Street, Leeds LS9 7TJ
YAPP

Angela Douglas
Psychodynamic Psychotherapist
5A Westgate, Otley, West Yorkshire
LS21 3AT
Tel: 01943 468443
YAPP

Yvonne Eadie
Cognitive Analytic Therapist
4 Alberta Avenue, Leeds LS7 4LX;
Specialist Psychotherapy Services,
Brunswick House, 299 Glossop Road,
Sheffield S10 2HL
Tel: 0114 271 6894/01532 622118
ACAT

K J B Edwards
Psychoanalytic Psychotherapist
2 Prospect Place, Bramley, Leeds
LS13 3JW
Tel: 01532 558220
LPDO

Dennis Flannery
Psychodynamic Psychotherapist
Dept of Psychotherapy, Southfield
House, 40 Clarendon Road, Leeds
LS2 9PJ
Tel: 0113 243 9000
YAPP

Michael Gartland
Psychodynamic Psychotherapist
Fall Hall, Waterside, Marsden,
Huddersfield HD7 6BU
HIP

Tim Gauntlett
Psychoanalytic Psychotherapist
'Waske Hall', 50 Skircoat Green,
Halifax HX3 0SA
Tel: 01422 341391
IPSS

Annika Gilljam
Psychoanalytic Psychotherapist
24 Eaton Road, Ilkley, West Yorkshire
LS29 9PU
Tel: 01943 602449
GUILD, YAPP

Jean Glover
Sexual and Marital Psychotherapist
The Rectory, Church Side, Methley,
Leeds LS26 9BJ
Tel: 01977 515278
BASMT

Susan Godsil
Analytical Psychotherapist
1A Oakwood Lane, Leeds LS8 2PZ
Tel: 0113 264285
YAPP

Helga Hanks
Family Therapist, Analytical
Psychotherapist
Dept of Psychology, St James Hospital,
Leeds LS9 7TF
Tel: 0113 283 7038
YAPP

Anne Harrow
Analytical Psychotherapist
3 Woodbine Terrace, Headingley, Leeds
LS6 4AF
Tel: 0113 278 6142
YAPP

Colleen Heenan
Analytical Psychotherapist
11 Milford Place, Bradford BD9 4RU
Tel: 01274 493125
YAPP

Jan Helbert
Group Analyst
173 Highgate, Heaton, Bradford,
W Yorks BD9 5PU
Tel: 01274 544259
IGA

C Anthony Hill
Cognitive Behavioural Psychotherapist
Horbury Health Centre, 2A Westfield
Road, Horbury, Wakefield, West
Yorkshire WF4 6LL
Tel: 01924 265555
BABCP

Sharon Jackson
Personal Construct Psychotherapist
Highdale Cottage, 217 Barnsley Road,
Denby Dale, W Yorks HD8 8TS
Tel: 01484 864824
CPCP

Maggy Jones
Family Therapist
Bay House Cottage, 118 Main Street,
Coronley, Nr Keighley, W Yorks
BD20 8NR
Tel: 01535 661531/01535 637202
AFT

Margaret Kay
Group Analyst
20 Kingswood Gardens, Leeds LS8 2BT
Tel: 01977 605500/01532 666147
IGA

Monica Ludolf
Hypno-Psychotherapist
4 Riviera Gardens, Chapel Allerton,
Leeds, Yorkshire LS7 3DW
Tel: 0113 262 2355
NRHP

Rosie Manton
Psychosynthesis Psychotherapist
Lower Small Shaw Farm, Pecket Well,
Hebden Bridge, W Yorks HX7 8RF
Tel: 01422 843 501
PET

Carol Martin
Psychodynamic Psychotherapist
Dept of Psychiatry and Behaviourial
Sciences, 15 Hyde Terrace, Leeds
LS2 9JT
Tel: 0113 275 1982
YAPP

Sally Mitchison
Group Analyst
41 Ash Grove, Headingley, Leeds
LS6 1AX
IGA

Philip Nolan
NLP Psychotherapist
67 Kaye Lane, Almondbury,
Huddersfield, West Yorks HD5 8XT
Tel: 01484 432847
ANLP

Ian H Oakley
Analytical Psychotherapist
Glen Royd, Birchcliffe Road, Hebden
Bridge, West Yorkshire HX7 9DB
Tel: 01422 843563
LPDO, YAPP

Annabel Page
Analytical Psychotherapist
18 Crossbeck Road, Ilkley, W Yorks
YAPP

David Richards
Cognitive Behavioural Psychotherapist
32 The View, Roundhay, Leeds, West
Yorkshire LS8 1HQ
Tel: 0113 235 6914
BABCP

Sally Rose
Psychoanalytic Psychotherapist,
Psychodynamic Psychotherapist
4 Victoria Road, Kirkstall, Leeds
LS5 3JB
Tel: 0113 245 5725/0113 274 5147
AAP, YAPP

Chris Rowan
Integrative Arts Psychotherapist
60 Victoria Road, Leeds LS6 1DL
Tel: 0113 274 3065
IATE

Carolyn Rowe
Psychodynamic Psychotherapist
Low Meadow, Hall Drive, Bramhope,
Leeds LS16 9JF
HIP

Celly Rowe
Analytical Psychotherapist
Dept of Psychotherapy, Southfield
House, 40 Clarendon Road, Leeds
LS2 9PJ
YAPP

Brian Sidey
Psychoanalytic Psychotherapist
38 Wellington Crescent, Shipley,
W Yorks BD18 3PH
Tel: 01274 599327
YAPP

Helen Sieroda
Psychosynthesis Psychotherapist
42 Hangingroyd Road, Hebden Bridge,
W Yorks HX7 6AH
Tel: 01422 842804
PET

Alisdair Stokeld
Psychoanalytic Psychotherapist,
Psychodynamic Psychotherapist
4 Victoria Road, Kirkstall, Leeds
LS5 3JB
Tel: 0113 274 5147
AAP, YAPP

Gabrielle Syme
Analytical Psychotherapist
Mount Farm House, Town Street,
Rawdon, Leeds LS19 6QJ
Tel: 0113 250 5700
YAPP

Nick Tanna
Group Analyst, Psychodynamic
Psychotherapist
17 Grey Gables, Blacker Lane,
Netherton, W Yorks WF4 4SS
Tel: 01742 682883/01924 280424
IGA, YAPP

Chris Trepka
Cognitive Psychotherapist
Ashgrove CMHC, 48 Ashgrove,
Bradford, West Yorkshire BD7 1BL
Tel: 01274 391671
BABCP

Marta Vaciago Smith
Child Psychotherapist, Psychoanalytic
Psychotherapist
Dept of Child & Family Psychiatry,
St James University Hospital, Leeds LS9;
21 Milnthorpe Drive, Wakefield
WF2 7HU
Tel: 0113 2433144 x 4292/01924
255629
ACP, YAPP

Jane Walford
Transactional Analysis Psychotherapist
2a Weetwood Lane, Far Headingley,
Leeds LS16 5LS
Tel: 01132 789953
ITA

Robin Walford
Transactional Analysis Psychotherapist
2a Weetwood Lane, Far Headingley,
Leeds LS16 5LS
Tel: 01132 789953
ITA

Daphne Wallace
Psychoanalytic Psychotherapist
Fulford Grange Hospital, Mickleford
Lane, Rawdon, Leeds LS19 6BA
LPDO

L Wattis
Psychodynamic Psychotherapist
11 Cherry Rise, Leeds LS14 2HJ
Tel: 0113 273 6076
WMIP

Libby Wattis
Psychoanalytic Psychotherapist,
Psychodynamic Psychotherapist
11 Cherry Rise, Leeds LS14 2HJ
Tel: 01132 736076
LPDO, YAPP

Joan Webb
Psychoanalytic Psychotherapist,
Psychodynamic Psychotherapist
23 Henconner Lane, Chapel Allerton,
Leeds LS7 2NX
Tel: 01132 623766
LPDO, HIP, YAPP

Lawrence Welch
Cognitive Analytic Therapist
4 Alberta Avenue, Leeds LS7 4LX
Tel: 01904 430370/0113 262 2118
ACAT

Catherine Welsh
Analytical Psychotherapist
54 Ridge End Villas, Leeds LS6 2DA
Tel: 0113 275 0153
YAPP

Christopher John Williams
Cognitive Psychotherapist
Level 5, Clinical Sciences Building,
St James's University Hospital, Beckett
Street, Leeds LS9 7TF
BABCP

WILTSHIRE

Ron Banks
NLP Psychotherapist
Middlehill House, Middlehill, Box,
Corsham, Wiltshire SN13 9QS
Tel: 01225 742230
ANLP

Elizabeth Ann Brown
Group Analytic Psychotherapist
Flat 30, Anthony Road, Swindon,
Wiltshire SN4 9HN;
c/o Swindon Counselling Service, 23
Bath Road, Swindon, Wiltshire
SN1 4AS
Tel: 01793 813918/01793 514550
IPC

Elizabeth Cartwright Hignett
Child Psychotherapist
Iford Manor, Bradford-on-Avon,
Wiltshire
Tel: 01225 863146
ACP

Jane Coleman
Psychoanalytic Psychotherapist
'Cotswold', 99 High Street, Marshfield,
Chippenham, Wiltshire SN14 8LT
Tel: 01225 891478
IPSS

Brenda Davis
Cognitive Behavioural Psychotherapist
Child & Family Therapy Service,
Trowbridge Family Health Centre, The
Halve, Trowbridge, Wiltshire
BA14 8SA
Tel: 01225 766161
BABCP

Janice De Souza
Cognitive Psychotherapist
31 Wood Street, Swindon, Wiltshire
SN1 4AN
Tel: 01793 491917
BABCP

Jenifer Elton Wilson
Integrative Psychotherapist
The Bakehouse, Thickwood, Colerne,
Nr Chippenham, Wilts SN14 8BN
Tel: 0117 976 3818/01225 743081
MET

Wendy English
Psychoanalytic Psychotherapist
87 Greencroft Street, Salisbury,
Wiltshire SP1 1JF
Tel: 01722 321323
LCP

Philippa Gardner
Cognitive Analytic Therapist
The Maltings, 3 Back Lane, Ramsbury,
Wiltshire SN8 2QH
Tel: 01672 521036
ACAT

Michael Green
Psychoanalytic Psychotherapist
'Cotswold', 99 High Street, Marshfield,
Chippenham, Wiltshire SN14 8LT
Tel: 01225 891478
IPSS

Giles Lascelle
Psychodrama Psychotherapist
3 Hythe Road, Old Town, Swindon,
Wilts SN1 3NZ
Tel: 01793 430701
BPDA

Kathy Leach
Transactional Analysis Psychotherapist
Townsend, Ogbourne St Andrew,
Marlborough, Wilts SN8 1SE
Tel: 01672 841254
ITA

Jane Mellett
Humanistic and Integrative
Psychotherapist
16 Tutton Hill, Colerne, Chippenham,
Wilts SN14 8DN
Tel: 01225 742163
BCPC, AHPP

V Middleton-Smith
Systemic Psychotherapist
1 Queensberry Road, Salisbury, Wilts
SP1 3PH
Tel: 01722 327602
KCC

Peter Millar
Analytical Psychologist-Jungian Analyst
13 Cotswold Community, Ashton
Keynes, nr Swindon, Wiltshire
SN6 6QU
Tel: 01285 862312
AJA

Pamela Mundy
Transactional Analysis Psychotherapist
Tannery House, 8 The High Street,
Downtown, Wiltshire SP5 3PJ
Tel: 01725 513023
ITA

Kirsty M G O'Brien
Cognitive Psychotherapist
Farmer Memorial Unit, Savernake
Hospital, London Road, Marlborough,
Wilts SN8 3HL
Tel: 01793 425 418
BABCP

Patricia Pidgeon
Systemic Psychotherapist
1 Queensberry Road, Salisbury, Wilts
SP1 3PH
Tel: 01722 327602
KCC

David Pocock
Family Psychotherapist
Child and Family Guidance Centre,
Wyvern House, Theatre Square,
Swindon SN11 0DX
Tel: 01793 642666
AFT

Olga Pocock
Analytical Psychotherapist
104 Tollgate Road, Salisbury, Wiltshire
SP1 2JW
Tel: 01722 320093
SIP

Sheila Pregnall
Psychodrama Psychotherapist
70 Kent Road, Swindon, Wilts
Tel: 01793 341899
BPDA

Otto Rheinschmiedt
Group Analyst
Chapel Plaister's Road, Chapel Plaister,
Wadswick Lane, Nr Corsham, Wilts
SN14 9HZ
Tel: 01225 811945/0171 794 2320
IGA

Lynn Rimmer
Psychoanalytic Psychotherapist
69 St Mark's Road, Salisbury, Wilts
Tel: 01722 330661
GUILD

Melissa Robb
Family Psychotherapist
79 Gloucester Road, Malmesbury,
Wiltshire SN16 0AJ
FIC

John Sharpe
Group Analyst
Clare Cottage, 23 West Dean, Nr
Salisbury SP5 1JB
Tel: 01794 340028
IGA

Anna Tham
Core Process Psychotherapist,
Autogenic Psychotherapist
Turleigh Farm, Turleigh, Nr Bath,
Wiltshire BA15 2HH;
50 Blenheim Crescent, Notting Hill
Gate, London W11 1NY
Tel: 0171 727 6382/01225 868221
BAFAT, KI

Cara Voelcker
Humanistic and Integrative
Psychotherapist
Avils Farm, Lower Stanton, Quinton,
Chippenham, Wilts SN14 6DA
Tel: 01249 720202
BCPC

Stephen Westman
Cognitive Behavioural Psychotherapist
Dept of Behavioural & Cognitive
Psychotherapy, 31 Wood Street, Old
Town, Swindon, Wiltshire SN1 4AN
Tel: 01793 873558/01793 491917
BABCP

John Whitwell
Group Analytic Psychotherapist
The Old Farmhouse, Cotswold
Community, Ashton Keynes, Nr
Swindon, Wilts SN6 6QU
Tel: 01285 861694
LCP

Debbie Williams-Conley
Cognitive Behavioural Psychotherapist
31 Wood Street, Old Town, Swindon
SN1 4AN
Tel: 01793 491917
BABCP

WORCESTERSHIRE

Veronica Ashwell
Hypno-Psychotherapist
40 Canada Way, Lower Wick,
Worcester, Worcestershire WR2 4ED
Tel: 01905 428764
NRHP

A Duine Campbell
Psychoanalytic Psychotherapist
(Jungian)
Home Farm, High Park, Droitwich,
Worcestershire WR9 0AG
Tel: 01905 771588
WMIP

Sally Denham-Vaughan
Gestalt Psychotherapist, Integrative
Psychotherapist
The Summer House, 127 Columbia
Drive, Lower Wick, Worcester
WR2 4XX
Tel: 01905 763333 x 33103
GPTI

Toni Gilligan
Gestalt Psychotherapist
22 Tileford Cottages, Long Lane,
Tileford, Nr Pershore, Worcs
WR10 2LA
Tel: 01386 561528
GCL

Nigel Groom
Psychoanalytic Psychotherapist
(Jungian)
The Gap, Saleway, Nr Droitwich Spa,
Worcestershire WR9 7JY
Tel: 01905 391470
IPC, WMIP

Gordon Law
Transactional Analysis Psychotherapist
5 Bawdsey Avenue, Malvern,
Worcester WR14 2EW
Tel: 01684 566268
ITA

Rita Newby
Psychoanalytic Psychotherapist
78 Victoria Avenue, Worcester
WR5 1ED
Tel: 01905 763552
CPP

Anne O'Leary
Group Analytic Psychotherapist
27 Bushley Close, Woodrow, Redditch,
Worcestershire B98 7TU
Tel: 01527 501565
IPC

Mary Reddie
Psychoanalytic Psychotherapist
The Landscape, 41 East Road,
Bromsgrove, Worcs B60 2NW
Tel: 01527 872055
WMIP

Kate Vickers
Psychosynthesis Psychotherapist
Village Cottage, Hopton Wafers,
Kidderminster, Worcestershire
DY14 0NB
Tel: 01299 271 336
IPS

OVERSEAS

AFRICA

Vera Burhmann
Analytical Psychologist-Jungian Analyst
Arnetis 307, Strand, RSA 7140
SAP

Alice Jacobus
Biodynamic Psychotherapist
7B Norfolk House, Main Road,
Kenilworth 7700, West Cape, South
Africa
BTC

Sheila Miller
Child Psychotherapist
5e Spinney Close, 17 Main Avenue,
Rivera 2193, South Africa
Tel: 00 127 646 9786
ACP

Diane Salters
Transactional Analysis Psychotherapist
15 Disa Road, Murdock Valley North,
Simons Town 7995, Republic of South
Africa
ITA

ASIA

Aiveen Bharucha
Child Psychotherapist
125 Wodehouse Road, Colaba,
Bombay 400005, India
ACP

Manek Bharucha
Child Psychotherapist, Psychoanalytic
Psychotherapist
125 Wodehouse Road, Colaba,
Bombay 400005, India
Tel: 00 91 22 215 1257
ACP, AAP, CPP

Bernard Wai Kai Lau
Cognitive Behavioural Psychotherapist
Room 703 Capitol Centre, Jardine's
Bazaar, Causeway Bay, Hong Kong
Tel: 852 25773996/852 25773900
BABCP

Leslie E C Lim
Cognitive Behavioural Psychotherapist
Institute of Mental Health, 10 Buangkok
Green, Singapore 1953, Republic of
Singapore
Tel: 00 65 385 0411
BABCP

Breda Noonan
Group Analyst
Columban Sisters, PO Box 2369,
Ozamiz City 9101, Philippines
IGA

Charles O'Brian
Family Psychotherapist
Dept of Applied Social Sciences, City
Polytechnic of Hong Kong, Tai Chee
Avenue, Kowloon, Hong Kong
IFT

Nia Pryde
Sexual and Marital Psychotherapist
14A Block 1, Tam Towers, 25 Sha Wan
Drive, Victoria Road, Hong Kong
BASMT

Dorcas Shuen
Psychoanalytic Psychotherapist, Group
Analytic Psychotherapist
42, RN 8, Fairview Park, Yuen Long,
NT, Hong Kong
Tel: 248 20308
LCP

AUSTRALASIA

Anne Brown
Jungian Child Analyst
11 Eckersley Court, Blackburn South
3130, Melbourne, Victoria, Australia
SAP

Brian Cade
Family Therapist
PO Box 386, Eastwood, New South
Wales, Australia 2122
Tel: 012 612 868 2606
AFT

Ann Cebon
Child Psychotherapist
8 Coombs Avenue, Kew, Victoria 3101,
Australia
Tel: 0171 794 3353/0061 398 533 114
ACP

Giles Clark
Analytical Psychologist-Jungian Analyst
1 Russell Street, Woollahra, Sydney,
NSW 2025, Australia
Tel: 02 386 0648
IGAP

Stefan Durlach
Integrative Psychotherapist
Flat 5, 40 Fletcher Street, Bondi, 2026
Australia
Tel: 02 308 705
RCSPC

Bill Farrell
Psychoanalytic Psychotherapist
PO Box 60297, Titirangi, Auckland
1007, New Zealand
Tel: 01244 679748
LPDO

Peter B Fullerton
Psychoanalytic Marital Psychotherapist,
Analytical Psychologist-Jungian Analyst
99 The Righi, Eaglemont, Victoria 3084,
Australia
Tel: 03 9455 2791/03 9459 5323
TMSI, SAP

Bruce Hart
Family Psychotherapist
4 Paruma Avenue, Birkdale, Auckland
10, New Zealand
Tel: 649 483 7892
AFT

Rachel M Henry
Child Psychotherapist
4 Wigram Road, Austinmer, NSW
2515, Australia
ACP

Julia Howell
Psychodrama Psychotherapist
59 Bandara Street, Morningside,
Brisbane, Q4170, Australia
Tel: 010 617 395 722
BPDA

Peter Hubbard
Psychosynthesis Psychotherapist
Institute of Psychosynthesis, 7 Farnol
Street, Auckland 5, New Zealand
Tel: 00 649625 9559
IPS

Pat Kenwood
Child Psychotherapist
51 Cole Street, Brighton, Victoria
3186, Australia
Tel: 00 61 359 62306
ACP

Sandra Kondos
Integrative Psychotherapist
Flat 5, 40 Fletcher Street, Bondi, NSW
2026, Australia
Tel: 02 308 705
RCSPC

Elana Leigh
Integrative Psychotherapist
158 Wellington Street, Bondi 2026,
Sydney, Australia
Tel: 02 300 9907
ITA, MET

Shirley Morrissey
Cognitive Behavioural Psychotherapist
Dept of Psychology and Sociology,
James Cook University, PO Box 6811,
Cairns 4870, Australia
Tel: 00 61 77 788 343/00 61 77 814 198
BABCP

Lynne Norris
Cognitive Behavioural Psychotherapist
75c Goodall Street, Hillsborough,
Auckland, New Zealand
Tel: 00649 625 8602
BABCP

Renata Ogilvie
Existential Psychotherapist
18 The Rampart, Castlecrag, NSW
2068, Australia
Tel: 02 99 06 88 44/02 99 67 20 20
RCSPC

Helen Palmer
Psychosynthesis Psychotherapist
Institute of Psychosynthesis, 7 Farnol
Street, Auckland 5, New Zealand
Tel: 00 649 625 9559
IPS

Anthony Peters
Personal Construct Psychotherapist
50 Cairnfield Road, Whangarei, New
Zealand
CPCP

George Rodwell
Analytical Psychologist-Jungian Analyst
PO Box 33-486, Takapuna, Auckland,
New Zealand
Tel: 649 623 1359
SAP

Ruth Schmidt-Neven
Child Psychotherapist
12 Cornell Street, Camberwell 3124,
Victoria, Australia
Tel: 00 618 304253/00 618 857777 (f)
ACP

Alison Strasser
Integrative Psychotherapist
251 Underwood Street, Paddington,
NSW 2021, Australia
Tel: 010 612 327 1693/02 363 5663
RCSPC

Lily Elizabeth Tindle
Cognitive Behavioural Psychotherapist
14 Cranwood Street, Kenmore 4069,
Queensland, Australia
Tel: 00 61 7 33788530/
00 61 7 33783156
BABCP

Henck P J G van Bilsen
Cognitive Behavioural Psychotherapist
75c Goodall Street, Hillsborough,
Auckland, New Zealand
Tel: 006496 258602
BABCP

Linda Viney
Personal Construct Psychotherapist
Department of Psychology, PO Box
1144, Wollongong University, NSW
2500, Australia
CPCP

Jaclyn Webber
Systemic Psychotherapist
PO Box 428, Deewhy 2099, Sydney,
Australia
KCC

EUROPE

Josta Bernstadt
Gestalt Psychotherapist
In der Hohl 32, 56170 Bendorf,
Germany
GPTI

Kate Bradshaw-Tauvon
Psychodrama Psychotherapist
Sveavagen 52 2tr, S 111 34 Stockholm,
Sweden
Tel: 0046 8 411 0420
BPDA

Jill Bright
Analytical Psychologist-Jungian Analyst
2 Alexander Place, Cork, Ireland
Tel: 353 28 21989/353 21 507360
BAP

Gerard Butcher
Cognitive Behavioural Psychotherapist
St John of God Hospital, Stillorgan, Co
Dublin, Ireland
Tel: 353 1 288 1781
BABCP

Elizabeth J Caird
Hypno-Psychotherapist
22 Cherrymount Park, Dublin 7, Irish
Republic;
8 Melford Avenue, Thornton Heath,
Surrey CR7 7RH
Tel: 0181 689 3601/00 3531 8389767
NSHAP

Hanne Campos
Group Analyst
Pasea San Gervasio 30, 08022
Barcelona, Spain
Tel: 010 34 3 247 5639
IGA

Victoria Canobbio
Primal Psychotherapist
Berlinerstrass 73, 14467 Potsdam,
Germany
LAPP

Anna Chesner
Psychodrama Psychotherapist
Kaiserholzstrasse 41, D80995 Munich,
Germany
Tel: 00 49 89 150 6521
BPDA

Kay Conroy
Psychosynthesis Psychotherapist
White House, Templeogue, Dublin 6,
Ireland
Tel: 00 3531 280 0626
IPS

Annalisa Corlando
Family Therapist
Via Giacinto Collegus No 57, 10138
Torino, Italy
AFT

Mira Dana
Psychoanalytic Psychotherapist
22 Shimshon Street, Haifa 34615, Israel
Tel: 00 9724 256130
WTC

Patricia de Hoogh-Rowntree
Analytical Psychologist-Jungian Analyst
The Garden House, Nottermorsweg 3,
7642 LM Wierden, The Netherlands
Tel: 00 31 546 573737/
00 31 546 577217
BAP

Sascha Donges
Psychosynthesis Psychotherapist
Schule fur Erwachsene,
Gundeldingerstrasse 280, Basel CH
4053, Switzerland
Tel: 00 4161 357975
PET

Mark Duberry
Integrative Psychosynthesis
Psychotherapist
6 Woodlands Avenue, Stillorgan, Co
Dublin, Ireland
Tel: 003531 2887216
RE.V

Livia Fischer
Integrative Psychosynthesis
Psychotherapist
Gyllenkrooksgatan 5, 412 82 Goteborg,
Sweden
Tel: 0046 31 205602
RE.V

Stephen Flynn
Psychodrama Psychotherapist
Carrig Na Floinn, Lavally, Mallow, Co
Cork, Eire
Tel: 010 35322 2193
BPDA

C Frey-Wehrlin
Analytical Psychologist-Jungian Analyst
Plattenstrasse 48, CH8032 Zurich,
Switzerland
SAP

Verity Gavin
Integrative Psychotherapist
Le Bastidon, Hameau de St Pierre,
St Martin de Castillon 84750, France
Tel: 90 75 10 65/90 75 25 71
RCSPC

Gabriella Grauso Calaresu
Child Psychotherapist
Via Cola di Rienzo 8, Milan 20144, Italy
Tel: 00 392 423 8627
ACP

Mary V E Grover
Psychoanalytic Psychotherapist
Ardralla, Church Cross, Skibbereen,
County Cork, Ireland
Tel: 00 353 28 38373
LCP

Christina Hagelthorn
Psychodrama Psychotherapist
Foreningsgaten 4, 411 27 Goteborg,
Sweden
BPDA

Caroline Harrison
Sexual and Marital Psychotherapist
RCSI Dept of OB/GYN, Rotunda
Hospital, Dublin 1, Ireland
Tel: 3531 8727599
BASMT

Pauline Hering-Josefowitz
Child Psychotherapist
12 Chemin Des Eglantieres, 1208
Geneva, Switzerland
Tel: 00 41 22 349 1230
ACP

Sister Columba Howard
Transactional Analysis Psychotherapist
St John of God Generalate, Summerhill
Heights, Summerhill Wrexford, Ireland
Tel: 053 42396
ITA

Brian Howlett
Sexual and Marital Psychotherapist
1B Belfield Court, Donnybrook, Dublin
4, Ireland
BASMT

Julian Ibanez
Psychoanalytic Psychotherapist
Alameda de Urquijo, NÏ94, NÏ1 DCHA,
48013 Bilbao, Spain
Tel: 00 344 4277340
AAP

Jennie Jarvis
Attachment-based Psychoanalytic
Psychotherapist
Grundhof 6, 79271 St Peter, Germany
Tel: 00 492 11680 1752
CAPP

Karina Kalderwaay
Psychosynthesis Psychotherapist
Ouderkerkdijk 204, 1096 cr
Amsterdam, Netherlands
Tel: 00 3120 692 9589
PET

Saeunn Kjartansdottir
Psychoanalytic Psychotherapist
'Asendi' 16, 108 Reykjavik, Iceland
Tel: 00 354 581 1148/00 354 553 9113
AAP

Meg Kleisen
Psychosynthesis Psychotherapist
Fransekampweg 1, 6721 MC,
Bennekom, Holland
Tel: 31 83 891 9236
IPS

Effie Layiou-Lignos
Child Psychotherapist
54 Aimono Street, Colonos, 10442,
Athens, Greece
Tel: 00 301 514 8123
ACP

Mikael Leiman
Cognitive Analytic Therapist
Raivonmaentie 7, 83500 Outokumpu,
Finland
Tel: 358 73 550 517
ACAT

Suzanne Maiello Hunziker
Child Psychotherapist
Via Dalmazia 16A, I-00198 Rome, Italy
Tel: 00396 85351420
ACP

Ingrid Masterson
Psychoanalytic Psychotherapist
'Alberta', Ardtona Avenue, Lower
Churchtown, Dublin 14, Ireland
Tel: 003531 2988 288
IPSS

Benig Mauger
Psychoanalytic Psychotherapist
69 Cowper Road, Rathmines, Dublin 6,
Ireland
Tel: 1 4970501
AGIP

Yaron Mazliach
Child Psychotherapist
PO Box 42, Gam Rashal, Herzelliya
46308
Tel: 00 9729 589978
ACP

Aine McCarthy
Sexual and Marital Psychotherapist
357 Howth Road, Raheny, Dublin 5,
Ireland
BASMT

Rita McCarthy
Analytical Psychologist-Jungian Analyst
39 Balally Terrace, Dundrum, Dublin
16, Ireland
Tel: 295 6002
AJA

Helen McCormack
Psychoanalytic Psychotherapist
Transito de los Gramaticos-3, 15703
Santiago, Spain
Tel: 00 34 981 572866
AAP

Hugh E McFadden
Cognitive Behavioural Psychotherapist
'Sancta Maria', Gortlee, Letterkenny,
Co Donegal, Ireland
Tel: 00353 742 1919
BABCP

Mary McGoldrick
Cognitive Behavioural Psychotherapist
St Patrick's Hospital, James's Street,
Dublin 8, Ireland
Tel: 00 3531 677 5423
BABCP

Maureen McGroary-Meehan
Sexual and Marital Psychotherapist,
Behavioural Psychotherapist
Donegal Community Services, East End
House, Clar Road, Donegal Town,
Ireland
Tel: 00 353 72 41351/00 353 73 21933
BASMT, BABCP

Angela Molnos
Group Analyst
H-4025 Debrecen, Hatvan u 1/A, 1 11h,
III, 10, Hungary
IGA

Chris Moutzoukis
Cognitive Behavioural Psychotherapist
63 Egnatia Street, 546 31 Thessaloniki,
Greece
Tel: 00 30 31 210 379/00 30 31 288 380
BABCP

Catherine Murray
Psychodrama Psychotherapist
Newtown House, Doneraile, Co Cork,
Eire
Tel: 00 353 222 4117
BPDA

Aine O'Connor
Primal Psychotherapist
The Garden Studio, 15 Morehampton
Road, Donnybrook, Dublin 4, Ireland
Tel: 00 3531 668 3123
LAPP

Mary O'Conor
Sexual and Marital Psychotherapist
The Albany Clinic, Clifton Court,
Lower Fitzwilliam Street, Dublin 2,
Ireland
Tel: 661 2222
BASMT

Julia O'Neill
Biodynamic Psychotherapist
Corabella, Ardfinnan, Clonmel, Co
Tipperary, Ireland
Tel: 00353 52 36512
BTC

Miceal O'Regan
Psychosynthesis Psychotherapist
Eckart House, 19 Clyde Road,
Ballsbridge, Dublin 4, Ireland
Tel: 00 3531 6684687
IPS

Bernadette O'Sullivan
Personal Construct Psychotherapist
2 Dungar Terrace, Northumberland
Avenue, Dun Laogharie, Co Dublin,
Ireland
Tel: 00 3531 284 3336
CPCP

Johanna Ohnesorg
Biodynamic Psychotherapist
Bachlerstrasse 62, CH-8046,
Switzerland
Tel: 0044 1 371 7647
BTC

Irene Oromi
Educational Therapist
C/Mallorca 239 2o, 08008 Barcelona,
Spain
Tel: 5897067
FAETT

Joachim Otto
Biodynamic Psychotherapist
Furnacetown, Feacle, Co Clare, Eire
BTC

Thelma Patricia
Psychoanalytic Psychotherapist,
Humanistic Psychotherapist
Flaskekrokken, Flaskebekk, 1450
Nesoddtangen, Norway
IPSS, AHPP

Rainer Pervöltz
Integrative Psychotherapist, Body
Psychotherapist
Wenzingerstr 28, 79291 Herdingen,
Germany
Tel: 07668 94532
CCHP

Franc Peternel
Group Analyst
Slovenceva 109, 61113 Ljubljana,
Slovenia
Tel: 010 061 302 899/
010 38 061 344521
IGA

Alessandra Piontelli
Child Psychotherapist
Largo Richini 1, 20100 Milan, Italy
Tel: 00 392 583 07193
ACP

Kirsten Prosch-Jensen
Systemic Psychotherapist
Bredgade 16, 4000 Roskilde, Denmark
Tel: 00 45 46326940
KCC

Danielle Roex
Psychosynthesis Psychotherapist
Zandpoortstraat 16, 9000 Gent,
Belgium
Tel: 00 3291 234543
IPS

Marjo Ruismaki
Systemic Psychotherapist
Majavatie 9L 40, Helsinki, 00800 HKI,
Finland
Tel: 90 789923
KCC

Margo Russell
Psychosynthesis Psychotherapist
PsykosyntesAkademin, Stora Nygatan
45, 2 tr, S-111 27 Stockholm, Sweden
Tel: 00 46 8 217 409
PET

Topsy Sandler
Systemic Psychotherapist
Skogalundsklippan 6 NB, 131 39 Nacka,
Sweden
Tel: 08 716 1692
KCC

Mary Sazanjoglou-Hitzos
Jungian Child Analyst
PO Box 21523, 55201 Panorama,
Salonika, Greece
Tel: 031 310 471
SAP

Els Schopman
Psychodrama Psychotherapist
Menadostr 49 B, 1095 TH Amsterdam,
Netherlands
BPDA

Marja Schulman
Child Psychotherapist
Visakoivuntie 23A, SF-02130 Espoo,
Finland
Tel: 00 35 80 4553712/
00 35 80 4558948 (f)
ACP

Brian Scott-McCarthy
Psychoanalytic Psychotherapist
Pigges Eye, South Schull, Schull, Co
Cork, Ireland
Tel: 00 353 21772622
AGIP

Gregoris Simos
Cognitive Behavioural Psychotherapist
24 Vas Georgiou Street, 546 40
Thessalonki, Greece
Tel: 0030 31 853 009/0030 31 838 755
BABCP

Anne-Charlotte Soderstrom
Psychoanalytic Psychotherapist
Ilmarigaten 10, C 44 00100 Helsinki,
Finland
Tel: 010 3588 440005
IPSS

Jill Stevens
Sexual and Marital Psychotherapist
11 Tivoli Terrace North, Don
Laoghaire, Co Dublin, Ireland
BASMT

Gerry Sullivan
Lacanian Analyst
14 The Belfry, Inchicore Road, Dublin
8, Ireland
Tel: 00 353 1 4544304
CFAR

Mehmet Sungur
Cognitive Behavioural Psychotherapist
Medical School of Ankara University,
Dept of Psychiatry, Cebeci-Ankara,
Turkey
Tel: 00 90 312 2851007/
00 90 312 3192160 x 697
BABCP

Froukje Tjepkema
Psychoanalytic Psychotherapist
Johan De Wittstraat 7 bis, 3581 XX
Utrecht, The Netherlands
Tel: 030 2333715
IPC

Yvonne Tone
Cognitive Behavioural Psychotherapist
St Patrick's Hospital, PO Box No 136,
James's Street, Dublin 8, Ireland
Tel: 01 677 5423
BABCP

Carole Turner
Transactional Analysis Psychotherapist
La Galera de Las Palmeras 119, 03590
Altea, Alicante, Spain
Tel: 00 346 584 6191
MET, ITA

Ingrid van Beek
Psychosynthesis Psychotherapist
Kooikershof 7, 5256 KD Heusden,
Holland
Tel: 31 20 676 5171
IPS

Diederik van Rossum
Psychosynthesis Psychotherapist
c/o Emmastraat 26, 1075 HV
Amsterdam, Holland
Tel: 31 20 676 5171
IPS

Margit Veje
Psychoanalytic Psychotherapist
Skt Pauls Gade 8B, St, 8000 Arhus C,
Denmark
Tel: 00 45 86 128530
AAP

Shirley Ward
Humanistic Psychotherapist
Curtlestown, Enniskerry, Co Wicklow,
Ireland
Tel: 013531 2862428
AHPP

IRELAND

Ger Murphy
Integrative Psychotherapist
23 Lower Albert Road, Sandy Cove,
Co Dublin, Ireland
Tel: 00 35 31 280 8989
MC

Mary O'Brien
Sexual and Marital Psychotherapist
6 West View, Church Road, Blackrock,
Cork, Ireland
BASMT

NORTH AMERICA

Dolores Bate
Gestalt Psychotherapist
1747 Gordon Avenue, West
Vancouver, BC, Canada V7V 1V4
Tel: 604 922 5793/604 925 2012 (f)
GPTI

Cynthia Carlson
Child Psychotherapist
2516E Newton Avenue, Milwaukee W1
53211, USA
ACP

Ellie Chalkind
Psychoanalytic Psychotherapist
46 Carolane Trall, Houston, Texas,
77024, USA
WTC

Luise Eichenbaum
Psychoanalytic Psychotherapist
WTC I, 80 East 11th, Suite 101, New
York 10003, USA
WTC

Franz Epting
Personal Construct Psychotherapist
9310 NW 10th Pl, Gainesville, Florida,
FL 32606, USA
CPCP

Deborah M Fish
Hypno-Psychotherapist
3437 W 2nd Avenue, Vancouver, BC,
Canada V6R 1J3
Tel: 604 737 7563
NRHP

Lois Harvey
Analytical Psychologist-Jungian Analyst
Carol Woods # 131, 750 Weaver Diary
Road, Chapel Hill, North Carolina,
27514 USA
SAP

Gloria Hope-Price
Group Analyst
44 Sunset Ridge, St James, Barbados,
BWI
Tel: 010 1 809 432 6425
IGA

Helen Lewis
Hypno-Psychotherapist
25 Tidy Island Blvd, Bradenten, Florida
34210, USA
NRHP

Rita Lynn
Group Analyst
622 North Linden Drive, Beverly Hills,
California 90210, USA
Tel: 310 285 0503
IGA

Mildred Marshak
Analytical Psychologist-Jungian Analyst
12257 Atrium Circle, Saratoga, CA
95070, USA;
313 Saratoga Avenue, Los Gatos, CA
95030, USA
SAP

Hem Phaterpekar
Psychoanalytic Psychotherapist
#116-8434 120th Street, Surrey, British
Columbia, V3W 7S2, Canada
Tel: 604 543 4449
LPDO

Noemie Rattray
Psychoanalytic Psychotherapist
45 Spice Hill Road, Warwick, WK03,
Bermuda
Tel: 441 238 2980
LCP

Tove Rognerud
Psychoanalytic Psychotherapist
c/o Alan Mason, Treasury Dept,
Government Admin Building,
Georgetown, Grand Caymen, British
West Indies
IPSS

Renee Roseman
Psychoanalytic Psychotherapist
104-430 River Avenue, Winnipeg,
Manitoba, R3L OC6 Canada
Tel: 204 474 0428
BAP

Mara Sidoli
Child Psychotherapist
4307 Massachusetts Avenue NW,
Washington DC 20016, USA
Tel: 001 202 362 1886
ACP

David Smolira
Hypno-Psychotherapist
6559 North Glenwood Avenue,
Chicago, IL 60623-5121, USA
NSHAP

Pamela Sorenson
Child Psychotherapist
2725 Hunt Country Lane,
Charlottesville, Virginia 22901-8989,
USA
Tel: 010 1180 49795669/010 1804
9715540 (f)
ACP

Helge Staby-Deaton
Child Psychotherapist
1 Mya Drive, Princeton, New Jersey
08540, USA
Tel: 001 609 924378
ACP

J R Wilson
Systemic Psychotherapist
108 Willards Way, Yorktown, Virginia
23693, USA
Tel: 1010 804 764 7801/1010 804 766
8029
KCC

SOUTH AMERICA

Doris Benrey
Child Psychotherapist
Fuente de los Angeles 16,
Techmachalco, Mexico 53950
Tel: 0052 589 7315
ACP

M L Montalbetti
Child Psychotherapist
Santander 147, Miraflores, Lima 18,
Peru
ACP

Andre Samson
Biodynamic Psychotherapist
Rua Baru 65, Sao Paulo, SP 04639-030,
Brazil
BTC

ALPHABETICAL LISTING

A

Shafika Abbasi (p.88)
C Abberley (p.134)
Elisabeth Abrahams (p.50)
Jan Abram (p.50)
Susanna Abse (p.50)
Stella Acquarone (p.65)
Madeleine Adam (p.19)
Eve Adams (p.28)
Ghislaine Adams (p.7)
Janet Adams (p.5)
Martin Adams (p.47)
Mary Adams (p.66)
Megan Adams (p.125)
Tessa Adams (p.82)
Stephen Adams-
  Langley (p.88)
Margaret Adcock (p.34)
Mary Addenbrooke (p.137)
Peter Addenbrooke (p.137)
Evelyn Adey (p.8)
Eve Adler (p.5)
Hella Adler (p.66)
James Agar (p.28)
Percy Aggett (p.47)
Joyce Agnew (p.27)
Ana Aguirregabiria (p.88)
Eileen Aird (p.127)
Bobbie Akinboro-
  Cooper (p.66)
Nigel Alabaster (p.82)
Gisela Albrecht (p.50)
Sylvia Albrighton (p.66)
Helena Alder (p.109)
Barrie Aldridge (p.27)
Janet Aldridge (p.137)
Erica Alexander (p.134)
Gina M V Alexander (p.82)
Paul T Alexander (p.38)
Sandra Alexander (p.50)
V V Alexander (p.66)
Tamara Alferoff (p.50)
Ian Alister (p.8)
Brenda Allan (p.50)
Kay Allan (p.28)
Nadia Allawi (p.88)
Lesley Allen (p.66)
Patricia Allen (p.96)
Patricia M Allen (p.117)
Tessa Allen (p.126)
Mary A Allinson (p.15)
Paul Allsop (p.50)
Christine Alnuaimi (p.38)
Talal Alrubaie (p.50)
Michelle Altman (p.45)
Jenny Altschuler (p.66)
Anne Alvarez (p.66)
Olivia Amiel (p.50)

Peter Amies (p.117)
Eleanor Anderson (p.34)
Elizabeth Anderson (p.50)
James Anderson (p.138)
Janet Anderson (p.24)
Judith Anderson (p.115)
Michael Anderton (p.66)
Chriso Andreou (p.88)
Elizabeth Andrew (p.89)
Robert Andry (p.50)
Nabil Anees (p.125)
Yon Anjali (p.17)
Ofra Anker (p.50)
Shakir Ansari (p.82)
Carol Anson (p.47)
Ivor Antao (p.7)
Louise Anthias (p.30)
Joy Appleby (p.105)
Sonia Appleby (p.82)
Janet Applegarth (p.42)
Richard Appleton (p.20)
Remy Aquarone (p.112)
Stephen Arcari (p.20)
C Ruth Archer (p.89)
Jacqueline Ardeman (p.109)
Alicia Arendar (p.50)
Seema Ariel (p.50)
Lynda Arkwright (p.42)
P K Armbruster (p.17)
Pamela Armitage (p.117)
Caroline Armstrong (p.96)
Derick Armstrong (p.89)
Brian Arnold (p.50)(p.51)
Katherine Arnold (p.51)
Lynn Arnold (p.96)
Rosemary Arnold (p.51)
Biddy Arnott (p.66)
Pamela Arriens (p.8)
A R Arthur (p.66)
Jane Arundell (p.24)
Yiannis Arzoumanides (p.96)
Robert Ash (p.1)
Lia Ashby (p.51)
Anne Ashley (p.127)
Jill Ashley (p.66)
Veronica Ashwell (p.141)
Freda Ashworth (p.42)
Elke Asmus (p.6)
Alexandra Asseily (p.96)
John Aston (p.33)
Bronwen Astor (p.127)
James Astor (p.96)
Loukas Athanasiadis (p.89)
Coral Atkins (p.82)
James Atkinson (p.126)
Paul Atkinson (p.47)
Brian Attridge (p.30)
Melloney Atuahene (p.30)

Peter Atwood (p.82)
Lesley Austin (p.66)
Neil Austin (p.66)
Shelagh Austin (p.1)
Mark Aveline (p.115)
Jenny Averbeck (p.109)
Corinne Aves (p.51)
Jocelyn Avigad (p.109)
Paul Aylard (p.1)
Anthony Ayres (p.82)
Kathleen Ayres (p.137)
Racheli Azgad (p.51)
Okeke Azu-Okeke (p.89)

B

Claire Bacha (p.105)
Roger Bacon (p.8)
Charles D Bactawar (p.34)
Steve Bagnall (p.117)
James Bailey (p.44)
Susanna Bailey (p.138)
Marie Baines (p.127)
Adrienne Baker (p.51)
Jan Baker (p.96)
Moke Baker (p.127)
Ruth Baker (p.127)
Sally Baldwin (p.134)
Gillian Ballance (p.34)
Tessa Balogh Henghes (p.51)
James Bamber (p.96)
Nickie Bamber (p.38)
Debbie Bandler
  Bellman (p.66)
Mary Banks (p.38)
Ron Banks (p.140)
Afrakuma Bannerman (p.51)
Anne Bannister (p.105)
Gill Bannister (p.47)
John Bannon (p.20)
Maureen Rahima
  Bannon (p.20)
Vivien Bar (p.51)
Talia Levine Bar-
  Yoseph (p.66)
Tessa Baradon (p.66)
Monica Bard (p.66)
Rosemary Bardelle (p.137)
Peter Barham (p.96)
Anne Baring (p.30)
Elizabeth Barker (p.96)
Gina Barker (p.51)
John Barker (p.44)
Lily Barker (p.121)
Bill Barnes (p.107)
Hugh Barnes (p.1)
Tricia Barnes (p.89)
Gillian Barnett (p.105)
Mary Barnett (p.20)

Ruth Barnett (p.66)
Gillian Barratt (p.51)
Sara Barratt (p.34)
James Barrett (p.134)
Jean Barrett (p.66)
Kate Barrows (p.1)
Paul Barrows (p.1)
Anne Barry (p.51)
Jill Barry (p.20)
Francesca Bartlett (p.51)
Harika Basharan (p.96)
George Bassett (p.115)
Dolores Bate (p.146)
Helen Bates (p.28)
Parizad Bathai (p.66)
Cecilia Batten (p.28)
Audrey Battersby (p.66)
Stefanie Baum (p.96)
Eva Bayley (p.127)
Gay Baynes (p.66)
Monica Baynes (p.15)
Jan D Beach (p.31)
Hilary Beard (p.82)
Mia Beaumont (p.51)
Joanna Beazley-
  Richards (p.20)
Jean B Bechhofer (p.23)
Amely Becker (p.66)
Dale Beckett (p.51)
Jennifer Beddington (p.51)
Julie C Beech (p.7)
Diane Beechcroft (p.115)
Naona Beecher-
  Moore (p.45)
M A Beedie (p.134)
Margaret Beer (p.127)
Deike Begg (p.89)
Ean Begg (p.89)
Agnes Beguin (p.96)
Harold Behr (p.51)
Chris Beighton (p.24)
Frances Bell (p.82)
Claire Bellenis (p.66)
Stella Bellis (p.19)
Susan Benbow (p.105)
Helen Bender (p.47)
Nicholas Benefield (p.11)
Haydene Benjamin (p.66)
Angela Bennett (p.51)
Gerald A Bennett (p.19)
Lesley Bennett (p.82)
Margaret Bennett (p.127)
Ross Bennett (p.31)
Judy Bennison (p.121)
Rita Benor (p.17)
Doris Benrey (p.147)
Jarlath Benson (p.115)
Pauline Benson (p.67)

Patrick Bentley (p.51)
Arnon Bentovim (p.67)
Bice Benvenuto (p.67)
Marie Beresford (p.51)
Edith Bergel (p.107)
Iris Berger (p.34)
Jocelyn Berger (p.89)
Lorna Berger (p.96)
Joseph Berke (p.51)
Linda Berman (p.11)
Josta Bernstadt (p.143)
Eileen Berry (p.31)
Juliet Berry (p.121)
Mary Berry (p.11)
Peter Berry (p.34)
Sally Berry (p.51)
Sally Kemmis Betty (p.89)
Judith Bevan (p.34)
Aiveen Bharucha (p.142)
Manek Bharucha (p.142)
Radha Bhat (p.127)
Vibha Bhatt (p.51)
Z Bhunnoo (p.38)
Jenny Biancardi (p.133)
Vicky Bianco (p.51)
Keith Bibby (p.89)
Tricia Bickerton (p.47)
Desmond Biddulph (p.89)
Paul Bielicz (p.107)
Geraldine
  Bienkowski (p.104)
John H Bierschenk (p.51)
Julie G Biggs (p.121)
Tessa Bilder (p.51)
Jane Bingham (p.24)
Linda Binnington (p.51)
Jane Bird (p.34)
John Bird (p.11)
Diana Birkitt (p.89)
Janice Birtle (p.134)
Nagy R Bishay (p.105)
Bernadine Bishop (p.67)
Patricia Bishop (p.82)
Peter Bishop (p.20)
David Black (p.67)
Dora Black (p.46)
Judith Black (p.82)
Margaret Black (p.42)
Nicholas J Black (p.31)
Pat Black (p.133)
Sandra Black (p.82)
Teresa J Black (p.44)
Ivy-Marie Blackburn (p.133)
John Blackburn (p.121)
Paul Blackburn (p.23)
Polly Blacker (p.121)
Renate Blackwood (p.127)
Caroline Blair (p.23)
Adrian Blake (p.38)
Nancy Blake (p.113)
Raymond Blake (p.109)
John Bland (p.82)
Roger Bland (p.67)
Evanthe Blandy (p.67)
Graeme Blench (p.38)

E Veronica (Vicky)
  Bliss (p.42)
Sonia Bliss (p.123)
Linda Bloch (p.117)
Valerie Blomfield (p.83)
Wolf Blomfield (p.89)
Irene Bloomfield (p.96)
David C Blore (p.115)
Kirsten Blow (p.118)
Colin M Blowers (p.20)
Derek Blows (p.38)
Anita Blum (p.67)
Arna Blum (p.67)
Miranda Blum (p.96)
Suzanne Blundell (p.107)
Cherry Boa (p.127)
David Boadella (p.46)
Janet Boakes (p.83)
Ian Boardman (p.14)
Daphne Boddington (p.31)
Joachim Boening (p.96)
Michaela Boening (p.97)
Roger Boff (p.127)
Antonia Boll (p.89)
Charmian Bollinger (p.46)
Elaine Bollinghaus (p.7)
G N Bolsover (p.113)
Jan Bolton (p.127)
Tom Bolton (p.107)
A R Bond (p.134)
Sharon Bond (p.47)
Valerie Bonnefin (p.67)
Kate Bonner (p.138)
Robert Bor (p.46)
Sheila Borges (p.89)
Dascha Boronat (p.11)
Su Borsig (p.67)
Camilla Bosanquet (p.97)
Christine Bostock (p.138)
Elizabeth Bostock (p.109)
Mary Boston (p.17)
Paula Boston (p.67)
Bryan Boswood (p.24)
Marie Botha (p.38)
David Bott (p.20)
Willie Botterill (p.97)
Victoria Botwood (p.97)
Jane Bould (p.31)
John Boulton (p.47)
Anne Bousfield (p.38)
Barry Bowen (p.114)
Rosalind Bowers (p.126)
Elizabeth Bowman (p.20)
Heather Bowman (p.52)
Jo Bownas (p.52)
Sally Box (p.1)
Suzanne Boyd (p.38)
Ebba Boyesen (p.97)
Gerda Boyesen (p.97)
Mona Lisa Boyesen (p.97)
Sue Bradbury (p.20)(p.21)
Catrin Bradley (p.52)
Jonathan Bradley (p.52)
Rex Bradley (p.52)
Kate Bradshaw-
  Tauvon (p.143)

Marion Brady (p.52)
Rosemary Braid (p.27)
Irene Brankin (p.24)
Maire Brankin (p.118)
Mari E Brannigan (p.28)
Pauline Brassington (p.127)
Eleanor Braterman (p.52)
Wendy Bratherton (p.8)
Anna Brave-Smith (p.52)
Jillyan Bray (p.134)
Stephen Bray (p.83)
Anne Brazier (p.124)
David Brazier (p.133)
Graham Breeze (p.125)
Clare Brennan (p.21)
Damian Brennan (p.52)
Joady Brennan (p.121)
Stan Brennan (p.52)
June Brereton (p.11)
John Brett (p.27)
Madelyn Brewer (p.118)
Michael Briant (p.8)
Steve Briant (p.8)
Jenny Bridge (p.127)
Johanna Brieger (p.8)
George Bright (p.97)
Jill Bright (p.143)
Elisabeth Brindle (p.39)
Marion Brion (p.47)
Charlie Brittain (p.83)
Clive Britten (p.52)
Stewart Britten (p.24)
Sue Brock (p.31)
Sasha Brookes (p.89)
Shaun Brookhouse (p.105)
Beverly Brooks (p.83)
Louise Brooks (p.11)
Lee Brosan (p.9)
Cornelia Brosskamp (p.21)
Sue Brough (p.125)
William Brough (p.115)
Vivian Broughton (p.123)
Anne Brown (p.142)
Avril Brown (p.115)
Carolyn Brown (p.116)
Dennis Brown (p.97)
Elizabeth Ann Brown (p.140)
Geoffrey Brown (p.5)
Gillian A Brown (p.127)
Lesley Brown (p.109)
Ray Brown (p.1)
Robin Brown (p.118)
Robin Gordon Brown (p.1)
Sara Brown (p.52)
Teresa Brown (p.28)
Thomas M Brown (p.104)
Toni Brown (p.127)
Elizabeth Browne (p.52)
Margaret Browne (p.97)
Maureen Browne (p.97)
Valerie Browne (p.127)
Claire Bruas-Jaquess (p.97)
Ann Bruce (p.83)
Clare Brunt (p.109)
Mervyn Brunt (p.33)
Pat Bryant (p.116)

Sandra Bryson (p.107)
Sarah-Jill Buchanan (p.127)
Linda Buckingham (p.83)
Richard Buckland (p.17)
Jackie Buckler (p.97)
Jane E Buckley (p.9)
M Buckley (p.105)
Marie-Noël (Billie)
  Buckley (p.89)
Mary Buckley (p.46)
Nicky Buckley (p.45)
Valerie Bucknall (p.39)
Julia Buckroyd (p.34)
Rosemary Budgell (p.5)
Diana Buirski (p.97)
Birgit Bukovics-
  Heiller (p.127)
Graham Bull (p.24)
Liz Bulmer (p.113)
Carol Bunker (p.39)
Nigel Bunker (p.39)
Jane Bunster (p.97)
Nigel Burch (p.67)
Charlotte Burck (p.67)
C W Burdett (p.113)
Suesanne Burgess (p.47)
Bernard Burgoyne (p.52)
Vera Burhmann (p.142)
Maggie Burlington (p.47)
John Burnard (p.89)
Tamara Burnet-Smith (p.6)
Joan Burnett (p.89)
John Burnham (p.134)
Alex Burns (p.67)
Elizabeth Burns (p.7)
Paula Burns (p.134)
Stephen Burr (p.138)
Ellora Polly Burridge (p.52)
William Burritt (p.28)
Joanna Burrows (p.11)
Susie Burrows (p.52)
Mary V Burton (p.67)
Michael Burton (p.21)
Monica Burton (p.109)
Simon Burton (p.112)
Dennis R Bury (p.52)
Malcolm Bush (p.127)
Don Busolini (p.34)
Christel Buss-
  Twachtmann (p.52)
Barbara Butcher (p.7)
Gerard Butcher (p.143)
Josie Butcher (p.11)
Catherine Butler (p.89)
John Butler (p.89)
Linda Butler (p.14)
Todd Butler (p.97)
Diana Butt (p.67)
Eric Button (p.44)
Sally Byford (p.9)
Catherine ByGott (p.52)
John Byng-Hall (p.67)
Sue Byng-Hall (p.34)
Carola Byring (p.67)
Dorothy Byrne (p.52)
Patrick J Byrne (p.128)

C

Jennifer Caccia (p.67)
Brian Cade (p.142)
Elizabeth J Caird (p.143)
Mary Cairns (p.39)(p.115)
J G Callaghan (p.42)
Harriet B Calvert (p.7)
Jane Calvert (p.134)
Angela Cameron (p.9)
Anna Cameron (p.52)
Iain Cameron (p.115)
Katherine Cameron (p.24)
Rod Cameron (p.52)
A Duine Campbell (p.141)
Christine Campbell (p.89)
David Campbell (p.52)
Donald Campbell (p.67)
Elizabeth Campbell (p.67)
Jane Campbell (p.118)
Margaret Campbell (p.118)
Aileen Campbell Nye (p.52)
John Campbell-
 Beattie (p.17)
Christina Campbell-
 Thomson (p.52)
Hanne Campos (p.143)
Maria Canete (p.67)
Lesley Cann (p.138)
Victoria Canobbio (p.143)
Diana Cant (p.39)
Rosemarie Carapetian (p.67)
Misha Carder (p.1)
Pietro Cardile (p.97)
Faye Carey (p.83)
Illana Cariapa (p.125)
Sonia Carlish (p.134)
John Carlisle (p.9)
Cynthia Carlson (p.146)
Theresa Carlson (p.67)
Nicholas Carolan (p.52)
Brede Carr (p.128)
Jean Carr (p.118)
Kate Carr (p.138)
Samantha Carr (p.9)
Helen Carroll (p.109)(p.128)
Barbara Carruthers (p.28)
Dianna Carruthers (p.31)
Carol Carsley (p.39)
Paula Carter (p.28)
Alan Cartwright (p.39)
Elizabeth Cartwright
 Hignett (p.140)
Kate Cartwright (p.39)
Charles Caruana (p.83)
Martha Carvajal-
 Ogden (p.128)
Richard Carvalho (p.67)
Ann Casement (p.97)
Jules Cashford (p.52)
Anne Casimir (p.53)
John Casson (p.42)
Sean Cathie (p.53)
J Heather Caulfield (p.125)
Geraldine Causton (p.39)
Prudence Cave (p.68)
Paul Caviston (p.53)

Anthony Cawley (p.107)
Deborah Cazalet (p.68)
Ann Cebon (p.142)
Ellie Chalkind (p.146)
David Challender (p.39)
Raymond T Challis (p.116)
Suzy Challis (p.125)
Laurena Chamlee-
 Cole (p.53)
Lynn Champion (p.68)
Anne Chancer (p.89)
Diana Chandler (p.83)
Mark Philip Chandler (p.24)
Philip Chandler (p.53)
Stanley Chandler (p.109)
Lilian Chandwani (p.68)
Michael Channon (p.128)
Maureen Chapman (p.24)
Sandy Chapman (p.47)
Claire Chappell (p.68)
Praxoulla
 Charalambous (p.53)
Anne Charvet (p.68)
Carola Chataway (p.97)
Anne Chatfield (p.53)
Jon Chatham (p.124)
Janine Cherry-
 Swaine (p.116)
Anna Chesner (p.143)
Karen Chessell (p.83)
Joyce Chesterton (p.118)
Nick Child (p.23)
Adrian Childs-Clarke (p.31)
Barbara Chilton (p.21)
Kathleen Chimera (p.89)
Giselle China (p.68)
Jacques China (p.53)
Freni Chinoy (p.128)
Sangamithra U D
 Choudree (p.97)
Jim Christie (p.28)
Conny Christmann (p.68)
Elphis Christopher (p.53)
Suzanne Clackson (p.5)
Tosin Clairmonte (p.21)
Catherine Clancy (p.97)
Miles Clapham (p.89)
Jo Ann Clapp (p.68)
Tony Clapp (p.109)
John Clare (p.97)
Louise Clare (p.5)
Alec Clark (p.114)
Christine Clark (p.39)
Giles Clark (p.142)
Margaret Clark (p.25)(p.128)
Nita Clark (p.109)
Elaine Clarke (p.11)
Isabel Clarke (p.31)
Peter R F Clarke (p.121)
Stephen Lawrence
 Clarke (p.15)
Susan Elizabeth
 Clarke (p.19)
Wendela Clarke (p.7)
Petruska Clarkson (p.97)
Patricia Claxton (p.6)

John Clay (p.89)
Evelyn Cleavely (p.109)
Alison Clegg (p.126)
Ian Clegg (p.45)
Sue Clements-
 Jewery (p.107)
Dorel Cleminson (p.83)
Richard Cleminson (p.83)
David Clendon (p.34)
Cairns Clery (p.90)
Sarah Clevely (p.17)
Andrea Clifford (p.31)
Jennifer Clifford (p.53)
Elaine Clifton (p.90)
S Clifton (p.31)
Andrea Clough (p.83)
Gillian Clover (p.34)
Christopher Clulow (p.68)
Rachel Clyne (p.1)
Sonia Coats (p.116)
Vivienne Cobden (p.34)
Marion Cochlin (p.97)
Christine Cochrane (p.97)
Margaret Cochrane (p.83)
Andrew Cockburn (p.68)
Anne Codd (p.5)
Mary Coghlan (p.118)
Stephen Cogill (p.98)
Barbara Cohen (p.34)
David Cohen (p.53)
Maggie Cohen (p.53)
Pauline Cohen (p.68)
Sylvia Cohen (p.53)
Vivienne Cohen (p.68)
Hans W Cohn (p.128)
Nancy Cohn (p.53)
Grace Coia (p.28)
Mireille Colahan (p.53)
Barbara Cole (p.21)
Martin Cole (p.135)
Shanti Cole (p.15)
Eva Coleman (p.137)
Jane Coleman (p.140)
Jane Coleridge (p.90)
Peter J Coles (p.31)
Prophecy Coles (p.90)
Walter Coles (p.90)
Gloria Collins (p.11)
Jane Collins (p.6)
Leila Collins (p.34)
Natalie Collins (p.47)
Jeffrey Collis (p.68)
Whiz Collis (p.1)
Anita Colloms (p.47)
Warren Colman (p.68)
Louise Colson (p.90)
Ingrid Coltart (p.98)
Stephen Colver (p.121)
Ann Combes (p.83)
Ann Conlon (p.90)
Isobel Conlon (p.138)
Christopher Connolly (p.68)
Beth Conroy (p.15)
Kay Conroy (p.143)
Susan Conway (p.21)
Jim Conwell (p.68)

Marie Conyers (p.25)
Robert Cooke (p.105)
Alan Cooklin (p.68)
Alison Cookson (p.133)
Suzanne Coombs (p.14)
Cassie Cooper (p.109)
Faye Cooper (p.121)
Graham Cooper (p.11)
Grahame F Cooper (p.135)
Hilary Cooper (p.68)
Howard Cooper (p.53)
Jan Cooper (p.6)
Jillian Cooper (p.53)
Margaret Cooper (p.15)
Penny Cooper (p.116)
Rebecca Cooper (p.47)
Robin Cooper (p.68)
Sara Cooper (p.53)
Suzanne Cooper (p.109)
Terry Cooper (p.53)
Tom Cooper (p.53)
Beta Copley (p.68)
Brian Copley (p.31)
Alexander Coren (p.118)
Enid Corker (p.126)
Annalisa Corlando (p.143)
Susan Corneck (p.83)
Maria Cornell (p.42)
Lou Corner (p.6)
Ursula Cornish (p.109)
Ita Coronas (p.90)
Jenny Corrigall (p.9)
Marilyn Corry (p.90)
Ronald Cosmo
 Luckcock (p.53)
Jan Costa (p.105)
John Costello (p.90)
Marie Costello (p.68)
Barbara Cottman (p.1)
Christopher
 Coulson (p.126)
Susan Coulson (p.53)
Stephen Coulter (p.115)
Theresa Coulter (p.68)
Valerie Coumont
 Graubart (p.90)
Susie Courtault (p.90)
Anita Courtman (p.109)
Mary Courtney (p.138)
Jan Cousins (p.83)
Patricia Coussell (p.137)
Kay Coussens (p.25)
Linda Coutts (p.39)
Jeni Couzyn (p.53)
Susan Cowan-Jenssen (p.53)
Pauline Cowmeadow (p.83)
Brenda Cox (p.124)
Christine Cox (p.21)
Mary Cox (p.15)
Murray Cox (p.6)
Philip Cox (p.47)
Jenny Coxwell-White (p.6)
Christina H Coyle (p.120)
Jenny Craddock (p.98)
Ian Craib (p.126)
James Craig (p.44)

William Cramer (p.14)
George Crawford (p.28)
Joan Crawford (p.47)
Stephen Crawford (p.68)
Kiki Crean (p.33)
Gordon Cree (p.83)
Verena Crick (p.109)
Dave Crisp (p.68)
J A Crisp (p.126)
Bill Critchley (p.53)
Gabrielle Crockatt (p.98)
Paul Cromarty (p.133)
Clare Crombie (p.47)
Terry Cromey (p.115)
Sheila Cromwell (p.34)
Jeremiah Cronin (p.39)
Didi Crook (p.98)
A S B Crosby (p.21)
John Cross (p.29)
Paddy Crossling (p.42)
Carol Crouch (p.25)
Michael Crowe (p.83)
Julia Crowley (p.53)
Catherine Crowther (p.54)
Paul Cubie (p.1)
Lynne Cudmore (p.68)
Deborah Cullinan (p.34)
Andrew Culliss (p.90)
Sylvia Cullum (p.126)
Peter Cummins (p.135)
Diane Cunningham (p.39)
Valerie Cunningham (p.39)
Annalee Curran (p.83)
M Curran (p.135)
Naomi Curry (p.44)
Marjorie Curtis (p.42)
Bernadette Curwen (p.39)
Ron Cushion (p.46)
Anne Cussins (p.109)
Jane Cutler (p.1)
Adrienne Cutner (p.42)
Gerard Cutner (p.29)
Grazyna Czubinska (p.48)

D

Josephine Dahle (p.31)
Brian Daines (p.121)
Penelope Daintry (p.98)
Caroline Dalal (p.98)
Farhad Dalal (p.54)
Anne M Dale (p.7)
Barbara Dale (p.69)
Carole Dale (p.121)
Rebecca Dalgarno (p.44)
Peggy Dalton (p.98)
Kevin Daly (p.69)
Mira Dana (p.143)
Hazel Danbury (p.128)
Catherine Daniel (p.48)
Gwyn Daniel (p.118)
Heather Daniel (p.54)
Diana Daniell (p.69)
Dorothy Daniell (p.34)
Frank Daniels (p.16)
Mo Daniels (p.31)
Orpa Daniels (p.54)

Susan Daniels (p.54)
Alan Danks (p.98)
Didier Danthois (p.69)
Gillian Darcy (p.34)
Arminal Dare-Bryan (p.90)
Guy Dargert (p.21)
Susannah Darling
  Khan (p.17)
Liv Darling (p.54)
Hazel Darnley (p.39)
Marie-Laure
  Davenport (p.54)
Sarah Davenport (p.105)
Tom Davey (p.21)
Ann David (p.54)
Anna David (p.48)
Julian David (p.17)
Adele Davide (p.69)
Maggie Davidge (p.98)
Leslie Davidoff (p.113)
Suzanne Davidoff (p.113)
Jennifer Davids (p.69)
Brian Davidson (p.46)
John Davidson (p.137)
Ann Davies (p.128)
Dilys Davies (p.44)
J Keith Davies (p.98)
Judy Davies (p.9)
Mairlis Davies (p.124)
Miranda Davies (p.29)
Peggy Davies (p.39)
Sheila Davies (p.1)
Arna Davis (p.34)
Brenda Davis (p.140)
Emerald Davis (p.90)
Helen Davis (p.69)
Jim Davis (p.105)
Joyce Davis (p.98)
P Davis (p.115)
Paul E Davis (p.137)
Valerie Davis (p.35)
Dilys Daws (p.69)
Jenny Dawson (p.17)
Joyce Dawson (p.39)
Linda Dawson (p.48)
Neil Dawson (p.69)
Peter Dawson (p.83)
Erica Day (p.1)
Laurie Day (p.128)
Lesley Day (p.110)
Michael Day (p.110)
Sally Day (p.110)
Mahendra Singh
  Dayal (p.135)
Patricia de Berker (p.128)
Paul de Berker (p.128)
Polly de Boer (p.54)
John De Carteret (p.121)
Marianne De Groot (p.7)
Penelope de Haas (p.69)
Patricia de Hoogh-
  Rowntree (p.143)
Heather de Leon (p.98)
Patrick de Mare (p.69)
Asun de Marquiegui (p.90)
Janice De Souza (p.140)

Felicity de Zulueta (p.54)
Marie De'ath (p.118)
Kieron Deahl (p.46)
Alicia Deale (p.83)
Paul Dean (p.110)
Sally Dean (p.110)
Guy Deans (p.44)
Judith Dear (p.98)
Barbara Kathleen
  Dearnley (p.83)
Mark Dearnley (p.128)
Elizabeth A Deeble (p.25)
Christine Deering (p.110)
Judith Dell (p.69)
Peter Delves (p.44)
Lindsey D Denford (p.83)
Sally Denham-
  Vaughan (p.141)
Ursula Deniflee (p.83)
Cara Denman (p.90)
Francesca Denman (p.90)
Brian Denness (p.16)
Diana Dennis (p.98)
Suzanne Dennis (p.90)
Peter Dent (p.44)
Marika Denton (p.69)
Hanora Desmond (p.21)
George Dewey (p.1)
Gianni Dianin (p.54)
Adrian Dickinson (p.69)
Paul Dickinson (p.107)
Johanna Maria
  Diepeveen (p.29)
Sedwell Diggle (p.9)
Rosemary Dighton (p.90)
Marisa Dillon Weston (p.98)
Bernard Dinneen (p.123)
John Dinwoodie (p.98)
Rosemary Dixon-
  Nuttall (p.21)
Damini Angeli
  Diyaljee (p.69)
Wendy Dobbs (p.69)
Mary Dobson (p.133)
Barbara Docker-
  Drysdale (p.29)
Raymond F Docking (p.112)
Elizabeth Dodge (p.84)
Elizabeth Anne
  Doggart (p.135)
Anne Doggett (p.69)
Geri Dogmetchi (p.69)
Yair Domb (p.54)
Gillian Donaldson (p.98)
Sascha Donges (p.144)
Laura Donington (p.90)
Gillian Donohoe (p.125)
Moira Doolan (p.39)
Pat Dooley (p.128)
Damien Doorley (p.69)
Rhoda Dorndorf (p.11)
Angela Douglas (p.138)
Dana Douglas (p.1)
Sue Douglas (p.118)
Gill Doust (p.54)
Jenny Dover (p.69)

Hilary Dowber (p.84)
Deirdre Dowling (p.128)
Emilia Dowling (p.69)
Gwynneth Down (p.69)
Elizabeth Doyle (p.107)
John Doyle (p.84)
Sue Draney (p.46)
Pim Draper (p.15)
Ros Draper (p.17)
Ora Dresner (p.46)
Iain Dresser (p.1)
Margaret Drew (p.48)
Alicja Drewnowska (p.98)
Christine Driver (p.54)
Helen Drucquer (p.121)
Lynne Drummond (p.90)
Gitta Drury (p.116)
Jan Dryden (p.124)
Windy Dryden (p.69)
Simon Du Plock (p.90)
Marc Du Ry (p.69)
Mark Duberry (p.144)
Alexandre Dubinsky (p.128)
Helene Dubinsky (p.69)
Dorothy M Duck (p.39)
Jennifer Duckham (p.128)
Moira Duckworth (p.98)
Alexander
  Duddington (p.70)
Nick Duffell (p.54)
Rosemary Duffy (p.48)
Kathleen Duguid (p.39)
Mary Duhig (p.118)
Sally Duncan (p.128)
Alec John Duncan-
  Grant (p.21)
Jenny Dunn (p.54)
Katie Dunn (p.116)
Mark Dunn (p.54)
Nicola Dunn (p.70)
Alan Dupuy (p.84)
Stefan Durlach (p.142)
Jane Dutton (p.54)
Pat Dyehouse (p.17)
Paula Dyer (p.31)
Andrea Dykes (p.128)
Arif Dyrud (p.70)
Margaret Dyson (p.9)

E

Yvonne Eadie (p.138)
Marje Eagles (p.70)
Marjorie Eagles (p.70)
Patricia East (p.45)
Judith Easter (p.70)
John Eaton (p.6)
Barbara Eccles (p.54)
Andrea K Edeleanu (p.128)
Robert J Edelmann (p.128)
Rose Edgcumbe (p.70)
Enid Edgeley (p.31)
Marjory Edgell (p.90)
Yvonne G
  Edmondstone (p.38)
Dagmar Edwards (p.70)
David Edwards (p.121)

Judith Edwards (p.90)
K J B Edwards (p.138)
Michael Edwards (p.90)
Jude Egan (p.35)
Stella Egert (p.84)
Susan Egert (p.54)
Judi Egerton (p.105)
Patricia Eglin (p.91)
Hella Ehlers (p.46)
Alyce Faye Eichelberger
  Cleese (p.98)
Luise Eichenbaum (p.146)
Bernd Eiden (p.98)
Clive Eiles (p.84)
Sue Einhorn (p.54)
Hetty Einzig (p.54)
Susan Eisen (p.54)
Heiner Eisenbarth (p.21)
Ivan Eisler (p.84)
Isabelle Ekdawi (p.84)
Penny Elder (p.54)
Martin Eldon (p.35)
Zack Eleftheriadou (p.54)
Judith Elkan (p.98)
Barbara Elliott (p.70)
Dena Elliott (p.98)
Lea K Elliott (p.29)
Lois Elliott (p.54)
Peter Elliott (p.38)
Sandra A Elliott (p.84)
Victoria Elliott (p.84)
Lynda Ellis (p.121)
Mary Lynne Ellis (p.54)
Michael Ellis (p.54)(p.55)
Jane Ellwood (p.28)
Anthony Elman (p.1)
Anne Elton (p.70)
Naomi Elton (p.25)
Jenifer Elton Wilson (p.140)
Louise Elwell (p.118)
Louise Emanuel (p.55)
Ricky Emanuel (p.70)
Louise Embleton-
  Tudor (p.121)
Frances Emeleus (p.29)
Mary Eminson (p.42)
Susan Emm (p.125)
Beckett Ender (p.133)
Christine Ender (p.112)
Wendy English (p.140)
Carole Epstein (p.55)
Frances Epstein (p.55)
Franz Epting (p.146)
Sheila Ernst (p.55)
Meg Errington (p.98)
Richard Errington (p.15)
Archibald Erskine (p.70)
Judith Erskine (p.84)
Richard Erskine (p.116)
Ruth Erskine (p.55)
Claude Esposito (p.137)
Delia Essex (p.107)
Suzanne Essex (p.1)
Mary Etherington (p.17)
G E Evans (p.16)
Joan Evans (p.70)

Ken Evans (p.116)
Mairi M Evans (p.116)
Michael Evans (p.35)
Ray Evans (p.128)
Richard Evans (p.137)
Roger Evans (p.70)
Tricia Evans (p.128)
Madeleine Everington (p.31)
John Eveson (p.35)
Arturo Ezquerro-
  Adan (p.70)

F

Anthony F Fagan (p.98)
Margaret Fagan (p.48)
Rufus Fagbadegun (p.42)
Merlyn Falkowska (p.35)
Alexandra Fanning (p.70)
Em Farell (p.55)
Nina Farhi (p.70)
Jeffrey Faris (p.124)
Nancy M Farley (p.39)
Christopher Farmer (p.11)
Eddie Farmer (p.91)
Graeme Farquharson (p.113)
Kay Farquharson (p.11)
Bill Farrell (p.142)
Margaret Farrell (p.9)
Shirley Faruki (p.48)
Ruth Fasht (p.110)
Keith Faull (p.126)
Ann Fausset (p.35)
Caroline Fawkes (p.55)
Antonio Fazio (p.70)
Keith Fearns (p.30)
Don Feasey (p.105)
Tish Feilden (p.1)(p.2)
Marilyn Feldberg (p.55)
Tom Feldberg (p.70)
Wendy Feldman (p.55)
Angela Fell (p.98)
John Fentiman (p.70)
Christopher Fenton (p.33)
Geoff Ferguson (p.55)
Mary Ferguson (p.42)
Heidi Ferid (p.70)
Valentina Fernandez (p.70)
Geraldine Festenstein (p.70)
Berthe Ficarra (p.70)
John C Field (p.137)
Nathan Field (p.55)
Rosalind Field (p.21)
Mike Fielder (p.70)
Karl Figlio (p.25)
Erica Filby (p.129)
Felicity Fincham (p.31)
David Findlay (p.84)
Rosalind Finlay (p.55)
Judith Firman (p.84)
Sue Firth (p.13)
Livia Fischer (p.144)
Deborah M Fish (p.146)
Sue Fish (p.99)
Anstice Fisher (p.2)
James V Fisher (p.70)
Linda Fisher (p.84)

Susan Fisher (p.99)
Geoff Fisk (p.45)
Freda Fitton (p.11)
Albina Fitzgerald-
  Butler (p.110)
Janet Fitzsimmons (p.35)
Dennis Flannery (p.138)
Jean Flannery (p.45)
Marj Fleming (p.55)
Patrick Fleming (p.129)
Peter Fleming (p.91)
Robert W K Fleming (p.84)
Joan Fletcher (p.84)
Elisabeth Flinspach (p.55)
Stephen Flynn (p.144)
Ann Foden (p.70)
Brenda Foguel (p.99)
Jane Foley (p.71)
Andrew Fookes (p.116)
Susan Ford (p.55)
Daniel Fordwour (p.118)
Barbara Forryan (p.34)
Jennifer Forssander (p.99)
Matthew Forster (p.21)
Angus Forsyth (p.15)
Laura Forti (p.55)
Jackie Fosbury (p.55)
Jane Fossey (p.2)
Angela Foster (p.71)
Paul Foster (p.107)
Michael Foulkes (p.123)
Alfred Fox (p.99)
Almuth-Maria Fox (p.25)
Annie Fox (p.35)
Fiona Fox (p.135)
Hugh Fox (p.16)
Jessica Fox (p.21)
Loretta Fox (p.55)
Margaret Fox (p.123)
Tom Foxen (p.11)
Richard France (p.129)
Anne Francis (p.31)
Frank Franklyn (p.71)
Fay Fransella (p.14)
Bobbie Fraser (p.23)
Daphne Fraser (p.39)
Lynett Fraser (p.99)
Diane Frazer (p.71)
Glenda Fredman (p.55)
Christopher Freeman (p.23)
David Freeman (p.40)
Linda Freeman (p.91)
Martin Freeman (p.99)
Pat Freeman (p.129)
Sue Freeman (p.55)
C Frey-Wehrlin (p.144)
Joe Friedman (p.71)
Debbie Friedman-
  Kempson (p.71)
Ann Froshaug (p.48)
Caroline Fry (p.99)
Marianne Fry (p.21)
Richard P W Fry (p.71)
Victoria G Fuller (p.91)
Peter B Fullerton (p.142)
Anne Furneaux (p.99)

Lena Furst (p.129)
Susan Fyvel (p.71)

G

Mark Gabbay (p.105)
Jill Gabriel (p.2)
Michael Gage (p.118)
Sue Gagg (p.20)
Maryline Gagnere (p.9)
William Galbreath (p.116)
Derek Gale (p.25)
Eogain Gallagher (p.21)
Jan Galloway (p.7)
Rus Gandy (p.91)
Steve Gans (p.71)
Margaret Gardiner (p.84)
Vicki Gardiner (p.9)
Fiona Gardner (p.2)
Peter Gardner (p.2)
Philippa Gardner (p.140)
Anne Garland (p.133)
Rita Garlovsky (p.121)
Alegra Garner (p.129)
Michael Gartland (p.138)
Pauline Garvin-
  Crofts (p.121)
Chris Gaskell (p.2)
Fiorella G Gatti-Doyle (p.91)
Pamela Gaunt (p.20)
Tim Gauntlett (p.138)
Christopher Gausden (p.40)
Verity Gavin (p.144)
Audrey Gavshon (p.71)
Pamela Gawler-
  Wright (p.48)
Heather Geddes (p.17)
Elizabeth Gee (p.55)
Hugh Gee (p.55)
Irene Gee (p.55)
Sheryle Geen (p.71)
Bryan W J Geldeard (p.12)
Eva Gell (p.2)
Sally Gell (p.118)
Michael Gent (p.116)
Valerie Gentry (p.9)
Dorothy George (p.71)
Evan George (p.99)
Pamela George (p.71)
Jackie Gerrard (p.35)
Himanshu Ghadiali (p.126)
Rita Ghent (p.126)
Golshad Ghiaci (p.71)
Jenny Gibson (p.48)
Melanie Gibson (p.99)
Barbara Gilbert (p.15)
Betty Gilbert (p.21)
Gillie Gilbert (p.55)
Maria Gilbert (p.99)
Sharon Gilbert (p.25)
Carol A Gilboy (p.7)
Katarina Gildebrand (p.71)
Pauline Gilkes (p.5)
Douglas Gill (p.71)
Patricia Gillan (p.14)
Timothy P Gillett (p.133)
Liliana Gilli (p.110)

Toni Gilligan (p.141)
Cath Gilliver (p.135)
Annika Gilljam (p.138)
Jeanne Gimblett (p.14)
Guy Gladstone (p.46)
S Gladwell (p.135)
Brian Glaister (p.129)
Tony Glanville (p.91)
Danya Glaser (p.46)
Claire Glasscoe (p.110)
Patricia Glasspool (p.31)
Maureen Gledhill (p.99)
Liza Glenn (p.99)
Jean Glover (p.138)
Julie Glynn (p.12)
Janet Glynn-Treble (p.6)
Lynne Goddard (p.21)
Godfrey Godfrey-
  Issacs (p.91)
Geraldine Godsil (p.99)
Susan Godsil (p.138)
Bonnie Gold (p.71)
Phyllis Goldblatt (p.55)
Ellen Golden (p.91)
Francoise Golden (p.99)
Sylvia Golden (p.55)
Pauline Golding (p.7)
John Goldman (p.99)
Pam Goldstein (p.110)
Elma Golsworthy (p.129)
Angelika Golz (p.17)
Lavinia Gomez (p.71)
Elizabeth Good (p.48)
Liz Good (p.71)
Simon Good (p.48)
John Goodchild (p.48)
Deborah Goodes (p.48)
Lesley Goodman (p.55)
Mary Goodman (p.126)
Anne Goodrich (p.29)
Gill Goodwillie (p.123)
Patricia Goodyear (p.135)
Peter Goold (p.31)
Michael GÖpfert (p.107)
Deidre Gordon (p.110)
Inger Gordon (p.21)
Jill Gordon (p.21)
Leila Gordon (p.9)
P Kenneth Gordon (p.31)
Paul Gordon (p.71)
Sheila Gordon (p.84)
Virginia Gordon (p.91)
Ian Gordon-Brown (p.99)
Rosemary Gordon-
  Montagnon (p.99)
Gill Gorell Barnes (p.71)
Joan Goring-Avery (p.25)
Graham Gorman (p.110)
Carry Gorney (p.71)
Arlene Gorodensky (p.71)
Kate Goslett (p.56)
Pat Gosling (p.2)
Thomas Goss (p.110)
Ewa Gottesman (p.129)
Robert Gottesman (p.129)
Sue Gottlieb (p.123)

Jane Gotto (p.123)
Geraldine Gould (p.44)
Brunhild Gourlay (p.35)
Kevin Gournay (p.35)
Marion Gow (p.56)
Myrna Gower (p.129)
David Gowling (p.29)
Jaya Gowrisunkur (p.105)
Carole Grace (p.99)
Olga Gracia (p.84)
Jane Gracie (p.29)
Hilary Graham (p.56)
Hilary E Graham (p.116)
Judy Graham (p.56)
Nancy Graham (p.91)
Anthony Grainger (p.44)
Eve Grainger (p 25)
Margaret Granowski (p.56)
Bob Grant (p.99)
Iona Grant (p.71)
Rosamund Grant (p.56)
Gabriella Grauso
  Calaresu (p.144)
John Gravelle (p.25)
Anne Gray (p.35)
Kati Gray (p.48)
Maggie Gray (p.24)
Nigel Gray (p.56)
Pete Gray (p.126)
Stephen Michael
  Gray (p.120)
Juliet Grayson (p.129)
Barry Greatorex (p.16)
Margaret Greaves (p.32)
Sarah Greaves (p.9)
Barbara A Green (p.12)
Eliott Green (p.40)
Esther Green (p.71)
June Green (p.110)
Margaret Green (p.56)
Michael Green (p.140)
Roberta Green (p.91)
Sylvia Green (p.2)
Viviane Green (p.71)
Cyril Green-
  Thompson (p.56)
Maurice Greenberg (p.99)
Alice Greene (p.46)
Frances Greenfield (p.99)
Terence Greenfield (p.12)
Sarah Greening (p.113)
Ian Greenway (p.116)
Angela Greenwood (p.25)
John Greenwood (p.91)
Judith Gregory (p.2)
Peter Gregory (p.32)
Julie Gresty (p.2)
David Grey (p.56)
Mary Griffin (p.84)
Anne Megan Griffiths (p.22)
Pamela Griffiths (p.99)
Sheila Griffiths (p.56)
Thelma Griffiths (p.6)
Roz Grigg (p.14)
Francoise Grimshaw (p.129)
Annie Grocott (p.29)

Nigel Groom (p.141)
Grete Gross (p.56)
Stephen Gross (p.56)
Vivienne Gross (p.56)
Virginia Grosser (p.129)
Mary V E Grover (p.144)
Shaun Growney (p.91)
Angela Gruber (p.35)
Sheena Grunberg (p.71)
Ingolf Gudjonsson (p.125)
Hazel Guest (p.9)
Nicola Guest (p.2)
Liz Guild (p.9)
John F Guilfoyle (p.72)
Anita Guiton (p.121)
Pamela Gulliver (p.91)
Gaye Gunton (p.35)
Madeleine Guppy (p.56)
Michal Gurion (p.35)
Rosalie Gurr (p.32)
Else Guthrie (p.105)
Liana Guy (p.118)

H

Jamie G H Hacker
  Hughes (p.25)
Roger Hacker (p.72)
Gideon Hadary (p.56)
Orna Hadary (p.56)
Janet Haddington (p.84)
Ray Haddock (p.122)
Nellie Hadzianesti (p.99)
Patricia Hagan (p.107)
Christina Hagelthorn (p.144)
Kitty Hagenbach (p.137)
Herbert Hahn (p.2)
Rex Haigh (p.6)
Ann Haine (p.72)
Stephen Haine (p.72)
David Hall (p.9)
Guy Hall (p.56)
Kelvin Hall (p.29)
Kirsty Hall (p.56)
Linda Hall (p.32)
Ruth Hallam-Jones (p.122)
Sharon Hallard (p.126)
Jeff Halperin (p.72)
William Halton (p.56)
Christine Hamblin (p.114)
David Hamblin (p.2)
Angela Hamilton (p.28)
Dorothy Hamilton (p.56)
Eira Hamilton (p.24)
Kim Hamilton (p.35)
Nigel Hamilton (p.99)
Sheila L L Hamilton (p.107)
Wallace Hamilton (p.28)
Paule Hamilton-
  Duckett (p.56)
Christine Hammond-
  Small (p.14)
Lesley Hampson (p.72)
Monica Hanaway (p.118)
Thomasz Hanchen (p.84)
Elizabeth Hancock (p.137)
Maureen Hancock (p.56)

Pauline Hancock (p.84)
Rima Handley (p.113)
S Handy (p.135)
Helga Hanks (p.138)
Ian G Hanley (p.115)
Marie Hanley (p.2)
Dorothy Hanna (p.84)
Chris Hannah (p.5)
Clare Hannah (p.5)
Francesca Hannah (p.12)
David J Hannigan (p.116)
Sr M Letizia Hannon (p.56)
Carol Hanson (p.72)
Linda Harakis (p.99)
Michael Harari (p.110)
Ursula Harben (p.112)
Mark Hardcastle (p.22)
Georgina Hardie (p.56)
Celia Harding (p.48)
Michael Harding (p.72)
Anne Hardman (p.107)
Peter Hardwick (p.19)
Liz Hardy (p.9)
Helena Hargaden (p.84)
Judy Hargreaves (p.56)
Nahum Harlap (p.72)
Ki Harley (p.56)
Biljana Harling (p.48)
Paul Harlow (p.91)
Peter Harmsworth (p.108)
Anita Harper (p.57)
Eric Harper (p.57)
Suzanne Harper (p.46)
Neil Harrington (p.27)
Bob Harris (p.2)
Dianne Harris (p.35)
Gerald A Harris (p.135)
Gordon Harris (p.118)
Michele Harris (p.99)
Nina Harris (p.135)
Paul David Gwyn
  Harris (p.28)
Tirril Harris (p.57)
Caroline Harrison (p.144)
Gillian Harrison (p.9)
Jane Harrison (p.57)
Susan Harrison (p.7)
Susan Harrison-Mayor (p.35)
Anne Harrow (p.138)
Bruce Hart (p.142)
Mary Anne Maclellan
  Hart (p.24)
Melanie Hart (p.91)
Robert Hart (p.129)
Sally Hart (p.112)
Wendy Hartman (p.57)
Trevor Hartnup (p.91)
Olivia Harvard-Watts (p.72)
Andrew Harvey (p.122)
Linda Harvey (p.25)
Lois Harvey (p.146)
Natasha Harvey (p.72)
Pam Harvey (p.35)
T A Harvey (p.135)
Beth Hashemi (p.129)
Nicola Haskins (p.57)

Alan Hassall (p.45)
Jon Hastings (p.2)
Kim Hastings (p.2)
Peter Hatswell (p.32)
Valerie Hatswell (p.32)
Nelly Hatzianesti (p.100)
Christopher Hauke (p.85)
Brigitte Haupts (p.100)
Susan Hauser (p.100)
Jolien Haveman (p.13)
Sheila Hawdon (p.2)
Peter Hawkins (p.2)
Jane Hawksley (p.135)
Ann Haworth (p.12)
Helen Haworth (p.42)
Peter Haworth (p.118)
Kit Haxby (p.22)
Susan Haxell (p.72)
Michael Hayes (p.91)
Pamela Hayes (p.129)
Gillian Hayhurst (p.40)
Eric Haynes (p.9)
Jane Haynes (p.72)
Mark Hayward (p.14)
Jeremy Hazell (p.125)
Jean Hazlehurst (p.108)
Christopher Headon (p.40)
Jean Headworth (p.45)
Marlene Heap (p.129)
Liesel Hearst (p.110)
Christine Heath (p.5)
John Heatley (p.129)
John Heaton (p.72)
Anita Heavens (p.129)
Anne Heavey (p.72)
Fran Hedges (p.85)
Korinna Hedinger-
  Farrell (p.129)
Karen Hedley (p.72)
Nick Hedley (p.29)
Colleen Heenan (p.138)
Karin Heinitz (p.100)
Elisabeth Heismann (p.57)
Jan Helbert (p.139)
Mary B Heller (p.13)
Kate Hellin (p.105)
Caroline Helm (p.91)
Judith Hemming (p.57)
Gillian Isaacs
  Hemmings (p.32)
Andrew Henderson (p.100)
John Henderson (p.48)
Pauline Henderson (p.57)
Theresa Hendra (p.38)
Begum Hendrickse (p.108)
Devam Hendry (p.25)
Evelyn R Hendry (p.85)
June Henley (p.129)
Dinea Henney (p.57)
Lindy Henny (p.91)
Marika Henriques (p.91)
John Henry (p.72)
Rachel M Henry (p.142)
Judith Henshaw (p.17)
Roger Hepburn (p.6)
Claudia Herbert (p.118)

Linda Herdman (p.137)
Pauline Hering-
  Josefowitz (p.144)
Steve Herington (p.48)
Zdenka Hermann (p.72)
Edward Herst (p.72)
Bridget Hester (p.114)
Agnes Birgit Heuer (p.100)
Gottfried Heuer (p.100)
Rachael Hewett (p.129)
Philip J Hewitt (p.40)
Julie Hewson (p.17)
Sue Hickman (p.5)
Hazel Hickson (p.48)
Rene Hiestand (p.40)
Judith Higgins (p.2)
Robert Higgo (p.108)
Helen High (p.57)
Judy Hildebrand (p.72)
Alison Hilder (p.57)
Brenda Hill (p.134)
C Anthony Hill (p.139)
Jenny Hill (p.121)
Penny Hill (p.118)
Val Hill (p.135)
Ruth Hiller (p.57)
Christine Hillman (p.137)
Jan Hillman (p.30)
Janet Hills (p.44)
John Hills (p.40)
Deborah Hindle (p.116)
Robert Hinshelwood (p.100)
Ruth Hirons (p.40)
Malka Hirsch-
  Napchan (p.72)
Hazel Hirst (p.44)
Paul Hitchings (p.100)
Nini Hitchman (p.91)
Linda M Hoag (p.123)
Astrid Hoang (p.48)
Elizabeth Hoare (p.112)
Ian Hoare (p.17)
Robin Hobbes (p.12)
Anita Hobbs (p.110)
Michael Hobbs (p.118)
Robert Hobson (p.105)
Amanda Hodd (p.14)
Barbara Hodges (p.17)
Jill Hodges (p.46)
Pauline Hodson (p.118)
Christine Retson
  Hogg (p.28)
Jo Hogg (p.57)
Elisabeth Holdaway (p.123)
John Holden (p.48)
Sarah Holden (p.85)
Elizabeth Holder (p.6)
Gisele Holender (p.57)
Louise Holland (p.9)
Penelope Holland (p.24)
Ray Holland (p.72)
Stevie Holland (p.57)
Sue Holland (p.22)
Avril Hollings (p.57)
Jannie Hollins (p.12)
Peter Hollis (p.91)

Max Holloway (p.2)
Kirsti E Holm (p.72)
Carol Holmes (p.57)
Jeremy Holmes (p.17)
Lynne Holmes (p.100)
Paul Holmes (p.57)
Betty Anne Holtrop (p.72)
Harriet Holve (p.129)
Marjorie Homer (p.13)
Peter Honig (p.35)
Peter Hood (p.25)
Patricia Hoogh-
  Rowntree (p.29)
Beatrice Hook (p.32)
John Hook (p.32)
Anne Hooper (p.72)
Christine M Hooper (p.32)
Gloria Hope-Price (p.146)
Jill Hopkins (p.123)
Vera M Hopkins (p.32)
Earl Hopper (p.72)
Ann Hopwood (p.91)
Jean Hopwood (p.129)
Michael Hopwood (p.129)
Faridoon Hormasji (p.25)
Alan Horne (p.105)
Ann Horne (p.72)
Pam Horrocks (p.126)
Roger Horrocks (p.100)
Daphne Hort (p.85)
Ralph Horton (p.110)
Tone Horwood (p.2)
Flora Hoskin (p.100)
John Hosking (p.57)
Gaie Houston (p.73)
Angela Howard (p.73)
Coral Howard (p.85)
Heather Howard (p.85)
Irene Howard (p.91)
Sister Columba
  Howard (p.144)
Marilyn Howe (p.134)
Patricia Howe (p.124)
Carolyn Howell (p.57)
David Howell (p.92)
Hilary Howell (p.16)
Julia Howell (p.142)
Kathleen Mary
  Howes (p.121)
David D Howie (p.30)
Brian Howlett (p.144)
Christina Howtone (p.25)
Judith Hubback (p.73)
Peter Hubbard (p.142)
Inge Hudson (p.57)
Marjorie Hudson (p.130)
Pauline Hudson (p.57)
Peter Hudson (p.14)
Margaret Hueting (p.22)
Ann Hughes (p.57)
Carol Hughes (p.85)
Jacqui Hughes (p.112)
L Hughes (p.14)
Lynette Hughes (p.105)
Patrick Hughes (p.6)
Margot Huish (p.35)

Anne J A Hume (p.28)
Margaret Humphrey (p.73)
David Humphreys (p.35)
Harold Humphries (p.57)
Maggie Hunt (p.57)
Anne Hunt Overzee (p.7)
Patricia Hunt (p.12)
Patricia A Hunt (p.122)
Margaret Hunter (p.92)
Joan Hurd (p.44)
Jennifer J Hurley (p.9)
Karolyn Hurren (p.15)
Anne Hurry (p.73)
Hannah Hurst (p.58)
Margaret Hurst (p.25)
Richard Huson (p.48)
Fakhir Hussain (p.130)
Anna K Huszcza (p.5)
Rosemary Hutchby (p.116)
Gary Hutchinson (p.2)
Peter Hutchinson (p.118)
Sylvia Hutchinson (p.73)
Eric Hutchison (p.9)
Dennis Hyde (p.130)
Keith Hyde (p.105)

I

Julian Ibanez (p.144)
George Ikkos (p.35)
Nida Ingham (p.130)
Sonia Ingram (p.92)
Antonia Inlander (p.58)
Lesley Ironside (p.22)
Nicholas Irving (p.113)
Susan Irving (p.92)
Sacha Alexi Irwin (p.73)
Toni-Lee Isaac (p.105)
Joy Isaacs (p.92)
Zelda Isaacson (p.73)
Chris Iveson (p.100)
Di Iveson (p.58)

J

Elisabeth Jackson (p.105)
Eve Jackson (p.58)
Judith Jackson (p.92)
Paul Jackson (p.32)
Sharon Jackson (p.139)
Emily Jacob (p.92)
Brian Jacobs (p.85)
Joe Jacobs (p.35)
Michael Jacobs (p.44)
Paula Jacobs (p.34)
Romey Jacobson (p.58)
Alice Jacobus (p.142)
Marianne Jacoby (p.58)
Silvia Jacon (p.73)
Glenys Jacques (p.48)
Roma Jacques (p.38)
Tony Jaffa (p.9)
Sally Jakobi (p.130)
Anthony James (p.46)
Christopher James (p.85)
Glenys James (p.3)
Jo James (p.73)

Pat James (p.3)
Jane Jameson Milner (p.108)
Eileen Jamieson (p.35)
Diana Jansen (p.133)
Penny Jaques (p.119)
Cecilia Jarvis (p.100)
Charlotte Jarvis (p.73)
Eileen Jarvis (p.92)
Jennie Jarvis (p.144)
Alison Jefferies (p.8)
Jinnie Jefferies (p.130)
Rosie Jeffries (p.3)
Martin Jelfs (p.46)
Beverley Jenkins (p.25)
Hugh Jenkins (p.85)
Sheila Jenkins (p.30)
Natasha Jenner (p.100)
Jenny Jennings (p.100)
Lyn C Jennings (p.58)
Einar D Jenssen (p.58)
Sue Jewson (p.44)
P H Jezard-Clark (p.3)
Bryan Jobbins (p.58)
Riva Joffe (p.73)
Carolyn H John (p.133)
Carlotta Johnson (p.133)
Duncan B Johnson (p.5)
Ellie Johnson (p.100)
Frank Johnson (p.133)
Michael Johnson (p.16)
Pat Johnson (p.3)
Camilla Johnson-Smith (p.6)
Linda Johnston (p.119)
Janice Johnstone (p.25)
John Jolliffe (p.73)
Arthur Jonathan (p.130)
Alan Jones (p.130)
Alun Jones (p.14)
Caroline Jones (p.108)
Dave Jones (p.49)
David Jones (p.92)(p.119)
Elsa Jones (p.125)
Helen Jones (p.22)(p.114)
Janet Jones (p.73)
Judith Jones (p.108)
Maggy Jones (p.139)
Margaret Jones (p.40)
Margaret Peggy Jones (p.130)
Marlene Jones (p.114)
Merryn Jones (p.85)
Nicole Jones (p.17)
Pamela Jones (p.40)
Richard Jones (p.44)
Ros Jones (p.22)
Sue Jones (p.16)
Jerome Devakumar
   Joseph (p.22)
Angela Joyce (p.58)
Philip Joyce (p.100)
Leonor Juarez (p.58)
Dorothy Judd (p.73)
Malcolm Judkins (p.43)

K

Fagie Kadish (p.73)
Maggie Kafton (p.100)

A Kahn (p.135)
Brett Kahr (p.73)
Karina Kalderwaay (p.144)
David Kalisch (p.17)
Matthew Kalitowski (p.46)
Jonathan Kanakam (p.6)
Ros Kane (p.49)
Nasim Kanji (p.36)
Myron Kaplan (p.73)
Catherine Kaplinsky (p.22)
Alexandra Karan (p.100)
Marcia Karp (p.17)
Stewart Katzman (p.58)
David L Kay (p.58)
Malcolm Kay (p.106)
Margaret Kay (p.139)
Agnes Keane (p.49)
Pamela Keane (p.92)
Anne Kearns (p.100)
Jacqueline Keating (p.119)
Ray Keedy-Lilley (p.58)
Paul Keenan (p.116)
Paul Stephen Keenan (p.108)
Duncan Kegerreis (p.100)
Susan Kegerreis (p.100)
Joyce Keith (p.130)
Bridget Kelly (p.40)
Caro Kelly (p.73)
Gillian Kelly (p.15)
Michael Kelly (p.58)
Philip Kelly (p.19)
Paul David Kemp (p.14)
Jo Reed Kendal (p.133)
Tim Kendall (p.122)
Margaret Kendrick (p.25)
David Kennard (p.114)
Des Kennedy (p.108)
Fiona Kennedy (p.38)
Helen Kennedy (p.24)
Kay Kennedy (p.27)
Michael Kennedy (p.100)
Christine Kennett (p.114)
Wendy Kennett-
   Brown (p.100)
Angela Kenny (p.58)
Marie Kenny (p.115)
Miranda Kenny (p.58)
Peter Kenny (p.15)
Jennifer Kenrick (p.73)
Pat Kenwood (p.142)
Patricia Kerkham (p.113)
Marilyn Kernoff (p.73)
Anna Kerr (p.85)
Jack Kerridge (p.85)
Petra Kerridge (p.17)
Judi Keshet-Orr (p.58)
Inge Kessel (p.58)
Kunderke Kevlin (p.3)
Olya Khaleelee (p.73)
Lee Kidd (p.58)
Brian Kiely (p.134)
Gundi Kiemle (p.43)
Ursula Kiernan (p.137)
Joyce Kilgour (p.12)
Mimi Kilgour (p.10)
Suna Kilich-Walpole (p.36)

William Kinbacher (p.100)
Diana Kinder (p.101)
Christine King (p.85)
Gillie King (p.119)
John J King (p.6)
Lucy King (p.10)
Madeleine King (p.36)
Michael King (p.14)
Laurence Kingsley (p.135)
Mary Kingsley (p.58)
Wendy Kingsnorth (p.110)
Alan Kirby (p.85)
Babs Kirby (p.92)
Kate Kirk (p.12)
Nick V Kirkland-
   Handley (p.12)
Robert Kirkwood (p.36)
Nicholas Kitson (p.92)
Jane Kitto (p.58)
Saeunn
   Kjartansdottir (p.144)
Laila Kjellstrom (p.24)
Josephine Klein (p.85)
Mavis Klein (p.73)
Richard Klein (p.58)
Wendy Klein (p.6)
Meg Kleisen (p.144)
Liebe Klug (p.10)
Jane Knight (p.46)
Michael Knight (p.73)
Jane Knowles (p.6)
Madeleine Knowles (p.49)
Valerie Knowles (p.58)
Jean Knox (p.119)
Marianna
   Koeppelmann (p.85)
Christiane Kohler (p.30)
Valli Kohon (p.73)
Claudius Kokott (p.110)
Peter John Kolb (p.92)
Marianne
   Kolbuszewski (p.92)
Sandra Kondos (p.142)
Achim Korte (p.101)
Jasna Kostic (p.58)
Reinhard Kowalski (p.6)
Sebastian Kraemer (p.74)
Sue Krzowski (p.74)
Sue Kuhn (p.3)
Pedro Kujawski (p.92)
Michael Kulyk (p.110)
Jane Kunkler (p.24)
Ann E Kutek (p.92)
Enno Kuttner (p.30)
Daniel Kwei (p.26)
Edna Kyrie (p.74)
Christine
   K Chemann (p.119)

L

Maggie La Tourelle (p.74)
Yig Labworth (p.58)
Frances Lacey (p.29)
Irene Lacey (p.134)
Jo Lacy-Smith (p.19)
Martine Lafargue (p.59)

Robert Lafon (p.130)
Regine Lallah (p.59)
Kirsten Lamb (p.43)
Daphne Lambert (p.10)
Florangel Lambor (p.22)
Lyn Lamplough (p.101)
Michael Lamprell (p.49)
Katalin Lanczi (p.40)
Patricia Land (p.59)
Margaret Landale (p.119)
Peter Lang (p.85)
Richard Lang (p.59)
Susan Lang (p.85)
Monica Langdon (p.85)
Roslyn Langdon (p.18)
Allen Langley (p.30)
Dorothy Langley (p.18)
Monica Lanyado (p.85)
M Laport-Steuerman (p.74)
Phil Lapworth (p.3)
Giles Lascelle (p.140)
Bernie Laschinger (p.110)
Judith Lask (p.85)
Barbara Latham (p.74)
Annie Lau (p.26)
Bernard Wai Kai Lau (p.142)
Gordon Law (p.141)
Heather Law (p.36)
James Lawley (p.101)
Virginia Katharine
   Lawlor (p.74)
E Lawrence (p.12)
Margaret Lawrence (p.92)
Christine Lawson (p.130)
Ruth Lawson (p.115)
Effie Layiou-Lignos (p.144)
Sandy Layton (p.92)
Myrna Lazarus (p.59)
Christine Le Brun (p.137)
Mary Lea (p.125)
Kathy Leach (p.140)
Peter Leakey (p.16)
Terry Lear (p.114)
John Leary-Joyce (p.36)
Judith Leary-Tanner (p.36)
Catherine Leder (p.74)
Tsafi Lederman (p.59)
Rushi Ledermann (p.22)
Adrienne Lee (p.116)
Denis Lee (p.12)
Graham Lee (p.101)
Helen Lee (p.116)
Joan M Lee (p.85)
John Lee (p.40)
Heather E Lee
   Messner (p.74)
Jennifer Leeburn (p.22)
Gareth Leeming (p.85)
Claire Leggatt (p.43)
Pam Lehrer (p.74)
Elana Leigh (p.142)
Tim Leighton (p.3)
Mikael Leiman (p.144)
Elizabeth Leiper (p.130)
Rob Leiper (p.40)
Norman Leitman (p.101)

Alessandra Lemma (p.59)
Susan Lendrum (p.106)
Graham Lennox (p.40)
Sara Leon (p.92)
Georgia Lepper (p.59)
Clare Lester (p.3)
Hilary Lester (p.85)
Sue Lethbridge (p.32)
Liisa Lettington (p.40)
Muriel Letts (p.59)
Mary Levens (p.101)
Brigitte Leveque (p.101)
Maria A Lever (p.106)
Maureen Lever (p.32)
Jackie Levitsky (p.74)
Patricia D Levitsky (p.74)
Colette Levy (p.74)
Clara Lew (p.10)
Melanie Lewin (p.40)
Vivienne Lewin (p.74)
Paul Lewington (p.10)
Helen Lewis (p.146)
Jo-Ann Lewis (p.26)
Ken Lewis (p.12)
Penny Lewis (p.110)
Philip Lewis (p.18)
Richard Lewis (p.92)
Ruth Lewis (p.130)
Bernd Leygraf (p.59)
Alan Lidmila (p.122)
Wendy Lidster (p.22)
Stuart Lieberman (p.130)
Lauren Liebling (p.59)
Raymond Lightbown (p.135)
Meira Likierman (p.74)
Davina Lilley (p.46)
Diana Lilley (p.12)
Leslie E C Lim (p.142)
Roger Linden (p.74)
Sophie Linden (p.74)
Marion Lindsay (p.106)
Caroline Lindsey (p.74)
Shirley Lingard (p.130)
Derek Linker (p.101)
Iris Linn (p.135)
Maxine Linnell (p.18)
Bill Lintott (p.10)
Gwenda Lippitt (p.32)
Mary Lister (p.92)
Christine Lister-Ford (p.13)
Jon Little (p.113)
Marie Little (p.22)
Martin Little (p.59)
Ray Little (p.101)
Sarah Littlejohn (p.106)
Ann Littlewood (p.12)
Britta Lloyd (p.101)
Helen Lloyd (p.135)
Patricia Lloyd (p.46)
Sandra Lobel (p.106)
Sydney Lobel (p.106)
Josephine Lock (p.101)
Gisela Lockie (p.124)
Susan Loden (p.101)
Michael Lodrick (p.74)
Del Loewenthal (p.92)

Patrick A Loftus (p.122)
Nancy Logue (p.19)
Peter Lomas (p.10)
Clive G Long (p.114)
Jennifer Long (p.19)
Joan Longford (p.16)
Joan Longley (p.86)
Suzanne Looms (p.130)
Judith Green Loose (p.46)
Maria Loret de Mola (p.59)
Julia Loudon (p.15)
Olivia Lousada (p.59)
Mollie Love (p.22)
Gaynor Lovell (p.74)
Karina Lovell (p.86)
Helena Lövendal-
  Sörensen (p.74)
James Low (p.74)
Judith Lowe (p.86)
Julie Lowe (p.125)
Ian Lowery (p.135)
David Loxley (p.122)
Lorne Loxterkamp (p.18)
Philippa Lubbock (p.92)
Carol Lucas (p.12)
Rosemarie Lucas (p.11)
Tina Lucas (p.111)
Dorothy Luciani (p.101)
Jochen Lude (p.101)
Monica Ludolf (p.139)
Francesco Lunardon (p.74)
Charles Lund (p.133)
Aidan Lunt (p.32)
Barbara Luthy (p.29)
Marianna Lutyens (p.119)
Nick Luxmoore (p.119)
Maria Lynch (p.111)
Mary Lynch (p.74)
Valerie Lynch (p.130)
Rita Lynn (p.147)
Kathleen Lyons (p.49)

M

Eileen MacAlister (p.43)
Norman D Macaskill (p.122)
Duncan Macdiarmid (p.92)
Alasdair Macdonald (p.20)
Helen F Macdonald (p.20)
Laurie Macdonald (p.86)
Catherine MacGregor (p.75)
Danuza Machado (p.75)
Catharine Mack
  Smith (p.119)
Christopher
  MacKenna (p.130)
I D Mackenzie (p.135)
Liz MacKenzie (p.44)
Nancy MacKenzie (p.22)
Jennifer Mackewn (p.3)
Hetty MacKinnon (p.28)
Sylvia Mackinnon (p.6)
Dorrie MacLean (p.101)
Enid MacNeill (p.122)(p.125)
Malcolm MacPherson (p.30)
Jeanne Magagna (p.46)
Valerie Magner (p.92)

Anne Maguire (p.43)
Claire Maguire (p.43)
Marie Maguire (p.92)
Janet Mahmood (p.133)
Suzanne Maiello
  Hunziker (p.144)
Begum Maitra (p.75)
Hanne Malcolm (p.120)
David Male (p.135)
Julius Malkin (p.49)
Renee Mallardo (p.59)
Michael Mallows (p.75)
Sue Malone (p.32)
Sean Maloney (p.18)
Mira Malovic-Yeeles (p.119)
Gertrud Mander (p.75)
Claire Manifold (p.75)
David Mann (p.86)
Pamela Mann (p.122)
Cordelia Mansall (p.75)
Rosie Manton (p.139)
Norma Anderson
  Maple (p.130)
Rosie March-Smith (p.19)
Deena Marcus (p.36)
Marietta Marcus (p.92)
Michal Margalit (p.93)
Frank Margison (p.106)
Peter Mark (p.59)
Angela Markham (p.3)
Desa Markovic (p.93)
Olivera Markovic (p.43)
Gaby Marks (p.59)
Helen Marks (p.108)
Shirley Marks-Pinfold (p.36)
Frances Marling (p.93)
Veronika Marlow (p.101)
Martin Marlowe (p.101)
Mario Marrone (p.75)
Patricia Marsden (p.93)
Veronica Marsden (p.111)
Peter Marsden-Allen (p.114)
Jennifer Marsh (p.86)
Mildred Marshak (p.147)
Antoinette Marshall (p.59)
Cherrith A Marshall (p.32)
Janet Marshall (p.130)
Jill Marshall (p.130)
Myra Marshall (p.122)
Patricia Marshall (p.115)
Susan Marshall (p.22)
Vivien Marshall (p.130)
Carol Marshallsay (p.59)
Nicholas Marshallsay (p.59)
Angela Martin (p.32)
Brandy Martin (p.111)
Carol Martin (p.139)
Christine Martin (p.75)
Edward Martin (p.86)
Gill Martin (p.114)
Stephen Martin (p.59)
Susan Martin (p.108)
Philippa Marx (p.75)
Helen Masani (p.22)
Peter A Masani (p.22)
Chandra Masoliver (p.101)

Barry Mason (p.75)
Kikan Massara (p.101)
Ingrid Masterson (p.144)
Alexsandra Mastilovic (p.93)
Marilyn Mathew (p.86)
Trevor J Mathews (p.26)
Greta Mattar (p.111)
Carol Matthews (p.101)
Carolyn Matthews (p.15)
Helen P Matthews (p.32)
Sharon Matthews (p.123)
Sheila Mattison (p.108)
Caroline Maudling (p.36)
Benig Mauger (p.144)
Brian Lawrence
  Maunder (p.86)
Brian Maxwell (p.130)
Adam May (p.30)
G May (p.135)
Kathryn May (p.43)
Robert Mayer (p.59)
Jessica Mayer-Johnson (p.59)
Henrietta Mayne (p.59)
Cynthia Maynerd (p.130)
Yaron Mazliach (p.144)
Elspeth McAdam (p.113)
Eileen McAleer (p.108)
Sue McAllister (p.43)
Brigitte McAndrew (p.32)
John McAuley (p.122)
Stewart McCafferty (p.59)
Meg McCaldin (p.43)
Anita McCann (p.36)
Damian McCann (p.36)
Aine McCarthy (p.144)
Rita McCarthy (p.144)
Meryl McCartney (p.36)
John McClure (p.59)
Una McCluskey (p.114)
Doris McColl (p.13)
Judith McConnach (p.36)
Helen McCormack (p.144)
Elizabeth
  McCormick (p.126)
Helen McCormick (p.12)
Sean McCoy (p.40)
Teresa McCreanor (p.101)
Noel McCune (p.115)
Moira McCutcheon (p.86)
Ian McDermott (p.75)
Paul McDermott (p.75)
David McDonald (p.6)
James McDonald (p.136)
Jennifer McDonnell (p.60)
Veronica McDouall (p.10)
Dennis McEldowney (p.101)
Patricia McEvoy (p.75)
Hugh E McFadden (p.145)
Alison M McFarlane (p.24)
Colin McGee (p.60)
Robin McGlashan (p.93)
Mary McGoldrick (p.145)
Graeme McGrath (p.106)
Tony McGregor (p.6)
Jan McGregor-
  Hepburn (p.115)

Maureen McGroary-
  Meehan (p.145)
Maureen McGuinness (p.5)
Brenda McHugh (p.75)
Jeannie McIntee (p.12)
Molly McKay (p.12)
Maggie McKenzie (p.60)
Bryce McKenzie-
  Smith (p.60)
Savi McKenzie-Smith (p.93)
Mary McKeon (p.60)
Andy McKeown (p.101)
Patricia McKeown (p.131)
Julienne McLean (p.75)
Paula McLeod (p.22)
Brendan McLoughlin (p.3)
Brendan Nicholas
  McLoughlin (p.86)
Brendan McMahon (p.16)
Gladeana McMahon (p.86)
Gaynor McManus (p.93)
Penny McMillan (p.86)
Stuart McNab (p.12)
Ann McNair (p.60)
Barbara McNamara (p.3)
Jennifer McNamara (p.13)
Janet McNaught (p.134)
Delcia McNeil (p.60)
June McOstrich (p.29)
Jane McQuillin (p.16)
Oliver McShane (p.101)
Damien McVey (p.108)
Betty Mead (p.60)
Christine Mead (p.102)
Rosaleen Meaden (p.93)
Sylvia Mears (p.86)
Monica Meinrath (p.111)
Mando Meleagrou (p.75)
Jane Mellett (p.140)
David Mellows (p.60)
Hilary Mellows (p.60)
Jane Melton (p.7)
Sheila Melzak (p.75)
Beckie Menckhoff (p.111)
Annette Mendelsohn (p.75)
Penny Mendelssohn (p.40)
Steven Mendoza (p.102)
Sallie Mercer (p.102)
Joan Meredith (p.106)
William Meredith-
  Owen (p.75)
Philip Messent (p.49)
Hans Jorg Messner (p.60)
Oriel Methuen (p.60)
Lisa Mettam (p.122)
Ann L Meza (p.60)
Jess Michael (p.60)
Suzanne Michaud-
  Lennox (p.111)
V Middleton-Smith (p.140)
David Midgley (p.13)
Julia Mikado (p.93)
Belinda Milani (p.36)
Irene Milburn (p.93)
Fiona Miles (p.86)
Gillian Miles (p.75)

David Millar (p.26)
Gerry Millar (p.86)
Peter Millar (p.140)
Sheila Millard (p.119)
Ann Miller (p.60)
Beth Miller (p.102)
John Miller (p.119)
John Andrew Miller (p.75)
Lisa Miller (p.75)
Liza Miller (p.114)
Lynda Miller (p.45)
Martin Miller (p.75)
Michael Miller (p.10)
Ori Miller (p.60)
Penny Miller (p.60)
Riva Miller (p.75)
Sheila Miller (p.142)
Sylvia Millier (p.93)
Malcolm Millington (p.76)
Judith Mills (p.18)
Frances Milne (p.24)
Pamela Milne (p.114)
Harry Milton (p.24)
John Mitchell (p.124)
Lesley Mitchell (p.106)
Louise Mitchell (p.102)
Richard Mitchell (p.36)
Ruth Mitchell (p.93)
Muriel Mitcheson
  Brown (p.3)
Sally Mitchison (p.139)
Adele Mittwoch (p.76)
Richard Mizen (p.102)
Elizabeth Model (p.76)
Cass Moggridge (p.29)
Carol Mohamed (p.122)
Terry Mohan (p.126)
Lucia Moja-Strasser (p.76)
Angela Molnos (p.145)
Jane Monach (p.122)
John Monk-Steel (p.106)
M L Montalbetti (p.147)
Isabel Montero (p.60)
Wendy Monticelli (p.86)
Barbara Moon (p.43)
Gordon Moore (p.133)
Jill Moore (p.18)
Julia Moore (p.76)
M C Moore (p.122)
Norah Moore (p.102)
Terry Moore (p.32)
Stirling Moorey (p.49)
Anni Moorhouse (p.102)
Flavia Morante (p.102)
Aslan Mordecai (p.60)
Kay Mordecai (p.60)
Anne Morgan
  (Mhlongo) (p.60)
Elizabeth Morgan (p.123)
H Morgan (p.76)
Jo Morgan (p.30)
Linda Morgan (p.136)
Mary Morgan (p.76)
Shirley P Morgan (p.133)
Sian Morgan (p.10)
William Morgan (p.133)

Richard Morgan-Jones (p.22)
Sue Morgan-Williams (p.36)
Lisa Morice (p.131)
Michael Morice (p.131)
Ann Morley (p.116)
Elspeth Morley (p.60)
Robert Morley (p.60)
Allan Morris (p.49)
Ann Morris (p.43)
Brenda Morris (p.86)
Clare Morris (p.102)
Elizabeth Morris (p.29)
Monique Morris (p.76)
Peter A Morris (p.36)
Shosh Morris (p.60)
Stephen Morris (p.29)
Susan Morrish (p.40)
Barbara Morrison (p.36)
Philippa Morrison (p.119)
Richard Morrison (p.60)
Shirley Morrissey (p.143)
Gillian Morton (p.60)
Mary Morton (p.45)
Richard Victor
  Morton (p.120)
Susan Moses (p.26)
Duncan Moss (p.10)
Bahman Mostaeddi (p.111)
Geoff Mothersole (p.22)
Anita Mountain (p.45)
Lesleen Mountjoy (p.131)
Chris Moutzoukis (p.145)
Cathy Moxon (p.126)
Theresa Moyes (p.126)
Ruth Muffett (p.76)
Diana Mukuma (p.86)
Nuala Muldoon (p.102)
Alan Mulhern (p.61)
Jean Mulvey (p.22)
Josephine Mulvey (p.32)
Jean Mundy (p.113)
Pamela Mundy (p.140)
Elisabeth Perriollat
  Munro (p.106)
Jon Munsey (p.18)
Stephen Munt (p.93)
Lesley Murdin (p.10)
Derry Murphy (p.119)
Ger Murphy (p.146)
Katherine Murphy (p.102)
Susan Murphy (p.86)
Catherine Murray (p.145)
John Murray (p.102)
Jean P Murton (p.40)
Beatrice Musgrave (p.93)
Graham Music (p.61)
Heather Musker (p.18)
June Mycroft-Miles (p.131)
Marion Myers (p.134)
Piers Myers (p.61)
Trish Mylan (p.125)

N

Elizabeth Nabarro (p.76)
Zenobia Nadirshaw (p.36)
Omar Nafie (p.76)

Robin Nagle (p.76)
Julia Naish (p.61)
Sue Nappez (p.93)
(Jennifer) Ruth
  Nathan (p.116)
Gill Nathan (p.76)
Jack Nathan (p.86)
Carol Naughton (p.10)
Trinidad Navarro (p.61)
Alan Naylor-Smith (p.36)
Charles Neal (p.76)
Lalage Neal (p.93)
Patricia Neate (p.93)
Michael Neenan (p.26)
Annie Nehmad (p.61)
Denis E Neill (p.12)
Julia Nelki (p.108)
Denise Nelson (p.49)
Margaret Nelson (p.10)
Maureen Nelson (p.11)
Judith Nesbit (p.49)
Antje Netzer-Stein (p.102)
Jaqui Nevin (p.12)
Chris Newbery (p.19)
Alison Newbigin (p.86)
Rita Newby (p.141)
Adrian Newell (p.126)
Alexander Newman (p.3)
Kenneth Newman (p.119)
David Newns (p.111)
John Newson (p.16)
Mary Newson (p.8)
Kathleen Newton (p.76)
Zah Ngah (p.61)
R Niblett (p.126)
P John Nicholas (p.134)
Christine Nicholson (p.22)
David W Nicholson (p.40)
Elizabeth Nicholson (p.18)
Jane Nicholson (p.106)
Eileen Nightingale (p.18)
Ruth Nissim (p.119)
Amelie Noack (p.61)
Jane Noble (p.61)
Marsha Nodelman (p.61)
Philip Nolan (p.139)
Breda Noonan (p.142)
Veronica Norburn (p.76)
Susan Norrington (p.76)
Lynne Norris (p.143)
Giuliana Norsa (p.111)
Joanna North (p.18)
Sheila Norton (p.45)
Kate Nowlan (p.124)
Elizabeth Noyes (p.76)
Peg Nunneley (p.113)
Alexander R Nuthall (p.123)
Georgiana Nye (p.3)
Turid Nyhamar (p.32)

O

Charles O'Brian (p.142)
Kirsty M G O'Brien (p.140)
Maja O'Brien (p.93)
Mary O'Brien (p.146)
Pat O'Brien (p.131)

Lesley O'Callaghan (p.76)
Pierce J O'Carroll (p.108)
Susan O'Cleary (p.76)
Victoria O'Connell (p.76)
Aine O'Connor (p.145)
Len O'Connor (p.76)
Michael O'Connor (p.32)
Nadia O'Connor (p.131)
Noreen O'Connor (p.61)
Mary O'Conor (p.145)
Tricia O'Dell (p.131)
Miranda O'Donnell (p.11)
Elizabeth O'Driscoll (p.49)
Karen O'Hara (p.29)
Anne O'Leary (p.141)
Carmen O'Leary (p.49)
Christopher J
  O'Neill (p.131)
Helen M O'Neill (p.114)
James O'Neill (p.93)
Julia O'Neill (p.145)
Miceal O'Regan (p.145)
Bernadette
  O'Sullivan (p.145)
Renee O'Sullivan (p.40)
Haya Oakley (p.76)
Ian H Oakley (p.139)
Madeleine Oakley (p.86)
Silvia Oclander Goldie (p.76)
Andrew Odgers (p.76)
Renata Ogilvie (p.143)
Margaret D Ohene (p.61)
Johanna Ohnesorg (p.145)
Rudolph Oldeschulte (p.102)
David Oldman (p.46)(p.47)
Christine Oliver (p.93)
Elizabeth Oliver-
  Bellasis (p.76)
Felicia Olney (p.76)
John E D Oram (p.122)
Ann Orbach (p.137)
Susie Orbach (p.77)
Eileen Orford (p.77)
Vanja Orlans (p.77)
Tom Ormay (p.77)
Irene Oromi (p.145)
Jane Orton (p.119)
Madeline Osborn (p.30)
James Osborne (p.126)
Lynda Osborne (p.131)
Dorothy Ostler (p.20)
Joachim Otto (p.145)
Nicola Overs (p.126)
Christopher Owen (p.61)
Ian Rory Owen (p.136)
Peter Owtram (p.131)

P

Louise Padgett (p.3)
Annabel Page (p.139)
Anne Page (p.102)
Jean Pain (p.10)
Shan Palanisamy (p.86)
Lesley Palgrave (p.40)
Sue Pallenberg (p.36)
Fiona Palmer Barnes (p.34)

Dorothy Palmer (p.137)
Helen Palmer (p.143)
Jane Palmer (p.77)
Lisa Elaine Palmer (p.8)
Stephen Palmer (p.86)
Nicholas Pamphlett (p.43)
Marion Panchkowry (p.8)
Simona Panetta-
  Crean (p.61)
Renos Papadopoulos (p.49)
Annabelle Paramour (p.5)
Will Parfitt (p.124)
Gabrielle Parker (p.102)
Mary Parker (p.93)
Michael Parker (p.26)
Niki Parker (p.41)
Rosie Parker (p.61)
Jane Parkinson (p.22)
Jillian Parkinson (p.16)
Judy Parkinson (p.86)
Phil Parkinson (p.93)
Penny Parks (p.127)
Val Parks (p.61)
Malcolm Parlett (p.3)
John Parr (p.7)
Meriel A Parr (p.36)
Glenys Parry (p.122)
Patrick Parry-
  Okeden (p.119)
Shanti Parslow (p.77)
Barbara Parsons (p.125)
Marianne Parsons (p.77)
Karen Partridge (p.131)
Miranda Passey (p.38)
Anna-Maria Patalan (p.77)
Stuart Paterson (p.61)
Thelma Patricia (p.145)
Anna Patterson (p.61)
Linda Patterson (p.3)
Diana Paulson (p.77)
Lesley Pavincich (p.93)
Jack Pawsey (p.87)
Chris Pawson (p.36)
Sheila Pawson (p.36)
Denis Payne (p.127)
Graham Payne (p.114)
Helen Payne (p.36)
John Payne (p.14)
Susan Peace (p.121)
George Pearce (p.61)
Rosalind Pearmain (p.49)
Cathy Pearman (p.131)
Jean Pearson (p.102)
Mary Peart (p.5)
R G Peckitt (p.137)
Jonathan Pedder (p.87)
Lena Pehrsson-
  Tatham (p.18)
Adrianna Penalosa (p.93)
Paul Pengelly (p.131)
Joyce Penn (p.26)
Sandy Penniceard (p.93)
Mary M Penwarden (p.41)
Brenda Peover (p.131)
Hara Pepeli (p.77)
David Percy (p.32)

Rosine Perelberg (p.77)
Ajit Perera (p.131)
Angie Perrett (p.122)
Michael Perring (p.47)
Christopher Perry (p.111)
Rose Persson (p.124)
Rainer Pervöltz (p.145)
Franc Peternel (p.145)
Anthony Peters (p.143)
Linda Peters (p.77)
Roderick Peters (p.93)
Sheila Peters (p.87)
Corinna Peterson (p.77)
Susan Pethen (p.122)
Belinda Pethick (p.131)
Clare Petrie (p.27)
Julie Petrie-Kokott (p.111)
Sharon Pettle (p.61)
Hem Phaterpekar (p.147)
Peter Philippson (p.106)
Adam Phillips (p.102)
Asha Phillips (p.111)
Laurie Phillips (p.20)
Marriane Phillips (p.41)
Sue Phillips (p.87)
Susan Phillips (p.117)
Judith Philo (p.61)
Janet Philps (p.5)
Ashleigh Phoenix (p.133)
Desmond Picard (p.77)
Rachel Pick (p.61)
Keith Pickstock (p.61)
Deborah Pickvance (p.122)
Patricia Pidgeon (p.141)
Stella Pierides (p.61)
Patrick Pietroni (p.77)
Sheila Pigott (p.117)
Margery Pike (p.37)
Allan Pimentel (p.102)
Edna Pimentel (p.61)
Christine Pinch (p.37)
Malcolm Pines (p.47)
Eliana Pinto (p.87)
Alessandra Piontelli (p.145)
Robin Piper (p.61)
Alix Pirani (p.3)
Eduardo Pitchon (p.62)
Ruth Pitman (p.62)
Christopher Pitt (p.108)
Stef Pixner (p.49)
Barbara Plant (p.33)
Sue Platt (p.77)
Rene Plen (p.49)
Angela Plotel (p.102)
John Plowman (p.30)
Polly Plowman (p.87)
David Pocock (p.141)
Olga Pocock (p.141)
Barbara Pokorny (p.111)
Michael Pokorny (p.77)
Jane Polden (p.113)
Cynthia Pollard (p.8)
Elena Pollard (p.77)
James Pollard (p.10)
Patricia Polledri (p.62)
Sheena Pollet (p.13)

Juliette Pollitzer (p.94)
Marie Pompe (p.87)
Nick Poole (p.106)
Robert Poole (p.102)
Sian Pope (p.3)
Sue Pople (p.37)
Barbara Porter (p.119)
David Porter (p.33)
George J Porter (p.45)
Ruth Porter (p.77)
Dusan Potkonjak (p.26)
Stephen Potter (p.106)
Andrew Powell (p.119)
Angela Powell (p.77)
Glyn Powell (p.111)
Sheila Powell (p.77)
Kevin Power (p.77)
Maria E Pozzi (p.37)
Werner Prall (p.77)
Sheila Pratt (p.131)
Sheila Pregnall (p.141)
Kristiane Preisinger (p.77)
Michael Preisinger (p.77)
Fern Presant (p.62)
Kay Preston (p.62)
Annie Price (p.77)
Susan Price (p.87)
Lois Prichard (p.131)
John Priestley (p.94)
Michael Pritchard (p.7)
Harry Procter (p.124)
Susan Proctor (p.115)
Alan Prodgers (p.106)
Barry D Proner (p.102)
Karen Proner (p.102)
Kirsten Prosch-
  Jensen (p.145)
Helen Proudley (p.114)
Celia M Prussia (p.14)
Nia Pryde (p.142)
Jane Puddy (p.77)
John Pugh (p.121)
Andrew Pullin (p.124)
Jane Purkiss (p.3)
Chris Purnell (p.123)

Q

Mary Quaine (p.94)
Barbara Quin (p.33)
Asher Quinn (p.94)
Eilish Quinn (p.78)
Michelle Quoilin-
  Lebrun (p.7)

R

Marie-Louise Rabe (p.131)
Judith Rabin (p.78)
Norman Rabin (p.78)
Patricia Radford (p.78)
Marty Radlett (p.62)
Frances Rae (p.41)
Maeja Raicar (p.26)
John E Ralphs (p.119)
Elizabeth Ram (p.62)
Margaret Ramage (p.94)

Sandra Ramsden (p.102)
Christopher Rance (p.87)
Margaret Randall (p.136)
Rosemary Randall (p.10)
R S Rani (p.94)
Prue Rankin-Smith (p.22)
Francesca Raphael (p.78)
Hilde Rapp (p.78)
Bernard Ratigan (p.117)
Harvey Ratner (p.102)
Tammy Ratoff (p.49)
Noemie Rattray (p.147)
Verity Ravensdale (p.78)
Jean Rawsthorne (p.106)
Caroline Raymond (p.94)
Beryl Ann Rayner (p.122)
Joan Rayson (p.45)
Judith Rea (p.62)
Celia Read (p.78)
Jane Read (p.103)
Tim Read (p.62)
Frances Reader (p.127)
Bill Reading (p.41)
Paula Reardon (p.94)
William Reavley (p.137)
Ruth Reay (p.8)
Mary Reddie (p.141)
Michael Reddy (p.8)
Peter Reder (p.94)
Joseph Redfearn (p.78)
Kenneth Redgrave (p.13)
Leon Redler (p.78)
Alex Reed (p.133)
Keith Reed (p.103)
Keith Reed-Jones (p.33)
Susan Rees (p.14)
Diane Rees-Roberts (p.111)
Christopher Reeves (p.38)
Stephen Regel (p.117)
Joan Reggiori (p.78)
Marie-Christine
   Réguis (p.63)
Marguerite Reid (p.94)
Rosamund Reid (p.131)
Susan Reid (p.78)
Rachel Reidy (p.8)
Herta Reik (p.78)
Stephen Reilly (p.114)
Sigurd Reimers (p.124)
Marina Remington (p.33)
Davina Rendall (p.119)
Sue Rennie (p.62)
Martine Renoux (p.62)
Mirjana Renton (p.78)
Lynette Rentoul (p.62)
Robert W Rentoul (p.136)
John Renwick (p.49)
Malcolm Retallick (p.14)
Jennie Reuvid (p.94)
Paulina Reyes (p.94)
Carmen Reynal (p.29)
Alun Reynolds (p.10)
Francois Reynolds (p.113)
Hilary Reynolds (p.131)
M J Reynolds (p.136)
Michelle Reynolds (p.26)

Otto Rheinschmiedt (p.141)
Sue Rhind (p.62)
Eric Rhode (p.103)
Maria Rhode (p.78)
Rev A Rhodes (p.106)
Paul Rice (p.26)
Christopher Richards (p.3)
David Richards (p.139)
Diana Richards (p.78)
Janet Richards (p.7)
Michael Richards (p.23)
Paul Richards (p.117)
Val Richards (p.62)
Anne Richardson (p.103)
Elizabeth Richardson (p.37)
Gillian Richardson (p.3)
Madeleine J
   Richardson (p.23)
Sue Richardson (p.13)
Susan Richardson (p.113)
Ian Rickard (p.30)
Marion Rickett (p.37)
Susan Ricketts (p.111)
Thomas N Ricketts (p.122)
Ann Riding (p.41)
Nick Riding (p.41)
Jane Ridley (p.131)
Gabrielle Rifkind (p.78)
Elizabeth J Riley (p.8)
Frederic Riley (p.18)
Janet Rimmer (p.111)
Lynn Rimmer (p.141)
Sheila Ritchie (p.62)
Mark Rivett (p.125)
Sandra Rix (p.26)
Melissa Robb (p.141)
Jeff Roberts (p.8)
Julie Roberts (p.114)
June Roberts (p.111)
Pauline Roberts (p.41)
Sylvia Roberts (p.62)
Chris Robertson (p.78)
Ewa Robertson (p.78)
Zuleika Robertson (p.18)
Carole Robinson (p.10)
Ferga Robinson (p.87)
Gary Robinson (p.16)
Hazel Robinson (p.78)
J G Robinson (p.28)
Jenny Robinson (p.136)
Judy Robinson (p.23)
Louise Robinson (p.124)
Mardi Robinson (p.26)
Margaret Robinson (p.33)
Marlene Robinson (p.47)
Martin Robinson (p.20)
Sue Robinson (p.103)
Mary Roddick (p.18)
Hilary C A M Rodger (p.103)
George Rodwell (p.143)
Danielle Roex (p.145)
Anne Rogers (p.5)
Cynthia Rogers (p.87)
Lesley A Rogers (p.41)
Maggie Rogers (p.103)
Tove Rognerud (p.147)

Estelle Roith (p.78)
Letizia Romano (p.62)
Liza Romisch-Clay (p.62)
G Romm-Bartfeld (p.78)
Alivia Rose (p.4)
Kevin Rose (p.78)
Sally Rose (p.139)
Sylvia Rose (p.136)
Wendy Rose (p.94)
Gillian Rose-Smith (p.33)
Renee Roseman (p.147)
Margaret Rosemary (p.122)
Maria Rosen (p.62)
Angela Rosenfeld (p.122)
J E Rosenthall (p.78)
Fiona Ross (p.87)
Julie Ross (p.43)
Miroslava Ross (p.103)
Susan M Ross (p.33)
Nicole Rossotti (p.37)
Jenner Roth (p.62)
Priscilla Roth (p.78)
Ruth Roth (p.79)
Alan Rowan (p.62)
Chris Rowan (p.139)
John Rowan (p.49)
Carolyn Rowe (p.139)
Celly Rowe (p.139)
Dorothy Rowe (p.62)
Jill Rowe (p.4)
Gail Rowland (p.41)
Helen Rowlands (p.125)
Geraldine Roy (p.136)
Jane Roy (p.8)
Philip Roys (p.119)
Robert Royston (p.62)
Robin Royston (p.41)
Rosette Rozenburg (p.103)
Val Rubie (p.33)
Peter Ruddell (p.87)
Marjo Ruismaki (p.145)
Boris Rumney (p.87)
Nigel Runcorn (p.16)
Richard Rusbridger (p.79)
Malcolm Rushton (p.79)
Gillean Russell (p.45)
Julian Russell (p.79)
Margo Russell (p.145)
Marion Russell (p.62)
Rosemary Russell (p.33)
Wilson Russell (p.28)
Mary Jane Rust (p.62)
Margaret Rustin (p.79)
Stanley Ruszczynski (p.79)
Sue Ryall (p.87)
A M Ryan (p.136)
Elizabeth Ryan (p.120)
Joanna Ryan (p.62)
Tom Ryan (p.62)
Murray Ryburn (p.134)
Joel Ryce-Menuhin (p.79)
Judy Ryde (p.4)
Brigitte Ryley (p.87)
Patsy Ryz (p.63)

S

Andrea Sabbadini (p.63)
Joseph Sadowski (p.37)
Nigel A Sage (p.131)
Jas Ananda
   Salamander (p.23)
Jonathan Salisbury (p.117)
Miriam Salles (p.63)
Gillian Salmon (p.87)
Gill Salter (p.33)
Diane Salters (p.142)
Adam Saltiel (p.63)
Gwyneth Sampson (p.122)
Andre Samson (p.147)
Andrew Samuels (p.63)
Carole Samuels (p.63)
Audrey Sandbank (p.131)
Peter Sanders (p.23)
Susie Sanders (p.94)
Topsy Sandler (p.145)
Julia Sarkic (p.87)
Patrick Savage (p.43)
Peter J D Savage (p.43)
Margaret Savill (p.94)
Sue Saville (p.63)
Albert Sawyer (p.106)
Ken Sawyer (p.30)
Noel F Sawyer (p.26)
Mary Sazanjoglou-
   Hitzos (p.145)
Celia Scanlon (p.106)
Jean Scarlett (p.79)
Maggie Schaedel (p.41)
Wendy Schaffer-
   Fielding (p.111)
Morton Schatzman (p.79)
Joy Schaverien (p.45)
Margot Schiemann (p.79)
Maureen Schild (p.79)
John Schlapobersky (p.63)
Ruth Schmidt-Neven (p.143)
Anneliese
   Schnurmann (p.79)
Lynn-Ella Schofield (p.94)
Tamar Schonfield (p.63)
Els Schopman (p.145)
Kay Schreiber (p.26)
Thomas Schroeder (p.16)
Heiner Schuff (p.103)
Marja Schulman (p.146)
Chuck Schwartz (p.94)
Joe Schwartz (p.79)
Brigitte Scott (p.33)
Charlie Scott (p.108)
Glenys Scott (p.10)
Anna Scott Hayward (p.18)
Jan Scott (p.133)
Janice Scott (p.103)
Michael Scott (p.26)(p.108)
Tricia Scott (p.49)
Jean Scott-Chinnery (p.132)
Brian Scott-
   McCarthy (p.146)
Michael Scovell (p.124)
Daphne Seaman (p.111)
Michael Seear (p.47)

Barbara Segal (p.79)
Ruth M Seglow (p.26)
Anthony Seigal (p.87)
Elizabeth Seigal (p.29)
Anne Selby (p.4)
Gina Selby (p.7)
Marilyn Selby (p.63)
Eva Seligman (p.79)
Philippa Seligman (p.125)
Ruth Selwyn (p.37)
Merkel Sender (p.79)
Adriana Seradi (p.63)
Marc A Serfaty (p.133)
Nicholas Michael
 Serieys (p.16)
Vivienne Serpell (p.10)
Irena Bruna Seu (p.79)
Michael Sever (p.15)
Michael Sevitt (p.132)
Janette G Sexton (p.13)
Vivienne Seymour
 Clark (p.18)
E John Seymour (p.33)
Carole Shadbolt (p.120)
Adella Shapiro (p.63)
Pury Sharifi (p.63)
Juliet Sharman (p.103)
Belinda Sharp (p.63)
John Sharpe (p.141)
Meg Sharpe (p.103)
Geraldine Sharples (p.108)
Maureen Shaw (p.41)
Ann Shearer (p.79)
Anne Shearer (p.8)
Christine Shearman (p.49)
Margaret Sheehan (p.87)
Maureen Sheehan (p.79)
Nuala Sheehan (p.4)
Brian Sheldon (p.132)
Helen Sheldon (p.43)
Angela Sheppard-
 Fidler (p.132)
Mannie Sher (p.63)
Dolores Sheridan (p.103)
Alison Sheriffs (p.38)
Arthur Sherman (p.79)
Peggy Sherno (p.37)
Deanne Sherriff (p.87)
Sue Sherwin-White (p.103)
G C Shetty (p.108)
Doreen Shewan (p.120)
Ellen Attracta Shields (p.103)
Christopher Shingler (p.87)
Geraldine Shipton (p.122)
Sunita Shipton (p.103)
H Shivakumar (p.63)
Diana Shmukler (p.79)
Peter Shoenberg (p.103)
Deborah Short (p.117)
Patricia Short (p.7)
Thomas R Shortall (p.111)
Bani Shorter (p.24)
Rosa Shreeves (p.103)
David Shrimpton (p.26)
Lindsay Shrubsole (p.134)
Dorcas Shuen (p.142)

Alan Shuttleworth (p.49)
Judy Shuttleworth (p.111)
Susan Sibley (p.24)
Dave Sichel (p.103)
Ronald Siddle (p.106)
Brian Sidey (p.139)
Mara Sidoli (p.147)
Helen Sieroda (p.139)
Charlotte Sills (p.103)
Franklyn Sills (p.18)
Maura Sills (p.18)
Mary Silmon (p.29)
Carl M Silverman (p.79)
Jennifer Silverstone (p.94)
Keith Silvester (p.79)
Tina Simmonds (p.79)
Alison Simmons (p.4)
Gloria Simmons (p.63)
Monty Simmons (p.63)
Dave Simon (p.38)
Gail Simon (p.63)
Gregoris Simos (p.146)
Fiona Simpson (p.120)
Ian Simpson (p.94)
Kevin J Simpson (p.15)
Michael J A Simpson (p.10)
Lyn Sims (p.5)
Valerie Sinason (p.79)
Fiona Sinclair (p.10)
Ilse Sinclair (p.4)
Iris Singer (p.111)
Claire Skailes (p.30)
Charmian Skinner (p.103)
Cheryl Sklan (p.112)
Robin Skynner (p.79)
Anna Sladden (p.37)
John Slade (p.49)
David Slattery (p.4)
Julia Sleeper (p.120)
Rachid Smail (p.94)
Imogen Smallwood (p.94)
Jonathan Smerdon (p.23)
Anne Smith (p.94)
Basil Smith (p.7)
Carole Smith (p.80)
Cora Smith (p.117)
David Smith (p.16)
David L Smith (p.87)
Donna Smith (p.4)
Eileen F Smith (p.125)
Eva Smith (p.120)
Flo M F Smith (p.108)
Gerrilyn Smith (p.80)
Gill Smith (p.4)
Gillian Smith (p.10)
Janet Smith (p.16)
Jonathan Smith (p.63)(p.103)
Judith Smith (p.80)
Margaret Smith (p.108)
Margaret E Smith (p.63)
Nick Smith (p.94)
Norah Smith (p.87)
Paddie Smith (p.113)
Peter Smith (p.63)
Richard Smith (p.26)
Ruthie Smith (p.63)

Susan Diane Smith (p.41)
Trevor E L Smith (p.87)
Val Smith (p.87)
David Smolira (p.147)
Penelope Smyly (p.94)
Randa Snow (p.94)
Patricia Snowden (p.132)
Brian Snowdon (p.94)
Milica Sobat (p.103)
Anne-Charlotte
 Soderstrom (p.146)
Hannah Solemani (p.63)
Hester Solomon (p.80)
Clare Soloway (p.63)
Barbara Somers (p.103)
Gwynnedd Somerville (p.49)
Joanne Sones (p.20)
Michael Sones (p.20)
Ann Ngan Soo (p.103)(p.104)
Pamela Sorenson (p.147)
Michael Soth (p.120)
Sarah Soutar (p.23)
Rosemary Southan (p.80)
John Southgate (p.80)
Clover Southwell (p.104)
Edna Sovin (p.80)
John Spalding (p.41)
Frances Sparkes (p.120)
Penny Spearman (p.41)
Liz Specterman (p.80)
Bebe Speed (p.136)
Mary Spence (p.87)
Dave Spenceley (p.43)
Janet Spencer (p.94)
Margaret Spencer (p.123)
Lyndsay Spendelow (p.50)
Marlene Spero (p.80)
Josefine Speyer (p.80)
Ernesto Spinelli (p.88)
Shirley Spitz (p.104)
Ken Sprague (p.18)
Graham S Spratt (p.43)
Jenny Sprince (p.115)
Kate Springford (p.23)
Suzanne Sproston (p.4)
Robin Sproul-Bolton (p.37)
Lawrence Spurling (p.80)
Terri Spy (p.95)
Natalie Spyer (p.80)
Nick Spyropoulos (p.37)
Brenda Squires (p.63)
Joyce Stableford (p.106)
Helge Staby-Deaton (p.147)
Linda Stacey (p.37)
Anthony Stadlen (p.80)
Amanda Stafford (p.115)
Barbara Stafford (p.80)
David Stafford (p.112)
Paul Stallard (p.4)
Christine Stanbury (p.15)
Sally Standart (p.134)
Elizabeth Standish (p.120)
Pamela Stang (p.104)
Elizabeth Stanley (p.104)
Martin Stanton (p.88)
Rick Stanwood (p.33)

Gordon Starte (p.132)
John Stathers (p.18)
Theresa Staunton-
 Soth (p.120)
Frances Stearman (p.112)
Maire Stedman (p.88)
Patricia Steel (p.26)
Sandra Steel (p.37)
Miriam Steele (p.80)
Dorothee Steffens (p.95)
Peter Stehle (p.80)
Yvonne Stein (p.63)
Monika Steiner (p.8)
David Stembridge (p.132)
June Stephens (p.117)
Lyn Stephens (p.30)
Erika Stern (p.117)
Janine Sternberg (p.80)
David B Steven (p.24)
Jean Stevens (p.14)
Jill Stevens (p.146)
Yvonne Stevens (p.4)
Alice Stevenson (p.41)
Bruce Stevenson (p.80)
F Beaumont
 Stevenson (p.120)
Judy Stevenson (p.50)
Kate Stevenson (p.64)
Jill Steward (p.120)
Angus Stewart (p.64)
Henry B Stewart (p.120)
Ian Stewart (p.117)
John Stewart (p.80)
June Stewart (p.108)
Angela Steyn (p.80)
Marion Stiasny (p.50)
Quentin Stimpson (p.33)
Karen Stobart (p.95)
Yael Stobezki (p.80)
Beverley Stobo (p.37)
Alisdair Stokeld (p.139)
Jean Stokes (p.95)
Jenny Stokes (p.136)
Eva Stolte (p.33)
Anthony Stone (p.80)
Barry Stone (p.33)
Martin Stone (p.80)
Miriam Stone (p.80)
Sandra Stone (p.80)
Christine Stones (p.4)
Susan Storring (p.112)
Joy Stovell (p.64)
Amarilla Stracey (p.95)
Gill Straker (p.104)
Ricardo Stramer (p.64)
Jenny Strang (p.45)
Susi Strang (p.13)
Alison Strasser (p.143)
Freddie Strasser (p.80)
Jacqueline Stratford (p.4)
Eddy Street (p.125)
Sabina Strich (p.120)
Cassandra Struthers (p.95)
Gillian Stuart (p.64)
Lilly Stuart (p.88)
John Sudbury (p.43)

Anita Sullivan (p.80)
Christopher Sullivan (p.81)
Gerry Sullivan (p.146)
Graeme Summers (p.43)
Margot Sunderland (p.64)
Michael Sunderland (p.104)
Mehmet Sungur (p.146)
Sue Sünkel (p.64)
Deborah Sussman (p.47)
Pauline Sutcliffe (p.104)
Elisabeth Sutherland (p.50)
Janet Sutherland (p.45)
Robert I Sutherland (p.112)
Adrian Sutton (p.107)
Deirdre Sutton-Smith (p.30)
Joan Swallow (p.18)
John S Swan (p.120)
Alison Swan Parente (p.64)
Joanna Swift (p.112)
Sue Swift (p.41)
Barbara C Swinburne (p.95)
Richard Swynnerton (p.64)
Gabrielle Syme (p.139)
Jan Symes (p.33)
Karin Syrett (p.104)
Ann Syz (p.81)
Heather Szabo (p.13)
Gerard Szary (p.13)
Kasia Szymanska (p.104)

T

Sue Taberner (p.13)
Adrian Tait (p.124)
Britt Tajet-Foxell (p.95)
Alan Talbot (p.26)
Richard Tan (p.64)
Alannah Tandy
   (Pilbrow) (p.95)
Daniel Tanguay (p.95)
Nick Tanna (p.139)
Claire Tanner (p.88)
Digby Tantam (p.123)
Peter Tapang (p.26)
Helen Tarsh (p.132)
Peter Tatham (p.18)
Idonea Taube (p.81)
Hanna Taussig (p.11)
Elizabeth Taylor (p.43)
Harvey Taylor (p.64)
Helen Taylor (p.18)
Jane Taylor (p.95)
Jill Taylor (p.112)
Jon Taylor (p.16)
Mary Taylor (p.50)(p.81)
Maye Taylor (p.107)
Patsy Taylor (p.108)
Susie Taylor (p.120)
Tony Taylor (p.33)
Vivienne Taylor (p.136)
Caroline Taylor-
   Thomas (p.81)
Chris Teng (p.27)
Shoshi Terry (p.64)
Rita Testa (p.81)
Rose Thacker (p.13)
Anna Tham (p.141)

Geoffrey Thiel (p.37)
Harriet Thistlethwaite (p.64)
Marjorie Thoburn (p.13)
Margaret Tholstrup (p.95)
Alyss Thomas (p.19)
Jenny Thomas (p.28)
Kerry Thomas (p.104)
Lennox Thomas (p.64)
Madeleine Thomas (p.124)
Nigel Thomas (p.81)
Penny Thomas (p.30)
Sandra Thomas (p.13)
Hilary Thompson (p.121)
Jeannie Thompson (p.117)
Joan Thompson (p.27)
Joy Thompson (p.19)
Paul Thompson (p.64)
Alan Thomson (p.45)
Jean Thomson (p.81)
Pat Thomson (p.123)
Simon Thomson (p.120)
Helen Thorley (p.123)
Chris Thorman (p.37)
Bill Thorndycraft (p.112)
Andy S Thornton (p.15)
Suzanne Thornton (p.132)
Ivan Thorpe (p.138)
Steven Ticktin (p.64)
Brenda Leo Tiller (p.16)
Penny Tillett (p.64)
Anthony Tilney (p.136)
S Timmann (p.37)
Lily Elizabeth Tindle (p.143)
Froukje Tjepkema (p.146)
Ian Tod (p.16)
Gillian Todd (p.11)
Margaret Todd (p.123)
Margaret Togher (p.27)
Eileen Toibin (p.64)
Jack Tollan (p.27)
Moya Tomlinson (p.23)
Penny Tompkins (p.104)
Susan Tompkins (p.37)
David A Toms (p.117)
Yvonne Tone (p.146)
Anne Tonge (p.41)
Harold Tonks (p.136)
Nick Topliss (p.88)
Maria Totman (p.41)
Harry Tough (p.115)
Patricia Touton-Victor (p.11)
Michael Townend (p.136)
Heather Townsend (p.81)
Pat Townsend (p.125)
Esme Towse (p.107)
Maggie Towse (p.107)
Joy K Toyne (p.41)
Barbara Traynor (p.112)
Clare Tredgold (p.23)
Barbara Tregear (p.11)
Chris Trepka (p.139)
John Trewhella (p.15)
Joanna Trosh (p.27)
Brian Truckle (p.136)
Shirley Truckle (p.136)
Frances Truscott (p.41)

Claude Tse (p.41)
Molly Tuby (p.95)
Keith Tudor (p.123)
Guinevere Tufnell (p.50)
Julia Tugendhat (p.104)
Daphne Tully (p.41)
David Tune (p.27)
Ann Tunwell (p.13)
Annie Turner (p.95)
Carole Turner (p.146)
Jane Turner (p.23)
Martin S Turner (p.28)
Michael Turton (p.43)
Iris Tute (p.4)
Brenda Mary Tweed (p.136)
Heidy Twelvetrees (p.41)
Stephen Tyrrell (p.19)
Robert Tyson (p.114)
Laurie Tytel (p.7)

U

Christine Uden (p.14)
Jay Upton (p.132)
Catherine Urwin (p.50)

V

Marta Vaciago Smith (p.139)
Chris Valentine (p.4)
Paola Valerio-Smith (p.88)
Fiona Vallance (p.136)
Pat Vallely (p.23)
Yvonne Vallins (p.132)
Ingrid van Beek (p.146)
Henck P J G van
   Bilsen (p.143)
Jan-Floris Van der
   Wateren (p.104)
Emmy van Deurzen-
   Smith (p.88)
Corrie Van Halm (p.23)
Carlien van Heel (p.81)
Paul van Heeswyk (p.88)
S Van Marle (p.136)
Diederik van Rossum (p.146)
Linda Van Schoor (p.13)
Douglas Van-Loo (p.42)
Arturo Varchevker (p.81)
Susan Vas Dias (p.50)
Tonie Vass (p.45)
Gethsimani Vastardis (p.64)
David Veale (p.64)
Maurice Veale (p.64)
Helen Veasey (p.132)
Margit Veje (p.146)
Rolf Veling (p.64)
Julia Vellacott (p.64)
Malathi Venki (p.20)
Christine Verduyn (p.107)
Paul Vernon (p.64)
Arlene Vetere (p.7)
Kate Vickers (p.141)
Salley Vickers (p.112)
Athina Villia-Gosling (p.136)
Christopher Vincent (p.81)
David Vincent (p.50)

Francis Vine (p.4)
Linda Viney (p.143)
Sheila Vipan (p.123)
Leslie Virgo (p.42)
Cara Voelcker (p.141)
Marina Voikhanskaya (p.11)
Jose von Buhler (p.33)
Valerie Vora (p.43)(p.44)

W

Karin-Marie Wach (p.88)
Margot Waddell (p.64)
Liz Wadland (p.112)
Susan Wagstaff (p.7)
Jane Walford (p.139)
Robin Walford (p.140)
Catriona Walker (p.117)
David Walker (p.42)
Jim Walker (p.138)
Judy Walker (p.65)
Lorraine Walker (p.104)
Mary J Walker (p.95)
Moira Walker (p.45)
Steven Walker (p.27)
Daphne Wallace (p.140)
Norma Wallace (p.132)
Diane Waller (p.23)
Sandra Walline (p.95)
Benjamin J Wallis (p.95)
Sue Walrond-Skinner (p.95)
Aine Walsh (p.95)
Belinda Walsh (p.16)
Eileen Walsh (p.104)
Stuart Walsh (p.44)
Peter J Walters (p.120)
Michael Walton (p.132)
Michael Wang (p.113)
Peter Wanless (p.81)
Kitty Warburton (p.5)
Barbara Ward (p.19)
Dawn Ward (p.23)
John Ward (p.112)
Keltie Ward (p.117)
Shirley Ward (p.146)
Shona Ward (p.30)
Eve Warin (p.81)
Judith Warin (p.19)
Barbara Warner (p.104)
Yvonne Warren (p.42)
Heather Warwick (p.11)
Sue Washington (p.44)
Hilary Waterfield (p.65)
Anne Waters (p.42)
Kathleen Waters (p.88)
Judy Watkins (p.30)
Eileen Watkins
   Seymour (p.81)
Andrea Watson (p.8)
Christine Watson (p.88)
Clare Watson (p.16)
Gay Watson (p.19)
Gordon Watson (p.95)
J P Watson (p.88)
Lindsay Watson (p.81)
Pauline Watson (p.15)
Roy Watson (p.134)

ORGANISATION MEMBERSHIP LISTS

AAP - Association of Arbours Psychotherapists

Jan Abram
Neil Austin
Joseph Berke
Sally Berry
Manek Bharucha
Sasha Brookes
Nicky Buckley
Nigel Burch
Mary Cairns
Anna Cameron
Rod Cameron
Christina Campbell-Thomson
Prudence Cave
Gianni Dianin
Anne Doggett
Pat Dyehouse
Hella Ehlers
Clive Eiles
Lois Elliott
Margaret Fagan
Alexandra Fanning
Caroline Fawkes
Susan Ford
Laura Forti
Deborah Goodes
Bob Grant
Iona Grant
Margaret Green
John Greenwood
Roger Hacker
Janet Haddington
Guy Hall
Kirsty Hall
Julian Ibanez
Bridget Kelly
Michael Kelly
Saeunn Kjartansdottir
Katalin Lanczi
Francesco Lunardon
Chandra Masoliver
Brigitte McAndrew
Helen McCormack
Isabel Montero
Elisabeth Perriollat Munro
Trinidad Navarro
Susan O'Cleary
Lesley Pavincich
George Pearce
Marriane Phillips
Stella Pierides
Angela Powell
Marie-Louise Rabe
Verity Ravensdale
Sally Rose

Tom Ryan
Marie-Christine Réguis
Andrea Sabbadini
Adam Saltiel
Maggie Schaedel
Morton Schatzman
Tamar Schonfield
Irena Bruna Seu
Peter Smith
Hannah Solemani
David Stafford
Alisdair Stokeld
Margit Veje
Karin-Marie Wach
Hilary Waterfield
Sonia Whittle

ACAT - Association of Cognitive Analytic Therapists

Shakir Ansari
Hilary Beard
Cherry Boa
Beverly Brooks
Sangamithra U D Choudree
Susan Elizabeth Clarke
Pauline Cowmeadow
Annalee Curran
Dilys Davies
Francesca Denman
Mark Dunn
Yvonne Eadie
Louise Elwell
John C Field
Jackie Fosbury
Philippa Gardner
Linda Harvey
Brigitte Haupts
Michael Knight
Sue Kuhn
Tim Leighton
Mikael Leiman
Liisa Lettington
James Low
Norma Anderson Maple
Martin Marlowe
Elizabeth McCormick
Jane Melton
Annie Nehmad
Lesley Palgrave
Glenys Parry
Cynthia Pollard
Rachel Reidy
Eva Smith
Yvonne Stevens
Claire Tanner
Judith Warin

Lawrence Welch
Virginia West
Angela Wilton

ACP - Association of Child Psychotherapists

Stella Acquarone
Bobbie Akinboro-Cooper
Anne Alvarez
Janet Anderson
Chriso Andreou
P K Armbruster
Katherine Arnold
James Astor
Corinne Aves
Tessa Balogh Henghes
Debbie Bandler Bellman
Tessa Baradon
Paul Barrows
Francesca Bartlett
Stella Bellis
Helen Bender
Haydene Benjamin
Doris Benrey
Aiveen Bharucha
Manek Bharucha
Evanthe Blandy
Suzanne Blundell
Mary Boston
Catrin Bradley
Jonathan Bradley
Stewart Britten
Linda Buckingham
Richard Buckland
Jane Bunster
Donald Campbell
Diana Cant
Cynthia Carlson
Elizabeth Cartwright Hignett
Ann Cebon
Lynn Champion
Janine Cherry-Swaine
Freni Chinoy
Maggie Cohen
Pauline Cohen
Nancy Cohn
Anita Colloms
Beta Copley
Susan Coulson
Jan Cousins
George Crawford
Kiki Crean
Verena Crick
Gabrielle Crockatt
Deborah Cullinan
Jennifer Davids

Miranda Davies
Dilys Daws
Linda Dawson
Yair Domb
Deirdre Dowling
Ora Dresner
Alexandre Dubinsky
Helene Dubinsky
Rosemary Duffy
Kathleen Duguid
Barbara Eccles
Rose Edgcumbe
Judith Edwards
Alyce Faye Eichelberger Cleese
Judith Elkan
Victoria Elliott
Jane Ellwood
Louise Emanuel
Ricky Emanuel
Carole Epstein
John Eveson
Wendy Feldman
Robert W K Fleming
Audrey Gavshon
Janet Glynn-Treble
Ellen Golden
Eve Grainger
Gabriella Grauso Calaresu
Viviane Green
Sheena Grunberg
Nicola Guest
Michal Gurion
Gideon Hadary
William Halton
Wallace Hamilton
Carol Hanson
Michael Harari
Nina Harris
Trevor Hartnup
Christine Heath
Caroline Helm
John Henderson
Rachel M Henry
Pauline Hering-Josefowitz
Helen High
Alison Hilder
Deborah Hindle
Jill Hodges
Elizabeth Holder
Louise Holland
Jannie Hollins
Ann Horne
Carol Hughes
Margaret Hunter
Anne Hurry
Margaret Hurst
Lesley Ironside
Judith Jackson

Joe Jacobs
Charlotte Jarvis
Dorothy Judd
Susan Kegerreis
Jennifer Kenrick
Pat Kenwood
Valli Kohon
Monica Lanyado
M Laport-Steuerman
Effie Layiou-Lignos
Sandy Layton
Meira Likierman
Judith Green Loose
Maria Loret de Mola
Lorne Loxterkamp
Dorothy Luciani
Mary Lynch
Catharine Mack Smith
Jeanne Magagna
Suzanne Maiello Hunziker
Christine Martin
Stephen Martin
Yaron Mazliach
Anita McCann
Meryl McCartney
Moira McCutcheon
Savi McKenzie-Smith
Mando Meleagrou
Sheila Melzak
Annette Mendelsohn
Julia Mikado
David Millar
Lisa Miller
Martin Miller
Sheila Miller
Elizabeth Model
M L Montalbetti
Lisa Morice
Michael Morice
Bahman Mostaeddi
Robin Nagle
Antje Netzer-Stein
Zah Ngah
Giuliana Norsa
Turid Nyhamar
Silvia Oclander Goldie
Rudolph Oldeschulte
Elizabeth Oliver-Bellasis
Eileen Orford
Niki Parker
Marianne Parsons
Miranda Passey
Mary M Penwarden
Adam Phillips
Asha Phillips
Janet Philps
Rachel Pick
Alessandra Piontelli
Eduardo Pitchon
Maria E Pozzi
Barry D Proner
Karen Proner
Patricia Radford
Sandra Ramsden
Susan Rees
Christopher Reeves

Marguerite Reid
Susan Reid
Mirjana Renton
Paulina Reyes
Eric Rhode
Maria Rhode
Susan Ricketts
J G Robinson
Marlene Robinson
Miroslava Ross
Priscilla Roth
Richard Rusbridger
Margaret Rustin
Patsy Ryz
Joseph Sadowski
Wendy Schaffer-Fielding
Ruth Schmidt-Neven
Anneliese Schnurmann
Marja Schulman
Barbara Segal
Ruth M Seglow
Ruth Selwyn
Sue Sherwin-White
Alan Shuttleworth
Judy Shuttleworth
Susan Sibley
Mara Sidoli
Valerie Sinason
Milica Sobat
Joanne Sones
Michael Sones
Pamela Sorenson
Jenny Sprince
Nick Spyropoulos
Helge Staby-Deaton
Miriam Steele
Janine Sternberg
Judy Stevenson
Marion Stiasny
Sandra Stone
Susan Storring
Deborah Sussman
Alison Swan Parente
Ann Syz
Rita Testa
Brian Truckle
Shirley Truckle
Frances Truscott
Catherine Urwin
Marta Vaciago Smith
Paul van Heeswyk
Susan Vas Dias
Gethsimani Vastardis
Margot Waddell
Mary J Walker
Andrea Watson
Felicity Weir
Ann Wells
Anastasia Widdicombe
Eleanor Wigglesworth
Gianna Williams
Ian Williamson
Gillian Wilson
Jilian Wilson
Peter Wilson
Linda Winkley

Isca Wittenberg
Margarita Wood
Therese M-Y Woodcock
Gillian Woodman-Smith
John Woods
Nicola Woodward
Marie Zaphiriou Woods

AFT- The Association for Family Therapy

Nigel Alabaster
Brenda Allan
Christine Alnuaimi
Jenny Altschuler
Richard Appleton
Jacqueline Ardeman
Hugh Barnes
Helen Bates
Kirsten Blow
David Bott
Barry Bowen
Anne Brazier
Gillian A Brown
Sandra Bryson
Joanna Burrows
Brian Cade
David Challender
Jon Chatham
Nick Child
Alec Clark
Cairns Clery
Barbara Cohen
Mireille Colahan
Jan Cooper
Annalisa Corlando
Stephen Coulter
Mairlis Davies
Michael Day
Moira Doolan
Mary Eminson
Suzanne Essex
Keith Faull
Hugh Fox
Margaret Fox
Pat Freeman
Richard P W Fry
Susan Fyvel
Mary Goodman
Myrna Gower
Hilary Graham
Pete Gray
Peter Harmsworth
Bruce Hart
Mark Hayward
John Hills
Amanda Hodd
Peter Hudson
Tony Jaffa
Eileen Jamieson
Linda Johnston
Maggy Jones
Marie Kenny
Joyce Kilgour
Michael King
Wendy Klein

Enno Kuttner
Irene Lacey
Myrna Lazarus
Denis Lee
Alasdair Macdonald
Angela Markham
Olivera Markovic
Peter Marsden-Allen
Una McCluskey
Noel McCune
Penny Mendelssohn
Liza Miller
Denis E Neill
Julia Nelki
Ruth Nissim
Barbara Parsons
Christopher Pitt
David Pocock
Ruth Reay
Mark Rivett
Mary Roddick
Audrey Sandbank
Patrick Savage
Philippa Seligman
Dave Simon
Lyn Sims
Donna Smith
Yvonne Stein
Jacqueline Stratford
Christine Verduyn
Arlene Vetere
Liz Wadland
Susan Wagstaff
Steven Walker
Sue Walrond-Skinner
Jeni Webster
Tara Weeramanthri
Bilha Weider
Ann Whatley
Jan White
Gerti Wilford

AGIP - Association for Group and Individual Psychotherapy

Elizabeth Anderson
Seema Ariel
Bronwen Astor
Irene Bloomfield
Sara Brown
Charles Caruana
Patricia Claxton
Anne Codd
Howard Cooper
Enid Corker
Susan Corneck
Philip Cox
John Cross
Diane Cunningham
Liv Darling
Ann Davies
Wendy Dobbs
Karl Figlio
Jean Flannery
Anne Francis

Diane Frazer
Margaret Gardiner
Liz Good
Stephen Haine
Dorothy Hamilton
Kim Hamilton
Anita Heavens
Ralph Horton
Harold Humphries
Antonia Inlander
Myron Kaplan
Angela Kenny
Christine K Chemann
Monica Langdon
Graham Lee
Claire Leggatt
Sue Lethbridge
Jo-Ann Lewis
Joan Longley
Benig Mauger
Bryce McKenzie-Smith
Betty Mead
John Andrew Miller
Lynda Miller
Judith Nesbit
Elizabeth O'Driscoll
Tom Ormay
Laurie Phillips
Michael Pokorny
Jane Polden
Marie Pompe
Annie Price
Sheila Ritchie
Anne Rogers
Rosette Rozenburg
Brian Scott-McCarthy
Adriana Seradi
Sarah Soutar
John Spalding
Rick Stanwood
Lyn Stephens
Eva Stolte
Cassandra Struthers
Harvey Taylor
Tonie Vass
John Ward
Nigel Wellings
Lindsay Wells
Christina Wieland
Sheila Wildash
Annette Wotton
Jessie Zentler

AHPP - Association of Humanistic Psychology Practitioners

Gina Barker
Amely Becker
Naona Beecher-Moore
David Boadella
Rosemary Braid
Clare Brunt
Tamara Burnet-Smith
Helen Carroll
Barbara Carruthers

Petruska Clarkson
Barbara Cole
Whiz Collis
Rebecca Cooper
Ita Coronas
Christopher Coulson
Guy Dargert
Paul Dean
Judith Dell
Bernd Eiden
Dena Elliott
Michael Ellis
Peter Fleming
Derek Gale
Guy Gladstone
Angelika Golz
Judy Graham
Hazel Guest
Maureen Hancock
Sally Hart
Peter Hawkins
Marika Henriques
Agnes Birgit Heuer
Roger Horrocks
Martin Jelfs
Camilla Johnson-Smith
Alan Jones
Dave Jones
David Jones
David Kalisch
Kay Kennedy
Judi Keshet-Orr
Alan Kirby
Babs Kirby
Roslyn Langdon
Catherine Leder
Sara Leon
Hilary Lester
Bernd Leygraf
Jochen Lude
Barbara Luthy
Rosie March-Smith
Jane Mellett
Richard Mitchell
Elizabeth Morris
Stephen Munt
Chris Newbery
Vanja Orlans
Mary Parker
Thelma Patricia
Helen Payne
Edna Pimentel
Alix Pirani
Kristiane Preisinger
Michael Preisinger
Alun Reynolds
John Rowan
Judy Ryde
Brigitte Ryley
Tricia Scott
Josefine Speyer
Terri Spy
Anita Sullivan
David Tune
Heidy Twelvetrees
Shirley Ward

Gill Westland
Eric Whitton
Nigel Williams
Courtenay Young

AJA - Association of Jungian Analysts

Hella Adler
James Bamber
Anne Baring
Frances Bell
John H Bierschenk
David Black
Antonia Boll
Catherine ByGott
Ann Casement
Jules Cashford
Nita Clark
Adele Davide
Damien Doorley
Moira Duckworth
Alexander Duddington
Andrea Dykes
Rosalind Finlay
David Freeman
Gottfried Heuer
Begum Maitra
Rita McCarthy
Julienne McLean
Peter Millar
John Miller
Alan Mulhern
John Newson
Amelie Noack
Fiona Palmer Barnes
Denis Payne
Martin Robinson
Robin Royston
Carl M Silverman
Gordon Starte
Jean Stokes
Martin Stone
Gillian Stuart
Karin Syrett
Chris Williams
Susan Williams

ANLP - Association for Neuro-Linguistic Programming

Alexandra Asseily
Melloney Atuahene
Ron Banks
Dale Beckett
Nancy Blake
Maire Brankin
Stephen Bray
Marion Brion
Sue Brock
Laurena Chamlee-Cole
Conny Christmann
Susan Conway
Dave Crisp

Sheila Cromwell
Frank Daniels
Kieron Deahl
Peter Delves
John Dinwoodie
John Eaton
Martin Eldon
Richard Errington
Anne Furneaux
Juliet Grayson
Shaun Growney
Thomasz Hanchen
Suzanne Harper
Pamela Hayes
Jo Hogg
Margaret Hueting
Michael Johnson
Mimi Kilgour
John J King
Edna Kyrie
Maggie La Tourelle
James Lawley
Peter Leakey
Graham Lennox
Philip Lewis
Roger Linden
Suzanne Looms
Judith Lowe
Laurie Macdonald
Michael Mallows
Ian McDermott
Judith Mills
Terry Mohan
Terry Moore
John Murray
Jean P Murton
Philip Nolan
Jean Pain
Penny Parks
Nick Poole
Sian Pope
Glyn Powell
Francois Reynolds
Paul Richards
Gail Rowland
Julian Russell
Anna Scott Hayward
Michael Seear
Mary Silmon
Susi Strang
Gerard Szary
Joan Thompson
Penny Tompkins
Francis Vine
Eileen Walsh
Eileen Watkins Seymour

AUTP - Association of University Teachers of Psychiatry

Jonathan Pedder

BABCP - British Association for Behavioural & Cognitive Psychotherapy

Paul T Alexander
Mary A Allinson
Michelle Altman
Peter Amies
Loukas Athanasiadis
Charles D Bactawar
Jan D Beach
Jean B Bechhofer
Julie C Beech
Gerald A Bennett
Pauline Benson
Z Bhunnoo
Geraldine Bienkowski
Nagy R Bishay
Nicholas J Black
Ivy-Marie Blackburn
John Blackburn
Caroline Blair
John Bland
E Veronica (Vicky) Bliss
David C Blore
Colin M Blowers
Mari E Brannigan
Lee Brosan
Thomas M Brown
Toni Brown
Mary Buckley
C W Burdett
Stephen Burr
Dennis R Bury
Gerard Butcher
Linda Butler
Illana Cariapa
Mark Philip Chandler
Adrian Childs-Clarke
Isabel Clarke
Stephen Lawrence Clarke
Susan Elizabeth Clarke
Peter J Coles
Louise Colson
Brian Copley
Christina H Coyle
Gordon Cree
Paul Cromarty
Terry Cromey
Bernadette Curwen
Rebecca Dalgarno
Kevin Daly
John Davidson
Brenda Davis
Paul E Davis
Janice De Souza
Alicia Deale
Elizabeth A Deeble
Lindsey D Denford
Elizabeth Anne Doggart
Gillian Donohoe
Pim Draper
Lynne Drummond
Windy Dryden
Alec John Duncan-Grant
Katie Dunn

Andrea K Edeleanu
Robert J Edelmann
Yvonne G Edmondstone
Peter Elliott
Sandra A Elliott
Nancy M Farley
Keith Fearns
Valentina Fernandez
Felicity Fincham
Linda Fisher
Angus Forsyth
Jane Fossey
Tom Foxen
Richard France
Christopher Freeman
Anne Garland
Carol A Gilboy
Patricia Gillan
Timothy P Gillett
Jeanne Gimblett
Brian Glaister
Elma Golsworthy
P Kenneth Gordon
Kevin Gournay
Maggie Gray
Stephen Michael Gray
Barry Greatorex
Jamie G H Hacker Hughes
S Handy
Ian G Hanley
David J Hannigan
Mark Hardcastle
Neil Harrington
Paul David Gwyn Harris
Andrew Harvey
Jolien Haveman
Evelyn R Hendry
Claudia Herbert
Linda Herdman
Rene Hiestand
C Anthony Hill
Kathleen Mary Howes
Anne J A Hume
Jennifer J Hurley
Anna K Huszcza
Sheila Jenkins
P H Jezard-Clark
Carolyn H John
Jerome Devakumar Joseph
Paul Stephen Keenan
Philip Kelly
Paul David Kemp
Fiona Kennedy
Brian Kiely
Peter John Kolb
Jane Kunkler
Bernard Wai Kai Lau
Ruth Lawson
Mary Lea
Maria A Lever
Ken Lewis
Leslie E C Lim
Clive G Long
Jennifer Long
Karina Lovell
Rosemarie Lucas

Norman D Macaskill
Helen F Macdonald
Julius Malkin
Trevor J Mathews
Helen P Matthews
Sharon Matthews
John McClure
Sean McCoy
Hugh E McFadden
Alison M McFarlane
Mary McGoldrick
Maureen McGroary-Meehan
Molly McKay
Brendan Nicholas McLoughlin
Gladeana McMahon
Lisa Mettam
Pamela Milne
Gordon Moore
Stirling Moorey
William Morgan
Peter A Morris
Shirley Morrissey
Richard Victor Morton
Duncan Moss
Chris Moutzoukis
Theresa Moyes
Zenobia Nadirshaw
Michael Neenan
Adrian Newell
Lynne Norris
Elizabeth Noyes
Alexander R Nuthall
Kirsty M G O'Brien
Pierce J O'Carroll
Helen M O'Neill
Shan Palanisamy
Lisa Elaine Palmer
Stephen Palmer
R G Peckitt
Ajit Perera
R S Rani
William Reavley
Stephen Regel
Marina Remington
Paul Rice
David Richards
Ian Rickard
Thomas N Ricketts
Ferga Robinson
Lesley A Rogers
Susan M Ross
Peter Ruddell
Nigel A Sage
Noel F Sawyer
Jan Scott
Michael Scott
Jean Scott-Chinnery
Marc A Serfaty
Nicholas Michael Serieys
Brian Sheldon
Deanne Sherriff
Thomas R Shortall
Ronald Siddle
Gregoris Simos

Rachid Smail
Trevor E L Smith
Graham S Spratt
Paul Stallard
Sally Standart
Henry B Stewart
Mehmet Sungur
John S Swan
Barbara C Swinburne
Kasia Szymanska
Britt Tajet-Foxell
Jon Taylor
Madeleine Thomas
Nigel Thomas
Andy S Thornton
Lily Elizabeth Tindle
Gillian Todd
Yvonne Tone
Michael Townend
Pat Townsend
Chris Trepka
Joanna Trosh
Claude Tse
Martin S Turner
Henck P J G van Bilsen
David Veale
Malathi Venki
Belinda Walsh
Peter J Walters
Michael Wang
Norman Webster
Stephen Westman
Zena J Wight
Dianne P Wilcox
Verina Wilde
Beck Williams
Christopher John Williams
Ruth M Williams
Steve Williams
Debbie Williams-Conley
Frank Wills
Fiona Wilson
Mary Wilson
Gill Wiltshire
Jacqueline Withers
Paul Woodcraft
Christine M J Wright
Robin Yapp
Katherine Young

BAFAT - British Association for Autogenic Training and Therapy

Rita Benor
Jane Bird
Valerie Bonnefin
Sarah-Jill Buchanan
Tamara Burnet-Smith
Brian Davidson
Alice Greene
Grete Gross
Nida Ingham
Nasim Kanji
Hetty MacKinnon

Janet Marshall
Christine Pinch
Jennie Reuvid
Anna Tham
Jane Whistler

BAP - British Association of Psychotherapists

Gina M V Alexander
Patricia Allen
Robert Andry
James Astor
Okeke Azu-Okeke
Gillian Ballance
Mary Banks
Afrakuma Bannerman
Gillian Barratt
Cecilia Batten
Jennifer Beddington
Stella Bellis
Nicholas Benefield
Angela Bennett
Lorna Berger
Wolf Blomfield
Elizabeth Bostock
Victoria Botwood
Marion Brady
Johanna Brieger
Jill Bright
Robin Gordon Brown
Jane E Buckley
Joan Burnett
Jean Carr
Kate Carr
Maureen Chapman
Sandy Chapman
Elphis Christopher
John Clay
Marion Cochlin
Christine Cochrane
Margaret Cochrane
Alexander Coren
Lou Corner
Barbara Cottman
Gerard Cutner
Hazel Danbury
Diana Daniell
Arna Davis
Dilys Daws
Paul de Berker
Patricia de Hoogh-
   Rowntree
Diana Dennis
Archibald Erskine
Nathan Field
James V Fisher
Susan Fisher
Ann Foden
Martin Freeman
Lena Furst
Elizabeth Gee
Hugh Gee
Betty Gilbert
Geraldine Godsil

Lesley Goodman
Rosemary Gordon-
   Montagnon
Anthony Grainger
Stephen Gross
Nellie Hadzianesti
Herbert Hahn
Jeff Halperin
Wallace Hamilton
Christine Hammond-Small
Georgina Hardie
Dianne Harris
Gordon Harris
Tirril Harris
Robert Hart
Nelly Hatzianesti
Jeremy Hazell
Dinea Henney
Edward Herst
Agnes Birgit Heuer
Philip J Hewitt
Ruth Hirons
Penelope Holland
Peter Hood
Patricia Hoogh-Rowntree
Earl Hopper
Irene Howard
Margaret Humphrey
Anne Hurry
Eric Hutchison
Susan Irving
Marianne Jacoby
Glenys James
Penny Jaques
Miranda Kenny
Josephine Klein
Ann E Kutek
Daphne Lambert
Rushi Ledermann
Joan M Lee
Jennifer Leeburn
Rob Leiper
Mary Lister
Britta Lloyd
Susan Loden
Maria Lynch
Christopher MacKenna
Dorrie MacLean
Mira Malovic-Yeeles
Marietta Marcus
Nicholas Marshallsay
Peter A Masani
Marilyn Mathew
Henrietta Mayne
Beckie Menckhoff
Gillian Miles
Adele Mittwoch
Aslan Mordecai
Kay Mordecai
H Morgan
Elspeth Morley
Robert Morley
David W Nicholson
Maja O'Brien
Peter Owtram
Patrick Parry-Okeden

Jean Pearson
Christopher Perry
Roderick Peters
Sue Phillips
Judith Philo
Desmond Picard
Ruth Pitman
Andrew Powell
Sheila Powell
John Priestley
Michael Pritchard
Barry D Proner
John E Ralphs
Joan Reggiori
Lynette Rentoul
Diana Richards
Elizabeth Richardson
Renee Roseman
Philip Roys
Rosemary Russell
Jean Scarlett
Elizabeth Seigal
Pury Sharifi
Mannie Sher
Peter Shoenberg
Michael J A Simpson
Cheryl Sklan
Anna Sladden
Basil Smith
Hester Solomon
Rosemary Southan
Ricardo Stramer
Kerry Thomas
Lennox Thomas
Paola Valerio-Smith
Paul Vernon
Christopher Vincent
Benjamin J Wallis
Eve Warin
Susan Wax
Sarah Weston
Jean Wetherell
Anastasia Widdicombe
Yvete Wiener
Serena Willmott
Jilian Wilson
Ruth Windle
Gillian Woodman-Smith
Bernadette Woolmer
Denise Yeldham
Hindle Zinkin

BASMT - British Association for Sexual and Marital Therapy

Shafika Abbasi
Eve Adler
Sandra Alexander
Brian Arnold
Tricia Barnes
Chris Beighton
Iris Berger
Mary Berry
Anita Blum
Daphne Boddington

Charmian Bollinger
Pauline Brassington
Elisabeth Brindle
Avril Brown
Jackie Buckler
Malcolm Bush
Josie Butcher
Paula Carter
Alison Clegg
Sue Clements-Jewery
S Clifton
Sonia Coats
Martin Cole
Jane Collins
Jeffrey Collis
Faye Cooper
Grahame F Cooper
Penny Cooper
Michael Crowe
Sylvia Cullum
Brian Daines
Marianne De Groot
Asun de Marquiegui
Marie De'ath
Guy Deans
Rosemary Dighton
Sally Duncan
Paula Dyer
Frances Emeleus
G E Evans
Tricia Evans
Kay Farquharson
Bobbie Fraser
Michael Gage
Jan Galloway
Jean Glover
John Goldman
Peter Gregory
Mary Griffin
John F Guilfoyle
Rosalie Gurr
Ruth Hallam-Jones
Eira Hamilton
Caroline Harrison
Susan Harrison
Jane Hawksley
Christopher Headon
Begum Hendrickse
Brenda Hill
Jan Hillman
Anita Hobbs
Elisabeth Holdaway
Anne Hooper
Marilyn Howe
Brian Howlett
Margot Huish
Patricia Hunt
Paul Jackson
Emily Jacob
Caroline Jones
Judith Jones
Joyce Keith
Judi Keshet-Orr
E Lawrence
Bernd Leygraf
Wendy Lidster

Raymond Lightbown
Patricia Lloyd
Sandra Lobel
Sydney Lobel
Nancy Logue
Julia Loudon
James Low
Sue Malone
Shirley Marks-Pinfold
Angela Martin
Kathryn May
Aine McCarthy
Doris McColl
Maureen McGroary-
  Meehan
Janet McNaught
Louise Mitchell
Ruth Mitchell
Jill Moore
M C Moore
Elizabeth Morgan
Josephine Mulvey
June Mycroft-Miles
Denise Nelson
Maureen Nelson
Mary O'Brien
Mary O'Conor
Miranda O'Donnell
Sue Pallenberg
Dorothy Palmer
Angie Perrett
Michael Perring
Barbara Plant
Rene Plen
Helen Proudley
Nia Pryde
Margaret Ramage
Joan Rayson
Jane Read
Frances Reader
Davina Rendall
Jennie Reuvid
Gillian Richardson
Madeleine J Richardson
Jane Ridley
Elizabeth J Riley
Frederic Riley
Sandra Rix
Jane Roy
Elizabeth Ryan
Gwyneth Sampson
Daphne Seaman
Anthony Seigal
Vivienne Serpell
Ilse Sinclair
Patricia Snowden
Elizabeth Stanley
Jill Stevens
Jan Symes
Sue Taberner
Jane Taylor
Marjorie Thoburn
Moya Tomlinson
Daphne Tully
Ann Tunwell
Jose von Buhler

Valerie Vora
Keltie Ward
Heather Warwick
Christine Watson
J P Watson
Lynne Webster
Eleanor Wheeley
Ruth Whittaker
Llynwen Wilson
Norman Wilson
Sue Wood
Kevan R Wylie
Christine Yawetz

BCPC - Bath Centre for Psychotherapy and Counselling

Whiz Collis
George Dewey
Sue Douglas
Anthony Elman
Tish Feilden
Kelvin Hall
David Hamblin
Jon Hastings
Kim Hastings
Peter Hawkins
Ian Hoare
Inge Kessel
Yig Labworth
Jo Lacy-Smith
Barbara Luthy
Rosie March-Smith
Jane Mellett
Chris Newbery
Jane Orton
Alix Pirani
Jane Purkiss
Ruth Roth
Judy Ryde
Anne Selby
David Slattery
Penny Thomas
Chris Valentine
Cara Voelcker
John Kirti Wheway

BPDA - British Psychodrama Association

Ana Aguirregabiria
Shelagh Austin
Anne Bannister
Jenny Biancardi
Jane Bould
Sue Bradbury
Kate Bradshaw-Tauvon
David Brazier
Teresa Brown
John Casson
Anna Chesner
Jan Costa
William Cramer

Carole Dale
Mo Daniels
Christopher Farmer
Stephen Flynn
Christina Hagelthorn
Peter Haworth
Barbara Hodges
Paul Holmes
Julia Howell
Peter Hutchinson
Jinnie Jefferies
Marcia Karp
Malcolm Kay
Gillie King
Kate Kirk
Laila Kjellstrom
Dorothy Langley
Giles Lascelle
Mary Levens
Olivia Lousada
Nick Luxmoore
Enid MacNeill
Cass Moggridge
Jon Munsey
Catherine Murray
Dusan Potkonjak
Andrew Powell
Sheila Pregnall
Barbara Quin
Jonathan Salisbury
Celia Scanlon
Els Schopman
Alison Simmons
Ken Sprague
Susie Taylor
Jeannie Thompson
Simon Thomson
Barbara Tregear
Stuart Walsh
Roy Watson
Sylvia Wheadon
Eve White
Paul Wilkins
Gill Williams
Sandra Wooding
Maureen Wright

BTC - The Gerda Boyesen Centre

Caroline Armstrong
Rosemary Bardelle
Elizabeth Barker
Stefanie Baum
Ebba Boyesen
Gerda Boyesen
Mona Lisa Boyesen
Cornelia Brosskamp
Sally Byford
Carola Byring
Martha Carvajal-Ogden
Richard Cleminson
Didi Crook
Didier Danthois
Valerie Davis
Ursula Deniflee

Heiner Eisenbarth
Merlyn Falkowska
Maryline Gagnere
Rus Gandy
Gillie Gilbert
Michele Harris
Susan Hauser
Karin Heinitz
Alice Jacobus
Helen Jones
Achim Korte
Tsafi Lederman
Lauren Liebling
Paula McLeod
Jean Mundy
Peg Nunneley
Julia O'Neill
Johanna Ohnesorg
Joachim Otto
Chris Pawson
Sheila Pawson
Michelle Quoilin-Lebrun
Miriam Salles
Andre Samson
Brigitte Scott
Sunita Shipton
Clover Southwell
Janet Sutherland
Daniel Tanguay
Jill Taylor
Jan-Floris Van der Wateren
Carlien van Heel
Deborah Webb
Joan Woodhill

CAPP - Centre for Attachment-Based Psychoanalytic Psychotherapy

Janet Adams
Anna Brave-Smith
Valerie Bucknall
Emerald Davis
Judith Erskine
Heidi Ferid
Marj Fleming
John Henry
Hazel Hickson
Stevie Holland
John Hosking
Hannah Hurst
Jennie Jarvis
John Jolliffe
Bernie Laschinger
Penny McMillan
Jess Michael
Penny Miller
Andrew Odgers
Jane Parkinson
James Pollard
Chris Purnell
Maeja Raicar
Sue Richardson
Val Rubie
Joe Schwartz

Iris Singer
John Southgate
Susan Vas Dias
Kate White
Laurie Jo Wright

CCHP - Chiron Centre for Holistic Psychotherapy

Sylvia Albrighton
Joachim Boening
Michaela Boening
Maureen Browne
Suzanne Cooper
Jenny Coxwell-White
Alicja Drewnowska
Bernd Eiden
Dena Elliott
Nigel Gray
Korinna Hedinger-Farrell
Janet Hills
Ray Holland
Lynne Holmes
Silvia Jacon
Gillian Kelly
Claudius Kokott
Margaret Landale
Gisela Lockie
Jochen Lude
Karen O'Hara
Rainer Pervltz
Julie Petrie-Kokott
Werner Prall
Paddie Smith
Michael Soth
Theresa Staunton-Soth
Bruce Stevenson
Amarilla Stracey
Shoshi Terry
David Tune
Max Wilkins

CCPE - Centre for Counselling & Psychotherapy Education

Tamara Alferoff
Jenny Averbeck
John Bannon
Maureen Rahima Bannon
Harika Basharan
Tessa Bilder
Charlie Brittain
Diana Buirski
Susie Burrows
Theresa Carlson
Peter Dawson
Hanora Desmond
Enid Edgeley
Susan Emm
Anthony F Fagan
John Fentiman
Jennifer Forssander

Alfred Fox
Annie Fox
Daphne Fraser
Pamela Gaunt
Pamela Griffiths
Thelma Griffiths
Angela Gruber
Kitty Hagenbach
Linda Hall
Nigel Hamilton
Anita Harper
Nicola Haskins
Brigitte Haupts
Carolyn Howell
Paula Jacobs
Roma Jacques
Jenny Jennings
Ros Jones
Maggie Kafton
Agnes Keane
Pamela Keane
William Kinbacher
Mary Kingsley
Lyn Lamplough
Brandy Martin
Paul McDermott
Patricia McKeown
Ann L Meza
Ori Miller
Sue Nappez
David Newns
Nadia O'Connor
Phil Parkinson
Clare Petrie
Allan Pimentel
Lois Prichard
Asher Quinn
Anne Richardson
Letizia Romano
Wendy Rose
Jas Ananda Salamander
Susie Sanders
Dolores Sheridan
Jonathan Smerdon
Richard Smith
Penelope Smyly
Quentin Stimpson
Yael Stobezki
Geoffrey Thiel
S Timmann
Pat Vallely
Meredith Wheeler
Wendy Winter
Diana Young
Raymond Young

CFAR - Centre for Freudian Analysis and Research

Vivien Bar
Bice Benvenuto
Graham Bull
Bernard Burgoyne
Margaret Campbell
Gillian Darcy

Marc Du Ry
Eric Harper
Michael Kennedy
Richard Klein
Danuza Machado
Hara Pepeli
Alan Rowan
Gerry Sullivan
Lindsay Watson

CPCP - Centre for Personal Construct Psychology

Joyce Agnew
Willie Botterill
Damian Brennan
Joady Brennan
Dennis R Bury
Catherine Butler
Eric Button
Cassie Cooper
A S B Crosby
Peter Cummins
Peggy Dalton
Alan Dupuy
Franz Epting
Ray Evans
Fay Fransella
Fiorella G Gatti-Doyle
Peter Goold
Francoise Grimshaw
Sharon Jackson
Helen Jones
Brenda Morris
Clare Morris
Derry Murphy
Bernadette O'Sullivan
Nicola Overs
Anthony Peters
Harry Procter
Nicole Rossotti
Dorothy Rowe
Gina Selby
Frances Sparkes
Helen Taylor
Joan Thompson
Alan Thomson
Chris Thorman
Linda Viney
David Winter

CPP - Centre for Psychoanalytical Psychotherapy

Katherine Arnold
Manek Bharucha
Diana Birkitt
John Boulton
Jonathan Bradley
Maureen Gledhill
Orna Hadary
Malka Hirsch-Napchan
Diana Jansen

Dorothy Judd
Florangel Lambor
Stuart Lieberman
Gwenda Lippitt
Rita Newby
Tom Ormay
Patricia Polledri
G Romm-Bartfeld
Richard Tan

CSP - Cambridge Society for Psychotherapy

Pamela Arriens
Steve Briant
Jenny Corrigall
Judy Davies
Michael Evans
Margaret Farrell
Valerie Gentry
Leila Gordon
Sarah Greaves
Lucy King
Liebe Klug
Clara Lew
Peter Lomas
Sian Morgan
Carol Naughton
Annabelle Paramour
Rosemary Randall
Carole Robinson
Vivienne Seymour Clark
Gillian Smith

CSPK - Centre for the Study of Psychotherapy (University of Kent)

Carol Bunker
Nigel Bunker
Mary Cairns
Alan Cartwright
Kate Cartwright
Diane Cunningham
Hazel Darnley
Rob Leiper
Bill Reading
Ann Riding
Nick Riding
Maggie Schaedel
Maureen Shaw

CTS - Centre Training School of Hypnotherapy and Psychotherapy

Shaun Brookhouse
Marjorie Curtis
Adrienne Cutner
Anne Hardman
Toni-Lee Isaac
Susan Martin
Damien McVey
Barbara Moon

Ken Sawyer
Joyce Stableford
Elizabeth Taylor
Jack Tollan
Sue Washington

FAETT - Forum for the Advancement of Educational Therapy & Therapeutic Teaching

Mia Beaumont
Ellora Polly Burridge
Anne Casimir
Claire Chappell
Andrea Clifford
Walter Coles
Catherine Daniel
Jenny Dover
Heather Geddes
Sally Gell
Angela Greenwood
Sr M Letizia Hannon
Helen High
Sacha Alexi Irwin
Lyn C Jennings
Helen Masani
Gillian Morton
Irene Oromi
Gillian Salmon
Marilyn Selby
Merkel Sender
Ann Ngan Soo
Idonea Taube
Penny Tillett

FIC - The Family Institute, Cardiff

Erica Alexander
Susan Benbow
John Brett
Brenda Cox
Paddy Crossling
Jeffrey Faris
Michael Foulkes
Sue Gagg
Hilary Howell
Sue Jones
Helen Marks
Cherrith A Marshall
Trish Mylan
James Osborne
Dorothy Ostler
Sigurd Reimers
Melissa Robb
Gary Robinson
Bebe Speed
Eddy Street
Jim Wilson

GCL - The Gestalt Centre, London

Amely Becker

Ita Coronas
Clare Crombie
Susannah Darling Khan
Maggie Davidge
Michael Ellis
Toni Gilligan
Lesley Hampson
Maureen Hancock
Flora Hoskin
Gaie Houston
John Leary-Joyce
Judith Leary-Tanner
Veronica Marsden
Jane Puddy
Alivia Rose
Peggy Sherno
Jonathan Smith
Heidy Twelvetrees
Maurice Veale

GCP - Guildford Centre for Psychotherapy

Bronwen Astor
Renate Blackwood
Patricia de Berker
Paul de Berker
Anne Francis
Beth Hashemi
Peter Hatswell
Valerie Hatswell
Harriet Holve
Jean Hopwood
Michael Hopwood
Sue Lethbridge
Valerie Lynch
Christopher MacKenna
Tricia O'Dell
Peter Owtram
Sheila Pratt
Rosamund Reid
Jean Scarlett
E John Seymour
Rick Stanwood
Eva Stolte
Vivienne Wilmot
Melanie Yallop

GPTI - Gestalt Psychotherapy Training Institute

Joy Appleby
Talia Levine Bar-Yoseph
Dolores Bate
Josta Bernstadt
Vivian Broughton
Lesley Brown
Todd Butler
Petruska Clarkson
Ita Coronas
Bill Critchley
Penelope Daintry
Jenny Dawson
Sally Denham-Vaughan

Dagmar Edwards
Ken Evans
Richard Evans
Sue Fish
Freda Fitton
Andrew Fookes
Marianne Fry
Maria Gilbert
Tony Glanville
Ian Greenway
Judith Gregory
Judith Hemming
Judith Higgins
Jacqui Hughes
Elisabeth Jackson
Glenys Jacques
Jane Jameson Milner
Philip Joyce
Anne Kearns
Caro Kelly
Des Kennedy
Helen Kennedy
Daniel Kwei
Elizabeth Leiper
Patricia D Levitsky
Philippa Lubbock
Liz MacKenzie
Jennifer Mackewn
Caroline Maudling
John Mitchell
Diana Mukuma
(Jennifer) Ruth Nathan
Vanja Orlans
Lynda Osborne
Malcolm Parlett
Peter Philippson
Malcolm Retallick
Margaret Rosemary
Janice Scott
Christine Shearman
Margot Sunderland
Michael Turton
Robert Tyson
Jonathan Whines
Guinevere Williams

GUILD - Guild of Psychotherapists

Tessa Adams
Mary Addenbrooke
Olivia Amiel
Pamela Armitage
Rosemary Arnold
Coral Atkins
Paul Atkinson
Anthony Ayres
Roger Bacon
Vivien Bar
Peter Barham
Mary Barnett
Jean Barrett
Jill Barry
Audrey Battersby
Peter Berry
Vibha Bhatt

Tricia Bickerton
Evanthe Blandy
Camilla Bosanquet
Rosalind Bowers
Michael Briant
Julia Buckroyd
Michael Burton
Elizabeth Campbell
Anne Chancer
Philip Chandler
Jacques China
Suzanne Clackson
Louise Clare
David Clendon
Sylvia Cohen
Nancy Cohn
Jane Coleridge
Natalie Collins
Stephen Colver
Suzanne Coombs
Sara Cooper
Jeni Couzyn
Jeremiah Cronin
Sue Draney
Jenny Dunn
Judith Easter
Susan Egert
Susan Eisen
Nina Farhi
Margaret Farrell
Berthe Ficarra
Matthew Forster
Caroline Fry
Rita Garlovsky
Annika Gilljam
Phyllis Goldblatt
Simon Good
Pat Gosling
Marion Gow
Rosamund Grant
Anne Gray
Kati Gray
Sarah Greaves
Anne Megan Griffiths
Annie Grocott
Virginia Grosser
Liana Guy
David Hall
Elizabeth Hancock
Olivia Harvard-Watts
Peter Hatswell
John Heaton
Marika Henriques
Linda M Hoag
Jill Hopkins
Daphne Hort
Angela Howard
Marjorie Hudson
Ann Hughes
Carlotta Johnson
Margaret Jones
Angela Joyce
Ros Kane
Alexandra Karan
Anna Kerr
Jack Kerridge

Sue Krzowski
Margaret Lawrence
Marie Maguire
David Mann
Jennifer Marsh
Irene Milburn
Michael Miller
Muriel Mitcheson Brown
Sian Morgan
Monique Morris
Shosh Morris
Elizabeth Nabarro
Alan Naylor-Smith
Elizabeth Nicholson
Jane Noble
Noreen O'Connor
Haya Oakley
Ann Orbach
John Payne
Rosalind Pearmain
Lena Pehrsson-Tatham
David Percy
Adam Phillips
Ruth Porter
Sheila Pratt
Susan Price
Judith Rea
Joseph Redfearn
Christopher Richards
Janet Richards
Val Richards
Marion Rickett
Lynn Rimmer
Zuleika Robertson
Hazel Robinson
Judy Robinson
Sue Robinson
Boris Rumney
Lynn-Ella Schofield
Glenys Scott
Anne Smith
Kate Springford
Lawrence Spurling
Adrian Tait
Hanna Taussig
Jay Upton
Yvonne Vallins
Helen Veasey
Salley Vickers
Marina Voikhanskaya
Judy Watkins
Lesley Wells
Roger Wells
Rosemary Westcott
Shirley Wheeley
Jean White
Gillian Wilce
Michael Wilson
Frances Mary Wooster
Chrysoula Worrall

HIP - The Hallam Institute of Psychotherapy

Lily Barker

Judy Bennison
Juliet Berry
Polly Blacker
G N Bolsover
Christine Bostock
J Heather Caulfield
Peter R F Clarke
John De Carteret
Helen Drucquer
David Edwards
Lynda Ellis
Michael Gartland
Ingolf Gudjonsson
Anita Guiton
Vera M Hopkins
Patricia A Hunt
Tim Kendall
Alan Lidmila
Ann Littlewood
Patrick A Loftus
David Loxley
Enid MacNeill
Pamela Mann
Myra Marshall
John McAuley
Joan Meredith
Jane Monach
John E D Oram
Susan Pethen
Deborah Pickvance
Beryl Ann Rayner
Carolyn Rowe
Geraldine Shipton
Eileen F Smith
John Sudbury
Sandra Thomas
Pat Thomson
Margaret Todd
Sheila Vipan
Joan Webb
Jean Willowes
Myra Woolfson

IATE - Institute for Arts in Therapy and Education

Graeme Blench
Paul Dean
Sue Fish
Jo James
Sara Leon
James Low
Francesca Raphael
Sue Rennie
Chris Rowan
Margot Sunderland
Veronica Wilson

IFT - Institute of Family Therapy

Margaret Adcock
Percy Aggett
Louise Anthias

Jill Ashley
Peter Atwood
Jocelyn Avigad
Steve Bagnall
Sara Barratt
Margaret Bennett
Arnon Bentovim
Vicky Bianco
Peter Bishop
Dora Black
Paul Blackburn
G N Bolsover
Robert Bor
Paula Boston
Anne Bousfield
Charlotte Burck
Elizabeth Burns
Diana Butt
John Byng-Hall
Sue Byng-Hall
Patrick J Byrne
David Campbell
Kathleen Chimera
Alan Cooklin
Ursula Cornish
Catherine Crowther
Paul Cubie
Ron Cushion
Barbara Dale
Gwyn Daniel
Neil Dawson
Elizabeth Dodge
Emilia Dowling
Gwynneth Down
Ros Draper
Jane Dutton
Stella Egert
Ivan Eisler
Anne Elton
Ruth Erskine
Claude Esposito
Erica Filby
Chris Gaskell
Irene Gee
Evan George
Danya Glaser
Claire Glasscoe
Gill Gorell Barnes
Nancy Graham
Vivienne Gross
Peter Hardwick
Gillian Harrison
Anne Heavey
Theresa Hendra
June Henley
Steve Herington
Judy Hildebrand
Peter Hollis
Peter Honig
Christine M Hooper
David Humphreys
Chris Iveson
Di Iveson
Brian Jacobs
Anthony James
Christopher James

Hugh Jenkins
Ellie Johnson
Elsa Jones
Marlene Jones
Madeleine Knowles
Sebastian Kraemer
Robert Lafon
Judith Lask
Annie Lau
Paul Lewington
Stuart Lieberman
Caroline Lindsey
Barry Mason
Robert Mayer
Cynthia Maynerd
Damian McCann
David McDonald
Brenda McHugh
Sallie Mercer
Philip Messent
Ann Miller
Riva Miller
Anni Moorhouse
Allan Morris
Charles O'Brian
Pat O'Brien
Len O'Connor
Shanti Parslow
Diana Paulson
Rosine Perelberg
Sharon Pettle
Margery Pike
Harvey Ratner
Margaret Robinson
Nuala Sheehan
Gerrilyn Smith
Nick Smith
Maire Stedman
Pauline Sutcliffe
Peter Tapang
Nick Topliss
Guinevere Tufnell
Annie Turner
Linda Van Schoor
Douglas Van-Loo
Barbara Warner
Kathleen Waters
Huguette Wieselberg
David Wilmot
Jeremy Woodcock

IGA - Institute of Group Analysis

Shafika Abbasi
Ivor Antao
Stephen Arcari
Biddy Arnott
Claire Bacha
James Bamber
Gillian Barratt
Harold Behr
Eileen Berry
Radha Bhat
Raymond Blake
Linda Bloch

Janet Boakes
Ian Boardman
Dascha Boronat
Bryan Boswood
Dennis Brown
Jane Campbell
Hanne Campos
Maria Canete
Anne Chatfield
Jim Christie
Tosin Clairmonte
Stephen Cogill
Vivienne Cohen
Murray Cox
Farhad Dalal
Patrick de Mare
Felicity de Zulueta
Marika Denton
Marisa Dillon Weston
Marje Eagles
Sue Einhorn
Barbara Elliott
Sheila Ernst
Arturo Ezquerro-Adan
Rufus Fagbadegun
Graeme Farquharson
Ruth Fasht
Geraldine Festenstein
Brenda Foguel
Victoria G Fuller
Liza Glenn
Bonnie Gold
Ewa Gottesman
Roberta Green
Maurice Greenberg
Ray Haddock
Rex Haigh
Sharon Hallard
Bob Harris
Liesel Hearst
John Heatley
Jan Helbert
Michael Hobbs
Sarah Holden
Beatrice Hook
John Hook
Gloria Hope-Price
Earl Hopper
Inge Hudson
Patrick Hughes
Sylvia Hutchinson
George Ikkos
Sonia Ingram
Margaret Kay
Duncan Kegerreis
Michael Kelly
David Kennard
Diana Kinder
Jane Knowles
Terry Lear
John Lee
Davina Lilley
Diana Lilley
Bill Lintott
Tina Lucas
Rita Lynn

Eileen MacAlister
Nancy MacKenzie
Norma Anderson Maple
Peter Mark
Mario Marrone
Brian Maxwell
Jessica Mayer-Johnson
Monica Meinrath
Sheila Millard
Sally Mitchison
Adele Mittwoch
Angela Molnos
Anne Morgan (Mhlongo)
Gill Nathan
Breda Noonan
Carmen O'Leary
Marion Panchkowry
Michael Parker
Anna-Maria Patalan
Franc Peternel
Malcolm Pines
Andrew Powell
Andrew Pullin
Christopher Rance
Tim Read
Herta Reik
Otto Rheinschmiedt
Gabrielle Rifkind
Jeff Roberts
Julie Roberts
Mardi Robinson
Cynthia Rogers
Angela Rosenfeld
Wilson Russell
Michael Scott
Michael Sevitt
John Sharpe
Ian Simpson
Robin Skynner
Val Smith
Marlene Spero
Robin Sproul-Bolton
F Beaumont Stevenson
Sabina Strich
Deirdre Sutton-Smith
Nick Tanna
Digby Tantam
Joy Thompson
Harry Tough
David Vincent
David Walker
Bernard Westcott
Julie Wetherill
Jeremy White
Gerhard Wilke
Sally Willis
James Wilson
Ewa Wojiechowska
John Woods
Tim Woolmer

IGAP - The Independent Group of Analytical Psychologists

Michael Anderton

Derick Armstrong
Ean Begg
William Burritt
Aileen Campbell Nye
Giles Clark
John Costello
Julian David
Joyce Davis
Cara Denman
Michael Edwards
Linda Freeman
Ruth Hiller
Eve Jackson
Jacqueline Keating
Pedro Kujawski
Anne Maguire
Frances Milne
Kenneth Newman
Renos Papadopoulos
Carmen Reynal
Joel Ryce-Menuhin
Chuck Schwartz
Ann Shearer
Bani Shorter
Janet Spencer
Peter Tatham
Molly Tuby
Lorraine Walker
Hildegard Weinrich
Michael Whan

IPC - Institute of Psychotherapy and Counselling

Gisela Albrecht
Kay Allan
Elizabeth Andrew
C Ruth Archer
Jane Arundell
Marie Baines
Moke Baker
Gill Bannister
Gay Baynes
Margaret Beer
Agnes Beguin
Jane Bingham
Arna Blum
Marie Botha
Elizabeth Ann Brown
Valerie Browne
Marie-Nd (Billie) Buckley
Brede Carr
Sean Cathie
Deborah Cazalet
Michael Channon
Maureen Chapman
Catherine Clancy
Jo Ann Clapp
Christine Clark
Jennifer Clifford
Vivienne Cobden
Ann Combes
Marie Costello
Stephen Crawford
Julia Crowley

Grazyna Czubinska
Heather Daniel
Alan Danks
Arminal Dare-Bryan
Joyce Dawson
Sally Day
Sally Dean
Rosemary Dixon-Nuttall
Pat Dooley
Christine Driver
Meg Errington
Eddie Farmer
Christopher Fenton
Sue Freeman
Melanie Gibson
Anne Goodrich
Nigel Groom
Pamela Gulliver
Paule Hamilton-Duckett
Celia Harding
Wendy Hartman
Natasha Harvey
Beth Hashemi
Lindy Henny
Astrid Hoang
John Holden
Marjorie Hudson
Janet Jones
Merryn Jones
Lee Kidd
Wendy Kingsnorth
Valerie Knowles
Regine Lallah
Michael Lamprell
Gareth Leeming
Colette Levy
Roger Linden
Michael Lodrick
Marianna Lutyens
Dorrie MacLean
Gertrud Mander
Patricia Marsden
Vivien Marshall
Philippa Marx
Carol Matthews
Brian Lawrence Maunder
Veronica McDouall
Mary McKeon
Brendan McLoughlin
Rosaleen Meaden
Sylvia Millier
Wendy Monticelli
Susan Moses
Lesley Murdin
Beatrice Musgrave
Lalage Neal
Kate Nowlan
Tricia O'Dell
Anne O'Leary
Rosie Parker
Judy Parkinson
Val Parks
Jack Pawsey
Sandy Penniceard
Rose Persson
Linda Peters

Sue Pople
David Porter
Kay Preston
Mary Quaine
Diane Rees-Roberts
Hilary Reynolds
Michael Richards
Pauline Roberts
Hilary C A M Rodger
Gillean Russell
Sue Saville
Juliet Sharman
Belinda Sharp
Charmian Skinner
Randa Snow
Gwynnedd Somerville
Pamela Stang
Jill Steward
John Stewart
Angela Steyn
Jean Stokes
Miriam Stone
Caroline Taylor-Thomas
Bill Thorndycraft
Froukje Tjepkema
Susan Tompkins
Anne Tonge
Aine Walsh
Anne Webster
Dorothea Elizabeth West
Penny Wigram
Sherly Williams
Suzanne Winders
Rob Wood
Martyn Wood-Bevan
James Wright
Melanie Yallop
Gaila Yariv
Tony Yates

IPS - Institute of Psychosynthesis

Ofra Anker
Jarlath Benson
Marie Beresford
Diana Chandler
Andrea Clough
Gillian Clover
Beth Conroy
Kay Conroy
Jane Cutler
Johanna Maria Diepeveen
John Doyle
Nick Duffell
Beckett Ender
Christine Ender
Joan Evans
Roger Evans
Debbie Friedman-Kempson
Dorothy Hanna
Jane Harrison
Michael Hayes
Karen Hedley
Nick Hedley
Sue Holland

Peter Hubbard
Richard Huson
Meg Kleisen
Reinhard Kowalski
Helena Lvendal-Srensen
Catherine MacGregor
Deena Marcus
Maureen McGuinness
June McOstrich
Christine Mead
Gerry Millar
Mary Newson
Miceal O'Regan
Helen Palmer
Cathy Pearman
Mary Peart
Sue Rhind
Danielle Roex
Maureen Schild
Christopher Shingler
Keith Silvester
Hilary Thompson
Maria Totman
Ingrid van Beek
Diederik van Rossum
Kate Vickers
Anne Welsh
Pamela Wolfe

IPSS - Institute of Psychotherapy and Social Studies

Nadia Allawi
Lesley Bennett
Patricia Bishop
Sandra Black
Anna Brave-Smith
Alex Burns
Paula Burns
Katherine Cameron
Lilian Chandwani
Karen Chessell
Giselle China
John Clare
Jane Coleman
Theresa Coulter
Susie Courtault
Andrew Culliss
Anne Cussins
Susan Daniels
Leslie Davidoff
J Keith Davies
Geri Dogmetchi
Hilary Dowber
Tom Feldberg
Heidi Ferid
Frank Franklyn
Tim Gauntlett
Guy Gladstone
Paul Gordon
Kate Goslett
June Green
Michael Green
David Grey
Anita Harper

Tone Horwood
Heather Howard
Riva Joffe
Leonor Juarez
Patricia Kerkham
Ursula Kiernan
Heather Law
Pam Lehrer
Muriel Letts
Marie Little
Antoinette Marshall
Ingrid Masterson
Dennis McEldowney
Colin McGee
Suzanne Michaud-Lennox
Flavia Morante
Veronica Norburn
Madeleine Oakley
Thelma Patricia
Norman Rabin
Hilde Rapp
Val Richards
June Roberts
Maggie Rogers
Tove Rognerud
Kevin Rose
Carole Smith
Jonathan Smith
Anne-Charlotte
  Soderstrom
Natalie Spyer
Monika Steiner
Joy Stovell
Sue Sünkel
Tony Taylor
Jim Walker
Robert M Young
Ali Zarbafi

ITA - Institute of Transactional Analysis

James Agar
Patricia M Allen
Joanna Beazley-Richards
Diane Beechcroft
Suzanne Boyd
June Brereton
Jenny Bridge
Mervyn Brunt
Birgit Bukovics-Heiller
Liz Bulmer
Pietro Cardile
Joyce Chesterton
Petruska Clarkson
Sarah Clevely
Robert Cooke
Mary Cox
Valerie Cunningham
Ann David
Peggy Davies
Jim Davis
Mary Etherington
Sue Fish
Jenny Gibson
Maria Gilbert

Katarina Gildebrand
Lynne Goddard
David Gowling
Eliott Green
Francesca Hannah
Helena Hargaden
Ki Harley
Biljana Harling
Judith Henshaw
Rachael Hewett
Julie Hewson
Hazel Hirst
Robin Hobbes
Sister Columba Howard
Nicholas Irving
Paul Keenan
Mavis Klein
Frances Lacey
Phil Lapworth
Gordon Law
Kathy Leach
Adrienne Lee
Elana Leigh
Melanie Lewin
Christine Lister-Ford
Ray Little
Carol Lucas
Jennifer McNamara
Jane McQuillin
David Midgley
John Monk-Steel
Susan Morrish
Geoff Mothersole
Anita Mountain
Pamela Mundy
Nicholas Pamphlett
Jillian Parkinson
John Parr
Susan Phillips
Juliette Pollitzer
Michael Reddy
Jenny Robinson
Sylvia Rose
Diane Salters
Peter Sanders
Carole Shadbolt
Christine Shearman
Diana Shmukler
Charlotte Sills
Fiona Simpson
Dave Spenceley
Alice Stevenson
Ian Stewart
Lilly Stuart
Graeme Summers
Sue Swift
Rose Thacker
Jenny Thomas
Anthony Tilney
Barbara Traynor
Keith Tudor
Carole Turner
Brenda Mary Tweed
Christine Uden
Corrie Van Halm
Jane Walford

Robin Walford
Shona Ward
Anne Waters
Martin Wells
Gill Wyatt

KCC - Kensington Consultation Centre

Lesley Allen
Eleanor Anderson
Carol Anson
Patrick Bentley
Sally Kemmis Betty
Judith Bevan
Jan Bolton
Sharon Bond
Jo Bownas
John Burnham
Simon Burton
Samantha Carr
Geraldine Causton
Anne Charvet
Carola Chataway
Caroline Dalal
Michael Day
Polly de Boer
Mark Dearnley
Rosemary Dighton
Raymond F Docking
Jude Egan
Isabelle Ekdawi
Naomi Elton
Ann Fausset
Glenda Fredman
Pam Goldstein
Gill Goodwillie
Inger Gordon
Virginia Gordon
Carry Gorney
Sheila Griffiths
Vivienne Gross
Chris Hannah
Clare Hannah
Ursula Harben
Pam Harvey
Gillian Hayhurst
Fran Hedges
Elisabeth Heismann
Sue Hickman
Elizabeth Hoare
Coral Howard
Pauline Hudson
Romey Jacobson
Eileen Jarvis
Wendy Kennett-Brown
Madeleine King
Peter Lang
Susan Lang
Penny Lewis
Ruth Lewis
Shirley Lingard
Martin Little
Gaynor Lovell
Desa Markovic
Alexsandra Mastilovic

Elspeth McAdam
Stewart McCafferty
Patricia McEvoy
Gaynor McManus
Ann McNair
V Middleton-Smith
Belinda Milani
Omar Nafie
Patricia Neate
Michael O'Connor
Margaret D Ohene
Christine Oliver
Gabrielle Parker
Karen Partridge
Adrianna Penalosa
Patricia Pidgeon
Kirsten Prosch-Jensen
Frances Rae
Peter Reder
Alex Reed
Sylvia Roberts
Marjo Ruismaki
Murray Ryburn
Topsy Sandler
Margaret Savill
Kay Schreiber
Philippa Seligman
Angela Sheppard-Fidler
Patricia Short
Gloria Simmons
Gail Simon
Margaret E Smith
Mary Spence
Kate Stevenson
Barry Stone
Mary Taylor
Chris Teng
Margaret Togher
Julia Tugendhat
Judy Walker
Ann Webb
Jaclyn Webber
Maria Wheeler
Gwyn Whitfield
Julia Wigglesworth
Michael Wilkins
Mary Wilkinson
J R Wilson
Teresa Wilson
Jenny Wimshurst

KI - Karuna Institute

Yon Anjali
Brian Attridge
Laura Donington
Deidre Gordon
Frances Greenfield
Julie Gresty
Roz Grigg
Anne Hunt Overzee
David Kalisch
Yig Labworth
Maxine Linnell
Sean Maloney
Heather Musker

Joanna North
Louise Padgett
Prue Rankin-Smith
Franklyn Sills
Maura Sills
John Stathers
Anna Tham
Alyss Thomas
Jane Turner
Gay Watson
Wendy Webber
Angela Willow
Bernard Wooder

LAPP - The London Association of Primal Psychotherapists

Victoria Canobbio
Susan Cowan-Jenssen
Einar D Jenssen
Jasna Kostic
Martine Lafargue
Heather E Lee Messner
Hans Jorg Messner
Marsha Nodelman
Aine O'Connor

LCP - London Centre for Psychotherapy

Shafika Abbasi
Stella Acquarone
Madeleine Adam
Evelyn Adey
Patricia Allen
Robert Andry
Sonia Appleby
Remy Aquarone
Alicia Arendar
Elke Asmus
Sally Baldwin
Nickie Bamber
Monica Bard
Ruth Barnett
James Barrett
Bernadine Bishop
Renate Blackwood
Wolf Blomfield
Elizabeth Bostock
Clare Brennan
Jennifer Caccia
Harriet B Calvert
Faye Carey
Nicholas Carolan
Praxoulla Charalambous
Tony Clapp
Margaret Clark
Christine Cochrane
Andrew Cockburn
David Cohen
Prophecy Coles
Ann Conlon
Marie Conyers
Marilyn Corry

Jenny Craddock
Ian Craib
James Craig
Dorothy Daniell
Patricia de Berker
Paul de Berker
Judith Dear
Christine Deering
Adrian Dickinson
Ora Dresner
Marjorie Eagles
Penny Elder
Jane Ellwood
Wendy English
Archibald Erskine
Madeleine Everington
Antonio Fazio
Geoff Ferguson
Nathan Field
Janet Fitzsimmons
Patrick Fleming
Daniel Fordwour
Angela Foster
Jessica Fox
Lynett Fraser
Martin Freeman
Ann Froshaug
Eogain Gallagher
Eva Gell
Pamela George
Jackie Gerrard
Maureen Gledhill
Godfrey Godfrey-Issacs
Francoise Golden
John Goodchild
Sheila Gordon
Robert Gottesman
Sue Gottlieb
Mary V E Grover
Madeleine Guppy
Ann Haine
Marie Hanley
Linda Harakis
Tirril Harris
Melanie Hart
Kit Haxby
Gillian Isaacs Hemmings
Zdenka Hermann
Robert Hinshelwood
Gisele Holender
Michael Hopwood
Irene Howard
Joy Isaacs
Beverley Jenkins
Natasha Jenner
Bryan Jobbins
Camilla Johnson-Smith
David Jones
Fagie Kadish
Olya Khaleelee
Suna Kilich-Walpole
Nicholas Kitson
Jane Kitto
Josephine Klein
Jackie Levitsky
Vivienne Lewin

Meira Likierman
Sophie Linden
Mollie Love
Marietta Marcus
Michal Margalit
Gaby Marks
Mario Marrone
Carol Marshallsay
Judith McConnach
Teresa McCreanor
Jennifer McDonnell
Jan McGregor-Hepburn
Sylvia Mears
David Mellows
Hilary Mellows
Steven Mendoza
Adele Mittwoch
Richard Morgan-Jones
Jack Nathan
Christine Nicholson
Susan Norrington
Victoria O'Connell
Susie Orbach
Tom Ormay
Brenda Peover
Belinda Pethick
Eliana Pinto
Robin Piper
Eduardo Pitchon
Barbara Pokorny
Michael Pokorny
Elena Pollard
Robert Poole
Kevin Power
Karen Proner
Eilish Quinn
Elizabeth Ram
Tammy Ratoff
Noemie Rattray
Celia Read
Michelle Reynolds
Eric Rhode
Estelle Roith
Maria Rosen
Robert Royston
Carole Samuels
Jean Scarlett
John Schlapobersky
Heiner Schuff
Ruth Selwyn
Dorcas Shuen
Jennifer Silverstone
Monty Simmons
Julia Sleeper
Judith Smith
Rosemary Southan
Edna Sovin
Penny Spearman
Suzanne Sproston
Anthony Stadlen
Barbara Stafford
Martin Stanton
Frances Stearman
David Stembridge
Angus Stewart
Ricardo Stramer

Michael Sunderland
Heather Szabo
Harvey Taylor
Mary Taylor
Harriet Thistlethwaite
Paul Thompson
Eileen Toibin
Clare Tredgold
Laurie Tytel
Arturo Varchevker
Rolf Veling
Julia Vellacott
Paul Vernon
Diane Waller
Vivien Webber
Patricia Wheeler
John Whitwell
James Wilson
Gillian Woodman-Smith
Ralph Woolf
Vernon Yorke
Vega Zagier Roberts

**LPDO - Liverpool
Psychotherapy Diploma
Organisation
(University of Liverpool)**

Janet Applegarth
Bill Barnes
Monica Baynes
Edith Bergel
Sandra Bryson
J G Callaghan
Suzy Challis
Elaine Clarke
Gloria Collins
Graham Cooper
Paul Dickinson
Rhoda Dorndorf
Elizabeth Doyle
K J B Edwards
Judi Egerton
Delia Essex
Bill Farrell
Mary Ferguson
Paul Foster
Mark Gabbay
Bryan W J Geldeard
Julie Glynn
Barbara A Green
Michael Gpfert
Patricia Hagan
Angela Hamilton
Sheila L L Hamilton
Ann Haworth
Bridget Hester
Robert Higgo
Alun Jones
Gundi Kiemle
Nick V Kirkland-Handley
Kirsten Lamb
Marion Lindsay
Claire Maguire
Sheila Mattison
Jeannie McIntee

Stuart McNab
Jaqui Nevin
Ian H Oakley
Hem Phaterpekar
Sheena Pollet
Stephen Potter
Celia M Prussia
Julie Ross
Charlie Scott
Janette G Sexton
Geraldine Sharples
G C Shetty
Kevin J Simpson
Flo M F Smith
Margaret Smith
June Stewart
Patsy Taylor
Helen Thorley
Daphne Wallace
Libby Wattis
Joan Webb
P G Wells
Anne Wheeler
Peter Wilkin
Pete Woodall
A E Woods
Rae Woodward

MC- Minster Centre

Elisabeth Abrahams
Helena Alder
Lynn Arnold
Jan Baker
Parizad Bathai
Sheila Borges
Heather Bowman
Jim Conwell
Valerie Coumont Graubart
Kay Coussens
Helen Davis
Nicola Dunn
Margaret Dyson
Louise Embleton-Tudor
Angela Fell
Rosalind Field
Elisabeth Flinspach
Jane Foley
Sheryle Geen
Lavinia Gomez
Margaret Granowski
John Gravelle
Susan Harrison-Mayor
Pauline Henderson
Max Holloway
Betty Anne Holtrop
Fakhir Hussain
Dennis Hyde
Alison Jefferies
Pat Johnson
Marianne Kolbuszewski
Richard Lang
Clare Lester
Richard Lewis
Sarah Littlejohn
Josephine Lock

Julia Moore
Barbara Morrison
Ger Murphy
Graham Music
Alison Newbigin
Lesley O'Callaghan
Jane Palmer
Stef Pixner
Sue Platt
Kristiane Preisinger
Fern Presant
Martine Renoux
Louise Robinson
Ruth Roth
Margot Schiemann
Adella Shapiro
Dave Sichel
Tina Simmonds
John Slade
Gill Smith
Clare Soloway
Sandra Steel
Joan Swallow
Leslie Virgo
Peter Wanless
Nigel Williams
Rosemary Wood-Bevan
Charlotte Wynn-Parry
Hymie Wyse
Margot Young

**MET- Metanoia
Institute**

Talia Levine Bar-Yoseph
Joanna Beazley-Richards
Su Borsig
Vivian Broughton
Lesley Brown
Todd Butler
Petruska Clarkson
Elaine Clifton
Bill Critchley
Valerie Cunningham
Penelope Daintry
Ann David
Peggy Davies
Laurie Day
Lesley Day
Paul Dean
Gillian Donaldson
Jenifer Elton Wilson
Ken Evans
Sue Fish
Freda Fitton
Jenny Gibson
Maria Gilbert
Katarina Gildebrand
David Gowling
Helena Hargaden
Ki Harley
Biljana Harling
Andrew Henderson
Paul Hitchings
Rosie Jeffries
Philip Joyce

Anne Kearns
Caro Kelly
Des Kennedy
Daniel Kwei
Frances Lacey
Phil Lapworth
Elana Leigh
Elizabeth Leiper
Norman Leitman
Christine Lister-Ford
Jennifer Mackewn
Valerie Magner
Andy McKeown
Jennifer McNamara
John Mitchell
Geoff Mothersole
Katherine Murphy
(Jennifer) Ruth Nathan
Lynda Osborne
Michael Perring
Susan Phillips
Barbara Porter
Keith Reed-Jones
John Renwick
Helen Rowlands
Janice Scott
Carole Shadbolt
Christine Shearman
Charlotte Sills
Gill Straker
Graeme Summers
Margot Sunderland
Margaret Tholstrup
Barbara Traynor
Keith Tudor
Carole Turner
Norma Wallace
Gill Wyatt

NAAP - Northern Association for Analytical Psychotherapy

Eileen Aird
Pat Black
William Brough
Iain Cameron
Alison Cookson
Margaret Cooper
Christine Deering
Mary Dobson
Sue Firth
Barbara Gilbert
Mary B Heller
Karolyn Hurren
Diana Jansen
Carlotta Johnson
Frank Johnson
Jo Reed Kendal
Joan Longford
Charles Lund
Malcolm MacPherson
Janet Mahmood
Patricia Marshall
Carolyn Matthews

Jan McGregor-Hepburn
Shirley P Morgan
Ann Morris
Graham Payne
Ashleigh Phoenix
Susan Proctor
Lindsay Shrubsole
Amanda Stafford
Christine Stanbury
Ian Tod
Pauline Watson

NRHP - The National Register of Hypnotherapists and Psychotherapists

Veronica Ashwell
Freda Ashworth
Kathleen Ayres
Julie G Biggs
Adrian Blake
Tom Bolton
John Butler
John Campbell-Beattie
Rosemarie Carapetian
Anthony Cawley
Raymond T Challis
Stanley Chandler
Barbara Chilton
Wendela Clarke
Grace Coia
Christine Cox
Suzanne Davidoff
Damini Angeli Diyaljee
Marjory Edgell
Shirley Faruki
Deborah M Fish
Albina Fitzgerald-Butler
Pauline Garvin-Crofts
Christopher Gausden
Michael Gent
Pauline Gilkes
Patricia Glasspool
Pauline Golding
Graham Gorman
Hilary E Graham
Terence Greenfield
Gerald A Harris
Mary Anne Maclellan Hart
Jean Hazlehurst
Roger Hepburn
Christine Retson Hogg
Faridoon Hormasji
David D Howie
Duncan B Johnson
Janice Johnstone
Christine King
Michael Kulyk
Allen Langley
Helen Lewis
Iris Linn
Monica Ludolf
Hanne Malcolm
Renee Mallardo
Jill Marshall

Greta Mattar
Adam May
Tony McGregor
Harry Milton
Lesleen Mountjoy
Christopher Owen
Jean Pain
Susan Peace
Joyce Penn
Sheila Peters
Angela Plotel
John Plowman
John Pugh
Caroline Raymond
Kenneth Redgrave
Susan Richardson
Julia Sarkic
Peter J D Savage
Michael Sever
Anne Shearer
Susan Diane Smith
Patricia Steel
David B Steven
Jean Stevens
Robert I Sutherland
S Timmann
Joy K Toyne
John Trewhella
Stephen Tyrrell
Peter M J Wesson
Kenneth Wingrove-Gibbons

NSAP - North Staffs Association for Psychotherapy

Anne Barry
Graham Breeze
Louise Brooks
Sue Brough
Rita Ghent
Alan Hassall
Cathy Moxon
Enid Whittam
Margaret Wiles
Kath Yates

NSHAP - National School of Hypnosis and Psychotherapy

Ghislaine Adams
Megan Adams
Talal Alrubaie
Claire Bellenis
Keith Bibby
Judith Black
Margaret Black
Roger Boff
Elizabeth Bowman
Eleanor Braterman
Suesanne Burgess
Monica Burton
Don Busolini
Barbara Butcher

Elizabeth J Caird
Misha Carder
Ian Clegg
Shanti Cole
Ronald Cosmo Luckcock
Linda Coutts
Anne M Dale
Bernard Dinneen
Dorothy M Duck
John Eaton
Pamela Gawler-Wright
Joan Goring-Avery
Geraldine Gould
Cyril Green-Thompson
Eric Haynes
Kirsti E Holm
Christina Howtone
Pamela Jones
Matthew Kalitowski
Jonathan Kanakam
Ray Keedy-Lilley
Margaret Kendrick
Christiane Kohler
Sylvia Mackinnon
Meg McCaldin
Jo Morgan
Linda Morgan
Christopher J O'Neill
George J Porter
Albert Sawyer
David Smolira
Brenda Leo Tiller
Dawn Ward

NWIDP - North West Institute for Dynamic Psychotherapy

Tessa Allen
Lynda Arkwright
Gillian Barnett
Linda Berman
Paul Bielicz
John Bird
Teresa J Black
M Buckley
Isobel Conlon
Maria Cornell
Sarah Davenport
Jaya Gowrisunkur
Else Guthrie
Helen Haworth
Kate Hellin
Robert Hobson
Alan Horne
L Hughes
Patricia Hunt
Keith Hyde
Malcolm Judkins
Susan Lendrum
Aidan Lunt
Frank Margison
Sue McAllister
Graeme McGrath
Lesley Mitchell
Jane Nicholson

Madeline Osborn
Alan Prodgers
Jean Rawsthorne
Rev A Rhodes
Helen Sheldon
Janet Smith
Adrian Sutton
Digby Tantam
Maye Taylor
Esme Towse
Maggie Towse

PA - Philadelphia Association

Racheli Azgad
Madelyn Brewer
Paul Caviston
Miles Clapham
Hilary Cooper
Robin Cooper
Marie-Laure Davenport
Heather de Leon
Mary Duhig
Mary Lynne Ellis
Mike Fielder
Joe Friedman
Steve Gans
Golshad Ghiaci
Douglas Gill
Paul Gordon
Liz Guild
Liz Hardy
Penny Hill
Joan Hurd
Lucy King
Barbara Latham
Christine Lawson
Del Loewenthal
James Low
Noreen O'Connor
James O'Neill
Haya Oakley
Leon Redler
Joanna Ryan
Fiona Sinclair
Joanna Swift
Patricia Touton-Victor
Heather Townsend
Gordon Watson
Paul Zeal

PET - Psychosynthesis & Education Trust

Eva Bayley
Naona Beecher-Moore
Deike Begg
Valerie Blomfield
Irene Brankin
Maggie Burlington
Rachel Clyne
Christopher Connolly
Anita Courtman
Sascha Donges

Dana Douglas
Arif Dyrud
Hetty Einzig
Marilyn Feldberg
Judith Firman
Loretta Fox
Sharon Gilbert
Liliana Gilli
Ian Gordon-Brown
Thomas Goss
Olga Gracia
David Hamblin
Pauline Hancock
Rima Handley
Devam Hendry
Christine Hillman
Nini Hitchman
Patricia Howe
Maggie Hunt
Cecilia Jarvis
Karina Kalderwaay
Marilyn Kernoff
Petra Kerridge
Kunderke Kevlin
Marianna Koeppelmann
Kathleen Lyons
Rosie Manton
Frances Marling
Fiona Miles
Eileen Nightingale
Georgiana Nye
Will Parfitt
Keith Pickstock
Janet Rimmer
Margo Russell
Alison Sheriffs
Helen Sieroda
Barbara Somers
Liz Specterman
Brenda Squires
Linda Stacey
Christopher Sullivan
Elisabeth Sutherland
Alannah Tandy (Pilbrow)
Barbara Ward
Diana Whitmore
Avril Wigham
Heather Williams
Vivienne Wynant

RCSPC - Regent's College School of Psychotherapy and Counselling

Martin Adams
Stephen Adams-Langley
Barrie Aldridge
Janet Aldridge
Yiannis Arzoumanides
John Aston
Lesley Austin
Adrienne Baker
Ruth Baker
Jocelyn Berger
Roger Bland

Miranda Blum
Margaret Browne
Rosemary Budgell
Angela Cameron
Christine Campbell
Carol Carsley
Dorel Cleminson
Hans W Cohn
Eva Coleman
Leila Collins
Jillian Cooper
Carol Crouch
Tom Davey
Anna David
Margaret Drew
Simon Du Plock
Stefan Durlach
Patricia Eglin
Zack Eleftheriadou
Frances Epstein
Em Farell
Almuth-Maria Fox
Peter Gardner
Fiorella G Gatti-Doyle
Verity Gavin
Dorothy George
Sylvia Golden
Elizabeth Good
Arlene Gorodensky
Carole Grace
Gaye Gunton
Monica Hanaway
Michael Harding
Nahum Harlap
Carol Holmes
Zelda Isaacson
Arthur Jonathan
Brett Kahr
Sandra Kondos
Virginia Katharine Lawlor
Christine Le Brun
Norman Leitman
Alessandra Lemma
Brigitte Leveque
Maureen Lever
Jon Little
Julie Lowe
Claire Manifold
Cordelia Mansall
Susan Marshall
Kikan Massara
Eileen McAleer
Lucia Moja-Strasser
Sue Morgan-Williams
Philippa Morrison
Nuala Muldoon
Susan Murphy
Piers Myers
Margaret Nelson
Renee O'Sullivan
Renata Ogilvie
Ian Rory Owen
Meriel A Parr
Judith Rabin
Marty Radlett
Paula Reardon

Liza Romisch-Clay
Ellen Attracta Shields
Imogen Smallwood
David L Smith
Lyndsay Spendelow
Ernesto Spinelli
Anthony Stadlen
Peter Stehle
Alison Strasser
Freddie Strasser
Richard Swynnerton
Suzanne Thornton
Ivan Thorpe
Steven Ticktin
Emmy van Deurzen-Smith
Michael Walton
Kitty Warburton
Yvonne Warren
Karen Weixel-Dixon
Frances Wilks
Claerwen Williams
Carol Wilson
Sarah Young
Nicholas Zinovieff

Re.Vision

Eve Adams
Lesley Brown
Helen Carroll
Joan Crawford
Suzanne Dennis
Mark Duberry
David Findlay
Livia Fischer
Anstice Fisher
Gary Hutchinson
Polly Plowman
Chris Robertson
Ewa Robertson
Sue Ryall
Roe Woodroffe

SAP - Society of Analytical Psychology

Mary Addenbrooke
Peter Addenbrooke
V V Alexander
Ian Alister
Biddy Arnott
Anne Ashley
James Astor
James Atkinson
Gillian Ballance
Desmond Biddulph
Derek Blows
Camilla Bosanquet
Wendy Bratherton
Johanna Brieger
George Bright
Clive Britten
Anne Brown
Geoffrey Brown
Elizabeth Browne

Claire Bruas-Jaquess
Ann Bruce
Jane Bunster
Vera Burhmann
John Burnard
Dorothy Byrne
John Carlisle
Richard Carvalho
Margaret Clark
Mary Coghlan
Ingrid Coltart
Catherine Crowther
Miranda Davies
Linda Dawson
Penelope de Haas
Sedwell Diggle
Jennifer Duckham
C Frey-Wehrlin
Victoria G Fuller
Peter B Fullerton
Vicki Gardiner
Alegra Garner
Elizabeth Gee
Hugh Gee
Himanshu Ghadiali
Liza Glenn
Jill Gordon
Rosemary Gordon-
  Montagnon
Brunhild Gourlay
Esther Green
Christine Hamblin
Michael Harari
Paul Harlow
Lois Harvey
Christopher Hauke
Susan Haxell
Jane Haynes
Marlene Heap
Edward Herst
Louise Holland
Ann Hopwood
David Howell
Judith Hubback
Sally Jakobi
Margaret Peggy Jones
Catherine Kaplinsky
Stewart Katzman
David L Kay
Robert Kirkwood
Jane Knight
Jean Knox
Daphne Lambert
Rushi Ledermann
Georgia Lepper
Derek Linker
Duncan Macdiarmid
Veronika Marlow
Mildred Marshak
Edward Martin
Robin McGlashan
Oliver McShane
William Meredith-Owen
Beth Miller
Richard Mizen
Norah Moore

Ruth Muffett
Jean Mulvey
Alexander Newman
Kathleen Newton
Anne Page
Simona Panetta-Crean
Christopher Perry
Roderick Peters
Corinna Peterson
Patrick Pietroni
Joseph Redfearn
Keith Reed
Susan Rees
George Rodwell
Fiona Ross
Malcolm Rushton
Andrew Samuels
Mary Sazanjoglou-Hitzos
Eva Seligman
Meg Sharpe
Margaret Sheehan
Maureen Sheehan
Arthur Sherman
H Shivakumar
Norah Smith
Brian Snowdon
Dorothee Steffens
Judy Stevenson
Karen Stobart
Alan Talbot
Jean Thomson
Sandra Walline
John Way
Marcus West
Jan Wiener
Margaret Wilkinson
Averil Williams
Ian Williamson
Mary Wilson
Robert Withers

SCPC - Stockton Centre for Psychotherapy and Counselling

Sarah Greening
Marjorie Homer
Christine Lister-Ford
Jennifer McNamara

SIP - Severnside Institute for Psychotherapy

Kay Allan
Robert Ash
Kate Barrows
Cecilia Batten
Sally Box
Ray Brown
Robin Brown
Robin Gordon Brown
Barbara Cottman
Miranda Davies
Sheila Davies

Barbara Docker-Drysdale
Iain Dresser
Lea K Elliott
Barbara Forryan
Fiona Gardner
Eva Gell
Pat Gosling
Sue Gottlieb
Jane Gracie
Sylvia Green
Annie Grocott
Herbert Hahn
Marie Hanley
Gordon Harris
Sheila Hawdon
Jeremy Hazell
Jeremy Holmes
Jill Hopkins
Glenys James
Nicole Jones
Carol Matthews
Barbara McNamara
Muriel Mitcheson Brown
Stephen Morris
Alexander Newman
Linda Patterson
Lena Pehrsson-Tatham
Olga Pocock
Christopher Richards
Martin Robinson
Jill Rowe
Michael Scovell
Elizabeth Seigal
Doreen Shewan
Basil Smith
Judith Smith
Suzanne Sproston
Elizabeth Standish
Christine Stones
Peter Tatham
Iris Tute
Abigail Wedderkopp
Alexandra Wilson
Paul Zeal

SPEC - Spectrum

Paul Allsop
Lia Ashby
Ross Bennett
Rex Bradley
Stan Brennan
Dianna Carruthers
Terry Cooper
Tom Cooper
Josephine Dahle
Erica Day
Gill Doust
Jan Dryden
Joan Fletcher
Jill Gabriel
Jane Gotto
Margaret Greaves
Judy Hargreaves
Avril Hollings
Maggie McKenzie

Delcia McNeil
Oriel Methuen
Richard Morrison
Julia Naish
Charles Neal
Stuart Paterson
Anna Patterson
Gillian Rose-Smith
Jenner Roth
Marion Russell
Gill Salter
Rosa Shreeves
Anthony Stone
Sarah Craven Webster
Kate Williams
Susan Willmott
John Witt

SPTI - The Sherwood Psychotherapy Training Institute

George Bassett
Carolyn Brown
Pat Bryant
Gitta Drury
Richard Erskine
Ken Evans
Mairi M Evans
Andrew Fookes
William Galbreath
Rosemary Hutchby
Christine Kennett
Caroline Maudling
Sheila Pigott
Diana Shmukler
Deborah Short
Cora Smith
Shirley Spitz
June Stephens
Erika Stern
Gill Straker
Jackie Watts
Heward Wilkinson
Kate Wilkinson

STTDP - South Trent Training in Dynamic Psychotherapy

Mark Aveline
James Bailey
Naomi Curry
Brian Denness
Geoff Fisk
Jean Headworth
Richard Jones
Helen Lee
Brendan McMahon
Mary Morton
Sheila Norton
Bernard Ratigan
Nigel Runcorn
Thomas Schroeder
David Smith

Catriona Walker
Clare Watson
Chris Whyte
Raymond Young

TMSI - Tavistock Marital Studies Institute

Susanna Abse
Linda Binnington
Elaine Bollinghaus
Sasha Brookes
Christel Buss-Twachtmann
Evelyn Cleavely
Christopher Clulow
Warren Colman
Patricia Coussell
Lynne Cudmore
Diana Daniell
Orpa Daniels
Barbara Kathleen Dearnley
James V Fisher
Peter B Fullerton
Pauline Hodson
Lynette Hughes
Dorothy Judd
Malcolm Millington
Mary Morgan
Elspeth Morley
Robert Morley
David Oldman
Felicia Olney
Paul Pengelly
J E Rosenthall
Stanley Ruszczynski
Eva Seligman
Helen Tarsh
Christopher Vincent
Kenneth Wright
Marion Yass

ULDPS - University of Leicester Diploma in Psychodynamic Studies

Peter Dent
Patricia East
Pam Horrocks
Michael Jacobs
Sue Jewson
Jenny Strang
Moira Walker
Sherly Williams

WMIP - West Midlands Institute of Psychotherapy

C Abberley
Judith Anderson
Nabil Anees
A R Arthur
John Barker
James Barrett
M A Beedie
Janice Birtle
Sonia Bliss
A R Bond
Jillyan Bray
Sue Brough
Mary V Burton
Jane Calvert
A Duine Campbell
Sonia Carlish
Grahame F Cooper
J A Crisp
M Curran
P Davis
Mahendra Singh Dayal
Lea K Elliott
Don Feasey
Barbara Forryan
Fiona Fox
Cath Gilliver
S Gladwell
Patricia Goodyear
Nigel Groom
T A Harvey
Jenny Hill
Val Hill
Linda M Hoag
Pat James
A Kahn
Peter Kenny
Laurence Kingsley
Helen Lloyd
Ian Lowery
I D Mackenzie
David Male
G May
Helen McCormick
James McDonald
Ann Morley
Marion Myers
R Niblett
P John Nicholas
Sheila Pratt
Margaret Randall
Mary Reddie
Robert W Rentoul
M J Reynolds

Geraldine Roy
A M Ryan
Joy Schaverien
Thomas Schroeder
David Shrimpton
Claire Skailes
Bebe Speed
Margaret Spencer
Jenny Stokes
Vivienne Taylor
David A Toms
Harold Tonks
Brian Truckle
Shirley Truckle
Fiona Vallance
S Van Marle
Athina Villia-Gosling
L Wattis
Jean Way
Sue Wheeler
Shirley Wheeley
H White
Sherly Williams
Linda Winkley
Joan Woodward
H Wright
Kath Yates

WTC - The Women's Therapy Centre

Mary Adams
Vivien Bar
Sally Berry
Clare Brennan
Nicky Buckley
Ellie Chalkind
Praxoulla Charalambous
Mira Dana
Marie-Laure Davenport
Marika Denton
Luise Eichenbaum
Sue Einhorn
Sheila Ernst
Eva Gell
Marion Gow
Iona Grant
Rosamund Grant
Esther Green
Margaret Green
Hazel Hickson
Inge Hudson
Sue Krzowski
Patricia Land
Marie Maguire
Mando Meleagrou

Carol Mohamed
Isabel Montero
Susie Orbach
Angela Powell
Sheila Ritchie
Mary Jane Rust
Ruthie Smith
Beverley Stobo
Deirdre Sutton-Smith
Alison Swan Parente
Margot Waddell

YAPP - Yorkshire Association for Psychodynamic Psychotherapy

James Anderson
Paul Aylard
Susanna Bailey
G N Bolsover
Kate Bonner
Christine Bostock
Lesley Cann
Kate Carr
Stephen Colver
Isobel Conlon
Mary Courtney
Brian Daines
Angela Douglas
Dennis Flannery
Annika Gilljam
Susan Godsil
Ingolf Gudjonsson
Helga Hanks
Anne Harrow
Colleen Heenan
Bridget Hester
David Kennard
Alan Lidmila
Carol Martin
Gill Martin
Una McCluskey
Ian H Oakley
Annabel Page
Stephen Reilly
Sally Rose
Celly Rowe
Brian Sidey
Alisdair Stokeld
Gabrielle Syme
Nick Tanna
Marta Vaciago Smith
Libby Wattis
Joan Webb
Catherine Welsh

ORGANISATION CONTACT ADDRESSES AND TELEPHONE NUMBERS

1. Analytical Psychology Section

Association of Jungian Analysts
Flat 3
7 Eton Avenue
London NW3 3EL
Tel: 0171 794 8711

Independent Group of Analytical
Psychologists
PO Box 1175
London W3 6DS
Tel: 0181 993 3996

Society of Analytical Psychology
1 Daleham Gardens
London NW3 5BY
Tel: 0171 435 7696

2. Behavioural and Cognitive Psychotherapy Section

British Association for Behavioural
and Cognitive Psychotherapies
c/o Harrow Psychological Health
Services
Dept. of Clinical Psychology
Northwick Park Hospital
Watford Road
Harrow HA1 3UJ
Tel: 0181 869 2325/6

3. Experiential Constructivist Therapies Section

Association for Neuro-Linguistic
Programming
48 Corser Street
Old Swinford
Stourbridge
West Midlands
DY8 2DQ
Tel: 01384 443935 / 01384 894145

Centre for Personal Construct
Psychology
Vigilant House
120 Wilton Road
London SW1V 1JZ
Tel: 0171 828 3445

4. Family, Couple, Sexual and Systemic Therapy Section

The Association for Family Therapy
Administrative Secretary
Mrs Pauline Matthews
18 Winnipeg Drive
Lakeside
Cardiff
CF2 6ET
Tel: 01222 753162

British Association for Sexual and
Marital Therapy
PO Box 62
Sheffield
S10 3TS
Enquiries by mail only

The Family Institute, Cardiff
105 Cathedral Road
Cardiff
CF1 9PH
Tel: 01222 226532

Institute of Family Therapy
24-32 Stephenson Way
London
NW1 2HX
Tel: 0171 391 9150

Kensington Consultation Centre
2 Wyvil Court
Trenchold Street
London
SW8 2TG
Tel: 0171 720 7301

5. Humanistic and Integrative Psychotherapy Section

Association of Cognitive Analytic
Therapists
Munro Clinic
Guy's Hospital
London
SE1 9RT
Tel: 0171 955 4822

Association of Humanistic Psychology
Practitioners
BCM AHPP
London WC1N 3XX
Tel: 0345 660326

Bath Centre for Psychotherapy and
Counselling
1 Walcot Terrace
London Road
Bath BA1 6AB
Tel: 01225 429720 / 01761 490149 /
01225 466635

British Psychodrama Association
8 Rahere Road
Cowley
Oxford OX4 3QG
Tel: 01865 715055

Centre for Counselling and
Psychotherapy Education
Beauchamp Lodge
2 Warwick Crescent
London W2 6NE
Tel: 0171 266 3006

Chiron Centre for Holistic
Psychotherapy
26 Eaton Rise
London W5 2ER
Tel: 0181 997 5219

The Gerda Boyesen Centre
Acacia House
Centre Avenue
London W3 7JX
Tel: 0181 743 2437

The Gestalt Centre, London
64 Warwick Road
St Albans
Herts AL1 4DL
Tel: 01727 864806

Gestalt Psychotherapy Training
Institute
2 Bedford Street
London Road
Bath BA1 6AF
Tel: 01225 482135

The Institute of Psychosynthesis
65a Watford Way
Hendon
London NW4 3AQ
Tel: 0181 202 4525

Institute of Transactional Analysis
BM Box 4104
London WC1 3XX
Tel: 0171 404 5011

The Institute for Arts in Therapy and
Education
The Windsor Centre
Windsor Street
London N1 8QL
Tel: 0171 704 2534

Karuna Institute
Natsworthy Manor
Widecombe in the Moor
Newton Abbot
Devon TQ13 7TR
Tel: 01647 221457

London Association of Primal
Psychotherapists
West Hill House
6 Swains Lane
London N6 6QU
Tel: 0171 267 9616

The Metanoia Institute
13 North Common Road
London W5 2QB
Tel: 0181 579 2505

The Minster Centre
1 Drakes Court Yard
291 Kilburn High Road
London NW6 7JR
Tel: 0171 372 6866 / 0171 372 4940

North Staffs Association for
Psychotherapy
34 High Street
Navenby
Lincoln LN5 0DZ
Tel: 01522 810940

Psychosynthesis and Education Trust
92/94 Tooley Street
London SE1 2TH
Tel: 0171 403 2100

Regent's College School of
Psychotherapy and Counselling
Regent's College
Inner Circle
London NW1 4NS
Tel: 0171 487 7406

Re.Vision
8 Chatsworth Road
London
NW2 4BN
Tel: 0181 451 2165

The Sherwood Psychotherapy
Training Institute
Thiskney House
2 St James Terrace
Nottingham NG1 6FW
Tel: 01602 243994

Spectrum
7 Endymion Road
London N4 1EE
Tel: 0181 341 2277 /0181 340 0426

Stockton Centre for Psychotherapy
and Counselling
77 Acklam Road
Thornaby on Tees
Cleveland TS17 7BD
Tel: 01642 649004

6. Hypnotherapy Section

British Association for Autogenic
Training and Therapy
Heath Cottage,
Pitch Hill, Ewhurst
Surrey GU6 7NP
General enquiries by mail only
For training enquiries:
Tel: 01923 675501

Centre Training School for
Hypnotherapy and Psychotherapy
145 Chapel Lane
Longton
Preston PR4 5NA
Tel: 01772 617663

The National College of Hypnosis and
Psychotherapy
12 Cross Street, Nelson
Lancs BB9 7EN
Tel: 01282 699378

The National Register of
Hypnotherapists and
Psychotherapists
12 Cross Street, Nelson
Lancs BB9 7EN
Tel: 01282 699378

National School of Hypnosis and
Psychotherapy
28 Finsbury Park Road
London N4 2JX
Tel: 0171 359 6991

7. Psychoanalytic and Psychodynamic Psychotherapy Section

Association of Arbours
Psychotherapists
6 Church Lane
London N8 7BU
Tel: 0181 340 7646

Association for Group and Individual
Psychotherapy
1 Fairbridge Road
London N19 3EW
Tel: 0171 272 7013

British Association of
Psychotherapists
37 Mapesbury Road
London NW2 4HJ
Tel: 0181 452 9823

Cambridge Society for Psychotherapy
1 Dean Drive
Cambridge CB1 4SW Enquiries by
mail only

Centre for Attachment-Based
Psychoanalytic Psychotherapy
12a Nassington Road
London NW3 2UD
Tel: 0171 794 4306

Centre for Freudian Analysis and
Research
60 Ivydale Road
London SE15 3BS
Tel: 0171 639 8289

Centre for Psychoanalytical
Psychotherapy
The Secretary
10 Blenheim Gardens
London NW2 4NS
Tel: 0181 450 4504

Centre for the Study of
Psychotherapy
Kent Research and Development
Centre
University of Kent
Canterbury CT2 7PD
Tel: 01227 764000 (Ext. 3691)

Guild of Psychotherapists
19b Thornton Hill
London SW19 4HU
Tel: 0181 947 0730

Guildford Centre for Psychotherapy
PO Box 63
Guildford
Surrey GU1 2UZ
Tel: 01483 560607

Hallam Institute of Psychotherapy
P.O. Box No. 1098
Sheffield S19 6YQ
Tel: 0114 2768555 (Ext. 4971)

Institute of Group Analysis
1 Daleham Gardens
London NW3 5BY
Tel: 0171 431 2693

Institute of Psychotherapy and
Counselling
607 The Chandlery
50 Westminster Bridge Road
London SE1 7QY
Tel: 0171 721 7660

Institute of Psychotherapy and Social
Studies
18 Laurier Road
London NW5 1SG
Tel: 0171 284 4762

Liverpool Psychotherapy Diploma
Organisation
Department of Clinical Psychology
Whelan Building
PO Box 147
Liverpool L69 3BX
Tel: 0151 794 5529

London Centre for Psychotherapy
19 Fitzjohn's Avenue
London NW3 5JY
Tel: 0171 435 0873

NAFSIYAT
278 Seven Sisters Road
London N4 2HY
Tel: 0171 263 4130

Northern Association for Analytical
Psychotherapy
Consulting Room
Post Office Cottage
Mickley
Stocksfield
Northumberland NE43
Tel: 01661 842727

North West Institute for Dynamic
Psychotherapy
c/o Dr Graeme McGrath
Gaskell House Psychotherapy Service
Swinton Grove
Manchester M13 0EU
Tel: 0161 273 2762

Philadelphia Association
4 Marty's Yard
17 Hampstead High Street
London NW3 1QW
Tel: 0171 794 2652

Severnside Institute for
Psychotherapy
Administrative Secretary
Vivien Hagen
11 Orchard Street
Bristol BS1 5EH
Tel: 01275 333266

South Trent Training in Dynamic
Psychotherapy
c/o Leicestershire Mental Health
Service
Dynamic Psychotherapy Service,
Humberstone Grange Clinic
Thurmaston Lane
Leicester LE5 0TA
Tel: 01162 460505

Tavistock Marital Studies Institute
Tavistock Centre
120 Belsize Lane
London NW3 5BA
Tel: 0171 435 7111

University of Leicester Diploma in
Psychodynamic Studies
Dept. of Adult Education
Vaughan College
St Nicholas Circle
Leicester LE1 4LB
Tel: 01162 517368

West Midlands Institute of
Psychotherapy
Uffculme Clinic
Queensbridge Road
Birmingham B13 8QD
Tel: 0121 449 0476

Westminster Pastoral Foundation
23 Kensington Square
London W8 5HN
Tel: 0171 937 6956

The Women's Therapy Centre
6-9 Manor Gardens
London N7 6LA
Tel: 0171 263 6200

Yorkshire Association for
Psychodynamic Psychotherapy
Dept. of Psychotherapy
40 Clarendon Road
Leeds LS2 9PJ
Tel: 0113 243 9000

8. Psychoanalytically-based Therapy with Children

Association of Child Psychotherapists
120 West Heath Road
London NW3 7TU
Tel: 0181 458 1609

Forum for the Advancement of
Educational Therapy and Therapeutic
Teaching
13 Highbury Terrace
London N5 1UP
Tel: 0171 226 8103

Institutional Members

Association of University Teachers of
Psychiatry
41 St Michael's Hill
Bristol
BS2 8DZ
Tel: 01179 303165

Tavistock Clinic
120 Belsize Lane
London NW3 5BA
Tel: 0171 435 7111

Universities Psychotherapy
Association
Centre for Psychotherapeutic Studies
16 Claremont Crescent
Sheffield S10 2TA
Tel: 0114 282 4931

Special Members

British Psychological Society
St Andrews House
48 Princess Road East
Leicester LE1 7DR
Tel: 01162 549568

Royal College of Psychiatrists
17 Belgrave Square
London SW1X 8PG
Tel: 0171 235 2351

Friends of the Council

British Association for Counselling
1 Regent's Place
Rugby
Coventry
CV21 2PJ
Tel: 01788 578328